S0-CPS-137

PANAMÁ
Caracas
VENEZUELA
LAS GUAYANAS
Bogotá
COLOMBIA
Quito
ECUADOR
Río Amazonas
PERÚ
BRASIL
Lima
Cuzco
Lago de Titicaca
La Paz
BOLIVIA
PARAGUAY
Asunción
Córdoba
Mendoza
URUGUAY
a Río de Janeiro
Santiago
Buenos Aires
ARGENTINA
Montevideo
CHILE
Cosimini

El Camino Real

UNDERSTANDING OUR SPANISH-SPEAKING NEIGHBORS

Book Two

EDITH MOORE JARRETT
Fillmore High School, Fillmore, California

HOUGHTON MIFFLIN COMPANY
BOSTON · NEW YORK · CHICAGO · DALLAS · ATLANTA · SAN FRANCISCO
The Riverside Press Cambridge

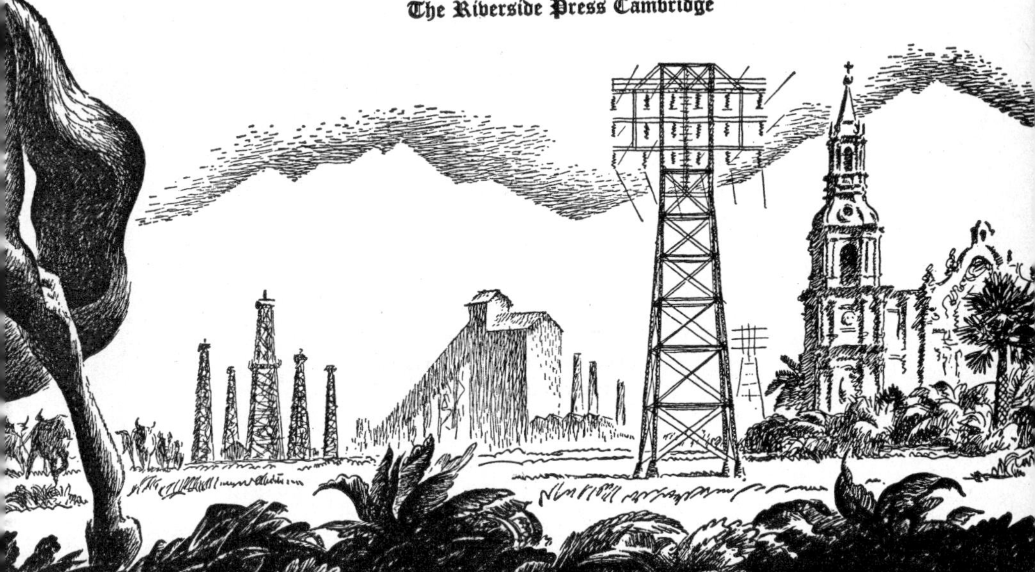

ACKNOWLEDGMENTS

THE author wishes to acknowledge her indebtedness for story material to the Lozano Publications of Los Angeles and San Antonio; to *Las Américas* of New York; to Sr. don Claudio E. Montealegre of the Junta Nacional de Turismo of San José, Costa Rica; to Sr. don Manuel Vieytez of the Circuito de Teatros Nacionales of San Salvador, El Salvador; and to Mrs. Alice Moore Milton for her original arrangements of the folksongs.

Appreciation for their reading and helpful criticism of the manuscript is due to Mrs. Beryl J. M. McManus, Hollywood High School, co-author of Book I; to Miss Nina Lee Weisinger, Department of Romance Languages, the University of Texas; to Miss Lilly Lindquist, Supervisor of Foreign Languages, Detroit, Michigan; to Miss Margaret R. Tupper, Washburn High School, Minneapolis; and to Doctor Leslie P. Brown, San Diego State College, San Diego, California. Thanks are due also to Professor G. Rivera of Harvard University for his careful checking of the Spanish text and exercises.

The Riverside Press
CAMBRIDGE · MASSACHUSETTS
PRINTED IN THE U.S.A.

CONTENTS

PART FOUR

¡Buen viaje!

More and more, these days, we realize the importance of getting better acquainted with our "Good Neighbors" to the south. It is not enough merely to trade with them. We must have an understanding and appreciation of the Latin-American temperament and point of view, and know their personal and national problems before we can become good neighbors ourselves.

To do this, we can hardly expect them to deal with us entirely in our language while we remain ignorant of theirs. Therefore while they study English — as they are required to do in their schools — we study Spanish, and in our second year we find much satisfaction in our fast-increasing ability to make use of it.

One year of Spanish in high school is barely an appetizer; two years can give you a foundation which will make it safe for you to be stranded in a town where no one knows English. But at best, two years' study of any language in school alone cannot make you speak it like a native. If you think of your Spanish only during class time, it will never be really yours; so make it a point to take it home with you each day. Try it on the family, practice it on the neighbors, look for it in your reading, and every time you meet a Spanish-speaking person, be bold and refuse to speak anything but his language, which will delight him and give you valuable experience.

In your second year of study, you take up many practical things. In your conversation exercises, you learn how to use the telephone, discuss your automobile, get along in hotels and restaurants, and read traffic signs and laundry lists. You even learn sports expressions and beauty-shop words, not to mention some amusing and popular slang. You learn, too, how to begin and end personal and business letters, which is much more of an art among Latin Americans than it is with us.

You become acquainted, in the stories you read, with Latin America's favorite writers, who give you word pictures of life in their countries in legends and fables and in tales of treasures and miracles, of romance and adventure.

And soon you will find yourself realizing that your elementary-school ideas of Latin America have broadened remarkably, for you learn that the culture and civilization of these countries is not crude or primitive, but in some respects — you may be embarrassed to find — more advanced than ours, because the sensitive and unhurried Latins of the educated classes have more of an appreciation of the fine arts than we practical and busy *norteamericanos* have. In literature, for instance, they know Spain's masterpieces, which we don't; they have as well our literary heritage from Europe, and then in addition they read our current best-sellers — often in the original English. This does not imply that they lack literature and art and music of their own, for they have a great deal which we are coming to appreciate as we at last look southward.

So as you begin your second journey along the old *caminos reales* that Spain built in Central and South America as well as in Mexico and our own country, you may expect to find as you go a great deal of enjoyment and profit in the language of the good neighbors who live by the side of the road.

¡Buen viaje! Pleasant journey!

Part One

Popular magazine covers from Spanish-speaking countries feature bright colors, pretty girls, and cartoons. From Mexico to Argentina, people read in their favorite magazines the same type of articles that we enjoy.

CAPÍTULO 1

Anuncios clasificados

Sometimes, after studying a foreign language in textbooks for a while, we become so wrapped up in its difficulties that we forget there really are people casually using that language in their everyday lives just as we use English. All over the Spanish-speaking world — and somewhere the sun is always shining on it — people are solving their personal problems day by day entirely in Spanish: calling the cat, playing games, buying their clothes, having parties, earning a living, going to movies, laughing over comic strips, reading the daily papers and advertising in them for just the same sort of things that we do.

To show you how much alike people are, whether they speak Spanish or English, here is part of a classified advertising section from a Mexican daily, including everything from Help Wanted to occult assistance in love affairs.

You will find that you can read much practical Spanish by guessing new words according to their context; so read each advertisement entirely through at least once to get the general idea, and then go back and fit in individual words that were not clear at first. Most of the words you may not know are given at the right. Since some of those which look like English are not in the general vocabulary, you will have to guess their meanings.

Of course all the names and addresses are fictitious; so don't try to answer any of the ads!

Anuncios Clasificados	classified ads
Tarifas: 1½ centavos la palabra en los días de la semana; 2 centavos la palabra los domingos. Nueve centavos la palabra por siete veces consecutivas. Cobro mínimo: veinte palabras. Todos los anuncios deben entregarse en las oficinas del periódico antes de las cuatro de la tarde.	**tarifa,** rate **cobro,** charge **mínimo,** minimum **entregarse,** to be delivered **periódico,** newspaper

Arrendamientos	arrendamientos, rentals
ALQUILO o vendo casa grande con cinco cuartos sin muebles. Luz y agua pagadas. Sr. Serrano, teléfono 13876.	**alquilar,** to rent **muebles,** furniture
$40 AL MES. Casa nueva con sala, tres recámaras, baño, cocina, comedor, garage. Informan Calle Primera, 295.	**recámaras,** bedrooms (*Mex.*) **informar,** to give information
SE ALQUILA casa amueblada de dos recámaras, agua caliente. Cerca de escuela. Informan Avenida Vera Cruz 865.	**amueblada,** furnished **avenida,** avenue
ALQUILO a familia honorable, bonita casa moderna, estilo estuco español de seis cuartos. Informa Sr. Benavente, Calle Ramona 743.	**estilo estuco,** stucco style
Empleos	**empleos,** employment, "help wanted"
SE NECESITA mujer para trabajo de casa, familia de tres. Cuarto, comida, o puede volver a casa de noche. $25 al mes. Llamen CA 13–476 entre las diez y las doce de la mañana.	**comida,** "board"
QUIERO MUCHACHO de diez y ocho años para trabajar en tienda y manejar automóvil. Tiene que hablar inglés y español. Llamen teléfono NA 8654.	**manejar,** to drive
NECESITO jardinero. Buen empleo, inmediatamente. Un día de descanso. Las Palmas 1419.	**descanso,** rest
HOMBRE DE BUENA PRESENCIA de veinte y dos a treinta años, para aprender a solicitar órdenes de casa en casa. Pequeño salario al empezar. Ocurran a las ocho y media de la mañana, Calle Reforma 598.	**presencia,** appearance **órdenes,** orders **ocurrir,** to apply
¡USTED PUEDE GANAR MÁS como experto en radio! Estudie en su casa este método	**método,** method

interesante y fácil. Sólo necesita saber leer y escribir. Aquí tiene la oportunidad de ser independiente, ganando en sus horas libres cuarenta a cincuenta dólares a la semana. Enseñamos la Radiomecánica, Sistemas de Amplificación para Oratoria, Radiocomunicación, Onda Corta, Radio en la Aviación, Cine Sonoro, Televisión, etc. ¡Pida Vd. nuestro libro gratis, hoy mismo! Escuela Nueva, Calle Pico 987.

libre, free
radiomecánica, radio mechanics
oratoria, public address
onda corta, short wave
cine sonoro, sound movies
gratis, free
hoy mismo, this very day

Compras Varias

COMPRAMOS ropa usada: abrigos, vestidos de seda, trajes sastre, sombreros, zapatos, medias de señora, etc.; pantalones, camisas, sacos, corbatas, zapatos de hombre. Pagamos los mejores precios. López Hermanos, Calle 7, 156.

compras varias, "wanted to buy"
abrigos, overcoats
seda, silk; **traje sastre,** suit
medias, stockings
camisa, shirt; **saco,** coat

Ventas Autos

¿VA USTED A COMPRAR un automóvil usado? ¡Tenemos el auto que Vd. busca!

¡Verdaderas Gangas!

¡Coches desde $68!

Aquí puede Vd. comprar un auto con toda confianza. Especial para esta semana:

'40 Fiat coupé, de apariencia y condición como nuevo, completamente reacondicionado, llantas nuevas, muy elegante. Sólo $158, en abonos fáciles. Pérez y Cía., Calle Sonora 365.

ventas autos, cars for sale
ganga, bargain
coche, car
confianza, confidence
llanta, tire
abono, payment
Cía. = Compañía

Ventas Varias

¡OPORTUNIDAD! Vendo muebles de mi casa: camas, mesas, sillas, sofá, tapetes, piano, estufa, tocadores, servicio de mesa, etc. Compre ahora, pague después. Sr. Carrillo, Avenida Jiménez, 941.

ventas varias, "for sale"
tapete, rug
estufa, stove; **tocador,** dresser

APR 2 1943

LA PRENSA

EDICION DE

BUENOS AIRES, SABADO 6 DE FEBRERO DE 1943

Dirección y Administración: Av. de

Rusos Llegaron al Mar de Azov y Avanzan Hacia las Ciudades de Kharkoff, Kursk y Rostoff

PAGINA 5

El Conde Ciano Dimitió su Cargo de Ministro de Relaciones Exteriores Italiano

PAGINA 4

Aumenta la Presión de las Fuerzas de los Estados Unidos en Territorio de las Islas Salomón

PAGINA 5

El Gobierno de Finlandia Estaría Dispuesto a Negociar la Paz con el de la Unión Soviética

PAGINA 5

La Intensidad de la Actual Sequía Sería Menor que la de los Años 1916 y 1937

PAGINA 7

TERRENOS en VENTA

PREST., HIPOTECAS, TITULOS y valores

AVISOS PARA CARNAVAL

ALHAJAS, BRILL., POLIZ., OBJ. de arte y antigüedades

COMPRA de MUEBLES, PIANOS, ropa y objetos varios

Comentarios

ESTADO DEL TIEMPO

Temperatura de ayer: mínima: 21.8°, a las 8.5; máxima, 33°, a las 16.5. Perspectivas para hoy: bueno y caluroso; luego lluvias ligeras, con leve descenso de temperatura. Para mañana: lluvias parciales y temperatura sobre la normal. Página 8.

Informaciones

Servicio Telegráfico

DEL INTERIOR

DEL EXTERIOR

Latin American newspapers usually do not go in for startling headlines like ours. Here is *La Prensa,* one of the world's outstanding journals, which gives classified ads on the front page.

SACRIFICO barato máquina de escribir por efectivo. ¡Si busca Vd. una ganga, vea ésta hoy! Calle Primera, 536.	**barato,** cheap; **máquina,** machine **efectivo,** cash
CAMBIO buen piano, casi nuevo, por automóvil en buenas condiciones. Informan después de las cinco de la tarde. Sra. García, Calle 22, 926.	**cambiar,** to exchange
¡GANGA! Una hermosa garantizada plumafuente puede ser suya por sólo 79¢. Le ponemos su nombre en la pluma en oro, absolutamente gratis. Escribe veinte mil palabras por contenido de tinta. Es una pluma que le gustará muchísimo. Pídala hoy mismo. Límite: dos a cada cliente. Calle Vallejo, 543.	**garantizada,** guaranteed **plumafuente,** fountain pen **por contenido,** "in one filling" **tinta,** ink **cliente,** customer
VENDO tienda de abarrotes con departamento de carnicería y legumbres. Bien equipada y buena clientela. Vendo a precio muy bajo. Informan Calle Hidalgo, 2300.	**abarrotes,** groceries (*Mex.*) **legumbres,** vegetables **bajo,** low

SE VENDE «lonchería», con dulcería y fuente para refrescos. Limpia, renta barata, precio bajo. Diez y ocho meses para pagar. Avenida Juárez, 441.

lonchería, lunch counter (*Mex.*)
dulce, sweet
refrescos, "soft drinks"
limpio, clean

¡ATENCIÓN! ¡Magnífica oportunidad! ¿Por qué pagar más cuando por menos puede Vd. tener lo mejor?

Nuestra casa y la de Vd.

LA CASA COLORADA

«La más barata»

Elegante ropa para toda la familia. Abra Vd. su cuenta en La Casa Colorada. Puede pagar sólo 75¢ cada semana. Abierta todas las noches.

¿Por qué comprar al contado, pudiendo comprar a crédito?

LA CASA COLORADA

Calle Figueroa, 405.

la de Vd., yours
colorado, red
cuenta, account
al contado, for cash

Personales

APRENDA VD. guitarra. Lecciones fáciles. Nunca es tarde para aprender. Pida nuestro catálogo gratis. Un dólar la hora. Venga a vernos hoy. Manuel Ávila, Avenida 23, 368.

gratis, free

SEÑOR sale el diez de noviembre para la capital de México en auto y quiere pasajero. Escriban Apartado D, este periódico.

pasajero, passenger
apartado, box

CABALLERO norteamericano, que quiere aprender a hablar español, desea alquilar cuarto en casa moderna con familia de habla española. Escriban a George Smith, Apartado X, este periódico.

caballero, gentleman

¡APRENDA VD. el inglés! Mi método es el más fácil y práctico. Vd. puede estudiar en su propia casa durante sus horas libres. Ésta es una magnífica

propio, own

oportunidad para ganar más dinero. Pida mi libro gratis. Sr. Luis Pedroza, Apartado 56A, este periódico.

PERDÍ el miércoles por la noche bolsa negra cerca del Teatro Fábregas. Si la persona que la halló me devuelve los documentos, puede tener el dinero que contenía. Sra. Inés Herrera, Avenida Flores, 273.

bolsa, handbag
devolver, to return
contener, to contain

SUBSCRÍBASE a este diario.

diario, daily

Miscelánea

¡TRIUNFE EN AMORES! Muchas personas son felices por medio de mis trabajos. Si desea Vd. obtener el amor de alguna persona, mándeme sólo el nombre y un dólar y tendrá Vd. su deseo inmediatamente. Si no manda dinero, no contesto. Sra. F. Gómez, Apartado 47, Palacios, Sinaloa, México.

triunfar, to win; **amor,** love
por medio de, by means of
obtener, to obtain
mandar, to send
tendrá, *fut. of* **tener**

¡AMORES, DINERO O ENFERMEDADES! Si tiene Vd. dificultades, Madame Sábelotodo puede ayudarle. Miles de personas satisfechas. Escriba o venga a verla. Teléfono NE 6540.

enfermedades, illnesses
dificultad, difficulty
Sábelotodo = Sabe + lo + todo
ayudar, to help

¿CREE USTED EN LA SUERTE? Lleve Vd. un par de legítimas piedras verdes. Se dice que los antiguos siempre llevaban consigo dos de estas piedras verdes, una para atraer la buena suerte en dinero, amor, negocios, trabajo, etc., y la otra para prevenir la mala suerte como pérdidas, enfermedades, dificultades, etc. Lleve un par de estas curiosas piedras. Cincuenta centavos por las dos, porte pagado. Satisfacción garantizada. Apartado 6B, Monterrey, Nuevo León, Mexico.

suerte, luck
par, pair, couple; **legítimo,** genuine
antiguos, ancients
atraer, to attract
negocios, business
prevenir, to prevent
pérdidas, losses
porte pagado, postage paid

PALABRAS IMPORTANTES[1]

These important words and expressions from the ads are some you had in first year, but which you may have forgotten. Make a short sentence or phrase using each one. (They are all in the general vocabulary.)

1 **antes de**	**domingo**	1 **mujer**	**sala**
2 **buscar**	3 **enseñar**	1 **nuevo**	3 **satisfecho**
1 **cada**	1 **entre**	2 **oro**	4 **semana**
2 **cerca de**	2 **feliz**	1 **palabra**	1 **sólo**
cocina	2 **ganar**	1 **pedir** (i)	4 **tienda**
2 **contestar**	2 **luz**	1 **perder** (ie)	1 **veces** (*pl. of* **vez**)
1 **cuarto**	1 **llevar**	2 **piedra**	2 **verdadero**
1 **deber**	1 **mejor**	1 **poder** (ue)	3 **vestido**
1 **después de**	1 **mes**	3 **ropa**	1 **volver** (ue)

EXPRESIONES

***de casa en casa** ***de habla española** ***de noche**
***en vez de** ***volver a casa**

¿VERDAD O NO?

According to what you read in the advertisements, are these statements true or false? (They are listed in the same order as the advertisements. Remember to guess familiar-looking words.)

1. La casa nueva se alquila por catorce dólares al mes. 2. La casa que está cerca de la escuela no tiene agua caliente. 3. Una familia de trece personas desea una mujer para trabajar. 4. Un muchacho tiene que hablar español y saber manejar un automóvil. 5. El hombre de buena presencia no va a tener salario al empezar. 6. Sólo es necesario saber leer y escribir para aprender la televisión con este método. 7. Los hermanos López compran sólo vestidos, zapatos y sombreros usados. 8. Se puede comprar un automóvil usado desde setenta y ocho dólares. 9. El señor Carrillo quiere el

[1] Note to teacher: The numbers refer to the frequency of the words according to the Buchanan List: 1 = 1–189; 2 = 190–500; 3 = 501–1000; 4 = 1001–1500. Asterisks on idioms in chapter vocabularies indicate that they are among the first two hundred of the Keniston List; in the general vocabulary words starred are those used in Book I.

dinero por sus muebles inmediatamente. 10. La señora García está en casa antes de las cinco de la tarde. 11. Vd. puede comprar tres plumas garantizadas por sólo setenta y nueve centavos cada una. 12. En la tienda de abarrotes, no se venden carnes ni legumbres. 13. En la «lonchería» se venden dulces, sodas, y comidas. 14. No se puede comprar a crédito en «La casa colorada». 15. El profesor de guitarra vende su catálogo por un dólar. 16. Un pasajero quiere salir en auto el diez de noviembre. 17. Una familia de habla española quiere alquilar un cuarto. 18. El método de aprender el inglés se puede estudiar en casa. 19. La señora Inés Herrera desea los documentos que tenía en su bolsa. 20. La señora F. Gómez contesta a todos si mandan dinero o no.

PREGUNTAS

These questions about the advertisements are divided into sections in order to help you answer them more easily. The meanings of many of the words are given only with the ads.

I. Arrendamientos, Empleos y Compras Varias

1. ¿Desea el señor Serrano vender su casa sin muebles? 2. ¿Tiene comedor la casa en la Calle Primera, número doscientos noventa y cinco? 3. ¿Tiene muebles una casa amueblada? 4. ¿Es mejor alquilar una casa a una familia honorable? 5. Si quiere Vd. trabajar en la familia de tres personas, ¿a qué hora debe Vd. llamar por teléfono? 6. ¿Por qué es necesario hablar inglés y español para trabajar en la tienda? 7. ¿Cuántos días tiene que trabajar el jardinero cada semana? 8. ¿Cuántos años debe tener el hombre de buena presencia? 9. ¿Cómo puede Vd. ser experto en radio? 10. ¿Quiénes compran ropa usada?

II. Ventas Autos y Ventas Varias

1. ¿Cuál es la ganga especial de Pérez y Cía. esta semana? 2. ¿Qué muebles quiere vender el señor Carrillo? 3. ¿Se puede comprar la máquina de escribir en abonos (*payments*) fáciles? 4. ¿Qué quiere la señora García en vez de su piano? 5. ¿Qué se puede poner gratis en la plumafuente? 6. ¿Se vende mucho en la tienda de abarrotes? 7. ¿Es «lonchería» una palabra española? 8. ¿Qué se vende en «La casa colorada»? ¿Se vende barato?

III. Personales y Miscelánea

1. ¿Es tarde para aprender a tocar (*play*) la guitarra? 2. ¿Qué quiere el señor que sale para México? 3. ¿Por qué quiere el caballero norteamericano alquilar un cuarto en una familia de habla española? 4. ¿Cómo pueden los mexicanos ganar más dinero? 5. ¿Qué perdió (*lost*) la señora Inés Herrera? ¿Dónde? 6. ¿Puede la señora F. Gómez verdaderamente darle a uno el amor de otra persona? 7. ¿Qué quiere hacer la Madame Sábelotodo para miles de personas?

ESTUDIO DE PALABRAS

I. In each group of five words there is one that does not belong. Which one is it?

semana	domingo	antes de	mujer	todo
mes	viernes	después de	muchacho	cama
inglés	miércoles	salir de	hombre	mesa
año	menos	cerca de	mejor	silla
hora	sábado	entre	caballero	piano

cocina	dólar	feliz	buscar	para
familia	centavo	bonito	creer	de
baño	poder	desde	llevar	sin
comedor	precio	fácil	gustar	mil
sala	pagar	malo	mejor	con

II. These words and most of their opposites are found in the advertisements. What are their opposites?

día	hallar	bueno	al contado	salir
comprar	caliente	sin	hombre	llamar
enseñar	buscar	grande	ir	más

III. What word in List B would you associate with each word in List A?

A		B	
baño	sombrero	mes	silla
cocina	ganar	estudiar	calle
hoy	mesa	dinero	mañana
semana	avenida	agua	después
escuela	ahora	comida	zapatos

IV. Count from 1 to 20 in Spanish; by tens from 10 to 100; by hundreds to 1000 (§ 100).[1]

V. Say these numbers in Spanish (§ 100):

26, 38, 184, 236, 1423; 19, 43, 162, 555, 2784; 15, 55, 190, 971, 5555

VI. Give these expressions of time in Spanish (§ 102):

1. it is one o'clock	4. it is 4:45	7. it is 10:35 P.M.
2. at one o'clock	5. at 6:50	8. it is 3:10 P.M.
3. it is 3:30	6. at 12:40	9. at 8:30 A.M.

REPASO DE VERBOS

I. If you have forgotten the present tense endings for the three conjugations, you will find familiar models in section 62 of the Appendix.

Conjugate in the present tense with subject pronouns (§ 106):

comprar, vender, escribir, trabajar, deber, vivir

II. Give the verb forms suitable for each subject pronoun, using the verbs **creer, deber, buscar, hallar, abrir,** *and* **pagar:**

1. yo *believe*	6. Vd. *believe*	11. Vds. *look for*
2. ellas *ought*	7. nosotros *pay*	12. nosotros *open*
3. tú *look for*	8. ellos *look for*	13. él *believes*
4. ella *finds*	9. yo *ought*	14. yo *find*
5. vosotros *open*	10. Vd. *pay*	15. ella *ought*

III. Review the formula for making polite commands in section 99, and give the first person singular and command of each of these verbs:

comprar	trabajar	contestar	pagar (§ 91)
vender	escribir	llamar	buscar (§ 92)
mandar	anunciar	abrir	enseñar

[1] **Sections with numbers above 61 are in the Appendix.**

IV. Give the infinitive of each of these verb forms; then translate them, noticing carefully whether they are present tense or commands:

1. Vd. abre
2. ¿compra Vd.?
3. vendemos
4. busque Vd.
5. ¿pagan?
6. contesta
7. pague Vd.
8. ¿cree Vd.?
9. debo
10. compras
11. venden
12. ¿llama?

HOW TO READ SPANISH

Who wants to spend an hour on any lesson, when he could prepare it as well or better in twenty minutes? There is a definite way to cut down your study time if you will adopt it. Now is the time to learn a new procedure or at least to improve on your former technique, because from now on, instead of the intentionally simplified sentences of Book I, you will gradually read the kind of Spanish that Spanish-speaking people enjoy using — long, involved sen-

Newsstand in Caracas, Venezuela, displays magazines and papers printed in Spanish, French, and English, since educated people of Latin America read several languages with no difficulty.

Gendreau

tences that are sometimes almost puzzles to solve. If you try to read this complicated Spanish word-for-word, as you could the easy stories in Book I, you will waste time and possibly become discouraged, thinking you don't know anything when you really do.

So, whether you see the reason for them or not, try these helpful hints:

1. *Read the whole sentence.* Read at least as far as the first punctuation mark (sometimes continue past a comma, but never past a semicolon), and decide what the sentence says, with the general story idea in mind. If it is all clear to you, go on. If it isn't, read it again, and even three times; often before the third reading the meaning will suddenly become clear without your looking up a word. If it doesn't, there is probably some certain key word holding you up. Find it, look up its meaning, being sure the meaning you select fits the sentence, and there you are! Other words which were vague will jump into place, and the sentence is conquered.

Incidentally, after you have looked up a word, *never* write it in your book. This is not entirely for the sake of the book, either, because when you read the story thereafter, your eye will jump the Spanish word completely, seeing only the English you have written in. This means that the Spanish word never has a chance to reach your brain and become a part of your vocabulary.

2. *Look for idioms.* Reading a whole sentence at a time, you will notice groups of words that must not be translated separately; if you read word by word, you flounder over these idioms and lose the thread of the story. Familiar words often change their meaning a great deal when in a combination; for example, ***dar las doce*** does not mean *to give the twelve,* which doesn't make sense, but *to strike twelve,* which does.

3. *Dodge the dictionary.* Never, never go blindly through a story looking up every unfamiliar word and writing it down before you begin to read. If you look up words only when all else fails, you can easily tell whether ***manzana***, in a particular sentence, means *apple* or *city block,* for it may mean either.

a. Look for cognates (words resembling English). By this time you know that many Spanish words are so much like English that you can guess them. In this book you will make a definite study of different types of cognates; after this study is completed, you should never try to find familiar-looking words in the dictionary. To keep you from absent-mindedly turning to the back of the book, many guessable words have been intentionally omitted. If you waste time looking for one of this kind and it isn't there, scold yourself for not having guessed in the first place!

b. Analyze long words. Long, unfamiliar words often tell you their meaning if you look at them closely and take them apart. It is easy to guess that ***un lavaplatos*** (***lavar,*** *to wash*; ***platos,*** *dishes*) means *a kitchen sink* or *a dishwasher*; ***un robachicos*** (***robar,*** *to steal*; ***chicos,*** *little ones*) simply has to mean *kidnapper.* Remember that the longer a word is, the easier it usually is to guess its meaning.

c. Look up familiar words when they don't make sense. When you find an old, familiar word that just doesn't fit, look it up! It probably has a new meaning in this particular story. For example, ***gato,*** *cat,* also means *automobile jack* or *money bag and the money kept in it;* ***blanco,*** *white,* also means *target.* You never can tell what a familiar word may turn out to mean!

4. *Rearrange word order.* Never hesitate to change the Spanish word order when you are struggling with a complicated sentence. When you know all the words and they still don't make sense, change them around until they do. No two languages use identical word order.

5. *GUESS!* When you travel in foreign countries where you do not know the language, in self-defense you soon become an expert guesser. Use the same technique in reading Spanish stories, and your teacher will never hold it against you if you make an intelligent guess that happens to be wrong.

¡Buena suerte!

CAPÍTULO 2

Costumbres de la raza

Spanish-speaking children, in whatever country they grow up, are taught the traditional courtesy of their race, as you can see by this newspaper article, which was written for Mexican boys and girls of your age. It appeared in a Mexican newspaper of Los Angeles, California, and gives a good review of Spanish customs. You should know or be able to guess most of the words.

Para los extranjeros, algunas de nuestras costumbres parecen muy raras. La mayor parte (*most*) de nuestras costumbres tienen su origen en el país que nos da la lengua, la historia y la religión. Ese país es España.

España, ante todo, nos enseña a ser caballeros, y como caballeros, aprendemos a usar con los nombres de las personas mayores de edad, el *don*.

Ningún otro país del mundo tiene una palabra tan cortés como el *don* que usamos nosotros los mexicanos.

Cuando decimos «don Fulano de Tal», significamos respeto, y somos caballeros. En español, cuando hablamos de una dama, nunca decimos «la señora García», sino «doña Juana García», para ser más corteses.

Hay otras fórmulas de cortesía que están de moda, aunque son muy antiguas. Cuando una persona nos pregunta el nombre, al darlo, siempre agregamos (*add*), — A sus órdenes, — o — Para servir a Vd.

Si una persona quiere saber la dirección de otra, un caballero siempre contesta, — Tiene Vd. su casa en la calle tantos más cuantos (*so-and-so*). — También, cuando nos referimos a nuestra casa, tenemos la costumbre de decir, — ¿Gusta Vd. pasar a su casa? — No decimos «mi casa». También, cuando una persona viene por primera vez a nuestra casa,

Black Star

Mexican beauties still wear for fiestas the traditional lace mantilla and high comb. These girls, at the opera, hang their bright Spanish shawls over the edge of their box.

es costumbre decir, — Ésta es su casa, — o — Tome Vd. posesión de su casa. — Con estas expresiones damos una prueba de hospitalidad y de amistad, pues se entiende que la casa de uno debe ser la casa del amigo también.

En nuestras cartas también somos corteses. Cuando dirigimos (*address*) una carta a un señor, no escribimos solamente «señor Juan López», sino, para ser caballeros, «señor don Juan López». Esto siempre demuestra el grado de educación que tiene la persona que escribe o que habla.

Cuando escribimos una carta a una persona de la misma ciudad, nuestra cortesía nos manda poner la fecha así:

«Su casa, 10 de marzo de 1945». Y en la carta decimos a un buen amigo, — Envío a Vd. un estrecho (*close*) abrazo.— Al terminar la carta escribimos, — Soy de Vd. su atento amigo y seguro servidor.[1]

En los países de habla española un niño siempre hace pasar primero por una puerta a un grande. Los extranjeros creen que esto es muy curioso, y dicen que nosotros los mexicanos siempre nos disputamos (*argue about*) la entrada. No es esto exactamente. Lo que hacemos es tratar de significar que damos el paso a una persona de mayor respeto.

Nosotros los mexicanos siempre damos la mano cuando encontramos a algún amigo. Si es un buen amigo, le damos un abrazo cordial, que significa amistad. Este abrazo sólo es costumbre en España y en los países de habla española, y los extranjeros creen que es muy curioso.

Nuestros niños, aunque viven en un país extranjero, no olvidan nuestras viejas y honrosas (*honorable*) costumbres. Sabemos que a veces éstas parecen demasiado exageradas aquí, pero, si nacemos mexicanos y si por nuestras venas (*veins*) corre sangre española, ¿por qué no seguir nuestras viejas costumbres? Así conservamos nuestra nacionalidad y nuestra dignidad de caballeros.

ADAPTED FROM *La Opinión* (LOS ANGELES)

Find These Expressions in the Story

1. No other country in the world 2. forms of courtesy which are in style 3. Most of our customs 4. one's house should be one's friend's house 5. I am, very sincerely yours 6. Spain, above all, teaches us to be gentlemen 7. We Mexicans always shake hands 8. with the names of older persons 9. sometimes these seem too exaggerated 10. a proof of hospitality and friendship 11. Spanish blood runs through our veins 12. which we Mexicans use

[1] I am your attentive friend and true servant; *that is*, very sincerely yours.

PALABRAS NUEVAS[1]

3	**abrazo**[2]	embrace		**nacionalidad**	nationality
	almorzar (ue)	to eat lunch	2	**paso**	right-of-way
3	**amistad** (*f.*)	friendship	3	**pronunciar**	to pronounce
3	**dama**[2]	lady	3	**prueba**	proof
3	**demostrar** (ue)	to show		**raza**	race
	dignidad	dignity		**referir** (ie, i)	to refer
3	**dirección**	address	2	**respeto**	respect
	exagerado	exaggerated	2	**sangre** (*f.*)	blood
3	**grado**	degree	4	**significar**	to mean, signify
	hospitalidad	hospitality			

Expresiones

*__ante todo,__ above all, before all
*__a veces,__ sometimes
dar la mano, to shake hands
fórmulas de cortesía, expressions of courtesy
¿gusta Vd.?, would you care to?
mayores de edad, older (persons)
por primera vez, for the first time

PARA COMPLETAR

Complete these sentences in Spanish according to the story. (A dash means one word; dots mean several.)

1. Muchas costumbres de México tienen su origen en ——. 2. Los hombres de habla española tratan de conservar su dignidad de ——. 3. Ningún otro país del mundo tiene una palabra tan cortés como el ——. 4. Cuando los mexicanos dan su nombre, siempre dicen, — .... 5. Cuando una persona viene por primera vez a la casa, es costumbre decir, — .... 6. Al encontrar a un buen amigo, es costumbre darle la ——. 7. Los extranjeros creen que dar ... es muy curioso. 8. Para terminar una carta es costumbre escribir, ...

[1] Note to teacher: Words in chapter vocabularies (except in optional chapters) are ordinarily those not used in Book I and difficult to guess. Many cognates used in early chapters are in the general vocabulary, but pupils should be encouraged to guess whenever possible.

[2] Nouns ending in *-o* are masculine and those ending in *-a, -dad,* and *-ción* are feminine unless otherwise marked. Nouns with other endings are marked (*m.*) or (*f.*).

PREGUNTAS

1. ¿Son muy corteses las personas de países de habla española? 2. ¿Cómo se demuestra el grado de educación de una persona? 3. ¿Está de moda la cortesía en nuestro país? 4. ¿Qué es costumbre decir en español a una persona que viene por primera vez a una casa? 5. ¿Cuándo dan la mano las personas de habla española? 6. ¿Siempre se disputan (*argue about*) la entrada los mexicanos? 7. ¿Quién debe pasar primero por una puerta? 8. ¿Corre sangre española por las venas (*veins*) de los mexicanos? 9. ¿Deben todos los hombres conservar su dignidad de caballeros? 10. ¿Cómo es costumbre terminar una carta en español? 11. ¿Cuál es la fecha?

REPASO DE VERBOS

I. Radical-changing verb models are conjugated in sections 86 and 87. *Conjugate in the present tense without subject pronouns:*

entender (ie), querer (ie), demostrar (ue), encontrar (ue)

II. Irregular verbs are listed alphabetically beginning with section 63. *If you need to, look up these verbs in order to conjugate them in the present tense:*

dar, ir, poner, salir, ser, tener

III. Read this story, replacing italicized infinitives with correct present tense verb forms. Tell the story in the first person.

Mi día

Ser alumno [1] de la Escuela Superior de ——. *Vivir* en la calle de ——, número ——.

Siempre *dormir* bien. Todos los días *tener* que levantarme a las siete. Cuando mi madre me *llamar,* yo *creer* que todavía *ser* de noche.

Comer mucho por la mañana porque *tener* mucha hambre. Después *ir* a la escuela. A veces *olvidar* mis libros y *tener* que correr porque no *querer* llegar tarde.

[1] There are words in this exercise which will have to be changed to the feminine if a girl answers.

Black Star

Smartly dressed young people of San José, Costa Rica, meet at teatime at a roof garden. It is considered correct for ladies not to wear hats in public in many Latin-American countries.

Cuando la profesora *pasar* lista, *contestar*, — Servidor. — La profesora *decir* que *ser* un buen alumno, a veces.

Al mediodía (*noon*) *volver* a casa para almorzar. Por la tarde *estudiar* más en la escuela, y después *jugar* al tenis con mis amigos. A las seis y media *comer* con buen apetito con mis padres y mis hermanos. Después éstos y yo *estudiar* nuestras lecciones, o todos *ir* al cine.

Así *pasar* el día.

IV. Change the story to Nuestro día, *using the proper forms of the verbs.*

V. Describe your day in Spanish without referring to the story.

VI. Give the first person singular and polite commands, singular and plural, of the following verbs. The ones starred do not follow the rule, and you may have to look them up.

poner, tener, contestar, correr, ver, comprar, salir, pagar*, buscar*, ir*, ser*, dar*

VII. Here are some bits of more or less serious advice! *Change the infinitives to the polite commands.*

Consejos para jóvenes

1. *Dormir* nueve horas.
2. No *hablar* mientras come.
3. No *poner* libros en el suelo.
4. Nunca *correr* en la casa.
5. *Estudiar* sus lecciones.
6. Siempre *comer* bien.
7. No *jugar* en la escuela.
8. No *olvidar* sus libros.
9. *Conservar* la salud (*health*).
10. *Tener* cuidado en la calle.
11. *Comer* con buen apetito.
12. *Volver* a casa a veces.
13. *Dar* la mano a sus amigos.
14. No *entrar* por la ventana.
15. No *dormir* en la clase.
16. *Ser* cortés con los grandes.
17. *Contestar* siempre, — A sus órdenes.

REPASITO

I. Complete in Spanish, being careful of the agreement of the adjectives (§ 103):

1. Aprenden *some* de nuestras costumbres. 2. Todos quieren ser *courteous.* 3. Contestamos a una carta *old.* 4. Escribo la *new* lección por *first* vez. 5. Creo que la *old* costumbre es muy *curious.* 6. Vivimos en la *same* ciudad. 7. Conservan *all* las costumbres.

II. Use the adjectives at the left to complete the sentences.

rojo	1. La casa es ——.
blanco	2. Escribimos la carta en papel ——.
azul	3. La casa tiene puertas ——.
negro	4. El mapa del país no es ——.
verde	5. El libro y el papel son ——.
amarillo	6. En la ciudad hay edificios y casas ——.
morado (*purple*)	7. La bandera y la pluma son ——.
azul, blanco	8. La bandera —— y —— es de Guatemala.

III. Complete in English (§ 103):

1. An adjective which modifies two masculine nouns must be —— ——. 2. An adjective which modifies two feminine nouns must be —— ——. 3. An adjective which modifies both a masculine and a feminine noun must be —— ——.

ESTUDIO DE PALABRAS

I. Spanish words which look like their English equivalents are called *cognates*. The Spanish endings ***-dad*** and ***-tad*** often correspond to the English *-ty*. *What do these cognates mean?*

atrocidad	nacionalidad	crueldad	curiosidad	habilidad
puntualidad	adversidad	unidad	sociedad	ciudad
libertad	majestad	prosperidad	oportunidad	formalidad

II. These words and their opposites were used in the reading. *What are the opposites?*

ir, ninguno, diferente, preguntar, llamar, nunca, menos, recibir

III. Make a list of courteous expressions found in the reading and practice using them.

PARA PRONUNCIAR

Can you understand this murdered "King's English"?
"Wassatchoogot?"
"Bookapotry fringlish."
"J'bring yurol jometry book?"
"Cudnfinditenny where. Jeechet?" [1]
"Notchet. Cmon, lesgogitta hoddog."

Startling as this example may seem, the idea we get from it is that people, in any language, do not space words as they are written, but in talking run them together more or less smoothly. Of course, a cultured pronunciation will not carry this linking and omission of letters to such an extreme, but it is always done to a certain extent.

When we speak or read Spanish, then, we must remember not to say, *la-persona-que-escribe-o-que-habla,* but *lapersona quescribeo quehabla.* When one word ends with a vowel and the next begins with a vowel, we must be especially careful to "link" them (even "overlap" them when they are the

[1] "Did you eat yet?"

Black Star

Mexican men in *charro* costume greet each other with the typical enthusiastic *abrazo*. Note the beautifully gold-embroidered costume of the gentleman in the background.

same) so that our Spanish pronunciation will be smooth. Our division of words into syllables as we pronounce them also differs from our division as we write them, for we really say *u-na-ni-mal* for *un animal.* The proper division into syllables will be automatic if we speak smoothly; so the thing to keep especially in mind at first is to link the vowels.

These sentences will help you practice. Read each one aloud several times, linking especially all words that are joined.

1. Ana ve un animal.
2. Beba aquella agua.
3. Y ya iba a alejarse.
4. Buscaba algo que no estaba allí.

5. Nunca encuentra una amiga.

6. Cada uno ha aprendido a hacer algo.

7. ¿Qué va a hacer esa alumna?

PARA LEER SIN ESTUDIAR[1]

I. ¿Sabía Vd. esto?

Los Ángeles, California, tiene más mexicanos entre sus habitantes que cualquier otra ciudad de la América del Norte menos la capital de México. La segunda ciudad de México es Guadalajara, con una población de unas 200.000 personas, y Los Ángeles tiene más habitantes mexicanos que Guadalajara.

II. Un chiste

El jefe (*boss*) — Venga Vd. acá (*here*).

El trabajador (*workman*) — ¿Qué quiere Vd.?

El jefe — Dígame Vd. ¿Por qué lleva Vd. sólo una tabla (*plank*), mientras los otros trabajadores llevan dos o tres cada uno?

El trabajador — Porque ellos son perezosos (*lazy*).

El jefe — ¿Perezosos?

El trabajador — Sí, señor. No quieren hacer tantos (*as many*) viajes como yo.

TEMA[2]

If you can write these sentences correctly in Spanish, you are well prepared. Watch for expressions that are not the same in Spanish and English (***dar la mano,*** *to shake hands*). Words in parentheses are to be put in, unless they are in *italics*.

1. Mexicans are very courteous. 2. Spain teaches them to be gentlemen. 3. When they speak of a lady, they do not say, "Mrs.

[1] Note to teacher: This easy plateau section may be used throughout the course for aural drill, by reading it aloud to the pupils with their books closed and checking their comprehension either in English or Spanish.

[2] Note to teacher: This exercise is optional. The PREGUNTAS, PARA PRONUNCIAR, and PARA LEER SIN ESTUDIAR sections may take its place. Words in parentheses are to be put in, unless in italics; words in brackets are to be omitted.

García," but "doña Juana García." 4. In no other country do they give the embrace which means friendship. 5. (The) foreigners say that a Mexican child always tries to give the right-of-way to a grown-up. 6. When a person writes a letter for the first time, he ends it, "Very sincerely yours." 7. My house is on so-and-so street. (*Express it the Spanish way.*) 8. This expression gives a proof of hospitality and (of) courtesy. 9. We Americans do not always shake hands. 10. Sometimes this (***esto***) seems very strange to (the) foreigners.

CAPÍTULO 3

Alumnos de los Estados Unidos

Spanish-speaking young people are curious about our lives just as we are about theirs, and this article, from a newspaper often read in Mexico, tells them about our elementary-school day. You will notice that the article is friendly, but not entirely accurate, which should make you realize that all you read about other countries may not be accurate either.

What customs do you find mentioned as being of interest because they are different from those in Mexican schools? Remember that there are many private schools in Spanish-speaking countries, some for boys and some for girls, for usually both do not attend the same school above the fourth grade.

Estamos en Chicago. Bob, el pequeño Bob, rubio, con los ojos azules, ha venido corriendo por la calle y ha encontrado a su amiga, Hazel.

Los dos gritan de alegría. No se han visto desde el viernes,

Black Star

Modern high school for girls in Mexico City uses the best of equipment in the geography classroom. Boys and girls are taught in separate classes.

y los niños norteamericanos,[1] que sienten como nadie (*no one else*) la felicidad de vivir (*joy of living*), la demuestran a cada instante.[2]

— Buenos días, Bob, — dice Hazel.[3] — Hemos llegado muy temprano. Aún no ha sonado la campana.

— ¡Tanto mejor! ¿Sabes? ¡Tengo un *job*!

«*Job*» es el nombre que se da en los Estados Unidos a todo pequeño trabajo remunerado (*paid*).

— ¿Sí? ¿Cuál es?

— Tengo que repartir (*deliver*) doce botellas de leche con mi bicicleta entre las siete y las ocho de la mañana.

— ¡Qué buena suerte! Mi hermano Jimmy también tiene un *job* para mañana. Si nieva esta tarde, mañana va a

[1] Notice that they call us *norteamericanos*, because in Spanish *americano* is generally used to mean a native of a Spanish American country.

[2] It's too bad, but we are known all over the world for our shrill voices and general noisiness. Spanish-speaking children are quieter on the street than American boys and girls.

[3] Would you speak so formally? They actually do!

limpiar banquetas (*sidewalks*) entre las ocho y las nueve. ¡Veinte y cinco centavos por hora! ¿Qué van Vds.[1] a hacer con tanto dinero?

— Vamos al cine el sábado. Tú puedes ir con nosotros.

De todas partes llegan los chicos a la escuela pública, la escuela gratuita (*free*), donde se educan (*are educated*) hasta los catorce años[2] todos los niños, ricos o pobres, de los Estados Unidos.

La escuela es blanca, con ventanas grandes. Está rodeada (*surrounded*) de magníficos jardines, con canchas (*courts*) de tenis, campo de fútbol y praderas (*lawns*) verdes. Parece un sanatorio.[3]

Todos los chicos se conocen desde el primer año de sus estudios, y al encontrarse tiran al aire alegremente sus

[1] The plural familiar, *vosotros*, is used only formally in Spanish America, and so *ustedes* serves as plural for both familiar and polite forms.

[2] *Catorce años* is the limit of compulsory education in their schools, not ours, for ours extends to eighteen years in some states.

[3] Did you ever think that your school with all its windows might look like a sanatorium to a foreigner?

Mexican schools, except the new ones, are often heavy, squat stone buildings with fewer windows than ours. The school yard is inside the patio, and may have little play equipment except basketball standards.

Learning to sew in a Mexico City girls' school presents the same problems as it does with us.

Black Star

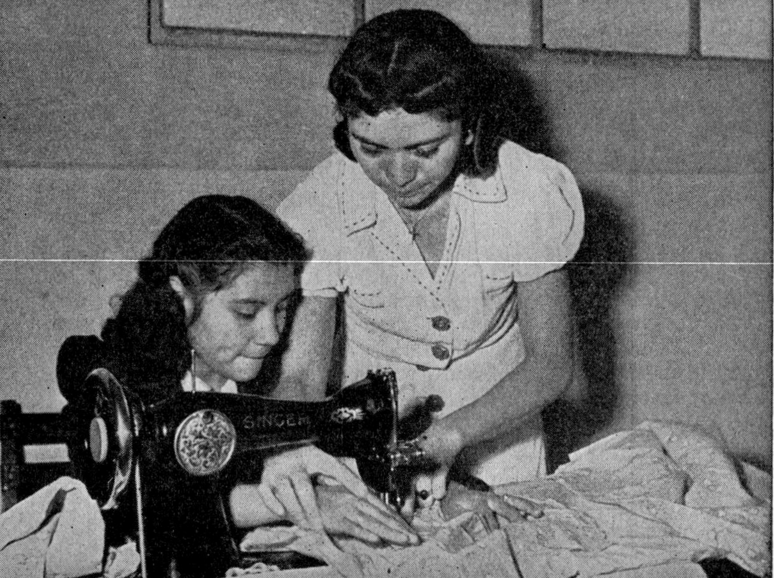

Black Star

Physiology lesson in a modern boys' school in Mexico City finds war posters competing with anatomy diagrams.

carteras.[1] Son las nueve menos cinco. Suena la campana. ¡Están preparados! Las nueve. Las puertas de la escuela están abiertas. Los niños entran en fila (*line*), y cada uno va con su clase.

Comienza la lección de literatura inglesa, composición y gramática. Cada alumno habla cinco minutos. Pasan cincuenta minutos. ¡A jugar!

Las diez. Otra vez la campana. Ahora comienza la lección de trabajo manual. En los Estados Unidos se considera el trabajo manual como una necesidad para la persona educada. Chicos y chicas son obreros (*workmen*) hábiles. Sus manos, que saben manejar (*handle*) la herramienta (*tools*) del carpintero, no son suaves y delicadas como las (*those*) de los niños europeos, sino ásperas (*rough*), fuertes y morenas.

Después del trabajo manual aún hay otra hora de clase, y

[1] Pupils in Spanish-speaking countries carry ***carteras*** (*briefcases*) or small satchels to school, containing their books, pencils, and papers, for they must furnish all their own supplies and have no lockers or desk space in which to leave them at school. The writer imagines that American pupils carry briefcases, too!

Black Star

Print shop in a Mexican boys' school teaches a practical trade as well as the "three R's."

a las doce menos diez salen de la escuela cientos de alumnos que corren a sus casas a tomar el *lunch.* A las dos [1] comienzan otra vez las clases. Se dan la geografía, historia, y aritmética, y más tarde, la mecanografía (*typing*) y estenografía (*shorthand*).[2]

Cuando dan las cuatro, las clases terminan. Si quieren, los alumnos pueden jugar una hora o más al tenis o al fútbol.

A las seis todos se despiden hasta el día siguiente, que es martes. Todos vuelven a casa, porque no hay alumnos internos (*boarding*) [3] en las escuelas de los Estados Unidos. Los padres y los hermanos mayores han vuelto a casa y los esperan para comer. Todos están contentos de encontrarse juntos después del trabajo del día.

ADAPTED FROM *La Opinión* (LOS ANGELES)

[1] Two hours for lunch! They have borrowed our word, but not our custom, for in Spanish-speaking countries people go home at midday for a leisurely meal. The writer apparently hasn't heard about our cold sandwiches and haste!

[2] It looks as if the writer has confused high school and grammar school here.

[3] Private institutions in Spanish-speaking countries are usually boarding schools where the pupils live for the whole term.

Find These Expressions in the Story

1. who feel the joy of living like no one else 2. all the children are educated up to fourteen years 3. At six o'clock they all say good-by until the following day 4. hand work is considered a necessity 5. The bell hasn't rung yet. 6. When it strikes four, the classes end. 7. between seven and eight A.M. 8. All are happy to be together 9. Children (young folks) are arriving from everywhere 10. upon meeting each other they throw into the air 11. hundreds of pupils leave school 12. Twenty-five cents an hour!

PALABRAS NUEVAS

1	**aún**	still, yet	3	**maestro**	teacher
	bicicleta	bicycle		**moreno**	brown
4	**campana**	bell	2	**necesidad**	necessity
2	**comenzar** (ie)	to commence		**nevar** (ie)	to snow
2	**fuerte**	strong	4	**rubio**	blond
	guapo	handsome	3	**sonar** (ue)	to ring
	hábil	skilled	3	**suave**	soft

EXPRESIONES

de alegría, for joy **por hora,** an hour **trabajo manual,** manual training

PARA COMPLETAR

1. Los niños americanos gritan de ——. 2. Algunos alumnos mexicanos no —— a casa todos los días porque —— en la escuela. 3. Al salir de la escuela, los alumnos —— —— hasta otro día. 4. No tenemos carteras (*briefcases*) porque no —— a casa todos nuestros —— y ——. 5. Los españoles creen que —— —— deben ser suaves y delicadas. 6. Muchos muchachos de nuestro país reparten (*deliver*) —— de leche por la mañana antes de —— a la escuela. 7. Pocos alumnos mexicanos son —— con los —— azules. 8. Los (*those*) que trabajan antes de ir a la escuela ganan —— centavos —— hora. 9. Con —— dinero, pueden ir al —— el sábado.

PREGUNTAS

1. ¿Dónde vive el pequeño Bob? 2. ¿Por qué gritan los dos niños? 3. ¿Qué trabajo tiene Bob con su bicicleta? 4. Describa Vd. la escuela de Hazel y Bob. 5. ¿Qué van a hacer los niños con tanto dinero? 6. ¿Por qué se conocen todos los niños? 7. ¿Qué llevan los alumnos mexicanos en sus carteras (*briefcases*)? 8. ¿Cuántos años tiene Vd. que asistir a la escuela? 9. ¿A qué hora se despiden los niños? 10. ¿Corre Vd. a casa a tomar el *lunch*? 11. ¿Qué nombre se da a todo pequeño trabajo? 12. ¿Estudia Vd. la estenografía (*shorthand*)?

REPASO DE VERBOS

I. Review the verbs which change the stem vowel **e** *to* **i** *in the present tense* (§ 88). *To what conjugation do they all belong? Conjugate orally:*

pedir, servir, vestir, seguir; poder, querer; sentir

First aid instruction has become very popular in the up-to-date schools of Mexico.

Black Star

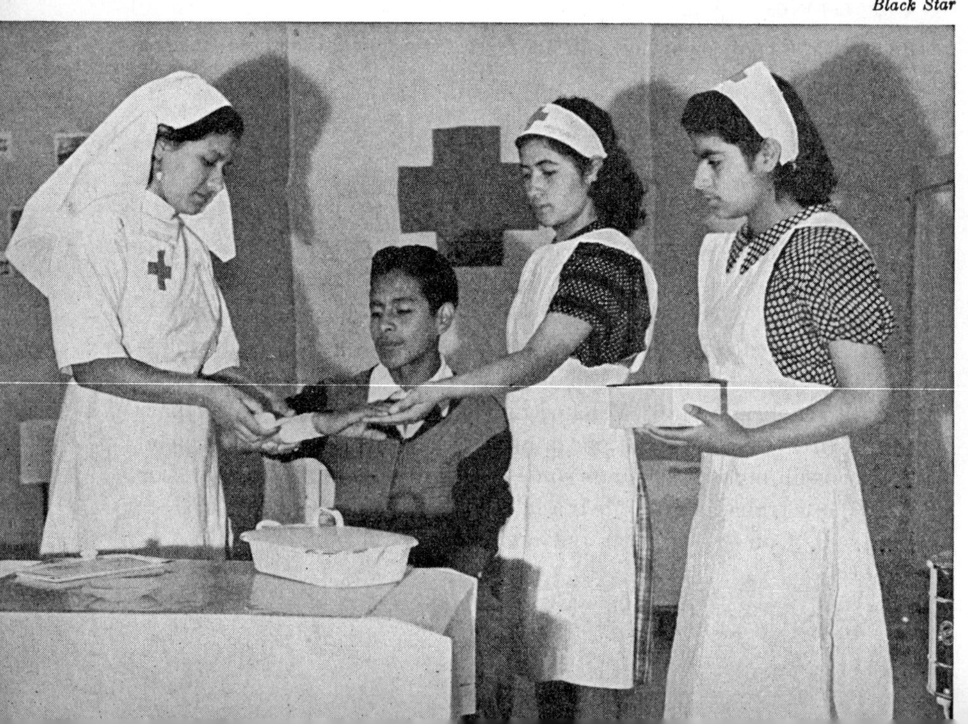

II. Review the reflexive pronouns in section 107. Conjugate in the present tense the verbs **levantarse, encontrarse,** *and* **despedirse.**

III. Among the irregular verbs listed beginning with section 63, find and review the present tense of:

estar, decir, venir, hacer, saber

IV. Translate the following forms of the verbs you have reviewed; then make the first ten plural:

1. pido
2. viste
3. Vd. sirve
4. me levanto
5. ¡levántese Vd.!
6. se encuentra
7. estoy
8. ella dice
9. vienes
10. hago
11. vengan Vds.
12. hacen
13. ¿dicen Vds.?
14. nos levantamos
15. se despiden

V. Review the present perfect tense in section 62 and irregular past participles in section 96; then complete these verb forms and translate:

1. *we have* leído
2. *they have* puesto
3. *I have* dicho
4. *he has* hecho
5. *you have* escrito
6. han *returned*
7. yo he *opened*
8. ha *seen*
9. ellas han *fallen*
10. hemos *seen*
11. han *read*
12. ¿ha *made* Vd.?

VI. Read this story, replacing the italicized infinitives with the proper present perfect tense verb forms, using the first person unless some other is indicated.

Mi vida

Vivir una vida activa. Siempre *tener* buena salud. *Pasar* la vida feliz porque nunca *estar* enfermo(-a). Siempre *comer* con buen apetito, tres veces al día.

Estudiar mucho en la escuela y *jugar* mucho los sábados. *Jugar* al tenis y al fútbol, y *tomar* lecciones de música.

Leer muchos libros y *escribir* muchos temas. La profesora me *decir* muchas veces, — Vd. *preparar* bien la lección.

Pero algunas veces *ser* un(-a) mal(-a) muchacho(-a). *Ir* al cine en vez de estudiar, y *tener* que quedarme después de la clase para terminar un ejercicio.

Así *pasar* mi vida hasta ahora.

ALGO NUEVO

1. Reciprocal Verbs

se han visto, *they have seen each other*
al encontrarse, *upon meeting each other*
se conocen, *they know each other*

Reflexive pronouns in the plural (*nos, os, se*) often have the meaning *each other* or *to each other* or *one another,* as you found in the reading.

EJERCICIO I. *Put into Spanish, following the models:*

1. We see each other.
2. You (*pl.*) know each other.
3. They meet each other.
4. We write to each other.
5. They speak to each other.
6. You (*pl.*) write to each other.

2. Review of Ser *and* Estar

EJERCICIO II. *Review the uses of* **ser** *and* **estar** *as outlined in section 122; then complete the following conversation, choosing* **es** *or* **está** *in each case, and justifying your choice:*

UN AMIGO NUEVO

— ¿Quién *is* aquel muchacho que *is* en su casa?
— *He is* mi amigo Alberto.
— ¿Dónde *is* su amigo ahora?
— *He is* en casa.
— *¿Is he* de España? (See § 123)
— No, *he is* de México.
— *¿Is he* un buen muchacho?
— Sí, y *he is* simpático también.
— *¿Is he* rubio?
— No, *he is* alto, moreno, y guapo.
— *¿Is he* cansado y enfermo?
— No, *he is* muy bien, gracias.
— *¿Is he* triste hoy?
— No, *he is* muy contento, como siempre.
— Entonces no *he is* viejo y pobre, ¿eh?

—— No, *he is* joven y rico, y tiene un nuevo automóvil con radio y todo.

—— ¡Ay, qué amigo tan bueno! Me gustaría muchísimo conocerle si tiene un automóvil con radio y todo. Vd. me invita a su casa a verle, ¿eh?

—— Con todo gusto.

3. New Uses of Ser

The major uses of ***ser*** which you have not had are these (§ 123):

Es de Chile. *He is from Chile.* (origin)
Es de oro, de papel. *It is of gold, of paper.* (material)
Es de Pedro. *It is Peter's.* (ownership)

EJERCICIO III. *Complete these sentences in Spanish, explaining why you use* **ser** *or* **estar.** (Where is the word *it*?)

El pupitre (*desk*) *is* de madera y hierro (*iron*). *It is* de la escuela. *It is* nuevo y bonito. *It is* para los alumnos de la clase.

It is cerca de la puerta. *It is* bastante grande. *It isn't* todo de madera. Una parte *is* de hierro. *It is* en el suelo; *it isn't* en el techo (*ceiling*). *It is* mío ahora.

Outdoor calisthenics for Mexico's physical fitness program have been popular in the schools for many years.

4. New Use of Estar

Los niños están preparados, *the children are prepared.*

In the reading you found *estar* used with a past participle to describe a condition. The past participle is then an adjective, and must agree with the subject of *estar* (§ 124–2).

EJERCICIO IV. *Complete in Spanish and explain each use of estar:*

1. Los libros *are written* en inglés. 2. Las ventanas *are open* por la noche. 3. La puerta *is closed* por la mañana. 4. La pluma *is broken* ahora. 5. La clase siempre *is prepared.* 6. La casa *is built* **(construir)** de madera. 7. La carta *is written* en buen papel.

EJERCICIO V. *Play the game called «¿Quién es o dónde está?»* One pupil leaves the room while the rest choose someone in the class to describe. The pupil who is "it," on returning to the room, asks either — *¿Quién es?* — or — *¿Dónde está?* —, and each pupil in turn must answer with a short sentence describing the pupil chosen. The last one to give a sentence before "it" guesses the correct answer then becomes "it."

5. Numbers, Days, and Months

EJERCICIO VI. *Obey these commands as you are called upon:*

1. Díganos Vd. la fecha de hoy (§ 101). 2. Diga Vd. los nombres de los días de la semana (§ 101). 3. Nombre Vd. los meses del año (§ 101). 4. Cuente Vd. de diez en diez hasta ciento (§ 100). 5. Cuente Vd. de ciento en ciento hasta mil (§ 100). 6. Mire Vd. el reloj y díganos la hora (§ 102). 7. Escriba Vd. la fecha de su cumpleaños. 8. Dénos Vd. el número de su casa, de su teléfono, o de sus zapatos. (**Número** means *size* as well as *number!*) 9. Díganos Vd. cuántos años tiene. 10. Díganos Vd. a qué hora se levanta por la mañana (§ 102).

EJERCICIO VII. *Diga Vd. en español con mucho cuidado* (§§ 101–102):

1. 200 public schools
2. 500 large classes
3. 700 good days
4. it is six o'clock sharp
5. on Thursday, Oct. 2nd
6. at ten minutes till two
7. on Sundays and Mondays
8. at ten-thirty sharp

ESTUDIO DE PALABRAS

I. You have probably noticed that the Spanish word endings ***-ía*** or ***-ia*** (***-io***) often correspond to the English endings *-y* or *-e,* and that the Spanish ending ***-ción*** means *-tion.*

What do these words mean?

providencia, infancia, astrología, constancia, historia, importancia, diccionario, estenografía, paciencia, lotería, colonia, ordinario, misterio, ración, corrupción, cultivación, inscripción, proporción, economía, acción, exploración, civilización, animación, puntuación, revolución, satisfacción, información, condición, aviación, comunicación, amplificación, sección, estación, dirección

II. Among these words find for each one an opposite or a synonym, or both:

pequeño	entrar en	enviar	noche	caerse
alegre	temprano	todavía	tarde	moreno
contento	enseñar	fuerte	poco	recibir
dar	volver	aún	terminar	ir
mucho	día	delicado	rubio	grande
mismo	joven	salir de	comenzar	diferente
aprender	levantarse	viejo	chico	

PARA PRONUNCIAR

I. Complete these statements (§ 135):

1. The sound of ***c*** before ***e*** and ***i*** is ——. 2. The sound of ***c*** elsewhere is ——. 3. The sound of ***z*** is always ——. 4. The sound of ***g*** before ***e*** and ***i*** is ——. 5. The sound of ***g*** elsewhere is ——. 6. The sound of ***j*** is always ——. 7. The sound of ***h*** is always ——.

II. Practice these words until you can pronounce them without hesitation. (Never mind their meanings!)

general, alhaja, generoso, cancela, gatazo, zozobra, gelatina, zanja, canalizo, gentil, cincel, almohada, gitano, ángel, goma, gimnasio, honorable, giro, hocicada, cenizas, hojalata, genial, zapatazo, ciudad, cuidado, ahijado

PARA LEER SIN ESTUDIAR

El hijo del indio

Un indio lleva a la escuela a su hijo pequeño, y dice al maestro, — Mi hijo Juanito quiere asistir a su escuela.

— Bueno, — contesta el maestro. — ¿Sabe leer el niño?

— Ni una letra, — responde el indio.

— ¿Sabe escribir su nombre?

— No sabe escribir nada.

— Entonces, amigo mío, — dice el maestro, — como no sabe nada, y es mucho trabajo enseñarle todo esto, tengo que cobrarle a Vd. (*charge you*) doce pesos.

— ¡Ay, caray! — exclama el indio. — Es mucho dinero. ¡Por doce pesos puedo comprar un burro!

— Pues, entonces, — dice el maestro, — compre Vd. ese burro, y ¡con éste tiene dos![1]

TEMA[2]

Escriba Vd. en español con mucho cuidado:

1. Today is Friday, Sept. 21, 19—. 2. It is 3:30 P.M., and I have to go (*return*) home to meet (**a**) my friends. 3. My watch is (of) gold, and my automobile is of many metals. 4. The radio is new and is my father's. 5. It is near the window, which is closed now. 6. The radio is of brown wood and has a clock that strikes the hour[s]. 7. When it strikes nine, we arrive from everywhere. 8. We have all known one another since (the) [age of] six years. 9. We have often gone to the movies instead of studying. 10. Our (***nuestras***) hands are not soft and delicate, but strong and brown.

[1] This is a pun, for a person who is "dumb" is called «***burro***».

[2] Words in brackets are to be omitted.

Spain in America

Texas' historic shrine, the Alamo Mission, was built to consolidate Spain's holdings in the north, and still lends its old Spanish atmosphere to bustling San Antonio's skyscrapers.

Galloway

COLUMBUS never knew what he had started.

Other explorers quickly followed his example and like him claimed territory for Spain in the New World. Three things led them tirelessly on — their desire for gold, for glory, and for spreading the gospel; so adventurers, soldiers, and priests made up the first great migration of Spaniards to the West, to be followed much later by settlers who brought their families to stay.

Since Columbus had landed originally in the West Indies, those palm-fringed tropical islands were the first to be explored and settled. So many Spanish galleons sailed to this Caribbean and Gulf area in their search for treasure that it is sometimes called the "Spanish Main," although the name properly refers to the mainland instead of to the sea.

Cuba and Santo Domingo — the latter called Hispaniola by Columbus — became the Spanish headquarters, and after Balboa had struggled across the jungles of Panama to discover the Pacific Ocean, the Isthmus, too, became a base for further discoveries.

It was less than three decades after Columbus' first voyage that rumors of Aztec treasure sent Cortés out from Cuba to conquer Mexico, and the amount of wealth that this conquest contributed to Spain surpassed even the wildest dreams of the expedition. Encouraged by such success, Alvarado slashed his way through the

Oldest house in the United States, St. Augustine, Florida, was built thirty-six years before English settlers landed at Jamestown. This was the eastern terminal of Spain's *Camino real.*

Sawders

jungle south of Mexico to conquer the Mayan tribes of Guatemala, while at the same time conquering Spanish armies went north from Panama into the rest of Central America. Pizarro, then living in Panama, turned south to conquer the Inca Empire of Peru, and soon two continents — three Americas — had acquired the Spanish heritage in language, architecture, religion, and customs, that makes them what they are today.

The North American mainland was the last section to be settled, although about the time that Balboa had reached Panama, Ponce de León had led some two hundred men to Florida in an attempt to found the first colony on the northern mainland. He was driven off by the fierce natives, and it was not until almost a half century later that St. Augustine, our oldest city, was finally founded by the Spaniards.

Mexico City, after its conquest by Cortés, replaced Cuba and Santo Domingo as the New World base for Spain, and northward from that capital the tide of exploration flowed to follow rumors of more wealth yet to be found. Thousands of small bands of men, their names now all but forgotten, came to the New World with their medieval firearms, a few horses, and some fierce fighting dogs, financing their own travels and hoping for gold and glory, but dutifully claiming for their king the territory they charted. Often

Oldest complete fortification of our country is Ft. Marion, at St. Augustine. Spaniards spent a hundred years building it, and it has never been taken in siege, although it has known four flags.

Sawders

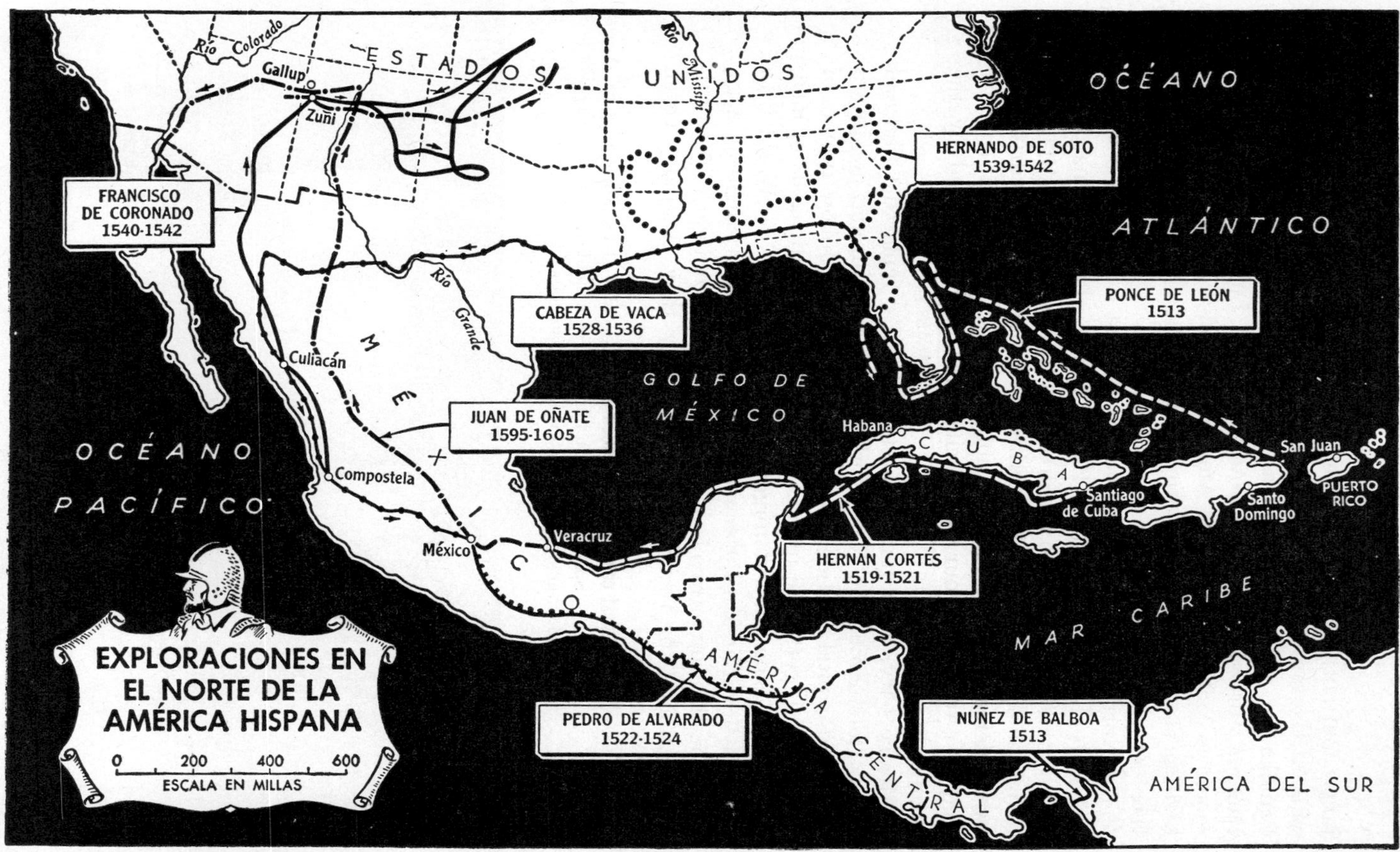
EXPLORACIONES EN EL NORTE DE LA AMÉRICA HISPANA
0
200
400
600
ESCALA EN MILLAS
OCÉANO ATLÁNTICO
OCÉANO PACÍFICO
GOLFO DE MÉXICO
MAR CARIBE
ESTADOS UNIDOS
MÉXICO
CUBA
AMÉRICA CENTRAL
AMÉRICA DEL SUR
Río Colorado
Gallup
Zuñi
Río Misisipí
Río Grande
Culiacán
Compostela
México
Veracruz
Habana
Santiago de Cuba
Santo Domingo
San Juan
PUERTO RICO
FRANCISCO DE CORONADO 1540-1542
HERNANDO DE SOTO 1539-1542
CABEZA DE VACA 1528-1536
PONCE DE LEÓN 1513
JUAN DE OÑATE 1595-1605
HERNÁN CORTÉS 1519-1521
PEDRO DE ALVARADO 1522-1524
NÚÑEZ DE BALBOA 1513

rumors led them on fruitless quests, and even Coronado with his great expedition, after exploring our country as far north as present-day Kansas, returned to Mexico City broken and disheartened because he had found no treasure in his two-year journey.

As these bands of men brought in their reports, patient priests went out over the same rough trails to carry the gospel to the Indians, and with them hardy colonists rode into the dusty wilderness on horseback and in oxcarts, driving their sheep and cattle before them.

It was then that St. Augustine, Florida, settled fifty-five years before the Pilgrims landed at Plymouth Rock, became the eastern terminal of the *camino real* which was to stretch across a continent. Santa Fe, New Mexico, founded eleven years before Plymouth Rock, was long the northern terminal of the *camino real* over which great pack trains from Mexico City brought supplies to the settlers and carried back products for Spain. San Antonio, Texas, was founded to protect the middle-western section of Spain's great holdings from the French who were threatening to encroach upon it from New Orleans. In all these cities and many others one still finds many signs of their Spanish heritage which even modern developments have not erased.

Then westward the tide of settlers flowed, and California, an almost desert country that blossomed at the touch of water, became a land of plenty for the Spanish aristocrats who traveled north from Mexico City to establish their great ranchos. Twenty-one adobe missions were built along the Pacific Coast to consolidate Spain's position in the West as well as to save the souls of the primitive California Indians. These missions became centers of culture, where the weary traveler was always welcome and where Spanish colonial life was at its pleasantest. Ships from Mexico relayed luxuries brought from Spain for the wealthy ranchers, and although the "latest styles" had often been a year or more on the way from Madrid, what did it matter to the happy Californians?

All during those colonial days, Mexico City was the heart of the New World on the North American mainland, and through that capital went all the trade and commerce of the vast territory united by the well-worn *camino real.* When, long afterward, the Mexican flag finally replaced the Spanish one, so well established was the Spanish heritage that little in the distant outposts was disturbed.

Then from the east came the descendants of the English colonists

Galloway

Olvera Street, Los Angeles, keeps its historic adobe houses and brick cellars as they were when the Dons and their damsels danced, although the many *puestos* remind one of modern Mexico.

Famous Spanish-Moorish courthouse of Santa Barbara, California, commemorates the romantic past of the once Spanish city. All new buildings must conform to the Spanish style of architecture of the early days.

Galloway

whose Anglo-Saxon civilization swept across the continent, replacing at last the Spanish rule from coast to coast. But to this day along the old *camino real* there still remains much to color our lives, as it does the lives of all Americans — North, South, and Central. Even now most of the names on the map of the entire Western Hemisphere are Spanish, and even across the United States one can trace the one-time possessions of Spain by the Spanish names that testify to the great chain of events started by one Christopher Columbus.

The next two chapters give you two pictures of those early Spanish days in our own country. Then in the following chapters you jump hundreds of years to stories of recent travels — that you might have made yourself — in modern Mexico and Guatemala, where modern civilization mingles happily with old Spanish colonial culture.

Interesting Books to Read

Conquistadores: RICHMAN, IRVING B.: THE SPANISH CONQUERORS. Yale University Press. (*History*) — BOLTON, HERBERT E.: THE SPANISH BORDERLANDS. (*History*)

New Mexico: OTERO, NINA: OLD SPAIN IN OUR SOUTHWEST. Harcourt, Brace. (*Quaint Spanish customs still in use*) — FERGUSSON, ERNA: OUR SOUTHWEST. Knopf. (*History and description*)

California: JACKSON, HELEN HUNT: RAMONA. Little, Brown. (*Fiction*) — BARTLETT, LANIER *and* VIRGINIA: ADIÓS. Morrow. (*Fiction*)

Lower California: FIERRO BLANCO, ANTONIO DE: THE JOURNEY OF THE FLAME. Houghton Mifflin. (*Fiction disguised as autobiography*)

CAPÍTULO 4

El misterio del norte

The Spanish explorers had sent so much gold back to Spain from Mexico and Peru that everyone was a little dizzy, and one expedition after another started out to look for more bonanzas farther to the north. Narváez, who headed an expedition to Florida that missed the boat back to Cuba, tried to make his way with his men along the coast to Mexico, which was supposed to be not far away. Of these travelers on this first transcontinental expedition along *El camino real*, only four survived: Cabeza de Vaca, the Moor Estebanico, and two others.

But these four had heard among the Indians some talk of gold to the north, and Cabeza de Vaca reported it to Viceroy Mendoza of Mexico City, who promptly encouraged Coronado to head an expedition to the unknown territory. Estebanico and Fray Marcos de Niza were to be the guides, but Estebanico had such a good time being a "big shot" among the Indians that he "got his signals mixed," and although pious Fray Marcos was sure he actually saw seven mysterious cities from a distance, what Coronado found when he got there was — well, read about the "mystery of the north"!

— ¡Siete ciudades hay, y todas de oro!

— ¡Siete ciudades hay, cada una tan grande como Sevilla!

— ¡Tienen casas de cinco pisos, con paredes de plata! [1]

— ¡Las calles son de oro, y todas las puertas son azules porque están cubiertas de turquesas!

— ¡Los indios andan por las calles vestidos de oro y la cabeza cubierta de adornos de oro!

— ¡Hasta los juguetes (*toys*) de los niños son de oro!

[1] One of Cortés' soldiers, during the conquest of Mexico years before, had been kidded when he excitedly reported that the Aztec houses were of silver, when what he actually saw was the sun shining on whitewashed adobe walls.

Todos los habitantes de la Nueva España[1] hablaban del misterio del norte.

Cabeza de Vaca había iniciado (*started*) los rumores, después de su famoso viaje a pie de la Florida a México.[2] Los indios le habían hablado de unos pueblos al norte donde había muchas riquezas. Pero Cabeza de Vaca nunca había visto las siete ciudades fantásticas.

En aquellos días era fácil creer rumores, y todos estaban listos (*ready*) para creer cualquier cosa. Pero todo era un gran misterio. Nadie sabía si de veras existían o no las siete ciudades maravillosas.

Entonces el Virrey (*Viceroy*) Mendoza, esperando hacerse rico y ganar la buena voluntad (*will*) del Rey de España, enviándole aún más riquezas, nombró a Francisco Vásquez de Coronado como capitán de una expedición. Con trescientos soldados, jóvenes de sangre noble, salió Coronado en busca

[1] New Spain was all of Mexico and all the territory north of it and west of the Mississippi, plus Florida.

[2] The first question they asked when they met their countrymen was, "What year is this?" only to find that they had been seven years on the road.

Modern Zuñi village of adobe looked to Fray Marcos de Niza four hundred years ago like one of the mysterious seven cities of Cíbola, with their "silver walls and turquoise doors."

Keystone

(*search*) de fama y fortuna. Le acompañó Fray Marcos de Niza, que había estado con Pizarro en el Perú, y como guía (*guide*) e intérprete (*interpreter*) de la expedición fué (*went*) Estebanico, el moro que había acompañado a Cabeza de Vaca en su viaje de siete años.

Llegados a Culiacán los españoles, Coronado mandó adelante a Fray Marcos y a Estebanico para buscar señas (*signs*) de la tierra rica que esperaban encontrar. Más tarde, Fray Marcos, que creía más que nadie en los rumores del oro, mandó más adelante a Estebanico. Al tener cualquier noticia de las riquezas que todos esperaban, este Estebanico debía enviar al padre una cruz. El tamaño (*size*) de esta cruz debía indicar la importancia del descubrimiento (*discovery*).

Este Estebanico había recibido tantas atenciones al llegar a la capital con Cabeza de Vaca que se creía muy importante. Vestido en una túnica (*robe*) roja con plumas de colores y campanillas de oro en los brazos y las piernas, se creía rey de los indios. Caminando a caballo, todo el día tenía música de flautas (*flutes*), tambores (*drums*) y chirimías (*pipes*) que sus indios tocaban para divertirle. Llevaba consigo una maraca (*gourd rattle*) cubierta de campanillas y plumas blancas y rojas. Esta maraca la usaba como emblema de su autoridad, y al llegar a un pueblo indio, la mandaba al jefe (*chief*) con sus exigencias (*demands*). En cada pueblo hacía el amor a las indias jóvenes y bonitas, e iba haciendo una colección de turquesas, conchas (*shells*), y pieles (*furs*) ricas.

Un día Fray Marcos de Niza recibió de Estebanico una cruz grande como un hombre, indicando que el moro había hallado riquezas enormes, y que Fray Marcos y Coronado debían seguirle inmediatamente. Salieron Fray Marcos y sus soldados, pero en pocos días, antes de poder alcanzar (*overtake*) al moro, recibieron la noticia de que los indios de las siete ciudades le habían muerto.[1]

Pero el valiente padre siguió adelante hasta llegar a un punto (*point*) desde donde podía ver a lo lejos las siete ciudades en una altura (*height*). Entonces volvió a Culiacán, donde

[1] Some say that his gourd rattle may have meant bad luck to those superstitious Indians, which certainly was unlucky for Estebanico.

Monkmeyer

Indian church of Isleta, New Mexico, was built over three hundred years ago by early Spanish settlers who followed Coronado's trail.

estaba Coronado, creyendo que el misterio se había resuelto.

Pero, ¿era verdad? Coronado y sus soldados siguieron a caballo por el desierto hasta llegar a las ciudades. ¡Cuál fué (*was*) su desilusión (*disappointment*) al encontrar sólo siete pueblos de adobe, en vez de siete ciudades de oro![1] Lo único de valor era el maíz (*corn*) que tenían los indios, y éste, para los soldados hambrientos (*hungry*), valía casi tanto como el oro que estaban buscando.

Fray Marcos, deshonrado y triste, volvió a México. Los dos, él y Estebanico, lo habían imaginado todo.

Adelante, siempre adelante, seguía caminando Coronado, creyendo siempre que pronto encontraría (*he would find*) las riquezas. Pero al fin se declaró vencido, y volvió a México, triste, enfermo, deshonrado.

El misterio del norte esta vez se había resuelto, y los rumores del oro habían resultado falsos.[2]

[1] The "seven cities" were the Zuñi villages of New Mexico not far from Gallup, which are still there. They are referred to today as "The Seven Cities of Cíbola."

[2] Broken-hearted and dishonored, Coronado never knew how famous his name would become because of his having explored and mapped the great unknown territory as far north as what is now Kansas. The wealth he sought was there, but in oil, agriculture, hidden minerals, cattle, cotton — and in the tourist trade of those who come now to see the historical country of the *conquistadores*. Coronado and those who followed him brought so much Spanish culture with them that to this day the State Legislature of New Mexico conducts its business in both Spanish and English.

PALABRAS NUEVAS

3 **adelante**	forward	3 **fama**	fame
adorno	ornament	**leyenda**	legend
3 **autoridad**	authority	4 **misterio**	mystery
brazo	arm	3 **nombrar**	to name
4 **caminar**	to travel	3 **resolver** (ue)	to solve
4 **campanilla**	little bell	(*p.p.*, **resuelto**)	
4 **combatir**	to fight	3 **riqueza**	wealth, (*pl.*) riches
4 **capitán**	captain	3 **soldado**	soldier
1 **consigo**	with him	**turquesa**	turquoise
Culiacán	city of Sinaloa, Mexico	3 **vencer**	to conquer
deshonrado	disgraced	2 **viaje** (*m.*)	journey

EXPRESIONES

***a lo lejos,** in the distance
declararse vencido, to give up
hacer el amor a, to make love to
lo único, the only thing
llegados a, having arrived at
mandar adelante, to send on ahead

PARA COMPLETAR

1. Se dice que había —— cubiertas de turquesas. 2. Cabeza de Vaca nunca había visto las siete —— de ——. 3. El Virrey Mendoza esperaba —— rico. 4. Fray Marcos de Niza mandó —— a Estebanico. 5. Una cruz grande debía indicar que había muchas ——. 6. Estebanico iba a ——, y todo el día tenía —— para ——. 7. El valiente —— podía ver a la distancia las —— ciudades. 8. Lo único de valor que encontró Coronado fué el —— de los indios. 9. Fray Marcos de Niza volvió a México muy ——. 10. Coronado no pudo —— las riquezas, y volvió a ——. 11. Todos los rumores habían resultado ——.

PREGUNTAS

1. Describa Vd. las siete ciudades. 2. ¿Quién hizo (*made*) un viaje a pie de la Florida a México? 3. ¿Por qué hizo este viaje? 4. ¿Cuántos años duró (*lasted*) el viaje? 5. ¿Quién acompañó a Cabeza de Vaca? 6. ¿Por qué se creía Estebanico muy importante?

7. ¿Qué quería hacer el Virrey Mendoza? 8. ¿Qué buscaba Coronado en el norte? 9. ¿Qué debía Estebanico enviar a Fray Marcos? 10. Describa Vd. el viaje de Estebanico. 11. ¿Quién resolvió el misterio de las siete ciudades? 12. ¿Cómo volvió Coronado a México?

REPASO DE VERBOS

I. Review the regular verb endings for the imperfect tense in section 62, also the imperfect tense of the only three that are irregular: *ser*, *ir*, and *ver* (§§ 79, 70, 85).

1. *Conjugate orally in the imperfect:*

estar, seguir, irse, ser, llevarse, haber

2. *Find in the story five examples of the imperfect tense where it means* used to *or* was — ing, *or where the tense is used for past description.*

II. Review the past perfect (pluperfect) tense of the model verbs in section 62. In what tense is the helping verb? What does *había* always mean in the past perfect?

Conjugate in the past perfect (§ 96):

decir, cubrir, volver, ver, poner, morir, hacer

III. What do you call the verb forms *caminando, haciendo, creyendo?* What is the sign of the gerund in English? How do you form the gerund in Spanish (§ 62)? Why is *creyendo* spelled with a ***y*** instead of an ***i*** (§ 97)?

Give the gerunds, with their meanings, of **ver, leer, buscar, caer, abrir, ir, oír, dar.**

ALGO NUEVO

6. Progressive Tenses

Estebanico iba haciendo una colección.
Estebanico kept making a collection.

seguía caminando Coronado
Coronado continued traveling

You have often found *estar* used with the gerund for the progressive tenses: *estamos estudiando, estaban hablando.*

The verbs *ir, andar,* and *seguir* are often used with the gerund for an even stronger progressive meaning, as you saw in the story. These forms give the idea of *keeping on, continuing,* or *progressing.*

EJERCICIO I. *Translate these expressions, showing as strongly as you can the idea of progression:*

vamos aprendiendo, sigue hablando, estaban leyendo, andan buscando, iban explorando, seguían trabajando, viene, voy [1]

7. New Use of the Gerund

aprendemos haciendo, *we learn by doing*

The gerund is often used alone with the meaning *by* or *while.* Remember never to use a preposition with a gerund. (*Before going,* **antes de ir;** *upon going,* **al ir.**)

EJERCICIO II. *Say in Spanish:* He learns by writing; they earn by working; he amuses himself by playing; we study while reading.

EJERCICIO III. *Translate these assorted verb forms carefully:*

1. encontrábamos	8. seguían	15. seguimos tocando
2. existían	9. estaban hablando	16. llegan
3. haciendo	10. tenga Vd.	17. digo
4. ¡Imagínese Vd.!	11. se despide	18. hemos puesto
5. eran	12. íbamos	19. vaya Vd.
6. visto	13. vuelvo	20. habíamos estado
7. nos escribíamos	14. ha cubierto	21. veían

8. Verbs with Changed Meanings

ir, *to go;* **irse,** *to go away;* **llevar,** *to carry;* **llevarse,** *to carry away*

Many verbs change their meanings when used reflexively, as these examples show. You will find both meanings in the dictionary at the back of the book.

[1] *Ir* and *venir* and other verbs of motion are never used progressively.

EJERCICIO IV. *Translate and show how the reflexive pronoun changes the meaning of the verbs in these sentences:*

1. El indio *dormía* en el camino; el indio *se dormía* porque estaba cansado. 2. La expedición *fué* (*went*) a Culiacán; la expedición *se fué* inmediatamente. 3. Pablo *come* temprano; Pablo *se come* las frutas. 4. El moro *puso* los adornos sobre la cabeza; el moro *se puso* los adornos de oro. 5. Los españoles esperaban *hacerse* ricos; para *hacer* esto, buscaban oro. 6. Coronado *se llevó* el maíz de los indios; el caballo de Coronado le *llevó* fácilmente. 7. Antonio *se levantó* para dar la lección; Antonio *levantó* la mano. 8. El niño *se llamaba* Enrique; el niño *llamaba* a Enrique.

9. Possessives

Review the long and short forms of the possessive adjectives and pronouns in sections 113–115.

EJERCICIO V. *Translate these expressions and explain why the long or short form is used:*

1. Mi hijo es rico. 2. Hijo mío, ¡dame el papel! 3. El papel es mío. 4. ¡Vida mía! (*Darling!*) 5. Un amigo mío ha llegado. 6. El mío está aquí. 7. Mis hermanas son bonitas.

Governor's Palace at Santa Fe, New Mexico, combines Pueblo Indian and old Spanish architecture in its beamed adobe construction. This was once the northern terminal of the *Camino real* from Mexico City.

Sawders

EJERCICIO VI. *Why is the definite article used with or in place of the possessive adjective in each of these sentences?*

1. *La* [1] hermana de Vd. es bonita. 2. Tengo *el* libro de ella. 3. *Los* nuestros son buenos. 4. *Los* de él son magníficos. 5. No llevamos plumas en *los* pies. 6. Los indios llevaban *la* (§ 113) cabeza cubierta de oro. 7. Sus manos son fuertes. (Why is the rule broken here? § 113) 8. Busco *el* mío. 9. Tiene *el* suyo.

EJERCICIO VII. *Complete in Spanish:*

1. *My* hermano está aquí.
2. *My son!* Dame la leche.
3. Ella tiene *her* dinero.
4. El dinero es *hers.*
5. *Our* lecciones son fáciles.
6. *Their* escuela es grande.
7. La escuela es *theirs.*
8. La casa blanca es *his.*
9. Nos lavamos *our faces.*[2]
10. Se lavan *their hands.*
11. Nos ponemos *our shoes.*
12. Nos ponemos *our hats.*[2]
13. Usan *their heads.*
14. Un amigo *of mine* viene.
15. ¿Es un amigo *of yours*?
16. No es *hers*, sino *his.*

ESTUDIO DE PALABRAS

I. The Spanish ending *-oso* often means *-ous* in English. *What do these cognates mean?*

curioso, famoso, maravilloso, furioso, vicioso, ansioso, misterioso, deseoso (*from* **desear**), precioso, valeroso, numeroso, monstruoso, delicioso, supersticioso, industrioso

II. These sentences are composed almost entirely of cognates. *Translate them rapidly at sight by guessing the meanings of the words.* Don't try to look them up!

1. En la literatura encontramos las fórmulas de cortesía que demuestran (***demostrar***) exactamente la educación y dignidad de los españoles, las que son bien conocidas. Con su hospitalidad los habitantes inmediatamente declaran su cultura. 2. En la clase

[1] Remember that the definite article may be used instead of the possessive adjective when an explanation follows.

[2] Singular because there is only one apiece. Also look up section 113 before doing sentences 9–12.

los mexicanos comienzan a estudiar las lecciones necesarias de composición, gramática, aritmética, geografía e historia. 3. Bob, muy contento, ha preparado su bicicleta para ir al sanatorio público con las botellas de leche para los niños delicados. 4. La maraca (*rattle*) del moro estaba cubierta de plumas, y era un emblema de su autoridad. 5. Los indios, adornados de una colección de turquesas enormes, acompañaban al moro con música de flautas mientras (*while*) éste exploraba la inmensidad del desierto. 6. ¡Imagínese Vd.! El valiente capitán de la famosa expedición de la conquista recibió una noticia de mucha importancia significando que había una fortuna maravillosa a lo lejos, e inmediatamente se resolvió el misterio fantástico del norte.

PARA PRONUNCIAR

I. The letters ***t, d, l,*** and ***n*** are formed in Spanish by placing the tongue farther forward in the mouth than when speaking English. Put your tongue so low against your upper front teeth that you could bite it, then smile, and you will get the Spanish sound. *Holding your face in that position, say these silly sentences with your best accent:* [1]

1. Tomás también tiene tinta para ti. 2. Anita no nombra a nadie en enero. 3. Lola nota lentamente el litro de lodo. 4. Don David da un duro a dos damas. 5. Nada te pide tanta atención. 6. Los tontos no tocan el piano ni cantan. 7. Adelante andaban los leones. 8. Tu tinta te tiñe de negro. 9. — Pita, pita, y caminando, — dice la letra.[2] 10. El nido del loro no era de lodo. 11. Dame linolué de Olinalá.[3] 12. Tantos tíos no tienen tiempo.

*II. Roll heavily **rr** or initial **r** as you pronounce carefully:*

Erre con erre en barril,
erre con erre en cigarros;
allá en el ferrocarril
rápidos corren los carros.

[1] Your teacher will translate them for you if you are curious.
[2] Words of a popular Mexican song.
[3] *Give me sweet-smelling wood from Olinalá* (Mexico).

III. Final *r* is a soft sound breathed and flipped off the end of the tongue with just a trifle of the roll of any other single *r*. Widen your mouth as if to smile and leave it open as you finish the sound. *Read aloud:*

¿Por qué tratar de ir? No hay nada que hacer. No podemos oír. Vamos a ver. Quiere venir. Va a salir sin querer. Favor de traducir y leer.

PARA LEER SIN ESTUDIAR

Always guess every word that looks the least bit like English.

I. ¿Sabía Vd. esto?

El nombre de Cabeza de Vaca tiene una historia muy curiosa. Se dice que hace (*ago*) varios siglos, cuando combatían los moros y los cristianos en España, un antepasado (*ancestor*) suyo, un hombre pobre, ayudó (*helped*) a los cristianos a hallar un paso por las montañas, indicándolo con la cabeza de una vaca. Así ganaron los españoles la batalla (*battle*), y el rey de España le dió título de noble al hombre pobre, dándole el nombre de Cabeza de Vaca.

II. La economía de Arturo

El padre de Arturo no estaba muy contento. Su hijo no salía bien en los exámenes de escuela, y siempre llevaba a casa notas (*grades*) muy malas porque no quería estudiar.

Un día el padre le dijo (*said*), — Hijo mío, si sales bien en los exámenes al fin del año, te compro una bicicleta nueva.

Arturo estaba muy contento con esta promesa (*promise*), porque quería mucho tener una bicicleta. Pero al niño le gustaba más jugar que estudiar, y seguía saliendo mal en sus clases.

Al fin del año su padre le dijo (*said*), — Arturo, lo siento (*regret*) mucho, pero tengo que decirte que los negocios (*business*) van tan mal ahora que no tengo el dinero para comprarte esa bicicleta.

Y respondió Arturo, — Eso lo sabía yo, papá, y he hecho todo lo posible para evitarle (*spare you*) el gasto (*expense*) de la bicicleta. He salido mal en todos mis exámenes.

TEMA

Escriba Vd. en español con mucho cuidado:

1. All the windows were covered with turquoises. 2. The Indians wore red feathers on their arms and legs. 3. Coronado had sent Fray Marcos on ahead in search of treasure. 4. The King of Spain was getting rich (*progressive*). 5. My son, what are you (*fam.*) looking for (*prog.*)? 6. They had never seen the seven golden cities. 7. They used to travel (**caminar**) on horseback through the desert. 8. The brave Spaniards did not put gold on their heads. 9. We learn by doing. Really? Yes, every day. 10. Don't go away, my friend. Make yourself at home.

CAPÍTULO 5

El fantasma de Punta Guijarros

The romantic days of the Dons in early California were an example of Spanish colonial living at its best. Priest and soldier had tamed a wilderness, and all along *El camino real*, with its hospitable missions stationed a day's horseback ride apart, lived the Spanish aristocrats on their great ranchos. For the Dons and their families it was a leisurely, pleasant life. There was dancing every Sunday after church, gay *caballeros* serenaded *señoritas* at their balconies, and everyone went on horseback to *fiestas* and *fandangos* (parties) at the various ranchos.

In those days there were many legends and superstitions of both Indian and Spanish origin, and "The Ghost of Cobblestone Point" (now called Point Loma, near San Diego), tells what one superstition is actually supposed to have done for the daughter of a Don in the one-time village of Southern California.

— ¿Viste a don Ramón en el pueblo? — preguntó doña Carmen a su criada, María, al encontrarla en el patio de la Casa Grande.[1]

— Sí, señorita, hace media hora, — contestó María, mirando la cara bonita de doña Carmen.

— ¡Ah! ¿Y qué dijo? Pero, ¡cuidado! Ese Pablo va a oírte. Ven (*come*) a mi cuarto y podemos hablar allí.

— Ese Pablo debe cuidar sus flores en vez de mirar siempre a la gente de razón,[2] — regañó (*scolded*) María, echándole (*giving*) una mirada indignada al jardinero malhumorado (*ill-humored*) que trabajaba en el patio. — ¡Debe saber que un jardinero no puede hacerle el amor a Vd.!

— ¡Chis (*sh*)! — dijo doña Carmen, cerrando la puerta de su cuarto. — ¿Qué dice don Ramón?

— Pues, señorita, — contestó María, — dice que tiene que verla a Vd. esta noche, y que es una cosa de mucha importancia. Dice que la esperará (*will await*) a las once en la Punta Guijarros.[3]

— ¡Ay, válgame Dios! — exclamó doña Carmen. — ¿Cómo puedo ir a la Punta? Bien sabe Ramón que nunca puedo salir de la casa de noche.

— Pues, señorita, — explicó la criada, — dice don Ramón que yo debo acompañarla, y así estará (*it will be*) bien.

— Y ¿Pablo? Si él me sigue, ¡ay de mí! Le tengo miedo.

— Ese jardinero no va a saber nada de esto. Lo que yo no quiero encontrar es aquel Fantasma de la Punta.

— ¡Fantasma! ¡Supersticiosa tú! — rió Carmen. — No hay fantasma en la Punta. Y si hay uno, la leyenda dice que existe para proteger a las damas inocentes.

[1] The "Big House" of a *rancho* or *hacienda* is always the owner's. Early California ranch houses were rambling affairs of adobe with the typical Spanish patio and balconies.

[2] ***Gente de razón,*** literally *people of reason*, is the name frequently given to the aristocrats by their inferiors in some Spanish-speaking countries. We might say "nice people." Of course the gardener was being very bold even to think that Carmen might notice him.

[3] A young lady's maid, by carrying messages to and from her lover, often plays Cupid for her even in these days, especially if the family disapproves of him.

— Pues, espero que sí. Entonces digo a don Ramón que le encontramos a las once, ¿eh?

— Sí, María. Y no digas nada de esto a nadie, ¿sabes?

— Bueno, señorita. — Y María salió del cuarto.

Pero no se fijó (*notice*) en que Pablo, trabajando en el patio, había estado muy cerca de la puerta....

Eran las once de la noche. Bajo la luz pálida (*pale*) de la luna, el risco blanco de la Punta se veía destacándose (*standing out*) sobre el mar. Abajo, las altas olas con su trueno (*thunder*) eterno se rompían contra las rocas. Una forma obscura apareció en la senda, y luego se escondió (*hid*) bajo los arbustos. La luna miraba, y esperaba.... Las olas seguían rompiéndose contra las rocas de abajo....

Dos mujeres aparecieron en la senda. — Ay, tengo miedo, — murmuró María. — Se dice que aquel fantasma siempre aparece en noches como ésta.

Point Loma, San Diego, was once called Punta Guijarros, and there in early California days the legendary ghost appeared after sunset. Here we see Point Loma across San Diego Bay.

— Pero, ¿dónde está Ramón? — preguntó ansiosamente Carmen, sin contestarle a María. — Dijo que estaría (*would be*) esperándome.

— Pronto vendrá (*will come*), — dijo María, y en seguida dió un grito de alarma. Un hombre había salido de los arbustos.

— Buenas noches, doña Carmen, — dijo la voz desagradable de Pablo.

— ¡Tú por aquí! — exclamó Carmen, indignada. — ¿Cómo te atreves tú a seguirme?

— Porque te quiero, — dijo Pablo con osadía (*boldly*), — y vengo a decirte que tienes que casarte conmigo y no con ese Ramón.

— ¡Casarme con un jardinero! — exclamó Carmen. — ¡Nunca! ¿No sabes que soy hija de don Guadalupe Reyes?

— Pero vas a casarte conmigo, — insistió Pablo. — Esta misma noche te vas conmigo, o mueres, ¿entiendes? Mira, hermosa, el risco es muy alto, ¿no? Es muy fácil caer de la Punta, y las olas no publican secretos.

— ¡Don Ramón vendrá (*will come*)! ¡Él me protegerá!

— Tu Ramón nunca vendrá más. Ya le he muerto, y tú, — tú vas conmigo. — Y se acercó a la dama aterrada.

— ¡Ay! ¡Ramón! — gritó Carmen desesperada (*despairingly*).

— No vale la pena de gritar, preciosa, — dijo Pablo riéndose. — Tu Ramón no puede oírte.

En este momento apareció en la senda detrás de Pablo una forma obscura, alta, envuelta (*wrapped*) en una capa (*cape*) larga. Iba acercándose cuando María la vió.

— ¡Ay, Dios mío! — gritó la criada. — ¡Es el Fantasma de la Punta!

Pablo volvió la cabeza. — ¡El fantasma! ¡Válgame Dios! — exclamó, aterrado.

— ¡Sí, y ahora eres tú el que va a morir! — gritó la supersticiosa María.

Pablo no podía escaparse por la senda, porque la forma misteriosa le cerró el paso. Aterrado, empezó a correr por el borde (*edge*) del risco. De pronto resbaló (*he slipped*) en la roca y comenzó a rodar (*roll*) hacia el precipicio. Los tres le miraban, paralizados, mientras el jardinero llegó al borde y desapareció sin poder salvarse. Grito tras grito podían oír a lo lejos, hasta que las altas olas se los tragaron (*swallowed*).

El fantasma había salvado a la dama inocente. Pero, ¿estaba hablando? Sí, el fantasma hablaba. — No tengas miedo, Carmen de mi alma. Soy Ramón. Pablo creía que me había muerto, pero sólo me hirió (*wounded*), y al fin pude (*succeeded in*) seguirle. ¿Estás bien, preciosa?

— Sí, perfectamente, — murmuró Carmen. — Y ¡cuánto debo a este «fantasma»!

PALABRAS NUEVAS

3 **(de) abajo**	below	**ola**	wave
ansiosamente	anxiously	**paralizado**	paralyzed
2 **aparecer**	to appear	4 **preciosa**	darling
arbusto	bush	**precipicio**	precipice
aterrado	terrified	**proteger**	to protect
2 **atreverse a**	to dare to	4 **punta**	point
dama	girl	**risco**	cliff
eterno	eternal	**roca**	rock
fantasma (*m.*)	ghost	3 **salvar**	to save
indignado	indignant	**senda**	path
3 **mirada**	look	3 **tras**	after

EXPRESIONES

a lo lejos, in the distance
cerrar el paso, to block one's way
de mi alma, darling
de pronto, suddenly
¡Dios mío!, for Heaven's sake!
estar bien, to be all right
hacer el amor a, to make love to
publicar secretos, to tell tales
valer la pena (de), to be worth while (to)
¡válgame Dios!, Heaven help (bless) me!

¿VERDAD O NO?

1. Doña Carmen era una criada vieja de la Casa Grande. 2. Pablo era un jardinero que trabajaba en el rancho de don Ramón. 3. Don Ramón quería encontrar a doña Carmen en la Punta. 4. Doña Carmen no podía salir de noche sin su criada. 5. Doña Carmen le tenía miedo al jardinero. 6. Aquella noche había luna y las olas eran muy altas. 7. Pablo llegó primero a la Punta y las esperó allí. 8. Doña Carmen quería casarse pronto con Pablo. 9. Pablo había muerto a don Ramón antes de ir a la Punta. 10. Cuando llegó don Ramón, Pablo creía que era el fantasma porque llevaba una capa (*cape*) larga.

PREGUNTAS

1. ¿Dónde vió María a don Ramón? 2. ¿Cuándo le vió? 3. ¿Oyó Pablo la conversación entre las dos? 4. ¿Debe un jardinero hacer el amor a la hija de un rico? 5. ¿Dónde quería don Ramón encontrar a doña Carmen aquella noche? 6. ¿A qué le tenía miedo María? 7. ¿A qué le tenía miedo doña Carmen? 8. ¿Quién llegó primero a la Punta? 9. ¿Quién estaba esperando a doña Carmen cuando llegó? 10. ¿Por qué siguió Pablo a doña Carmen?

REPASO DE VERBOS

I. Review the preterite tense of regular verbs in section 62. Using the verbs **cerrar, ver, salir,** *give these preterite forms:* [1]

he closed, they saw, she left, we closed, you saw, they left, you closed, he saw, we left, I closed, I saw, I left

[1] Next to the present, the preterite is the tense most often used, so you should learn it well.

II. Review the following irregular preterites in the list of irregular verbs beginning with section 63:

tener, ser, estar, ir, dar, venir, poner, hacer, decir, saber, poder, querer, traer (*to bring*)

III. Review the preterite tense and gerund (which matches it) of the III RC[1] *verbs* **pedir** *and* **dormir** (§§ 88, 89). *Give also the gerund and the preterite tense of* **morir, vestir, servir, seguir.**

Review the preterite and gerund of **caer** (§ 64). *Give the same forms for the verbs* **oír, leer,** *and* **creer.**

Learn the preterite and gerund of **reír,** to laugh (§ 75).

IV. Give the meanings of these verb forms. Translate the imperfect by "used to" or "was — ing," to show that you know its significance.

1. durmiendo	7. tuvimos	13. dimos	19. riendo
2. durmieron	8. eran	14. viniendo	20. salíamos
3. iba	9. estábamos	15. cerraban	21. cayendo
4. supo	10. creyendo	16. dijeron	22. rió
5. oyeron	11. pidió	17. iban leyendo	23. puso
6. volvían	12. trajo	18. oyó	24. decían

V. Since in radical-changing verbs ***e*** > ***ie*** *or* ***i****, and* ***o*** > ***ue*** *or* ***u****, from what infinitives do these verbs come?*

rieron, cierras, empiezan, muere, comienza, se despide, riendo, diciendo, siguieron, vuelven, durmiendo, vistió, sirvieron, vino, murió, almuerzas, sirviendo, cuente Vd., demuestra, pida Vd., juegan

10. The Imperfect and Preterite Tenses

EJERCICIO I. *Review the uses of the imperfect and preterite tenses in section 128, and tell which of these tenses you need for each of these infinitives and why:*

1. Alfredo *traer* una carta a la Casa Grande esta misma noche. 2. El caballero *salvar* a la dama inocente. 3. Todos los días María *ver* a don Ramón. 4. María le *tener* miedo al fantasma. 5. Las olas *ser* muy altas. 6. Don Ramón *venir* a la Casa Grande a veces. 7. — Buenas noches, — *decir* una voz. 8. *Ser* las once de la noche

[1] "III RC" means "third-conjugation radical-changing."

cuando el jardinero de pronto *caer* del risco. 9. Antonio siempre *comer* con buen apetito. 10. Pablo *cuidar* las flores cuando *llegar* María. 11. La mujer nunca *mirar* al jardinero. 12. La criada *dar* un grito cuando *ver* al fantasma.

ALGO NUEVO

11(a). A New Use of the Preterite

Estuvimos allí cuatro meses, *we were there four months.*
Dormimos ocho horas, *we slept for eight hours.*

A past occurrence, even though it may have lasted quite a long while, if in any way limited by an expression of time, takes the preterite tense. We may call this the "preterite of definite duration." [1]

EJERCICIO II. *Translate these sentences and explain why the verbs are preterite or imperfect:*

1. El viaje duró siete años. 2. Entonces yo estudiaba en Madrid, pero más tarde estudié un año en Chile. 3. La criada me sirvió mucho tiempo. 4. La criada me servía todos los días. 5. El jardinero siempre miraba a doña Carmen. 6. Aquella mañana la miró. 7. Ella nunca le miró. 8. Sabía bien la lección. 9. Al fin supo la noticia.[2] 10. Conocía a doña Carmen. 11. Conoció a la joven en el rancho.[2]

11(b). A New Use of the Imperfect

Creía que no podía escaparse, *he thought he could not escape.*

Verbs of believing, knowing, thinking, wishing, and being able are frequently used in the imperfect tense because they express a state or condition rather than an action.

[1] Sometimes called the "preterite of perspective of time."

[2] Some verbs have a slightly different meaning in the preterite: ***sabía*** (*he used to know*), ***supo*** (*he found out, learned*); ***conocía*** (*he was acquainted with*), ***conoció*** (*he met, became acquainted*); ***podía*** (*he was able*), ***pudo*** (*he succeeded in*).

EJERCICIO III. *Translate these sentences and explain the tense of each verb:*

1. El hombre sabía que estaba enfermo, y deseaba salir, pero no podía. 2. Creía que la mujer quería salvarle. 3. Tenía miedo, pero no podía correr. 4. Conoció a Ramón en San Diego, donde supo que Pablo había ido a la Punta, pero pudo salvar a su amiga.

12. Adjectives Used as Nouns

un hospital para los enfermos, *a hospital for the sick*
tengo el rojo, *I have the red one*

Adjectives are often used alone as nouns. Sometimes it is necessary to supply the word *one* in order to make a good English translation.

EJERCICIO IV. *Translate carefully, noticing how adjectives are used as nouns:*

1. Los ricos tienen automóviles. 2. Los pobres usan un burro. 3. El grande es de usted; el rojo es de ellos. 4. La primera parte no vale nada; la otra es preciosa. 5. Los jóvenes juegan mucho. 6. Los míos [1] no estaban en casa. 7. Los nuestros [1] fueron al pueblo. 8. Déme Vd. el chico y el verde.

13. Negatives

Review this list of negative words and expressions:

nada	nothing, anything	**yo no**	not I
nadie	no one, anyone	**ni yo tampoco**	nor I either
ninguno	no, none, any	**sin nada**	without anything
nunca	never, ever	**más que nadie**	more than anyone
ni . . . ni	neither . . . nor	**más que nunca**	more than ever

EJERCICIO V. *Complete in Spanish, using the negative words or expressions given in the preceding list:*

1. No llego *never* tarde a la escuela. 2. Carlos no tenía *neither* casa *nor* automóvil. 3. ¿Quiere Vd. irse en vez de comer? *Not I.*

[1] ***Los míos,*** *my "folks."* These possessive pronouns are often used in colloquial speech to refer to one's people.

Neither do I (*nor I either*)! 4. No podemos vivir *without anything.* 5. *No one* se atreve a reír en la clase de español. 6. Ese hombre es más desagradable que *anyone.* 7. No veo a *any* criada. 8. No digas *anything* de esto a *anyone.* 9. No vieron *anyone* en el patio.[1] 10. Ella *never* dice *anything* cuando no tiene *anything* que decir.

ESTUDIO DE PALABRAS[2]

Many Spanish cognates differ from English in the following ways:

1. Nouns and adjectives are like English except that they add an **-a, -o,** or **-e:** *marcha, costo, aire.* Others change a final **-e** to **-o** or **-a:** *artículo, completo, cultura.*

2. Spanish words have no double consonants except **cc** and sometimes **nn** (**ll** and **rr** are considered single letters): *inteligente, necesario, oficial.*

3. Spanish **f** is used instead of English **ph:** *fonógrafo, teléfono.*

4. Spanish **t** is used instead of English **th:** *Arturo, aritmética.*

5. Spanish initial **s** followed by a consonant is preceded by **e:** *estudio, especial.*

6. Spanish **c** is used instead of English **ch:** *cristiano.*

7. Spanish **i** is used instead of English **y:** *sistema, bicicleta.*

8. Many common Spanish verbs merely replace a final English **-e** with **-ar, -er,** or **-ir:** *escapar, explorar, dividir;* others simply add the infinitive ending to the English: *demandar, inventar, formar.*

Keeping these changes in mind, tell what the following words mean without looking them up. (If you cover the initial **e** before **s** it is easier to see what the word looks like.)

telefonear, curar, admirar, estenógrafo, establo, fotografía, típico, competir, completar, imaginar, catedral, método, mito (*myth*), fan-

[1] ***Nadie*** takes the "personal ***a***" when it is an object.

[2] From this point on you will find many cognates omitted from the general vocabulary, and you will be expected to guess them because of their similarity to English. It would be a good idea to turn now to the first page of the Spanish-English dictionary and note the types of words you should be able to recognize according to the list there.

tasma, especial, esfera, estudioso, micrófono, escaldar, comparar, escándalo, tipo, observar, determinar, espacio, escarlata, autor, conservar, coincidir, causar, espléndido, estación, estilo

PARA PRONUNCIAR

I. Spanish ***b*** and ***v*** are pronounced the same. As initial letters, beginning a breath group, they have almost the sound of English ***b****: veinte.* They have this sound also when preceded by ***n*** or ***m*** (the ***n*** turns to ***m***): *invierno* (pronounced *imbierno*), *pan bueno* (pronounced *pambueno*). In other words, ***nb*** or ***nv* > *mb*.**

Between vowels they are soft (say ***b*** without closing your lips): *sabe, la vaca.*

San Juan Capistrano is one of the best preserved and most beautiful of the old Spanish missions which were built along the California coast a day's horseback journey apart.

Sawders

II. Spanish ***nm*** becomes ***mm***, which is much easier to pronounce: *inmenso, un modo.*

III. Spanish ***d*** between vowels is voiced *th* as in *though*: *todo, cada.* At the end of words ***d*** is so soft that it is almost silent: *verdad.* ***D*** is most like English ***d*** when initial or after ***m, n, l,*** and ***s:*** *donde, aldea, desde.* All three sounds of ***d*** are found in *dividid.*

IV. Spanish ***s*** is always hissed as in *this*, except before several consonants, the commonest of which are ***d*** and ***m:***[1] *rosa, presidente; mismo, desde, es decir.*

V. Pronounce carefully, watching for examples of all the preceding rules. (Your teacher will translate the sentences if you cannot.)

1. Dame un momento en Madrid. 2. Dividid el durazno duro. 3. Cada dama bebe un vaso de vino. 4. «Dame un besito para vivir más contento yo.»[2] 5. Desde el balcón se veía al mismo barbero. 6. Inmediatamente vamos a ver un milagro. 7. Usted es inmortal, ¿no es verdad? 8. También toman más pan en el invierno. 9. Todos saben mandar las rosas al presidente. 10. Rosita tiene una vaca barata en mi establo. 11. «Sobre las olas» es una canción de la misma clase. 12. Se convirtió en un buen mozo.

PARA LEER SIN ESTUDIAR

This is a story told in Mexico. Guess all the words that look like English!

EL TURISTA MEXICANO

Un mexicano que no sabía hablar inglés vino a los Estados Unidos para hacer una visita. Fué a una ciudad grande, donde vió muchos edificios y casas y mucha gente.

Entró en una tienda (*store*) magnífica, y preguntó a un empleado (*employee*), — ¿De quién es esta tienda?

[1] The others are *b, v, g, l,* and *n.*

[2] Words of a popular Mexican folksong.

El empleado, que no entendía el español, dijo, "*What'd you say?*"

El mexicano respondió, — ¡Ah! ¡Es del señor Juan Chusé! ¡Qué nombre tan curioso! ¡Muy rico debe ser el señor si esta tienda es suya!

Siguió andando por la calle, y vió un hospital magnífico. Entró en el hospital y preguntó a un empleado, — ¿De quién es este hospital?

El empleado, que no entendía el español, dijo, "*What'd you say?*"

— ¡Ah! — respondió el mexicano. — ¡El hospital también es del señor Juan Chusé! ¡Muy bueno debe ser el señor si tiene un hospital para los pobres enfermos!

Entonces el mexicano salió a la calle, y de pronto vió allí un gran accidente. Un señor había muerto, y el mexicano preguntó a un pasajero (*passerby*), — ¿Quién murió?

El otro, que no entendía el español, respondió, "*What'd you say?*"

— ¡Ay, qué lástima! — exclamó el mexicano. — ¡Un señor tan rico y tan bueno como el señor Juan Chusé, que tiene un hospital y una tienda, ha muerto! ¡Qué lástima!

Told by Emelia Pulido (*Michoacán*)

TEMA

Escriba Vd. en español con mucho cuidado:

1. A week ago we went to look at the high waves. 2. We were afraid neither of the cliff (*risco*) nor of the waves. 3. "You do not have to marry me," laughed the servant in a disagreeable voice. 4. Hearing the voice, they believed that he had killed (*a*) his friend. 5. Suddenly the servant fell into (*a*) the sea, and there he died. 6. At last either the woman or the girl gave a cry. 7. The night was dark, but the people (*sing.*) began to run toward the sea. 8. The young folks sang for two hours beneath the moon. 9. They never heard so much noise on the ranch. 10. No one ever (never) says anything to anyone. (*Watch the negatives!*)

CAPÍTULO 6

Buen viaje

Modern Mexico is sometimes called "a foreign land but a step away," and when you go there you'll find it just that. As soon as you cross the border, even if you are familiar with Spanish culture, you sense a new atmosphere in the courteous speech of a charming people. In the country landscape you see kindly old Spanish church towers peering over distant trees, and oxen plowing in stone-walled fields, or you come to an up-to-date hacienda with tractors and modern farming methods. In the small towns you find Spanish plazas and fountains, and beside them, modern radio shops and basketball courts. In the cities you exclaim first over a smart avenue of pretentious stores, then you wander down a narrow street of ancient buildings that once saw viceroys pass. You go delightedly mad buying for almost nothing the baskets and pottery and silver jewelry made by patient craftsmen. You get the afternoon siesta habit and don't mind having dinner at nine o'clock (after you learn to take afternoon tea), and soon find yourself adopting the leisurely Spanish style of living that makes Mexico a different and attractive world to the hurried *norteamericano.*

After Jimmie Jones (that was actually his name) had taken two years of high-school Spanish and had heard his teacher talk about Mexico nearly every day, it's not strange that he finally coaxed his family into driving to Mexico City during summer vacation. "Mom" didn't know any Spanish and was afraid of bandits, "Dad" knew enough words to get into difficulties, and "Sis" wanted to eat everything she saw.

Jimmie practically had to conduct the tour, and as he went he wrote up their adventures in Spanish as a souvenir of his trip. And all the things he tells about really did happen!

Lunes, veinte y seis de junio.
Nuevo Laredo, Nuevo León, México.

¡Al fin estamos en México! Esta mañana cruzamos la frontera. En la aduana (*customs house*) registraron (*inspected*) nuestro equipaje, pero no tuvimos que pagar derechos (*duty*).

Cambiamos unos cheques de viajero (*travelers' checks*) por dinero mexicano. El tipo de cambio (*rate of exchange*) fué 4.80 pesos por cada dólar. Me equivoqué (*made a mistake*), porque le dije al cambiador (*money-changer*) que quería cambiar diez «dolores». El pobre hombre trató de no reírse de mí, pero cuando yo cambié la palabra a diez «dólares», los dos nos echamos a reír. *Dad* se burla de mi *high-school Spanish*, porque no sabe que es muy fácil equivocarse.

Mexican visitors are allowed to cross the International Bridge at Laredo, Texas, as long as their identification cards are in order. Uncle Sam's immigration officers are always on duty.

Galloway

El inspector de inmigración miró nuestras tarjetas (*cards*) de turista, y *Dad* tuvo que firmar un papel. El inspector, que no hablaba inglés, le dió su plumafuente verde con que firmarlo. *Dad* sabe unas pocas palabras de español, y dijo al escribir su nombre, — Una pluma muy buena. — Y el inspector, con cortesía mexicana, contestó, — La pluma es de Vd., señor. — *Dad* no sabía la costumbre, y creyendo que el inspector en efecto le había dado la pluma, dijo, — Muchas gracias, — y se la llevó.[1] Yo tuve que pedirle la plumafuente y devolvérsela al atónito (*astonished*) inspector. ¡Creo que nunca dirá eso a otro turista!

Sis cambió un dólar por pesos en la frontera, y va comprando cosas que comer. Ya ha comprado un tostón de cacahuates (*peanuts*) y dulce de calabaza.[2] ¡Siempre está comiendo!

Mañana compraré un billete de lotería. Espero ganar un premio.

Martes, veinte y siete de junio.
Monterrey, Nuevo León.

Hallamos muy bueno el Camino Nacional No. 1 hasta Monterrey. Hay buenas estaciones de servicio en todas partes, y la gasolina cuesta veinte y dos centavos el litro.[3] Nos parece muy curioso hablar de litros de gasolina, de kilómetros[3] en vez de millas (*miles*), y de «kilos»[3] en vez de libras (*pounds*), pero pronto nos acostumbraremos.

Hay muchas señales de tránsito, y cuando *Dad* vió una que decía «Velocidad máxima (*speed limit*) 80 kilómetros por hora», creía que indicaba millas, e iba muy de prisa hasta que *Mom* miró el velocímetro (*speedometer*).

Estamos en un campo de turistas, muy moderno y cómodo.

[1] ***se la llevó,*** *carried it off.* The Spanish custom is to present an article to a person who has admired it, saying, "It is yours." The "gift" is to be graciously refused with the answer, "It couldn't have a better owner," but Dad didn't know that!

[2] ***dulce de calabaza,*** *pumpkin candy.* Candied fruits, pumpkin, cactus, and even sweet potato are favorite ***dulces*** of Mexico.

[3] Units of measurement used in Spanish-speaking countries are liters (about a quart), kilometers (5/8 of a mile), and kilograms, «kilos», (2 1/5 pounds).

Black Star

Mexico's Camino Nacional No. I crosses roaring streams on modern steel bridges and climbs towering cactus-studded mountains with a high-gear road that is a triumph of engineering.

Monterrey tiene casas modernas, y también casas muy típicas de México, con balcones, rejas (*barred windows*), y patios. Algunas calles son estrechas y se permite el movimiento de vehículos en solamente una dirección. Una vez *Dad*, que estaba manejando el coche, no vió la flecha (*arrow*) que indicaba el tránsito, y entró en una calle estrecha. Unos niños empezaron a gritarnos, — ¡Contra tránsito! ¡Contra tránsito!

Mom espera (*expects*) ver un bandido (*bandit*) o una revolución detrás de cada árbol, pero no los hay. Pero sí [1] hay muchos guardias en motocicletas (*motorcycles*), todos vestidos de uniforme, y muy guapos.

Compré dos billetes de lotería.

[1] ***sí hay**, there certainly are.* ***Sí*** is often used just for emphasis.

Galloway

Mexico City's most luxurious hotel (with prices to match) fronts on the Paseo de la Reforma, the wide avenue that cuts from the heart of the city to Chapultepec Castle.

Viernes, treinta de junio.
México, D.F.[1]

Estamos en un hotel moderno que tiene garage, cuartos con baño de agua caliente día y noche, teléfono, muebles bonitos y camas cómodas. Hay un ascensor (*elevator*), y las comidas son buenas. No tomamos los cuartos con asistencia (*board*), porque es más interesante comer en distintos restaurantes.

La capital tiene rascacielos (*skyscrapers*) modernos, así como edificios pintorescos (*picturesque*) y muy antiguos. Ya no se permiten en las calles principales los bueyes (*oxen*), los burros, los pordioseros ni los vendedores, porque hay tanto movimiento de vehículos. Hasta hay *parking meters*, como en los Estados Unidos. *Dad* estacionó el coche cerca de uno demasiado tiempo, y cuando volvió, miró y exclamó, — ¡Al-

[1] ***D.F., Distrito Federal,*** like our D.C. (District of Columbia), is the area immediately surrounding the capital. When south of the border, say *México* for the city, and call the country *la República*. No one there ever says *la Ciudad de México.*

guien se ha robado las placas (*license plates*)! — Y fué a la delegación (*police station*) a informar a la policía. Al llegar, le dijeron que las placas estaban allí, y que tendría que pagar una multa (*fine*) para recobrarlas (*recover*). Pero cuando *Dad* explicó que era turista, le dieron las placas gratis, porque son muy corteses con los turistas.

Mom va comprando curiosidades para usar como premios en su *bridge club*. Dice que lo mexicano está de moda, y le compra algo a cada vendedor. Hoy estaba regateando (*bargaining*) con una vendedora de deshilados (*drawnwork*), y dijo, — Es mucho. — La vendedora, que creía que todos los turistas eran muy ricos, respondió, — Señora, Vd. vivirá y morirá, y nunca podrá gastar todo el dinero que tiene. — ¡Ella no sabe la verdad!

Sis compró unos mangos,[1] plátanos,[1] y una paleta helada.[1] Compré otro billete de lotería. Los otros no salieron.

Sábado, primero de julio.
México, D.F.

Hoy es el cumpleaños de *Sis*, y todos fuimos al Restaurant Prendes para celebrarlo. *Sis* tiene once años. Yo le dí una cajeta de Celaya [2] porque le gustan los dulces. *Mom* había mandado hacer un pastel de cumpleaños (*birthday cake*),[3] y había comprado una vela grande porque no sabía dónde hallar velitas. En la calle encontramos a un vendedor de gardenias, y *Dad* compró dos docenas por un tostón para adornar la mesa. Aquí son muy baratas las gardenias.

Cuando estábamos sentados a una mesa en el restaurant, el mesero nos trajo el pastel, lo puso en el centro de la mesa, y salió para traer la sopa. *Mom* puso la vela, la encendió (*lit*), y luego arregló las gardenias alrededor (*around*) del pastel. De

[1] A ***mango*** is a tropical fruit; ***plátano*** is *banana* in Mexico, although ***banana*** is a Central American word; and a ***paleta helada*** is a slab of fruit-ice frozen on a stick.

[2] A ***cajeta de Celaya*** is a small round wooden box filled with a soft sticky candy made of milk, sugar, and flavoring.

[3] Layer cake is not a Mexican "idea," but you can get anything in the capital! Some Americanized Mexicans now have birthday cakes, especially for a girl's fifteenth birthday.

Galloway

Open-air flower market of Mexico City sells enormous funeral wreaths which are often made entirely of gardenias.

pronto nos fijamos en que todo el mundo estaba mirándonos curiosamente, y en ese momento volvió el mesero con la sopa.

— ¡Dios mío! — exclamó, poniéndose muy pálido (*pale*) y casi dejando caer la sopa. — ¿Quién ha muerto?

¡Entonces nos enteramos de (*learned*) que en México las velas grandes se usan para el luto (*mourning*), y que no se usan las gardenias sino en los entierros (*funerals*)!

¡*Sis* nunca olvidará este cumpleaños!

PALABRAS NUEVAS

burlarse de	to make fun of	**manejar**	to drive
3 **cambiar**	to change, exchange	**mesero**	waiter
		milla	mile
4 **coche** (*m.*)	car	**Monterrey**	town of northeast Mexico
cómodo	comfortable		
3 **cruzar**	to cross	**No.**	*abbr.* for **número**
devolver (**ue**)	to return	**Nuevo Laredo**	border town across from Laredo, Texas
equipaje (*m.*)	luggage		
estacionarse	to park		
3 **fijarse en**	to notice	**pastel** (*m.*)	cake
firmar	to sign	3 **robar**	to steal
frontera	border	**tostón** (*m.*)	50¢ (Mexican slang)
guardia	policeman	**tránsito**	traffic

Expresiones

***así como**, as well as	**lo mexicano**, that which is Mexican
buen viaje, pleasant journey	**los dos**, we both
campo de turistas, tourist camp	**mandar hacer**, to have made
echarse a, to begin to	**señales** (*f.*) **de tránsito**, traffic signs
***en efecto**, in fact	

VIAJANDO EN MÉXICO

(*Estudio de palabras*)

In this chapter you have had many words and expressions you need for traveling in Spanish-speaking countries. Here are some additional ones you might like to know, which you will need for the questions: [1]

I. En el hotel

cuarto doble; sencillo	double room; single
cuarto interior; exterior	inside room; outside
agua corriente	running water
el botones (*buttons!*)	the bellboy
toallas; jabón (*m.*)	towels; soap
manta (frazada)	blanket
dar una propina a	to tip
la recamarera (*Mex.*)	the maid
la llave	the key
¿Hay cartas para el señor ——?	Is there any mail for Mr. ——?

II. Manejando un automóvil (*coche*)

engrasar; lavar	to grease; to wash
cambiar el aceite	to change the oil
llantas	tires
tener un pinchazo	to have a puncture
tener una llanta tronada	to have a blowout
se sentó una llanta	a tire went flat (*sat down!*)
reparación; componer	repairs; to fix
chófer (*m.*)	chauffeur
choque (*m.*)	accident, collision
placas	license plates

[1] Note to teacher: Optional section. These expressions are not given in the general vocabulary unless they are used again in later chapters, but are listed in the index as "travel expressions," etc.

III. Señales de tránsito

Mexican car owners pay a tax on each gallon of gasoline, which is spent for road-building. The National Highway No. 1, from Laredo to Mexico City (760 miles) is the main road, although there are others from Mexico City to Guadalajara (422 miles), to Vera Cruz (205 miles), and to Acapulco (285 miles). The Mexico section of the projected International Highway from Alaska to Buenos Aires, along the West Coast, is rapidly being built, and all completed roads are well marked and maintained.

These signs have been learned by thousands of tourists who have driven to Mexico.

Alto (*on red light*)	Stop (halt)
Siga (*on green light*)	Go (continue)
¡Alto, Vea, Oiga!	Stop, look, listen!
Camino transitable	Passable road
Peligro	Danger
Tome Vd. su derecha	Keep to the right
Seguridad ante todo	Safety first
TRÁNSITO (arrow)	Direction of traffic
Guarde Vd. su distancia	Keep your distance (*on bus*)
Maneje Vd. con cuidado	Drive carefully
Empalme	Junction

IV. En la frontera

Make a list of the expressions in Jimmie's diary that he learned crossing the border. Head it *En la frontera.*

PREGUNTAS

These questions on each section of Viajando en México include the words and expressions used in Jimmie's diary as well as the new ones listed.

I. ***En el hotel.*** 1. ¿Le gustaría más un cuarto exterior o uno interior? 2. ¿Qué se da al botones cuando lleva el equipaje? 3. ¿Es necesario tener jabón y toallas en un cuarto de baño? 4. ¿Es cos-

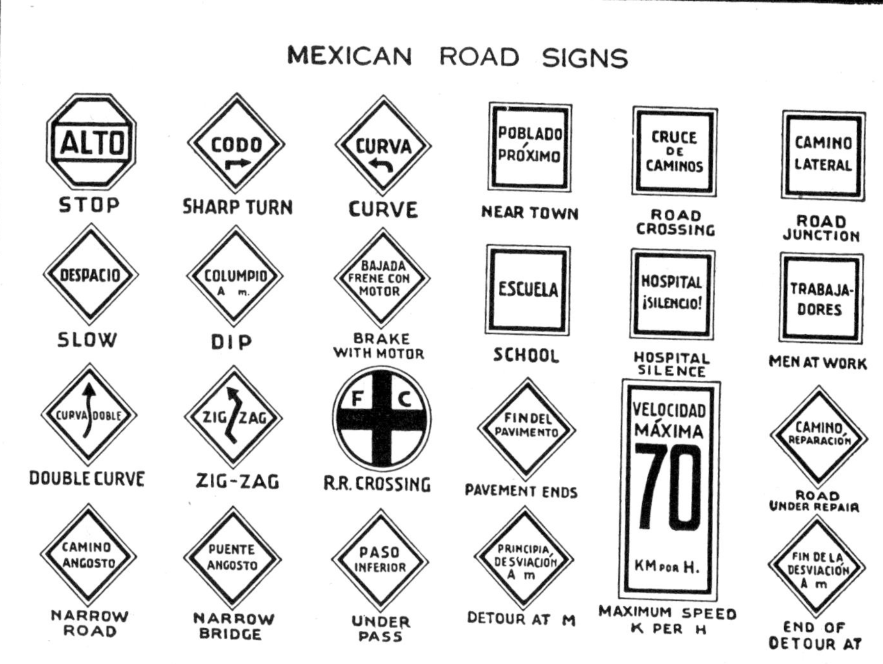

tumbre cerrar con llave (*to lock*) el cuarto en un hotel? 5. ¿Le gustaría a Vd. un cuarto con asistencia o sin ella?

II. ***Manejando el automóvil.*** 1. ¿Será necesario cambiar el aceite cada dos mil millas? 2. ¿Se puede estacionarse mucho tiempo en cualquier (*any*) calle? 3. ¿Le gustaría a Vd. tener un pinchazo en un viaje? 4. ¿Es fácil tener un choque si el chófer maneja sin tener cuidado? 5. ¿Cuántas llantas es costumbre tener para un coche? 6. ¿Es necesario tener placas en un coche?

III. ***Señales de tránsito.*** 1. ¿Qué significa la luz verde? ¿La luz roja? 2. ¿Es costumbre en México tomar la derecha o la izquierda? 3. ¿Dónde se ve la señal «¡Alto, vea, oiga!»? 4. ¿Hay peligro siempre en un camino transitable? 5. ¿Es peligroso cruzar la calle contra el tránsito? 6. ¿Cuál es la velocidad máxima en algunos caminos de México?

REPASO DE VERBOS

I. Review the future tense of the following verbs (beginning with section 63) and give the first person singular of each and its meaning:

decir, haber, hacer, poder, poner, querer, saber, salir, tener, venir

II. Using the same verbs, give the following forms:

we shall say, they will come, he will know, she will leave, I shall have (possess), they will make, you will put, he will want, we shall be able, you will say, I shall leave, she will put

III. Review the regular conditional tense endings in section **62**; *then give the first person singular conditional tense of each of the verbs in Exercise I and its meaning. Notice that the conditional tense has the same stem as the future.*

IV. Using the same verbs, give the following forms:

you would make, they would tell (say), she would put, they would be able, we would know, he would leave, I should wish, we should have (possess), he would come, you would know

V. Review the present tense of the irregular verbs **caer, oír, traer, reír, conocer, traducir, coger,** beginning with section 63. *Give the first person singular of each; then from it form the singular polite command and translate it.*

You have now reviewed all the common verbs which are irregular in the present tense.

ALGO NUEVO

14(a). ***Future of Probability***

¿Dónde está Pedro? No sé; estará (*he is probably*) **en casa.**
¿Qué hora es? No sé; serán (*it is probably*) **las doce.**
¿Cuántos años tiene? No sé; tendrá (*he is probably*) **veinte.**

The future tense, instead of meaning *will* or *shall*, often means *probably*. In such cases present action or condition is indicated instead of future.

EJERCICIO I. *Complete in Spanish:*

1. *They are probably* en la capital. 2. *He probably travels* a pie. 3. *It is probably* necesario manejar con cuidado. 4. *He probably doesn't want* permitirlo. 5. ¿Qué hora *can it be* (*is it probably*)?

6. ¿Cuántos años [old] *do you suppose he is* (*has he probably*)? 7. *He probably knows* (**conocer**) muy bien el camino. 8. ¿Dónde *can he be* (*is he probably*)?

14(b). Conditional of Probability

¿Dónde estaba Pedro? No sé; estaría (*he was probably*) **en casa.**

¿Qué hora era? No sé; serían (*it was probably*) **las doce.**

In the same way, the conditional tense is used to show past probability.

EJERCICIO II. *Change the future verbs you used in* Ejercicio I *to the conditional tense and translate.*

ALGO QUE REPASAR

15. Direct Object Pronouns

EJERCICIO III. *Review the list of direct object pronouns in section 108, then give these words in Spanish as the object of the verb* **ve**:

her, it (*m.*), it (*f.*), them (*f.*), you (*m. pol.*), you (*f. pol.*), thee, me, us, him (*two ways*), them (*m.*)

EJERCICIO IV. *Review the rule for the position of object pronouns in section 110; then complete these sentences in Spanish, explaining the position of each object pronoun in relation to the verb.* (Watch out for accents!)

1. *Dad* tuvo que firmar *it* (**papel**). 2. El inspector dió *it* a *Dad*. 3. *Sis* siempre está comiendo *them* (**dulces**). 4. Iremos a ver *it* (**la capital**). 5. El guardia inteligente quería explicar *it* (*two ways*). 6. Poniendo *it* sobre la mesa, se fué de prisa. 7. Todo el mundo estaba mirando *us* (*two ways*). 8. Traiga *me* Vd. la plumafuente. 9. No traiga *me* Vd. la gasolina. 10. Mire *it* Vd. (**camino**) antes de cruzar *it*.

16. The Infinitive after Prepositions

al volver, *upon* (*on*) *returning*; **antes de comer,** *before eating*

An infinitive is usually the only verb form that can follow a preposition in Spanish. In English such an infinitive is translated by a gerund.

EJERCICIO V. *Complete these sentences in Spanish and translate:*

1. *Upon beginning* el viaje, cambiaremos nuestro dinero. 2. *On account of* (**por**) *being* cansados, fuimos al hotel. 3. *Without seeing* el coche, no cruzaríamos la calle. 4. *Without looking at* el velocímetro, ella estaría contenta. 5. *On account of being afraid,* no viajaremos a pie. 6. *Without going* a México, sería difícil aprender sus costumbres. 7. *After changing* la llanta (*tire*), saldremos para Monterrey. 8. *Upon trying to* encontrar la casa de Juan, perdimos el camino. 9. *Before winning* un premio, sería necesario comprar un billete de lotería.

Modern restaurants spring up along the Mexican section of the Pan American Highway. Mural paintings here promote international friendship by picturing Uncle Sam in the Mexican National dance.

Black Star

PARA PRONUNCIAR

Review the rules for accentuation in section 137, then, following them closely, read aloud these Aztec sentences, slowly at first, then faster, to see if you can guess what they mean:

— ¿Ju aryú? ¿Juai aryu leit? ¿Uilyu espic tumí?
— Ol rait. ¿Juat duyu uantu no?
— ¿Du yusi Tami? ¿Juat uil jiséi? — ¿Jucantel?
— ¿Juai aryú somín? Yumecmi uántugo jom nau.
— Aim sari. Ay uil gotú.[1]

PARA LEER SIN ESTUDIAR

La turista y el diccionario

Un día mientras Jimmie estaba en un restaurant en México, vió en una mesa cercana (*nearby*) a una turista que por lo visto (*apparently*) no sabía el español. Estaba buscando palabras en su diccionario, y tratando de explicar al mesero con las manos lo que quería.

Al fin la señora terminó la comida, buscó más palabras en su diccionario, y llamó al mesero.

— ¿Mande Vd.? [2] — dijo el mesero al llegar a su mesa.

— Como mucho, — dijo la turista.

— Ah, ¡me gusta muchísimo! — respondió el mesero, e hizo una reverencia (*bow*).

— ¡Como mucho! — repitió la turista.

— Sí, señora, — respondió el mesero. — Me da mucho gusto saber que la comida fué buena.

— ¡Como mucho! — dijo otra vez la turista, con voz cada vez más irritada (*annoyed*).

— Pero señora, — empezaba el mesero confundido (*puzzled*), cuando llegó a la mesa Jimmie, que había oído la discusión.

[1] It looks more like Aztec than English, doesn't it? But it's only English written in Spanish phonetics, and means: "*Who are you? Why are you late? Will you speak to me?*" "*All right. What do you want to know?*" "*Do you see Tommy? What will he say?*" "*Who can tell?*" "*Why are you so mean? You make me want to go home now.*" "*I'm sorry. I will go too.*"

[2] *¿Mande Vd.?* is a polite way to answer when an older person or someone in a superior position calls you or when you have not heard what he has said.

— La señora quiere saber cuánto le debe por la comida, — explicó Jimmie al mesero. Pronto se arregló la cuenta (*bill*), y la turista salió muy satisfecha.

¿Cómo había sabido Jimmie lo que trataba de decir la turista? Pues, la señora había buscado en su diccionario la palabra *how*, luego la palabra *much*, ¡cuando quería saber decir *how much!*

TEMA

1. At last I shall go to Mexico by the National Highway. 2. Upon arriving, I shall change my dollars for pesos. 3. I shall try to drive carefully in the streets, where there is much traffic. 4. We should lose the road without reading them (*signs*). 5. The hotels will be modern and comfortable, with hot and cold water. 6. We shall go to various restaurants on Sundays. 7. Everyone will be looking at us, because we shall wear gardenias. 8. (The) Mexicans don't wear them, but we shall buy them often because they are cheap. 9. It would be easy to make mistakes in Spanish without studying it. 10. She is probably eleven years old on July seventh.

CAPÍTULO 7

Aventuras en México

Jimmie and his family could not be in Mexico long without discovering its Aztec heritage. All around them were Aztec names: Chapultepec (*Grasshopper Hill*), Xochimilco (*Flower Garden*), Teotihuacán (*Place of the Gods*). From a distance looked down upon them Popocatépetl (*Smoking Mountain*) and Ixtaccíhuatl (*Sleeping Woman*), the two famous volcanoes with their romantic legend. The Americans learned that many Mexican foods — chocolate, chile, *tortillas*, tomatoes, avocados — had been introduced to the European world by the Spaniards, who obtained them from the Indians. They explored Aztec-style open-air markets full of simple but beautiful things; they heard the clucking Náhuatl language of the Indians who still live in Xochimilco. And they finally realized that one reason Mexico is so different from the United States is that most of the people are at least partly of Indian blood, for instead of segregating or killing off the Indians, as our ancestors did, the Spaniards intermarried with them and formed the Mexican people.

Domingo, dos de julio.

Esta mañana dimos un paseo en coche hasta el Bosque de Chapultepec,[1] como toda la «gente de razón», para ver y ser vistos. En el Paseo de la Reforma [1] parecía haber una gran procesión, con todos los automóviles llenos de gente vestida de domingo. Había también muchos señores a caballo, todos vestidos de charro.[2] Al bajar del automóvil para visitar el Castillo (*Castle*) de Chapultepec, encontramos a un ciego que nos preguntó, — ¿Les pongo un ojo al coche,[3] señores? — Todo estaba bien cuando volvimos, y le pagué quince centavos. Cuando se los dí, nos dijo, — Vayan Vds. con Dios, señores.

Fuimos a Xochimilco esta tarde, a los «jardines flotantes (*floating*)» que ya no flotan. Allí tomamos una canoa grande

[1] Chapultepec Forest is a natural group of moss-bearded old cypress trees surrounding Chapultepec Castle on its two-hundred-foot hill. The ***Paseo de la Reforma,*** *Reform Drive,* was once called the ***Paseo de Carlota,*** after the French Empress who ordered the wide avenue slashed through the heart of the city to the Castle, three miles away.

[2] The ***charros,*** *horsemen,* usually belong to the Charro Association, which pledged itself years ago not to let the picturesque colonial costume die out.

[3] "*Shall I keep an eye on your car?*" A strange thing for a blind man to say! In some parts of the city it is customary to pay small boys a few *centavos* to watch your car while it is parked.

Brown Bros.

Fountain of Don Quixote, Chapultepec Park, is a favorite meeting place on Sunday mornings. The Spanish tile fountain, bookcases, and benches from Seville were a gift to Mexico from Spain.

con una mesa y cuatro sillas, y tomamos un *lunch* mientras nuestro canoero (*boatman*), indio azteca, nos llevaba por todos los canales. Éste habló náhuatl (la lengua azteca) con otros indios, pero conmigo habló español. Me contó la leyenda de la bandera mexicana,[1] y yo se la conté a la familia en inglés.

Vimos a muchos indios trabajando en sus jardines, donde crecían juntos maíz (*corn*) con claveles, frijoles con pensamientos (*pansies*), calabazas con margaritas (*daisies*). Cada una de las canoas, llenas de gente alegre, tenía un nombre interesante. Aquí tiene Vd. algunos: «Amor eterno», «El submarino de la niña», «Por ti muero, amor mío», «La perla de Leonardo», «La maravilla de Pablo Díaz», «Si estoy durmiendo, estoy soñando contigo», «Mi corazón te adora, angel mío», «Soy feliz sobre las olas del lago (*lake*)», y «Ni me presto (*lend*) ni me doy, soy de Roberto Solís». La nuestra

[1] The legend says that the Aztecs wandered south (via California!) until they found the sign they were searching for — an eagle perched upon a cactus eating a rattlesnake — and there they founded their city, although the Valley of Mexico was practically a marsh then. Legend says that the eagle was sitting on the rock where Chapultepec Castle now stands.

se llamaba «Me gusta estar en las olas del mar», y ¡el mar está a distancia de doscientas millas o más! ¡*Dad* dice que al parecer todos los indios de Xochimilco son poetas!

Mom compró un ramito grande de violetas y otro de claveles por veinte y cinco centavos. *Sis* por poco se cayó al agua, comprando unas pepitas tostadas de calabaza[1] a una vendedora que nos siguió en su canoa chica.

Martes, cuatro de julio.

Nos sorprendió mucho saber que se celebra aquí el cuatro de julio. El periódico más grande tiene toda una página con un grabado (*picture*) de colores de Jorge Wáshington con la bandera norteamericana. (Nuestra bandera se llama aquí «las barras y las estrellas».) ¡Hasta habrá una corrida de toros (*bullfight*) especial para celebrar nuestro día de independencia!

[1] ***pepitas tostadas de calabaza,*** *toasted pumpkin seeds,* are shelled, buttered and salted.

Flower-decorated barges float quietly along the canals between Xochimilco's "floating gardens," where corn and carnations or beans and pansies grow sociably together.

Black Star

Sawders

Chapel of the Well, at the shrine of Guadalupe, attracts visitors from all over Mexico. The waters of the sulphur spring bubbling up inside the chapel are supposed to cure any illness.

Por la tarde visitamos el Volador,[1] donde se vende toda clase de cosas usadas. Por un tostón compré un cuchillo de campo usado, muy viejo, que tiene un rótulo (*inscription*) que dice, «No vivo sin tu amor». El vendedor tenía otros cuchillos con inscripciones interesantes. Aquí tiene Vd. algunos: «Defenderé tu honra (*honor*)», «¡Viva México y mi dueño!», «Yo soy su rey, desgraciados», «Soy amigo de los hombres y enemigo de los traidores (*traitors*)», y «A quien pica (*bites*) esta víbora (*snake*), no hay remedio en la botica (*drugstore*)».

Un policía [2] que vió mi cuchillo de campo me dijo que no me permitiría llevarlo en el cinturón (*belt*) como una arma

[1] The *Volador,* a fascinating market full of second-hand junk like the Flea Market of Paris and the Rag Market of London, took its name from the Aztec flying game with which the end of their fifty-two-year "century" was celebrated. When the market's location was changed not many years ago, the name became «*El nuevo antiguo volador*»!

[2] ***La policía*** means *police force*; ***el policía*** means *policeman.*

(*weapon*), sino en la mano, como una curiosidad, porque soy extranjero, y los extranjeros no pueden portar (*carry*) armas.

En un puesto de loza (*pottery*) vimos muchos jarros (*jugs*) adornados con expresiones curiosas, por ejemplo: «Un regalito a mi amiguita Lucita», «María, María, dame tu amor», «Piensa en mí, chula (*beautiful*)», «Acuérdate de mí», «Quiéreme mucho», y «Dame un besito». Al parecer, los indios creen que es una tontería hacer un artículo de uso diario sin adornarlo.

Sis compró unos frijoles salteadores,[1] ¡pero espero que no tratará de comérselos!

Viernes, siete de julio.

Esta mañana fuimos a visitar la Villa (*town*) de Guadalupe, llamada oficialmente la Villa Madero.[2] Allí vimos la famosa iglesia que tiene la pintura (*painting*) de la Virgen de Guadalupe,[2] Santa Patrona (*Patron Saint*) de México. También visitamos la Capilla del Pozo (*Chapel of the Well*), donde brota (*gushes*) el agua milagrosa. Se dice que quien bebe de esta agua tendrá que volver a México, pero sé que yo querré volver sin beberla.

Sis compró unas gorditas de la Virgen,[3] y se las comió. Se vendían muchas velas cerca de la iglesia, ¡pero *Mom* no las compró!

De la Villa Madero salimos para las pirámides de San Juan Teotihuacán, las cuales (*which*) son más antiguas que las de Egipto. La Pirámide del Sol tiene la altura de un edificio de veinte pisos, cubre trece acres de tierra, y está hecha enteramente de adobe. Nadie sabe quién la construyó ni cuándo,

[1] ***frijoles salteadores,*** *jumping beans,* jump because a larva inside them moves. They are sometimes used for games, or as one curio store advertises, "to predict who will win the presidential chair!"

[2] Names of towns in Mexico are sometimes changed to honor national heroes. The Virgin of Guadalupe appeared miraculously painted upon an Aztec Indian's cloak on December 12, 1531, and has been the Patron Saint of Mexico ever since. Recently she was adopted as the Patron Saint of all Spanish America.

[3] *gorditas de la Virgen* are fat little cookies baked on a charcoal brazier out in the streets near the church.

pero los aztecas tenían un templo encima de ella. Hoy día no hay sino turistas en la cima.

Subimos la escalera (*stairway*), seguidos de chamacos ("*kids*") que trataban de vendernos unos «ídolos (*idols*) aztecas», más o menos nuevos. Al llegar a la cima, yo le conté a la familia algo de la historia de las pirámides, y pensando en lo que había pasado allí, todos nosotros, hasta *Sis*, guardamos silencio un rato. Aquí, en efecto — pensábamos — bajo nuestros mismos pies, estaba la pirámide enorme con su origen perdido en el misterio de miles de años.... Aquí, en este mismo lugar, sacrificaban (*sacrificed*) los aztecas a sus víctimas.... Aquí mismo, habían puesto en sus altares con sus ceremonias antiguas las «rojas frutas de las águilas»....[1]

Y en ese momento llegó un grupo de músicos (*musicians*) con sus guitarras, violines, y un saxófono, se sentaron en aquella pirámide antigua, ¡y empezaron a tocar una pieza de *swing* norteamericano!

[1] The "red fruits of the eagles" was the poetic name given by the Aztecs to the hearts torn from their living victims for their gods.

Age-old Aztec calendar, now in the Mexico City Museum, was more accurate than its European contemporary. The face represents the Sun God, the four rectangles the four seasons.

Gendreau

PALABRAS NUEVAS

3 **acordarse de** (**ue**)	to remember	2 **enemigo**	enemy
3 **adorar**	to worship	**flotar**	to float
3 **altura**	height	3 **grupo**	group
barra	stripe, bar	4 **página**	page
4 **beso**	kiss	4 **pieza**	piece
calabaza	pumpkin	**pirámide** (*f.*)	pyramid
canoa	canoe, barge	2 **sírvase**	please (*formal*)
3 **ciego**	blind (man)	3 **soñar** (**con**)	to dream (of)
cima	summit	3 **sorprenderse**	to be surprised
clavel (*m.*)	carnation	4 **tontería**	foolishness
3 **desgraciado**	unlucky		

Expresiones

***al parecer,** apparently
cuchillo de campo, knife carried as a weapon
dar un paseo, to go for a ride *or* drive
guardar silencio, to be quiet
por poco se cayó, almost fell
ser de, to belong to
toda clase de, all kinds of
vaya(n) Vd(s). con Dios, polite way to say good-by
vestido de domingo, dressed in Sunday best

PREGUNTAS

1. ¿Para qué dió la familia de Jimmie un paseo por el Bosque de Chapultepec? 2. ¿Cómo estaban vestidos los señores que iban a caballo? 3. ¿Qué quería hacer el ciego? 4. ¿Qué hizo la familia en los «jardines flotantes (*floating*)»? 5. ¿Qué lengua habló el canoero (*boatman*) con los otros indios? 6. ¿Qué crecía en los jardines? 7. ¿Cómo se llamaban algunas canoas? 8. ¿Qué leyó Jimmie en los cuchillos usados? 9. ¿De qué estaban adornados los jarros (*jugs*)? 10. ¿Qué querían vender los chamacos ("*kids*") que estaban cerca de la pirámide? 11. ¿Quiénes llegaron a la cima de la pirámide mientras estaban allí Jimmie y su familia? 12. ¿Qué empezaron a tocar los músicos (*musicians*)?

REPASO DE VERBOS

I. Review the preterite of the model third-conjugation radical-changing verb ("III RC verb") *sentir* in section 90. *Conjugate orally like it the verbs* **pedir, servir,** *and* **seguir.**

II. Review the similar preterite of *dormir* in section 89, and *conjugate* **morir** *like it. Then give the gerund of each verb in Exercises I and II.* Which preterite forms does the gerund resemble?

III. Review the preterite of *leer* in section 97. *Conjugate like it the verbs* **caer, oír,** *and* **creer,** *and give their gerunds.* How many accents are there?

Verbs ending in ***-uir*** are conjugated in the same way, except that they have only the two usual accents.

Conjugate **construir** *and* **huir** (*to flee*), *and give the gerunds; then complete this statement:* Unaccented ***i*** between two vowels changes to — in the —— tense and ——.

ALGO NUEVO

17. Familiar Commands, Singular

piensa en mí, *think of me;* **acuérdate de mí,** *remember me*

The only commands you have used until now are the polite forms, which require the "opposite vowel": *beber, beba Vd.; pasar, pase Vd.* The new ones, however, are familiar commands, and are formed differently. For a regular familiar command, use the third person singular present tense with the pronoun *tú,* or *tú* may be understood:

pensar, piensa tú; dar, da tú; oír, oye tú

EJERCICIO I. The only irregular commands you will be likely to need are the following, which must be learned. *Translate each one.*

decir	di (tú)	salir	sal (tú)
hacer	haz (tú)	ser	sé (tú)
ir	ve (tú)	tener	ten (tú)
poner	pon (tú)	venir	ven (tú)

18. Position of Object Pronouns

dime, *tell me* **hazlo,** *do it* **siéntate,** *sit down*
dile, *tell him* **vete,** *go away* **ponte,** *put on*

Object or reflexive pronouns are always attached to such commands, because these forms are used only in the affirmative. In Chapter 10 you will study negative familiar commands.

EJERCICIO II. *Give these commands in both the polite and familiar forms, singular only:*

1. put it	6. give me	11. drink it
2. come out	7. tell me	12. sit down
3. be careful	8. think of me	13. get up
4. come here (**acá**)	9. do it	14. visit him
5. go away	10. remember me	15. be good

19. Familiar Commands, Plural

tener, tened (vosotros); **salir, salid** (vosotros)

The plural of familiar commands is regular for every verb in the language. Simply replace the infinitive ***-r*** with a ***-d***, and add *vosotros,* which may also be omitted.

These forms are rarely used, however, since in Spanish America the plural familiar is replaced by *Vds.* Even in speaking to children you would say «*Vds.*» instead of «*vosotros*».[1] The forms with *vosotros* are used in making speeches.

20. Present Tense Used for Mild Commands

Vd. me lo dice, *will you please tell it to me.*

[1] Note to teacher: No drill is given here on the plural familiar command, since its use is rare. (Cf. Keniston, *Spanish Syntax List.*)

An interesting use of the present tense is for mild commands, when a simple statement takes it for granted that the person addressed is willing to do what is requested. This usage is found mainly in familiar conversation.

EJERCICIO III. *Translate these sentences as statements, then as commands:*

1. Vd. contesta a la gente. 2. Vd. me lo trae, ¿eh? 3. Vds. buscan a las mujeres y les dicen donde estamos. 4. Tú vas a la ciudad, ¿eh? 5. Tú le explicas la leyenda. 6. ¿Me hace el favor de ir?

21. The "Personal a*"*

EJERCICIO IV. *Review the rule for the "personal* **a**" *in section 127; then complete these sentences in Spanish, telling why you did or did not use the "personal* **a**" *in each.* (¡Tenga Vd. cuidado!)

1. Veo *John.* 2. Visitamos *our friends.* 3. Ella adora *Paul.* 4. Yo defendería *my mother.* 5. Miran *the girls.* 6. Las señoritas miran *the flowers.* 7. Vimos *many Indians.* 8. Encontraron *a blind man.* 9. El ciego cuidaba de *the car.* 10. Mi hermanita se comió *the beans.* 11. En el camino vimos *a beautiful horse.* 12. Mira tú *Mary.*

22. Indirect Object Pronouns

EJERCICIO V. *Review the list of indirect object pronouns in section 109 and complete these sentences in Spanish:*

1. Cuenta la leyenda *to him, to her, to us.* 2. Dan las flores *to her, to you, to them* (*f.*). 3. Escriben las cartas *to you, to me, to them* (*m.*).

23. Two Object Pronouns

cuando se los dí, *when I gave them to him*

EJERCICIO VI. *Review the rule for this construction in section 111 and complete these sentences:*

1. When there are two object pronouns, one direct and one indirect, the — comes first. 2. If both begin with *l,* the indirect

Sawders

Popocatépetl, the Aztecs' "Smoking Mountain," lifts his snowy head above the Valley of Mexico. Spanish soldiers during the Conquest descended into its crater to obtain sulphur for their gunpowder.

object pronoun, — or —, must be changed to —. 3. If one is a reflexive pronoun, the — pronoun comes first.

EJERCICIO VII. *Translate carefully.* (Little words are much harder to translate than big ones!)

1. Me las vendió. 2. Se lo dió a ella. 3. Nos la dijo. 4. No quería decírselo. 5. Después de leérselo a ella, me fuí. 6. Estaban diciéndoselo a ellos. 7. Me lo preguntó. 8. Se lo comió. 9. Se las llevaron. 10. Nos los dieron. 11. Dímelo. 12. Dámelo tú. 13. Démelo Vd. 14. Tráiganosla Vd. 15. Se lo dije a Vd.

EJERCICIO VIII. *Write in Spanish:* [1]

1. He gives it to me. 2. He gives it to us. 3. He gives them to me. 4. He gives it to him. 5. He gives it to her; to you. 6. He gives them to her; to you. 7. He gives them to them; to you (*pl.*).

EJERCICIO IX. *Now rewrite the sentences in Exercise VIII, using* **está dando** *for the verb instead of* **da.** Where do you put the object pronouns? (There are two possible positions.)

[1] Write them backwards. Write *da* first, put *lo* before it, then *me* in front of that. Later you can think faster and write them in order as you go. This is a good exercise to repeat frequently.

EJERCICIO X. *Now rewrite the same sentences, using* **quiere dar** *for the verb.*

ESTUDIO DE PALABRAS

I. Review the demonstrative adjectives and pronouns (§§ 116, 117) and complete in Spanish:

1. *This* casa es más bonita que *that one* (*over there*). 2. Yo quiero *that one* (*near you*), pero ella quiere *that one* (*over there*). 3. *This* clase estudia más que *that one* (*yours*). 4. *These* cosas son de Luis, pero *those* (*over there*) son de Pedro. 5. *The latter* (**el indio**) me lo dijo. 6. Ví *the latter* (**Juana**) en el camino. 7. *This* mañana *that* animal nos siguió a casa.

II. Here are more traffic signs which Jimmie found in Mexico. *By guessing, choose from List B the meaning for each one in List A.*[1]

A	B
1. Crucero tranvías	*a.* For pedestrians
2. Tome Vd. su derecha	*b.* No parking here
3. Sírvase no estacionarse aquí	*c.* No overpass
4. Sírvase tomar su derecha	*d.* Streetcar crossing
5. Evite Vd. choques	*e.* Please keep to your right
6. Para peatones	*f.* No admittance (passing)
7. No hay paso	*g.* Avoid accidents
8. Se prohibe estacionarse aquí	*h.* School zone
9. No voltear a la izquierda	*i.* Please don't park here
10. Límite de bulevar	*j.* For persons
11. Evite accidentes	*k.* Slow
12. Zona de escuela	*l.* No left turn
13. Se prohibe pasar	*m.* Please turn to the left
14. Despacio	*n.* No trespassing
	o. Turn to your right
	p. Avoid collisions
	q. End of boulevard

[1] Note to teacher: Optional exercise. Some of these expressions are not found in the vocabulary, since they are not used elsewhere.

III. Using the verbs in the following list, complete the sentences. With their reflexives and prepositions, they are sometimes hard to manage. *(¡Cuidado con los verbos!)*

parecerse a, reírse de, ponerse, fijarse en, acostumbrarse a, mandar hacer, dejar caer, burlarse de, tratar de, bajar de

1. Yo *resemble* mi madre. 2. Todos *will laugh at* mí. 3. Ella *became* (*turned*) pálida de pronto. 4. Ellos *will pay attention to* esto. 5. Ellos *became accustomed to* las comidas. 6. Ella *ordered* un vestido nuevo *made*. 7. Vd. *will drop* la sopa. 8. Él *would make fun of* ellos. 9. Nosotros *shall try to* manejar con cuidado. 10. Siempre *we get out of* el coche de prisa.

PARA LEER SIN ESTUDIAR

¿SABÍA VD. ESTO?

1. ¡La «Casa blanca» de México lleva el nombre de un insecto! «Chapultepec», palabra azteca, significa *Grasshopper Hill*, porque había muchos saltamontes (*grasshoppers*) allí en los días de los aztecas.

2. Los aztecas inventaron el chocolate, y sus nobles lo bebían en tazas (*cups*) de oro. Los pobres nunca podían beberlo. El cacao (*cocoa*) valía tanto que las pepitas (*seeds*) servían de dinero entre los aztecas, aunque tenían bastante oro y plata.

3. Los indios aztecas tenían, hace muchos siglos (*centuries*), un calendario más perfecto que el nuestro. El principal, que hoy día está en el Museo (*Museum*) Nacional, es de piedra, tiene doce pies de altura, y tiene en el centro una cara que representa el sol. Así se llama muchas veces la «Piedra del Sol».

4. El Emperador de los aztecas, Moctezuma II, podía tener pescado (*fish*) fresco del mar todos los días, aunque vivía a distancia de casi trescientas millas del océano. Los indios corrían como en un *relay* desde la costa hasta la capital, llegando en veinte y cuatro horas con el pescado fresco envuelto (*wrapped*) en hojas (*leaves*) grandes de plátano (*banana tree*).

TEMA

1. This morning we shall go for a ride like everyone. 2. Carnations and beans were growing together in the gardens which no longer floated. 3. Those families were eating while the boatman (*canoero*) took them along the canals. 4. When we gave it to him, he said to us, "Thank you very much." 5. My sister bought some beans from (*a*) the vendor and ate them up quickly. 6. At that moment the Indians almost fell into the water. 7. The blind man was sleeping on the street near the church. 8. We saw those tourists on top of the Pyramid of the Sun, but these were buying knives. 9. The Aztecs knew how to read and write, but the Spaniards destroyed (*destruir*) their books. 10. She laughed at me when I told her so (*lo*). 11. Give it to me (*fam.*), and I will take it to him after reading it to her.

CAPÍTULO 8

Optional Chapter [1]

Tres cuentos para contar al hermanito

Spanish-speaking people like to tell these simple stories. You should be able to read them without looking up any words but the few new ones listed at the end of the reading. (They are not in the general vocabulary unless you are going to need them in a later chapter.)

I. PEPE REPEPE [2] Y SU PÁJARO

Una mañana Pepe Repepe estaba en su patio. Un pájaro

[1] Note to teacher: This chapter may be omitted in order to finish Chapter 9 by the end of the first quarter if there is not time for both. Chapter 9, however, should be completed, since it is a final review of Chapters 1–7 inclusive.

[2] *Pepe Repepe, Joe "Jo-jo,"* a whimsical coined surname.

voló a un árbol, y se quedó allí. Pepe Repepe vió que el pájaro se durmió.

Pepe Repepe se dijo, — Aquel pájaro está durmiendo. Buscaré una piedra y se la tiraré. El pájaro caerá al pie del árbol. No podrá volar, y lo atraparé. Lo pondré en una jaula (*cage*) en el patio. El gato lo mirará y se irá sin comerlo. Al principio el pájaro estará muy triste. Pero pronto estará más contento, y empezará a cantar. Todo el mundo dirá, «¿De quién es ese pájaro que canta tan bien?»

— Contestaré, «Este pájaro es mío, porque yo lo atrapé.»

— Todo el mundo querrá comprar el pájaro que canta tan bien. Lo venderé por mucho dinero. Con el dinero compraré una honda (*sling*). Con la honda atraparé muchos pájaros. Todos sabrán cantar bien y los venderé todos. Con el dinero me compraré un caballo blanco. Daré muchos paseos a caballo, y todo el mundo dirá, «¿Quién es aquel muchacho que va a caballo?»

Pepe Repepe cogió una piedra y levantó el brazo para tirarla. Dijo, — ¡A la una![1] ¡A las dos!

Y cuando iba a decir, — ¡A las tres! — el pájaro voló, gritándole a Pepe Repepe, — ¡Bienteveo! ¡Bienteveo![2]

ADAPTED FROM *La Prensa* (SAN ANTONIO)

II. EL SAPITO BIEN EDUCADO

Érase que se era (*once upon a time there was*) un sapito bien educado y muy cortés. Siempre se levantaba muy temprano, porque si no, ¿cómo diría a la gente, — Buenos días?

Nunca cantó de día ni de noche, este sapito bien educado, para no molestar a los vecinos.

Y por ser tan bien educado, el pobre sapito estaba triste y flaco (*thin*), porque a la hora de comer esperaba a que le sirviesen (*serve*) sin pedirlo, y nadie le servía nada.

[1] When you count, "One, two, three, go!" in Spanish, you must say ***a la una, a las dos,*** etc.

[2] A ***bienteveo*** is a brightly colored and noisy bird of the Argentine pampas. What does the word mean, literally?

Y cuando, con uno de sus amigos, encontraba un buen gusano (*worm*), siempre decía, — ¡Sírvase Vd.![1] ¡Primero usted! — Y el otro no le dejaba nada.

A veces se quedaba sin comer porque no podía comer como se debe: sin abrir demasiado la boca. ¡Y todos saben que los sapos, grandes o chicos, tienen que abrir demasiado la boca!

A veces las piernas del pobre sapito bien educado se le cansaban mucho (*became very tired*), porque nunca se sentó delante de un sapo mayor. Y siempre daba el paso a los mayores de edad.

Una vez se puso muy triste y empezó a llorar porque no tenía sombrero. ¿Por qué quería sombrero? Porque quería saludar (*greet*) a la gente, quitándose el sombrero y diciendo, — Servidor de usted.[2]

Un día se sentó en el camino muy triste. — ¿Vale la pena? — se dijo. — ¿Vale la pena ser tan bien educado? ¿No sería mejor ser como los otros?

Y en eso vió que alguien venía por el camino. Como era tan bien educado, inmediatamente dió un gran salto (*jump*) y luego otro, para dar el paso.

Su cortesía tan rápida le salvó la vida. Pues, ¡quien venía era una víbora (*snake*)!

— ¡Vale la pena! ¡Vale la pena! — se dijo el sapito bien educado. Y después nunca se comió una mosca (*fly*) sin decirle primero, — Dispense Vd. (*excuse me*).

ADAPTED FROM *La Prensa* (SAN ANTONIO)

III. LA FLOR DE NOCHEBUENA

Era Navidad, y la pobre muchacha india estaba muy triste. No tenía dinero. No tenía nada que dar al Niño Jesús. Todas sus amigas iban a llevar regalos a la iglesia

[1] ***sírvase*** is not *please* in this case, but *help yourself.*

[2] ***Servidor de usted,*** *at your service* (sometimes ***a sus órdenes*** or ***para servir a usted***), is a polite expression used especially when telling one's name.

para el Niño en la Nochebuena, y sólo ella no tenía nada que darle.

Muy triste, salió al patio para buscar flores que llevar a la iglesia. Pero allí no crecía ni una florecita. Solamente había un arbusto verde, muy feo, sin flores ni nada más que hojas grandes.

La pobre indita[1] se sentó en el patio sin flores y empezó a llorar. Sus lágrimas cayeron en las hojas grandes del arbusto verde.

Después de llorar un rato, la pobre indita se levantó para entrar en su casa. Y allí, cerca de ella ¡vió que el arbusto verde tenía hojas rojas, hojas magníficas! ¡Las lágrimas que habían caído en las hojas verdes, las habían vuelto (*turned*) rojas!

[1] *indita* = *indi(a)* + *ita.*

Sarapes — Indian blankets — attract tourists with their bright colors. Most of these are woven in modern designs, instead of the traditional tribal patterns which the Indians make for themselves.

Galloway

Entonces, ¡sí que tenía la pobre indita un regalo para el Niño Jesús! Su regalo era el más bonito de todos, y desde entonces por Navidad algunas hojas de este arbusto siempre se ponen rojas, y la planta se llama la «flor de Nochebuena» de México.

Ésta es la leyenda de la flor que simboliza la Navidad para nosotros también, porque un señor norteamericano, Joel Poinsett,[1] la encontró creciendo en México y la trajo a nuestro país, donde la llamamos la *poinsettia*.

PALABRAS NUEVAS [2]

	atrapar	to catch	4	**molestar**	to annoy
2	**boca**	mouth		**Navidad**	Christmas
2	**cantar**	to sing		**Nochebuena**	Christmas Eve
2	**coger**	to pick up	4	**pájaro**	bird
4	**cuento**	story	1	**¿de quién?**	whose?
2	**delante de**	in front of	2	**quitarse**	to take off
	dispense Vd.	excuse (me)		**sapo**	toad
3	**feo**	ugly		**sapito**	sap(o) + ito
3	**hoja**	leaf	3	**vecino**	neighbor
3	**lágrimas**	tears	3	**volar (ue)**	to fly (away)
2	**llorar**	to cry			

Expresiones

*__al principio,__ at first
bien educado, well behaved
de día, by day
en eso, at that moment
por Navidad, at Christmas
se debe, one ought to

NO ES VERDAD

Change these statements about the stories to make them true:

[1] Joel Poinsett was the United States Ambassador to Mexico in 1825.

[2] Note to teacher: Since this is a "plateau" chapter (that is, a chapter without any new grammar points and concerned mainly with review and use of materials already covered), all words not yet used in Book II are given here, but are repeated in vocabularies if introduced later, since this chapter will be omitted by many classes.

I. 1. El pájaro cayó al pie del árbol. 2. El gato se comerá el pájaro. 3. Todo el mundo dirá, — Este pájaro es mío. 4. Pepe dará muchos paseos a pie. 5. Pepe creía que el pájaro empezaría a gritar. 6. Todos los pájaros sabrían contar muy bien.

II. 1. El sapito se levantaba muy tarde por la mañana. 2. El sapito gritaba de día y de noche. 3. Comiendo con un amigo, siempre decía, — ¡Primero yo! 4. Siempre se sentaba delante de los mayores de edad. 5. El sapito empezó a llorar porque vió una víbora (*snake*). 6. Los sapos se comen las víboras. 7. Su cortesía le salvó solamente el sombrero. 8. No vale la pena ser cortés y bien educado.

III. 1. La indita quería llevar un regalo a una amiga suya. 2. En el patio crecía un arbusto verde con muchas florecitas. 3. El regalo de la indita era el más feo de todos. 4. La violeta simboliza para nosotros la Navidad. 5. La flor de Nochebuena existió primero en nuestro país. 6. Las lágrimas de cualquier persona vuelven (*turn*) rojas a las hojas.

LO CONTRARIO

The opposites of these expressions were used in the stories. *If you do not know them already, see if you can find them.*

1. estará más triste
2. terminará
3. nadie dirá
4. este pájaro es de Vd.
5. los compraré todos
6. un caballo negro
7. un sapito muy descortés
8. se levantaba muy tarde
9. alguien le servía algo
10. poniéndose el sombrero
11. se sentó detrás de los mayores
12. para cerrar el paso
13. la indita tenía mucho que dar
14. el arbusto bonito y rojo
15. el regalo más feo de todos
16. ningunas amigas iban a llevar regalos
17. aquí crecían muchas florecitas

PREGUNTAS

I. 1. ¿Qué hizo el pájaro en el árbol? 2. ¿Vió Pepe el pájaro? 3. ¿Qué iba a buscar Pepe? 4. ¿Qué haría Pepe con la piedra?

5. ¿Qué haría el gato? 6. ¿Estaría muy contento el pájaro al principio? 7. ¿Cómo podría Pepe comprar un caballo? 8. ¿Qué le dijo el pájaro al volar?

II. 1. ¿Por qué se levantaba temprano el sapito? 2. ¿Por qué estaba flaco el sapito? 3. ¿Qué decía siempre a sus amigos? 4. ¿Tienen los sapos que abrir demasiado la boca? 5. ¿Por qué lloró el pobre sapito? 6. ¿Valía la pena ser tan bien educado?

III. 1. ¿Por qué estaba triste la muchacha india? 2. ¿Qué iban sus amigas a llevar a la iglesia? 3. ¿Crecían muchas flores en el patio? 4. Cuando cayeron las lágrimas en las hojas verdes, ¿qué pasó? 5. ¿Quién tenía el regalo más bonito para el Niño Jesús?

REPASO DE VERBOS

I. Here is a synopsis model using all the verb forms you have had this semester, with their meanings:

Synopsis Model	
INFINITIVE	**cantar,** to sing
GERUND	**cantando,** singing
PAST PARTICIPLE	**cantado,** sung
PRESENT	**canto,** I sing
POLITE COMMAND	**cante Vd.,** sing
FAMILIAR COMMAND	**canta tú,** sing
IMPERFECT	**yo cantaba,** I used to sing, was singing
PRETERITE	**canté,** I sang
FUTURE	**cantaré,** I shall sing
CONDITIONAL	**yo cantaría,** I should sing
PRESENT PROGRESSIVE	**estoy cantando,** I am singing
PAST PROGRESSIVE	**yo estaba cantando,** I was singing
PRESENT PERFECT	**he cantado,** I have sung
PAST PERFECT	**yo había cantado,** I had sung
COND. PERFECT [1]	**yo habría cantado,** I should have sung

[1] The future perfect is so rarely used that drill is not necessary.

1. Complete the conjugation of each tense to be sure you know all the endings.

2. Copy the outline without the verb forms and fill in the proper forms of these verbs, using the first person singular except for the commands (§ 63 ff.):

buscar (*watch spelling of pol. com. and pret.*)
dar (*irreg. in pres. and pret.*)
caer (*watch pres., p.p., and ger.*)
dormir (*III RC: watch pret. and ger.*)
ir (*very irreg.; no progressive*)
decir (*¡Cuidado!*)

3. Now do the same with the reflexive verbs **sentarse (ie)** *and* **irse.** Where do the reflexive pronouns stand with each kind of verb form?

II. Give the infinitives and translate these assorted verb forms carefully. Remember that it makes lots of difference whether "a bear *is* chasing me" or "a bear *was* chasing me"!

se sentaron	cayendo	estaba durmiendo	quería
voló	se irá	no dirían	dirán
nos dormimos	sabríamos	nos poníamos	íbamos
había caído	habrían puesto	buscarán	cayó
eran	vieron	queremos	venderé
decías	viendo	querremos	vendré
dijo	se comió	podremos	vendí
dime tú	han hecho	podemos	trajeron
no se caiga Vd.	pusieron	podíamos	trayendo
ven conmigo	ponte tú	podríamos	salid
ten cuidado	comed vosotros	contábamos	dando

ESTUDIO DE PALABRAS

I. ¿Verdad o No? [1]

1. Sin la gasolina, no habría mucho tránsito en las avenidas modernas. 2. El saxófono, el violín, y el piano son instrumentos de orquesta. 3. Un poeta azteca escribió algunos versos para una niña en un submarino. 4. La historia de los canales de los aztecas es

[1] This exercise is made up almost entirely of cognates used before, many of which are not in the vocabulary.

solamente un rumor y nadie quiere creerla. 5. Sería imposible cruzar montañas por un paso. 6. Una dama inocente, dando gritos de alarma, cayó del risco. 7. La expedición oyó rumores falsos de la importancia de las siete ciudades. 8. Las víctimas eran sacrificadas en los altares de los templos. 9. Todos los habitantes de los Estados Unidos son chinos. 10. La superstición da importancia a los remedios de los indios.

II. Words of a "family" are related because they have the same ancestry. *Starting with the first word of each group, can you guess the meanings of the related ones?* Many of them are not in the general vocabulary; therefore you will have to rely on your imagination!

1. ***dos:*** doce, docena 2. ***calor*** (*heat*): caliente, calentar, calorífero 3. ***nombre:*** nombrar, nominación 4. ***número:*** numeroso, numérico, numeral, numéricamente 5. ***desear:*** el deseo, deseoso 6. ***casa:*** casarse con, un casado, un casamiento 7. ***pez*** (*fish*): pescar, pescador, el pescado, caña de pescar, la pesca (*catch*) 8. ***comer:*** comedor, comida, comestibles 9. ***favor:*** favorable, favorecer, favorito, favoritismo 10. ***cantar:*** canción, cancionero (*book*), el canto, cancionista, cantante, cantador 11. ***bueno:*** bondad, bondadoso 12. ***escribir:*** escribiente, escritor, escritorio, escritura (*handwriting*) 13. ***día:*** diario, diariamente 14. ***feliz:*** felizmente, felicitar (*congratulate*), felicidades, felicitación 15. ***amar*** (*to love*): el amor, amable, amabilidad, amante, amador

PARA DIVERTIRSE

«¿Qué hizo Fulano?»

In this game (1) the ***Jefe*** (*chief*) gives a command to ***Fulano;*** (2) ***Fulano*** tells what he is doing as he does it; and (3) the class tells the same thing *about* him. Then (4) the ***Jefe*** asks, "What did ***Fulano*** do?"; (5) ***Fulano*** tells what he did; and (6) the class repeats.

Por ejemplo:

1. Jefe — Fulano, póngase Vd. delante de la clase.
2. Fulano — Me pongo delante de la clase.

3. Clase — Fulano se pone delante de la clase.
4. Jefe — ¿Qué hizo Fulano?
5. Fulano — Me puse delante de la clase.
6. Clase — Fulano se puso delante de la clase.

Other commands to use in the same way (or you may make up some funny ones of your own):

1. Pase Vd. a la puerta. 2. Escriba Vd. su nombre en la pizarra. 3. Vuelva Vd. a su asiento. 4. Ponga Vd. la mano derecha cerca del ojo. 5. Cierre Vd. su libro. 6. Siéntese Vd. en el suelo. 7. Póngase Vd. cerca de un amigo suyo. 8. Siéntese Vd. cerca de una muchacha bonita. 9. Levántese Vd. 10. Ponga Vd. el pie derecho detrás del pie izquierdo. 11. Ponga Vd. las manos encima de la cabeza. 12. Abra Vd. la boca.

PARA LEER SIN ESTUDIAR

Estos chistes son fáciles de leer.

1. — ¡Papacito! ¡Este libro dice que hay animales que cambian de piel (*fur*) todos los años!

— ¡Silencio! ¡Tu madre puede oírte!

2. El pordiosero — ¡Tenga Vd. compasión de un pobrecito ciego!
El señor — Pero Vd. no es ciego.
El pordiosero — Yo no, pero mi perro (*dog*) sí.

3. — ¿Llora Vd. porque se han perdido sus gallinas (*hens*)?

— Sí, señor. Anoche (*last night*) dejé abierta la puerta del gallinero (*henhouse*).

— ¿Y se las robaron?

— No, señor. Cada una se fué a la casa de su antiguo dueño.

4. — ¿Quién protegió a Cristóbal Cólon?
— Isabel la Católica.
— ¿Qué le dió?
— Sus alhajas (*jewels*), porque Colón no tenía dinero.
— ¿Y por qué no tenía dinero la reina (*queen*)?
— Porque sería fin de mes.

5. — En esta casa los vecinos pueden ver por esta ventana todo lo que se hace dentro (*within*).

— Bien, señora, tapemos (*let us cover up*) la ventana.

— Entonces, ¿cómo podré yo ver lo que hacen los vecinos?

6. Pasajero tímido — Dígame, piloto, los aeroplanos como éste, ¿se caen con frecuencia?

Piloto — No, señor, se caen solamente una vez.

7. Manuel — ¡Ah, señorita, esta noche me llegaré a su balcón y le cantaré una bonita serenata (*serenade*)!

Consuelo — Hágalo. Y yo le dejaré caer una flor.

Manuel — Ah, ¿en un momento de amor?

Consuelo — No, en una maceta (*flowerpot*).

8. — ¿Ya sabes lo que pasó en un túnel que está entre México y Vera Cruz?

— No, ¿qué pasó?

— Un tren.

9. Pancho — ¿Cómo es que ese hijo tuyo, tan mal educado, tiene un ojo morado ("*black*")?

Pedro — Fué ese hijo tuyo, tan bien educado, que le tiró una flor [1] con maceta (*flowerpot*) y todo.

TEMA

1. One day Joe was sleeping (*prog.*) near a tree. 2. A bird fell at the foot of the tree. 3. The cat caught (***coger***) the bird and ate it up. 4. Whose bird is it? It is the cat's, now. 5. Everyone knows that the bird will sing no longer. 6. The little toad used to say to (the) people, "Good morning." 7. He never sat down without taking off his hat. 8. Someone was beginning to cry without opening his mouth too much. 9. Is it worth while to be courteous and well behaved? 10. She will have nothing to take to the church. 11. Her red flowers were the prettiest of all. 12. She brought the "Christmas Eve flower" to our country.

[1] To "throw a flower" usually means to "pay a compliment," but not in this case!

CAPÍTULO **9**

Quarterly Review

A Guatemala por avión

Jimmie's unexpected trip south to Guatemala by plane was a real thrill. In four and a half hours he flew over jungles and mountains from Mexico City to Guatemala City, a trip that would have taken a week on the temperamental little train connecting the two neighboring countries which used to be one.

During the trip the plane steward told Jimmie that after Cortés explored Mexico and conquered the Aztecs, he sent Pedro de Alvarado to do the same thing among Guatemala's Mayan Indians, and the whole territory became New Spain. But Guatemala had seceded from Mexico about a hundred years ago, he said, and since then each had grown up in its own way.

In spite of Guatemala's high percentage of Indian population, the steward told Jimmie, he could expect to find a remarkably clean and efficiently run country, where he would see no bullfights because the animals were too valuable to kill, where traffic officers would be standing under umbrellas at every street intersection, and where it would cost him five dollars to throw a chewing gum wrapper into the gutter!

This country, he went on to say, is the only civilized place in the Western Hemisphere where colorful Indians still live just as they did four hundred years ago. But when Jimmie got there, he found that quite a few of them had learned to say, "Okay!"

Sawders

Highland lakes of rugged Guatemala are ringed with volcanoes, some active and some extinct. In villages scattered over the uplands Indian tribes live much as they did before the conquest.

Lunes, diez de julio.
México, D.F.

¡Ay, qué suerte tan buena! ¡Mi billete de lotería ganó un premio de mil pesos! Todo el mundo me pregunta cómo voy a gastar el dinero, el cual equivale a (*is worth*) casi doscientos dólares, y eso lo sé sin tener que pensarlo. ¡*Dad* me ha dado permiso (*permission*) para hacer un viaje por avión a Guatemala! No será barato, porque un dólar vale solamente un quetzal,[1] pero tendré bastante dinero.

Martes, once de julio.
A bordo (*on board*) del avión entre México y Guatemala.

Salimos del aeropuerto esta mañana a las siete y media.

[1] The *quetzal*, a jungle bird with long green tail feathers, is the national symbol of Guatemala because it refuses to live in captivity. The bird is found pictured everywhere, and even the monetary unit is called a *quetzal*. One *quetzal* is worth one American dollar, because Guatemala is a prosperous little country.

Somos catorce personas en un «DC 2». Pasamos cerca de los volcanes «Popo» e «Ixta»,[1] cubiertos los dos de nieve como siempre. Hace dos horas alcanzamos (*overtook*) en el aire un viejo avión de carga (*freight*) «Ford Trimotor», que lleva expreso aéreo entre la capital y Yucatán, porque no hay ferrocarril. Nos agradó (*pleased*) ver debajo de nosotros el viejo avión, que parecía estar suspendido sobre la selva (*jungle*), porque volaba mucho más despacio que el nuestro.

Ahora volamos sobre la tierra verde y montañosa que es Guatemala, con volcanes por todas partes. Desde el aire podemos ver que muchos volcanes pequeños tienen dentro de su cráter una milpa (*cornfield*) que nunca se podría ver desde la tierra. ¡Hemos descubierto un secreto de los indios!

Miércoles, doce de julio.
Ciudad de Guatemala.

Me gusta Guatemala. Desde mi cuarto en el hotel puedo oír tocar en el patio la orquesta (*orchestra*) de marimba.[2] Pero

[1] «Popo» and «Ixta» are the pet names people give the Mexican volcanoes Popocatépetl and Ixtaccíhuatl.

[2] The *marimba*, a wooden xylophone which came from Africa, is Guatemala's most popular instrument. Some are so large that it takes seven men to play them.

La Aurora Airport at Guatemala City welcomes the air traveler by broadcasting semi-classical music. Guatemala City is five thousand feet above sea level, where the climate is delightful.

Gendreau

toca música moderna de México y de los Estados Unidos, porque hay poca música indígena (*native*) del país. Voy a comprar la única canción (*song*) guatemalteca, llamada «El leñador» (*woodcutter*), que han tocado.

Las comidas son excelentes, y en el menú del desayuno (*breakfast*) hallé la palabra «mosh»,[1] que demuestra la influencia norteamericana.

Todos los guatemaltecos son muy amigos de los Estados Unidos y muchos hablan inglés porque es obligatorio estudiarlo en las escuelas, o porque se han educado en las universidades de mi país. Hablando con una muchacha en el hotel, le pregunté cuánto tiempo tendría ella que estudiar mi lengua, y respondió tristemente, — Señor, ¡hasta que lo aprenda! [2]

Aquí los productos principales son las bananas y el café. Vendiéndonos tanto café, los guatemaltecos tienen bastante dinero para comprar nuestros automóviles y otras cosas. Ellos mismos también toman mucho café, y cuando le invitan a uno a «tomar te» (*tea*), ¡sirven café!

Viernes, catorce de julio.
Antigua, Guatemala.

Hoy hice un viaje en automóvil por tres de las cuatro capitales de Guatemala, y mañana veré la otra, camino de (*on the way to*) Chichicastenango. En la primera capital, Tecpan, los indios molestaron tanto a los españoles que éstos pronto se la devolvieron y se fueron.[3]

Cuando visité la segunda capital, Santiago de los Caballeros (ahora llamada Ciudad Vieja), encontré solamente una pared del palacio del conquistador Alvarado. Esta ruina está en el patio de una escuela moderna, y los niños la usan para jugar a la pelota (*handball*), sin pensar que allí, hace cuatro-

[1] *«mosh»*, *mush*, is the Guatemalan word for any kind of American breakfast food!

[2] *aprenda,* a subjunctive form you have not studied yet. Translate it as it sounds best.

[3] Today Tecpan is a sleepy Indian town, the only reminder of the Spaniards being the great church with the Hapsburg coat of arms in its ceiling.

Chichicastenango Indian, descendant of the Mayas, plays an old-style marimba in the patio of the Mayan Inn. The drawings on the wall behind him are Mayan writing copied from ancient stone carvings.

cientos años, murieron todos los habitantes de la ciudad en una inundación (*flood*).[1] Sobre la ruina hay una placa (*plaque*) que dice:

> Detened el paso (*stop*), viajeros. Esto es lo único que hoy queda del palacio de los Conquistadores de Guatemala. Aquí perecieron (*perished*) la sin ventura (*luckless*) doña Beatriz de la Cueva y once damas de su corte (*court*) en la catástrofe de la ciudad el 8 de septiembre de 1541.

Estoy ahora en la tercera capital, Antigua Guatemala, que tuvo más suerte, porque duró más de doscientos años. En el año de 1700 era una de las tres ciudades más grandes de todo

[1] The story goes that when Doña Beatriz, Alvarado's wife, heard of his death on his way north to look for the Seven Cities of Cíbola, she proclaimed herself Captain-General of the Kingdom of Guatemala, and ordered the entire city to be painted black in mourning for him. People complained that it was wrong to use such deep mourning for even a *conquistador*, but before the orders were carried out, rain began to fall. For nine days and nights it poured; then an earthquake broke open the crater of Mt. Agua, and down rushed the flood that wiped out the entire city. Nothing remains today but one wall of Doña Beatriz' chapel.

Gendreau

Market-day in Chichicastenango finds the great plaza filled with Indians who have walked for many miles to exchange their produce, just as their ancestors did hundreds of years ago.

el Nuevo Mundo. Tenía una universidad y cien iglesias hermosísimas. Pero esta ciudad magnífica, tres años antes de nuestra Declaración de Independencia, fué destruida por unos terremotos, cuando murió mucha gente y se derrumbaron (*tumbled down*) casi todas las casas. Entonces el Rey de España mandó construir otra capital — la de hoy — a distancia de unas veinte y cinco millas, y casi toda la gente fué a la ciudad nueva.

Hoy día Antigua es una ciudad de ruinas pintorescas, donde viven unos 8.000 habitantes esperando a los turistas que vienen a ver lo que hizo el terremoto hace muchos años. Lo curioso es que desde entonces, aunque no ha habido otro terremoto en Antigua, en Guatemala ha habido muchos.

Domingo, diez y seis de julio.
Chichicastenango, Quiché, Guatemala.

En la capital ví muchos indios, pero aquí en «Chichi» casi todos son indios. Hoy es «día de plaza»,[1] como siempre lo ha sido, y toda la plaza se ha convertido en un gran mercado (*market*), donde todos compran y venden cosas. Los indios hacen telas maravillosas, y hasta los hombres las usan en sus vestidos de colores.

Se dice que los indios son muy honrados, y éste es un cuento que alguien me contó de ellos.

Un señor que compraba telas a los indios hacía muchos viajes a caballo por las montañas para visitarlos. Un día, hallando que llevaba demasiadas cosas consigo, dejó al pie de un árbol en un pueblo indio su cámara (*camera*), su escopeta (*gun*), y una manta (*blanket*). Al volver varios días después, halló allí sus cosas como las había dejado. Cogiéndolas,

[1] Market day, a pre-conquest custom found in all countries where there are many Indians, is the social and commercial event of the week for the lower class. Whole families carry their products thirty miles to market without a whimper.

Guatemala City, because of earthquakes, has many low buildings, although taller earthquake-proof structures have recently been built. Each street corner is policed night and day by a soldier traffic officer.

Galloway

dijo a un indio viejo que estaba cerca, — Dígame, señor, ¿por qué no se robó nadie estas cosas?

Y el indio, mirándole con sorpresa, le contestó, — Pues, señor, ¡no es costumbre!

¡Y creemos que somos nosotros los civilizados!

PALABRAS NUEVAS [1]

aéreo	air (*adj.*)	**guatemalteco**	Guatemalan
aeropuerto	airport	**honrado**	honest
avión (*m.*)	plane	3 **montaña**	mountain
por avión	by plane	**obligatorio**	required
3 **café** (*m.*)	coffee	**pintoresco**	picturesque
2 **coger**	to pick up	**tela**	cloth
convertir (ie, i)	to convert	1 **tercero**	third
4 **cuento**	story	**terremoto**	earthquake
2 **descubrir**	to discover	3 **volar** (ue)	to fly
3 **destruir**	to destroy	**volcán** (*m.*)	volcano
3 **durar**	to last		

NO ES VERDAD

Change these sentences to make them true.

1. Un dólar vale casi cinco quetzales. 2. El avión para Guatemala sale del aeropuerto a las siete y media de la noche. 3. Un secreto de los indios se puede ver solamente desde el camino. 4. El instrumento típico de Guatemala es la guitarra. 5. La niña tendrá que estudiar nuestra lengua solamente un año. 6. Los productos más importantes de Guatemala son los automóviles. 7. Los guatemaltecos toman mucho te por la tarde. 8. Los españoles pronto devolvieron su segunda capital a los indios porque éstos los molestaron tanto. 9. Todos los habitantes de Ciudad Vieja murieron en un terremoto. 10. Antigua está cerca de la capital moderna, y ya no vive nadie allí. 11. Los indios se llevaron todas las cosas del señor que viajaba a caballo.

[1] Note to teacher: Since this is a plateau chapter, *all* words not given before in Book II (except in optional Chapter 8) are given here in order to make the story easier to read.

REPASO DE PALABRAS IMPORTANTES

I. Find in List B a word which is the opposite of or may be contrasted with each word in List A; then reverse the process, starting with List B.[1]

A			B		
todo	levantarse	entrar en	vivir	mal	nunca
dar	llamar	después de	nuevo	leer	porque
mujer	salir	día	rico	recibir	llevarse
desde	mano	entonces	bajo	hombre	diferente
hoy	más	éste	nada	viejo	pie
escribir	mío	grande	antes de	pierna	venir
joven	mismo	hermano	allí	entonces	pequeño
poco	morir	¿por qué?	sin	noche	responder
aquí	alguien	quedarse	hasta	sentarse	alguno
bien	ninguno	siempre	aquél	menos	dar
brazo	viejo	sobre	mañana	mucho	hallar
con	pedir	traer	llegar	salir	irse
nada	perder	volver	suyo	ahora	ir
ahora	pobre	ir	nadie	hermana	algo

II. Find in List B a synonym for or a word that is translated the same as each word in List A.[2]

A			B		
hermoso	sobre	dejar	pero	luego	chico
entonces	comenzar	feliz	viejo	tomar	contestar
pequeño	hallar	beber	encontrar	bonito	contento
responder	andar	antiguo	mandar	permitir	empezar
enviar	su	sino	suyo	encima de	ir

III. Find in List B a word which is the opposite of or may be contrasted with each word in List A.[3]

[1] Note to teacher: Most of these words are in Buchanan's first 189.

[2] Note to teacher: Most of these words are in Buchanan's first 500.

[3] Note to teacher: Most of these words come between 189 and 500 in the Buchanan list.

A			B		
abrir	coger	derecho	bueno	recibir	escribir
antiguo	comenzar	empezar	temprano	detrás de	morir
bajar de	amigo	comprar	luna	terminar	tierra
bastante	contestar	enviar	cerrar	hallar	reír
beber	delante de	feliz	negro	correr	dejar caer
andar	nacer	ganar	lejos de	subir a	preguntar
blanco	sol	leer	enemigo	nuevo	completar
buscar	tarde	llorar	izquierdo	demasiado	vender
cerca de	enfermo	mar	triste	comer	perder

IV.[1] Here are some Spanish compound nouns, made by combining two or more familiar words. *Analyze each one and show how it comes to have the meaning given.* Notice that a compound word made of verb + noun is usually masculine, regardless of its ending.

el hazmerreír (*clown*), el salsipuedes (*box canyon; intricate design*), los dimes y diretes (*argument; act of bargaining*), Blancanieves (*name of the heroine of a fairy tale*), el robachicos (*kidnapper*), el rompecabezas (*puzzle*), el matasiete (*bragging person*), el limpiatodo (*scouring powder*), el sábelotodo (*cocky person*), el buscapiés (*firecracker on the ground*), el paraguas [2] (*umbrella*), el parasol (*sunshade*), el paracaídas (*parachute*), el lavamanos [3] (*wash bowl*), el lavaplatos (*dishwasher*), el casamóvil (*house trailer*), el ciempiés (*centipede*), la puertaventana (*shutter*), el imperdible (*safety pin*), la guardarropa (*wardrobe*), el saltamontes [4] (*grasshopper*), el saltaburro (*leapfrog*), el saltaparedes (*a wild youth*), el cumpleaños [5] (*birthday*)

REPASO DE MODISMOS (*Idioms*) [6]

Complete each of these sentences with one or more of the idioms listed at the left.

[1] Optional exercise.

[2] ***parar**, to stop*

[3] ***lavar**, to wash*

[4] ***saltar**, to jump*; ***monte**, bush*

[5] ***cumplir**, to fulfill*

[6] Note to teacher: These idioms are of high frequency, being listed in Keniston's first 200.

a casa
a la vez
a lo lejos
ante todo
a pie
aquí tiene Vd.
así como
a veces
dejar caer
de prisa
de veras
en casa
en efecto
está bien
hace dos años
hace mucho tiempo
hoy mismo
la mayor parte de
muchas veces
no hay más que
otra vez
por la noche
por todas partes
sí (que)
tener que
tener miedo de (a)
todo el mundo
todos los días
ya no

1. No vamos *home* en automóvil, sino *on foot.*
2. *This very day* oigo *in the distance* una voz.
3. Juan *dropped* la sopa y se fué *quickly.*
4. *Two years ago* busqué *everywhere* a mi amigo.
5. La madre *is afraid of* los bandidos, pero *everyone* sabe que no los hay.
6. — Seguridad *first* (*before all*) — me dice mi padre *every day.*
7. *Most of* la gente *have to* trabajar.
8. Nosotros, *as well as* nuestros amigos, *sometimes* no estamos *at home.*
9. *Here is* una leyenda que me contaron *often* en México.
10. — *All right* — dijo el turista, dándole *at the same time* un peso.
11. — *Certainly* tengo dinero, — repondió. — *A long time ago* que me lo dieron.
12. *No longer* hay conquistadores en Guatemala. *There are only* indios en «Chichi».
13. *Again* tengo que estudiar *at night.*
14. — *¿Really?* — dijo el hombre. — ¡No lo habría creído!
15. No me dijo que no podría ir; *in fact,* me dijo que quería ir.

REPASO DE VERBOS

I. Copy the model synopsis outline in Chapter 8 and study the verb forms given there, even if you have already had that chapter.

II. Then fill in your outline with the proper forms of the three regular verbs **ganar, comerse,** *and* **permitir.**

III. Now complete the conjugation of each tense orally to be sure that you know all the endings.

IV. Most of the following verbs are irregular, and will be found alphabetically listed beginning with section 63 of the appendix. *Conjugate them in the tenses indicated.*

Pres.: **ser, estar, irse, venir, oír**
Imperf.: **ser, ir, ver, dar**
Pret.: **oír, dormirse, servir, dar, ir, tener, decir**
Future: **poner, decir** Conditional: **poder, venir**
Pres. Prog.: **traer** Past Prog.: **decir**
Pres. Perf.: **decir, volver, entrar**
Past Perf.: **hacer, poner, dar**
Cond. Perf.: **ver, comer, caer**

V. Give singular polite and familiar commands of each of these verbs:

decir, salir, tener, oír, hacer, poner, venir, comprar, ir, ser, contar (ue), dar

VI. Give the gerund and past participle of each of these verbs (§ 96):

cubrir, reír, morir, poder, escribir, decir, pedir, leer, oír, cantar

VII. If you can give instantly the meanings of these forms, taken from the verbs you reviewed in the preceding exercises, you are well prepared. Remember that an incorrect translation of a verb form may be quite startling, for instance, if you should say, "I *am* a baby," instead of "I *was* a baby"!

1. se comió
2. permiten
3. he ganado
4. soy
5. éramos
6. oyen
7. oyeron
8. pondrán
9. Vds. podrán
10. están trayendo
11. estaba durmiendo
12. he dicho
13. ella había hecho
14. habrían visto
15. estamos
16. íbamos
17. se durmió
18. dirán
19. vendríamos
20. han vuelto
21. habías puesto
22. habría comido
23. me voy
24. veías
25. sirvieron
26. he entrado
27. fueron
28. habrían caído
29. dábamos
30. dieron

VIII. To give verb forms correctly and rapidly in Spanish is difficult but extremely important. If you can figure out these forms quickly and correctly, you are well on your way toward speaking Spanish fluently.

1. we ate "up"
2. we are (***ser***)
3. they used to be
4. she permits
5. they have earned
6. he is bringing
7. she should come
8. I was sleeping
9. he had put
10. you used to see
11. you hear
12. I should have seen
13. you had eaten
14. he heard
15. we are going away
16. you will be able
17. I would have fallen
18. they have said
19. we were giving
20. he has returned
21. we shall put
22. they have entered
23. she had made
24. he is (***estar***)
25. he served
26. we used to go
27. you went
28. I went to sleep
29. we gave
30. he will tell

REPASO DE COSAS NUEVAS [1]

I. If you can complete these statements, you know your rules of grammar. Then, if you can give the example correctly in Spanish, you know how to apply the rule. Each dash stands for one word. (Look up the section references if you cannot remember the missing words.)

1. An adjective which modifies a masculine and a feminine noun must be —— ——. (§ 103) [2]

*The man and the woman are **tall**.*

[1] Note to teacher: This exercise combines the TEMA with the grammar review, and even if the TEMA is not ordinarily assigned, it should be used here.

[2] Sections with numbers above 61 are in the Appendix.

Monkmeyer

Mother and daughter of the Guatemalan highlands wear identical dresses of hand-woven cotton in bright-colored traditional designs, with necklaces of old Guatemalan coins no longer in use.

2. The plural —— pronouns often mean *each other* or *one another.* (§ 107)

Peter and Albert write to each other, but Albert and I see each other every day.

3. To form a polite command, take the —— person singular of the —— tense, if it ends in ——; remove the ——, add the —— vowel and ——. (§ 99)

Go to the store, buy some beans, and return quickly.

4. To form the singular of familiar commands, use the —— person singular of the —— tense and add ——. (§ 17)

Buy the book, read ten pages, and write the new words.

5. *Ser* is always used to tell —— or ——; *estar* is always used to tell ——. (§ 122)

Louis is a good boy. He is my brother. He is at home now.

6. *Ser* is used to express ——, ——, and —— (§ 123); *estar* is used with the —— to form —— tenses. (§ 124)

The book is of white paper; it is from Chile; it is near the woman; it is Robert's, and we are studying (prog.) *it.*

7. The —— forms of the possessive adjective precede the noun; the —— forms follow it or the verb ——. (§ 113, § 114)

My friend is not here now. My friend, don't go away! He is a friend of yours.

8. The definite article is always used with *mío*, etc., except when it follows its —— or the verb ——. (§ 115)

My letter is on the chair; his is near yours, theirs are on that table, and she has hers.

9. The article is used instead of the possessive adjective with —— of —— and —— of the ——, unless it is the —— word of the sentence. (§ 113)

We put on our hats;[1] *he buys his shoes. Her dress is pretty, and she takes care of her hands.*

10. Object pronouns —— the verb unless it is an ——, ——, or —— ——, then they —— it and are —— to it. (§ 110)

Bring me the letter and I will read it. I can't. George is reading (prog.) *it, and wants to finish it now.*

11. When there are two object pronouns, the —— always precedes the ——, or a reflexive —— any other. (§ 111)

Bring it (letter) to me and I will read it to you. George wants to read it to her first. Why are you showing (prog.) *it to him?*

12. The —— pronouns must be used after prepositions, although they are translated the same as the —— object forms. (§ 112)

We used to see the house; we saw it every day; we entered it each week.

13. Adjectives may be used alone as ——, often requiring the word —— to be used in the translation. (§ 12)

The big one is yours; I want the red one. The young people used to sing, and the old ones listened.

14. When the —— object of a verb is a —— person, an —— animal, or a pronoun referring to a ——, it must be preceded by ——. (§ 127)

No one has seen John's horse, but everyone saw John two days ago. We will look for Raymond because we don't see anyone here.

15. If a negative word stands *before* the verb, it is not necessary to use ——. —— negatives are good Spanish, but not good English. (§ 13)

No one ever (never) says anything when he hasn't anything to say.

[1] Only one hat apiece!

16. The —— tense often expresses present probability. (§ 14)

What is Peter doing without saying anything? He is probably studying. Is he ten years old? No, he is probably twelve.

17. An —— is the only verb form commonly used after a preposition. (§ 16)

After looking at the hotel, we shall ask for a room. Before going to Guatemala, it would be necessary to win a prize. Upon looking for her, we found her on the street without knowing where she was.

18. A past occurrence limited by an expression of time takes the —— tense. (§ 11 a)

We studied [for] a year. They slept [for] ten hours.

19. Verbs which express a state or condition rather than an action are frequently used in the —— tense. (§ 11 b)

We were afraid, but we couldn't run. He wanted to leave, but he was ill.

II. Turn back to section 23, Exercises VIII, IX, and X, and see if you can write those tricky sentences quickly and accurately now.

PARA LEER SIN ESTUDIAR

¿SABÍA VD. ESTO?

Jimmie saw in a bookstore window in Guatemala these familiar English books published in Spanish for Spanish-speaking people. Can you identify them? (Guess; don't look up words!) Only the first word of a title is capitalized in Spanish, unless all the letters are capitals.

Viajes de Gúlliver, Oliverio Twist, Viajes de Marco Polo, Tres obras (*works*) de Shakespeare, Los tres mosqueteros, Las mil y una noches, Blancanieves y los siete enanos (*dwarfs*), El mercader de Venecia (por Shakespeare), Veinte mil leguas de viaje submarino, Los últimos días de Pompeya, Una historia de dos ciudades, La vuelta al mundo en ochenta días, Lo que el viento se llevó ("G.W.T.W.")

EL LEÑADOR[1]

[1] Unfamiliar words used in the song: **leñador,** *woodcutter;* **ahí no más,** *right over there;* **leña,** *firewood;* **catrín,** *elegant;* **pollón,** *clever;* **calzón rayado,** *striped trousers;* **bendito,** *blessed.*

1.
2.
diós. En el ca - mi - diós. Tie-ne ra - zón, tie-ne ra -
zón el Jo - se - ci - to . . . . . tie - ne ra - zón, tie - ne ra -
zón el muy ben - di - to . . . . . Pues pa-ra es-tar pues pa-ra es -
tar con su Ma - rí - a . . hay que en-tre - gar, an - tes que
na-da, la le - ña al pa - trón. Tie-ne ra - trón.
1.
2.

Part Two

Around the Spanish Sea

Palm-fringed tropical islands greeted Spanish explorers and conquerors who anchored their creaking galleons in the warm blue seas and gulfs that lie between the Americas.

Black Star

Foto Flatau, Panama

Mossgrown old Spanish fort of Porto Bello, Panama, looks out over a harbor used by Columbus in 1502. Drake was buried at sea off the Bay of Porto Bello.

In the days of the Spanish conquerors and explorers, many a creaking Spanish galleon anchored near the tropical isles and coasts of the warm blue seas and gulfs that lie between the West Indies and the meeting of the three Americas. Lusty treasure-seekers from Spain scattered over this area the names of their saints and homeland cities, and many of the islands and almost all of the countries bordering this "American Mediterranean," as we sometimes call it, still bear Spanish names. Mexico, Guatemala, Honduras, Nicaragua, Costa Rica, and Panama face east on the fabled sea (El Salvador has only a western seacoast); Colombia and Venezuela look north from South America, and in the green crescent of islands that swings north from Venezuela to Florida are Puerto Rico, Santo Domingo, and Cuba, all early centers of the Spanish culture that still colors them.

Romantic tales of great treasures carried to Spain from this region stir us even now, but no less valuable are the treasures of today that modern civilization finds on its tropical coasts. The "Banana Republics," we often call the Central American group, but we could as well call most of them "Coffee Republics," for although neither bananas nor coffee grew there until the Spaniards

CENTROAMÉRICA
y ANTILLAS
0 100 200 300 400 500
ESCALA EN MILLAS
ESTADOS UNIDOS
MÉXICO
México
GOLFO DE MÉXICO
OCÉANO PACÍFICO
MAR CARIBE
Habana
CUBA
ISLAS BAHAMAS
ANTILLAS MAYORES
Santiago de Cuba
JAMAICA
HAITI
SANTO DOMINGO
Ciudad Trujillo
San Juan
PUERTO RICO
ANTILLAS MENORES
MARTINICA
TRINIDAD
Caracas
VENEZUELA
COLOMBIA
Bogotá
Cartagena
PANAMÁ
Panamá
San José
COSTA RICA
NICARAGUA
Managua
HONDURAS
Tegucigalpa
EL SALVADOR
San Salvador
GUATEMALA
Guatemala
HONDURAS BRITÁNICA
ISLA DEL COCO

came, those two crops constitute today two of the principal exports that they send to us. In addition, their cocoa trees supply chocolate for our breakfasts and our sweet shops; their fields of waving cane yield the sugar that goes with it, and the tropical trees of their steaming jungles give us valuable medicines and precious hardwoods.

All these countries, from Mexico south around the inland sea and back to Cuba, have many things in common aside from their crops and climate. All have a similar history and speak Spanish because of their heritage; all are friendly to the United States and buy our manufactured goods, show our movies, and adopt our sports and popular music and styles. And all, even those which use oxcarts even now because many of their roads are still poor, are unconcernedly air-minded, and the daily freight and passenger planes which swoop down to their hibiscus-flowered airports are as commonplace to them as the thundering trucks on our highways are to us.

For all their similarities, these republics differ from each other, too. Mountainous Costa Rica, like Colombia, is one of the purest democracies on earth, an "oasis of peace" with a hard-working

Clearing the jungle for a banana plantation in Costa Rica is a real job. Tough vines as big as small tree trunks climb the tropical timber to reach for the sunlight.

Armstrong Roberts

white population, mostly of the middle class, that believes in more schools than police stations.

Colombia, facing the Spanish sea from the mainland, is the oldest democracy on the South American continent, and is proud of her co-educational universities, her high political standards, and her freedom of speech.

Some of the countries encircling the Spanish sea, quite unlike these two, are not democracies, like Honduras, Guatemala, and El Salvador; while others, like Venezuela and Mexico, are growing toward modern democracy as fast as complicated social conditions will permit.

Each country has its own individuality. For various reasons, Nicaragua and Mexico, along with Cuba and Panama, seem to show most clearly the influence of the United States, but even in Venezuela, which was until recently little concerned with Uncle Sam, you will see a sign reading, "*Perros calientes, 25¢. No pague más.*"

Honduras has many problems, since its whole life is dependent upon shipping bananas that spoil in a matter of hours; El Salvador, the first to finish its section of the Pan American Highway, is crowded and cosmopolitan and sophisticated, while Nicaragua is sparsely settled, but with people who are gay and sociable.

Many of these countries accept American money as readily as their own; they all teach English in their schools, and many of the wealthier people send their boys to us for their higher education. They depend on our Monroe Doctrine for protection, and we depend on them for many things we need, not the least of which is their friendship and cooperation.

When you travel in peace times by lazy freighters from port to port around the old Spanish sea, or crisscross it in the silver planes that fly from peninsula to island to mainland, you soon realize the interdependence of North and Central and South America. You see that, even if the treasures from the Caribbean are no longer chests of "pieces of eight," there still remain treasures of no less value to us, and that they are one sure link between us and the modern Spanish sea.

The following eight chapters give you legends, history, fiction, and current events of the countries around this area.

Keystone

Wayside shrine in the Venezuelan Andes invites the traveler to stop and say a prayer. The rider covers himself and his saddle with a waterproof *poncho* to shed the rain of mountain storms.

Morro Castle still guards the entrance to Havana's warm harbor, just as it did when the Spaniards built it in 1589. Modern Havana is a city where the new merges with the old.

Armstrong Roberts

Interesting Books to Read

Central America: ROTHERY, AGNES EDWARDS: CENTRAL AMERICA AND THE SPANISH MAIN. Houghton Mifflin. (*By the lady who puts so much human interest into her travel stories that they are very easy to read*) — FRANCK, HARRY, *and* LANKS, HERBERT: THE PAN AMERICAN HIGHWAY. Appleton-Century. (*Excellent pictures and interesting description*) — GUNTHER, JOHN: INSIDE LATIN AMERICA. Harpers. (*The book that explains all Latin America to us as it has not been explained before*) — EARLY, ELEANOR: LANDS OF DELIGHT. Houghton Mifflin. (*Travel tales*) — RECK, DAISY: PUERTO RICO AND THE VIRGIN ISLANDS. Farrar and Rinehart. (*Travel and description*)

Colombia: NILES, BLAIR: COLOMBIA, LAND OF MIRACLES. Grosset and Dunlap. (*Impressions of the rugged country of Colombia*) — GUNTHER, JOHN: INSIDE LATIN AMERICA.

Venezuela: FERGUSSON, ERNA: VENEZUELA. Knopf. (*Told by one who is an excellent and understanding guide*) — GUNTHER, JOHN: INSIDE LATIN AMERICA.

CAPÍTULO **10**

Tesoros y leyendas de tesoros

Pieces of eight!

Chests of jewels! Silver bars!

Pearls, and emeralds, and a golden throne!

The *conquistadores* came for treasure, and treasure they found. Over every green, palm-fringed island of the Caribbean they swarmed; deep into every mile of mainland from Florida to Panama they penetrated in their search for wealth. Here unbelievable tales came true; here treasure from north and south gathered at Panama and Cartagena and poured into ships bound for Spain.

Tales of easy riches spread, and over to the Spanish sea flocked buccaneers — English, French, Dutch — to lie in wait for the gold-laden Spanish galleons and to seize the treasure for themselves. Then pirate highjacked pirate, and the game went on, sometimes all being losers when none survived to claim the loot they had buried on a forgotten isle.

In colonial days family jewels and plate were mortared into thick stone walls for safe-keeping; in later times of revolution people hid their valuables in the same way and sometimes died without telling the secret of the hiding place. There is scarcely a town but what has its legend of treasure still to be found, and in some of them the search has been successful. So it is that from the days of the missing Aztec treasure to a matter-of-fact item in yesterday's newspaper, all around the Spanish sea there still persist rumors of wealth to be had for the finding.

— Moctezuma [1] tiene en su palacio un trono (*throne*) de oro, tan grande como una casa, — dijo doña Marina [2] a Cortés. — Tiene esmeraldas, y joyas de oro, y hasta estatuas de oro. Los he visto todos, y pronto serán nuestros.

Esto lo creía Cortés, y también lo creían todos sus soldados. Pero nunca hallaron ni trono, ni esmeraldas, ni joyas. ¿Dónde estaría el tesoro?

Nadie lo sabía. Algunos dijeron que los aztecas lo habían enterrado todo, otros que lo habían echado a las aguas del Lago Xochimilco,[3] y otros que lo habían llevado a una caverna de las montañas. De todos modos, todavía queda escondido.

Esta leyenda es solamente una de las que se cuentan en todos los países de habla española que rodean (*surround*) el Mar Caribe y el Golfo (*Gulf*) de México, y lo maravilloso es que de vez en cuando se encuentra algo de valor.

[1] Moctezuma II, Emperor of the Aztecs when Cortés conquered them, lived in a luxury of which the Spaniards never dreamed.

[2] Doña Marina was the Aztec girl who became Cortés' interpreter and helped him conquer her people.

[3] Lake Xochimilco is the site of the "floating gardens" which you read about in Chapter 7.

Gendreau

Old Panama's most famous ruin dates from the days when pirate Henry Morgan destroyed the city and carried away the riches which had come there for Spain from all over the New World.

Son cuatro los principales tesoros que se han descubierto en México: el primero en una casa de Toluca, el segundo en una casa de la capital que derribaron (*tore down*) para construir en su lugar el Palacio de Hierro;[1] el tercero bajo una escalinata (*stairway*) de un hotel de Puebla, y el cuarto en una residencia vieja donde actualmente está el Mercado Abelardo Rodríguez.[2]

En general, los tesoros se escondían en las paredes gruesas de piedra, en cuevas, o se enterraban en cofres (*chests*) de hierro o en botijos (*jars*). Se dice que el que entre[3] en una cueva en las montañas cerca de Tepic, Nayarit, a las doce de una noche de luna, oirá la voz de un fantasma que guarda un tesoro, y que siempre dice, — Llévatelo todo o no te lleves nada.

México no es el único país de leyendas de tesoros, porque en

[1] The Iron Palace is a five-story department store in Mexico City, where wrought-iron lace railings surround each gallery overlooking the patio in its center.

[2] The market was named for a president of Mexico who was educated in Arizona.

[3] *que entre*, a subjunctive form of *entrar* which you have not had yet. Translate it as it sounds best.

toda Centroamérica las hay también. Éste es un artículo que apareció en un periódico del año de 1931:

GRAN TESORO DESCUBIERTO

DE VALOR DE ₡300.000.000

SAN SALVADOR, 10 de abril de 1931. El 26 del marzo pasado descubrió un tesoro un marino (*sailor*) inglés, William P. Fox, en una pequeña isla cerca del Puerto Piñón. Fué escondido allí hace muchos años por un bisabuelo suyo, famoso pirata inglés, y aun en estos tiempos de inmensas fortunas es un verdadero tesoro, pues vale, según los peritos (*experts*), más de trescientos millones de colones.[1]

El señor Fox tuvo el permiso del gobierno de esta república para buscar el tesoro de su bisabuelo, teniendo en su posesión un plano antiguo.[2]

El Panamá antiguo, en los tiempos coloniales, era la ciudad por donde pasaban casi todas las riquezas del Nuevo Mundo camino de España. Del Perú llegaban galeones cargados del

[1] The "dollars" of El Salvador are *colones*, so called after Cristóbal Colón.

[2] Adapted from *La Voz de la Colonia*, Santa Paula, California.

Gaillard Cut in the Panama Canal, though it appears narrow, is wide enough for two ocean liners to pass in safety. Constant dredging keeps the canal free from sliding earth.

Gendreau

oro de los incas.[1] De Panamá se llevaba todo esto por el istmo (*isthmus*) en mulas, para volver a cargarse en otros galeones con destino a España. Por esto Panamá era saqueado de vez en cuando por los piratas. Uno de ellos fué el pirata Henry Morgan, que al fin destruyó enteramente la rica ciudad. De esto provienen leyendas de tesoros enterrados, que permanecen bajo las ruinas.

Cartagena, Colombia, y San Juan, Puerto Rico, también tienen sus cuentos de tesoros, porque con la enorme riqueza de oro, perlas, y esmeraldas que encontraron los españoles, estas ciudades llegaron a ser puertos (*ports*) importantes en el comercio colonial. Sir Francis Drake supo esto, y a pesar de los muros (*walls*) gruesos de Cartagena, la saqueó.

De todas estas leyendas, la más interesante es la de la Isla del Coco, posesión de Costa Rica en el Pacífico. Una leyenda de tres siglos ha atraído (*attracted*) a sus costas una expedición tras otra en busca del tesoro más grande del mundo. Se sabe por cierto que el pirata Morgan hizo varios viajes a esta isla, que Drake mismo llegó hasta allí, y se cree que Thompson, pirata que saqueó a Lima, en el Perú, en los tiempos coloniales llevó a la isla las joyas y el dinero que robó.

No hace muchos años que el famoso automovilista, Sir Malcolm Campbell,[2] trató de hallar la fortuna que, según se cree, vale más de cien millones de dólares.

Dijo Sir Malcolm, después de volver sin la fortuna, — Todavía creo que hay tesoro. Tengo un plano que indica que, al hallar cierto lugar, hay que dar cierto número de pasos hasta encontrar un agujero entre las piedras en donde meter una barra de hierro. Según el plano, esta barra servirá para mover una piedra grande y abrir la entrada de una caverna en donde se hallará el tesoro bajo la custodia de una gran estatua de oro de la Virgen y el Niño Jesús.

Pero Sir Malcolm no consiguió hallar el agujero, porque una enorme cantidad de tierra había caído sobre el lugar.

[1] The Incas were the rulers of the Indians Pizarro found high in the Andes when he conquered Peru.

[2] Sir Malcolm Campbell set many automobile speed records in this country.

Y éste es un artículo reciente de periódico:

SAN JOSÉ, COSTA RICA, 9 de marzo de 1940. Una expedición de buscadores (*seekers*) de tesoros bajo la dirección de James Forbes y Fred Lewis de California salió hoy en el yate (*yacht*) *Ranger* con destino a la Isla del Coco, en el Pacífico.

Unos soldados de Costa Rica los acompañan para observar sus operaciones. Tendrán constante comunicación por radio con San José.

¿Hay tesoros en la isla?
¡Quién sabe! [1]

PALABRAS NUEVAS

4	**actualmente**	at present
	agujero	hole
1	**aun**	yet
	automovilista (*m.* and *f.*)	motorist
	bisabuelo	great-grandfather
3	**cantidad**	quantity
3	**cargar (de)**	to load (with)
	coco	coconut
3	**conseguir (i)**	to succeed in
3	**costa**	coast
	custodia	custody
3	**destino**	destination
	esmeralda	emerald
	galeón (*m.*)	galleon
3	**gobierno**	government
	grueso	thick
	hierro	iron
3	**isla**	island
	permanecer	to remain
	provenir (de)	to come from, to originate
	plano	chart
	saquear	to plunder

EXPRESIONES

a pesar de, in spite of
camino de, on the way to
con destino a, en route to
***dar un paso,** to take a step
***de todos modos,** at any rate
***de vez en cuando,** from time to time
***hace muchos años que,** it has been many years since
llegar a ser, to become
***por cierto,** for certain, certainly
***por esto,** for this reason
volver a (ue) + inf., to (do) again

[1] Parts of the story are adapted from *La Prensa,* San Antonio, Texas; other information was furnished by the Junta Nacional de Turismo de Costa Rica. Costa Rica amiably permits treasure hunters to dig up uninhabited Cocos Island as they wish, guaranteeing nothing but fine fishing when they tire of digging. Several presidents of the United States have gone there for the good fishing.

¿VERDAD O NO?

Change the sentences that are false to make them true.

1. Muchos creían que los piratas habían enterrado su tesoro bajo el Lago Xochimilco. 2. Los tesoros en general se escondían en agujeros en los caminos. 3. El famoso automovilista no consiguió hallar el tesoro más grande del mundo porque perdió su plano. 4. Una expedición salió para buscar la riqueza escondida en la cueva cerca de Tepic. 5. El pirata Morgan saqueó la ciudad de

Dancing El tamborito — the Little Drum — in Panamanian fiestas, one must wear the traditional costumes. The lace of the girl's dress is made by hand in old designs; the man's shirt is hand embroidered.

Lima y se llevó muchas joyas y mucho dinero. 6. Los soldados de Costa Rica tenían que buscar el tesoro de los aztecas bajo un hotel. 7. Los conquistadores encontraron muchas esmeraldas y el trono de oro de Moctezuma. 8. En Costa Rica un dólar se llama un quetzal. 9. Todos los países de habla inglesa tienen leyendas de riquezas escondidas. 10. El soldado que guarda el tesoro siempre dice, — Llévatelo todo o no te lleves nada. 11. El Salvador es el país más grande de Centroamérica. 12. La Isla del Coco está en el Atlántico y es posesión de Guatemala.

REPASO DE VERBOS

I. Review the familiar commands in sections 17 and 19, and complete this story in Spanish:

— *¡Give me* la manzana, Rosita! — gritó Juanito.

— *¡I don't want to!* — contestó Rosita. — ¡Es *mine!* *¡Be careful*, o *I am going to* decírselo a mamá!

— *¡Tell it* a mamá, si quieres! — *said* Juanito.

— Juanito, *come* acá, — dijo la señora, — y *tell me* la verdad. ¿Por qué riñen (*quarrel*) los dos?

— Porque Rosita es *the worst girl in the* mundo.

— Juanito, te he dicho *a million times* que no debes exagerar, — *said* la señora. — ¿Qué hizo Rosita?

— Pues, *we were playing* a Adán y Eva (*Adam and Eve*), y en vez de *giving me* una parte de la manzana, ¡ella *was eating it* (*prog.*) toda!

ALGO NUEVO

24. Negative Familiar Commands ("*Don't*")

Llévatelo todo o no te lleves nada.
Take it all or don't take anything.

The familiar (second person) commands you have been reviewing may be used only in the affirmative. In order to say *don't*, you must use an entirely different form, which is the second person of the present subjunctive tense.

25. Present Subjunctive Tense

This new tense is called the present subjunctive, from which come all polite commands and all negative familiar commands.

PRESENT SUBJUNCTIVE MODELS [1]		
ganar	**responder**	**vivir**
I (may) earn, etc.	*I (may) answer, etc.*	*I (may) live, etc.*
(yo) **gane**	(yo) **responda**	(yo) **viva**
ganes	**respondas**	**vivas**
gane	**responda**	**viva**
ganemos	**respondamos**	**vivamos**
ganéis	**respondáis**	**viváis**
ganen	**respondan**	**vivan**

EJERCICIO I. *Referring to the models, see if you can answer these questions:*

1. Is the "opposite vowel" used for present subjunctive endings? 2. What is the stem? (The same as for a polite command.) 3. Which two persons are the same? How will you often have to distinguish them? 4. If you put ***Vd.*** after the third person, what form do you have? 5. Give the polite commands, singular and plural, that are taken from this subjunctive conjugation. 6. What are the familiar commands of these verbs (§§ 17, 19)? Are they found in the models? 7. Put ***no*** before the second person singular of each subjunctive verb and add (***tú***): ***no ganes*** (***tú***).[2] Now you have the negative familiar command form, *don't*, which is actually part of the subjunctive.

EJERCICIO II. Here are the various singular command forms for ***cantar:*** [3]

[1] The present subjunctive is the fourth most important tense in Spanish. Only the present, preterite, and imperfect indicative are used more often.

[2] *Tú* is usually omitted in the negative.

[3] Note to teacher: Since *cantad* and *no cantéis* are not used in Spanish America for informal speech, drill is not given on the plural. According to Keniston, such forms as *sentaos*, also, are so rare that there is no place for them in second-year study.

Armstrong Roberts

Post office in San José, Costa Rica, faces a plaza filled with semi-tropical verdure. People seen along the clean, paved avenues wear dark clothing instead of the white cotton worn at lower altitudes.

INF.	POLITE COMMAND	NEGATIVE POL. COM.	FAMILIAR COMMAND	NEGATIVE FAM. COM.
cantar	**¡Cante Vd.!**	**¡No cante Vd.!**	**¡Canta tú!**	**¡No cantes (tú)!**
to sing	*Sing!*	*Don't sing!*	*Sing!*	*Don't sing!*

Using the above outline, give the four commands and their meanings for the verbs **pasar, correr,** *and* **combatir.**

26. Irregular Present Subjunctives

The present subjunctive of irregular verbs comes from the first person present stem, if it ends in **-*o*,** just as the polite command does:

decir: digo: diga Vd.; present subjunctive: **diga, digas, diga; digamos, digáis, digan.**

EJERCICIO III. *First give the infinitive, the first person present indicative, and the polite command; then conjugate in the present subjunctive each of the following verbs:* **pasar, correr, combatir, hacer, poner, salir, tener,** *and* **venir.**

EJERCICIO IV. *Referring to the present subjunctive forms of the verbs in Ejercicio III, make an outline of commands as in Ejercicio II.* (Be careful about the singular familiar form!)

27. Present Subjunctive of Radical-Changing Verbs

Radical-changing verbs of the first and second conjugations have the same stem changes in the subjunctive as in the indicative.

contar: cuente, cuentes, cuente; contemos, contéis, cuenten

28. First Person Commands

The first person plural of the subjunctive often means *let us*: ***comamos***, *let's (let us) eat.*

EJERCICIO V. *Say in Spanish:*

Let's put, let's leave, let's run, let's sing, let's not make, let's count, let's begin, let's not return.

Let us can also be expressed by ***vamos a:***

vamos a comer, *let's eat* (**Vámonos** is idiomatic for *let's go.*)

EJERCICIO VI. Here are some proverbs, sayings adapted from proverbs, and parts of songs which use the familiar verb forms. *Translate them, give the infinitive of each verb, and explain why the commands are or are not in the subjunctive.*

1. No firmes carta, si no la lees; no bebas agua si no la ves. 2. No dejes para mañana lo que puedes hacer hoy. 3. A caballo regalado ("*gift*"), no le mires el diente. 4. Llévatelo todo o no te lleves nada. 5. No llores por tu Pancho. 6. Canta y no llores. 7. Dime con quien andas, y te diré quien eres. 8. Cuida de los centavos, (por)que los pesos se cuidarán solos. 9. Dime que sí, no digas (que) no. 10. Entre padres y hermanos no metas tus manos. 11. Estrellita (*little star*), baja y dime si (él) me quiere un poco.

29. Nouns Used as Adjectives

un sombrero de papel, *a paper hat*

Nouns cannot be used as adjectives in Spanish as they are in English, but must have the preposition **de** before them.

EJERCICIO VII. *Complete these sentences in Spanish:*

1. Sir Malcolm esperaba hallar una *gold* estatua. 2. Los españoles tenían muchas *silver* barras. 3. Es necesario meter una *iron* barra en el agujero para mover la *stone* puerta. 4. La tienda más grande de México se llama el *Iron* Palacio. 5. Un pirata famoso tenía una *wooden* pierna.

REPASITO

I. Review in section 105 the list of adjectives which may be shortened; then complete these sentences, explaining why you used the full or shortened form each time.

1. Según el *first* hombre, no hay tesoros allí. 2. Descubrieron la *first* isla, y más tarde la *third* [*one*]. 3. ¡No encontró *no* oro! 4. ¿Quería esconderlo el *bad* pirata? 5. El *good* [*one*] no robó nada a (*from*) nadie. 6. No podríamos comer *one hundred* man-

Costa Rica's coastal slopes are covered with dense tropical forests which give way to fertile pastures where cattle thrive. Timber and cattle are the chief products of the province of Guanacaste.

Armstrong Roberts

zanas. 7. El *great* hombre, Cristóbal Colón, descubrió muchas islas. 8. ¿Era Colón un *large* hombre?

II. Review in section 119 the comparison of adjectives and complete these sentences in Spanish:

1. La leyenda duró *more than* doscientos años. 2. Panamá era *the richest city in* el Nuevo Mundo. 3. Los turistas fueron al *best restaurant in* la capital. 4. Soy *taller than* Vd., pero Vd. es *older than* yo. 5. El tesoro valía *as much as* el galeón. 6. Los piratas habían escondido *more* tesoros *than* los conquistadores. 7. ¡Ella es *exceedingly beautiful*! 8. María es *my prettiest* hermana. 9. ¡Qué *large* hombre! (*What a man so large!*) 10. ¡*What a beautiful* caballo! (*What a horse so beautiful!*)

III. When adjectives of nationality are used for languages, they usually require the definite article except after ***hablar, de,*** and ***en*** (§ 125–6.) They are all masculine.

Complete in Spanish:

Spanish es más fácil que *English*. Ya hemos aprendido *English*, y ahora estamos estudiando *Spanish*. Después de completar nuestro estudio de *Spanish*, queremos aprender a hablar *French*. En *French* hay muchas letras que no se pronuncian, pero en *Spanish* se pronuncian todas las letras menos la ***h***. *Spanish* es un poco más fácil que *French*, y *Latin* (**latín**) es la lengua más difícil de todas. *Spanish, French, Italian, Portuguese* (**portugués**) *and Rumanian* (**rumano**) provienen de *Latin*,[1] así todas se llaman lenguas romances, porque los romanos hablaban *Latin*.

IV. Review the prepositional pronouns in section 112, then complete these sentences in Spanish:

1. Si encuentro el tesoro, compraré muchas cosas con *it*. 2. Echaron el oro a las aguas del lago; *they threw it into them*. 3. No quiere salir del país; *he doesn't want to leave it*. 4. Escondieron los tesoros en las paredes; *they hid them in them*. 5. No entre Vd. en la cueva a las doce; *don't enter it*. 6. El artículo apareció en el periódico; *it appeared in it*. 7. La Isla del Coco es posesión de Costa Rica; es posesión de *it*. 8. Pasaban por las ciudades antiguas;

[1] Use the article here because the word ***idioma*** (*language*) is understood.

Galloway

San Felipe, ancient Spanish fort, is only one of the many that still overlook picturesque Cartagena, little changed since the days of the pirates and buccaneers of the Spanish Main.

they passed through them. 9. Entre *them* estaba el pirata Morgan. 10. Las riquezas permanecen bajo *them* (las ruinas). 11. Según *them* (los peritos, *experts*), el tesoro vale millones de colones. 12. Parece que el tesoro no es para *us,* sino *for them.*

ESTUDIO DE PALABRAS

I. Here are the idioms you have had with ***vez,*** *time. Select one of them to complete each sentence, using each idiom only once.*

otra vez algunas veces a veces de vez en cuando a la vez en vez de una vez por primera vez tres veces al día

1. Se han descubierto tesoros —— —— —— ——. 2. No se puede cantar y comer —— —— ——. 3. Sir Malcolm volvió a casa —— —— —— hallar las riquezas. 4. —— —— los trabajadores encontraron dinero escondido en el lugar del Palacio de Hierro. 5. Cabeza de Vaca cruzó el continente a pie —— ——

——. 6. —— —— el hierro vale más que el oro. 7. Según la leyenda, el fantasma de Tepic dice —— ——, — Llévatelo todo. 8. Es costumbre comer —— —— —— ——. 9. Después de fracasar (*fail*), hay que tratar —— ——.

II. ***Por*** has many meanings. Those you have already had in this book are *by*, *for*, *in*, *through*, *along*, *in exchange for*, *on account of*. Which of these meanings is correct in each sentence? [1]

1. Nos despertamos por la mañana. 2. Le damos nuestros dólares por pesos. 3. Pasamos por la puerta y damos un paseo por la calle. 4. Por estar cansados, dormimos una siesta por la tarde. 5. El tesoro fué escondido por los piratas, y quedó allí por dos siglos.

PARA LEER SIN ESTUDIAR

¿Sabía vd. esto?

1. La expedición Forbes-Lewis descubrió en la Isla del Coco una piedra marcada con una "K" y una flecha (*arrow*) que en su plano indica el lugar del tesoro de Lima. Pero el tesoro no se encontrará pronto, porque durante la guerra (*war*) el gobierno ha prohibido nuevas exploraciones.

2. Henry Morgan llegó a ser caballero de Inglaterra (*England*) después de ser pirata por mucho tiempo, y pasó muchos años de su vida gozando de (*enjoying*) las riquezas que había robado en el Nuevo Mundo.

3. Colombia es la tierra de esmeraldas, y en la capital, Bogotá, hay un cuarto lleno de estas piedras verdes, pero nadie puede verlas porque hay seis llaves (*keys*) diferentes para la puerta, y seis personas las tienen. Así, sin estar presentes todas las seis, nadie puede abrir la puerta.

4. Las esmeraldas de Colombia valen un millón de dólares la libra (*pound*).

[1] Note to teacher: Further treatment of *por* (and *para*) is found in Chapter 19.

TEMA

1. One must take ten steps to the right in order to discover the first treasure. 2. In spite of discovering the island, the captain's son did not succeed in finding [any] gold. 3. The largest treasure in the world is buried on Cocos Island, according to the old legend. 4. At any rate it is harder than ever (never) to find a fortune in a cave. 5. Certainly the pirate himself would not succeed in finding it now. 6. Two centuries ago they buried it near the mountain. 7. The Iron Palace is not a place in which (**donde**) iron is sold. 8. It is many years since Morgan destroyed the wealthiest city in the New World. 9. Run (*fam.*) to your mother; don't come here. Do it immediately and don't wait! 10. "Come here, son, and tell me the truth," said Mrs. Núñez. 11. "That is the reddest apple I have seen, and Rosita is eating it all!" answered Johnny.

CAPÍTULO *11*

La Carretera Panamericana del Pacífico

In normal times we *norteamericanos* on wheels think nothing of driving across the continent, and many of us have learned more geography from our automobile windows than we ever learned from a book. Fifty thousand of our family cars whirled down to Mexico City the first year after the *Camino Nacional No. 1* was opened; and from there on to the Panama Canal it is only as far as from New York to Los Angeles. So imagine how fast we'll get acquainted firsthand with our other good neighbors when the Pan American Highway from Alaska to Buenos Aires is completed!

Over the trail from the frozen north, made by Mayan, Aztec and Incan tribes as they wandered south before the dawn of

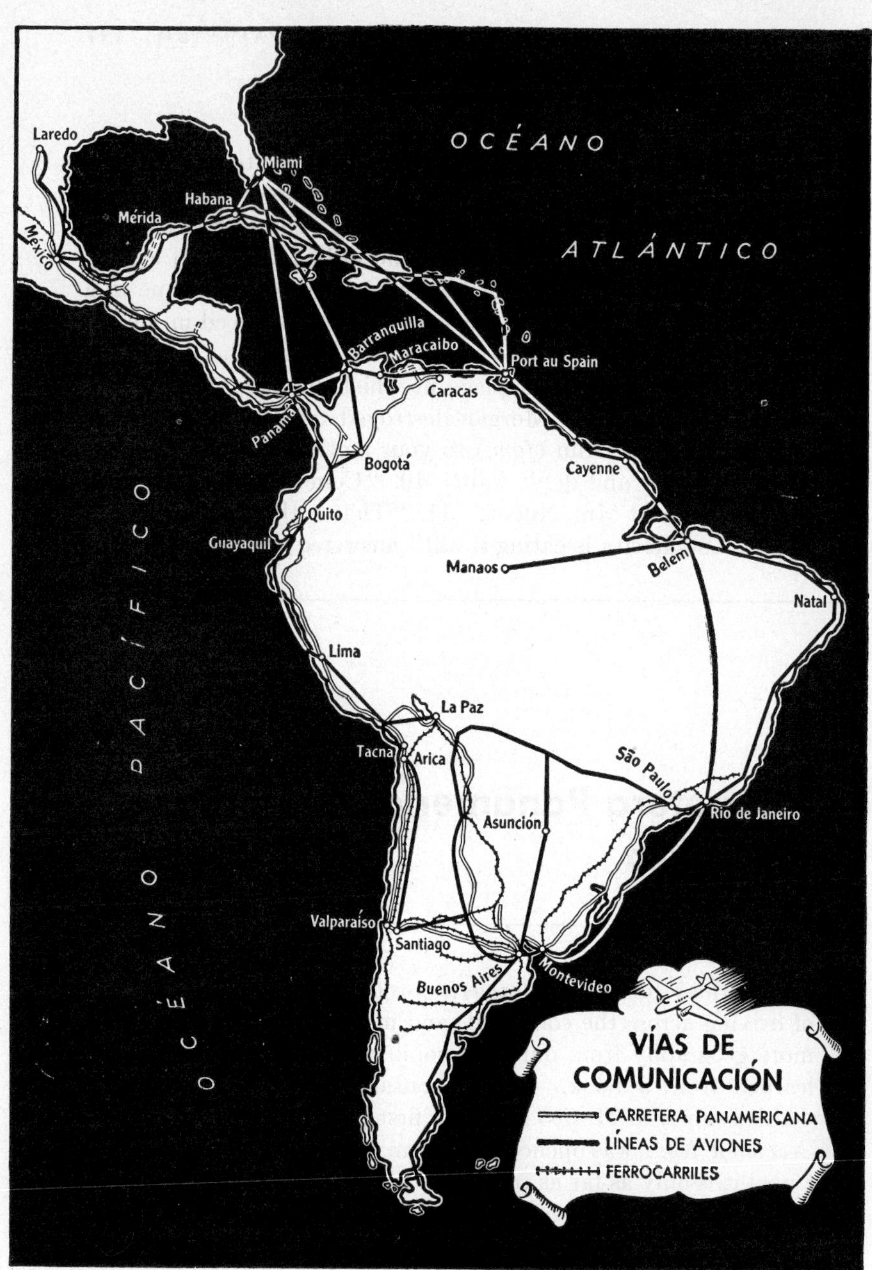

OCÉANO
ATLÁNTICO
OCÉANO PACÍFICO
Laredo
Miami
Habana
Mérida
México
Barranquilla
Maracaibo
Port au Spain
Caracas
Panamá
Bogotá
Cayenne
Quito
Guayaquil
Manaos
Belém
Natal
Lima
La Paz
Tacna
Arica
São Paulo
Rio de Janeiro
Asunción
Valparaíso
Santiago
Buenos Aires
Montevideo
VÍAS DE COMUNICACIÓN
CARRETERA PANAMERICANA
LÍNEAS DE AVIONES
FERROCARRILES

history, we will then be able to drive on the longest continuous motor road in the world. And all along those thousands of miles we will meet but two principal languages — English and Spanish, — something unheard-of in any other part of the globe.

When we turn homeward again we'll carry souvenirs from many Spanish-speaking countries — perhaps *yerba mate* tea and a silver *bombilla* from Argentina, an Araucanian silver dish from Chile, tiny silver llamas and a soft alpaca fur robe from Peru, carved wood bowls and figures from Ecuador, an emerald from Colombia, hand-woven cotton tapestry from Guatemala . . .

But our most important souvenir of all will be a better understanding of these remarkable neighbors of ours, for only then can we truly appreciate those modern civilizations to the south.

¡Imagínese usted! Todos los días de su vida, vamos a suponer, usted llega a la escuela montado en un burro, caminando por una senda estrecha, un viaje tan largo y penoso (*painful*) para usted como para el burro. Usted camina así porque no hay otro método de llegar. Sí hay automóviles en las ciudades, pero en el campo, ¿qué vale un automóvil sin caminos buenos?

Pues, un día llega usted a la escuela en un gran avión color de plata, que vuela por el aire y le lleva a su destino en poco tiempo. ¡Y todavía no ha viajado usted nunca en automóvil por un camino de campo pavimentado!

Así se puede describir el cambio dramático de la transportación en muchos países de Centroamérica y de la América del Sur. «De Burro a Avión» [1] podría simbolizar el progreso moderno, porque todos los países están unidos ahora con una red (*network*) de aerovías (*airways*).

«Ahora sí el mundo es chico», dice una famosa compañía de aerovías en su mapa de ruta (*route*). Sobre desiertos, ciénagas (*swamps*), montañas, y selvas vuelan los aviones de plata,

[1] «*De Burro a Avión*» is the name painted on the side of a wagon seen in the streets of Bogotá, the capital of Colombia, which was one of the first countries to begin using planes to reach cities perched high in the Andes.

Sawders

Pan American Highway in Mexico climbs high into the sierras and passes near the Nevado de Toluca. The road sign shows that this spot is fifty-two kilometers from Mexico City.

llevando consigo pasajeros y carga, mulas y maquinaria (*machinery*).

Por supuesto, este método de transportación cuesta mucho, y hay personas que no pueden pagar tanto. Así es que en el año de 1923 empezaron todos los países del Hemisferio Occidental a pensar en una carretera internacional del Pacífico, entre Fairbanks, Alaska, y Buenos Aires, Argentina, que sería de unas 14.000 millas de largo, y que uniría quince repúblicas. [1]

[1] The Pan American Highway continues on from Buenos Aires to Uruguay and Brazil. There is also a branch going to Paraguay. And, of course, we must not forget Canada, our neighbor to the north. Thus nineteen countries in all will be connected by the Highway.

Todos nuestros «buenos vecinos» desean que pronto se termine [1] esta carretera importantísima para hacer posible el turismo (*touring*), así como la transportación de productos. Hasta se ha fundado (*founded*) una Federación Interamericana de Clubs Automovilistas, para poder cruzar más fácilmente las fronteras. Esta federación podrá dar al automovilista un librito que le permitirá pasar fácilmente de un país a otro, porque no quiere que se moleste [2] el viajero en cada frontera.

Pero entretanto vamos a ver cómo es actualmente este camino larguísimo.[3] Por el ochenta por ciento de la distancia, ya se han construido caminos, aunque algunos sirven solamente en tiempo seco. El tramo por la costa occidental de México hasta la frontera guatemalteca es transitable (*passable*), aunque todavía no está completamente pavimentado.

En Guatemala ya está construido todo el camino, aunque la

[1] *se termine*, a subjunctive form which is explained in this chapter. Translate it as it sounds best.

[2] *moleste*, see footnote 1.

[3] As it was in 1943. The United States loaned millions of dollars to various countries for bridges and road construction in order to speed the work along.

Oxcart traffic, to leave room for cars, keeps well to the right on Guatemala's dusty country roads, a part of the Pan American Highway. The driver always walks ahead of the patient oxen, which follow wherever he goes.

Sawders

parte entre la capital y El Salvador no es muy buena. El Salvador terminó su tramo hace poco, y Honduras ha completado la tercera parte de su sección. En Nicaragua todavía faltan unas cien millas, las cuales se pueden terminar dentro de tres años.

Los Estados Unidos han prestado (*loaned*) a Costa Rica $4.000.000 para construir su tramo difícil, el cual pasará por las montañas y no se podrá terminar en mucho menos de cuatro años.

En Panamá faltan algunas millas para llegar a la frontera de Costa Rica, y al sur del Canal el camino desaparece en la selva impenetrable. Si es imposible construirlo allí, será preciso llevar los automóviles por barcas (*ferries*) entre Cristóbal, Panamá, y algún puerto de Colombia, donde hay ya camino transitable durante todo el año, como se ve en el mapa. Este tramo se llama la «Carretera Simón Bolívar».[1]

Al sur de Colombia, el Perú es el único país que ha terminado su tramo, y ya lo ha pavimentado, porque el camino sigue la costa y no hay montañas que cruzar.[2] En Chile tuvieron que construir el camino por un desierto donde no se encuentran ni siquiera (*not even*) cactos (*cacti*), y luego hay que cruzar los Andes con sus nieves de invierno y sus alturas inolvidables. Una cosa interesante es que en todos estos países[3] uno toma la derecha como aquí, pero al llegar a la frontera entre Chile y la Argentina, en los Andes donde está el famoso «Cristo de los Andes»,[4] el que maneja tendrá que tomar la izquierda, porque es costumbre en la Argentina. ¡Uno puede imaginarse la confusión del tránsito en aquel camino montañoso!

Actualmente el Club Automovilista Argentino está organizando una carrera (*race*) de automóviles, el «Gran Premio de

[1] Simón Bolívar is the George Washington of South America, and statues of him on a prancing bronze horse stand in almost every plaza.

[2] Peru is very proud of having finished its section first, and prints maps of it on many government pamphlets.

[3] Except Panama.

[4] The "Christ of the Andes" is a huge bronze statue of the Redeemer which stands on the boundary line between Chile and Argentina to watch over the peace that the two countries have promised will always abide between them.
The road across the Andes is blocked with snow over half the year.

Souvenirs from the Pan American Highway are Otavalo Indian figures (right) and bamboo Pan pipes from Ecuador; Quichua Indian dolls from Peru; and carved mahogany plaque in Mayan design from Guatemala.

More souvenirs are Ecuadorean bowl, Indian figures, and tagua nut medallions; Argentinian *bombilla* and gourd (center); tiny knives and silver dish from Chile; Bolivian fish and spoon pins; and silver llamas from Peru.

las Américas», entre Buenos Aires y Nueva York para celebrar la unidad interamericana. Dos caravanas, una del norte y la otra del sur, se encontrarán en Bogotá, Colombia, al completarse la carretera.

¿Se ha hecho ya este viaje por los dos continentes? Sí, «créase o no (*believe it or not*)», cuatro hermanos argentinos, José, Felipe, Benito y Ernesto Mallo,[1] en 1941 manejaron un viejo «Dodge» desde Buenos Aires hasta Wáshington, D.C., por buenos y malos caminos, tardándose 230 días en el viaje. Lo hicieron para traer la buena voluntad a nuestra América, y para llamar la atención a la necesidad de terminar pronto la Carretera Panamericana. ¡Imagínese su alegría cuando la Compañía Dodge les regaló un coche nuevo para su viaje de vuelta!

Sin duda, dentro de poco todos los «Jimmies» de nuestras escuelas estarán pidiendo a sus padres que vayan [2] a Buenos Aires en sus vacaciones. ¿Por qué no?

PALABRAS NUEVAS

3	**cambio**	change	4	**puerto**	port
3	**carga**	freight	4	**regalar**	to present
	carretera	highway	3	**seco**	dry
	inolvidable	unforgettable		**selva**	jungle
	montañoso	mountainous		**tramo**	section
	pavimentar	to pave	2	**unir (se)**	to unite, join
2	**preciso**	necessary			

Expresiones

***entretanto,** meanwhile
hace poco, not long ago
Hemisferio Occidental, Western Hemisphere
la tercera parte, one third
millas de largo, miles long
por ciento, per cent
***viaje de vuelta,** return trip

[1] *Mallo* is pronounced somewhat like *Mazho* in Argentina, where all *ll*'s are given a *zh* sound (resembling the *z* in *azure*). How would an Argentinian say *Calle Allende?* What would be the difference between the Mexican and the Spanish pronunciations? (§ 4)

[2] *vayan,* see footnote 1 on page 151.

¿VERDAD O NO?

Referring to the map of **Vías de Comunicación** *and the story, decide whether these statements are true or not.*

1. La Carretera Panamericana ya está pavimentada en los Estados Unidos. 2. Todo el Camino Nacional No. 1 entre Laredo y la capital de México sirve solamente en tiempo seco. 3. Es posible manejar un coche entre Panamá y Colombia ahora en tiempo seco. 4. México tiene menos caminos pavimentados que Nicaragua. 5. El tramo del Perú es mejor que el tramo del Ecuador. 6. Sería fácil cruzar la frontera entre México y Guatemala en coche. 7. Es imposible cruzar los Andes sin avión. 8. Chile tuvo que pavimentar más millas de camino que el Ecuador. 9. La distancia entre Buenos Aires y México es más grande que la distancia entre México y Vancouver. 10. Sería preciso cruzar los Andes para ir de Santiago de Chile a Buenos Aires. 11. La Carretera Panamericana sigue la costa occidental de la América del Sur.

Crossing the Andes in Peru, the railroad track leaps across the gorges from tunnel to tunnel, and the Pan American Highway switches back and forth beneath it across the Rimac River.

Sawders

ALGO NUEVO

30. More Subjunctives

Review the present subjunctive forms given in sections 25 and 26.

EJERCICIO I. *Conjugate these verbs in the present subjunctive tense* (§ 63 ff.):

conocer, caer, costar (ue), traer, oír, perder (ie), seguir (i), volver (ue), sentarse (ie)

31. Irregular Present Subjunctives

Six common verbs whose first person singular present indicative does not end in ***-o*** have the following present subjunctive forms (§ 63 ff.):

dar: dé	**haber: haya**	**saber: sepa**
estar: esté	**ir: vaya**	**ser: sea**

Remember that the same stem is kept throughout the conjugation:

vaya, vayas, vaya; vayamos, vayáis, vayan

EJERCICIO II. *Continue the conjugation of these verbs in the present subjunctive.*

32. III RC Subjunctives

Third conjugation radical-changing verbs have the usual stem changes, except that the first and second persons plural have the **e** > **i** or **o** > **u** change we found in the third person preterite:

sentir: sienta, sientas, sienta; *sintamos, sintáis,* sientan
pedir: pida, pidas, pida; *pidamos, pidáis,* pidan
dormir: duerma, duermas, duerma; *durmamos, durmáis,* duerman

EJERCICIO III. *Conjugate in the same way* **morir, servir, preferir, seguir,** *and* **vestir.**

EJERCICIO IV. Here is a list of assorted verb forms, including commands and present indicative and subjunctive tenses. *Give the infinitive of each one, identify it, and tell what it means, translating each subjunctive with* may: **coma,** he may eat.

1. vengan
2. me siento
3. salgamos
4. ten tú
5. no tengas (tú)
6. viene
7. haga
8. sal tú
9. venid vosotros
10. ella vuelva
11. ponte
12. diga Vd.
13. cueste
14. dime tú
15. yo tenga
16. cuentan
17. conozcamos
18. no cantes (tú)
19. siga Vd.
20. no te pongas
21. sirvamos

33. The Subjunctive after Verbs of Causing [1]

In the story you found these new uses of the present subjunctive:

Desean que pronto se termine esta carretera.
They want this highway to be finished soon.

no quiere que se moleste el viajero
doesn't want the traveler to be annoyed

Jimmie pedirá a sus padres que vayan
Jimmie will ask his parents to go

Subjunctive verb forms, as well as being used for all polite commands and negative familiar commands, have other usages which are very common in everyday Spanish. The difficulty for us is that since we use the subjunctive very little in English, we have to become accustomed to expressing ourselves differently in Spanish.

The subjunctive is usually the subordinate (secondary) verb in the sentence, not the main verb.[2] Nearly always it is pre-

[1] Note to teacher: The following presentation of the subjunctive is based upon Keniston's *Spanish Syntax List*, a study of syntax frequency, and stresses mainly usages of proven high frequency.

[2] The word "indicative" comes from the Latin verb *indico, indicare* which means *to point out*, and the indicative, therefore, indicates or points out facts. The word "subjunctive" means *subjoined;* that is, attached and subordinate to.

Sawders

Small town in the Peruvian Andes shows old Spanish influence in the overhanging balconies of its houses. The Pan American Highway follows the gorge of the Rimac River far into the mountains.

ceded by some word which causes it to be subjunctive, and if you think carefully, you can see that there is usually something *doubtful* about the matter.

For example, when I say *I want you to go,* whether you go or not is up to you, and, although I expect to *cause* you to go, you may decide not to do it.

In Spanish *I want you to go* cannot be expressed as in English. You must say *I want that you go,* and then the *sub*ordinate verb *go* is a *sub*junctive:

quiero (main verb) **que Vd. vaya** (subordinate verb)

In a case like this we say that ***vaya*** is a subjunctive because it follows a verb of causing. This is the most common use of the subjunctive, and the commonest verbs of causing are ***querer*** and ***decir.*** (Of course if we say *I want to go,* ***quiero ir,*** there is no subjunctive because there is no change of subject.)

REMEMBER:	The subjunctive is used after verbs of causing if there is a change of subject.

The four most common verbs of causing, which *must* take the subjunctive, if there is a change of subject, are:

querer	**decir**	**pedir**	**desear**
to want	*to tell*	*to ask*	*to want*

Four other common verbs of causing — "exceptions" — which may take the subjunctive but more often do not, are:

dejar	**hacer**	**permitir**	**mandar** [1]
to let, allow	*to make*	*to permit*	*to command*

If you do not want to use the subjunctive with these four exceptions, use the infinitive:

Paco no permite que entren, *or,* **Paco no les permite entrar**
Frank doesn't permit them to enter

Three other verbs of causing which usually take the subjunctive, but which are less common, are:

aconsejar	**preferir** (ie)	**rogar** (ue)
to advise	*to prefer*	*to beg*

EJERCICIO V. *Translate these sentences, first exactly as they stand, then as we would ordinarily say them, and tell why the subjunctive is or is not used in each case.*

If you "diagram" such sentences, by putting an arrow after each verb of causing and underlining the subjunctive verb, you will be able to understand them better: **Quiero > que Vd.** ***vaya.***

1. Quiero que Vd. vaya. 2. Le digo a Juan que entre. 3. No deseamos que Pablo vuelva. 4. Le pide a su padre que lo compre. 5. No me dejan entrar. 6. No dejan que yo entre. 7. Quiero que todos lo sepan. 8. Le aconsejo que esté allí. 9. Me dice que se lo dé. 10. Nos mandan ir. 11. Mandan que vayamos. 12. Ella prefiere que María no salga. 13. Ruega a su padre que vaya a

[1] And sometimes ***aconsejar,*** *to advise.*

casa. 14. ¿Quiere Vd. que yo le diga la verdad? 15. Me dicen que tenga cuidado.

EJERCICIO VI. *Complete these sentences in Spanish, using the subjunctive if it is required.* Notice that in Spanish you usually cannot say "me to go" or "John to come," but must change the statements to "that I go" or "that John come."

1. Juan quiere *me to go.* (*What extra word must you use?*) 2. Deseo *John to come.* 3. Le pide a su padre *to return.* 4. Me dice *to study.* 5. Le permitimos *to read* (*two ways*). 6. No le deje Vd. *to fall* (*two ways*). 7. Me manda *to enter* (*two ways*). 8. Quiero *you to know* a mi amigo. 9. Desean *us to hear* la música. 10. Quiere *you to bring it.* 11. Le dice *not to lose* el premio. 12. Le aconsejamos *not to leave* sin pagar. 13. Preferimos *to sleep* en casa. 14. Me pide *to sleep* en casa. 15. Ella quiere *me to make* el viaje. 16. No quiere *me to arrive* tarde.

EJERCICIO VII.[1] It might seem to you that such a roundabout way of expressing oneself would be used only in literary

[1] Optional exercise or to be read at sight.

South of Lima the Pan American Highway slashes through sandy desert wastes where it rains so rarely that not even cactus grows, and great dunes pile up between the mountains and the sea.

Sawders

form, but that is not the case. Everyone, educated or not, uses the Spanish subjunctive in everyday speech, and it is found even in the comic strips and in signs.

Here are some signs and advertisements from different Spanish-speaking countries which show how common this usage is. *Translate them and explain why the subjunctive is used in each one, guessing new words that resemble English.*

1. Si desea Vd. que le quiera su novia (*sweetheart*), cómprele chocolates «Gloria». (Candy store ad, Mexico) 2. ¿Le gustan las flores? No permita Vd. que las tomen. (Santa Lucía Hill, Santiago de Chile) 3. El Hotel San Marcos recomienda a todos que hagan uso de este servicio. (Lima, Peru) 4. Le invitamos cordialmente a que visite nuestro Salón de Exhibición. (Córdoba, Argentina) 5. Recomendamos a todos los votantes (*voters*) que voten «no». (San Juan, Puerto Rico) 6. Queremos que nuestro servicio dé gusto a nuestra clientela. (Hotel in Mexico) 7. Le rogamos que fije Vd. en este aviso (*notice*) y que envíe el pago (*payment*) de su subscripción. (Mexican newspaper)

34. Impersonal Uno and Se

no se puede describir, *one cannot describe*
uno puede imaginarse, *one may imagine*
se dice, *it is said, they say*
uno toma la derecha, *one turns to the right*

Se and ***uno*** are often used with third person verbs to express an indefinite subject. ***Uno*** is used with reflexive verbs where ***se*** is not possible.

EJERCICIO VIII. *Complete in Spanish:*

1. Desde la ventana *one sees* la montaña. 2. *One can* entender que cuesta mucho volar en avión. 3. *They say* que nuestros buenos vecinos desean que visitemos su continente. 4. *One never knows* qué pasará en una celebración grande. 5. ¿*May one* entrar por esta puerta? 6. Por aquí *one may not pass.* 7. ¿Qué *ought one* hacer? 8. ***One ought to*** **tomar la derecha.**

EJERCICIO IX. *Translate freely:*

1. ¿Se le ofrece algo? (Polite way to offer assistance) 2. Preguntando se llega lejos. 3. Del árbol caído se saca leña (*firewood*). 4. Riendo se va aprendiendo. 5. Poco a poco se anda lejos. 6. Con pan y vino se anda el camino.

ESTUDIO DE PALABRAS

I. Here are some idioms with ***tener*** which you have had in your first or second year Spanish course. *Choose one to complete each sentence, using each idiom only once. Change the verb to any form you wish.*

tener prisa, tener miedo (de), tener calor (*or* frío), tener que, tener —— pies de altura, tener la bondad de, aquí tiene Vd., tener —— años, tener hambre (*or* sed), tener razón

1. Todos *have to* estudiar para aprender. 2. Josecito *is right*; hay que entregar la leña al patrón. (*Song*, El leñador) 3. Hoy día nadie *is afraid to* volar en avión. 4. La hermanita de Jimmie *is eleven years old* el siete de julio. 5. *Please* mirar el mapa de la carretera nueva. 6. En los Andes los indios *are cold* en el invierno. 7. Quien come poco, *is hungry*. 8. En el viaje de vuelta, *we are always in a hurry* porque queremos llegar a casa. 9. El cortés inspector dijo, — *Here is* mi pluma para firmar el papel. 10. En algunas partes de los Andes, hay picos (*peaks*) que *are twenty thousand feet high*.

PARA LEER SIN ESTUDIAR

I. ¿SABÍA VD. ESTO?

1. El «Cristo de los Andes» fué hecho del metal de los cañones (*canons*) de Chile y la Argentina, con que los dos países habían combatido por muchos años. Al terminar su disputa, hicieron la estatua de sus cañones y prometieron (*promised*) no combatir nunca más.

2. En Panamá se pueden comprar curiosidades de casi todos los países del mundo, porque por el Canal pasan vapores (*steamers*) de todas partes.

3. Costa Rica tiene el gobierno más democrático del mundo. El presidente puede viajar sin protección, nunca hay revoluciones, y hay más maestros (*teachers*) de escuela que soldados.

II. Unos chistes

1. El hombre que tiene hambre — Oiga, mesero. Hoy quiero comer muy bien. ¿Qué me aconseja Vd.?

El mesero — Le aconsejo que vaya a otro restaurant.

2. Un pobre entra en un restaurant y habla con el dueño.

— Hace tres días que no como, señor.

— Lo siento.

— Tengo muchísima hambre.

— Y ¿qué quiere Vd. que yo le haga?

— ¡Ah, Vd. tiene el corazón noble! ¡Hágame un plato de frijoles con tortillas!

TEMA

1. We all want our parents to go to South America. 2. They want us to go, too. 3. The Andes are more than 14,000 feet high in the Uspallata Pass (***Paso de Uspallata***) where stands (***está***) the Christ of the Andes. 4. Of course, in the winter there is much snow on the road. 5. One-third of the highway through Panama is not paved yet. 6. Within a few years we shall be able to reach Buenos Aires, believe it or not. 7. In most of these countries it is necessary to turn to the (take one's) right. 8. We advise you to leave without waiting [any] more. 9. Do you want me to make the return trip without flying? 10. We ourselves prefer to enter, but we don't want you to lose the time. 11. Don't let the horse fall! 12. They invite us cordially to visit them.

CAPÍTULO 12

La leyenda de Xochiquetzal[1]

El Salvador, about the size of Maryland, is the smallest country of Central America, but an enterprising one with many cultured people who speak several languages and have seen the world. The country is dotted with volcanoes, and plagued with earthquakes, but coffee plantations climb boldly up crater sides so steep that the coffee pickers sometimes tie themselves to the shade trees to keep from falling off the farms!

In spite of its very visible Spanish heritage from Extremadura and Andalusia, as shown by its architecture, markets, oxcarts, and guitars, El Salvador is not a sleepy *mañana* country, for its girls play basketball, its boys play soccer, and everyone takes an active interest in government affairs. El Salvador was the first Central American country to finish its share of the Pan American Highway, possibly because Salvadoreans drive cars themselves and appreciate good roads.

The Aztecs in pre-colonial days had penetrated even to this part of Central America; so it is not surprising to find old Aztec names and legends still common. This tale of mysterious Lake Ilopango, where not so long ago some islands disappeared during an earthquake, tells how the ancient peoples tried superstitiously to prevent such catastrophes. Here it is, a legend of two boys and a girl of about your age, who lived in

[1] If in Aztec, ***Xochimilco*** means *flower garden* and ***quetzal*** is a ***bird***, what does ***Xochiquetzal*** mean?

There is a shop in Mexico City called Xochicalli. ***Calli*** in Aztec means ***house***. What kind of shop is it?

El Salvador before the Spaniards came. Remember — in a legend anything can happen and usually does!

1

— ¡Qué azules están las aguas del Ilopango[1] esta tarde! — dijo Atlox, sentado bajo una vieja higuera a la orilla del lago con su hermano Atonal y su amiguita, Xochiquetzal.

— Sí, el azul es el color favorito de la diosa del lago, — contestó Atonal, ocupado en comer uno de los zapotes[2] que los tres muchachos habían cogido en el bosque.

— ¿Crees que de veras haya[3] diosa en el fondo (*bottom*) del lago? — preguntó Xochiquetzal.

— ¿Cómo no? — respondió Atonal. — Mi padre dice que sí. Dice que si sube el nivel de las aguas, es cierto que vendrá un terremoto, porque esto quiere decir que la diosa quiere otro sacrificio.

— A mí todo eso no me parece verdad, — dijo Atlox. — ¿Por qué querría una diosa un sacrificio de cuatro muchachas bonitas? No creo que tengan razón los sacerdotes.

— Espero que no tengan razón, — dijo Xochiquetzal riéndose, — porque ¿no soy yo una de las muchachas de la edad en que se sacrifican?

— Y una de las más bonitas, también, — dijo Atlox, mirándola con afecto.

— ¡Miren Vds.! — exclamó Atonal, de pronto. — ¿No está más alto el nivel del agua esta tarde? ¡Aquel árbol antes estaba más lejos del lago, y ahora casi está en el agua!

— ¡Es verdad! — murmuró Xochiquetzal, mirándolo fascinada (*fascinated*). — ¡Ay, Atlox, tengo miedo! ¡Temo que venga un terremoto!

[1] Ilopango is a lake twelve kilometers from San Salvador, the capital of El Salvador. Many families have summer homes there.

[2] The ***zapote***, *sapota*, is a delicate tropical fruit with a thin green skin and sweet, buttery flesh. The ***chico zapote*** tree furnishes the chicle which makes our chewing gum.

[3] ***haya***, present subjunctive of ***hay***. This is a new use of the subjunctive which is presented in this chapter. Translate it as it sounds best.

En ese instante sonó a lo lejos el toque (*roll*) de los teponaztles.[1]

— ¡Oigan Vds.! ¡Los teponaztles! — exclamó Atlox. — ¡Quiere decir que algo importantísimo va a pasar en el templo!

— ¡Quiere decir que los sacerdotes se han fijado en el nivel de las aguas, y que va a haber sacrificio a la diosa del lago! — dijo Atonal. — Y tú, Xochi, tú eres la más bonita y la más —

— ¡Cállate! — mandó Atlox a Atonal. — Nuestra Xochi no será sacrificada! No permitiremos que se la lleven!

Pero los teponaztles sonaban cada vez más cerca, hasta que al fin llegaron a donde los esperaban, temblando, los tres jóvenes aterrados....

2

Xochiquetzal vivía en el palacio real, con las otras tres hermosas vírgenes. Todos los días los criados les daban vestidos nuevos; todos los días les servían comidas ricas; todos los días les tocaban música. Porque era costumbre tratar de mantener (*keep*) contentas a las desgraciadas, pues ellas habían de pedir a la diosa del lago clemencia (*mercy*) para los demás.

Pero entretanto, Atlox y Atonal se ponían cada vez más tristes. Echaban de menos la voz dulce de Xochiquetzal; echaban de menos a su amiguita en sus paseos por los bosques donde los tres habían pasado tantos ratos alegres.

— No pueden sacrificar a nuestra Xochi, — dijo Atlox tristemente. — No creo que tal sacrificio pueda impedir (*prevent*) los terremotos.

— Si hay diosa o si no la hay, no quiero que echen al agua a Xochi, — dijo Atonal, — pero ¿cómo podríamos salvarla? Somos muchachos —

— Sí, somos muchachos, pero fuertes, y ligeros, y listos. ¡Es preciso hacerlo! Oye, Atonal, te diré cómo la vamos a salvar....

[1] A *teponaztle* is an Aztec drum made from a section of tree trunk and often carved to represent a crouching animal.

Y la vieja higuera escuchó las dos voces jóvenes, y la brisa las oyó, y las aguas azules del lago al pie del árbol sonrieron bajo el sol, oyendo la idea de los dos....

3

Llegó el día del sacrificio. Del palacio real, al toque (*roll*) triste de los teponaztles, salieron los sacerdotes con las cuatro hermosas vírgenes, todas vestidas de blanco. A ambos lados de Xochiquetzal caminaban en la procesión Atlox y Atonal, silenciosos, velando (*watching over*) a la pequeña figura blanca.

Al fin llegó la procesión a un risco en la orilla del Ilopango. Se oyó otro toque (*roll*) de los teponaztles, y los sacerdotes cogieron a Xochiquetzal para echarla a las olas. Pero en el instante en que iban a dejarla caer, Atlox y Atonal la arrebataron (*snatched*) de sus manos y huyeron con ella por el bosque.

¡Y en ese instante empezó a temblar la tierra! La gente, aterrada, cayó de rodillas para pedir perdón a la diosa, y

Coffee pickers in Costa Rica strip the cherry-red berries from the trees. The volcanic ash of Costa Rica's soil grows mild coffees to be blended with those of heavier flavor from other countries.

Keystone

San Salvador's cathedral cannot be of heavy stone construction because of the frequent earthquakes. As in most Latin-American countries, a national hero sits his bronze horse on a pedestal in the plaza.

nadie siguió a los tres jóvenes que huyeron, huyeron, hasta llegar a la otra orilla del lago donde no vivía nadie. Allí iban a quedarse, sin volver nunca a su pueblo.

Pero los sacerdotes estaban furiosos. — Han huido, — dijeron, — pero no se escaparán. Mandaremos a nuestros soldados que los sigan y los devuelvan al palacio, y entonces veremos lo que pasa. . . .

Por el bosque los iban buscando los soldados, y al fin, llegando a la otra orilla del lago, uno de ellos vió a lo lejos el vestido blanco de Xochiquetzal.

— ¡Allí están! — exclamó, y todos empezaron a correr hacia los jóvenes.

Atlox y Atonal, aterrados, vieron venir a los soldados. ¡Cómo salvar a su querida amiga!

— ¡Diosa del lago! — gritó Atonal, desesperado. — ¡Salva de los soldados a nuestra inocente Xochiquetzal! ¡Ella no tiene la culpa! ¡Hazla agua,[1] hazla una parte de tu lago azul!

Y en ese instante desapareció Xochiquetzal, y las olas del lago sonrieron dulcemente.

Pero, ¿qué pasaba con los jóvenes leales (*loyal*)? Poco a poco se iba convirtiendo Atlox en una higuera verde al lado del lago, y poco a poco iba desapareciendo Atonal, convirtiéndose en la brisa suave que acariciaba (*caressed*) las hojas verdes de la higuera y las olas azules del Ilopango.

Y cuando llegaron los soldados, ya no estaban allí los tres amigos. Solamente había el árbol, la brisa, y el lago azul....

PALABRAS NUEVAS

4	**alegrarse** (de)	to be glad (to)	2	**huir**	to flee
2	**ambos**	both		**lago**	lake
4	**bosque** (*m.*)	forest	3	**ligero**	swift
	brisa	breeze		**nivel** (*m.*)	level
2	**callarse**	to be quiet	4	**orilla**	shore
3	**convertir** (se) (en) (ie, i)	to change (into)	4	**sacerdote** (*m.*)	priest
			2	**seguro**	sure
	diosa	goddess		**silencioso**	silent
1	**haber de**	to be to, must	3	**sonreír** (i)	to smile
	higuera	fig tree		**teponaztle** (*m.*)	wooden drum

Expresiones

a ambos lados, on both sides
al otro lado, on the other side
***caer de rodillas,** to fall on one's knees
***cada vez más, gradually**
***con afecto,** affectionately
***dice que sí,** he says so
***echar de menos,** to miss
***querer decir,** to mean

¿VERDAD O NO?

Change the sentences that are false to make them true:

1. Ilopango era el nombre de un lago que ya no existe. 2. Xochi-

[1] *Hazla agua,* "*Turn her into water...*"

quetzal y sus dos amigos vivieron en Costa Rica. 3. Éste es el cuento de un incidente que pasó después de la conquista de los aztecas por los españoles. 4. Muchas veces los tres jóvenes habían dado paseos por el bosque. 5. Aquella tarde las aguas del Ilopango habían subido. 6. Era costumbre echar al agua del lago tres muchachas bonitas para impedir (*prevent*) los terremotos. 7. Antes del sacrificio, las cuatro víctimas vivían en el palacio real sin nada que comer. 8. Xochiquetzal nunca temía los terremotos. 9. La gente echaba al agua a las jóvenes para hacerlas contentas. 10. «Xochiquetzal» quiere decir «Flor-pájaro» en la lengua de los aztecas. 11. Los tres amigos vivieron felices a la otra orilla del lago sin ser descubiertos por los soldados.

PREGUNTAS

1. ¿Qué cogieron los tres amigos en el bosque? 2. ¿Creían ambos muchachos en la diosa del lago? 3. ¿Qué significaba el toque (*roll*) de los teponaztles? 4. ¿Se fijaron los sacerdotes en el nivel de las aguas? 5. ¿Cómo pasó Xochiquetzal los días antes del sacrificio? 6. ¿Echaron de menos los muchachos a su amiguita? 7. ¿Por qué cayó de rodillas la gente cerca del lago? 8. ¿A dónde huyeron los tres jóvenes? 9. ¿Tenía razón Atlox cuando dijo que la diosa no querría un sacrificio? 10. ¿Cree Vd. que termine felizmente el cuento?

REPASO DE VERBOS

I. Give the infinitives of these present tense verbs, tell whether they are indicative or subjunctive, and translate, using may *to show a subjunctive meaning.* (You *must* learn to recognize the subjunctive when you meet it!)

1. hacemos	6. den	11. ¡pague Vd.!	16. durmamos
2. pidamos	7. hagan	12. conozca	17. dormimos
3. pedimos	8. venimos	13. vayáis	18. traigan
4. busquen	9. empiece	14. yo sea	19. salen
5. buscan	10. Vd. pague	15. haya ido	20. pida

II. Give the first person present subjunctive of each of these verbs, preceding it with **que yo,** *and tell what it means, using* may *in the translation.* Example: **que yo ponga,** that I may put.

1. poner	5. estar	9. contar	13. perder
2. pedir	6. hacer	10. tener	14. saber
3. conocer	7. dormir	11. llegar [1]	15. ser
4. ir	8. pagar [1]	12. buscar [1]	16. haber

III. Using the list of verbs in Exercise II, give the singular polite command for each one except the last. Example: **ponga Vd.**

IV. Using the same list of verbs, give the familiar singular commands, affirmative and negative. Example: **pon tú; no pongas.**

V. With the same list of verbs, give the first person plural subjunctive and translate, using let us (let's) *in the translation.* Example: **pongamos,** let's put.

ALGO NUEVO

35. The Subjunctive after Expressions of Emotion

In the reading you found these new uses of the present subjunctive:

Espero que no tengan razón.
I hope they are not right.

Temo que venga un terremoto.
I am afraid an earthquake may come.

The subjunctive is used after expressions of emotion or feeling (to be glad, sorry; to hope, fear, etc.) when there is a change of subject.

If there is no change of subject, the infinitive is used:

Espero ir mañana.
I hope to go tomorrow.

[1] Be sure your spelling gives the correct sound! (§§ 91, 92)

You may "diagram" these sentences as you did those with verbs of causing, to show yourself why you need a subjunctive: **Espero > que Vd. vaya.**

REMEMBER: The subjunctive is used after expressions of emotion if there is a change of subject.

The five most common expressions of emotion are:

esperar	**ser lástima**	**temer**	**alegrarse de**	**sentir**
to hope	*to be a pity*	*to fear*	*to be glad (to)*	*to regret*

EJERCICIO I. *Translate these sentences, first exactly as they stand; then (if there is any difference) as we would ordinarily say them in smooth idiomatic English. Tell why the subjunctive is necessary in each case:*

1. Esperamos que Vds. vayan. 2. Temo que no tengan tiempo. 3. ¡Es lástima que ese alumno no estudie! 4. Siento que Vd. no venga a mi casa. 5. Me alegro de que Vd. no haya estado [1] enfermo. 6. Los profesores siempre quieren que estudiemos. 7. Nos aconsejan que leamos cada lección. 8. Nuestros padres prefieren que salgamos bien en nuestros exámenes. 9. Voy a pedir a mis padres que me den una plumafuente si salgo bien. 10. Pida Vd. a su padre que le dé una también. 11. Pero no le mande Vd. que se la dé, porque no es costumbre.

EJERCICIO II. The main verbs in these sentences often cause a subjunctive. *Translate and explain why the subjunctive is not used in these cases.*

1. Mi madre me hace estudiar cada noche. 2. No me permite ir al cine sin preparar mis lecciones. 3. Siento muchísimo no saber la lección, pero me molesta escribirla. 4. ¿Espera Vd. salir bien en los exámenes? 5. Me alegro de poder hacerlo. 6. Temo caer si cruzo la calle contra tránsito.

[1] The present perfect subjunctive is made by changing the helping verb (***he, has, ha,*** etc.) to the subjunctive form ***haya, hayas, haya,*** etc. The past participle does not change.

EJERCICIO III. *Copy the sentences of Ejercicio I and "diagram" each one to show how the subjunctive is caused by the main verb.* Example: Esperamos > que Vds. vayan.

36. The Subjunctive after Expressions of Doubt

In the reading you found these new uses of the subjunctive:

¿Crees que haya diosa en el lago?
Do you believe there is a goddess in the lake?

No creo que tengan razón.
I don't believe they are right.

The subjunctive is used after any expression that shows doubt in the mind of the speaker, just as it is used with verbs of causing and emotion when there is a change of subject.

> REMEMBER: The subjunctive is used after expressions of doubt if there is a change of subject.

The most common expressions of doubt (although none of them are found so often as verbs of causing or emotion) are: [1]

no creer	**¿cree Vd.?**	**no estar seguro de**
not to believe, think	*do you believe?*	*not to be sure*

Can sentences of this type be "diagrammed" like the others we have had?

EJERCICIO IV. *Translate these sentences, showing by the skeptical tone of your voice that you are doubtful about the matter!*

1. ¿Cree Vd. que Fulano haya estudiado su lección? 2. No creo que pueda leerla sin estudiar. 3. La profesora no está segura de que la haya preparado. 4. Y Fulano no cree que la lección sea difícil. 5. ¿Creen los otros alumnos que sea preciso escribirla? 6. No, no creen que sea preciso, aunque sería mejor escribirla.

[1] Note to teacher: *Dudar* and *negar* are so rarely found, according to Keniston, that it is unnecessary to mention them here.

EJERCICIO V. *Put the verbs in these sentences into Spanish, avoiding the subjunctive wherever it is permissible:*

1. Quiero *you to go.* (Can you usually say *you to go*?) 2. Me aconseja *to come.* 3. Nos piden *to pay.* 4. Los manda *to sleep.* 5. Espero que ellos *have gone.* 6. Temo que ella *may not arrive.* 7. Mi madre me deja *go* al cine. 8. Mi padre no me permite *return* a casa muy tarde. 9. ¡Qué lástima que ellos *have not studied*! 10. Nos alegramos de que ellos *are looking for it.* 11. Siento muchísimo que Vd. no *know* a mi amigo. 12. Le he dicho *not to sing.*

37. The Spanish Neuter

1. Neuter demonstrative pronouns

You have been using neuter pronouns, without realizing what they were, in such expressions as:

Eso no parece verdad. *That doesn't seem true.*
¿Sabía usted esto? *Did you know this?*
esto quiere decir, *this means*

As you know, all Spanish nouns are either masculine or feminine in gender; therefore, since pronouns must agree in gender with the nouns to which they refer, neuter pronouns cannot be used to replace or to refer to nouns. The neuter demonstrative pronouns, ***esto, eso,*** and ***aquello,***[1] always refer to a *whole idea,* rather than to any one word.

2. Neuter article ***lo***

You have found ***lo*** used with adjectives to express an idea:

lo mexicano está de moda, *that which is Mexican is in style*
lo curioso es, *the curious thing* (about the matter) *is*
lo único de valor, *the only thing of value*

The neuter article ***lo*** used in this way with an adjective

[1] *Aquello* is rarely used; *eso* is the most common of the three.

makes an abstract noun of the adjective and refers, as the neuter always does, to a *whole idea.*

3. Neuter relative ***lo que***

You have often found the neuter relative pronoun *lo que*, meaning *that* or *what* (*that which*):

> **Veo todo lo que hacen los vecinos.**
> *I see all that the neighbors do.*
>
> **¿Sabes lo que pasó en un túnel?**
> *Do you know what happened in a tunnel?*
>
> **Lo que hacemos es dar el paso.**
> *What we do is to give the right-of-way.*

When *which, what,* or *that* refers to an idea rather than to some definite noun, ***lo que*** instead of ***que*** must be used.

REMEMBER: Any Spanish neuter refers to a WHOLE IDEA.

EJERCICIO VI. *Translate these sentences freely, expressing the neuter idea as clearly as possible.* (You will often find such expressions in reading Spanish literature.)

1. Favor de cuidarme todo esto mientras busco al capitán. 2. ¡Fíjense Vds. en esto! ¡Es muy importante no olvidarlo! 3. Eso no me gustaba. 4. Todos hicieron lo mismo. 5. Lo mío no está aquí todavía. 6. Dé Vd. lo contrario de estas palabras. 7. Quiero hacer todo lo bueno. 8. — Un cinco por lo que piensas. — Eso no es posible. 9. Esto es lo fácil de la lección. 10. ¿Es esto lo que quería Vd.? — ¡Eso sí que es!

ESTUDIO DE PALABRAS

You have had these idioms with ***a***. *Choose one to complete each sentence, using each idiom only once.*

a la vez, a ver, a las cuatro, a la izquierda, a caballo, a casa, a lo lejos, a pie

1. — *¡Let's see!* — dijo el extranjero, — ¿Dónde estará la casa? 2. Todos pidieron permiso para ir *to the left.* 3. Mi hermana rió cuando me vió *on horseback.* 4. Vimos volar *in the distance* el avión de plata. 5. Voy *home* para sentarme en una silla cómoda. 6. Si no hay caminos ni aviones ni animales, es preciso viajar *on foot.* 7. Oímos música bajo el balcón *at four o'clock* de la mañana. 8. ¿Qué haré? Me falta dinero, y *at the same time* tengo hambre.

REPASITO

Una conversación por teléfono

Complete these sentences, using the proper form of **ser** *or* **estar** *in the present tense unless some other tense is indicated:*

1. ¿Quién *is it*? 2. *It is* su amigo, Pepe. 3. ¿Dónde *have you been?* 4. *I have been* en el pueblo. 5. *¿Is George studying* (*prog.*) ahora? 6. No, *he's* enfermo. 7. Siento que *he is* enfermo, y espero que pronto *he is* mejor. 8. Dígale que *to be* allí a las diez. 9. Oiga. Vd. tiene un reloj, ¿verdad? *¿Is it* de plata? 10. No, *it is* de oro. *It used to be* de mi tío, y me lo dió. 11. *¿Is it* un buen reloj? 12. Sí, *it is* muy bueno. *It is* de oro. 13. Si Vd. *are* en casa mañana, iré a ver su reloj. 14. ¡Qué bueno! *Be* aquí a las once. Adiós.

PARA LEER SIN ESTUDIAR

I. ¿Sabía vd. esto?

En los países de habla española las calles principales de las ciudades generalmente tienen más de un nombre. Por ejemplo, en México una de las antiguas calzadas (*causeways*) de los aztecas actualmente lleva siete nombres distintos (*different*): Calzada de Tacuba, Ribera (*Strand*) de San Cosme, Puente (*Bridge*) de Alvarado, Avenida Hidalgo, Calle de Tacuba, Calle de Guatemala, y Calle Manuel Negrete. ¡Así uno puede perderse fácilmente!

II. Chiste

Un sudamericano, viajando por los Estados Unidos, entró en una tienda para comprar un par (*pair*) de calcetines (*socks*). No pudo explicar lo que quería comprar, porque no hablaba inglés. El dependiente (*clerk*), que no hablaba español, le enseñó una cosa tras otra, tratando de averiguar (*find out*) lo que quería, y al fin le enseñó un par de calcetines.

Viéndolos, el sudamericano exclamó, muy contento, — ¡Eso sí que es!

Y el dependiente le dijo, un poco fastidiado (*annoyed*), "*Well, why didn't you spell it before?*"

TEMA

1. Do you believe there is a bird in that tree? 2. That doesn't seem necessary to me. 3. That tree was farther from the forest, but now it is beside it (*él*). 4. The two young fellows gradually became more sad. 5. She always missed her two friends when she went for a walk. 6. They don't want the goddess to throw her into the lake. 7. No one followed the soldiers when they fled to the other shore. 8. She isn't to blame! Make her a part of the old tree! 9. Little by little she was disappearing (*prog.*) into the waves of the lake. 10. How do we know all this? Our father said so. 11. This means that the people are not right.

CAPÍTULO 13

El tesoro de Buzagá

Colombia, which faces north on the Caribbean Sea as well as west on the Pacific, is traditionally known as the emerald country and the home of El Dorado — the fabulous Indian chief who covered himself with gold dust.

But modern Colombia is more than a land of gold and emeralds. It was the first country in the world to have a commercial air line and many of its people are cultured and smartly dressed. According to other Spanish Americans, the Colombians speak the finest Spanish in the New World. They also speak other languages fluently, study English conscientiously, and are familiar with North American newspapers. In fact, they know more about North American culture than North Americans know about that of South America. Businessmen are said to write poems between conferences, and everyone reads and discusses the world's most famous literature — classical and modern.

With such a cultured people, it is not strange that Colombia has many noteworthy authors. Here you read an amusing tale by Enrique Otero D'Costa, a famous modern historian of Colombia, who in addition to writing histories tells fascinating legends of his country.

En la muy noble ciudad de Tunja [1] vivía cierto honrado vecino llamado Lope Badillo, el cual era empedrador (*street*

[1] Tunja is a good-sized city of Colombia, not far from Bogotá, on the Simón Bolívar Highway.

paver). Decir empedrador es decir pobre, y este Lope era tan pobre que cuando su mujer le lavaba su único pantalón (*trousers*), tenía él que quedarse en cama por no tener otro.

El deseo de hacer fortuna le molestaba, y pasaba las horas pensando en el mejor medio de conseguir esto, sin poder ganar cosa alguna en muchos años.

Pero cierto día la suerte de Lope Badillo le hizo contar su deseo a una india vieja que sabía muchos secretos del país, y ella ofreció llevarle a un brujo que vivía en un lugar lejano y que guardaba un tesoro escondido.

Ya listos para la aventura, una mañana salieron de Tunja Lope y la india. Al fin llegaron los dos a unas verdes cumbres, desde donde le mostró la india el lejano bohío (*Indian hut*) del brujo. De allí volvió la vieja a Tunja, temiendo morir si se acercaba más al misterioso lugar.

Nuestro Lope continuó su viaje por una senda empinada, hasta acercarse al bohío (*hut*) de su corazón. Se acercó con mucha cautela (*caution*), miró por la puerta abierta, y vió

Christopher Columbus Avenue is usually one of the better streets of a Latin-American city, as here in Bogotá, Colombia. And any Andean town has a backdrop of high-piled, rugged mountains.

Monkmeyer

en el fondo del cuarto a un indio viejo, flaco (*thin*) y seco, sentado en el suelo.[1]

Sus ojillos [2] brillantes miraban fríamente a Lope. ¡Aquel viejo sería el brujo!

Mas en lugar de enojarse, el viejecillo[2] le preguntó a Lope muy cortésmente en qué podía servirle.

— Me gustaría que me mostrase algo, — le dijo Lope. — Ya lo sabrá Vd., viéndome llegar por esta senda tan mala.

— Je, je, — rió el viejecillo, — o mucho me equivoco, o buscas el tesoro de Buzagá.

— Vd. no se equivoca.

— Serás satisfecho. Es posible que halles [3] el tesoro ahora, porque hay luna nueva. Será preciso que hagas un viaje largo, pero vale la pena, porque el tesoro vale mucho.

Tras largo caminar por el bosque, tomaron una empinada cuesta, cansándose bastante y en poco tiempo bajo el sol ardiente. De pronto se detuvo el brujo, diciendo que no podía seguir adelante, y se sentó en la senda, mostrando así que no pensaba dar un paso más.

Para no perder el tesoro, Lope ofreció llevar al viejecillo sobre los hombros. Le tomó como San Cristóbal [4] al Santo Niño Jesús, y siguieron adelante.

Pero, ¡quién lo creyera! [5] ¡El viejo pesaba más que una montaña! Hasta los dientes de Lope le sudaban (*perspired*) por aquella cuesta arriba. Al fin quiso sentarse para descansar, pero el viejo gritó, — ¡Mal, mal! ¡Descansando, perderás la suerte! ¡Con el encanto de este tesoro es preciso que me lleves sin descansar ni detenerte en el camino!

El pobre de Lope tuvo que continuar cuesta arriba. Pero, al mirar hacia el horizonte (*horizon*), vió que en vez de acer-

[1] Many Indian tribes prepare their dead for burial in a sitting position with knees to chin.

[2] The diminutive *-illo* or *-cillo* is not so likely to be flattering as *-ito*. So the reader knows at once that the old Indian isn't *simpático*.

[3] This is a new use of the subjunctive which you will study in this chapter.

[4] Saint Christopher, the patron saint of travelers, is supposed to have carried the Christ Child across a river on his back.

[5] *Pero, ¡quién lo creyera!* *But, who would have believed it!*

Sawders

Colombia's coffee, of heavy body and delicate flavor, is used largely for blending with that of other regions. Inspectors in this modern country check samples frequently to make sure that quality is maintained.

carse a la cumbre, iba alejándose cada vez más.

— O me equivoco o aquella cumbre se va alejando, — dijo Lope.

— Ji, ji, ji, — rió el brujo. — Ya llegaremos, horitita [1] llegaremos a ganar el orito. ¡Ji, ji, ja, ja! ¡Orito, orito, y algunitas esmeraldillas! ¡Qué de riquezas! ¡Ya lo verás, ya lo verás!

Lo que vió Lope en aquel momento fué que la cumbre ya no se veía. El camino, como por encanto, se había estirado (*stretched*) tanto que su final ahora desaparecía a lo lejos.

El pobre de Lope empezaba a creer que sin duda aquel viaje tenía mala pata.[2] Deteniéndose, le dijo al viejo que se bajase.

Mas el brujo volvió a reírse, y dijo, — ¡Arre, arre, que ya

[1] ***horitita,*** *right now.* Notice how the *viejecillo* puts a diminutive on the end of almost every word!

[2] ***tenía mala pata,*** *was unlucky.* ***Pata*** means leg and foot of an animal or object, and is used in many colloquial expressions, such as *to put one's foot in it* (***meter la pata***).

vamos llegandito! Está aquí, aquí cerquita, — y le dió unos talonazos (*kicks*) como a una mula.

— ¡Qué cerquita ni qué nada! [1] — respondió Lope, enojándose mucho. Y cogió una piedra pesada y con ella golpeó (*struck*) al brujo en la cabeza.

¡San Miguel [2] nos valga! La piedra rebotó (*rebounded*) contra Lope Badillo como si fuera [3] de caucho (*rubber*), echándole al suelo con el viejo, el cual todavía iba a hombros, riéndose más que nunca.

— ¡Pues diablito tenemos! — pensó Lope. ¡No faltaba más!

Sacando un frasquillo (*little bottle*) de agua bendita (*blessed*) que siempre llevaba, Lope la echó sobre el brujo, invocando (*calling on*) a la vez a San Miguel. ¡Santo remedio!

El viejo cayó al suelo como un árbol seco, y fué rodando (*rolling*) cuesta abajo, echando chispas (*sparks*) como una fragua (*forge*) de herrero (*blacksmith*), hasta llegar al fondo del cañón (*canyon*) con el ruido de un gran trueno (*thunderclap*).

Lope, dando las gracias a Dios por haberse escapado, bajó al fondo para mirar al muerto. ¡Cuál no fué su sorpresa al ver que aquel «viejo» se había convertido en un cadáver (*corpse*) seco, muerto hacía muchísimos años! El cuerpo había sido tomado como morada (*dwelling place*) por el diablo mismo, para llevarse al camino infernal a los hombres honrados que no querían más que hacerse ricos.

Y huyendo de allí, volvió a la ciudad el bueno de Lope, a seguir empedrando (*paving*) calles, curado de andar buscando lo que no se le había perdido.

ADAPTED FROM ENRIQUE OTERO D'COSTA (*Colombia*)

[1] *Nearby, nothing!* (Slang.)

[2] *¡San Miguel nos valga!* *St. Michael bless us!* St. Michael is supposed to have defeated the Devil in hand-to-hand combat.

[3] *como si fuera, as if it were.* A subjunctive usage which you have not studied yet.

PALABRAS NUEVAS

3	**alejarse** (de)	to go farther away		**equivocarse**	to be mistaken
	brujo	wizard	2	**fondo**	bottom, depths; back (of a room)
3	**cansarse**	to get tired			
	cuesta	hill	4	**hombro**	shoulder
4	**cumbre** (*f.*)	peak	4	**lejano**	distant
3	**descansar**	to rest	1	**mas**	but
4	**diablo**	devil	1	**mismo**	himself (*new meaning*)
	empinado	steep	2	**pesar**	to weigh
	enojarse	to become angry	2	**pesado**	heavy

Expresiones

a hombros, on his back
¡cuál no fué su sorpresa!, how surprised he was!
cuesta abajo, down hill
cuesta arriba, up hill
***no faltaba más,** that was the last straw

PREGUNTAS

1. ¿Cómo sabe Vd. que era muy pobre Lope Badillo? 2. ¿Quién le dijo cierto día un secreto del país? 3. ¿Acompañó a Lope la

Modern Colombia boasts of buildings quite unlike those of traditional Spanish style, like this new children's theater in Bogotá.

Monkmeyer

india hasta el lugar misterioso? 4. ¿Era muy guapo el brujo? 5. ¿Cómo era? 6. ¿Cómo recibió el viejecillo a Lope? 7. ¿Qué era preciso que hicieran? 8. Al cansarse, ¿qué hizo el viejecillo? 9. ¿Cómo era preciso que Lope llevase al viejecillo? 10. ¿Qué pasó cuando Lope golpeó (*struck*) al brujo con una piedra? 11. ¿Qué supo Lope entonces? 12. ¿Cómo se salvó Lope? 13. ¿Qué, en efecto, había sido aquel «viejo»?

PARA COMPLETAR

Find the proper ending in List B to complete each sentence which begins in List A.

A	B
1. Le molestaba a Lope el deseo de	*a.* se enojó mucho.
2. Mientras su esposa lavaba su ropa, Lope	*b.* siguiese adelante.
	c. hacer fortuna.
3. La india ofreció llevarle a un	*d.* se quedaba en cama.
4. Lope le pidió a la india que	*e.* lugar lejano.
5. Lope no temía que la india	*f.* cuesta empinada.
6. Era posible que Lope y el brujo	*g.* muriese si iba más cerca.
7. Lope tuvo que subir a una	*h.* se bajase.
8. Era preciso que Lope le	*i.* daba las gracias a Dios.
9. En vez de acercarse, la cumbre	*j.* encontrasen el tesoro.
10. Cuando el viejo no quiso bajar, Lope	*k.* iba alejándose.
	l. llevase a hombros.
11. Lope le dijo al viejecillo que	*m.* se detuviese.
12. El viejecillo le dijo a Lope que	*n.* le mostrase el camino.

REPASO DE VERBOS

I. Here is a review of some common verbs which are irregular or unusual in the present subjunctive, with a few regular ones included for practice, for sometimes we drill so much on the hard ones that we forget the easy ones.

The numbers refer to these or similar verbs in the Appendix. Those not numbered are regular or are listed alphabetically beginning with section 63.

Galloway

Street cleaner in a small Andean town of Colombia parks his patient oxen by leaning the ox goad against the yoke fastened to their horns.

Give the first person singular present indicative of each verb and its corresponding present subjunctive form. Example: ***hacer: hago: haga***

REGULAR: bajar, abrir, cerrar, celebrar, firmar, vender, costar
IRREGULAR: dar, estar, ir, haber, saber, ser
IRREGULAR INDICATIVE STEM: caer, conocer (95), decir, hacer, huir (97), oír, poner, salir, tener, traer, venir, ver
ORTHOGRAPHICAL-CHANGING: buscar (92), coger (93), comenzar (94), empezar (94), llegar (91), pagar (91), sacar (92), seguir (78)
III RC: morir (89), dormir (89), pedir (88), sentir (90), servir (88), vestir (88)

II. Give the infinitive of each of these forms and tell whether it is indicative or subjunctive:

1. oigamos 2. conozca 3. paguen 4. salimos 5. demos 6. pongamos 7. hacen 8. dice 9. durmamos 10. dormimos 11. traiga 12. huyen 13. abráis 14. hace 15. servimos 16. sirvamos 17. tenga 18. cueste 19. cae 20. empiecen 21. saque 22. dé 23. vengamos 24. veamos

ALGO NUEVO

38. The Past (Imperfect) Subjunctive Tense

Here are the past subjunctive conjugations, which always use for their stem the third person plural of the preterite tense.

tener: tuvieron: tuviese (-ra) **dormir: durmieron: durmiese (-ra)**
hacer: hicieron: hiciese (-ra) **caer: cayeron: cayese (-ra)**

There are two ways to conjugate any verb in the past subjunctive, and you may generally use either one. (In Spanish America the ***-ra*** form is more popular.)

The same sets of endings serve for both ***-er*** and ***-ir*** verbs.

Past Subjunctive Models			
ganar *I (might) earn, etc.*		**responder** *(and -ir verbs)* *I (might) answer, etc.*	
gan ase	**gan ara**	**respond iese**	**respond iera**
gan ases	**gan aras**	**respond ieses**	**respond ieras**
gan ase	**gan ara**	**respond iese**	**respond iera**
gan ásemos	**gan áramos**	**respond iésemos**	**respond iéramos**
gan aseis	**gan arais**	**respond ieseis**	**respond ierais**
gan asen	**gan aran**	**respond iesen**	**respond ieran**

EJERCICIO I. *Referring to the models, try to answer these questions:*

1. How can you tell an ***-ar*** ending from an ***-er*** or ***-ir*** ending? 2. Are the ***-se*** and ***-ra*** endings exactly alike except for those two letters? 3. Which person has a written accent in all four sets of endings? 4. What stem is always used to form all past subjunctive tenses? 5. Which two persons are alike in each of the four sets of endings? 6. What English word often translates a past subjunctive?

EJERCICIO II *Give the third plural preterite of each of these verbs; then the first person singular past subjunctive of both the* **-se** *and* **-ra** *forms.* Example: **venir: vinieron: viniese, viniera**

1. haber	6. decir [3]	11. estar [4]	16. creer
2. querer	7. traducir [3]	12. saber	17. huir
3. dar [1]	8. traer [3]	13. servir	18. oír
4. poder	9. cantar	14. pedir	19. poner
5. ir [2]	10. comer	15. leer	20. ser [2]

39. Using the Past Subjunctive Tense

In the story you found the following new verb forms:

Me gustaría que Vd. me mostrase.
I should like for you to show me.

Le dijo al viejo que se bajase.
He told the old man to get down.

The subordinate verbs *mostrase* and *bajase* in these sentences are in the past subjunctive tense because the verbs that cause the subjunctive are in the past instead of in the present.

Notice the difference in these pairs of sentences:

Quiero que Vd. vaya; quería que Vd. fuese.
I want you to go; I wanted you to go.

Le pido a Vd. que salga; le pedí a Vd. que saliese.
I ask you to leave; I asked you to leave.

There are two ways to tell whether to use the present or past subjunctive:

[1] This *-ar* verb has *-er* endings in both preterite and past subjunctive!

[2] There is no *i* following the *u* anywhere in this past subjunctive conjugation.

[3] Verbs with a *j* in the preterite have no *i* following the *j* anywhere in this conjugation.

[4] This *-ar* verb takes *-er* endings in the past subjunctive.

1. If the English says *may*, use the present subjunctive; if it says *might*, use the past.

REMEMBER:	May = present Might = past

2. If neither English *may* nor *might* is used, as in *I asked you to go*, watch the main verb and use the same tense for the subjunctive that you find in the indicative.[1]

REMEMBER:	Present follows present. Past follows past.

EJERCICIO III. *Change these sentences from the present to the past tense and translate:*

1. Quiere [2] que yo le diga la verdad. 2. Nos pide que se lo demos al dueño. 3. Esperan que lleguemos temprano. 4. Es lástima que no oiga bien. 5. Me dicen que lo ponga aquí. 6. ¿Cree Vd. que ella sepa el camino? 7. No creo que lo hayan celebrado todavía. 8. ¿Teme Vd. que ella caiga? 9. Queremos que nos den bastante dinero. 10. Les pido a Vds. que no duerman en la clase. 11. ¿Espera Vd. que tengan tiempo? 12. ¿Quiere Vd. que yo compre la casa?

40. Subjunctive after Impersonal Expressions

Es posible que halles el tesoro.
It is possible for you to find the treasure.

Será preciso que hagas un viaje largo.
It will be necessary for you to make a long trip.

Es posible and *será preciso* are "impersonal expressions" because the subject of each is not a person, but *it*.

An impersonal expression usually is followed by the sub-

[1] Note to teacher: More detailed instructions will be given as they are needed.

[2] Remember that verbs of believing, wishing, etc. are usually in the imperfect because they do not express an action (§ 128).

junctive when the subordinate verb has an expressed subject; otherwise, an infinitive may be used instead. Compare these sentences:

Es posible que Vd. vaya; es posible ir.
Es preciso que yo estudie; es preciso estudiar.

The most common impersonal expressions are:

es posible	**puede ser**	**es preciso**	**es mejor**
it is possible	*it is possible*	*it is necessary*	*it is better*

Others used less frequently are **es necesario,** *it is necessary;* **es probable,** *it is probable;* **es importante,** *it is important.*

Impersonal verbs which sometimes take the subjunctive are:

importar	**convenir** (ie)
to be important	*to be fitting* or *proper*

> REMEMBER: The subjunctive is often used after impersonal expressions.

Why are the impersonal expressions ***es verdad*** and ***es cierto*** (*it is certain*) not followed by the subjunctive?

EJERCICIO IV. *Translate these sentences carefully, watching the tenses closely, and tell why the subjunctive is or is not used each time.* These may be "diagrammed" like the other subjunctive sentences you have had: Es posible> que Juan vaya.

1. Es posible que Arturo no me pague. 2. Es necesario que me dé pronto el dinero. 3. Espero que él no haya perdido mi dólar. 4. Me dijo que iba a la ciudad. 5. Pero no quería que yo le acompañase. 6. Yo le dije que pidiese el dinero a su padre. 7. Me contestó que era preciso que su padre pagase primero sus cuentas (*bills*). 8. ¿Cree Vd. que Arturo haya ganado más dinero desde entonces? 9. Puede ser que haya buscado un empleo (*job*). 10. Es mejor que trabaje un poco para ganar dinero. 11. Ese Arturo cree que no es preciso trabajar mucho. 12. Me gustaría que me pagase esta semana.

41. Diminutives

ojillos, *little eyes*; **viejecillo,** *little old man*; **cerquita,** *very near*

You have already learned to use the diminutive endings ***-ito*** and ***-cito*** (***-ecito***), which often add a flattering or affectionate meaning to a word. Now you find ***-illo*** and ***-cillo*** (***-ecillo***), which may signify dislike or contempt, or at least a lack of importance.[1]

There are many other diminutive endings in Spanish, but these are the most common, especially in the everyday speech of women, children, and old people. They give color or character when used in stories or plays.

EJERCICIO V. *Translate these words, showing in any way you can the additional meaning given them by the diminutive endings:*

nuevecito, ahorita, todito, Juanito, un centavito, amiguito mío, una mesilla, una mesita, en un momentito, una mexicanita, una viejecita, un animalito, un animalillo, cerquita, chiquito, poco a poquito, papacito, mamacita, caballito del diablo (*dragon fly*), adiosito

ESTUDIO DE PALABRAS

I. HABLANDO POR TELÉFONO[2]

Read this telephone episode without trying to look up even strange words. If you cannot guess some of them, look at the list of telephone expressions in Exercise II for clues:

(*Un señor descuelga el receptor*)
LA CENTRAL — ¿Qué número?
EL SEÑOR — Señorita, favor de darme el número 26–47.
LA CENTRAL — (*Después de un rato*) No contestan.

[1] There is no rule to tell you when to use ***-ito*** instead of ***-cito*** or ***-illo*** instead of ***-cillo***. It is just one of those things you pick up from hearing and reading the language.

[2] Note to teacher: Exercises I and II are optional, since new words found here are not used again unless introduced in the regular way.

EL SEÑOR — Otra llamada, señorita, por favor.

LA CENTRAL — La línea está ocupada.

EL SEÑOR — Entonces favor de comunicarme al número 45–32, larga distancia, Toluca.

UNA VOZ — ¡Bueno! [1]

EL SEÑOR — ¡Bueno! ¿Hablo con la señorita doña Fulana de Tal?

LA VOZ — No, señor. Le han dado el número equivocado. (*Cuelga el receptor.*)

EL SEÑOR — (*A la central*) Oiga, señorita. Sírvase ponerme en comunicación con el número 45–32.

UNA VOZ — ¡Bueno!

EL SEÑOR — ¿Quién habla?

LA VOZ — Cuarenta y cinco treinta y dos.

EL SEÑOR — ¿Está doña Fulana?

LA VOZ — Espere un momento. (¡Señorita! ¡La llaman a Vd. al teléfono!)

LA SEÑORITA — (*Después de un rato*) Bueno.

EL SEÑOR — Querida mía, ¿quiere Vd. casarse conmigo?

LA SEÑORITA — Con todo gusto. ¿Quién habla?

II. Find out how to say these telephone expressions by looking carefully through the story. These are not all exact translations, so — *¡cuidado!*

1. The line's busy 2. long distance 3. You have the wrong number. 4. You're wanted on the phone. 5. Who's speaking? 6. Hello! (*two ways*) 7. Ring again, please. 8. They don't answer. 9. Number, please. 10. to take down the receiver 11. to hang up the receiver 12. to telephone 13. Is this Miss So-and-so? 14. Please give me 45–32. 15. Please connect me with 45–32.

III. Tell what these words and expressions mean and why they take the subjunctive:

1. querer 2. ¿creer? 3. esperar 4. es posible 5. no creer 6. es lástima 7. puede ser 8. pedir 9. sentir 10. aconsejar 11. es preciso 12. temer 13. desear 14. es necesario 15. dejar 16. decir

[1] In some Spanish-speaking countries they say — *¡Aló!*

REPASITO

I. Conjugate these verbs in the preterite and imperfect indicative:

buscar, venir, hacer, llegar, caer, poner, ir

II. Using the same verbs, give in Spanish the preterite tense forms unless the English says used to *or* was — ing, *which indicates the imperfect:*

1. I looked for 2. we came 3. he used to make 4. he put 5. he fell 6. I arrived 7. he arrived 8. they were falling 9. we used to go 10. they went 11. you used to put 12. they were arriving 13. he came 14. they made 15. we were coming

III. The italicized infinitives in this story should all be in the imperfect or preterite tenses. *Remembering that the imperfect is used for the stage setting,* "used to" *or* "was — ing," *and the preterite for the action that takes place, change the italicized infinitives to the proper forms.*

Domitilo, un criado mexicano de once años, *vivir* y *trabajar* en casa de la señora Alvarado en Bogotá, Colombia.

En la misma casa *visitar* una señorita norteamericana, que *querer* aprender a hablar español. Muchas veces la señorita *hablar* con Domitilo, pero en vez de tutearle (*speak in the second person*), como *deber*, le *decir* «usted». Ella *saber* bien que no *deber* hablar así con un niño, especialmente cuando éste *ser* criado, pero le *ser* muy difícil aprender la segunda persona de los verbos.

Pues, un día la señorita *estar* en su cuarto, y *llamar* a Domitilo. — Tráigame Vd. un cuchillo, por favor, — le *decir*. — Quiero comerme esta piña (*pineapple*).

Domitilo la *mirar* y *pensar*, — Si ella me dice «usted», eso quiere decir que los dos somos iguales (*equal*). Si somos iguales, yo no debo servirla a ella. — Y le *contestar*, — Vd. puede hallar los cuchillos en el comedor, — y *irse* sin traerle uno.

La señorita *enojarse* mucho, cuando lo *entender* todo. Así, no *decir* nada, y *ir* al comedor a buscar el cuchillo.

Al día siguiente, habiendo aprendido bien su lección, la señorita *llamar* a Domitilo y le *decir*, — Tráeme tú un cuchillo, por favor.

Y ¿qué *hacer* Domitilo? Pues *contestar* al momento y con mucho respeto, — Sí, señorita, con todo gusto. — ¡Y le *traer* el cuchillo!

IV. Just to be sure you understood the story while you struggled with the verbs, answer these three questions:

1. Why did the visitor use *usted* to Domitilo at first? 2. Why didn't he bring her the knife the first time? 3. Why was he so polite the second time?

PARA LEER SIN ESTUDIAR

Here is a clever little song from Colombia, the words of which were written by one of that country's favorite poets, Rafael Pombo, who died in 1912. Many of his verses are taught in the schools there, and everyone knows them by memory.[1]

LA VIEJECITA

RAFAEL POMBO Arr. by ALICE MOORE MILTON

[1] Here are the words whose meanings you may not know: ***érase***, *once there was;* ***tortas***, *cakes;* ***caldo***, *broth;* ***ranchito***, *hut;* ***fuera de***, *except;* ***huerta***, *orchard;* ***dorada***, *gilded;* ***cortes***, *styles;* ***mal***, *illness;* ***arrugas***, *wrinkles;* ***encorvada***, *bent over;* ***quejarse***, *complain;* ***lograr***, *succeed in;* ***disfrutar***, *enjoy;* ***pobrezas***, *poverty.*

car - nes, fru - tas, dul - ces, tor - tas, hue - vos, pan y pez. Be - bía
de u - na ca - sa gran - de con su huer - ta y su jar - dín. Nun - ca

cal - do, cho-co - la - te, le - che, vi - no, te y ca - fé, y la po-bre no en-con-
tu-vo en que sen-tar - se si - no si - llas y so - fás, ni o-tra ca - ma que u-na

Coro
tra - ba que co - mer ni que be - ber.
gran-de más do - ra-da que un al - tar.
Tra la di - ra, tra la li - ra, tra la

di - ra, tra la li. Tra la di - ra, tra la li - ra, tra la di - ra, tra la li.

3. Y esta pobre viejecita
no tenía que vestir
sino trajes de mil cortes
y de telas mil y mil.
Y esta pobre viejecita
cada año, hasta su fin,
tuvo un año más de vida
y uno menos que vivir.

4. Se murió de mal de arrugas
ya encorvada como un tres,
y jamás volvió a quejarse
ni de hambre ni de sed.
Duerma en paz y Dios permita
que logremos disfrutar
las pobrezas de esa pobre
y morir del mismo mal.

RAFAEL POMBO (*Colombia*)

TEMA

1. It is necessary for you to go. 2. What did he say to you? 3. He said it was necessary for you to go. 4. Why don't you ask him to do it? 5. I asked him to do it not long ago, but he didn't want to. 6. I'm glad you are going, at any rate, because I want you to bring me some candy (*pl.*). 7. You ought to buy [some] bread and eggs, too. 8. We lack tea and coffee, but I hope there is [some] bread. 9. Lope was so poor that he had to stay in bed while his wife washed his trousers. 10. Lope wanted the Indian woman to show him the hut (***bohío***) of the wizard (***brujo***). 11. The old lady was afraid the wizard might kill her.

CAPÍTULO 14

El gran Libertador

When we think of Venezuela, which looks northward toward the Caribbean Sea, we usually think of two things: Bolívar and oil, for Simón Bolívar, Latin America's greatest hero, was born in Venezuela, and oil put it on the map of the world's commerce. And if you have ever been there, you will also think of a five-cent candy bar that costs thirty cents, and a ten-cent cake of soap that sells for eighty, for Venezuela has the highest prices in the world!

A modern democratic nation for the last few years, Venezuela was for twenty-seven years almost the personal property of a cruel dictator who finally died of old age. Since his death in 1935, the country has restored free speech and personal liberty, signed a treaty fixing the long-disputed boundary line between Venezuela and Colombia, and started a remarkable program of education, especially in country schools. Along with education there has been developed a sports program featuring soccer, basketball, baseball, wrestling, and swimming, so that boys and girls your age in Caracas, the capital, enjoy many of the same things you do.

However, there is still much of old Spain to be found in patios and plazas, in the language, and in the customs of strict chaperonage, of bullfighting, and of having a national lottery; for, although Bolívar freed the country from Spain, nothing can ever take away its Spanish heritage.

Here is the story of Venezuela's favorite son and why no one today can forget him.

¡Bolívar! ¡Bolívar! ¡El gran Libertador!

Por toda la América del Sur se encuentra este nombre dado a plazas, a hoteles, a teatros, y a las monedas nacionales de dos países.[1] Un ferrocarril antiguo,[2] en Venezuela, y una carretera moderna,[3] en Colombia y el Ecuador, llevan el nombre. En las estampillas de correo y en los billetes de banco de Venezuela se ve la estatua del héroe, siempre montado en un caballo pisador (*prancing*) de bronce (*bronze*),[4] como si Bolívar nunca hubiese ido [5] a pie.

[1] The "dollar" of Venezuela is the *bolívar*, while in Bolivia ten *bolivianos* make a *bolívar*. Bolivians usually call their *bolivianos* «*billetes*», and English-speaking people shorten that to "bills."

[2] The oldest railway in the country, its track is only two feet wide.

[3] You read about the Carretera Simón Bolívar, which is to be part of the Carretera Panamericana del Pacífico, in Chapter 11.

[4] The horse usually stands upon his hind legs, and people of each country show you their statue and tell you proudly that this is the "only one" with the horse and rider so delicately balanced that the sculptor did not need to provide a third support to keep them from falling!

[5] There are some new uses of the subjunctive in this chapter.

Simón Bolívar, with his love for fine clothes, poetry, and gay parties, was at the same time a hard general who spared neither himself nor others in his fight for his country's freedom.

Pan American Union

Gendreau

Venezuela — Little Venice, the Spanish explorers named the new country when they found Indian huts built on stilts along the coast. Many of the old Indian villages have been replaced by thriving oil towns.

Si fuese [1] usted un sudamericanito, estudiando la geografía de los países de la América del Sur, tendría que aprender que éste es el nombre de un país (Bolivia), de una provincia del Ecuador, y de un estado de Venezuela cuya capital se llama Ciudad Bolívar (¡donde el hotel principal lleva el mismo nombre!). Además, aprendería que hay en varios estados de Venezuela cinco distritos (*districts*) que se llaman Bolívar; que en Colombia hay un departamento [2] y tres poblaciones de este nombre, y que en el Ecuador hay un Puerto Bolívar.

Hasta en Lima, capital del Perú, hay otra Plaza Bolívar, y además un Gran Hotel Bolívar. En Quito, capital del Ecuador, el cine más grande se llama el Bolívar; en la Argentina hay estatuas del Libertador, y — aunque Vd. no lo crea — también en nuestra Nueva York, en el Parque (*Park*) Central, hay otra estatua de este Bolívar, obsequio (*gift*) de Venezuela a los Estados Unidos en el año de 1921.[3]

[1] There are some new uses of the subjunctive in this chapter.

[2] Some countries, such as Guatemala and Colombia, are divided into *departamentos*, corresponding to our states.

[3] Nine years later the United States gave Venezuela a statue of Henry Clay, and so a plaza was named for it. Caracas has a George Washington Plaza, too.

No hay en el mundo otro nombre dado a tantos lugares en tantas tierras tan lejanas unas de otras. Hasta el nombre de Jorge Wáshington, nuestro «Libertador», aunque se ha dado a nuestra capital y a uno de nuestros estados, no se encuentra en tantos lugares.

Nosotros, pensando honrar a Simón Bolívar, decimos que es «el Jorge Wáshington de la América del Sur», mientras los sudamericanos, pensando honrar a Jorge Wáshington, dicen que es «el Simón Bolívar de los Estados Unidos». Pues, ¿quién fué este Simón Bolívar, cuyo nombre todavía se usa tanto, más de cien años después de su muerte?

Fué el libertador de seis países, que entonces no eran más que posesiones coloniales de España. Durante casi trescientos años estas posesiones enviaban oro y tesoros a los reyes españoles, que cada vez pedían más.[1]

Este Simón Bolívar nació en Caracas, capital de Venezuela, cinco años después de nuestro «*Valley Forge*». Fué educado en Europa, y se casó cuando muy joven con una divina muchacha que murió poco tiempo después. Esto entristeció tanto a Bolívar que nunca volvió a casarse. En cambio, para olvidar su tristeza, iba haciendo viajes de un país a otro, hasta a los Estados Unidos. Aquí conoció a Lafayette y a Enrique Clay, quienes se hicieron buenos amigos suyos, y aquí supo también lo que había hecho Wáshington por nuestro país.

Fué a México también, y es una cosa curiosa que actualmente el cuarto en que durmió Bolívar se conserva allí exactamente como estuvo entonces, para que sea reliquia (*relic*) del hombre que más tarde se hizo tan famoso.

Al fin decidió el joven lo que quería hacer. Fué en Roma que juró no descansar ni casarse nunca hasta que hubiese libertado de España a su patria, y desde aquel momento, pasó la vida combatiendo contra los españoles hasta conseguir esta libertad.

[1] You have no idea what a struggle it was to free enormous South America from Spain's domination, for after more than three centuries she had no intention of letting her New World possessions get away from her.

Bolívar was helped in his tremendous task by San Martín, who started in Argentina and worked north. You will read more about him later.

Para hacer esto, una vez cruzó los Andes con sus soldados, lo que no se creía posible.[1] Dos veces tuvo que huir de los españoles, pero cada vez volvió a combatir contra ellos. Una vez, al regresar a Caracas después de una victoria gloriosa, fué recibido como un héroe. Las calles estaban cubiertas de flores y tocaban las bandas, mientras su coche entró en la ciudad, tirado, no por sus caballos, sino por doce señoritas hermosísimas de las familias más soberbias (*proud*).

Bolívar siempre llevaba consigo un guardapelo (*locket*) que contenía un mechón (*lock*) del pelo de Jorge Wáshington, el cual le había enviado la familia de Wáshington. Lafayette había sugerido (*suggested*) que los Wáshington hiciesen esto, porque él sabía lo mucho que Bolívar veneraba (*honored*) la memoria del libertador norteamericano.

Libertar a seis países [2] del yugo (*yoke*) de España fué al-

[1] San Martín also crossed the Andes, farther south.

[2] They were five countries then: Venezuela, Colombia, Peru, Bolivia (once part of Peru), and Ecuador. At that time Panama was a part of Colombia.

Candy vendors of Caracas, Venezuela, line the sidewalks with their tempting displays of goodies made locally or imported from the United States or Europe. A five-cent candy bar costs thirty cents!

Gendreau

go de suma importancia, pero la fama de Simón Bolívar no depende enteramente de eso. Lo importante con que había soñado fué unir a estos países, junto con la Argentina y Chile, en una gran federación de estados unidos sudamericanos, como había hecho Wáshington en el norte.[1]

No consiguió realizar este sueño, porque fué un sueño del porvenir (*future*), y las jóvenes repúblicas no estaban listas para tal unión. Así murió expatriado (*in exile*) el gran Libertador, creyendo que había fracasado (*failed*) en el trabajo de su vida, y gritando en su delirio (*delirium*) a su criado,

— ¡José! ¡Trae el equipaje! ¡Nos vamos! ¡Aquí ya no nos quieren!

Lo triste es que cien años después, en el centenario (*centennial*) de su muerte (1930), la República de Venezuela, para honrar aun más al héroe de un continente, ¡declaró cancelada toda la deuda (*debt*) externa! Y en una gran fiesta, celebrada por nueve países de habla española, se oía una y otra vez,

— ¡Viva Bolívar! ¡Viva el gran Libertador!

PALABRAS NUEVAS

1	**cuyo**	whose		**libertador**	liberator
	depender de	to depend on		**libertar a**	to liberate
	entristecer	to sadden	3	**patria**	native country
	estampillas de correo	postage stamps		**regresar**	to return
3	**honrar**	to honor		**Roma**	Rome
3	**jurar**	to swear	4	**sumo**	greatest
2	**libertad** (*f.*)	liberty			

Expresiones

dar a, to face

lo mucho que, how much

poco tiempo después, a short time after

una y otra vez, time after time

[1] Bolívar would be very happy today if he could attend one of our Pan American Conferences because he dreamed of such a union of all the American nations many years ago. In fact, he called such a conference, which was held at the Isthmus of Panama in 1826.

PARA COMPLETAR

1. Muchos lugares llevan el nombre de ——. 2. Este héroe de —— países se llama el —— —— del sur. 3. Su estatua se ve en muchas ——, con el Libertador siempre —— ——. 4. Hace más de —— años que Bolívar libertó de España a estas posesiones. 5. En los Estados Unidos Bolívar conoció a —— y a —— ——. 6. Juró no —— ni —— nunca hasta que hubiese ganado la libertad para su país. 7. Una vez llegó a Caracas en un coche tirado por —— ——. 8. La posesión favorita de Bolívar era un guardapelo (*locket*) que la familia de —— le había dado. 9. El gran sueño de Bolívar era —— a todos los países del sur en una federación. 10. Bolívar —— creyendo que había fracasado (*failed*) completamente. 11. Cien años después, Venezuela —— al héroe del continente con una gran ——.

¿VERDAD O NO?

Change the sentences that are false to make them true.

1. Por todos los Estados Unidos se encuentra el nombre de Bolívar. 2. El nombre de nuestro libertador se ha dado a más lugares que el nombre de Bolívar. 3. Hasta hay teatros, plazas y ferrocarriles que llevan el nombre. 4. Las monedas nacionales de tres países se llaman bolívares. 5. Simón Bolívar nació en Caracas, capital de Colombia. 6. Nunca se casó porque su novia (*sweetheart*) murió muy joven. 7. En México todavía se conserva como estuvo entonces el cuarto en que durmió Lafayette. 8. Dos veces el héroe tuvo que huir de los caballos. 9. Había soñado con unir a todos los países de habla española. 10. Mientras estaba muriéndose, mandó a su criado que le trajese el equipaje para irse. 11. Ya no se honra en Venezuela la memoria de Bolívar.

REPASO DE VERBOS

I. Give first person plural present and past subjunctive of the verbs haber, dar, saber, ir, buscar, pagar, venir, poner, caer, decir, dormir, servir, sacar, *and* poder.

II. Translate these assorted verb forms, using may *to indicate present subjunctive and* might *to indicate past subjunctive:*

1. salgan	6. dé Vd.	11. lleguen	16. fueran
2. salen	7. que Vd. dé	12. llegara	17. fueron
3. saliesen	8. vemos	13. llegará	18. serán
4. traiga Vd.	9. veamos	14. estuvieron	19. dijo
5. que Vd. traiga	10. oyó	15. estuvieran	20. diga

III. Put these forms into Spanish:

1. I used to put	10. that you may see
2. we were sleeping	11. that she may tell
3. we slept	12. that we might go
4. he will leave	13. we may have paid
5. they continued	14. I might have seen
6. he said	15. she will return
7. that we may go	16. he has heard
8. that I might be	17. you will come
9. that he may put	18. Go away! (*two ways*)

ALGO NUEVO

42. The Future Subjunctive Tense

This tense has practically disappeared from the Spanish language, and is rarely found now except in proverbs and legal expressions. It is formed like the past subjunctive ***-se*** form, except that ***r*** is substituted for ***s*** throughout:

cantare, cantares, cantare; cantáremos, cantareis, cantaren
hiciere, hicieres, hiciere; hiciéremos, hiciereis, hicieren

Since you will have no use for this tense, you will not find it used in exercises in this book except once for recognition.

43. Sequence of Tenses

Quiere que yo vaya, *he wants me to go.*
Ha querido que yo vaya, *he has wanted me to go.*
Quería que yo fuese, *he wanted me to go.*
Había querido que yo fuese, *he had wanted me to go.*

You have learned that in general, a present subjunctive tense follows a present indicative, and a past follows a past. Compound tenses follow the same rule, a present perfect being considered a present tense and a past perfect a past tense.

Other tenses to consider are the future indicative, which is listed with the present tenses, and the conditional, which is listed with the past. So a complete general outline of the sequence (following) of tenses looks like this:

	Main Verb	*Subjunctive Verb*
REMEMBER:	Present Present Perfect Future Commands	Present (or Present Perfect)
	Past Past Perfect Conditional	Past (or Past Perfect)

There are exceptions to this rule, but in such cases it is usually safe to follow the English wording. Example: **Siento que muriese Ramón,** *I am sorry* (present) *that Raymond died* (past).

EJERCICIO I. *What subjunctive tense (if one were to be used) would ordinarily follow each of these indicative verbs?*

pide	aconsejó	esperaré	había mandado
sentían	he querido	sería preciso	me alegro de
deja	temía	es posible	será lástima
¿creía Vd.?	pediría	dígale Vd.	temeríamos
diría	siento	han buscado	¿no cree Vd.?

44. The Subjunctive in Adverbial Clauses

1. After conjunctions expressing time:

hasta que hubiese libertado a su patria, *until he had freed his country*

No iré antes que vuelva, *I shall not go before he returns.*

The subjunctive is used after conjunctions expressing time (temporal conjunctions), when indefinite future time is implied or expressed. If past time is implied, the verb is in the indicative.

To say "future time is implied" does not necessarily mean that the main verb will be in the future tense, as you can see from this conversation:

JUAN — Esperaré hasta que llegue María.
PEDRO — (*A Alfredo*) — ¿Qué dijo Juan?
ALFREDO — Juan dijo que esperaría hasta que llegase María.

Although the verb *llegase* is in the past tense, Mary has not arrived yet. When Alfred quotes John, he repeats the sentence, putting it all into the past, but still implying future time.

Some of the most common conjunctions of time are:

cuando	**antes que** [1]	**mientras (que)**	**hasta que** (*or* **a que**)	**en cuanto**
when	*before*	*while*	*until*	*as soon as*

[1] *Antes que* (sometimes *antes de que*) always takes a subjunctive.

Bolívar's home, in Caracas, is an architectural gem as well as a patriotic shrine. The wealthy Liberator spent most of his fortune fighting for his country's freedom from Spain.

Galloway

REMEMBER:	The subjunctive is used after conjunctions expressing time *if* indefinite future time is implied.

"Diagram" sentences of this type by putting an arrow after the word which causes the subjunctive and underlining the subjunctive verb, which shows you what you are doing:

cuando > venga; antes que > vaya

2. After other conjunctions:

aunque Vd. no lo crea, *although you may not believe it*
para que sea reliquia, *in order that it may be a relic*

The subjunctive is used after some other conjunctions if the subordinate verb expresses something which may not have happened yet.

The most commonly used conjunctions of this kind are:

para que [1]	**aunque**	**sin que** [1]
in order that	*although, even if*	*unless, without*

Other conjunctions of this kind, but much less commonly used, are:

a fin de que [1]	**de manera que**	**con tal (de) que** [1]
so that	*so that*	*provided that*

3. After other words:

como Vd. quiera, *as you wish*
iré adonde vaya Vd., *I will go where (ever) you go*

Some adverbs often take the subjunctive because they imply the idea of something doubtful. Those frequently found are:

como, *as* (a) **donde,** *where, wherever*

4. Subjunctive after *si:*

Si fuese Vd. sudamericano, tendría que aprenderlo.
If you were a South American, you would have to learn it.

[1] This always takes a subjunctive.

Gendreau

Oil derricks of Maracaibo, Venezuela, bring up the "black gold" that makes the country's prices the highest in the world.

The past subjunctive (never the present) is used after *if* when it expresses a condition that is not true ("contrary-to-fact"). In this case the *other* (main) verb in the sentence, whether it comes first or last, is in the conditional tense. Learn the model sentence **si yo fuese Vd., yo estudiaría,** and follow the model for all such sentences.

REMEMBER:	Use the past subjunctive after ***si*** in contrary-to-fact sentences.

5. Subjunctive after ***como si:***

como si nunca hubiese ido a pie, *as if he had never walked*
como si estuviera cansado, *as if he were tired*

Como si, which always takes the past subjunctive, is found even more frequently than *si* alone, although often it does not express something that is not true. We call this an "imaginative comparison."

EJERCICIO II. *Make a list of all the words in section 44 which cause the subjunctive, with their meanings, and use the list for reference as you do the remaining exercises of this chapter.*

EJERCICIO III. *Translate these sentences and give the reason for each use of the subjunctive:*

1. Cuando Diego venga a verme, iremos a nadar en el río (*river*). 2. Iríamos al lago si no hiciera tanto frío. 3. Antes que vayamos, tendremos que comer. 4. Para que lleguemos a casa temprano, saldremos pronto. 5. Pero no podremos salir hasta que venga José. 6. Mientras esperemos[1] a José, empezaremos a comer. 7. En cuanto llegue José, le invitaremos a acompañarnos. 8. No esperaremos a que llegue, si no viene pronto. 9. Si Rosita no tuviese miedo del agua, la invitaríamos a ir también. 10. Es posible que ella pueda aprender a nadar. 11. ¡Pero Rosita dice que nunca entrará en el agua hasta que sepa nadar! 12. Así estará segura de que nunca se ahogará (*drown*).

EJERCICIO IV.[2] These uses of the subjunctive are very common, as you will see when you read these advertisements, proverbs, song titles, sayings, etc., from several Spanish-speaking countries.

Translate and tell why the subjunctive is used in each case.

1. Ford Servicio Donde Vaya (Guatemalan advertisement)

2. «Cuando ya no me quieras» (Mexican song title)

3. «Hasta que llueva en Sayula, buena suerte te dé Dios». (Mexican saying wishing good luck for a long, long time)

4. — Que (*may*) Dios me bendiga (*bless*) hasta que llegue a donde haya gente. (Said reprovingly if no one says «*Salud*» when a person sneezes)

5. — Mientras yo lleve la nariz (*nose*) sobre la boca (*mouth*), nunca tomaré pulque (*cactus juice drink of Mexico*). (Implying that the speaker wouldn't touch *pulque*!)

6. — Sírvase (*help yourself*) como si estuviese en su propia casa. (Said at the table to a guest, in Puerto Rico)

[1] Notice that ***esperar*** may mean *hope* or *wait* (*for*); so be sure to choose the meaning that fits.

[2] Optional exercise.

7. Donde fueres, haz como vieres. (Proverb)

8. «Piden pan y no les dan;
piden queso y les dan un hueso (*bone*).
Se sientan a llorar en la puerta del zaguán (*entrance*),
a que suenen las campanas, — ¡Pan! ¡Pan! ¡Pan!»
(Verse for jumping rope, Mexico)

9. «México en una laguna (*lagoon*),
Guadalajara en un llano (*plain*);
yo voy a comer una tuna (*cactus pear*),
aunque me espine (*pricks*) la mano.» (Mexico)

10. «Si tuviera cuatro vidas, cuatro vidas serían para ti.» (Mexican song)

11. Antes que te cases, mira lo que haces. (Proverb)

12. — Si hubiese tenido más suerte, ese bandido habría sido tan famoso como Pancho Villa. (Said about Manuel Lozada, a Mexican bandit)

13. Favor de apagar (*put out*) la luz cuando ya no la necesite. (Sign in hotel, El Salvador)

EJERCICIO V. *Put the italicized infinitives into Spanish and explain why you use a subjunctive, when you do.*

1. Cuando *ir* Vd., yo le acompañaré. 2. ¿Qué dijo Vd.? — Dije que cuando *ir* Vd., le acompañaría. 3. Mientras yo le *esperar*, descansaré aquí. 4. ¿Qué quiere Vd. que *hacer* Alberto? 5. Dije que quería que Alberto *estudiar*, aunque no le *gustar*. 6. En cuanto lo *saber* Enrique, irá a casa. 7. Si *tener* más tiempo, yo sé lo que haría. 8. ¿Qué *hacer* Vd. si *poder*? 9. Si yo *ser* Vd., trataría de manejar mejor. 10. El Libertador juró que mientras *vivir*, no dejaría de (*stop*) combatir contra los españoles. 11. Si Bolívar *haber* tenido más suerte, no *haber* muerto pobre y triste. 12. Bolívar murió pobre, como si *haber* nacido sin un centavo. 13. Wáshington quería que su patria *ser* libre. 14. José, su criado, le dijo a Bolívar, — Adonde *ir* Vd., yo iré también.

ESTUDIO DE PALABRAS

I. You have had many verbs formed by adding a prefix to another verb, such as *cubrir, descubrir; volver, devolver,* etc.

Since it is sometimes confusing to conjugate the longer verbs unless you know them thoroughly, it is well to practice with them.

Give the meaning of the original verb and its derivative, and then the first person singular present indicative, third person plural preterite, and gerund of each one. Example: **seguir,** *to follow*; **conseguir,** *to obtain*; **consigo, consiguieron, consiguiendo**

parecer: aparecer, desaparecer
cubrir: descubrir
poner: suponer, reponer (*to replace*)
volver: devolver, revolver
tener: detenerse, contener
reír: sonreír
venir: convenir
seguir: perseguir (*to pursue*)
pedir: despedirse
escribir: describir
volar: trasvolar (*to fly across*)
mostrar: demostrar

II. The longer the word, the easier it is to guess! *Locate the most familiar part of each of these words and explain their derivation:*

anochecer, entristecer, acercarse a, alejarse de, saludable, casarse con, encerrar, verdadero, dormitorio (*bedroom, dormitory*), libertador, inolvidable, increíble (*unbelievable*), sombrerería (*a store*), mandamiento (*commandment*), enfermedad, encima de, acostumbrarse

III. You cannot guess short words; you just have to know them. *What do these words or combinations mean?*

se lo, me la, nos los, te las, para él, sin ella, le — a Vd., la — a Vd., el mío, la suya, la de él, el de ella, se las — a Vd., os la, te lo, a las tres, nos (*three meanings*), les — a ellas, les — a Vds., su — de Vd., el — de ellas, éste, esto (*What gender?*)

REPASITO

Complete in Spanish:

1. Enséñeme Vd. la página; *show it to me.* 2. No me acuerdo de la fecha; *I don't remember it.* 3. Los enemigos no le robaron las

esmeraldas; *they did not steal them from him.* 4. Me pidió el dinero; *he asked me for it.* 5. ¿Por qué no quieren devolverme el cuchillo; *why don't they want to return it to me?* 6. Lafayette quería que los Wáshington diesen el pelo a Bolívar; *he wanted them to give it to him.* 7. Enrique pide que yo le compre los dulces; *he asks me to buy them for him.* 8. Alberto ofrece traer a Rosita la carne; *he offers to bring it to her.* 9. No debemos burlarnos de nuestros amigos; *we ought not to make fun of them.* 10. Vamos a entrar en el restaurant; *let's enter it.*

PARA LEER SIN ESTUDIAR

I. ¿Sabía vd. esto?

El guardapelo (*locket*) que la familia Wáshington envió a Bolívar, y que el Libertador siempre llevaba consigo, fué exhibido (*exhibited*) en el Edificio de Venezuela de la Feria Mundial (*World's Fair*) de Nueva York en 1939.

II. Chistes

The subjunctive may not seem funny to you, but it is so common in Spanish that it appears in many jokes! An uneducated person may misuse *ser* and *estar*, but he usually gets his subjunctives right, strange as that may seem to us.

1. — Pues, ¿Vd. es socialista?
   — Ciertamente.
   — Entonces, si tuviera Vd. dos caballos, ¿me daría uno?
   — Sin duda alguna.
   — Y si tuviera dos casas, ¿me daría una también?
   — Con el mayor gusto.
   — Y si tuviera dos gallinas (*hens*), ¿me daría una?
   — ¡Ah, eso no!
   — ¿Y por qué aquello sí y esto no?
   — Porque tengo dos gallinas.

2. — ¡Si tú supieras el dolor que sentí al perder mi perro!
   — ¿Estaba enfermo?
   — No, estaba pasado de moda.

3. — Mire, mamá. Si compra Vd. un piano para mi hermana, cómpreme para mí una bicicleta.

— ¿Y por qué quieres tú una bicicleta?

— Para dar un paseo cuando ella toque el piano.

4. El acreedor (*creditor*) — Pero, al menos, dígame Vd. si puedo esperar que me pague.

El deudor (*debtor*) — Sí, hombre, sí. Le doy permiso para que me espere.

(Pun on two meanings of *esperar*)

5. Un joven que va en coche dice al chófer, — No vaya Vd. tan despacio. ¿No sabe Vd. que me voy a casar? ¿Quiere Vd. que llegue tarde a casa de mi novia (*fiancée*)?

— Dispense (*excuse me*) Vd., caballero. Iba despacio para que tuviera tiempo de considerarlo.

TEMA

Watch for subjunctives, and when you find one, be sure to put it in the proper tense! To "diagram" the sentences may help you. The words are common ones, so that you can concentrate on the verb forms rather than on the vocabulary.

1. When George comes, tell him to wait for us. 2. Did you ask him to bring the flowers? 3. No, but I will tell him to do it now. 4. It will be necessary for us to listen well if we want to hear the car when he comes. 5. If I wanted to hear it, I would wait in the garden. 6. It would be better for you to sit down here. 7. What a pity that the flowers have not come yet! 8. I could not arrange them until they arrived unless I were a wizard (***brujo***). 9. He lets us wait as if he were a king. 10. Do you believe he is going to ask her to go? 11. I should like for her to go with me, even if (*although*) George may have a better car. 12. She will be glad that I have asked her to go, believe it or not (*even if you do not believe it*)!

CAPÍTULO 15

Cuentos de Puerto Rico

On his second voyage in 1493, Columbus stepped onto a tropical island in the West Indies, planted the flag of Spain in the sand before a few puzzled *borinqueño* Indians, and christened the place San Juan Bautista in honor of the Crown Prince of his country.

Ponce de León was with Columbus that day, and fifteen years later came back from Santo Domingo to be the first governor of the flowering little island that now belongs to the United States. He called the landlocked bay Puerto Rico — "rich harbor," and the name has come to be that of the entire territory, while the capital city, situated on a small island inside the bay, now bears the name of San Juan. Ponce de León had the rebellious *borinqueños* pretty well subdued when he heard rumors of a Fountain of Youth somewhere on the mainland and left for Florida on the quest that led him to his death.

Spain neglected Puerto Rico for some time, and it took an attack by the English Sir Francis Drake to make the Spanish king realize the danger of losing the island and order funds sent over from Mexico City for its defense. With the money, work was completed on *El Morro*, the great gray stone fortress that rears up on the northern point of the capital island with its feet in the sea.

Fort San Cristóbal, now four hundred years old, had already been built at the other end of San Juan, and today its sentinel towers still peer suspiciously at the horizon. Between the two great fortresses is the surprisingly Americanized and skyscrapered little city, where polite people insist on speaking to the visitor what they fondly believe is English.

For some reason, San Cristóbal Castle, as it is sometimes called, seems to have monopolized all the local legends, and although Uncle Sam makes sure that it is the neatest old Spanish ruin that ever scratched a visitor's shoe, the place manages to retain an air of mystery.

Here are two of the tales told to every visitor who scrambles over its time-stained ramparts and into its subterranean galleries.

I. El milagro de San Cristóbal

Hace unos cuantos siglos que llegó a San Juan un sacerdote, y en seguida hizo una inspección del Castillo de San Cristóbal, donde había de cuidar de la capilla [1] del santo del mismo nombre. Por las murallas, por las galerías subterráneas, desde una garita hasta otra, fué el buen padre, insistiendo en que todo fuese arreglado bien.

Al fin llegó a la cisterna inmensa debajo de la fortaleza. La cisterna contenía el agua de lluvia que iba cayendo durante todo el año sobre las azoteas (*flat roofs*) del Castillo, y que se guardaba allí para que a la ciudad nunca le faltase agua.

¡Cuál no fué la sorpresa del buen padre al ver que allí, dentro de la cisterna, había una pintura del santo patrón del Castillo, una pintura de San Cristóbal mismo, colgada en la obscuridad donde nadie podía verla!

— ¡Qué barbaridad! — exclamó el buen padre, y mandó a uno de sus soldados que sacase la pintura y la llevase a la capilla de la fortaleza, para colgarla en la pared.

Pero, ¡cosa curiosa! Al día siguiente no llovió ni una gota, ni al otro día tampoco. Pasaron semanas, y no caía lluvia. Poco a poco iba agotándose (*diminishing*) el agua de la cisterna. Todos los habitantes, desesperados, fueron a las iglesias y empezaron a rezar (*pray*). Todos ayunaron (*fasted*), y pidieron a sus santos que enviasen la lluvia. Pero en vano. No llovía ni una gota . . .

[1] Every old Spanish fort has a chapel dedicated to the patron saint of that particular place. Ammunition storage tunnels are dedicated to Santa Bárbara, the saint who guards soldiers from danger against explosives.

Galloway

El Morro, the great stone fortress of San Juan which the Spaniards began in 1539, was the last word in fortifications. The sentry box is just like the "haunted" one of the story.

Pues bien, un día vieron los soldados que se había acabado casi toda el agua. ¡Qué hacer!

Aquella noche, de pronto empezó a llover. Toda la noche siguió lloviendo, y poco tiempo después estaba llena la cisterna inmensa.

Pero los soldados, al ir a misa aquella mañana para dar las gracias a sus santos, se fijaron en que faltaba una cosa en la capilla. ¡Ya no estaba en su lugar la pintura de San Cristóbal! Había desaparecido de la pared, y con un terror supersticioso, cada uno salió a buscarla. Por todas las galerías subterráneas iban buscando, y al fin, ya listos a declararse vencidos, uno de ellos abrió la trampa (*trap door*) de la cisterna, y ¡a la luz de su vela vió, en su lugar antiguo, la pintura famosa! ¡Era un milagro! ¡San Cristóbal había vuelto a velar su cisterna para que no faltase agua!

Y hasta la fecha, todavía está allí la pintura, dentro de la obscuridad de la cisterna, y en todo Puerto Rico no hay nadie que se atreva a sacarla,[1] por valiente que sea.

II. La garita encantada

Por todas las murallas del Castillo de San Cristóbal hay garitas de piedra, en donde velaban los soldados día y noche la costa de la isla, temiendo que los piratas viniesen a robar las riquezas guardadas allí mientras que esperaban buques (*ships*) que las llevasen a España.[2]

Una de éstas se llama «la garita encantada», porque hace unos cien años, en una noche obscura mientras llovía a cántaros (*pitcherfuls*), desapareció un centinela (*sentinel*). ¿Qué habría pasado? Parecía imposible que hubiese podido bajar o caer al mar al pie de la garita, caída de unos cien pies, y no había otra manera de salir sin ser visto.

— ¡Será el diablo que se le ha llevado! — se dijeron los soldados supersticiosos, y cada uno se imaginó poder percibir el olor de azufre (*brimstone*) en la garita.[3]

Después de eso, por valiente que fuese, ni un soldado se atrevía a pasar la noche allí, y al fin se cerró el túnel que conducía a la garita, y ésta quedó abandonada.

¿Qué habría pasado? Pues, muchos años después, el soldado «perdido», ya muy viejo, fué encontrado en una finca de la isla, y lo explicó así:

— Yo era muy joven, y estaba enamorado de una bonita

[1] Nowadays visitors can see the great cistern and its moldy old painting with the aid of a flashlight.

[2] Once in Spanish days a storm drove the "Silver Fleet," loaded with millions of dollars worth of treasure, into the harbor at San Juan, and everyone was nervous until it left again, for fear Drake would come in to attack it and sack the town for good measure.

[3] In those days, when so many scientific facts were yet undiscovered, it was easy for people's imaginations to run away with them.

señorita de Caguas [1] a quien había conocido en una fiesta en San Juan. Ella tuvo que volver a su pueblo, y yo no pude acompañarla, siendo soldado con tres años más que servir al rey. Solito en la garita, noche tras noche, no podía pensar en otra cosa que en esa encantadora joven. No había nadie que pudiese ayudarme, pero «donde una puerta se cierra otra se abre». En una noche obscura, dejando allí mi uniforme y mi escopeta para que nadie me reconociese más tarde, bajé milagrosamente por el risco con la ayuda de una cuerda (*rope*), nadé por las olas hasta llegar a la playa (*beach*) donde había escondido otras prendas de vestir, y al fin conseguí llegar a esta finca, donde vivía mi querida. Aquí nos casamos, y aquí he pasado la vida. ¿Encantada la garita? No, aunque todos dijeron que sería imposible escapar, «los hechos son más seguros que las palabras». Solamente el amor me ayudó, y «el amor vence siempre».[2]

Pero la garita todavía se llama «encantada», y cualquier turista que busque recuerdos de Puerto Rico los encuentra pintados todos con la vista de aquella garita, ¡marca (*trade-mark*) moderna de la isla!

PALABRAS NUEVAS

1	**acabarse**	to be finished, "all gone"		**garita**	sentry box
			4	**gota**	drop
	ayuda	aid	3	**hecho**	fact
4	**caída**	drop, fall		**milagro**	miracle
	capilla	chapel		**muralla**	wall
	castillo	castle		**nadar**	to swim
3	**conducir**	to lead	4	**obscuridad**	darkness
3	**enamorado de**	in love with	4	**olor** (*m.*)	odor
4	**encantador**	charming		**percibir**	to perceive
	finca	farm	4	**velar**	to watch (over)
	fortaleza	fortress			

[1] Caguas is a little town in the interior of the island.

[2] Spanish is rich in proverbs and some people believe they can prove anything by quoting a suitable proverb.

EXPRESIONES

agua de lluvia, rainwater
en vano, in vain
hasta la fecha, up to the present time
***por — que,** however
prenda de vestir, article of clothing
¡qué barbaridad! how ridiculous!
***unos cuantos,** a few

PARA COMPLETAR

I. EL MILAGRO DE SAN CRISTÓBAL

1. Cada fortaleza española tiene una —— para el santo del mismo nombre. 2. Debajo del Castillo había una —— inmensa. 3. El padre halló dentro de la cisterna una —— de ——, santo patrón de la fortaleza. 4. El padre le dijo a un soldado que —— la pintura a la capilla. 5. Después de eso, no —— ni una gota. 6. Cuando alguien devolvió la pintura a la ——, empezó a ——. 7. Hasta la fecha la pintura —— —— allí.

II. LA GARITA ENCANTADA

1. Las garitas están construidas de ——. 2. Los españoles las construyeron porque temían que los piratas —— a robar los tesoros. 3. Los soldados —— creían que el —— se había llevado al centinela (*sentinel*). 4. El soldado «perdido» se había escapado con la —— de una cuerda (*rope*), y había ido a la —— de su amiga. 5. «Los —— son más seguros que las ——.» 6. «Donde una puerta —— ——, otra —— ——.» 7. La marca (*trademark*) moderna de —— —— es «la garita ——».

¿VERDAD O NO?

Change the sentences that are false to make them true.

I. EL MILAGRO DE SAN CRISTÓBAL

1. La cisterna debajo de la fortaleza contenía agua del mar. 2. La pintura famosa era de Santa Bárbara, protectora de los soldados. 3. Después que el padre mandó llevar la pintura a la capilla, cayó mucha lluvia. 4. Los habitantes fueron a las iglesias para

pedir a San Cristóbal que volviese. 5. Era un milagro cuando Santa Bárbara volvió a velar su cisterna.

II. La garita encantada

1. Los soldados velaban la costa día y noche, porque temían que desapareciese la pintura. 2. El centinela (*sentinel*) desapareció un día mientras llovía mucho. 3. Era muy fácil bajar por el risco para salir de la garita. 4. Al fin la garita quedó abandonada porque ya no había peligro (*danger*) de que viniesen piratas. 5. El soldado que desapareció quería asistir a una fiesta en Caguas. 6. Se llevó consigo su escopeta y su uniforme para poder usarlos más tarde. 7. El cuento termina felizmente. 8. El emblema moderno de Puerto Rico es la Isla del Coco.

REPASO DE VERBOS

I. Give the infinitives of these present subjunctive verbs; then change them to the same person of the past subjunctive. Example: **vayan: ir, fuesen**

1. sepa	6. pidamos	11. traiga	16. cuente
2. hagamos	7. Vd. duerma	12. pidan	17. salgan
3. sean	8. ella llegue	13. esté	18. canten
4. paguemos	9. yo venga	14. dé	19. abra
5. empiecen	10. tengan	15. vaya	20. ganes

II. Substitute the correct verb form for each italicized infinitive. Every time you use a subjunctive, explain why it was necessary:

1. Si Vd. *saber* que iba a ganar, jugaría a la lotería. 2. Si yo *tener* más tiempo, *ir* a visitar a mi amigo. 3. Aunque Vd. no lo *creer*, es la verdad. 4. Cuando Alberto *venir* a verme, le llevaré al cine. 5. Si ese bandido *haber* tenido suerte, *haber* llegado a ser rico. 6. Sírvase Vd. como si *estar* en su propia casa. 7. Si yo *tener* cuatro vidas, todas *ser* para ti. 8. Tendré que estudiar esta lengua hasta que yo la *aprender*. 9. Mientras yo *vivir*, siempre tendré por Vd. mucho afecto (*affection*). 10. Me alegro de que *haber* llegado mis padres. 11. Lope le pidió a la india que le *mostrar* el camino. 12. Lope le dijo al viejecito que *bajarse*.

ALGO NUEVO

45. The Subjunctive in Adjective Clauses

1. After an indefinite antecedent

You found this new use of the subjunctive in the stories:

buques que las llevasen, *ships which might carry them*

When an adjective (relative) clause has an indefinite antecedent, the verb *in* the clause must be in the subjunctive.

You may have to review your English grammar in order to understand "adjective clauses." Here are some points to help you identify them:

a. An adjective clause is introduced by one of the relative pronouns *who, which, what,* or *that* (***que*** in Spanish).

b. An adjective clause takes the place of an adjective:

an *intelligent* pupil (adjective)
a pupil *who is intelligent* (adjective clause)

c. The word which the adjective clause modifies or describes (or to which the relative pronoun refers) is called the antecedent (*pupil*).

In using Spanish we must analyze a sentence rather carefully in order to locate the antecedent and decide whether it is definite or indefinite. Try "diagramming" such sentences in the following way:

I am looking for a pupil (who is intelligent).

Put parentheses around the adjective clause beginning with *who, which, what,* or *that* and underline the verb in the clause. Then put an arrow pointing back from the relative pronoun to the antecedent, which this time is *pupil*. Then ask yourself, "Is that some *definite* pupil or just any (*indefinite*) pupil who is intelligent?" If the answer is "indefinite," you know that the verb you underlined is to be in the subjunctive; if the answer is "definite," you need no subjunctive. Do you need a subjunctive in the preceding example when you say it in Spanish?

2. After a negative

no hay nadie que se atreva, *there is no one who dares*
no había nadie que pudiese ir, *there was no one who could go*

When an adjective or relative clause is preceded by a negative, the verb in the clause is always in the subjunctive.

These sentences can be "diagrammed" in the same way, and you will often find the arrow pointing at the negative word itself: **No hay nada (que me guste),** *there isn't anything that I like.*

Notice that when the antecedent is negative, it is automatically indefinite as well.

3. After ***lo que*** (*whatever*) when indefinite

haga Vd. lo que quiera, *do what(ever) you wish* (indefinite)
ví lo que hizo, *I saw what he did* (definite, therefore no subjunctive)

Lo, being neuter and referring to a whole idea, is often an indefinite antecedent. When it is definite it does not require the subjunctive.

4. After ***por — que*** (*however*) [1]

por valiente que sea, *however brave he may be*
por valiente que fuese, *however brave he might be*

The expression ***por — que,*** *however,* always takes the subjunctive. Notice the English *may* or *might* in order to tell which tense to use, or follow the main verb.

EJERCICIO I. *Copy these English sentences, "diagram" them like the example in Part One of this section, and analyze each one in order to decide whether or not there would be a subjunctive in Spanish and where.* Do not try to translate the sentences into Spanish.

[1] ***Quienquiera,*** *whoever,* takes the subjunctive in the same way (***quienquiera que sea,*** *whoever he may be*), but this expression is not often found, according to Keniston's study.

1. I want a book that is new. (A certain definite book or just any new book?) **2.** You have a book that is old and torn, haven't you? **3.** I don't want any book that is torn. **4.** You bought one that was in good condition. **5.** Any pupil who has a good book ought to take care of it. **6.** Books that are dirty and torn show somebody's carelessness. **7.** People who drop books on the floor are making a mistake. **8.** Nobody likes a book that is a wreck. **9.** No pupil who throws books is a good citizen. **10.** I'll try to do whatever you want. **11.** Have you heard enough about people who destroy books? **12.** Yes, I want to talk about something that is more interesting. **13.** Well, let's talk about the game that we played yesterday. **14.** All right. It was the best game (that) we have had! **15.** I don't like games which are not exciting.

EJERCICIO II.[1] These advertisements, proverbs, etc., from Spanish-speaking countries, show how common this use of the subjunctive is. *Translate each one ("diagram" it if that will help) and explain why there is a subjunctive.*

1. Gratificaré (*award*) con $10 a quien me devuelva perro "*fox terrier*" chico de color negro con patas (*paws*) blancas. ("*Lost*" *advertisement*)
2. «El que tenga un amor, que (*let*) lo cuide». (*Mexican song*)
3. Niños que sepan andar pagarán pasaje (*fare*). (*Sign in street car, Mexico*)
4. Se prohibe pasar con perros que vayan sueltos (*loose*). (*Sign in Chapultepec Park, Mexico City*)
5. Radios desde $70 hasta $1000 con los plazos (*payments*) que Vd. quiera. (*Radio ad, Chile*)
6. Entregamos (*deliver*) los muebles el mismo día que se compren. (*Furniture store ad, Nicaragua*)
7. No tengo padre, ni madre, ni perro que me ladre (**ladrar,** *to bark*). (*Proverb*)
8. Pida lo que quiera; nosotros lo tenemos. (*Department store ad, Puerto Rico*)
9. No hay día que no llegue. (*Proverb*)
10. No hay mal que cien años dure. (*Proverb*)
11. El que haga daño (*damage*) a los arbolitos tendrá Q5 multa (*five* **quetzales** *fine*). (*Sign in park, Guatemala*)

[1] Optional exercise.

EJERCICIO III. *Complete these sentences in Spanish, watching carefully to see whether or not the verbs should be in the subjunctive.*

1. El soldado que *estar* «perdido» bajó por el risco. 2. El padre quería que la pintura *quedarse* en la capilla. 3. El padre reconoció al santo que *encontrar* en la cisterna. 4. No hay murallas que no *ser* de piedra. 5. No había nadie que *saber* dónde estaba la pintura. 6. No hay muchos que *creer* que es un milagro. 7. Los españoles esperaban que *llover*. 8. No hay puerta que no *poder* abrirse con el dinero. 9. No hay libertador que *haber* muerto felizmente. 10. El hombre que *descansar* mucho en el camino nunca llega a tiempo. 11. La señora que *haber* perdido su perro está muy triste. 12. Busco una moneda que *valer* cinco colones. 13. Bolívar tuvo un sueño que nunca *realizarse* (*past*). 14. ¿Ha visto Vd. una población que *tener* muchas estatuas de héroes?

ESTUDIO DE PALABRAS

I. Give the Spanish for each of these words and expressions. Why are they important?

in order that, when, although, as if, to hope, to command, to allow, to be glad of, until, as soon as, however, to be necessary, to regret, to tell, to be possible, to ask, to advise

II. Here are some useful idioms using **hacer**. *Complete each sentence with one of them, using each idiom only once.*

hace buen (mal) tiempo, hace calor, hace fresco, hace frío, hace muchos años, hace poco, hacer un viaje, hace viento, hacer preguntas, hacer el oso, haga Vd. el favor de, hacer daño a

1. Los piratas escondieron el tesoro en la isla *many years ago*. 2. Cuando se termine la Carretera Panamericana, yo *will take a trip* a Santiago de Chile. 3. El avión puede volar bien aunque *it is windy*. 4. Damos un paseo en la plaza cuando *it is good weather*. 5. Si *it is cold*, nos ponemos el abrigo (*overcoat*). 6. En Guatemala los niños *do not damage* los arbolitos. 7. Vamos a nadar en el río cuando *it is warm*. 8. Los alumnos no consiguen aprender sin

asking questions. 9. En muchos países de habla española los jóvenes *make love* debajo del balcón. 10. *Please* traerme un cuchillo, Domitilo. 11. *Not long ago* una expedición fué a buscar la riqueza. 12. En Puerto Rico muchas veces *it is not cool* porque es una isla tropical.

III. Turn back to Exercise II on page 104, and review the word families. Here are more of the same kind to try to guess. The first word is always one you have had unless it is translated.

1. **vía** (*way*): viaje, viajar, viajero, aerovía 2. **cambio:** cambiar, intercambio, cambista 3. **libre:** libertar, libertad, libertador, liberalmente, liberalidad 4. **lejos de:** lejano, alejarse de 5. **cerca de:** cercano, acercarse a, una cerca (*fence*) 6. **cien(to):** centenario, centavo, por ciento, centenares 7. **triste:** tristeza, entristecer, tristemente 8. **salud:** saludar, saludable, salutación, saludos 9. **cinco:** quince, cincuenta, quinientos 10. **noche:** anoche (*last night*), anochecer, nochebuena, nocturno, nocturnal 11. **aprender:** aprendedor, aprendiz 12. **mano:** manojo (*handful*), manecilla (☞), manejar, maniatar (*handcuff*), manicuro, manifactura, manuscrito, manualmente

REPASITO

I. In Capítulo 7 you had some important exercises on the use of two object pronouns which you may have found difficult at the time, but which should be easier now. *Turn back to page 93 and do again Ejercicios VIII, IX, and X.*

II. ***Gustar, faltar, molestar,*** and ***importar*** are often used in the third person, with the English object used as the Spanish subject:

me gustan las manzanas (*apples are pleasing to me*), *I like apples*

Notice that if the English object (*apples*) is plural, the Spanish verb is plural. Notice also that you usually find the definite article with the noun subject, because it often means, for instance, *apples in general.*

Using the four verbs **gustar, faltar, molestar,** *and* **importar,** *complete the following sentences in Spanish, reversing the word order in English first if that helps:*

1. *I like* correr (*to me it is pleasing*). 2. *We like* nadar en el río. 3. ¿*Do you like* bailar (*to dance*)? 4. *I like* el pan blanco. 5. *I like* las tortillas, también. 6. ¿*Do you like* los frijoles? 7. *You lack* dinero, ¿verdad? 8. *I don't care* (*it doesn't matter to me*). 9. *It bothers me* no tener bastante dinero. 10. *We lack* agua. 11. ¿(*Does*) la obscuridad *bother you*? 12. No, pero una garita encantada *would bother me.* 13. ¿*Who cares* (*to whom is it important*)? 14. *They lack* el tiempo para ayudarnos.

PARA LEER SIN ESTUDIAR

¿SABÍA VD. ESTO?

1. Hace muchos años, el gobernador (*governor*) de Puerto Rico fué Teodoro Roosevelt, hijo. Al llegar a la isla, empezó a estudiar el español, encontrándolo bastante difícil. Tenía que dar discursos (*speeches*) en español ante la gente, y un día dijo, sin saber lo que estaba diciendo, ¡que él era «la madre» de cuatro hijos!

Otro día, presentando a un amigo suyo que era soltero (*bachelor*), ¡dijo que era «solitaria», lo que quiere decir *tapeworm*!

2. De todas las Américas, Puerto Rico tiene la iglesia más antigua en uso continuo, y también tiene la iglesia más pequeña del mundo.

3. Puerto Rico es la única parte de los Estados Unidos que pisó (*set foot on*) Colón; es uno de los primeros lugares descubiertos por él, y la última colonia que perdió España en el Hemisferio Occidental.

4. Letreros (*signs*) que se ven en San Juan, Puerto Rico:

No entre. Hay perros.
Cuidado con el trolley
Esta tienda aire-acondicionada
No pise la grama (*grass*).
Cooperar es ser patriota.
No pare (*stop*) su coche aquí.
Vendemos a plazos (*payments*).
Pise Vd. con cuidado.

TEMA

1. A few centuries ago there was a painting inside a cistern in (*of*) Puerto Rico. 2. In order that the priest might see the painting, he had to carry a candle. 3. The soldiers asked him not to return the painting to the chapel. 4. They noticed that something was lacking. What could have happened (*cond. of probability*)? 5. There is no one who dares to return to the sentry-box (*garita*), however strong he may be. 6. About a hundred years ago a soldier met a pretty girl at a fiesta. 7. It seemed impossible that he could escape without being seen. 8. He didn't want anyone to recognize him later. 9. Any tourist who goes to Puerto Rico sees the modern emblem of the island everywhere. 10. One may speak whatever he wishes, even if he prefers Spanish.

CAPÍTULO **16**

Tierra de temporal[1]

Most Spanish-American countries are largely Catholic, for that was the religion brought over by the *conquistadores.* The beautiful statues of saints and virgins in their colonial churches, now hundreds of years old, seem very real to the Indians who were taught the new religion, and they consider these saints as personal friends who try to help them.

[1] ***Tierra de temporal,*** *dry-farming land.* One of the main foods of Mexico is corn, and if it does not rain to insure a good crop, there is much suffering.

In Zapopan, a little town of Jalisco, Mexico, from which the padres set out to found the missions of our Western States, the famous Virgin of Zapopan is taken each year for a tour of the neighboring churches. In Peru a certain Virgin of an Andean Indian village goes on an annual trip to nearby Pisac, accompanied by music, and when she gets there, the Indians dance for her in front of the church. And in Guatemala, where the Indians still live practically as they did four hundred years ago, they often go to the village church and scold a favorite saint severely for having allowed some disaster to happen.

This particular anecdote is told around Guanajuato, Mexico, where "they say" it really happened, but the same plot is found in similar stories in several Latin-American countries. You will find it told here in almost the very words of the Mexican author, who wrote a book of farm life stories; so at last you are able to read genuine literature in Spanish!

— Si no llueve cuando llene (*is full*) la luna, están perdidas las labores, muchachos...

— No hay que perder la esperanza. Anoche estuvo relampagueando (*lightning*) un rato.

— El maíz empieza a secarse.

— Todo porque tenemos tierras de temporal. Ojalá pudiésemos regarlas...

Con frecuencia examinaban el cielo ardiente. Ni una nube. Desde que sembraron (*sowed*), apenas se había caído una gota de lluvia.

— En otras partes la agricultura se garantiza (*guarantee*) con una presa (*dam*).[1]

— Sólo nosotros tenemos que esperar la lluvia... ¡Tierra de temporal!

— Tenemos cerca el río y las aguas se van para abajo sin servirnos de nada.

— ¡Hacer una presa (*dam*) y meter el agua cuesta millones!

Ni una nube. Parecía que la estación de calores iba a

[1] Dams have been built at government expense in many parts of Mexico during the last few years to solve the drought problem.

durar para siempre. Un sol tan rojo por la mañana como por la tarde. Un cielo azul. Los campos secos. Las palomas, descansando bajo el maíz.

La idea salvadora (*saving*) se le ocurrió de pronto a alguien:

— Vayamos al pueblo para pedir que nos presten uno de los santos más milagrosos. Hace años, cuando se necesitaba la lluvia, así lo hacían quienes eran más creyentes (*believing*) que nosotros.

— Es verdad. Traían un santo y lo llevaban a pasear por los campos en demanda de lluvia.

— Se le hace fiesta con bailes, y luego, una vez que se ha realizado (*been performed*) el milagro, se devuelve el santo con una cantidad de dinero para la iglesia.

— ¡Si solamente se nos hubiera ocurrido antes!

Ese mismo día varios de los campesinos fueron al pueblo. Ya en presencia del cura, explicaron el motivo de su viaje: la falta de lluvia, las labores a punto de perderse, la necesidad de la fe...

— Quisiéramos pedir prestado uno de los santos más milagrosos, y lo llevaremos con música, tendremos un baile, y después de llevarlo a pasear por los campos para que vea nuestra situación, se lo devolveremos con dinero...

— Está bien, — dijo el cura. — Ojalá que les haga un milagro. — Y les prestó un Cristo de tamaño (*size*) natural y túnica (*tunic*) roja.

Bajo el sol ardiente, los campesinos bajaban por la cuesta que conduce del pueblo a los ranchos, cada uno ayudando a llevar el santo. Los animaba la música, que, a la cabeza de la procesión, hacía salir a las puertas de las casas a más de una mujer, llena de curiosidad.

En cuanto llegaron, fueron directamente a los campos de labor. Y el santo fué llevado a pasear por entre los surcos (*furrows*), y uno de los hombres le puso en las manos una caña (*stalk*) seca de maíz, para que percibiera mejor que faltaba la lluvia. Por la noche todos los vecinos hicieron un baile [1]

[1] The dance would not be a social affair like ours, but a series of ancient Indian dances done by men who had learned the ritual from their fathers. They would

Sawders

Santiago — St. James — on his horse is a favorite saint of the Indians in Andean towns, and always attends their fiestas.

para honrar aun más la visita de la divinidad.

Y el milagro no tardó mucho en realizarse (*being performed*). A eso de la medianoche, bajo un cielo lleno de nubes, bastó un trueno (*thunderclap*) para que empezaran a caer las gotas de lluvia. Los que bailaban, bailaron aun más. Los músicos tocaron con más animación. Y después, a cada trueno (*thunderclap*) del cielo, la multitud respondía con gritos de alegría. Iba cayendo la lluvia a cántaros (*pitcherfuls*), y parecía que el cielo trataba de resarcir (*make up*) por la falta de lluvia. A la vez, hacía un fuerte viento, y pronto empezó a correr el agua hasta en los lugares más secos de los ranchos.

Pero con la luz del día cesó el entusiasmo: la lluvia y los vientos habían destruido casi completamente los campos,

be dressed in quaint, colorful costumes and accompanied by primitive flutes and drums and sometimes gourd rattles. The music usually consists of a few phrases repeated for hours, or until the dancers are exhausted.

sin dejar en pie una sola caña (*stalk*) de maíz.

Las lamentaciones (*wails*) se parecían a las que se habían oído por la falta de lluvia:

— Si no tuviéramos tierras de temporal... Si pudiéramos regarlas, para sembrar (*sow*) antes que llegasen los vientos...

Y mientras miraban y lamentaban la destrucción de la lluvia y del viento, el santo había quedado solo en el cuarto desierto donde tuvo lugar el baile.

Después de llorar y lamentarse lo suficiente, resignados con (*to*) su suerte, los campesinos pensaron en llevar el santo al pueblo.

Este viaje fué muy distinto del viaje del día anterior. Sin música y sin entusiasmo llevaron la divinidad al pueblo. Cuándo llegaron a la presencia del cura, éste les dijo,

— Ya ví que el santo les hizo el milagro. Llovió toda la noche, ¿verdad?

— Es verdad, pero ahora quisiéramos que Vd. nos prestase a la Virgen.

— ¿A la Virgen? ¿Para qué la quieren, hijos míos?

— ¡Para que vaya ella a ver la destrucción que hizo su santísimo hijo anoche!

ADAPTED FROM GREGORIO LÓPEZ Y FUENTES (*Mexico*)

PALABRAS NUEVAS

3 **animar** to cheer up
anoche last night
2 **apenas** hardly
2 **bastar** to be enough
3 **cesar (de)** to cease
Cristo Christ
4 **cura** (*m.*) priest
3 **distinto de** different from
2 **esperanza** hope
2 **fe** (*f.*) faith
maíz (*m.*) corn
3 **nube** (*f.*) cloud
3 **ocurrir** to occur
ojalá (que) oh that, would that
3 **prestar** to lend
regar (ie) irrigate
secar(se) to dry (up)
3 **tardar en** to be long in

Expresiones

a punto de, on the point of
***con frecuencia,** frequently
***en pie,** standing
estación de calores, hot season
lo suficiente, sufficiently
llevar a pasear, to take for a walk
no servir de nada, to be good for nothing
para abajo, down below
***para siempre,** forever
***pedir prestado,** to borrow
tener lugar, to take place
tierra(s) de temporal, unirrigated or dry-farming land(s)

PREGUNTAS

1. ¿Temían los campesinos perder su maíz? 2. ¿Había caído mucha lluvia durante la estación de calores? 3. ¿Por qué no había presa (*dam*) en el río? 4. Al fin, ¿qué idea se le ocurrió a uno de ellos? 5. ¿Dónde estaba el santo que querían pedir prestado? 6. ¿Quería el cura prestarles el santo? 7. Describa Vd. la procesión entre la iglesia y los ranchos. 8. ¿Para qué puso uno de los campesinos una caña (*stalk*) de maíz en las manos del Cristo? 9. ¿Tardó mucho en realizarse (*being performed*) el milagro? 10. ¿Se alegraban los campesinos de que lloviese? 11. ¿Qué hacían mientras llovía? 12. ¿Qué vieron a la luz del día? 13. ¿Devolvieron la divinidad a la iglesia? 14. ¿Para qué querían pedir prestada a la Virgen? 15. ¿Quisiera Vd. (§ 46, 2) ver uno de los bailes indios? 16. ¿Bailaron los indios como nosotros? 17. ¿ Para qué bailan los indios para sus santos? 18. ¿ Por qué salían muchas mujeres de la puerta de su casa? 19. Describa Vd. la tempestad que llegó durante el baile.

¿VERDAD O NO?

Change the sentences that are false to make them true.

1. Los campesinos tenían que regar sus tierras. 2. En algunas partes de México hay presas (*dams*) para conservar el agua preciosa. 3. Los campesinos fueron al pueblo para pedir prestado el dinero para construir una presa (*dam*). 4. El sol estaba tan amarillo por la mañana como por la noche. 5. Al devolver el santo, era costumbre dar una cantidad de maíz a la iglesia. 6. El cura no quería que los campesinos se llevasen el santo. 7. Hacía mucho frío mientras bajaban por la cuesta. 8. Hacía mucho viento durante la tempestad

(*storm*). 9. Cuando llegó la luz del día, los campesinos estaban más contentos que nunca. 10. Dieron las gracias al cura por el milagro. 11. El viaje de vuelta al pueblo se parecía mucho al del día anterior. 12. Dijeron que querían pedir prestada a la Virgen para que ella trajese más lluvia.

REPASO DE VERBOS

I. Review the future and conditional tenses in Chapter 6 if you need to; then give these expressions in Spanish:

1. I shall tell him so. 2. They will leave. 3. He will come here. 4. Shall you have time? 5. She will put it on. 6. They won't know it. 7. Will he be able to go? 8. You would have gone. 9. He wouldn't know. 10. It wouldn't occur to me. 11. Will it last long? 12. It will not be enough. 13. Will you lend it to me? 14. It won't be long now. 15. Will the dance take place? 16. He won't borrow it.

II. Using these verbs in the order in which they are given, make a series of short sentences describing your daily activities, heading them: **Lo que hago todos los días.** (What tense shall you use?)

levantarse, desayunarse, salir, ir, encontrar, reírse, jugar, comer, acostarse

III. Using the same verbs, head your list: **Lo que hice ayer.**

IV. Using the same verbs, head your list: **Lo que haré mañana.**

V. Make a series of sentences headed: **Lo que haría si pudiese,** *using the verbs* comprar, ir, tener, comer, dar.

VI. Make a series of sentences headed: **Lo que quiero que Vd. haga,** *using the verbs* prestar, dar, callarse, reírse de, molestar. (What's the catch?)

ALGO NUEVO

46. The Last New Subjunctive Usages

1. With *ojalá* (*que*)

ojalá pudiésemos regarlas
if we could only (might be able to) irrigate them

ojalá que les haga un milagro
I hope he works (may work) a miracle for you

The word ***ojalá,*** *would that,* comes from a short Moorish prayer (*enxo allah*) meaning "May Allah will it!" Since there was always some doubt as to whether or not Allah would grant the plea, the word is still followed by the subjunctive. It may or may not be used with *que*; the tense follows the English *may* or *might*; and the translation may be almost anything you like that expresses the idea of longing for the event to happen.

In spoken Spanish ***ojalá*** is often found alone as an exclamation:

— **Espero verle a Vd. el año que viene.**
— **¡Ojalá** (*I hope you may*)! [1]

2. In softened (polite) statements

quisiéramos pedir prestado uno, *we should like to borrow one*
quisiéramos que Vd. nos prestase, *we should like you to lend us* (*we wish you would lend us*)

The verbs *querer* and sometimes *deber* [2] are used in the ***-ra*** form of the past subjunctive to express an idea more politely. Instead of saying "we want to borrow one (and we don't mean maybe)," it is more polite to say "we should like to borrow one (if you don't mind)."

This is one case in which a subjunctive can start a sentence with nothing preceding it to cause the subjunctive.

[1] Then the cautious speaker usually adds, — *Si no morimos...*

[2] ***Debiera, I ought to*** (implying that I probably won't) is less often found. In its place ***yo debía*** is often used.

The conditional tense expresses the same idea:

nos gustaría pedir prestado uno, *we should like to borrow one*

If *quisiera* itself is a verb of causing and therefore the main verb in the sentence, in what tense must the subordinate verb be?

REMEMBER: ***Quisiera*** is more polite than ***quiero.***

3. Subjunctive of uncertainty after *perhaps*

quizás (**acaso, tal vez**) **pueda ir conmigo mañana**
perhaps he may go with me tomorrow

The subjunctive is used after any of the three words or expressions meaning *perhaps* (**quizás, acaso,** and **tal vez**), when future time is implied.

EJERCICIO I.[1] *Translate these sentences heard or seen in Spanish-speaking countries and explain their use of the subjunctive:*

1. Donde cortes (*cut*) un árbol, planta otro, y cuando veas que alguien destruye un árbol sin razón, debes protestar. (*Sign in Mazatlán, Mexico*) 2. — ¡Si supieras lo que Elena dijo de ti! (*Heard on the street in San José, Costa Rica*) 3. Cuando Vd. ofrezca o asista a una fiesta, envíenos los detalles (*details*). (*Society column in newspaper, Caracas, Venezuela*) 4. Sírvase hacer la lista de su ropa, de otra manera tiene Vd. que aceptar la que hagamos. (*Laundry list in hotel, Mexico City*) 5. No respondemos (*responsible*) por artículos que se encojan (***encogerse,*** *to shrink*). (*Same laundry list*) 6. «Si fueran falsas mis palabras, en un momento se olvidarían.» (*Rhyme from children's game, Chichicastenango, Guatemala*) 7. — Deseo un par de zapatos que sean grandes por dentro (*inside*) y chicos por fuera (*outside*). (*Joke, Mexico*) 8. «¡Cuánto me gusta una mujer bonita que sea delgadita (*slender*) y que tenga chiquito el pie!» (*Mexican song*) 9. «Yo la convidé (*invited*) que se fuera a pasear conmigo; me dijo que la esperara, en

[1] Optional exercise.

la esquina (*corner*) de la Roca (*a store*).» (*Same song*) 10. «Yo quisiera llorar, pero no tengo más llanto (*tears*).» (*Mexican song*) 11. Fué, es, y siempre será su mejor amiga cuando la necesite. (*Medicine ad, San Antonio, Texas*) 12. No hay mal que dure cien años. (*Proverb*)

EJERCICIO II. *Complete these sentences in Spanish:*

1. *I should like to* asistir a la fiesta. 2. ¿*Would you like to* asistir a ella también? 3. Si Vd. *wish,* puedo llevarle en mi coche. 4. Enrique *would like* pedir prestado mi coche, para llevar a Elena, pero no quiero prestárselo. 5. *I wish you would* (§ 46, 2) nos *accompany* para que nosotros *enjoy ourselves* más. 6. Por interesante que *may be* la fiesta, sin amigos, no hay nada que hacer. 7. No quiero asistir sin que alguien *go* conmigo. 8. Dolores dice que no va a casarse hasta que *she is thirty years old.* 9. Rosita dice que ella no va a tener treinta años hasta que *she gets married.* 10. Dolores dice que *she would like* saber la manera de hacer feliz a su futuro esposo. 11. Rosita le dice que la mejor manera es *not to marry him.*

12. La esposa: — *I should like* que en el santo de mamá tú le *give* algo eléctrico.

El esposo: — ¡Con todo gusto! ¡Voy a mandar que ellos le *bring* una silla!

EJERCICIO III. *Complete in Spanish:*

1. Diego quiere *me to go, you to sing, her to sleep, them to eat, him to be still.* 2. Diego quería *me to go, you to sing, her to sleep, them to eat, him to be still.* 3. José me dice *to begin, to leave, to come, not to forget, to bring it.* 4. José me dijo *to begin, to leave, to come, not to forget, to bring it.* 5. Temo que Vd. *may fall, may tell it, may not know him, may follow me.* 6. Yo temía que Vd. *might fall, might tell it, might not know him, might follow me.* 7. Le diré la verdad para que *he may hear it, may believe it, may not lose anything.* 8. Se lo diría todo, si *I had* más tiempo, si *I were* Vd., si *I knew how,* si *I were* allí. 9. Aunque yo se lo *tell,* se lo *write,* se lo *send* y se lo *give,* Pablo no sabrá nada. 10. Es preciso que Juanito lo *bring,* lo *study,* lo *look at* y lo *learn.*

ESTUDIO DE PALABRAS

Here are more expressions concerning weather. (You reviewed some in Chapter 15.) Remember that *hace* is used for invisible weather phenomena (*hace viento*), and *hay* for visible conditions associated with weather (*hay lodo*). *After you have studied the expressions, answer the questions.*

hay lodo, it is muddy
hay polvo, it is dusty
hay neblina, it is foggy
hay luna, it is moonlight
hay (*or* **hace**) **sol,** it is sunny
relampaguear, to lighten

tronar (**ue**), to thunder; **trueno,** thunderclap
helar (**ie**), to freeze; **hielo,** ice
nevar (**ie**), to snow; **nieve** (*f.*) snow
llover (**ue**), to rain; **lluvia,** rain

1. ¿Hay mucho lodo en una carretera pavimentada? 2. ¿Hay luna cuando llueve? 3. ¿Hay sol cuando nieva? 4. ¿Hay mucho polvo en una calle que no está pavimentada? 5. ¿Es fácil ver el camino mientras hay mucha neblina? 6. ¿Le gusta a Vd. oír los truenos? 7. ¿Hiela muchas veces en el verano? ¿en el invierno? 8. ¿Está Vd. muy contento mientras que está relampagueando? 9. ¿Tiene Vd. miedo cuando hay luna? 10. ¿Quiere Vd. que llueva mañana? ¿que nieve?

REPASITO

I. Complete these sentences in Spanish:

1. *His* es el *good one.* 2. ¿Dónde está *hers*? 3. *Yours* está cerca. 4. *The bad* camino conduce al pueblo. 5. Ha perdido el *first* diente. 6. Pronto perderá el *third one.* 7. Se ve *some* grupo de campesinos. No veo *any.* 8. ¿No tiene Vd. *one*? Tome *one* de *mine.* 9. El *great* Libertador se llamaba Simón Bolívar. 10. — Tenemos *one hundred* cosas que comer. — ¿Qué son? — — Frijoles.

II. Select the words or expressions from this list which may take the subjunctive, and tell why or when they do:

pedir, temer, tomar, es posible, para que, quizás, antes de, donde, sí, por — que, es mayor, sentar, ¿creer?, porque, es mejor, creer, alegrarse de, mientras, hablar, ojalá, lo que, querer, cuando, como si, aunque, sin, sin que, es preciso, hasta, hasta que, tal vez

PARA LEER SIN ESTUDIAR

To complete our brief swing around the Spanish Sea, here is some easy reading about Santo Domingo and Cuba, the only two Spanish-speaking countries of the Caribbean which we have not covered.

Santo Domingo's slogan is "The Land Columbus Loved Most," and Cuba advertises itself as "The Sugar Bowl of the World."

I. Santo Domingo (República Dominicana)

Colón fundó (*founded*) en esta isla (que hoy contiene Santo Domingo y Haiti) el primer pueblo del Nuevo Mundo, y lo llamó La Isabela en honor de la Reina (*Queen*) de España.

La capital, Santo Domingo (hoy Ciudad Trujillo), tenía cerca de la mar hasta hace poco el mismo árbol (la ceiba[1]) que sirvió de atadero (*hitching post*) para los barcos (*boats*) de Colón. Cuando fué pavimentada la calle hace unos años, murió el árbol, y hoy día se ve en su lugar un árbol igualito, hecho de cemento.

Santo Domingo fué el punto de partida (*starting point*) de casi todos los conquistadores del Nuevo Mundo. Salieron de allí Cortés para México, Ponce de León para Puerto Rico, Balboa para el Océano Pacífico, y Pizarro para el Perú.

Los restos (*remains*) de Colón están hoy en la catedral — la más antigua del Nuevo Mundo — aunque Sevilla afirma que allí descansan.[2] Pero una cosa que Santo Domingo no menciona es que en el cuarto viaje de Colón, ¡los habitantes de la isla no le permitieron entrar en el puerto durante una tempestad (*storm*)!

La República Dominicana es actualmente moderna y progresiva, y su capital es una de las ciudades más limpias del mundo. Hay buenos caminos, luz eléctrica, calles pavimentadas, y tiendas

[1] A *ceiba* tree furnishes the kapok with which we fill cushions.

[2] Seville, authorities have decided, has the remains of Columbus' son instead of those of Columbus himself.

Keystone

Tomb of Christopher Columbus is treasured in the old cathedral in Ciudad Trujillo, capital of Santo Domingo.

modernas. Tiene una Avenida de Jorge Wáshington por la orilla del mar, también una Avenida Simón Bolívar.

La influencia norteamericana se ve en las palabras inglesas que se emplean, como el autobús, el Country Club, el Restaurant Hollywood, la Tienda de Souvenir (que vende «libros y magazines»), y el «Beauty Pálor». ¡Y se acepta nuestro dinero, que se llama «el grínback»!

II. Cuba

«La perla de las Antillas» y «la cesta (*basket*) de frutas de los Estados Unidos», es como se llama aquella isla cerca de la Florida. Descubierta por Colón, hoy día tiene una mezcla (*mixture*) de lo español y lo norteamericano. Su capital, la Habana, fué un puerto importante del Nuevo Mundo, y todavía se puede ver el Morro, fortaleza inmensa que construyeron los españoles en 1589.

Se ve mucha influencia norteamericana en los juegos — el fútbol, el béisbol, y el básket — pero también juegan al jai alai.[1] Muchos hablan inglés, o emplean palabras inglesas. En su español se oyen palabras de la lengua *siboney* que hablaban los indios, tales como tabaco, canoa, y huracán (*hurricane*).

Casi todos van vestidos de blanco, porque hace calor; las mujeres pueden votar, y el producto principal es el «oro blanco», que es el

[1] *Jai alai* is the Basque handball game which originated in northern Spain.

azúcar. Tienen edificios magníficos, entre ellos muchos clubs de deportes (*sports*), así como *night clubs* para turistas, a quienes llaman «patos (*ducks*) de Florida». Lo peor de Cuba es que todos creen que cada «pato» tiene un millón de dólares, y los cubiches ("*kids*") le siguen todo el día, tratando de venderle algo, porque se acepta nuestro dinero con todo gusto.

Así es la tierra donde nació la rumba.

TEMA

1. The lack of rain was bothering the farmers. 2. The corn was drying up (*prog.*) because hardly a drop had fallen. 3. Suddenly a good idea occurred to someone. 4. They would go to borrow a miraculous saint in order that he might save the corn. 5. They would take him for a walk so that he might see the fields. 6. They would play music for him and dance to amuse him. 7. At about midnight it began to rain, and the water ran in the driest places. 8. If they could make the rain stop before the wind arrived, they would be happy. 9. If only (***ojalá que***) the winds might not come! We should like to see that happen. 10. Hardly a stalk (***caña***) of corn was standing. 11. They wanted her to see what had happened.

The new capitol building in Havana faces the Prado, a central parkway connecting three beautiful tropical plazas.

Armstrong Roberts

CAPÍTULO 17

Optional chapter[1]

Dos cuentos para contar al hermanito

There are many little tales in Spanish which are told over and over as we retell our old favorites. The difference is that in Spanish, these stories, instead of being fiction, are likely to be based upon history, for Spanish-speaking people take a much more personal interest in their country's past than we do, and talk about it over the teacups as readily as we do the latest gossip.

The first story in this chapter is an old Mexican tale about Moctezuma's spoons and is sometimes told slyly without giving away the secret, to tease one who does not know the custom of the country. Moctezuma, you probably remember, was the Emperor of the Aztecs when Cortés arrived in 1519 to start his conquest of Mexico. Moctezuma was a cultured, intelligent man, worthy to rule over his vast dominions, and had it not been for unusual circumstances, the Spaniards would probably never have stood a chance against the Aztecs and their Mayan neighbors.

The second story, about the *quetzal's* red feathers, is told in Guatemala, and is a combination of truth and legend. Another legend about the same bird says that once all *quetzales* sang beautifully, but that not one has ever even chirped since the death of Tecún Umán, the valiant chief of the Mayas.

[1] Note to teacher: This plateau chapter may be omitted in order to finish Chapter 18 by the end of the first semester if there is not time for both. Chapter 18, however, should be completed, since it is a final review of Chapters 10–16 inclusive.

I. Las cucharitas de Moctezuma

Al acercarse Cortés a Tenochtitlán, capital del imperio azteca, salió a su encuentro un embajador del Emperador Moctezuma. Cortés, tratando de convencer (*convince*) al azteca de que su pueblo debía aceptar pacíficamente (*peacefully*) la dominación de los españoles, empezó a decir al embajador algo de las glorias de España.

— Soy, — dijo Cortés, — del gran Imperio de España, país el más poderoso del mundo. El Imperio de mi Emperador da al océano como si fuese a su propio patio.

— El Imperio de mi Emperador, — respondió el embajador azteca, — da a dos océanos.

— Nadie, — dijo Cortés, — lleva puesto el sombrero en la corte de mi Emperador.

— Nadie, — contestó el azteca, — entra en la corte de mi Emperador con los zapatos puestos.[1]

— Nadie, — dijo Cortés, — se sienta en presencia de mi Emperador.

— Nadie, — repondió el azteca, — levanta los ojos en presencia del mío.

— Mi Emperador, — dijo Cortés, — vive en un palacio en donde hasta las cortinas (*curtains*) son de oro.

— El mío, — contestó el azteca, — en su palacio, duerme en una cama de oro y come en una mesa de oro.

— Oiga Vd., — dijo Cortés. — Eso no es nada. El Emperador de España es tan rico que los platos en su mesa son de oro y plata. Hasta las cucharitas con que come son de oro.

— Eso no es nada, — respondió el azteca. — Comiendo en su palacio, mi Emperador nunca emplea dos veces la misma cucharita. Con cada bocado que toma, usa otra cucharita, nueva y limpia.

Esto sorprendió tanto a Cortés que no tuvo más que decir.

[1] Aztec nobles, when they brought messages to Moctezuma, put on humble clothing and never addressed him directly or looked at his face.

Modern Mexican silver jewelry is made in pre-conquest designs. The parrot is Aztec, the solemn gentleman is a Tlaxcalan hero, the rings bear idol faces, and the reclining figure is a Mayan god.

Y no supo hasta que llegó a Tenochtitlán que el listo azteca se había burlado de él. Porque el Emperador Moctezuma, como todos los aztecas, acostumbraba usar como cucharita un pedazo de tortilla, que se comía con cada bocado.

Y hasta la fecha los indios de México siguen usando como entonces «una cucharita nueva y limpia con cada bocado».[1]

II. Las plumas rojas del quetzal

Como ya sabe Vd., la moneda nacional de Guatemala se llama el quetzal, porque este pájaro raro es el emblema de la libertad, y los guatemaltecos aman sobre todo la libertad. «Esmeralda con alas» llaman a su pájaro, o «orquídea (*orchid*) que vuela», y dicen que su larga cola es el arco iris (*rainbow*) de paz para su pueblo.

Pues, se dice que este pájaro hermosísimo, esta «esmeralda

[1] *Tortillas* — corn-meal pancakes — were invented by the Mayas, copied from them by the Aztecs, and are today the bread of the poor in Mexico and Central America, although even well-to-do people like them.

del tamaño (*size*) de una paloma», era una vez enteramente verde, aunque hoy tiene en el pecho plumas rojas. Ésta es la historia de las plumitas rojas, que todavía cree cada indio maya.

Pedro de Alvarado,[1] cruel conquistador que ayudó a Cortés en la conquista de México, fué más tarde a Guatemala, donde pensó vencer a los mayas. Estos indios, viendo venir a los extranjeros blancos con sus caballos, y creyendo que hombre y caballo eran uno, sabían que sería muy difícil ganar una batalla contra ellos.

Tecún Umán, jefe valiente de los indios, salió al encuentro del conquistador español, y con la ayuda de los intérpretes (*interpreters*) aztecas que acompañaban a Alvarado, pudo hablar con él. Entendiendo al fin que no había esperanza de evitar un conflicto, le propuso (*proposed*) el jefe maya que él y Alvarado combatieran solos, y que el que ganase fuese desde aquel momento rey de todas las tierras de los mayas. Esto les salvaría la vida a muchos soldados, tanto españoles como mayas, y al valiente Tecún Umán le parecía mejor perder una vida que muchas.

Alvarado aceptó la propuesta (*proposition*) de Tecún Umán, y empezó el combate. El capitán español iba montado en su caballo hermoso, y vestido en toda la armadura (*armor*) tradicional de los conquistadores. Tecún Umán, al contrario, iba a pie sin armadura

Miniature quetzal bird, emblem of liberty in Guatemala, is made of carved wood covered with green and red feathers.

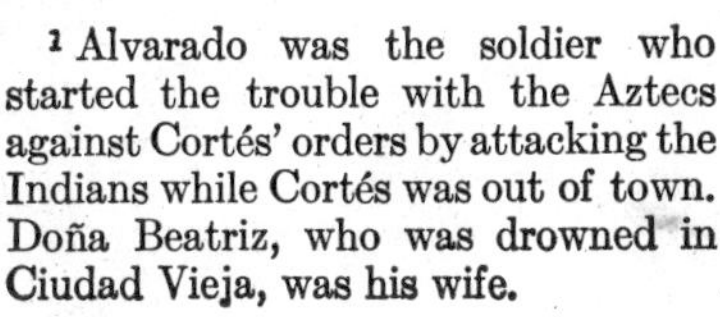

[1] Alvarado was the soldier who started the trouble with the Aztecs against Cortés' orders by attacking the Indians while Cortés was out of town. Doña Beatriz, who was drowned in Ciudad Vieja, was his wife.

alguna. Sobre la cabeza revoloteaba (*fluttered*) un quetzal, emblema de libertad, que había aprendido a acompañar siempre al jefe maya.[1]

Éste, creyendo que caballo y soldado eran uno, trató de matar al caballo, y pronto consiguió hacerlo. Pero, ¡cuál no fué su sorpresa al ver que, muerto el caballo, el jefe español podía combatir a pie como él! Esto le sorprendió tanto que en ese momento Alvarado consiguió matar el quetzal que volaba sobre la cabeza del maya. Tecún Umán, aterrado al ver caer el pájaro sagrado (*sacred*), trató de cogerlo, y en ese instante Alvarado le dió la estocada (*thrust*) mortal, hiriéndole (*wounding*) en el pecho con su lanza. La sangre que brotó (*burst*) del corazón del maya tiñó (*stained*) de rojo el pecho del quetzal verde que tenía en las manos, y murieron los dos juntos, terminando así para siempre el conflicto entre mayas y conquistadores.

Y desde entonces, todos los verdes quetzales, como símbolos de la muerte del valiente Tecún Umán, el cual había tratado

[1] The chief always carried a *quetzal* with him, sometimes one made of gold and emeralds, sometimes a live one trained to perch on his head or shoulder. Wooden masks worn by Indian dancers in Guatemala today represent Tecún Umán with two *quetzales* perched on his head, their curling green tails forming his bright mustache.

Modern Guatemalan silver jewelry recalls the past. The heavy ring represents Tecún Umán, last chief of the Mayas; the bracelet tells the story of the conquest and ends with the usual quetzal.

de salvarles la vida a sus soldados, tienen plumas rojas en el pecho.[1]

PALABRAS NUEVAS[2]

	el ala (*f.*)	wing	4	**imperio**	empire
2	**amar**	to love	4	**jefe** (*m.*)	chief
	bocado	bite, mouthful		**lanza**	lance
	cola	tail		**maya** (*m.* or *f.*)	Maya, Mayan
3	**corte** (*f.*)	court	2	**paz** (*f.*)	peace
	cuchara (-ita)	spoon	2	**pecho**	breast
	embajador (*m.*)	ambassador	3	**pedazo**	piece
	emperador (*m.*)	emperor	3	**poderoso**	powerful
2	**esperanza**	hope	2	**pueblo**	people
3	**evitar**	to avoid		**símbolo**	symbol

Expresiones

***al contrario**, on the contrary

puesto, "on" (article of clothing)

tanto — como, as well as

salir a su encuentro, to come out to meet him

NO ES VERDAD

Change the statements that are false to make them true.

I. 1. Cortés salió al encuentro de Moctezuma. 2. El embajador azteca le dijo a Cortés algo de las glorias de su tierra. 3. Nadie llevaba los zapatos puestos en la corte del Emperador de España. 4. El Rey de España comía con cucharitas de plata. 5. El Emperador Moctezuma usaba un cuchillo nuevo y limpio con cada bocado. 6. Cortés sorprendió mucho al azteca con sus cuentos de España.

[1] The story of the battle between Alvarado and Tecún Umán is true, regardless of the part about the red feathers! The place where the combat took place, with the Spanish and Mayan troops looking on, is now called Quezaltenango — *town of the quetzal* — and is one of Guatemala's largest cities.

[2] Note to teacher: Since this is a plateau chapter, *all* words not yet used in this book are given here, but are repeated in vocabularies if introduced later, since this chapter will be omitted by some classes.

II. 1. La moneda nacional de Guatemala lleva el nombre de su emblema de libertad. 2. El quetzal es un pájaro hermosísimo con una cola roja. 3. Los mayas creían que sería fácil ganar la batalla contra los españoles. 4. Alvarado propuso (*proposed*) que el jefe maya combatiera con él. 5. Tecún Umán iba montado en una mula, y trató de matar primero a Alvarado. 6. Tecún Umán cogió el pájaro sagrado (*sacred*) cuando se cayó. 7. La sangre del maya tiñó (*stained*) de rojo las alas del pájaro.

PREGUNTAS

I. 1. ¿A dónde fué Cortés? 2. ¿Quién salió a su encuentro? 3. ¿Por qué le dijo Cortés al embajador algo de las glorias de España? 4. ¿Le dijo el embajador a Cortés algo de las glorias de su tierra? 5. ¿Qué clase de cama tenía el Emperador azteca? 6. ¿Qué clase de cucharitas tenía el Rey de España? 7. ¿Qué clase de cucharitas tenía el Emperador azteca?

II. 1. ¿Cómo se llama la moneda nacional de Guatemala? 2. ¿Por qué usan los guatemaltecos un pájaro como emblema? 3. ¿Cómo llaman a su pájaro? 4. ¿Quién era Pedro de Alvarado? 5. ¿Qué creían los indios al ver los caballos? 6. ¿Quién era el jefe de los mayas? 7. ¿Qué propuso (*proposed*) Tecún Umán? 8. ¿Para qué propuso esto? 9. ¿Qué acompañaba al jefe maya? 10. ¿Cómo consiguió Alvarado matar a Tecún Umán? 11. ¿Por qué tiene el quetzal plumas rojas en el pecho?

REPASO DE VERBOS

I. Conjugate in the present subjunctive: **pedir, dormir, costar.**

II. Conjugate in the past subjunctive: **ser, decir, tener, amar.**

III. Conjugate in the conditional: **hacer, decir, amar.**

IV. Conjugate in the preterite: **evitar, prestar, cesar.**

V. Copy this verb synopsis outline, noticing the relationship of the tenses opposite each other, and complete it with the proper forms of **cargar, hacer,** *and* **leer,** *using the third person plural:*

Infinitive —— Gerund ——	Past Participle ——
Present Indicative ——	Present Subjunctive ——
Preterite Indicative ——	Past Subjunctive —— (*-se*)
Imperfect Indicative ——	Past Subjunctive —— (*-ra*)
Future Indicative ——	Conditional Indicative ——
Present Perfect Indicative ——	Present Perfect Subjunctive ——
Past Perfect Indicative ——	Past Perfect Subjunctive ——

VI. Give the infinitive and meaning of each of these verb forms, using may *to show a present subjunctive,* might *to show a past subjunctive, and* used to *or* was — ing *to show the imperfect indicative:*

cante	supo	quería	vuelan	descubriese
canté	diésemos	caigo	ponga	desapareció
destruyendo	dijésemos	cayó	suponga	seguiré
hicieron	sonrió	demos	tenían	conseguiré
hicieran	sonrío	dimos	contenían	ven tú
supe	querría	vuelcn	cubriese	no vengas

ESTUDIO DE PALABRAS

¿VERDAD O NO?[1]

1. El héroe nacional de una república siempre vive en un palacio que cuesta millones de dólares. 2. El progreso dramático de la transportación por el aire se ve con frecuencia en los mapas del hemisferio. 3. La unidad interamericana debe ser una tradición en los dos continentes americanos. 4. El santo patrón de los campesinos salvó sus labores sin la destrucción de sus ranchos. 5. El soldado se escapó sin su uniforme por el túnel subterráneo. 6. En consecuencia de las gloriosas victorias de Simón Bolívar, todo un continente se da cuenta de (*realize*) la importancia de su nombre. 7. El camino panamericano nos dará transportación internacional

[1] This exercise is made up almost entirely of cognates used in Chapters 9 to 16 inclusive, many of which are not in the vocabulary.

para los productos y los turistas. 8. El ganar su libertad pacíficamente les fué completamente imposible a los indios supersticiosos. 9. La multitud llevó su divinidad directamente a sus ranchos con el fin de salvar la situación. 10. El famoso automovilista estaba en posesión de un plano de operaciones para descubrir el tesoro tradicional.

PARA DIVERTIRSE

«Hagan ustedes esto»

Make polite commands of these phrases and choose a leader to give them to the class to perform. The pupils may be divided into two groups, standing by their desks, and all who do not obey instantly must sit down. That side wins whose members remain standing the longest. If the action specified by the command is impossible, the players should pretend to do it, anyway. If the leader makes some of the commands negative, he will catch those who perform the action when they shouldn't.

For variation, the leader may say, — *Quiero que Vds. cierren los libros,* — etc., using the subjunctive instead of a direct command.

cerrar los libros, cerrar los ojos, sentarse en el suelo, tocar la guitarra, levantarse, montar a caballo, abrir el libro, volar como un pájaro, dar dos pasos, lavarse la cara, no dar un paseo, meter el lápiz dentro del libro, sacar el lápiz del libro, prestar su lápiz a su vecino, devolver el lápiz, ofrecer un papel a su vecino, pedir prestado un libro, dormirse en pie, tocar el piano, manejar un automóvil, no tocar el violín, dejar caer un papel, no sonreír, pintar el suelo, caer de rodillas, beber una botella de leche, comer una tortilla, ponerse el sombrero

PARA LEER SIN ESTUDIAR

Chistes

1. — La semana pasada le dije algo a mi esposa, y desde entonces no me ha dicho una palabra.

— ¿Sabe Vd. lo que le dijo? Quisiera decírselo a mi esposa también.

2. — ¿Puede Vd. prestarme dos pesos?
— Solamente tengo uno.
— Bien, pues me deberá Vd. el otro.

3. — La bolsa (*pocketbook*) o la vida.
— Tome la bolsa. Pero hágame Vd. el favor de darme un recibo (*receipt*), porque mi mujer no creerá que me hayan robado.

4. Una señora dió a su hijo un pastel para que lo partiera (*divide*) con su hermana, diciéndole, — El pedazo más pequeño es siempre para aquél que parte.
El niño pensó un momento, y dándole el pastel a su hermana, dijo, — Tú puedes partirlo.

5. Una señora — Guardia, por lo que estoy oyendo, en este edificio estará tocando la Banda Municipal, ¿verdad?
El guardia — No, señora. Es una exposición (*show*) de perros.

6. — Su sueldo (*wages*) será de doscientos pesos, y antes de un año ganará el doble.
— Perfectamente. Entonces volveré dentro de un año.

7. — El texto que Vd. acaba de comprar, — dice el dependiente (*clerk*) al estudiante, — hará tan fácil el estudio de matemáticas que tendrá Vd. que estudiar sólo la mitad (*half*) del tiempo de antes.
— Magnífico, — responde el estudiante. — Entonces déme Vd. otro.

8. — ¿Tuvo Vd. alguna vez un accidente?
— Sí. Al pasar por un túnel no dí un beso a la hija, sino a la madre.

9. — Sí, señor, tengo setenta y siete años.
— Vd. debe ser el habitante más viejo de este pueblo.
— No, señor, mi padre tiene noventa y seis años.
— ¡Dios mío! Me gustaría verle.
— No puede ser, señor. Acaba de salir en bicicleta para visitar a mi abuelo.

TEMA

1. Cortés approached the Aztec capital on horseback. 2. An ambassador came out to meet him and told him that he should go away. 3. Cortés answered him as if he were a king. 4. The Aztec told him not to enter with his shoes on. 5. "That is nothing," said the Spaniard. "Even the teaspoons of my king are golden." 6. The Aztec had no more to say, because Cortés had made fun of him. 7. Alvarado later went to the land of the Mayas, which is now called Guatemala. 8. These Indians did not believe the Spaniards were gods. 9. The brave chief wanted Alvarado to fight alone. 10. Tecún Umán succeeded in killing the horse, but Alvarado killed the "emerald with wings."

CAPÍTULO **18**

Quarterly review

Cuentos que saben todos

Just as we, with our English heritage, have heard all our lives certain classical stories of our mother tongue, so all educated Spanish-speaking people learn the classics of their language. Children in Latin-American schools read the same Aesop's fables that we do, as well as the fables of their own race that date back to the earliest days of the literature of Spain.

These two popular stories and the poem, by famous Spanish authors of long ago, are found in the elementary readers used in

Bogotá and Medellín, Colombia, and are familiar to practically all school boys and girls in Spanish America.

They have been changed slightly, to make them easier for you, but on the whole they are much as they appear in the readers.

I. AGUDEZA (*cleverness*) DE UN LABRADOR

Un rústico labrador, deseoso de ver al rey, pensando que éste era más que hombre, pidió su salario y se despidió de su amo (*employer*). Yendo a la corte, con el largo camino se le acabó el dinero.

Llegado a la corte y habiendo visto al rey, viendo que era hombre como él, se dijo, — ¡Oh, por vida mía! Para ver a un hombre he gastado todo lo que tenía, y no me queda sino medio real.[1]

Tanto se enojó que le empezó a doler una muela, y con el hambre que tenía, no sabía qué hacer, porque decía, — Si yo me saco la muela, y pago este medio real, quedaré muerto de hambre; si me como el medio real, todavía me dolerá la muela.

En ese momento llegó a una pastelería donde vió muchos pasteles apetitosos.

Y por casualidad vinieron a pasar por allí dos criados del rey, quienes, viéndole mirar con tanto anhelo (*longing*) los pasteles, le dijeron, — Campesino, ¿cuántos pasteles podrías tú comer en una comida?

— Por Dios, — contestó el labrador, — me comería quinientos.

Dijeron los criados, — ¿Quinientos? ¡Líbrenos Dios del diablo (*Heaven help us*)!

El labrador respondió, — ¡De poco tienen miedo vuestras mercedes! [2]

[1] A *real* was originally a silver Spanish coin, but the name is now applied to various small coins of many Latin-American countries, especially those around the Caribbean area.

[2] ***vuestras mercedes,*** *your honors.* From *vuestra merced* came the modern *usted,* which takes the third person as the original form did. The farmer apparently uses this polite form sarcastically here, for later he uses the familiar.

Ellos dijeron que no, y él que sí,[1] y al fin dijeron, — ¿Cuánto apuestas?

— ¿Cuánto apuesto? Apuesto a que si no me los como, vosotros podéis sacarme esta primera muela, — y les mostró la que le dolía.

Contentos con la apuesta, pidieron pasteles los dos, y el labrador empezó a satisfacer el hambre que tenía. En cuanto hubo comido bastante, se limpió la boca y dijo, — Yo he perdido, señores.

Los otros dos, burlándose de él, llamaron a un barbero [2] y le sacaron la muela, aunque el labrador fingió (*pretended*) oponerse (*object*).

Burlándose de él, decían a los que estaban presentes, — ¿Habéis visto a este tonto campesino, que para comer bastantes pasteles nos dejó sacarle una muela?

Respondió el labrador, — Sois vosotros los tontos, que yo estaba muriendo de hambre y de esta muela que toda la mañana me dolía.

Al oír esto, todos empezaron a reírse de la burla (*joke*) que el labrador les había hecho a los dos, y éstos pagaron los pasteles y se fueron.

ADAPTED FROM JUAN DE TIMONEDA (*Spain*)

II. FANTASMAS QUE ROBAN PERAS

Había un viejo que tenía un peral, y todos los años le robaban las peras sin que consiguiese saber quiénes eran los ladrones. Desesperado, una noche de luna determinó esconderse y esperarlos.

A eso de la medianoche, vinieron unos estudiantes [3] vestidos de fantasmas, con velas en las manos y cestas (*baskets*) en los hombros, y caminaron en procesión hacia el peral cantando en tono de prefacio: [4]

[1] *Ellos dijeron que no, y él que sí,* *They said they weren't, and he said they were.*

[2] Barbers in medieval times pulled teeth and attended to minor ailments.

[3] University students in old Spanish literature are traditionally poor and up to some mischief.

[4] The *prefacio* is the first part or prologue of a mass.

Andar, andar,
hasta llegar al peral.
Cuando éramos vivos
andábamos por estos caminos;
y ahora que estamos muertos,
andamos por estos desiertos.
¿Hasta cuándo durarán nuestras
penas (*punishment*)?
Hasta que las cestas (*baskets*)
estén llenas.

— ¡Ay! — dijo el viejo, — éstas son las almas de los que me han robado las peras, que están haciendo penitencia. Que (*let*) descansen en paz. — Y se fué a acostar.

ADAPTED FROM FERNÁN CABALLERO (*Spain*)

III. EL BURRO FLAUTISTA

If you have difficulty in rearranging the words of the poem so that you understand it, read and compare with it the prose paraphrase opposite, which tells the same story in a simpler manner.

You may wish to memorize the poem, for it is very well known, and one often hears in Spanish the expression, "like the donkey that played the flute," meaning that someone has accidentally succeeded when he was not expected to.

Esta fabulilla
salga bien o mal,
me ha ocurrido ahora
por casualidad.

(Por casualidad me ha ocurrido esta fábula pequeña, que puede salir bien o mal.)

Cerca de unos prados
que hay en mi lugar,
pasaba un borrico
por casualidad.

(Por casualidad un burro pasaba por unos prados [*meadows*] que hay cerca del lugar en donde vivo.)

Una flauta en ellos
halló, que un zagal
se dejó olvidada
por casualidad.

(Por casualidad un burro halló una flauta que un zagal [*shepherd*] había olvidado y había dejado allí.)

Acercóse a olerla
el dicho animal,
y dió un resoplido
por casualidad.

(El dicho animal se acercó a la flauta a olerla, y por casualidad dió un resoplido [*snort*].)

Por la flauta el aire
hubo de pasar
y sonó la flauta
por casualidad.

(El aire tenía que pasar por la flauta, que sonó, por casualidad.)

— ¡Oh! — dijo el borrico.
— ¡Qué bien sé tocar!
¡Y dirán que es mala
la música asnal!

(— ¡Oh! — dijo el burro. — ¡Qué bien sé tocar! ¡Y nadie debe decir que la música de un burro es mala!)

Sin reglas del arte
borriquitos hay,
que una vez aciertan
por casualidad.

(Sin saber las reglas del arte, hay burritos que algunas veces aciertan [*succeed*], por casualidad.)

IRIARTE (*Spain*)

PALABRAS NUEVAS

	apetitoso	appetizing	4	**ladrón** (*m.*)	thief
	apostar (ue) (a)	to bet		**muela**	tooth
	apuesta	bet		**oler (ue)**	to smell
	borrico	donkey		**pastel** (*m.*)	pastry
3	**corte** (*f.*)	court	2	**paz** (*f.*)	peace
	deseoso	desirous		**pastelería**	pastry shop
1	**dicho**	aforesaid		**penitencia**	penance
	doler (ue)	to ache, pain		**pera**	pear
	flauta	flute		**peral** (*m.*)	pear tree
	flautista (*m.* or *f.*)	flute-playing, flute-player	1	**quinientos**	500
			3	**regla**	rule
4	**labrador**	working man, farmer	3	**satisfacer**	to satisfy

EXPRESIONES

por casualidad, by chance
***por Dios,** for goodness' sake
por vida mía, on my life

PARA COMPLETAR

Complete with as many words as you find necessary.

I. 1. El campesino deseaba ver al rey porque... 2. El viaje fué tan largo que gastó... 3. En la corte supo que el rey... 4. Si comprase algo que comer con su dinero, todavía... 5. Por casualidad dos criados le vieron... 6. El labrador dijo que si los tuviese, podría comer... 7. Apostó una muela contra... 8. Los criados creían que el campesino había perdido la muela porque... 9. Cuando el labrador lo explicó, todos empezaron a...

II. 1. Todos los años el viejo perdía... 2. Una noche decidió... 3. Los estudiantes estaban vestidos de —— con... 4. El viejo, al oír su canción, creía que...

III. 1. Un borrico estaba en... 2. Allí halló... 3. Con su resoplido (*snort*), el borrico consiguió... 4. El burro creía que sabía...

REPASO DE PALABRAS IMPORTANTES

I. Tell what shorter words give you a clue to the meaning of each of these words:

deseoso, pastelería, apetitoso, peral, estudiante, una apuesta, flautista, dolerá, descubierto, bisabuelo, terremoto, enterrar (ie), campesino, medianoche, desesperado, libertad, tristeza, acercarse a, caminar, lejano, deshonrado, siguiente, enamorado, reconocer

II.[1] These compound nouns combine two or more familiar words. *Analyze each one and show how it gets its meaning.* What is the usual gender of nouns composed of a verb and a noun? (Page 116.)

cuentagotas (*medicine dropper*), tragadieces[2] ("*juke box,*" Mexico), traganíquel ("*juke box,*" Panama), pisapapeles (*paperweight*), siempreviva (*everlasting flower*), matamoscas (*fly swatter*), fijapelo ("*wave set,*" beauty shop), guardapelo (*locket*), guardapolvo (*smock always worn by Argentine school children*), Miraflores (*a suburb in Lima, Peru*), aeropuerto (*airport*), anteojos (*eyeglasses*), descansabrazo (*armrest, in car*), limpiabotas (*bootblack*), parabrisa[3] (*wind-*

[1] Optional exercise. [2] *tragar, to swallow* [3] *parar, to stop*

shield), limpiaparabrisa (*windshield wiper*), quedirán (*public opinion*), salvavidas (*life preserver*), rompeolas (*breakwater*), calientacamas (*bed-warmer*), ganapán (*drudge*), matapolvo (*light rain*), padrenuestro (*Lord's Prayer*), pasatiempo (*pastime*), sacamuelas (*quack dentist*), quehacer doméstico (*household task*), cubrecama (*bedspread*, Chile), sobrecama (*bedspread*, Mexico)

III. Find in List B the opposite of each word or phrase in List A. These are trickier than they look!

A	B
1. todo el mundo va	1. muy poco
2. noche de luna	2. descubrirlo
3. camino de	3. prestar
4. hace muchos años	4. sacar de
5. meter en	5. en el viaje de vuelta
6. pedir prestado	6. actualmente
7. esconderlo	7. no va nadie
8. una enorme cantidad	8. mucha obscuridad
9. montar a caballo	9. callarse
10. al norte	10. juntos
11. dar un paseo	11. no acordarse de nada
12. distinto a	12. nunca
13. en pie	13. igualito
14. para siempre	14. ir a pie
15. ofrecer algo	15. quedarse en casa
16. no olvidar nada	16. sentado
17. alejarse de	17. no aceptar nada
18. solos	18. acercarse a
19. ambos	19. ni uno ni otro
20. gritar	20. al sur

IV. Find in List B a synonym for each word or phrase in List A.

A	B
1. hay que ir	1. hace cien años
2. volver a comer	2. hasta
3. hace un siglo	3. camino internacional
4. aún	4. necesito dinero

5. aun
6. llegar a ser
7. carretera panamericana
8. regresar
9. me falta dinero
10. a la vez
11. unos cuantos
12. acabar
13. sacerdote
14. querer decir
15. temer una cosa
16. la brisa
17. muy listo
18. está muy ocupado
19. llueve
20. nunca se equivocaba

5. unos pocos
6. cura
7. tener miedo de algo
8. inteligente
9. está lloviendo
10. tiene mucho que hacer
11. siempre tenía razón
12. el viento
13. significar
14. terminar
15. al mismo tiempo
16. volver
17. ponerse
18. todavía
19. es preciso ir
20. comer otra vez

REPASO DE VERBOS

I. Conjugate in the present subjunctive: **traer, sacar, contar, morir.**

II. Conjugate in the past subjunctive: **hacer, leer, ir, contener.**

III. Conjugate in the preterite: **dar, contestar, creer, pagar.**

IV. Conjugate in the future: **decir, tener, pasar.**

V. Give the gerunds for: **pedir, dormir, traer, quedarse, irse.**

VI. Give the familiar commands, singular and plural of: **tener, venir, salir, hacerlo, poner, gastar, pensar, decirme, traerle.**

VII. Give the negative familiar commands in the singular of the verbs in Exercise VI.

VIII. Copy the verb synopsis outline in Exercise V on page 247 and complete it with the proper forms of **decir, caerse,** *and* **saber,** *using the first person singular.* Can you explain why certain tenses are placed opposite each other in the outline?

IX. Translate these verb forms as quickly and accurately as you can, using may *to show a present subjunctive and* might *to show a past subjunctive.* Remember that nothing is worth less than an incorrectly translated verb!

1. llegué
2. llegue
3. consiguió
4. supongamos
5. sonaron
6. soñaron
7. cesasen
8. pidió prestado
9. durará
10. hubiésemos ido
11. yéndose
12. hayan declarado
13. supusiese
14. habría pintado
15. contuvieron
16. fíjese Vd.
17. devolvimos
18. tiemblen
19. se detuvo
20. hemos hecho
21. deténgase Vd.
22. conviene
23. sonreímos
24. éramos
25. ¡detente tú!
26. lavad
27. reconozca
28. ¡no te rías!
29. se han puesto
30. ¡llévate tú!

X. Put these verbs into Spanish as quickly as you can. (What tenses do *may, might, would, will, used to,* and *was — ing* indicate?)

1. we may go 2. they used to give 3. he might sleep 4. he might have slept 5. they fell 6. she would know 7. I have put 8. he is reading (*prog.*) 9. they came 10. he heard 11. they would have made 12. I will tell 13. she has been 14. we might give 15. I paid for 16. sleeping 17. he will have 18. we might walk 19. going away 20. he has told 21. we might put 22. they may arrive 23. you would be able 24. serving 25. we might come 26. I saw 27. you brought 28. hearing 29. they have brought 30. he made

XI. If each of these verb forms were the main verb in a sentence containing a subjunctive, in what tense would the subjunctive verb probably be? (§ 43)

pida, esperaba, temen, ¿cree Vd.?, quería, es posible, sería mejor,

ha sentido, no habían creído, me gustaría, quisiera, puede ser, mandó, dirá, esperan, será lástima, pidieron, dejó, había pedido, aconsejamos, querría, ha sido preciso, me alegro de, permitiría, hará

REPASO DE COSAS NUEVAS[1]

I. If you can complete these statements, you know the rules of grammar. Then, if you can give the example correctly in Spanish, you know how to apply the rule. (A dash stands for one word; dots stand for several.)

1. Familiar commands may be used only in the ——. The negative form comes from the —— —— tense. (§§ 24, 25)
Bring me (fam.) *a teaspoon. Don't bring me a knife.*

2. The stem for the present subjunctive is the —— person —— —— if it ends in ——. (§ 26)
poner: pongo: (*pres. subjv.*) ——; ***salir:*** ——: ——; ***caer:*** ——: ——; ***hacer:*** ——: ——; ***contar:*** ——: ——; ***reír:*** ——: ——

3. To say *let us* (*let's*), use the —— person —— of the —— —— tense. (§ 28)
Let's sing now. No, let's eat, or let's buy something.

4. A Spanish noun used as an adjective must be preceded by ——. (§ 29)
I don't want a paper hat; I want a gold watch.

5. When adjectives of nationality refer to languages, they take the definite article except after ——, ——, and ——. (§ 125, 6.)
Spanish is easier than French, and we learn Spanish easily.

6. The prepositional pronouns have the same meanings as the —— —— pronouns, but must always be used after a ——. (§ 112)
We are going with him. Do you see him? They are going with me if they can find me.

7. The six common verbs whose present subjunctive stem cannot come from the first person present indicative are: . . . (§ 31)
I may go; we may know; he may be (two verbs); *they may give; you may have eaten.*

[1] Note to teacher: This exercise combines the TEMA with the grammar review, and even if the TEMA is not ordinarily assigned, it should be used here.

8. III RC present subjunctive forms are irregular in the —— and —— persons ——. (§ 32)

Let us ask; we may sleep; they may regret.

9. In Spanish, instead of *I want you to go,* one actually says ... (§ 33)

He wants us to go; them to sing; her to study.

10. The subjunctive is used after verbs of —— if there is a —— of ——. (§ 33)

We want to learn; we want you to learn.

11. Four verbs of causing which may or may not take the subjunctive are ... (§ 33)

He lets us enter; they command us to work; she makes him return; we permit her to go. (Write two ways.)

12. To say the impersonal *one* or *they,* use —— or —— with a —— person verb. (§ 34)

They say that one may enter.

13. The subjunctive is used after —— of emotion if there is a —— of ——. (§ 35)

I hope you go; we are glad he is here; they regret he is ill.

14. Any expression of —— causes the subjunctive. (§ 36)

Do you believe he has it? I don't believe he can do it.

15. Any Spanish neuter refers to a —— ——. (§ 37)

What I have is mine. Is this what you want? That certainly is it!

16. The stem for the past subjunctive tense is always the —— person —— of the —— indicative tense. (§ 38)

poner: pusieron: *(past subjv.)* ——; ***dormir:*** ——: ——; ***traer:*** ——: ——; ***oír:*** ——: ——; ***dar:*** ——: ——; ***decir:*** ——: ——

17. The two ways to tell whether to use the present or past subjunctive tense are ... (§§ 39, 43)

He wants them to read; he wanted them to read. He hopes she may go; he hoped she might go.

18. An impersonal expression may take a —— verb or an —— verb in the subordinate clause. (§ 40)

It is necessary for us to eat (two ways).

19. The diminutive endings ***-illo*** and ***-cillo*** are —— flattering than ***-ito*** and ***-cito***. (§ 41)

an ugly little animal, a cute little animal; the unpleasant little old man; the nice little old man

20. The subjunctive is used after conjunctions showing —— when —— time is implied. (§ 44, 1)

I shall leave when he comes; I'll wait until he arrives.

21. Other common conjunctions that often take the subjunctive are ——, ——, and ——. (§ 44, 2)

We intend to work in order that we may earn money.

22. The only subjunctive tense used after ***si*** is the ——, and the other verb in the sentence must then be in the —— tense. (§ 44, 4)

If I were you, I should not leave yet.

23. To express an "imaginative comparison," use —— —— with the —— subjunctive. (§ 44, 5)

He talked as if he were a king!

24. When the antecedent of an adjective clause is ——, the verb in the clause must be a ——. (§ 45, 1)

We are looking for a dog that is intelligent.

25. There is automatically a subjunctive in an adjective clause which follows a ——. (§ 45, 2)

I don't see anyone who has a big hat.

26. Words meaning *whatever, however,* and *whoever* may take the ——. (§ 45, 3, 4)

However important he may be, and whoever he may be, he can't come into my house!

27. ***Quisiera*** is more polite than ——. (§ 46, 2)

I should like to have it, if it is possible. I should like for you to give it to me.

PARA CONTESTAR SIN ESTUDIAR[1]

Answer these personal questions with your book closed, as your teacher gives them.

1. ¿Cómo se llama Vd.? 2. ¿Dónde vive Vd.? 3. ¿Cuántos años tiene Vd.? 4. ¿Cuál es la fecha? 5. ¿Qué día es hoy? 6. ¿Qué hora es? 7. Si tuviese Vd. un millón de dólares, ¿qué compraría? 8. Si tuviese Vd. más tiempo, ¿qué haría? 9. ¿Hace muchos años que estudia Vd. el español? 10. ¿Quién es el alumno más alto de esta clase? 11. ¿Quién es el hijo mayor de su familia? 12. ¿Por qué no asiste Vd. al cine todas las noches?

[1] **Note to teacher: This exercise may be used for an aural comprehension test.**

PICA, PERICO

"Peck, Little Parrot" is an old Mexican folk song that everyone knows. As it is being sung, two boys often step forward and beat time to it with their feet in a shuffling *zapateado* (forward right, step left beside it; backward right, step left beside it), clasping their hands behind them and holding their heads down as they face each other.

The words mean: "Lady, your little parrot wants to take me down to the river, but I tell him no because I would die of cold. Peck, peck, peck, little parrot; peck, peck, peck the sand; peck, peck, peck, little parrot; peck, peck, peck my sister."

ART. by ALICE MOORE MILTON

2. Quisiera ser periquito
pa' ver la tierra caliente,
y allí echarte flores
sin que lo sepa la gente.

Would that I were a little parrokeet
To see the tropical land
And there to throw you flowers
Without anyone's knowing it.

Part Three

CAPÍTULO 19

I. El caballo de Cortés

Stories of Cortés and his conquest are still heard throughout Mexico and Central America, for with the coming of the Spaniards everything was changed. The Indians, although intelligent, were as puzzled by the weapons, armor, and animals of the invaders as we would be by an expedition from Mars.

This story about Cortés' horse is told by a Guatemalan, but the same plot, with some variations, has been used by other modern writers.

Remember that the Aztecs were the Indians of the Mexican highlands, while the Mayas lived on the peninsula of Yucatán as well as in Guatemala and Honduras. The Mayas were the older people, whose astounding culture was copied by the Toltecs, and later by the Aztecs of Central Mexico.

En la gran plaza del templo del dios Kukulkán,[1] en Tayazal, capital del reino de los Itzaes,[2] hay una animación nunca vista.

El pueblo no está reunido ahora para pedir a Kukulkán que haga llover, sino para rogarle que dé a los sacerdotes la manera de resolver la enorme desgracia que ha caído sobre los Itzaes desde el mismo día en que llegó el hombre blanco.

Hace poco pasó por Tayazal, con destino a tierras de Copán,[3] el conquistador Hernán Cortés. Éste se encontraba en

[1] Kukulkán is a Mayan name for Quetzalcóatl, the "Fair God" of the Toltecs and Aztecs who promised to return some day. The name means "Feathered Serpent," and the god is represented by carved stone rattlesnakes with feathers.

[2] The Itzas were the Mayas who, before the Conquest, left what is now Yucatán (a State of Mexico) and went south into Petén, Guatemala. It has been suggested that one reason for their leaving was the failure of their crops due to their ignorance of soil conservation.

[3] Copán is in Honduras, near the Guatemalan border, and is known for its ruins of a once great Mayan city.

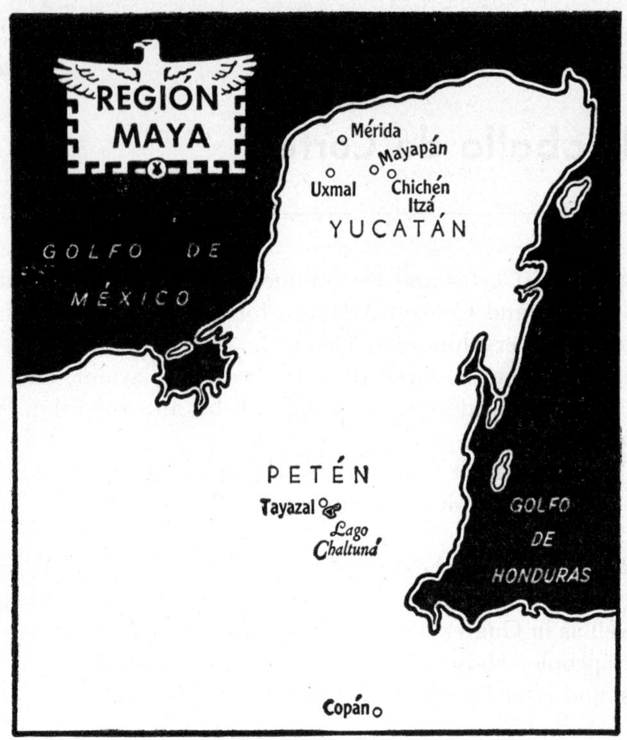

Tayazal cuando se puso enfermo su caballo. Esperó varios días a que éste mejorara, pero como no podía pasar más tiempo allí, dejó su caballo al cuidado del Canek,[1] diciéndole que en el viaje de vuelta vendría a buscarlo, y que ¡ay de él si no lo hallaba vivo, y sobre todo, curado su mal!

El Canek mandó a sus criados que cuidaran al caballo como si fuera una persona de sangre real. Él mismo iba a verlo, tres y más veces al día; y él mismo mandó que no se le diera al sagrado caballo sino oro de (*as*) alimento. Pensaba el rey,

— A los españoles les gusta el oro más que nada; dicen que cura un mal de que todos sufren;[2] así al caballo le gustará también el oro y éste lo curará.

[1] Canek is the Mayan word for King.

[2] The Spaniards told the Aztecs and Mayas that they all suffered from a heart ailment that only gold could cure! The Indians had never seen horses or any large animals before; so they weren't very good veterinarians!

A todas horas le llevaban el alimento de oro, pero siempre el caballo lo rehusaba (*refused*). Sin embargo, se le dejaba allí, pues todos creían que tarde o temprano habría de comerlo.

Un día, con gran sorpresa del Canek, hallaron el caballo muerto. El rey, aterrado, llamó a sus sacerdotes para saber qué podían hacer para devolverle la vida al animal. Le aconsejaron que hiciese sacrificios a los dioses a fin de que ellos le dieran la fórmula para resolver el caso.

Hacía un tiempo hermosísimo. A la plaza llega el Canek en su litera (*litter*) de oro llevada en los hombros de esclavos. El rey lleva en una mano un quetzal hecho de esmeraldas y rubíes y en la otra el delicado cuchillo de jade con el cual ha de hacer los sacrificios. . . .[1]

Las ceremonias terminan; los dioses han dado al gran sacerdote un mensaje (*message*) que ha de salvar al pueblo de la ira (*anger*) de Cortés. Del palacio se ve salir esa tarde un criado, que lleva unos rollos escritos y que se dirige a las tierras de Chichén Itzá.[2]

* * *

Ha pasado un mes. En el palacio real está sentado, cerca de una cortina que parece esconder algo, el maya Siguán, que no es de las tierras de Itzá. Vienen a sacarle de su meditación dos hombres. Son el Canek de los Itzaes, y el gran sacerdote de Tayazal.

Siguán no les dice una sola palabra.

El primero en hablar es el Canek. — Siguán, hoy es el último día, y hemos venido a ver tu obra. De ella depende tu vida y aun la felicidad futura de tu pueblo.

Siguán da dos pasos hacia atrás, sin volver la espalda a los señores, y con manos que tiemblan, descorre (*draws back*) la cortina.

[1] At this particular ceremony the story says five boys and five girls were sacrificed by having their hearts torn out.

[2] Chichén Itzá, in the jungles of Yucatán, is a city of the Mayas which was abandoned before the Spaniards came. Today visitors go by car to see its stupendous pyramids and temples, and the sacred well into which sacrificial victims were thrown. Since the ancient Mayas were great stone-carvers, it seems natural that the King should send to Chichén Itzá for an expert.

Ante los ojos atónitos (*astonished*) del Canek y de su sacerdote, se presenta una fiel imagen de un caballo blanco, hecha de piedra.

— Tu obra es admirable, Siguán, — dice el rey. — Has hecho honor al pueblo de Chichén Itzá, y tu trabajo te salva la vida. Pero el caballo no tiene vida. ¿Quién se la dará?

— No os preocupéis (*worry*), mi rey y mi señor, — dice el sacerdote. — Los dioses también me dieron la fórmula para hacer esto. Para darle vida, es preciso meter el caballo de piedra, en una noche de luna, en las aguas del lago Chaltuná,[1] y dejarlo en ellas hasta que los dioses le den vida.

Esa noche, por rara coincidencia, había luna, y la mara-

[1] Lake Chaltuná is now called Lake Flores, and there the Mayas built their last city before the Spanish Conquest.

Stone-faced Temple of Kukulcán, the "feathered serpent," towers above the jungles of Yucatán where once flourished the Mayan city of Chichén Itzá. An even older pyramid is hidden within it.

Gendreau

Gendreau

Reclining Mayan god of stone guards the restored Temple of the Warriors in deserted Chichén Itzá. Behind him stand two great "feathered serpent" columns, tails up and mouths open.

villosa escultura (*sculpture*) del caballo blanco, al cual dieron el nombre de «tzimimchac»,[1] haciéndolo divino, fué sacada del palacio sin que nadie lo supiera, y llevada a las orillas del Chaltuná, en cuyas aguas transparentes fué metida, según los consejos de los dioses.

* * *

Han pasado generaciones y generaciones . . . Hernán Cortés, para suerte del Canek y de su pueblo, no volvió jamás a Tayazal de los Itzaes. Y entre las aguas tranquilas del Chaltuná, esperando aún que un dios llegue a darle vida, se dice que está el tzimimchac blanco, que hasta hoy se puede ver cuando baja el nivel de las aguas del lago. . . .[2]

ADAPTED FROM FRANCISCO BARNOYA GÁLVEZ (*Guatemala*)

[1] *Tzimimchac* is one spelling of the Mayan word for horse-god, which they called it because they could not believe the creature to be a mere animal.

[2] "They say" it's still there!

II. El gato guardián

Some of the new words in the poem are not in the vocabulary, but are explained by the prose paraphrase. Compare the two versions and you will understand the poem.

Find in the paraphrase another way to say *ratoncillesco, por los contornos de, gobiernos dignos y timoratos, e hízola el gato* (§ 48), *refresco, que nadie pesca de improvisto, pillo.*

Un campesino que en su cocina
guardaba un queso de nochebuena,
oyó un ruidito ratoncillesco
por los contornos de su refresco.

(Un campesino que guardaba un queso de nochebuena [*Christmas Eve*] en su cocina, oyó un ruidito de ratones cerca de su alimento, el queso.)

Y pronto, pronto, como hombre
listo
que nadie pesca de desprovisto,
trájose el gato para que en vela
le hiciese al pillo la centinela.

(Y pronto, como hombre listo, que siempre sabe resolver sus problemas, llamó al gato para que hiciese la centinela [*act as sentinel*] y para que velase el queso y cogiese al ladroncillo.)

E hízola el gato con tal suceso,
que ambos marcharon — ratón y
queso.
Gobiernos dignos y timoratos,
donde hay quesos no mandéis gatos.

RAFAEL POMBO (*Colombia*)

(Y el gato la hizo tan bien que desaparecieron ambos — el ratón y el queso. De esto aprendemos que los buenos gobiernos nunca deben mandar otros a guardar tesoros, porque esto sale como el gato que guardaba el queso.)

PALABRAS NUEVAS

	alimento	food	3	**felicidad**	happiness
2	**caso**	case, situation	3	**imagen** (*f.*)	image
3	**consejo**	advice	4	**mal** (*m.*)	illness
	cortina	curtain	4	**mejorar**	to get better
4	**curar**	to cure	2	**obra**	work (of art)
3	**desgracia**	misfortune	4	**reino**	kingdom
4	**esclavo**	slave	4	**sagrado**	sacred

EXPRESIONES

al cuidado de, in care of
***sin embargo,** nevertheless, however
hacia atrás, backward
para suerte de, fortunately for
***sobre todo,** especially
con gran sorpresa de, to the great surprise of
volver la espalda a, to turn one's back on

PREGUNTAS

1. ¿Por qué había mucha animación en la plaza? 2. ¿Quería el pueblo que su dios hiciese llover? 3. ¿Quién había pasado por Tayazal con destino a Copán? 4. ¿Qué pasó con su caballo? 5. ¿Qué mandó Cortés al rey maya? 6. ¿Trató el Canek de salvarle la vida al caballo? 7. ¿Por qué no comió el caballo el alimento que le dieron? 8. ¿Por qué le dieron alimento de oro? 9. ¿Por qué quería el rey devolverle la vida al animal? 10. ¿Qué hicieron para saber qué hacer? 11. ¿De dónde era Siguán? 12. ¿Qué hizo Siguán? 13. ¿Qué hicieron los sacerdotes con el caballo de piedra? 14. ¿Le dieron vida los dioses? 15. ¿Está el caballo allí todavía? 16. ¿Qué guardaba un campesino en su cocina? 17. ¿Para que llamó al gato? 18. ¿Por qué desapareció el queso?

REPASO DE VERBOS

I. In section 98 you will find a list of verbs which take certain prepositions, either before a following infinitive or with an object. *Complete each of these sentences with the proper preposition, and translate:*

1. La felicidad depende —— la salud. 2. Anoche soñé —— mi abuelo. 3. Los galeones estaban cargados —— tesoros. 4. No tarde Vd. —— hacerlo. 5. El rey dejó —— hablar. 6. Lope se alejó —— la montaña. 7. Querría acercarse —— la casa. 8. Mis amigos no se ríen —— mí. 9. Y yo no me burlo —— ellos. 10. Se despidió —— sus padres. 11. Fíjese Vd. —— esto. 12. No me atrevo —— hacerlo. 13. Empezamos —— curarle. 14. Trataron —— curar al caballo. 15. Mi hermano no se parece —— mí. 16. Siempre pensamos —— esto. 17. ¿Se acuerda Vd. —— la fecha? 18. Nos acostumbramos —— todo. 19. Vamos —— honrarle. 20. Viene —— vernos. 21. Aprenderemos —— bailar. 22. La profesora nos enseñará —— bailar. 23. Doña Carmen se casó —— don Rafael. 24. Nos gusta jugar —— béisbol.

II. Using these expressions, make a list of sentences headed: **Lo que yo quisiera que hiciese Vd.** In what tense will the subordinate verbs have to be?

traerme un cuchillo, llamarme por teléfono, ir a casa, preparar la comida, cambiar este peso, callarse, limpiar la casa, decirme la verdad, volver temprano

ALGO NUEVO

47. Uses of Por *and* Para

por dos siglos, *for two centuries*
por ser tarde, *because it is (was) late*
listo para la aventura, *ready for the adventure*
para no perder tiempo, *in order not to lose time*

Por and ***para*** both mean *for* and *by*, but each has many other meanings as well.

1. *For* is expressed by ***por*** when it means:
   a. a certain length of time: **por tres años,** *for three years*
   b. in exchange for: **dar uno por otro,** *to give one for another*
   c. for the sake of: **lo hizo por su país,** *he did it for his country*

For is expressed by ***para*** when it means:

a. destination: **salió para Chile,** *he left for Chile*
b. purpose: **una cuchara para sopa,** *a soup spoon*

2. *By* is expressed by ***por*** when it means:

a. manner: **viaja por ferrocarril,** *he travels by rail*
b. a person by whom something is done: **fué vendido por Juan,** *it was sold by John*

By is expressed by ***para*** when it means:

a. with a time limit: **prepárelo para el lunes,** *prepare it by Monday;* **para las dos,** *by two o'clock*

3. Other meanings of ***por:***

through: **miró por la puerta,** *he looked through the door*
times: **tres por cuatro son doce,** *three times four are twelve*
per: **seis por ciento,** *six per cent*
on account of, or because (+ *inf.*): **por estar cansado, no salí,** *I did not go out because I was tired (on account of being tired)*
along: **andaba por la calle,** *he walked along the street*

Idioms with ***por:*** Twenty-seven of the two hundred most common idioms in the Spanish language begin with ***por.*** Of these, you have already had over half and you will have many of the remaining ones in this book.

4. Other meanings of ***para:***

in order to: **estudia para aprender,** *he studies in order to learn*
to: **cuentos para contar,** *stories to tell*

Idioms with ***para:*** **estar para,** *to be about to;* **para siempre,** *forever;* **¿para qué?,** *for what purpose;* **servir para,** *to be good for.*

EJERCICIO I. *Translate and explain why* **por** *or* **para** *is used in each of these phrases; then read each aloud several times so that your ear will become accustomed to the sound.*

más por su dinero
para estar bien de salud
cambio piano por automóvil
son cinco para las diez (5 *till* 10)

cuentos para niños
«clavelitos para ti» (*words of song*)
un cinco por lo que piensas
gracias por las flores
Compre Vd. su regalo para Carmen. (*Sign in store*)
«Para Vigo me voy» (*song title*)
Para muestra (*sample*), basta un botón (*button*). (*proverb*)
por falta de lluvia
tres pesos por docena
¡Vote Vd. por Fulano!
en un dos por tres (*in a jiffy*)
estoy loco por ti
no lo deje Vd. para mañana
una cuchara para sopa
Por la boca muere el pez (*fish*). (*Proverb*)
Velocidad máxima, 80 km. por hora
está para irse
vamos por avión
cupón para subscripción
lo hizo por amistad
por todo el país

EJERCICIO II. *Put into Spanish, referring to the preceding examples if you need help:*

1. shoes for children 2. I am about to finish 3. on account of leaving early 4. a pencil box 5. by Wednesday 6. for six years 7. to give $5 for a dog 8. the flowers are for you 9. we leave for the city 10. they travel by plane 11. we eat to live 12. for the sake of my father

48. Literary Word Order

trájose el gato, *he brought* (*in*) *the cat*
hízola el gato, *the cat did it*

You have learned never to attach object pronouns to conjugated verbs, but you will find in reading literary selections that authors often do it, especially at the beginning of a sentence or after a mark of punctuation. This form is used only in writing, and as far as you are concerned (not having a poetic license!) you need never use it, although you must learn to recognize it. Can you explain the accent?

EJERCICIO III. *Change the order of verb and pronoun in these sentences, and translate:*

1. Súpolo la tía del joven. 2. Púsose enfermo el caballo. 3. Aconsejáronle que hiciese sacrificios. 4. Háblale el rey al conquistador. 5. Al volver al palacio, dióle la fórmula para hacer esto. 6. Todos se fueron; viólos pasar el indio.

ESTUDIO DE PALABRAS

These words are Spanish-American adaptations of ours, showing the North American influence in other countries. *Can you understand them?*

BASEBALL TERMS: béisbol, un teic-yur-beis, el ompayer, un jonrón, llegar a jom, aut, estraic, tim, estraic-aut (*also called* pónchaut), un jit, llegar seif a primera, robar un base, un doble play, el pícher, el cácher (*A fielder is called* jardinero.)

AUTOMOBILE: el espidómetro, el cloch, los breques, el carburador, una troca, un autobús, un carro, un chófer

FOODS: el biftec (bife *in Argentina*), el mosh (*breakfast food*), el budín (*Chile*), el sandwich, panqueques (*Chile*), el lonche

MISCELLANEOUS: Popeye el Marino, el mitín, el líder, flirtear, bailar el fox, foxtrotear, el saisín (*trip for tourists*), los tiquets, el eswich (*for electric lights*), el pijama, el ménager de hotel, místeres (*Colombian name for North Americans*), aló (*telephone*)

REPASITO

I. Review the use of impersonal **uno** *and* **se** (*§ 34*), *and complete these sentences in Spanish:*

1. *One ought to* esperar un poco. 2. *They say* que murió el caballo. 3. *One cannot* entrar sin pagar. 4. *One forgets* fácilmente de vez en cuando. 5. Riendo, *one keeps on* aprendiendo. 6. *One sees* que no hay nada que hacer.

II. Answer these questions in the negative if they are affirmative, and vice versa. (§ 13)

1. ¿Tiene Vd. algo que hacer? 2. ¿Ve Vd. a alguien? 3. ¿Come Vd. carne? 4. ¿Quiere Vd. pluma o lápiz? 5. ¿Baila Vd. el fox algunas veces? 6. ¿Vuelve Vd. temprano a casa siempre? 7. ¿No tiene Vd. ningún dinero? 8. ¿No quiere Vd. nada que comer? 9. ¿No viene nadie ahora? 10. ¿No lleva Vd. ni dinero ni boleto (*ticket*)?

PARA LEER SIN ESTUDIAR

I. ¿Sabía Vd. esto?

México fué el primer país del Hemisferio Occidental que tuvo carretas (*carts*), porque los indios nunca habían sabido hacer la rueda (*wheel*). Un carpintero español que llegó con Cortés hizo las primeras carretas, y cuando no había caballos para tirar de ellas, los indios las empujaban (*pushed*). Por muchos años, ir en carreta fué un medio de transporte (*transportation*) prohibido a los indios.

II. Chiste

Un ingeniero (*engineer*) norteamericano, construyendo un ferrocarril en México hace algunos años, trataba de explicarle a un indio cómo le serviría un tren.

— ¿Cuánto tiempo necesita Vd. para llevar al mercado (*market*) sus productos? — preguntó el ingeniero.

— Con mi burro, tres días, — respondió el campesino.

— ¡Eso sí que es! — exclamó el norteamericano. — Con este ferrocarril, podrá Vd. llevar sus productos al mercado y volver el mismo día.

— Muy bien, señor, — dijo el indio. — Pero, ¿qué hago los otros días?

TEMA

1. The people have met to ask that the gods make [it] rain. 2. Since the very day on which the horse became ill, it has not rained. 3. The Mayas hoped it would get better, but it died. 4. Then the king called his slaves and ordered them to make a stone horse. 5. They took golden food to this stone horse, believing that he must eat it. 6. The king offered him a jade knife and an emerald bird as gifts. 7. The horse had brought a great misfortune to the Mayas, especially when it died. 8. That night they gave it the name of «*tzimimchac*», and put it into the waters of the lake. 9. It was moonlight, and they did it without anyone's knowing it. 10. There it remains to this day, where one can see it from time to time. 11. What a sad story!

The Andean Countries — and Paraguay

Andean pass, at altitude of 15,000 feet, gives a good view of the tortuous mountain road. Where once pack mules and llamas carried all the freight, busses now climb zigzag grades.

Sawders

PIZARRO, as you have heard, was copying Cortés and the conquest of Mexico when he left Panama for a Peru that was then almost a myth. His discovery and conquest of the great Incan civilization high in the Andes brought Spanish culture to the mountain regions of South America, from which it spread over the remainder of the modern Spanish-speaking countries of the continent.

Of all the countries of the southernmost America, those which reach up into the Andes are the most different, geographically speaking, from ours. Those which once made up the Incan Empire — Ecuador, Peru, and Bolivia — are often called the Andean countries, but they share with the Caribbean countries of Colombia and Venezuela the dominating geographical feature of the continent — that immense, overpowering chain of mountains with its inescapable influence on climate, peoples, products, and even history.

Climate in these South American countries is not a matter of latitude, or distance from the equator, as it is with us, but one of altitude, or height above sea level. Each of the Andean countries, even inland Bolivia, has its torrid zone, either along the seacoast or inland east of the Andes. Where there is rainfall, this torrid zone is a tropical jungle; where there is not, the hot country is desert. The temperate zone begins at three or four thousand feet above sea level, and the frigid zone is still higher, where eternal snows always whiten the mountains. At each level the climate is almost the same the year around, with no seasonal changes as we know them.

In all these Andean republics except Peru, the capital city has been located inland, high above the zone of tropical heat, and in most cases, only seaports and towns necessary for the exploitation of tropical industries are found in the often unhealthful lowlands, for human beings prefer to live in the pleasant "eternal spring" of the temperate altitudes.

Thus it is that the towering Andean heights dominating these countries have separated one from another, divided the countries themselves into independent sections, defied railroads and highways with their precipices and gorges, and stubbornly turned history this way and that with their unbelievable size. Mount Aconcagua, the highest peak of the Andes, is nearly 24,000 feet high; Chimborazo, in Ecuador, is over 20,000; and the capitals of all the Andean countries except Peru's Lima are over 3000 feet above sea level, with La Paz, Bolivia, claiming the honor of being the world's highest capital, at 11,000 feet. Their inaccessibility, due to this mountainous terrain,

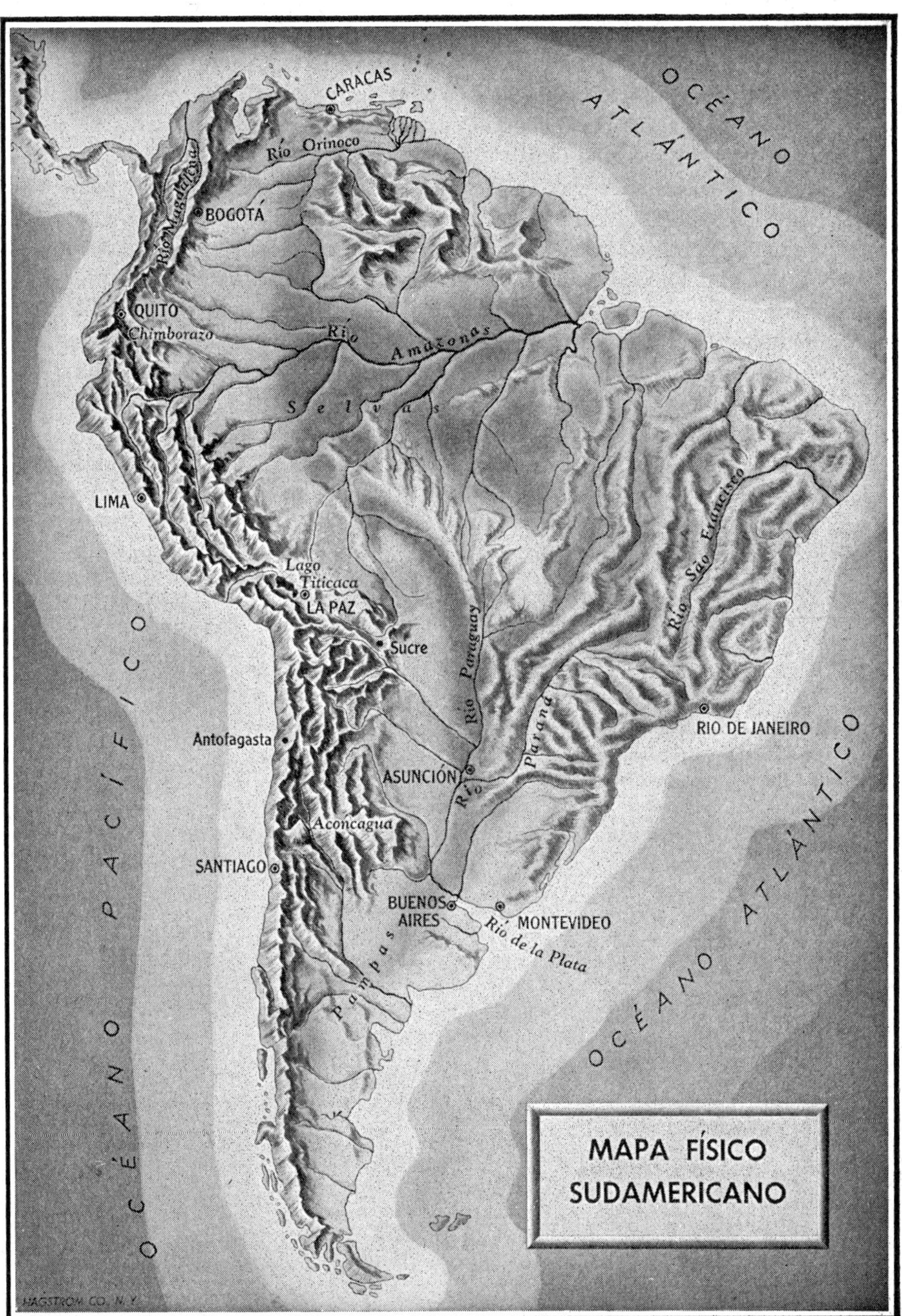

CARACAS
OCÉANO ATLÁNTICO
Río Orinoco
Río Magdalena
BOGOTÁ
QUITO
Chimborazo
Río Amazonas
Selvas
LIMA
Lago Titicaca
LA PAZ
Sucre
Río Paraguay
Río São Francisco
OCÉANO PACÍFICO
Antofagasta
ASUNCIÓN
Río Paraná
RIO DE JANEIRO
Aconcagua
SANTIAGO
BUENOS AIRES
MONTEVIDEO
Río de la Plata
Pampas
OCÉANO ATLÁNTICO
MAPA FÍSICO SUDAMERICANO
HAGSTROM CO., N. Y.

has kept many of these cities, like Quito in Ecuador and Bogotá in Colombia, colonial in appearance and spirit until only yesterday, when modern airplanes conquered chasms and cliffs and carried in on silver wings a new century of progress.

So, as the condor sees them from the heights, the Andean countries look much alike, and their Spanish heritage gives them many things in common in their language, customs, architecture, and religion. But look at them more closely and you will find them quite varied in their characteristics. Colombia, as you have read, is democratic and intellectual and free; Ecuador, which bestrides the equator from which it receives its name, is very religious and has many economic problems, the latter because the cacao trees which once furnished its chief export crop are now blighted. Ecuador is also very Indian, and many of its people still live much as they did in colonial days. Even though Ecuador's Indians are poor, they are able to raise their own food, and so they are less likely to suffer extreme want than those of the Andes farther away from the equator.

Aristocratic Peru, its beautiful Lima in colonial times the roman-

Highest capital in the world, La Paz, Bolivia, lies at the bottom of a valley over a thousand feet deep, where the climate is always cool because of the altitude — eleven thousand feet.

Sawders

Along Andean trails travel herds of snobbish-looking llamas, the camels of the mountains, carrying their small loads. Once wild, all have been domesticated, and are often household pets of the Indians.

tic Spanish capital of the southern New World, is wealthier. In the rich valleys of the coastal plains life is pleasant, and charming and cultured people live there, many of them graduates of San Marcos, the oldest university on the continent. At the same time, in the cold highlands of the Andes above them live many illiterate descendants of the Indians of the Incan Empire, knowing and caring so little about such things as modern civilization and self-government that the ruling class can do little either with or for them. This Indian problem, which apparently no one knows how to solve, is the current headache of many Latin-American countries, for how can they be truly democratic when so many of their inhabitants are content to live on in the primitive fashion of pre-conquest days?

Locked high in the Andes, without a coastal plain like Peru's to make life easier with its luxuriant crops, is chilly, barren Bolivia with its great Indian population whose life among the tin and copper mines at that breath-taking altitude is hard at best. A war with Chile over the boundary line in 1883 lost for Bolivia her Pacific seaport with its wealth of nitrate; another in the nineteen-thirties with Paraguay lost thousands of acres in the sparsely populated lowland jungle east of the Andes. Today the tourist in Bolivia sees plump, rosy-cheeked Indian women or *cholas* dressed in bright colors, cheerfully doing much of the hard work because their men have died in battle.

Dropping down from the Andes on the east we find rural Paraguay, even more a "land of women" than is Bolivia, but a tropical and agricultural country instead of one where life is cold and uncomfortable. Economically and culturally almost entirely dependent upon powerful Argentina, this country, that in colonial times locked itself in and refused to deal with outsiders, is now trying to overcome the handicaps of its warlike history and make itself as modern as it is pleasant and picturesque. There is no Indian problem here, for the intelligent and independent Guaraní Indians of the region absorbed the Spaniards rather than being dominated by them, and although Paraguay has its economic difficulties, its people are charming and intelligent.

Each country has its own set of economic, political, and social problems, along with its own individual personality. And all of them, whether they perch upon the backbone of the Andes or nestle in the lowland jungle, have in their people the common heritage of language and courtesy and dignity that we are learning to expect in our study of our good neighbors.

In the following chapters you will read tales of these countries in legends and fables, history and fiction.

Two-man-power threshing machine in the Andes of Peru depends on the chilly breeze to separate the wheat from the chaff. It is always cold at this altitude of twelve thousand feet.

Sawders

Sawders

Andean highway traffic near La Paz often runs into the heavy wet fogs which hang over the mountains, and which make the narrow road very dangerous.

Interesting Books to Read

Incas and the Conquest: NILES, BLAIR: PERUVIAN PAGEANT. Bobbs-Merrill. (*The story of Peru reviewed so that its history is as interesting as fiction*) — MAGOFFIN *and* DAVIS: THE ROMANCE OF ARCHEOLOGY, ch. XIII. Doubleday, Doran. (*Lives of the Indians of the Incan Empire before the conquest*) — NILES, BLAIR: DAY OF IMMENSE SUN. Bobbs-Merrill. (*Fiction wrapped up in Peru's Incan days*) — ROTHERY, AGNES: SOUTH AMERICAN ROUNDABOUT. Dodd, Mead. (*The story of the conquest vividly told*)

Peru: WILDER, THORNTON: THE BRIDGE OF SAN LUIS REY. Grosset and Dunlap. (*Fiction based on Peru's colonial days*) — CARR, KATHERINE: SOUTH AMERICAN PRIMER. Reynal and Hitchcock. (*Modern customs and people*)

Ecuador: VON HAGEN, V. W.: ECUADOR, THE UNKNOWN. Oxford University Press. (*A naturalist-explorer wanders around this fascinating country*)

Bolivia: OVERBECK, ALICIA: LIVING HIGH. Appleton-Century. (*Tales of life in the mining towns of Bolivia*)

Paraguay: CRAIG, C. W.: PARAGUAYAN INTERLUDE. Stokes. (*Scenes of Paraguayan life*)

CAPÍTULO 20

La cadena de oro del Titicaca[1]

It is impossible to visit or read about the Andean countries that straddle that stupendous mountain chain without running into stories of the Incas and their Empire, although not a living person bears that name now.[2] The dizzily high cold Empire of the "People of the Sun," efficiently and paternally governed from its capital, Cuzco, once stretched over two thousand miles along the Andes from the equator south as far as modern Argentina. To this day Ecuador, Bolivia, and Peru have a great Indian population in the descendants of the Incan tribes, mainly the Quichuas and Aymarás.

People who trimmed buildings with gold because they thought it a thing of beauty instead of something to spend were bound to be hunted out by the Spaniards. One rumor that nearly drove the conquerors wild after the conquest was the one whispered about the missing chain of the Incas. The story went that an Incan Empress had once had made in honor of her son, Huayna Capac, a huge golden chain which weighed thousands of pounds, and which was used to enclose the great square of Cuzco during festivals. Even our prosaic histories tell how it was supposed to have been thrown into a lake near Cuzco at the time of the conquest, and how forty Spaniards

[1] Lake Titicaca is the highest large navigable lake in the world — a cold blue sea over 12,000 feet up in the Andes between Peru and Bolivia, with cozy little lake steamers puffing across it daily.

[2] The ruler of the Empire was known as *The Inca.* Members of the ruling family and their descendants were commonly called *Incas.* Their empire consisted of the many tribes whom they conquered and ruled, all called *Incans.*

and two hundred Indians worked three months draining the lake and searching for it — but never found it.

This story, by a modern Peruvian, tells why they didn't succeed, and why no one ever will.

I

Todos sabían en la hacienda que Paucar, el viejo capataz (*overseer*), había oído de los labios de sus padres cuentos maravillosos del tiempo del Imperio, pues no era raro ver, a la caída de la tarde, sentarse a los indios alrededor de él cuando cesaban sus labores, para escuchar atentos las palabras que salían de su boca en su lengua nativa: el quichua.[1] Pero bastaba que uno de nosotros se acercara un poco, para que cesara el cuento y sólo se percibiera el mascar (*chewing*) de la coca.[2]

Era a mí, el hijo menor del patrón, a quien había visto desde niño, al que Paucar tenía más afecto.

— Paucar, — había preguntado yo al viejo, — ¿qué es lo que cuentas a los peones (*laborers*)?

— Cosas viejas, niño.

— Y ¿por qué callas cuando yo me acerco?

— No callo, niño; es que se acaba el cuento.

La respuesta no me satisfacía. — Paucar, cuéntame a mí también esas cosas viejas.

Y después de hacerme rogar un rato, varias veces Paucar me dejaba oír, en la monótona (*monotonous*) dulzura (*sweetness*) de la lengua quichua, episodios de una vida enteramente nueva para mí, y que la llegada (*arrival*) de los españoles había destruido.

[1] *Quichua* (sometimes spelled *quechua*) was the language of the Incas and it is still spoken by the Indians of Peru.

[2] In the cold, barren highlands of Peru and Bolivia the Indians make life bearable by chewing coca leaves with lime, for, since coca leaves contain cocaine, this deadens the feeling of cold and hunger, and makes them able to work beyond the usual limits of physical endurance.

Sawders

Light boats made of rushes skitter across chilly Lake Titicaca like leaves before the wind. Even horses are sometimes carried across the great lake on these *balsas*.

II

Los diarios que llegaban de la Capital [1] trajeron a la hacienda una feliz noticia. Hablaban de unos papeles recién encontrados que pertenecían a uno de los primeros conquistadores. En ellos el español contaba que había oído una conversación entre dos indios que dijeron que en el Lago Titicaca, situado (*situated*) a pocas leguas (*leagues*) de nosotros, se hallaba sumergido (*submerged*) un enorme tesoro: una cadena de oro puro, en la que cada eslabón (*link*) formaba la mano de un hombre. Era esto algo maravilloso. — ¿Quién sería el afortunado que conseguiría hallar el tesoro? — era la pregunta con que terminaba la gran noticia.

[1] The capital mentioned is Lima, Peru.

Como bandada (*band*) de pájaros emigrantes, vino de Lima un gran número de personas que hacían preguntas a cualquier indio que se pusiese a su paso. Yo mismo, al oír la noticia, pensé que podía ser mío el tesoro. ¿Quién mejor que Paucar podía darme la clave (*key*) de aquel misterio?

Mas en vano yo le hacía preguntas, porque su única respuesta era, — No puedes hallar el tesoro, niño. Paucar no puede dártelo.

En mi cabeza nació una idea: tal vez una promesa (*promise*) cerraba la boca de Paucar, pero yo le haría hablar. Bien recordaba que hacía muchos años, cuando murió la mujer de Paucar, su pena fué tan grande que bebió mucha chicha,[1] pidió prestada una quena,[2] tocó muchos «tristes»,[3] y habló de cosas que yo jamás había oído.

III

El techo (*ceiling*) de la habitación era bajo. Llovía torrencialmente afuera, y dentro, cuatro o cinco parroquianos (*customers*) bebían su chicha en silencio.

Al entrar, vimos en el fondo, casi perdido en la sombra, a un indio viejo.

— Por fin le encontramos, — murmuré al oído de mi compañero.

Ambos arrogantes e impetuosos, como buenos españoles, teníamos que andar con cautela (*caution*) si queríamos arrancar del indio su secreto. — Vamos, Paucar, ¿quieres tomar una copa (*"drink"*) conmigo?

— Con gusto, niño. — Yo era ya un hombre, pero él seguía llamándome «niño» siempre.

[1] *Chicha* is an ancient Indian drink made from fermented corn and sometimes flavored with fruit juices. Even North Americans who live in the Andes learn to like it.

[2] A *quena* is an Indian flute made originally from a long slender bone, which the lonely Andean llama-herder uses to while away the hours.

[3] A «*triste*» is a certain kind of mournful song heard in the Argentine as well as among the Andean Indians. On the Argentine pampas it is accompanied by a guitar instead of a *quena*.

Después de la primera copa bebimos otra a la salud de mi compañero, e inevitablemente la tercera a la salud de Paucar, y luego otra y otra. — Es el momento, — pensé yo, y le pregunté, — Paucar, cuéntame del tesoro del Titicaca... ¿Cómo fué aquello?

Volviéndose rápidamente, me miró...

— No lo encontrarán, — murmuró, — y por lo tanto, no podrán llevárselo. Fué allá, en los últimos tiempos del Imperio, cuando Huayna Capac era Emperador, y su poder (*power*) iba extendiéndose cada vez más con sus victorias. Y después de las guerras, cuando nació su hijo, el futuro Soberano, los guerreros que habían combatido con el Emperador y que le amaban formaron la gran cadena de oro puro que fué echada al lago sagrado en conmemoración de tan glorioso día.

— Pero, ¿en qué lugar la echaron? — pregunté.

— No la encontrarán nunca, porque los hombres blancos sólo llaman oro al rubio metal,[1] y la cadena fué de algo más que oro.

— ¿De qué fué, entonces?

Como si no hubiese oído mi pregunta, continuó. — Me parece como si aún oyera el cuento que me contó mi padre, como a él el suyo.[2] Fué una mañana de sol. Todos los guerreros con sus tributos salieron al lago sagrado, formando con sus balsas una cadena de orilla a orilla. Y todas las balsas ardieron (*burned*) a la vez, mientras los quipucamayos[3] trenzaron (*braided*) el blanco cordón (*cord*) que significaba el nacimiento del nuevo Soberano. Y fué echada al Lago Sagrado la cadena de oro purísimo que ofrecieron los guerreros al Padre Sol: oro de corazones que se echaron al agua en

[1] The "personal *a*" is used here only to show which word is the object of the verb.

[2] ***como a él el suyo,*** *as his* (*told it*) *to him.*

[3] ***quipucamayos,*** *quipu keepers.* The ancient Incas did not know how to read or write, but kept accounts and even recorded some history with bunches of knotted strings called *quipus.* Different colors and kinds of knots and spaces meant certain things, although only trained persons could read the story. Here the legend seems to indicate that braiding in a white cord means the birth of an heir to the Emperor.

agradecimiento (*gratitude*) por el nacimiento del nuevo Soberano.[1]

— Es ésta la leyenda del Lago Titicaca, que guarda el secreto de su inmenso tesoro: una cadena de oro purísimo en que cada eslabón (*link*) fué un hombre, y que nunca le podrá ser arrebatada (*taken away*).

Y su voz se apagó (*died out*) suavemente, como la luz se extingue cuando muere el día...

ADAPTED FROM LUISA FONSECA RECAVARREN (*La Crónica, Lima, Peru*)

PALABRAS NUEVAS

3	**afecto**	affection	4	**imperio**	empire
	afuera	outside	3	**labio**	lip
3	**arrancar**	to draw out		**nacimiento**	birth
4	**atento**	attentive	3	**oído**	ear (inner)
	balsa	reed boat		**patrón** (*m.*)	boss
4	**cadena**	chain	3	**pertenecer**	to belong
	emperador	emperor		**quichua** (*m.*)	Indian of Peru; the language he speaks
	extinguirse	to die away			
2	**guerra**	war	4	**respuesta**	answer
	guerrero	warrior	4	**soberano**	sovereign
3	**habitación**	room	*	**vamos**	come
4	**hacienda**	large ranch			

EXPRESIONES

a su paso, in their way
de sol, sunny
***por fin,** at last
***por lo tanto,** therefore

PREGUNTAS

1. ¿Qué hacían los labradores a la caída de la tarde? 2. ¿Por qué callaba Paucar siempre al acercarse los niños españoles? 3. ¿Cuál era la noticia de los periódicos? 4. ¿Qué hizo un gran nú-

[1] To throw oneself into Lake Titicaca is certain death, for the water is so icy and the air so rare that no one can swim in it. Although the Quichua Indians cross it daily in their light *balsas*, they never attempt to learn to swim.

mero de personas? 5. ¿Quería Paucar decir el secreto del tesoro? 6. ¿Qué le dieron a Paucar para hacerle hablar? 7. ¿Cómo celebraron los indios el nacimiento del futuro soberano? 8. ¿Se puede nadar en las aguas del Lago Titicaca? 9. ¿De qué se formó la cadena famosa? 10. ¿Por qué fué echada en el lago sagrado? 11. ¿Por qué dieron la vida los guerreros?

¿VERDAD O NO?

Change the statements that are false to make them true.

1. Paucar no había oído nada de los labios de sus padres. 2. Los indios se sentaban alrededor de él para escuchar cuentos en español. 3. Varias veces Paucar contaba al niño cosas viejas. 4. Los diarios de la Capital trajeron a la hacienda la noticia de la conquista. 5. Muchos habitantes de Lima fueron a buscar la cadena. 6. Paucar sabía el secreto del misterio. 7. Después de beber mucha chicha, Paucar quería ir a buscar la cadena. 8. Los guerreros que habían combatido con Huayna Capac le amaban muchísimo. 9. Los españoles llamaban oro al rubio metal. 10. Los guerreros se echaron de sus balsas al agua, pero todos sabían nadar. 11. La «cadena de oro» todavía se halla bajo las aguas del Lago Titicaca.

REPASO DE VERBOS

I. See how quickly you can give the infinitives of these verbs:

doy, salga, hizo, vinieron, vieron, vendré, venderé, quiso, hecho, oyendo, dicho, iba, cojo, río, supongo, devuelto, conviniese, persiguieron, demuestran, descubierto, desaparecía, sonriendo, contuvo, convendrá, se despidió, descrito, resuelto, consigo

II. Tell the tense or form of each verb in Exercise I.

III. En español:

I begin to eat, I hope to eat, I am going to eat, I can't eat, I have learned to eat, I come to eat, I dare to eat, I prefer to eat, I want to eat, I dream of eating

ALGO NUEVO

49. *Feminine* el *and* un

el agua, el hambre, un alma

El is used with feminine nouns beginning with stressed ***a*** or ***ha***, because it sounds better, just as we say *an apple* instead of *a apple.* Before such a noun ***una*** usually becomes ***un.*** This does not change the gender of the noun, and adjectives modifying it must be feminine. What articles will be used in the plural?

EJERCICIO I. *Complete in Spanish:*

1. *the* agua *cold* 2. *the* aguas *cold* 3. *the* amistad *sacred* 4. *the* águila (*eagle*) *blind* 5. *an* alma *precious* 6. *the* aventura *last* 7. *an* abuela *tall* 8. *the* hambre *first* 9. *the* alegría *daily* 10. *the* álgebra *daily* 11. *the* Alhambra *beautiful* 12. *an* arte *new* [1]

[1] *Arte* may be either masculine or feminine.

Aymará Indian shepherd amuses himself by playing simple tunes on the ancient *quena,* originally made of a human leg bone. His knitted cap and woolen blanket are necessary for warmth.

"One-man band" in the Bolivian Andes wears a fiesta headdress of ostrich plumes and plays monotonous melodies on ancient Aymará pipes as he beats his drum.

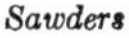

Sawders

50. *Uses of the Definite Article* [1]

a. **el año pasado**	*last year* (with a modified expression of time)
b. **son las diez**	*it is ten o'clock* (telling the hour)
c. **me gustan las manzanas**	*I like apples* (noun used in a general sense)
d. **es el señor Méndez**	*it is Mr. Méndez* (with a title except in direct address)
e. **el pobre de Lope**	*poor Lope* (name modified by adjective except in direct address)

As shown above the definite article is used in Spanish in many cases where it is omitted in English.

EJERCICIO II. *Referring to the examples listed above, give the letter of the example which is the model for each of these expressions:*

1. el mes que viene 2. Es la hermosa María. 3. a eso de las once 4. Prefiere el oro a la plata. 5. Buenos días, señor López. 6. la semana próxima 7. El pan es necesario. 8. ¿Le gustan a Vd. los cuentos? 9. El capitán Cortés llegó. 10. Ví al atento Pedro.

51. *Omission of the Indefinite Article* [2]

no tengo pluma	**sin reloj**	**no hay manera de ir**
I haven't a pen	*without a watch*	*there isn't a way to go*

After a negative, the indefinite article is often omitted.

EJERCICIO III. *Translate, showing the lack of the indefinite article in Spanish:*

[1] Note to teacher: The omission of the definite article with nouns in apposition is not stressed because Keniston's study shows it to be used much more often than omitted.

[2] Note to teacher: The use of the indefinite article with modified or unmodified predicate nouns (*es alumno, es un alumno; es buen alumno, es un buen alumno*), according to Keniston's study, has no set rule which makes it worthy of study at this stage.

Likewise, there is no set rule for the omission of the indefinite article with nouns in apposition, for it is used in one-third of the cases studied and omitted in the remainder, apparently at the discretion of the writer.

Sawders

Potosí, the "Silver Mountain" of Bolivia, from which the Spaniards took untold fortunes in colonial days, still towers over its cold little Andean town, one of the highest in the world.

1. No tenemos caballo. 2. No podemos ir sin automóvil. 3. No hay soldado sin uniforme. 4. ¿Por qué no lleva Vd. sombrero? 5. Ya no tengo sombrero ni gorra (*cap*).

EJERCICIO IV. *Translate the preceding sentences again, using* any *instead of the missing article.* How, then, do you often express the idea "any" in Spanish? (There isn't any "any"!)

ESTUDIO DE PALABRAS

Complete with one of the three words or groups of words suggested:

1. Yo era el hijo (*menos, menor, mayor*) del patrón. 2. Los indios se sentaban (*fuera del, encima del, alrededor del*) viejo Paucar. 3. El patrón (*lavó, llevó, llegó*) el diario a la hacienda. 4. Fué preciso llevar al viejecito sobre (*las hambres, los hombres, los hombros*). 5. Cuando (*hay polvo, hay luna, llueve*) uno se protege del agua. 6. Para cruzar los Andes en avión, hay que (*velar, valer, volar*) muy alto. 7. Después de pedir prestado el dinero, tendremos que (*volver,*

regresar, devolver) lo. 8. Nos preguntó (*cuanto, cuento, cuánto*) dinero teníamos. 9. A veces hace mucho (*veinte, viento, vano*) durante una tempestad. 10. Los domingos, los que tienen automóvil dan un (*paso, peso, paseo*).

REPASITO

I. Complete in Spanish (§ *29*):

1. Los indios de los Andes viven en *stone houses.* 2. Los conquistadores buscaban *the gold chain* en el lago. 3. Los niños se comieron *the candy hearts.* 4. Delante de la ventana había una *silk curtain.* 5. En la *Coconut Island* se dice que hay escondido un tesoro. 6. Antes de buscarlo, hay que tener *government permission.* 7. Solamente un *miracle man* podría encontrarlo. 8. Un *freight plane* lleva muchas cosas de un país a otro en Centroamérica. 9. *Clay bottles* se encuentran en las tumbas (*tombs*) de los antiguos indios de la costa del Perú. 10. El *day train* llega a eso de las ocho de la noche. 11. Los españoles guardaban sus monedas en una *iron box.*

II. Complete each sentence in Spanish:

1. Dijo *some* palabras en la lengua quichua. 2. La gente *French* rara vez habla quichua. 3. En la *same* habitación había *one hundred* personas. 4. Yo recordaba *a certain* incidente en la vida del viejo. 5. Yo no era el hijo *oldest* del patrón, sino *the youngest.* 6. Con la *last* copa de chicha, empezó a hablar. 7. Fué con *little* gusto que escucharon sus palabras. 8. Dijo que *several* guerreros se habían echado al agua. 9. *None* de ellos sabía nadar en las aguas frías. 10. *Such a* cosa no podría pasar en nuestro país.

PARA LEER SIN ESTUDIAR

Unas cosas interesantes acerca de Bolivia

Bolivia era antiguamente una parte de la República del Perú, pero se le dió este nombre después de ganar la independencia, cuando Simón Bolívar mismo escribió la nueva constitución.

La capital de Bolivia, La Paz,[1] es la capital más alta del mundo,

[1] Sucre is actually the capital, but La Paz is the center of activities and is usually called the capital.

Sawders

Bolivian halfbreeds at the "Fiesta of Little Things" in La Paz sell miniature good-luck charms representing anything the buyer may wish.

aunque está situada al fondo de un valle profundo (*deep*). Tiene una altura de unos 11.000 pies sobre el nivel del mar.

Bolivia es un país donde más de la mitad (*half*) de los habitantes son indios, muchos de los cuales todavía hablan la lengua quichua, como los indios del Perú. También es una «tierra de mujeres», porque murieron tantos hombres en la guerra del Chaco [1] con el Paraguay entre 1932 y 1935.

Las indias de Bolivia llevan hasta diez y seis faldas (*skirts*) de colores vivos, con una blusa (*blouse*) de otro color y un mantón (*shawl*) también de diferente color. El sombrero que lleva cada india es un hongo (*derby*) de color obscuro, y les gusta tanto este sombrero que ni siquiera se lo quitan (*take off*) dentro de la casa.

Para prender (*pin*) el mantón, las indias usan prendedores (*pins*) de plata o de cobre (*copper*), en forma de cucharita o de pez (*fish*), emblema de la buena suerte en Bolivia.

Hay tantas llamas en Bolivia que se ve una hasta en el escudo (*coat of arms*) nacional, pero se prohibe que entren estos animales dentro los límites de la capital, porque estorban (*hinder*) el tráfico.

[1] The Chaco is a lowland region between Bolivia and Paraguay, and was claimed by both countries. War was about to begin again in 1938, but all South America protested so loudly at breaking the peace of the continent that delegates finally settled the matter peaceably at Buenos Aires.

Las minas de plata del Potosí, con sus extraordinarias riquezas, han dado al mundo la expresión «vale un Potosí», que quiere decir que algo vale muchísimo. También hay minas de cobre (*copper*), y de éste hacen los indios objetos útiles, usando los mismos métodos que usaban los filisteos (*Philistines*) hace muchos siglos.

TEMA

1. Paucar was an old Quichua who worked on the hacienda. 2. The other Indians used to sit down around him and listen to the old things (that) he told. 3. But when I went near, he always stopped talking. 4. Last week we read in the daily [paper] that a golden chain had been thrown into the lake. 5. The man who should find it would be the richest man in (the) Peru. 6. I wanted Paucar to tell me the secret, but he would not (was not willing to). 7. We hoped that he would drink enough *chicha* to make him talk. 8. But instead of talking, poor Paucar borrowed a *quena* and played «*tristes*» all day. 9. At last we invited him to go with us to the sacred lake. 10. There we crossed silently to the other shore over the cold water. 11. Treasure stories are often heard in countries with an old civilization.

El Misti, Peru's favorite volcano, is a perfect snow-capped cone which guards the city of Arequipa.

Sawders

CAPÍTULO 21

La conquista del Perú

It's a long story of how Pizarro made his way to Peru and finally reached the Empire of the Incas in the high Andes. What happened when he arrived is much like the story of the conquest of Mexico, for luck and superstition made it possible for a few hardy Spaniards and their horses to capture the Inca Emperor, Atahualpa, and to conquer the intelligent and well-armed people of an empire far more vast than that of the King of Spain.

This is the story as it is told to Spanish-speaking young people, who hear about it from the time they enter the first grade, as we do our tales of the Pilgrims, Miles Standish, Captain John Smith, and Pocahontas.

Pizarro, impaciente por saber el recibimiento que podría esperar de Atahualpa, que estaba en Cajamarca,[1] envió dos embajadores españoles a invitarle a comer con él al día siguiente, rogando a Su Majestad que les dijese dónde debían arreglar sus cuarteles (*barracks*).

Atahualpa respondió que estaba observando un ayuno (*fast*) que duraría hasta la mañana siguiente, pero que entonces tendría el gusto de visitar a Pizarro, y que entretanto, sus huéspedes (*guests*) podían ocupar el tambo (*inn*) [2] real en la gran plaza de la ciudad.

[1] Atahualpa was holding court at Cajamarca just then, although his capital was Cuzco, which he had just taken from his brother.

[2] All along the ancient Incan highways that led along the Andes from the equator far to the south, were inns, called *tambos*, where travelers might stay.

Gran sorpresa causó a los indios ver a aquellos hombres vestidos de acero (*steel*), manejando caballos que veían por primera vez, y les parecía que hombre y caballo eran un solo ser. Se sorprendieron más aún cuando vieron que este monstruo (*monster*) podía descomponerse (*come apart*), y cuando observaron que los caballos tascaban (*champed*) los frenos (*bits*), creían que se alimentaban con metales y les presentaban oro para que comieran.

La espléndida corte del Inca,[1] con sus cincuenta mil soldados, convenció a los embajadores de Pizarro de que sería imposible conquistar a los incas, y regresaron al campamento (*camp*) muy tristes.

Pero Pizarro no se declaró vencido, e hizo su plan de acción. Harían un ataque repentino y se apoderarían del Inca en medio de sus soldados. Para facilitar el plan de Pizarro, Atahualpa le envió un embajador para decirle que la mayor parte de sus soldados le acompañarían, pero sin armas.

Al día siguiente, poco antes de la puesta del sol, empezó a pasar la procesión real. Primero venía un grupo de lacayos (*footmen*) que limpiaban el camino, cosa que hacían siempre cuando viajaba el Inca. Luego seguían los heraldos, que anunciaban la aproximación (*approach*) del soberano; luego los nobles y príncipes de sangre real, y por último, el Inca, rodeado de guardias, con su palanquín (*litter*) real adornado de ricas plumas y planchas (*sheets*) de oro y plata. El monarca estaba sentado en un trono de oro, ricamente vestido, y llevaba un collar de esmeraldas y brillantes muy grandes.

Cuando la procesión llegó a la plaza de Cajamarca, Atahualpa, viendo que nadie salía a recibirle, preguntó, — ¿Dónde están los extranjeros?

— Se esconden de miedo, — le contestaron los suyos.

Pero en ese instante, un sacerdote español salió a la plaza con un crucifijo (*crucifix*) en una mano y la Biblia en la otra. Acercándose al Inca, le habla [2] de la verdadera fe, pide al

[1] "The Inca" was the official name of the ruler only.

[2] In an exciting story, the present instead of the past tense is often used for actions, to make them more vivid.

Inca que abrace el cristianismo y que se declare vasallo (*vassal*) del Emperador de España.

Todo esto lo traducía Felipillo,[1] mientras Atahualpa escuchaba, al principio con curiosidad, después con desdén, y finalmente con violenta indignación.

— Yo soy el príncipe más grande de la tierra, y no seré vasallo de nadie, — exclamó, echando al suelo la Biblia que el padre le había dado, porque no sabía nada de libros.

Pizarro, comprendiendo el peligro, da la señal [2] convenida, y salen los españoles. El ruido de los arcabuces (*guns*) y cañones, de las trompetas, y de los caballos llena de miedo a los indefensos peruanos, que huyen como si fuesen víctimas de un terremoto o de una maldición (*curse*) del cielo.

[1] Felipillo was the official interpreter.

[2] The signal was — *¡Santiago!* The old Spanish war cry was *¡Santiago y cierra España!* in honor of Spain's patron saint, St. James.

Llama pack trains of Peru, with their small, neat loads, still cross Andean rivers on crude suspension bridges like those the Incas built hundreds of years ago.

Sawders

Sawders

Streets of Cuzco show clearly how Spaniards wrecked Incan buildings during the conquest and afterwards rebuilt on top of the ruins. Which were the better builders — Incas or Spaniards?

Los nobles que en vano habían formado con sus cuerpos un escudo (*shield*) para defender al Inca, cayeron como soldados valientes en sus puestos, y Atahualpa fué hecho prisionero por los españoles. Uno de ellos trató de dar muerte al Inca, pero Pizarro le defendió, prefiriendo hacerle prisionero.

El listo Inca había observado que a los españoles les gustaba el oro. Prometió al conquistador darle por su libertad todo el oro que deseara. Poniéndose de pie en la prisión, Atahualpa dijo, haciendo una marca en la pared hasta donde pudo alcanzar, — Yo llenaré de oro el cuarto hasta esta altura, y dos veces de plata el cuarto inmediato (*next*).

Pizarro aceptó el ofrecimiento de Atahualpa.[1]

Adapted from E. Rosay, *Mi primera historia del Perú*

[1] At the time, Pizarro probably intended to keep his word, but later decided it was too dangerous to let Atahualpa live, and so had him strangled after the ransom had been collected. While he was a prisoner, Atahualpa learned to speak Spanish and play chess and card games with his guards.

PALABRAS NUEVAS

2	**alcanzar**	to reach	**embajador** (*m.*)	ambassador
3	**anunciar**	to announce	**monarca** (*m.*)	monarch
3	**el arma** (*f.*)	weapon	3 **peligro**	danger
	ataque (*m.*)	attack	3 **príncipe** (*m.*)	prince
	Biblia	Bible	**repentino**	sudden
	brillante (*m.*)	diamond	3 **rodear (de)**	to surround (with)
2	**comprender**	to comprehend	1 **ser** (*m. noun*)	being
4	**convencer de**	to convince	4 **soberano**	sovereign
	desdén (*m.*)	disdain		

In addition to the English meanings for the following new words, a few Spanish words which you have already had are given here to show you the derivation of the new ones.

3 **abrazar** (**brazo**), to embrace
alimentarse con (**alimento**), to feed on
apoderarse de (**poder**, *power*), to overpower
4 **conquistar** (**conquistador**), to conquer
cristianismo (**Cristo**), Christianity
facilitar (**fácil**), to make easy
indefenso (**defender**), defenseless
llenar de (**lleno de**), to fill with
ofrecimiento (**ofrecer**), offering
peruano (**Perú**), Peruvian
recibimiento (**recibir**), reception
2 **verdadero** (**verdad**), true

Expresiones

***al principio**, at first
dar muerte a, to kill
en medio de, in the midst of
la puesta del sol, sunset
los suyos, his people
ponerse de pie, to stand up
***por último**, finally

PARA COMPLETAR

1. Pizarro invitó a Atahualpa a .... 2. Atahualpa contestó que no podía porque .... 3. Los indios creían que los caballos comían metales, y .... 4. Los embajadores de Pizarro estaban convencidos de que no podrían .... 5. En la procesión real había grupos de .... 6. Un sacerdote español llevaba .... 7. Felipillo había aprendido a .... 8. Los indios huyeron porque tenían miedo del ruido de .... 9. Los nobles trataron de .... 10. El listo Inca sabía bien que ....

PREGUNTAS PERSONALES

1. ¿Le gusta a Vd. hallarse en peligro? 2. ¿Se levanta Vd. a la puesta del sol? 3. ¿Está Vd. rodeado de enemigos? 4. ¿Le tendría Vd. miedo a un caballo al verlo por primera vez? 5. ¿Quisiera Vd. alimentarse de oro? 6. ¿Puede Vd. convencer a su profesor de que no es necesario tener exámenes? 7. ¿Tiene Vd. la costumbre de abrazar a sus amigos como lo hacen los españoles? 8. ¿Sabía Vd. traducir fácilmente esta lección? 9. ¿Comprende Vd. siempre lo que ve? 10. ¿Es Vd. un ser humano?

REPASO DE VERBOS

Make these verb forms plural (if possible), and translate:

dije, sabrá, yo duerma, yo tuviese, Vd. fué, salgo, trayendo, sé, llegué, sigue tú, leído, voy, ten tú, saqué, dijo, dicho, dí, traigo, ha visto, yo pida, hable, yo sacase, irá, yo daría, soy, traduzco, estuvo, cayó, sintiendo, habría puesto, pusieses, dieras, ven tú

ALGO NUEVO

52. *Hace Meaning* For[1]

Hace un mes que no le *veo*, *I have not seen him for a month.*

Hace mucho tiempo que *estudiamos* el español, *we have been studying Spanish for a long time.*

When an action or state has begun in the past and is still continuing in the present, *for* is expressed by ***hace,*** with the other verb in the sentence in the present tense (*veo, estudiamos*). What tense do we use in English, when translating the sentence?

EJERCICIO I. *Translate these sentences, first, exactly as they are written; then as we say them in everyday English:*

1. Hace un año que aprendemos a hablar español. 2. Hace dos años que tenemos la misma profesora. 3. Hace dos días que es-

[1] Note to teacher: *Hacía* in this construction is so rare, according to Keniston, that it is not presented here.

tudiamos este capítulo. 4. Hace treinta minutos que estamos en esta clase. 5. Hace cinco minutos que tratamos de leer este ejercicio. 6. Hace dos minutos que miro esta frase.

EJERCICIO II. *Complete these sentences in Spanish, being sure* not *to use the exact translation of the verbs.* (Why?)

1. Hace cuatro siglos que los españoles *have lived* en la América del Sur. 2. Hace mucho tiempo que los indios *have tried to* aprender el español. 3. Hace cien años que los españoles *have been looking for* la cadena de oro. 4. Hace cuatrocientos años que la cadena *has been* bajo las aguas del lago. 5. Hace muchos años que los Incas *have not lived* en el Cuzco.

53. Use of Lo *for* Le

Lo ví en el camino, *I saw him on the road.*
Lo envié a la tienda, *I sent him to the store.*

You have learned to use ***lo*** for *it* (*m.*). Not everyone who uses Spanish, however, follows this form, for many writers use ***lo*** for *him.* In your own speech and composition, continue to use the usual form, as you have been taught, but since you will be reading stories whose authors use ***lo*** instead of ***le,*** you should be able to recognize this usage.[1]

EJERCICIO III. *Translate these sentences, showing that you realize the different meanings that can be intended by* **lo.**

1. No lo veo ahora. 2. Lo defendió. 3. Lo enviamos a la casa. 4. ¿Lo vió Vd. esta mañana? 5. No, pero lo ví ayer. 6. Lo ví sobre la mesa grande.

ESTUDIO DE PALABRAS[2]

I. ***Para las muchachas.*** (*Se prohibe a los muchachos leer esto. Ellos deben leer el Número II.*)

[1] Less commonly, one may find ***le*** used for ***lo*** (*it,* m.) and ***la*** for ***le*** (*to her*).

[2] Optional section, since words used here are not repeated unless introduced in the regular way.

Sawders

Beautiful Spanish colonial church of Arequipa now finds itself just across the brick-paved street from a modern drygoods store.

Secretos de belleza

Los hombres admiran un cutis (*skin*) suave. El cutis mal cuidado esconde su belleza y juventud. Cada día hay que limpiar el cutis con agua tibia (*warm*) y jabón (*soap*) puro, para prepararlo para cualquier otro tratamiento (*treatment*) de belleza que Vd. quiera emplear. Si desea Vd. corregir (*correct*) un cutis seco, aplíquese (*apply*) una crema buena. Esto lo hace suave y fresco y sirve como base para los polvos. Así su cutis no se afectará con el aire, el polvo, ni el sol.

Para su maquillaje (*make-up*), use Vd. colorete claro (*light*), obscuro o brillante, semejante (*like*) a la tez (*complexion*) individual. El lápiz para los labios debe ser de un color que atraiga (*attracts*) irrestiblemente a los hombres. Debe permanecer (*remain*) sobre los labios por muchas horas, y este secreto lo conocen las mujeres atractivas.

Las damas elegantes saben que las manos expresan su femineidad, y para tenerlas suaves, hay que usar una crema todos los días. Para hacer adorables las manos, úsese en las uñas (*nails*) un esmalte (*enamel*) que dé una nota de buen gusto, y distinción a las manos.

Un lavado con champú de huevo una vez por semana mantiene (*keeps*) el pelo limpio, brillante, y firme, y prolonga la duración de su permanente.

Sólo con todo este cuidado, puede una dama acercarse más al corazón de él.

(*Beauty expressions as used in Santiago de Chile*)

Words resembling others you know: ***belleza*** (*bello*), ***juventud*** (*joven*), ***colorete*** (*color*), ***femineidad*** (*femenino*), ***lavado*** (*lavar*)

Find these expressions in the article:

1. with warm water and soap
2. any other beauty treatment
3. apply a good cream
4. as a powder base
5. for your make-up
6. the lipstick
7. use on your nails
8. a washing with egg shampoo
9. the duration of your permanent
10. to come closer to *his* heart

II. ***Para los muchachos.*** (*Las muchachas no deben leer esto, sino el Número I.*) Guess any word that looks or sounds familiar!

Kid Yucatán, el nuevo ídolo boxístico, pudo noquear a Babe Azteca

La última función boxística que ha de celebrarse en la Arena Nacional resultó en una gloriosa exhibición.

La causa fué un muchacho que vino de Yucatán, que se ha convertido en el ídolo de los fanáticos.

Durante el segundo raund Babe envió a la lona (*canvas*) el yucateco en dos ocasiones, pero éste se levantó para tirar (*knock down*) cinco veces a Babe, siendo la última para la cuenta (*count*) de los diez segundos en el cuarto raund.

El Kid Yucatán primero le dió un derecho al solar plexus, luego un gancho (*hook*) izquierdo en la boca. Para el cuarto raund, le metió un ópercut, y la cosa estaba perdida para Babe, aunque peleó como los hombres. La quinta vez que fué a la lona ya no hubo remedio. Muchos minutos pasaron para que se repusiera (*come to*) después del nócaut.

Al terminar, el público echó al ring una buena cantidad de dinero para el campeón.

En la semifinal, Monterrey Kid perdió a manos de Paco López, no pudiendo con el ponch de Paco, que hizo un buen comeback.

(*Sports expressions as used in Mexico*)

New words: ***poder con,*** *to be able to "take"*; ***quinto,*** *fifth;* ***ya no hubo remedio,*** *all was lost* (*there was no longer a remedy*); ***pelear,*** *to fight*

Make a list of sports expressions borrowed from English.

REPASITO

Complete in Spanish:

1. Los domingos llevamos *our* traje nuevo.[1] 2. Nos ponemos *our best hats* [2] para ir a la iglesia. 3. Limpiamos *our* zapatos (botas) como si fuésemos limpiabotas. (*Guess!*) 4. Los niños llevan *white shirts* y *long trousers*. 5. Las niñas llevan *uniforms* en las escuelas de Guatemala. 6. Para tener buena salud, hay que cuidar bien *our* [3] *bodies*.[2]

7. ¿Le duelen *your teeth*? 8. No, pero *my eyes* me duelen. 9. ¿Se lavaron Vds. *your hands and faces*? 10. Sí, y también nos limpiamos *our teeth*. 11. ¿Se pusieron Vds. *your shoes*? 12. Sí, nos pusimos *our shoes*. 13. Y nos quitamos *our hats* al entrar en la casa. 14. Levanten Vds. *your right hands* si saben contestar. 15. Elena, llevas demasiado lápiz en *your lips*. 16. Niña, no te pongas la pluma en *your mouth*. 17. Cuéntense Vds. *your fingers* (**dedos**). 18. ¿Puede Vd. contarse *your teeth*? 19. Todos *my teeth* son muy buenos. 20. *Mine*, también. 21. Y vemos bien con *our eyes*, y oímos bien con *our ears* (*sing.*).

[1] Why singular?

[2] Singular or plural?

[3] **Do you actually say "our"?**

PARA LEER SIN ESTUDIAR

¿Sabía Vd. esto?

1. La moneda nacional del Perú se llama el «sol», porque los incas antiguos adoraban el sol.

2. La ocarina, instrumento musical muy popular hoy día entre los niños, fué inventada por los incas del Cuzco, centenares (*hundreds*) de años antes de la llegada de los españoles.

3. La «papa (patata) irlandesa (*Irish*)» tiene su origen en los Andes, donde hace muchos siglos que la cultivan los indios.

4. En Lima, capital del Perú, hoy día tienen una carrera (*race*) de caballos todos los años, llamada la «clásica Atahualpa», en memoria del último emperador inca.

5. En Chile hoy se vende en las tiendas una marca (*brand*) popular de aceite (*oil*) para cocinar (*cook*), llamado «Aceite Inca»; en México un aceite popular se llama «Aceite Conquistador».

6. Una vez los indios estaban para hacer prisionero a Pizarro, cuando uno de sus soldados se cayó del caballo. Esto sorprendió tanto a los indios, — que creían que hombre y caballo eran un solo ser, — que dejaron de perseguir (*pursue*) a los españoles y éstos consiguieron escaparse sin dificultad.

7. En la tierra de los incas no había hierro, y Pizarro tuvo que mandar hacer para sus caballos herraduras (*horseshoes*) de plata pura.

TEMA

1. The Incas lived in the Andes before the Spaniards came. 2. They had roads with bridges (**puentes**), and could receive news of any part of the Empire within a short time. 3. They believed that gold was something beautiful. 4. Everyone had to work, but all had plenty to eat and there were no beggars (**pordioseros**) or thieves. 5. When an Indian left his house, he put a stick (**palo**) against the door to show that he was not at home, and no one would [used to] enter. 6. Anyone who did not tell the truth was punished severely. 7. When an Inca Emperor died, his palace remained as it was, and the new Emperor had a new palace built. 8. No one knew how to read or write, but the *quipucamayos* knew how to count and record (**indicar**) their history with *quipus*.

CAPÍTULO 22

La camisa de Margarita

Lima, in the good old Spanish colonial days, was practically owned by the viceroys sent over from Spain, who brought with them their wealthy and more adventurous friends. The city thus became a court in itself, with as much pomp and splendor as Madrid.

In style and fashion there was a great deal of rivalry among the aristocratic *limeñas*, and in trying to outdo each other, they managed to dress more richly than the colonial dames of any other Latin-American city. People who visited Lima were astounded when they saw the ladies' gold-embroidered gowns, trimmed with fine imported laces. Even the slaves wore silk, and the men dressed in gay and elaborate outfits topped with colorful long capes.

The ladies of Lima were supposed to stay demurely in their own patios, and even their balconies were shuttered with dark wooden lattice work through which they could see but not be seen by the passersby. One of their colonial innovations in dress, however, unexpectedly brought them a great deal of freedom, for it covered them so completely that they could go out upon the street without being recognized. This was the modest *saya y manto,* a long skirt and a large shawl that covered head, shoulders, and face so well that one could never be sure whose bright eye was peeping through the small open space left by the shawl.

Ricardo Palma, a modern writer of Peru, became so interested in the life, customs, and traditions of the colonial days that he found out all he could and wrote stories about them —

partly true and partly imaginary — which are enjoyed by people all over Spanish America. He liked to find the origin of quaint sayings, and in this story of the eighteenth century he tells why the people of Lima still say, "as expensive as Margaret's *camisa*." [1]

Probable es que algunos de mis lectores (*readers*) hayan oído decir a las viejas de Lima, cuando quieren exagerar el valor de un artículo, — ¡Qué! ¡Si esto es más caro que la camisa de Margarita Pareja!

Pues, esta Margarita Pareja era la hija favorita de don Raimundo Pareja, caballero de Santiago.[2] La muchacha era una de esas limeñas que por su belleza hacen al mismo diablo persignarse (*cross himself*). Tenía un par de ojos que eran como dos torpedos cargados de dinamita (*dynamite*), y que hacían explosión sobre el alma de los galanes limeños.

Llegó por entonces de España un guapo joven, llamado don Luis Alcázar. Vivía con un tío rico, don Honorato, que era más altivo que el Cid.[3] Mientras el joven esperaba la ocasión de heredar la fortuna de su tío, nuestro don Luis vivía tan pelado [4] como un ratón, teniendo que comprarlo todo al fiado para pagar cuando mejorase la fortuna.

En la procesión de Santa Rosa [5] conoció don Luis a la linda Margarita. La muchacha le llenó el ojo y le flechó (*pierced*) el corazón. La [6] echó flores,[7] y aunque ella no le contestó ni sí ni no, dió a entender con sonrisitas y demás armas del arsenal femenino que el galán era plato muy de su gusto.

[1] Today **camisa** means a *shirt*, but in olden days it was also the name of the garment that was the great-grandmother of the modern slip or underskirt.

[2] A *caballero de Santiago* was a knight of an old military order of Spain.

[3] *El Cid* was Spain's national hero who used to fight the Moors.

[4] ***tan pelado como un ratón***, *as hairless (penniless) as a mouse.* A pun on the two meanings of *pelado.*

[5] Santa Rosa is the Patron Saint of Lima, and on her day there is a great procession attended by everyone, rich or poor.

[6] For this use of ***la***, see footnote 1 on page 303.

[7] "To throw flowers" in Spanish means to pay a compliment. It is considered perfectly correct for gentlemen to make audible, flattering comments about a pretty girl as she passes, and, in fact, a *señorita* thinks she is not attractive if the men say nothing!

Sawders

Spanish-Moorish type home on the Paseo Colón in Lima is one of the city's most beautiful houses. The statue in the parkway is typical of the Latin-American's love for the fine arts.

Como los novios olvidan que existe la aritmética, don Luis creyó que su pobreza no sería obstáculo, y fué a ver al padre de Margarita y le pidió la mano de su hija.

A don Raimundo no le gustó la petición, y le dijo al galán que Margarita era aún muy niña para tomar marido, a pesar de sus diez y ocho mayos. Pero no era esto la verdad. Era que don Raimundo no quería ser suegro de un pobretón;[1] y se lo dijo en confianza a uno de sus amigos, que fué con el chisme (*gossip*) a don Honorato. Éste, con lo altivo que era,[2] se enojó muchísimo.

— ¡Qué barbaridad! ¡Decir que no a mi sobrino! ¡Muchacho más gallardo no lo hay en todo Lima! ¡Tal insolencia no la he visto en mi vida! — gritó el tío altivo.

Entretanto, Margarita lloró y se arrancó el pelo, y si no amenazó con envenenarse (*poison herself*), fué porque todavía no se habían inventado los fósforos (*matches*). Perdía colores

[1] ***pobretón,*** *a very poor person.*

[2] ***con lo altivo que era,*** *haughty as he was.*

y carnes, hablaba de hacerse monja (*nun*), y gritaba, — ¡O de Luis o de Dios! [1]

Alarmóse su padre, llamó médicos y curanderas (*practitioners*), y todos declararon que la única medicina que podía salvarla no se vendía en la botica.

O casarla con el joven de su gusto, o llevarla al cementerio (*cemetery*). Tal fué el *ultimátum* médico.

Don Raimundo (¡al fin padre!), olvidándose de coger capa [2] y bastón, salió como loco para la casa de don Honorato, y le dijo,

— Vengo a que consienta Vd. en que mañana mismo se case su sobrino con Margarita, porque si no, la muchacha se nos muere.

— No puede ser, — contestó con desdén el tío. — Mi sobrino es un pobretón, y lo que Vd. debe buscar para su hija es un hombre que tenga mucha plata.

El diálogo fué borrascoso (*stormy*). Cuanto más rogaba don Raimundo, más se subía el tío a la parra,[3] y el padre ya iba a declararse vencido cuando dijo don Luis,

— Pero, tío, no somos cristianos si matamos a quien no tiene la culpa.

— ¿Tú estás satisfecho?

— De todo corazón, tío.

— Pues bien, muchacho. Consiento en darte gusto, pero con una condición, y es ésta: Don Raimundo me ha de jurar que no regalará un ochavo [4] a su hija ni la dejará un real en la herencia (*inheritance*).

— Pero, hombre, — insistió don Raimundo. — Mi hija tiene veinte mil duros de dote (*dowry*).

— Renunciamos a la dote. La niña vendrá a casa de su marido con nada más que lo que lleve puesto.

[1] *I belong either to Louis or to God!* Girls disappointed in love often became nuns.

[2] ***capa y bastón:*** The traditional gentleman of colonial Lima wore a long cape and carried a walking stick.

[3] ***más se subía el tío a la parra,*** *the higher the uncle climbed up the grapevine,* i.e., *the angrier he got.*

[4] An *ochavo* was an old brass coin of little value.

— Permítame entonces darla los muebles y la ropa de novia.

— Ni un alfiler (*pin*). Si no le gusta, dejarlo y que se muera la chica.

— Sea Vd. razonable, don Honorato. Mi hija necesita llevar siquiera una camisa para reemplazar (*replace*) la que lleva puesta.

— Bien. Consiento en que le regale la camisa de novia.

Al día siguiente don Raimundo y don Honorato se dirigieron muy temprano a la iglesia, y dijo el padre de Margarita ante el altar, — Juro no dar a mi hija más que la camisa de novia. Y don Raimundo Pareja cumplió su promesa, porque ni en vida ni en muerte dió después a su hija cosa que valiera un real. Pero los encajes (*laces*) de Flandes (*Belgium*) que adornaban la camisa de la novia costaron dos mil setecientos duros, y el cordoncillo (*cord*) que ajustaba (*drew up*) el cuello (*neck*) era una cadena de brillantes, de valor de treinta mil.

Convengamos en que fué muy merecida (*deserved*) la fama que tiene la camisa de Margarita Pareja.

Adapted from Ricardo Palma (*Peru*)

Postoffice in Lima uses cast iron colonial lions' heads for outdoor mailboxes. After all, why not have mailboxes that are interesting as well as useful?

Sawders

PALABRAS NUEVAS

3	**amenazar**	to threaten
	botica	drugstore
	camisa	slip, underskirt
	caro	expensive
3	**confianza**	confidence
4	**consentir** (ie, i)	to consent
2	**dirigirse a**	to go to
4	**galán** (*m.*)	courtier
	gallardo	gallant
	heredar	to inherit
2	**marido**	husband
3	**par** (*m.*)	pair
	renunciar	to renounce
	***si**	why (*in exclamation*)
3	**siquiera**	even, at last
	suegro	father-in-law

New Words Related to Others You Know

altivo (**alto**), haughty
3 **belleza** (**bello**), beauty
3 **cargado de** (**carga**), loaded with
limeño (**Lima**), person of Lima
2 **muerte** (*f.*) (**morir, muerto**), death
pobreza (**pobre**), poverty
sonrisa (**sonreír**), smile

Expresiones

al fiado, on credit
cuanto más — más, the more — the more
***por entonces,** at the time
ropa de novia, trousseau

¿VERDAD O NO?

Change the statements to make them true if they are false.

1. Margarita era una limeña con ojos hermosísimos. 2. La linda muchacha vivía con su tío. 3. Don Luis tendría mucho dinero cuando muriera su tío. 4. Don Luis conoció a la linda Margarita en la iglesia. 5. Él le echó flores, lo que no le gustaba a ella. 6. Don Luis, al pedirle la mano, olvidó que no tenía mucho dinero. 7. Don Raimundo no permitió que Margarita se casase con don Luis porque ella era muy joven. 8. Doña Margarita quería morir si no podía casarse con su novio. 9. Los médicos dijeron que la medicina para salvarla se vendía en la botica. 10. El tío consintió con mucho gusto en que su sobrino se casase con la muchacha. 11. La niña recibió veinte mil duros de dote (*dowry*). 12. La camisa de Margarita valía una fortuna.

PREGUNTAS PERSONALES

1. ¿Es Vd. el hijo favorito de su familia? 2. ¿Tiene Vd. un par de ojos como dos torpedos? 3. ¿Compra Vd. siempre al fiado para pagar más tarde? 4. ¿Quisiera Vd. olvidar que existe la aritmética? 5. ¿Tiene Vd. diez y ocho mayos? 6. ¿Llora Vd. y se arranca el pelo cuando alguien no quiere darle una cosa? 7. ¿Compra Vd. muchas medicinas en la botica? 8. ¿Quiere Vd. casarse con un hombre (una señorita) que tenga mucha plata? 9. ¿Se dirige Vd. a la escuela muy temprano? 10. ¿Cuándo no contesta Vd. ni sí ni no?

REPASO DE VERBOS

I. Find at least six verbs in the story which are in the subjunctive mood, and explain the reason for each one.

II. Make a sentence containing each of these verbs, using them in the preterite tense:

(yo) abrazar (§ 94)	(it) pertenecer	(él) saber
(Vd.) prometer	(nosotros) curar	(Vd.) ponerse
(ella) recordar	(nosotros) reunirse	(Vds.) traer

III. Make a series of sentences headed: **Lo que hice ayer,** *using the following verbs:* dirigirse, decidir, comprender, traducir, no recordar, sufrir, volver, descansar, dormirse, soñar con

IV. Complete each of these sentences in three ways, using the proper form of each of the verbs suggested and whatever more you wish to add:

1. Mi padre no consiente en que yo (*comprar, ir, visitar*). 2. Quiero un (-a) novio (-a) que (*ser, tener, saber*). 3. No volveré a hablarle hasta que Vd. me (*ayudar, prestar, ofrecer* [§ 95]). 4. Le ayudaré para que Vd. no (*perderse, tener, dejar caer*).

ALGO NUEVO

54. Dative of Interest

La muchacha se nos muere, *the girl (will) die ("on us").*
Ella se comió la manzana, *she ate the apple.*

Spanish often uses an extra indirect object pronoun, sometimes impossible to translate into English, which shows the interest a person has in a matter. You will probably not be using this form in your own compositions, but you should be able to recognize it and appreciate its significance in the stories you read.

EJERCICIO I. *Locate the "dative of interest" in each of these sentences:*

1. Se me cayó un cuchillo. 2. El río se le llevó la casa. 3. Quería comérselo. 4. ¡No me mate el gato! 5. Se me olvidó la cosa. 6. ¿Se le ofrece a Vd. algo? 7. Se me murió el perro.

High-school boys of Lima dress more formally for school than we do. Only the older boys wear long trousers. Note the unusual type of architecture of their modern school building.

Galloway

55. *Dative of Separation*

Le compró al indio una esmeralda, *he bought an emerald from the Indian.*

Le pidió al extranjero un peso, *he asked the stranger for a dollar (asked for a dollar from the stranger).*

Several verbs (among them ***pedir, sacar, quitar*** [*to take away*], ***robar, comprar***), take an indirect instead of a direct object, when they convey the idea of separating someone from something.

Permitir, preguntar, and ***decir*** also take an indirect instead of a direct object when referring to persons or animals.

EJERCICIO II. *Translate these sentences and explain the use of the indirect object in each one:*

1. Le compré al hombre un reloj de oro. 2. Le quitó el plato al niño. 3. Le pidió un duro a Elena. 4. Les preguntamos a los jóvenes qué quieren. 5. Le dicen a Elena que no debe irse. 6. No permiten a los perros entrar en la casa. 7. ¿Qué le compró Vd. a Juan? 8. ¿Va Vd. a quitarle la cadena al indio? 9. Le robaron su caballo al español. 10. Le sacó el diente al campesino.

ESTUDIO DE PALABRAS

I. Give an English word which is related to each of these Spanish words, but which is not an actual translation.

Example: **árbol** means *tree* and looks like *arbor.*

aplicado, volver, periódico, pensar, padre, negocio, madre, dormir, cantar, vender, edificio, morir, fácil, cielo, alto, vecino, ante, premio, perder, mayor, menor, diente, mano

II. Group these words in five lists of related subjects, heading your lists with the first five:

labio, imperio, queso, camino, quetzal, dólar, brazo, reino, kilómetro, oído, calabaza, soberano, moneda, colón, peso, príncipe, boca, frontera, emperador, viajero, pera, carretera, frijoles, pelo, pastel

III. Conteste Vd. en español:

¿Para qué sirve: el pelo, la boca, la voz, el corazón, la mano derecha?

¿Para qué sirven: los oídos, los ojos, los dientes, las manos, los brazos, las piernas?

IV. Here are words for some other parts of the body. Complete the sentences, using each word only once. (They are not in the general vocabulary unless used again.)

nariz (*f.*), *nose*
frente (*f.*), *forehead*
barba, *chin* (*beard*)
tronco, *trunk*
mejilla, *cheek*
oreja, *ear*
dedos, *fingers* (*toes*)
cuello, *neck*

1. El hombre tiene la —— muy alta.
2. El gato no tiene las —— tan largas como el burro.
3. La —— está sobre la boca.
4. Las señoritas usan colorete en las ——.
5. Los hombres tienen barba en la ——.
6. En el —— llevamos un collar de perlas.
7. Dentro del —— hay muchos órganos.
8. Con los —— podemos tocar las cosas.

REPASITO

I. Complete in Spanish:

1. ¿Saben *your "folks"* dónde está Vd. ahora? 2. No, *mine* no lo saben, pero voy a decírselo pronto. 3. ¿Ha traído Vd. *your* cuchillo? 4. No tengo *mine,* sino *his.* 5. No quiero *his,* sino *hers.* 6. *Ours are* muy grandes. 7. Ellos no quieren *theirs.* 8. ¿Dónde está *yours*? 9. *Mine* está en casa con *John's.* 10. ¿Es éste *hers*? 11. No, ése es *his.* 12. Ese joven es un amigo *of mine.* 13. ¿Es un amigo *of yours* también? 14. No, pero quisiera *to know him.*

II. Answer these questions, using the proper form of the suggested words in your answers.

1. ¿Para qué le dió Vd. los frijoles? (*para que, comer*)
2. ¿Para qué estudió Vd. este capítulo? (*para que, salir bien*)
3. ¿Cuándo irá Vd. al lago? (*tener tiempo*)
4. ¿Hasta qué hora esperará Vd. a Alberto? (*por tarde que, venir*)
5. ¿Cómo se sentó Enrique? (*como si, estar cansado*)
6. ¿Qué quisiera Vd. que yo hiciese? (*sentarse en el suelo*)

7. ¿Cuándo saldrá Vd.? (*no, antes que, llegar, el tren*)
8. ¿Le dará Vd. el premio si lo gana? (*por bueno que, ser, no*)
9. ¿Qué haría Vd. si tuviese mil duros? (*hacer un viaje*)
10. ¿Qué quiere Vd. que hagamos? (*ir en avión*)

III. Answer these questions, using pronouns instead of nouns in your answers.

1. ¿Le dió el padre a Margarita un regalo muy caro? 2. ¿Le dió Margarita a Luis una sonrisa? 3. ¿Le pidió la mano de la linda muchacha? 4. ¿Le dijo don Raimundo a un amigo suyo por qué no le gustó la petición? 5. ¿Le echó flores Luis a Margarita? 6. ¿Se vendía en la botica la medicina para la niña? 7. ¿Le dió mucho dinero el padre a su hija? 8. ¿Le permitió el tío a don Raimundo que le regalara los muebles a su hija?

PARA LEER SIN ESTUDIAR

I. ¿Sabía Vd. esto?

1. Lima, llamada «Ciudad de los Reyes», nunca ha tenido rey. Se llama así porque fué fundada por Pizarro en el Día de los Reyes Magos (*Wise Men*), el seis de enero.

2. Una condesa (*countess*) de los tiempos coloniales de Lima, esposa de un virrey del Perú, le dió al mundo la quinina. Estaba enferma del paludismo (*malaria*) de que sufrían mucho los españoles, cuando un viejo indio le trajo un pedazo de la corteza (*bark*) de un árbol, y con él le hizo una medicina que la curó. Desde entonces se le ha dado a este árbol el nombre de «chinchona»,[1] porque la señora se llamaba la Condesa de Chinchón.

3. Aunque nunca llueve en Lima, crecen las plantas y las flores sin necesidad de regarse. Esto se debe a que durante seis meses del año hay tanta neblina que nada se seca.

4. No había gatos en el Nuevo Mundo hasta que los trajeron los españoles. Los primeros gatos llegaron a Lima en el año de 1537, y se vendían por doscientos duros cada uno.

5. Cerca de Lima hoy día se ve al lado de un camino un monumento de piedra, encima del cual están los restos (*remains*) de un automóvil destrozado (*destroyed*) en un choque en que murió bas-

[1] Sometimes spelled *cinchona*.

tante gente. En este monumento, construido por el Club Rotario, se ven las palabras «Despacio se va lejos», para hacer pensar a todos en lo peligroso que es manejar demasiado de prisa un automóvil.

II. Chistes

1. — Sí, Rosita de mi alma, la quiero tanto que cuando nos casemos vamos a estar solititos. Ojalá que ni los de su familia vengan a vernos.

2. — ¿Se casaría Vd. con un hombre tonto que tuviese mucho dinero?

— ¿Cuánto tiene Vd.?

3. Inés — Mañana tenemos fiesta en casa. Tendré veinte y un años.

Lucita — ¡Qué coincidencia! Yo los tendré también.

Inés — Sí, pero yo los tendré por primera vez.

TEMA

1. The handsome young man had to buy everything on credit. 2. He met the prettiest girl in Lima in the church. 3. He wanted to marry her, but his uncle didn't like it, in spite of her beauty. 4. The latter became very angry, and kept shouting, "Why, this cannot be!" 5. Her father wanted her to marry any man who had much money. 6. It was possible that this might kill one who was not to blame. 7. The more Don Raimundo shouted, the more the bride wept. 8. She wanted at least her furniture and trousseau. 9. He finally consented that she take away her furniture. 10. The doctors didn't know the only thing that might save her. 11. They answered neither yes nor no, and she left the house as [if] crazy. 12. Such is Margaret's story.

CAPÍTULO 23

El alacrán de fray Gómez

Colonial Lima was long the capital of all Spanish South America, for the culture of old Spain entered the continent through Peru and Pizarro's city ruled the colonies. Some of Lima's old Spanish homes with their haughty stone escutcheons and dark, carved wood balconies still stand, and visitors always go to see the colonial Torre Tagle Palace, where a carved lion bowsprit from some forgotten galleon still extends from a wall into the tiled patio, just as it did when viceroys hung their scales from it to weigh out gold for the king.

In Lima there was founded the first University of the New World, San Marcos, and there the colonial grandees held out for the Spanish kings after most of the rest of the colonies had gained their independence. These Spaniards were traditionally wealthy, but even though circumstances sometimes took away their fortunes, they were proverbially haughty, and there is many a story of a poor but proud Castilian who could never forget his "blue blood."

Among Ricardo Palma's tales of colonial Lima, we find many about priests, for the Church played a great part in bringing Spanish culture into the New World. "For God and gold" Spain conquered the Americas, and it is natural that there should be as many sixteenth-century stories of miracles as of treasures.

This typical colonial story, told in the whimsical style of Peru's favorite writer, is the tale of a poor but proud Castilian and the well-loved Brother Gómez, who performed his miracles so modestly as to be almost absent-minded about them at times.

Cuando yo era muchacho, oía con frecuencia a las viejas exclamar, hablando del precio de una alhaja, — ¡Esto vale tanto como el alacrán de fray Gómez!

Este fray Gómez era un padre que hizo en mi tierra milagros sin darse cuenta de ellos y como quien no quiere la cosa.

Sucedió que un día iba el padre por un puente, cuando un caballo arrojó sobre las piedras al jinete. El infeliz quedó en el suelo con la cabeza rota, y echando sangre por boca y narices.

Fray Gómez se acercó al hombre, le dió una bendición (*blessing*), y sin más médico ni más botica, el jinete se levantó tan fresco como si no hubiera sucedido nada.

— ¡Milagro, milagro! ¡Viva fray Gómez! — exclamaron los espectadores (*spectators*). Y en su entusiasmo trataron de llevar en triunfo (*triumph*) al padre. Éste, para evitarlo, corrió a su convento y se encerró en su celda.

Hay quien dice que fray Gómez, para escaparse, voló por

Lima's colonial Torre Tagle Palace is an architectural treasure with its dark, carved wooden beams and turned window grills. The one-time viceroys' palace is now the Ministry of Foreign Affairs.

los aires desde el puente hasta su convento. Yo ni lo niego ni lo afirmo. Puede que sí y puede que no.[1] Escribiendo de maravillas, no gasto tinta en defenderlas ni en refutarlas.

Aquel día estaba fray Gómez en vena de (*in a mood for*) hacer milagros, pues cuando salió de su celda fué a la enfermería, donde encontró a San Francisco Solano víctima de un furioso dolor de cabeza. Fray Gómez le dijo,

— Su reverencia está muy débil, y debe comer siquiera un poco.

— Hermano, — contestó el santo, — no tengo apetito.

Pero tanto insistió fray Gómez, que el enfermo, para evitar discusiones, le pidió lo que era imposible conseguir.

— Pues, mire, hermanito, sólo comería con gusto un par de pejerreyes.

Fray Gómez metió la mano derecha dentro de la manga (*sleeve*) izquierda, y sacó un par de pejerreyes tan fresquitos que parecían acabados de [2] salir del mar.

— Aquí los tiene su reverencia. Voy a prepararlos. — Y con los benditos (*blessed*) pejerreyes quedó San Francisco curado como por encanto.

Me parece que estos dos milagritos que he contado no son los únicos, pero dejo en mi tintero otros muchos [3] para seguir con el del alacrán.

Estaba una mañana fray Gómez en su celda cuando oyó llamar a la puerta.

— Entre, hermanito, — dijo el padre.

Y entró en la humildísima celda un individuo (*individual*) mal vestido, pero en cuya cara se veía la proverbial honradez del castellano viejo.

— Siéntese, hermano, y dígame lo que le trae por acá, — dijo fray Gómez.

— Es el caso, padre, que yo soy hombre bueno...

— Eso se sabe, y deseo que siga así.

— Y es el caso que soy zapatero, que tengo una familia

[1] ***Puede que sí y puede que no,*** *maybe so and maybe not.*

[2] ***parecían acabados de salir,*** *looked as if they had just come out.*

[3] ***otros muchos,*** *many others.* This order with *otro* is often found.

grande, y que en mi comercio no gano mucho, aunque no por falta de honradez e industria en mí.

— Me alegro, hermano, que a quien honradamente trabaja, Dios le ayuda.

— Pero es el caso, padre, que hasta ahora Dios se me hace el sordo.

— No desespere, hermano, no desespere.

— Pues es el caso que a muchas puertas he llegado pidiendo un préstamo de quinientos duros, y todas las he encontrado cerradas. Y anoche me dije a mí mismo, — ¡Ea! [1] Buen ánimo y vete a pedirle el dinero a fray Gómez, que si él lo quiere, pobre como es, medio encontrará para sacarte del apuro (*difficulty*). Y es el caso que aquí estoy porque he venido, y ruego que me preste esa suma por seis meses.

— ¿Cómo ha podido imaginarse, hijo, que en esta triste celda encontraría esa fortuna?

— Es el caso, padre, que yo no sabría responderle, pero tengo fe en que no me dejará ir sin el dinero.

— La fe lo salvará, hermano. Espere un momento.

Y mirando las desnudas (*bare*) paredes de su celda, vió un alacrán que caminaba tranquilamente sobre el marco (*sill*) de la ventana. Fray Gómez arrancó una página de un libro viejo, dirigióse a la ventana, cogió al alacrán, lo envolvió en el papel, y volviéndose hacia el castellano, le dijo, — Tome, buen hombre, y empeñe (*pawn*) esta alhajita. Pero no olvide devolvérmela dentro de seis meses.

El zapatero le dió las gracias, se despidió de fray Gómez, y más que de prisa se dirigió a la tienda de un usurero.

La joya era espléndida, verdadera alhaja de reina, por decir lo menos. Era un prendedor (*brooch*) en forma de alacrán. El cuerpo era una magnífica esmeralda sobre oro, y la cabeza era un grueso brillante con dos rubíes por ojos.

El usurero, al ver la alhaja, ofreció al castellano dos mil duros por ella, pero nuestro español insistió en no aceptar más que quinientos duros por seis meses.

Con este capitalito prosperó tanto el castellano en su comer-

[1] *¡Ea! Buen ánimo . . . Come, come! Cheer up . . .*

cio, que al fin del plazo (*time*) pudo desempeñar (*redeem*) la joya, y envuelta en el mismo papel, se la devolvió a fray Gómez.

Éste tomó el alacrán, lo puso sobre el marco (*sill*) de la ventana y dijo, — Animalito de Dios, sigue tu camino.

Y el alacrán empezó a andar libremente por las paredes de la celda.

Adapted from Ricardo Palma (*Peru*)

PALABRAS NUEVAS

	alacrán (*m.*)	scorpion		**jinete** (*m.*)	horseman
	alhaja	jewel		**narices** (*pl.* of **nariz**) (*f.*)	nostrils
3	**castellano**	Castilian	2	**negar** (ie)	to deny
	celda	cell		**pejerrey** (-es) (*m.*)	mackerel
4	**débil**	weak		**puente** (*m.*)	bridge
3	**envolver** (ue)	to wrap		**refutar**	to refute
3	**envuelto**	wrapped	2	**suceder** (con)	to happen (to)
	fray (*m.*)	brother		**tinta**	ink
3	**fresco**	fresh		**usurero**	money-lender

New Words Related to Others You Know

4 **desesperar** (**esperar**), to despair
3 **encerrar** (**cerrar**), to lock up
enfermería (**enfermo**), infirmary
honradez (*f.*) (**honrado**), honesty
honradamente (**honrado**), honestly
3 **infeliz** (**feliz**), unhappy
préstamo (**prestar**), loan
3 **reina** (**rey**), queen
tintero (**tinta**), inkwell
zapatero (**zapato**), shoemaker

Expresiones

***aquí (los) tiene (Vd.),** here (they) are
***darse cuenta de,** to realize, pay attention to
echar sangre, to bleed
hacerse el sordo, to play deaf
lo menos, the least

PREGUNTAS

1. ¿Quién era fray Gómez? 2. ¿Qué hizo el caballo? 3. ¿Se rompió un brazo el jinete? 4. ¿Fué amado siempre fray Gómez?

5. ¿Qué tenía San Francisco Solano? 6. ¿Quería San Francisco de veras un par de pejerreyes? 7. ¿Qué deja Ricardo Palma en su tintero? 8. ¿Qué quería pedir prestado el zapatero? 9. ¿Se los dió fray Gómez? 10. ¿Le devolvió el zapatero el alacrán dentro de seis meses?

PREGUNTAS PERSONALES

1. ¿Quisiera Vd. hacer milagros en la clase? 2. ¿Ha pasado Vd. alguna vez por un puente? 3. ¿Es Vd. buen jinete? 4. ¿Le gustaría a Vd. volar a casa por los aires? 5. ¿Tuvo Vd. ayer un fuerte dolor de cabeza? 6. ¿Qué comería Vd. con gusto en este momento? 7. ¿Duerme Vd. en una celda humilde? 8. ¿Puede Vd. hacerme un préstamo de quinientos duros? 9. ¿Ha arrancado Vd. muchas páginas de su libro de español? 10. ¿Prospera Vd. siempre en su comercio?

REPASO DE VERBOS

I. Give the first person singular present subjunctive of each of these verbs:

dar, saber, haber, ser, estar, ir, buscar, pagar, empezar, coger, conocer, valer, traer, caer, oír, seguir, dormir, pedir, servir

II. Give the first person plural past subjunctive of each of these verbs:

haber, andar, decir, saber, poner, hacer, ir, dar, venir, querer, poder, traer, ser, tener, dormir, seguir, vestir, caer, oír, creer

III. Give the preposition which is often used with each of these verbs, and translate. If you miss one, say it aloud with the verb several times so that your ear will become accustomed to the sound. (§ 98)

depender, soñar, cargar, tardar, dejar, reírse, fijarse, despedirse, atreverse, llenar, parecerse, pensar, acordarse, rodear, ir, venir, dirigirse, tratar, acabar, casarse

ALGO NUEVO

56. The True Passive

La cadena fué echada al agua, *the chain was thrown into the water.*

El Inca fué hecho prisionero por Pizarro, *the Inca was captured by Pizarro.*

The passive voice is formed in Spanish by some tense of the verb ***ser*** plus the past participle, which agrees with the subject like any adjective. The tense most often used in the passive is the preterite: ***la lección fué escrita por el niño.***

The passive voice is usually avoided. The reflexive substitute is used in its place (***se echó la cadena al agua***) when the agent is not expressed and when the subject is not personal. (§ 58)

Shoppers' delight in Lima is this modern arcade of smart shops protected from the dripping fog by a glass roof, for although it rarely rains, there is sunshine only half the year.

Sawders

True Passive

REMEMBER: Use ***ser*** + past participle for *action.*

With the passive, *by* is most often expressed by ***por.***[1]

EJERCICIO I. *Translate these sentences and tell whether their verbs are active or passive:*

1. Atahualpa fué invitado a comer por Pizarro. 2. Los aztecas y los incas fueron vencidos por los españoles. 3. La joya no fué vendida por el zapatero. 4. El usurero le prestó el dinero. 5. El dinero fué prestado por el usurero. 6. Los españoles vencieron a los indios. 7. El tesoro fué escondido por los piratas. 8. Los piratas escondieron sus tesoros. 9. Una conversación entre dos indios quichuas fué oída por un soldado. 10. El soldado oyó una conversación entre dos indios quichuas. 11. El Inca fué defendido por sus nobles antes de ser hecho prisionero por Pizarro. 12. Los nobles le defendieron valientemente.

EJERCICIO II. *Complete these sentences in Spanish, being careful to make the past participles agree with the nouns they modify:*

1. Los cuentos *were written* por Ricardo Palma. 2. Estos cuentos *are read* por todos los sudamericanos. 3. El dinero *was loaned* por el usurero. 4. La joya *was made* por un moro. 5. El alacrán *was changed* en una joya hermosísima. 6. Los caminos del Inca *were cleaned* por sus criados. 7. El Inca *was surrounded* por guardias. 8. La Biblia *was thrown* al suelo por Atahualpa. 9. Las cosas viejas *were told* por Paucar. 10. La vida feliz de los quichuas *had been destroyed* por los conquistadores.

EJERCICIO III. *Compare the use of* **estar** *plus the past participle with the true passive* (§§ 4; 123; 124–2).

[1] Note to teacher: According to Keniston, the use of *de* with a mental action is so rare that it need not be presented here.

REMEMBER:	Use *estar* + past participle for *description*, but not for *action*.

Now complete these statements:

1. The true passive expresses ——, not ——. 2. *Estar* with a past participle shows a —— or ——. 3. The tense most often used for the passive is the ——. 4. The past tense of *estar* most often used with the past participle is the ——. (*What tense is used for past description?*)

EJERCICIO IV. *Complete these sentences with the proper tense of* **ser** *or* **estar**, *being careful to choose the correct verb:*

1. La estatua del caballo *was* hecha de piedra. 2. La imagen *was* hecha por un maya llamado Siguán. 3. El caballo de piedra *was* sacado del palacio durante la noche. 4. *It was* llevado a las orillas del lago por los sacerdotes. 5. La capital *was* rodeada de [1] árboles. 6. La capital *was* rodeada por los guerreros. 7. La historia *was* contada por Ricardo Palma. 8. La historia *was* escrita. 9. La estatua *is* adornada de joyas. 10. El lago *is* situado a poca distancia de la hacienda. 11. La cadena nunca *was* hallada.

REPASITO

I. Write the story of «El alacrán de fray Gómez» *in your own words, using simple "first-grade" sentences so you will not make mistakes.* For example, you might begin: Fray Gómez era un padre. Hizo muchos milagros. Un día vió a un hombre a caballo. El caballo ... *etc.*

II. Do the same thing orally, without using your paper, each pupil giving one sentence. You will have to understand what everyone says in order to know what to tell when it is your turn.

[1] Some verbs, such as *rodear*, *acompañar*, and *seguir*, take *de* instead of *por* if condition and not action is implied.

TEMA

1. The old Castilian lived in Lima in the days of *fray* Gómez. 2. It happened that one day he fell from his horse. 3. But his broken head was cured by *fray* Gómez with no (**sin**) medicine, as if nothing had happened. 4. The old man had a headache and was very weak, but he had a good appetite. 5. He put on his new shirt, which was not torn. 6. His nephew saw him, and told him to be careful. 7. At first he did not realize the danger. 8. But he picked up the scorpion, and it became a jewel. 9. It was worth more than $500, but he asked for only a small loan. 10. It was wrapped in a piece of paper, and thus he returned it.

ESTUDIO DE PALABRAS[1]

I. When a brown-eyed waitress in a quaint Mexican Indian costume sets this breakfast menu down in front of you, you know that you are in the famous *Casa de Azulejos* (House of Tiles), or Sanborn's Restaurant, in Mexico City. The girl does not speak English, and it's up to you to guess as best you can in order to get your breakfast.

Choose a good, filling meal and figure out how much it will cost you if a dollar is worth five *pesos*. (The prices are given in *pesos*.) And don't forget to leave at least ten per cent for a tip for the pretty waitress!

(A tip for you is that the following items are to be found somewhere on the menu: strawberries, scrambled eggs, bacon, puffed wheat, cinnamon toast, raisin bread, Spanish omelet, (rolled) oats, grapefruit, soft-boiled ("warm") or fried eggs, fresh pineapple, chocolate with whipped cream, French toast with syrup or honey, hot biscuits.)

If you haven't the faintest idea what an item is, you will have to read Exercise II in order to find out, for most of the words are not in the dictionary. Note the American influence in this restaurant which is popular with American tourists.

[1] Optional section, since words used here are not repeated unless they are introduced in the regular way.

Salón de Refrescos Sanborn

MENÚ

Servicio: 7:30 a 21:30

DESAYUNO

FRUTAS	Fresas con crema	.75	Jugo de naranja	.40
	Piña fresca	.40	Jugo de jitomate	.40
	Plátano con crema	.50	Toronja (1/2)	.30
HUEVOS	Huevos fritos, al plato, tibios o revueltos, con jamón americano			1.50
	Huevos fritos, al plato, tibios o revueltos, con tocino americano			1.00
	Huevos poché en pan tostado			.80
	Tortilla de huevos a la española			1.50
	Huevos rancheros			1.00
CEREALES	Arroz inflado	.50	Corn flakes	.50
	Trigo inflado	.50	Avena	.50
	Crema de trigo	.50	Grapenuts	.50
CAFÉ, TE, *etc.*	Café con crema o leche caliente			.40
	1 taza de café con azúcar y crema			.25
	Café solo, chico			.20
	Póstum con crema o leche caliente			.40
	Te con crema, leche caliente o limón			.40
	Chocolate con crema batida			.50
	Leche, botella			.25
PAN	Pan blanco con mantequilla			.30
	Pan negro con mantequilla			.30
	Pan tostado			.30
	Rollos de Viena			.30
	Muffins de huevo			.30
	Bizcochos calientes			.30
	Pan de pasas			.40
	Pan tostado de canela			.50
	Tostado francés con jarabe o miel			1.00
	Hot cakes con jarabe o miel			.50
	Waffles con jarabe o miel			.60

II. Estas frases describen algunos alimentos del menú. Si Vds. las entienden, será fácil leerlo.

1. Las ***fresas*** son frutas rojas y pequeñas en forma de corazoncitos. En la Argentina, se llaman frutillas. 2. Los ***huevos al plato*** se cuecen (*bake*) en un plato, con mantequilla (*butter*). 3. Los ***huevos tibios*** algunas veces se llaman «huevos pasados por agua». 4. Los ***huevos revueltos*** se baten (*beat*) antes de cocerse (*cooking*). 5. Los ***jitomates*** de México se llaman tomates en la América del Sur. En México los jitomates son grandes y rojos, y los tomates son pequeños y verdes. 6. Una ***toronja*** se parece a una naranja, pero es más grande, menos dulce, y amarilla en vez de «color de naranja». 7. Los ***plátanos*** de México se llaman *bananas* en la América Central. 8. La ***piña*** es una fruta grande y dulce con hojas (*leaves*) largas. Crece en los países tropicales, sobre todo en las Islas Hawai. 9. Los ***huevos rancheros*** tienen una salsa (*sauce*) muy picante ("*hot*") que no les gusta a todos los norteamericanos. 10. El ***trigo*** sirve para hacer el pan. 11. Los chinos comen mucho ***arroz.*** 12. El ***jarabe*** y la ***miel*** son muy dulces. La miel es hecha por insectos pequeños que vuelan por los aires.

III. Conteste Vd. en español, mirando el menú si es necesario, porque las palabras nuevas no están en el vocabulario.

1. ¿Toma Vd. crema con la piña fresca? 2. ¿De qué color es el jugo de jitomate? 3. ¿De qué color son los plátanos? 4. ¿Cuál es más dulce, — la toronja o la miel? 5. ¿Cuál le gusta a Vd. más, — el jamón o el tocino? 6. ¿Toma Vd. azúcar y crema con el trigo inflado? 7. ¿Toma Vd. limón con una botella de leche? 8. ¿Toma Vd. mantequilla con el pan tostado? 9. ¿Es muy rico el chocolate con crema batida? 10. ¿Sabe Vd. por qué los mexicanos toman el café con leche caliente, mitad (*half*) y mitad? (*¡El café es muy fuerte!*) 11. ¿Prefiere Vd. el pan blanco al pan negro? 12. ¿Cómo toma Vd. el te?

PARA LEER SIN ESTUDIAR

¿Sabía Vd. esto? [1]

En los países de habla española, se encuentran nombres de alimentos que nos parecen muy curiosos. Así como nosotros tenemos

[1] Words in this story which are not in the general vocabulary are found in the menu and exercises based upon it.

el "*hot dog*," ellos tienen sus nombres igualmente interesantes.

Por ejemplo, los frijoles «a pie» en México son cocidos (*boiled*); «a caballo» quiere decir que son fritos (*fried*). Un huevo poché algunas veces se llama «huevo montado» o «a caballo».

El «cabello (*hair*) de ángel» es una clase de *vermicelli* que se usa en la sopa. «Media luna» es una clase de rollo o bizcocho. Los «panqueques» no se sirven en el desayuno, sino en la comida, como postre (*dessert*), en Chile y en el Perú.

Las «flautas» que se sirven en la comida son nuestros "*bread sticks*."

Y la «sopa de arroz», aunque de veras es sopa en el Paraguay, no lo es en México, donde es un plato de arroz seco con pollo. El mismo plato en España se llama «arroz a la Valenciana», y en Puerto Rico se llama «asopao».

Todos los pasteles chicos y las galletas (*cookies*) de México se llaman «fruta del horno (*oven*)». ¡Pero lo más curioso es que nuestro "*jelly roll*" en México lleva el nombre de «niño envuelto»!

CAPÍTULO 24

El abanico

This story of how a wise Marquis made his choice of a bride from among many beautiful girls is one that could have happened in Spain at almost any time, or in Mexico or South America during colonial days when most important people had titles.

The interesting thing about the story is that the same system of choosing a wife would work today, here as well as in a Spanish-speaking country, and whether the girls were countesses and duchesses or not. So girls, read it and learn how to get your man!

El Marqués estaba resuelto a casarse, y había dado esta noticia a sus amigos. La noticia corrió con la velocidad del relámpago (*lightning*) por toda la alta sociedad, porque el Marqués era un gran partido (*catch*), como se decía entre la gente de mundo. Tenía treinta y cinco años, un gran título (*title*), mucho dinero, era muy guapo, y estaba cansado de correr el mundo.

Con la noticia de aquella resolución, no le faltaban atenciones, pero pasaban los días, y las semanas, y los meses, y el Marqués no había escogido a la dama de su corazón.

— Pero, hombre, — le decían sus amigos, — ¿cuándo vas a decidirte?

— Es que no encuentro todavía la mujer que busco.

— Será porque tienes pocas ganas de casarte, pues hay muchas muchachas. ¿No es muy guapa la Condesa del Iris?

— Se ocupa demasiado de sus joyas y de sus trajes; cuidará más de un collar de perlas que de su marido.

— ¿Y la Duquesa (*Duchess*) de Luz Clara?

— Mucha belleza; pero sólo piensa en divertirse. Me dejaría moribundo (*dying*) en la casa por no perder una función del Real,[1] y abandonaría a un hijo enfermo para asistir al baile de una Embajada (*embassy*).

— Y la Marquesa (*Marchioness*) de Nevada, ¿no es guapísima y un modelo de virtud?

— Ciertamente; pero es más religiosa de lo que un marido necesita. Ningún cuidado, ninguna pena, ninguna enfermedad de la familia le impediría pasar toda la mañana en la iglesia.

[1] The "Teatro Real" might indicate that the story is one of Spain, for there is one in Madrid.

— Vamos, tú quieres una mujer imposible.

— No, nada de imposible. Como fruto de mi experiencia, sé que para formar juicio acerca de las mujeres, se deben observar sus acciones insignificantes. Como dice el refrán antiguo, para muestra (*sample*) basta un botón. Ya veréis cómo la encuentro, porque el que quiere casarse no busca belleza completa.

Una noche se daba un gran baile en la Embajada de Inglaterra. Los salones estaban llenos de hermosas damas y gallardos caballeros, todos flor y nata [1] de las clases más aristocráticas de la sociedad. El Marqués estaba en el comedor, adonde había llevado a la joven Condesita de Valle de Oro, una muchacha de veinte años, inteligente, simpática y distinguida (*distinguished*), pero que no llamaba la atención por su belleza.

La joven Condesa vivía sola con su padre, noble caballero, estimado por todos los que le conocían.

La Condesita, después de tomar una taza de te, conversaba con algunas amigas antes de volver a los salones.

— Pero, ¿no estuviste anoche en el Real? Cantaron admirablemente el Tannhauser [2] — le decía una de ellas.

— Pues, mira; me quedé vestida, porque tenía muchos deseos de oír la ópera. Ya tenía el abrigo puesto, cuando la criada me dijo que Leonor estaba muy grave. Entré a verla, y ya no me atreví a separarme de su lado.

— Y esa Leonor, — dijo el Marqués, — ¿es alguna señora de la familia de Vd.?

— Casi, Marqués; es el aya (*governess*) que tuvo mi mamá, y como nunca se ha separado de nosotros y me ha querido tanto, yo la veo como de mi familia.

— ¡Qué abanico tan precioso traes! — dijo a la Condesita una de las jóvenes que hablaban con ella.

— Ah, sí. Estoy encantada con él y lo cuido como a mi

[1] *flor y nata, flower and cream.* The "upper crust," we might say.

[2] Tannhauser is one of Wagner's operas, known to all cultured Spanish-speaking people as well as it is to us.

tesoro más precioso. Es un regalo que me hizo mi padre el día de mi santo.[1] Me lo compró en París.[2]

— ¡A ver, a ver! — dijeron todas, y se acercaron a la Condesita, que, con infantil (*childish*) satisfacción, desplegó (*unfolded*) a sus ojos el abanico, que verdaderamente era una maravilla del arte.

En este momento, uno de los criados que cuidadosamente cruzaba entre las señoras llevando en las manos una enorme bandeja (*tray*) con helados, tropezó, y sin poderse valer (*help himself*), vino a chocar con (*run into*) el abanico abierto, haciéndolo pedazos, y poco faltó para que los fragmentos hirieran la mano de la Condesita.

— ¡Qué bruto (*dumb*)! — dijo una señora mayor.

— ¡Qué hombre tan animal! — exclamó un caballero.

— Parece que no tiene ojos, — dijo una chiquilla.

Y el pobre criado, rojo de vergüenza, apenas podía balbucear (*stammer*) una disculpa (*excuse*) ininteligible.

— No se apure (*worry*) usted, — dijo la Condesita con la mayor tranquilidad; — no tiene usted la culpa, sino nosotros, que estamos aquí estorbando (*obstructing*) el paso.

Y reuniendo con la mano izquierda los pedazos del abanico, tomó con la derecha el brazo del Marqués, diciéndole con la mayor naturalidad (*naturalness*), — Están tocando un vals, y yo lo tengo comprometido (*promised*) con usted. ¿Me lleva usted al salón de baile?

— Sí, Condesa, pero no bailaré con usted este vals.

— ¿Por qué no?

— Porque en este momento voy a buscar a su padre para decirle que mañana mismo iré a pedirle a usted por esposa,[3] y dentro de ocho días, iré a saber la decisión.

[1] Remember that a person's birthday is usually his Saint's Day.

[2] If the story were told of Mexico, the fan would be Chinese, for most luxuries came from the Orient in Mexico's colonial days, and nowadays treasured family heirlooms are mostly of Chinese make.

After Carlotta and Maximilian came to Mexico, in 1864, it became more fashionable to have French luxury goods.

[3] The old Spanish custom, still followed in most Spanish-speaking countries, is for the suitor to ask the girl's father, not the girl, for her hand.

Tres meses después, se celebraron aquellas bodas, y en un rico marco (*frame*) bajo cristal, se mostraba en uno de los salones del palacio de los nuevos casados el abanico roto.

ADAPTED FROM VICENTE RIVA PALACIO (*Mexico*)

PALABRAS NUEVAS

abrigo	coat	3 **herir** (ie, i)	to wound
4 **bodas**	wedding	3 **impedir** (i)	prevent
botón (*m.*)	button	**Inglaterra**	England
collar (*m.*)	necklace	3 **juicio**	judgment
4 **condesa**	countess	**Marqués**	Marquis
4 **cristal** (*m.*)	glass	3 **pedazo**	piece
2 **deseo**	desire	4 **salón** (*m.*)	hall
3 **estimado**	esteemed	4 **valle** (*m.*)	valley
4 **función**	performance	2 **virtud** (*f.*)	virtue
2 **grave**	ill		

EXPRESIONES

gente de mundo, aristocracy

hacer pedazos, to break in pieces

ocho días, a week

poco faltó para que, very nearly

***tener ganas de,** to feel like (*inclined to*)

¿VERDAD O NO?

Change these statements to make them true if they are false.

1. El Marqués no dijo a nadie que estaba resuelto a casarse. 2. Nadie quería casarse con él. 3. Cada madre quería que su hija se casase con el Marqués porque era muy joven. 4. En poco tiempo el Marqués escogió a la dama de su corazón. 5. El Marqués quería una mujer que ante todo fuese bella. 6. La Condesa del Iris se ocupaba demasiado de sus joyas y de sus trajes. 7. La Duquesa de Luz Clara nunca pensaba en divertirse. 8. La Marquesa de Nevada nunca asistía a la iglesia. 9. «Para muestra basta un botón» quiere decir que hay que observar las acciones insignificantes. 10. La Condesita de Valle de Oro llamaba la atención de todos por su belleza. 11. La Condesita se puso muy enojada cuando el criado

hizo pedazos su abanico. 12. El Marqués quería casarse con la Condesita porque ella se enojaba fácilmente.

PREGUNTAS

1. ¿Por qué estaba resuelto el Marqués a casarse? 2. ¿Sería el Marqués un buen marido para alguna muchacha afortunada? 3. ¿Por qué no escogió una esposa pronto? 4. ¿Quería ante todo una esposa guapa? 5. ¿Dónde encontró el Marqués a la Condesita de Valle de Oro? 6. ¿Cuántos años tenía la Condesita? 7. ¿Por qué no había asistido ella al Teatro Real? 8. ¿De dónde vino el abanico que traía la Condesita? 9. ¿Qué llevaba el criado en las manos? 10. ¿Tenía él la culpa cuando se rompió el abanico? 11. ¿Era muy cortés la Condesita? 12. ¿Por qué se casó el Marqués con la Condesita?

Equador's colonial monasteries and churches are among the most beautiful in the world. This patio of San Francisco in Quito is still enjoyed by the quiet friars who live there.

Sawders

PREGUNTAS PERSONALES

1. ¿Está Vd. resuelto (-a) a casarse? 2. ¿Está Vd. cansado (-a) de correr el mundo? 3. ¿Tiene Vd. ganas de comer ahora? 4. ¿Cuándo tiene Vd. pocas ganas de comer? 5. ¿Se ocupa Vd. demasiado de sus trajes? 6. ¿Cuida Vd. bien de sus posesiones? 7. ¿Piensa Vd. mucho en divertirse? 8. ¿Le gustaría a Vd. asistir a un gran baile? 9. ¿Cuándo toma Vd. una taza de te? 10. ¿Tiene Vd. muchos deseos de oír una ópera? 11. ¿Tiene Vd. el abrigo puesto en este momento? 12. ¿Recibió Vd. muchos regalos en su cumpleaños? 13. ¿Come Vd. muchos helados? 14. ¿Le gusta a Vd. hacer pedazos una cosa de valor?

REPASO DE VERBOS

I. Give the past participle of each of these verbs (§ 96 or general vocabulary):

caer, dar, decir, hacer, ir, oír, poner, querer, reír, ser, traer, ver, volver, abrir, cubrir, escribir, morir, romper, resolver, leer

II. Translate these compound verb forms and tell the tense of each:

hemos caído, había dicho, habrán abierto, habrían roto, he visto, habíamos resuelto, han puesto, habría vuelto, habrá sido, había traído, habéis ido, habías dado, yo habría hecho, ha reído, Vd. había leído

III. Using the verbs in Exercise I, give these compound forms:

I had seen, you have returned, she has covered, they had written, he would have gone, they will have heard, have you brought?, we had opened, we should have opened, she has laughed, I should have told, he had done, they have put, we had wanted, you have broken, I have resolved

ALGO NUEVO

57. The Infinitive after Ver *and* Oír

oyó decir a las viejas, *he heard the old women say*

The infinitive is used after ***ver*** and ***oír,*** just as after the exceptions among the verbs of causing (***me hizo estudiar,*** *he made me study*).[1]

EJERCICIO I. *Write in Spanish:*

we saw them dance, they heard us sing, I heard her speak, we hear him answer, she will see us leaving, they would hear him enter, he saw her going away, I can't hear him read, we don't want to see them dancing, everyone has heard the old women say

58. Reflexive Substitute for Passive

se devolvió la joya, *the jewel was returned (returned itself)*
se ven las palabras, *the words are seen (see themselves)*

Spanish-speaking people prefer this reflexive substitute for the passive, and use it especially in speaking of things, for then the meaning cannot be mistaken. (***Se invitó*** might be intended to mean *he was invited,* but could be understood as *he invited himself.*)

REMEMBER:	Use the reflexive substitute for the passive except when speaking of persons.

EJERCICIO II. *Translate these sentences first literally, as if reflexive; then as they are intended, as passive.* Example:

Se dice, *it says itself = it is said.*

1. Se vendieron los gatos en Lima. 2. Siempre se hacía así. 3. Se llenó el cuarto de oro. 4. Se le dió este nombre a Bolivia en

[1] The gerund may also be used, as in English.

Sawders

Blood of Spanish grandees flows in the veins of this proud old Ecuadorian who inherited from his forefathers the proverbial dignity of the *conquistadores*.

honor de Bolívar. 5. Se vendió el sombrero por dos pesos. 6. Se prohibe entrar. 7. Se acabó el cuento. 8. Se encontraron los papeles en una casa antigua. 9. Se halló un tesoro en la isla. 10. Se echó la cadena al lago. 11. Se oyó el cuento. 12. Se cierran las puertas a las diez. 13. Se envolvió la alhaja en el papel. 14. Se ven estas palabras en el monumento.

EJERCICIO III. *Write in Spanish, using the reflexive substitute instead of the true passive:*

1. Los perros *were bought* en Madrid. 2. Lima *was given* este nombre en el año de 1535. 3. La cadena *was lost* hace muchos siglos. 4. Las voces *were heard* durante la noche. 5. La puerta del hotel *will be closed* a las diez. 6. La historia *is told* todos los días. 7. *It is said* que ya no hay incas. 8. El caballo *was left* con los indios. 9. Siempre *it is done* así. 10. La leyenda *was finished* antes que llegué.

ESTUDIO DE PALABRAS

These commonly used idioms are from Chapters 10–23. *Find the one which completes each sentence, using each idiom only once.* They are all in the general vocabulary.

dar un paso	decir que sí	sobre todo
hace muchos años que	echar de menos	al principio
de todos modos	por bueno que	por último
por esto	a punto de	por fin
entretanto	en pie	por lo tanto
caer de rodillas	para siempre	aquí tiene Vd.
cada vez más	pedir prestado	darse cuenta de
con frecuencia	sin embargo	

1. La función era buena, *at any rate.* 2. El criado *fell to his knees* para reunir los pedazos de cristal. 3. Le preguntó si quería bailar, y *finally* ella consintió. 4. El Marqués *realized* que había hallado a una joven muy simpática. 5. Los hombres admiran la belleza, pero *especially* admiran la virtud. 6. La criada estaba tan grave que no podía *take a step.* 7. Todos estaban *standing.* 8. Estaba *on the point of* salir. 9. La condesa *gradually* se enojaba. 10. Es muy difícil escoger un marido, *therefore* hay que tener cuidado. 11. Los campesinos *borrowed* un santo. 12. *For many years* el Marqués escoge una buena esposa. 13. *At first* no tenían deseos de ver el abanico. 14. *However good* sea, no me gustará. 15. *For this reason,* el salón estaba lleno de gente. 16. — ¿Es verdad? — *He says so.* 17. — *Here is* su abanico, Condesa, — dijo el Marqués. 18. *Meanwhile,* la Condesa tomó una taza de te. 19. Los muchachos *missed* a su joven amiga. 20. Dijo que la amaría *forever.* 21. No creían que sucediese un milagro; *nevertheless,* sucedió uno. 22. *Finally* llegó al valle. 23. Las señoritas asistían al baile *frequently.*

REPASITO

Translate freely, not word-for-word, these expressions from stories you have read:

rogó que le dijesen, los dos parecían un solo ser, se declaró vencido, la mayor parte de ellos, esto siempre se hacía, se esconden de miedo, no seré criado de nadie, trató de dar muerte al Inca, hace poco pasó por la ciudad, esperó a que éste mejorara, ¡ay de él si no venía!, les gusta más el oro que nada, le aconsejaron que hiciese sacrificios, da dos pasos hacia atrás, ¿quién se la dará?, sin que nadie lo supiera, se acaba el cuento, cuéntame a mí algo, no puede dártelo, ¿cómo fué aquello?, ¡Si esto es muy caro!, le echó flores, a pesar de sus diez y ocho mayos, alarmóse su padre, la muchacha se nos muere, cuanto más tiene más quiere

PARA LEER SIN ESTUDIAR

Cosas interesantes acerca del Ecuador

¡Imagínese Vd. un país donde las orquídeas (*orchids*) cuestan cinco centavos cada una! Éste es el Ecuador, donde el costo de la vida es el más barato del mundo, aunque el país está bastante cerca de Venezuela, donde el costo es el más caro.

Es el único país del mundo que ha tomado su nombre de su situación geográfica, y su capital, Quito, es la ciudad más antigua del Hemisferio Occidental. Escondida entre los volcanes de los Andes, Quito lleva todavía su aire de los tiempos coloniales, porque hasta la llegada de los aviones, era muy difícil llegar a ella. Allí hay una universidad fundada (*founded*) cincuenta años antes de nuestra Universidad de Harvard, y allí hay iglesias magníficas construidas por los españoles. Es el país más artístico de todos, y cada convento o cada iglesia es un museo (*museum*) con obras de arte que valen un Potosí.

Guayaquil, puerto del Ecuador, es una ciudad moderna con avenidas (*avenues*) anchas y plazas tropicales. Allí se reunieron Simón Bolívar y San Martín durante la guerra de la independencia, lo cual se conmemora (*commemorate*) con un monumento en el Malecón (*avenue along the sea wall*).

Hay contrastes hasta entre los indios. Algunos, como los jíbaros, son primitivos, viviendo en las selvas y buscando la cabeza de un enemigo para encogerla (*shrink*) en sus ceremonias antiguas. Otros indios, como los otavalos, son pacíficos, simpáticos y guapos, y los más limpios de todas las Américas. Usan sombrero de ala (*brim*) ancha en la cual llevan sus cosas, y sus prendas de vestir son de colores vivos.

Entre los productos del Ecuador se cuentan los sombreros «Panamá»,[1] que verdaderamente no se hacen en Panamá; el cacao (*chocolate bean*), que se llama «Pepa (*seed*) de Oro» porque vale tanto; y el tagua (*vegetable ivory*), del cual se hacen nuestros botones.

Atahualpa era el Inca de Quito cuando salió para el Cuzco a conquistar el reino de su hermano, Huáscar. Se dice que Cotopaxi, cerca de Quito, y el más alto volcán activo del mundo, echó al aire un pedazo inmenso de su pico (*peak*) en el día en que los españoles mataron a Atahualpa. Hasta hoy, se puede ver el pedazo cerca del volcán, y se llama «Cabeza del Inca».

¿Sería interesante visitar al Ecuador? ¡Ojalá pudiéramos hacerlo!

[1] In Spanish, they are called *sombreros de jipijapa* from the name of the plant from which they are made.

"Finest Panama hat weaver in the world," her fellow craftsmen call this girl of Ecuador. A fine hat like this one may be months in the making and sell for several hundred dollars.

Gendreau

TEMA

You may be surprised at the everyday conversations you can carry on in Spanish by now. Here is what two boys said to each other when they met on the street, and they could have said it all in Spanish if they had tried.

Translate the conversation freely, expressing the *idea* rather than giving it word-for-word. Expressions in italics are not to be translated literally, but by the Spanish expressions of similar meaning in the list at the end of the exercise. For example, "I'm out of money" means "I lack money," which takes the verb *faltar*.

Do you use quotation marks in writing conversation in Spanish?

"Hello! *How's everything?*"

"*Same as always.* Tell me the news."

"I don't know *a thing.*"

"*Neither do I.* Going to the dance next Saturday?"

"Can't. I have to stay home and take care of my little brother while *my folks* go to a meeting."

"*That's too bad!* I can't go, either. But let's go to the *show* tonight."

"Well, *I'd like to,* but I don't *feel like* going tonight. *I'm out of* money."

"Where's your bicycle?"

"Johnny borrowed it and *wrecked it.* He *ran into* an automobile."

"*He did!* Did it hurt him?"

"No, but it made me *feel like* telling him *a few things.*"

"*I should say it would!* Where'd you *get* that hat?"

"Bought it at the five and ten."

"*I thought so.* *I got* mine there, too."

"Well, *I'll be seeing you.*"

el cine	*tener ganas de	*creer que sí
hacer pedazos	conseguir (i)	cuatro cosas
*¿Qué tal?	como siempre	ni yo tampoco
hasta la vista	faltar	¡Qué lástima!
mis padres	¡Verdad!	me gustaría ir
*¡Ya lo creo!	nada	chocar con (*collide with*)

CAPÍTULO 25

La leyenda del ñandutí

"And Paraguay and Uruguay," we used to say, naming the South American republics.

But there ought to be a law against mentioning those two countries in the same breath, for they are perhaps as unlike each other as any two countries of South America.

About 1870, Paraguay's spunky Spanish-Guaraní inhabitants fought Argentina, Brazil, and Uruguay all at the same time, and when the smoke of battle had cleared away, most of the Paraguayan "soldiers" were found to be women who had taken the places of men who had been killed in battle. Ever since then, Paraguay has been underpopulated and women and children have had to help run the country. Boys your age, for example, instead of playing basketball, may stand long hours of duty as traffic officers in their capital, Asunción.

Asunción still has its ancient Spanish cobblestoned streets and flagstoned sidewalks, its markets, plazas, and patios. Orange trees grow in the parkways, great flame trees scatter scarlet petals on the ground, and jasmine perfumes the air.

The great Paraná River meanders past the capital and on down to Buenos Aires, and watching the stars from the deck of the cozy river boat you find the Southern Cross sometimes ahead of you and sometimes behind you as the river twists and turns, first through the jungle and then through the endless pampas farther south.

And you could never go to Paraguay and come away without a piece of that exquisite spiderweb lace called *ñandutí*, and someone would be sure to tell you this story of how it was first made.

Guazú era un bello y joven indio guaraní. Vivía con sus padres en una humilde cabaña (*cabin*) que éstos habían construido en la más hermosa parte del bosque paraguayo.

Todos los días la madre de Guazú se sentaba con él bajo la sombra de una palmera, y le enseñaba el amor y la bondad, no sólo para con los seres humanos sino también para con los animales y las plantas, — que tienen, — le decía — alma y corazón como los hombres.

Con esta educación, su hijo pronto fué considerado modelo de buen corazón. Además de bueno, era muy obediente. Jamás ponía mala cara cuando su madrecita le mandaba hacer alguna cosa.

Un día su madre le pidió que fuera hasta una fuente del bosque a traerle un cántaro de agua.

El joven la obedeció, yéndose con su cantarito al hombro. Había terminado de llenarlo cuando vió que en las aguas de la fuente se estaba ahogando una delicada ñandutí (arañita blanca). Recordó que su madre le había enseñado a ser bueno para con los animales, y con un ramito, salvó de morir ahogada a la ñandutí.

— Gracias, Guazú, — dijo el insecto al verse fuera de peligro, — por haberme salvado la vida. Con esta acción has demostrado ser un muchacho bueno. Jamás olvidaré este servicio. Si algún día necesitas de mí, ya sabes que me tienes a tus órdenes.[1]

La araña estaba para irse, pero Guazú le dijo, — No quiero que te vayas, ñandutí. Eres tan bonita que quiero llevarte a vivir conmigo.

— Si tú lo deseas, — le respondió, — estoy lista para irme contigo.

En este momento apareció sobre ellos una sombra enorme. Era el águila con sus enormes alas, que quería llevarse a la arañita. Empezó, entonces, una lucha entre el águila y Guazú, que al fin consiguió matar al ave grande, pero a consecuencia de la lucha, le quedó el hombro cubierto de sangre.

[1] In Spanish you always tell a person politely that you are *a sus órdenes*.

Había vuelto a la fuente para lavar sus heridas (*wounds*), cuando vió allí a una linda muchacha, que le dijo,

— No te preocupes (*worry*) por esto, Guazú. Déjame lavar el hombro, y pronto mejorarás.

La muchacha que le habló era una joven llamada Picazú. Era tan morena como la tierra paraguaya, tan bella como los jazmines [1] de las tierras guaraníes, y tan bondadosa y tierna como no había otra.

Era tal la belleza de la joven, que desde ese día el corazón de Guazú quedó prisionero de sus encantos.

Todas las tardes se reunían los jóvenes a soñar con el día en que pudieran llegar a formar un hogar (*home*) como el de sus padres. Pero cuando Guazú le dijo a Picazú que había tomado la decisión de que sus padres la pidieran en matrimonio,[2] de sus bellos ojos cayeron lágrimas.

— ¿Por qué lloras, alma mía? — preguntó Guazú.

— Es que cuando tus padres pidan mi mano a los míos, no la obtendrán.

Y así sucedió, porque cuando los padres de Guazú pidieron la mano de la muchacha, los de ella les dijeron que, por haber muchos pretendientes, solamente la darían a aquél que trajera a su hija el mejor regalo de bodas.

Entonces los pretendientes de Picazú empezaron su busca (*search*) del regalo más digno de la encantadora joven.

Uno de ellos hizo las más preciosas joyas, entre ellas un collar hecho con estrellas que robó al cielo.

Otro, buscando hasta en los rincones (*corners*) del bosque, le trajo las más bellas flores, e hizo con ellas una preciosa corona (*crown*).

Otro tejió (*wove*) los más complicados (*elaborate*) trajes, tiñendo (*dyeing*) las telas con el tinte de las flores.

Solamente Guazú, que era quien más la amaba, no hallaba un regalo digno de ella.

Temiendo perderla, decidió ir al bosque para ver si éste le

[1] The jasmine is Paraguay's national flower. Being lowland and close to the Torrid Zone, the country is full of flowers all the year around.

[2] What Paraguayan marriage custom do you find in this story? How does it compare with the old Spanish custom? (Chapter 23)

daba un buen consejo. Allí estaba sentado bajo la sombra de un árbol, cuando sintió en la mano un suave toque (*touch*), y se dió cuenta de que era la ñandutí, que le dijo:

— En una ocasión, Guazú, me salvaste la vida. Nunca lo he olvidado. Y en prueba de mi gratitud, ahora vengo a recompensar (*reward*) tu buen corazón.

Guazú sonrió al escuchar su voz. — ¿Cómo puede ser, — pensó, — que esta ñandutí sea capaz (*capable*) de darme un regalo que me permita ganar la mano de mi amada?

Pero el agradecido insecto hilaba, hilaba, hilaba (*kept spinning*), con hilos (*threads*) de plata que arrancaba a los rayos de la luna. Se durmió Guazú, pero la ñandutí trabajaba, trabajaba, trabajaba.

Terminó su obra a la misma hora en que salía el sol, y puso en manos de Guazú algo verdaderamente maravilloso que triunfó (*triumphed*) sobre las flores, las joyas y las telas que habían llevado los otros pretendientes.

Lo que la arañita blanca entregó al joven fué la primera pieza que se ha hecho en el Paraguay de esa bella tela, que

Ñandutí lace fan shows exquisite spiderweb needlework of the Guaraní Indians of Paraguay.

Sawders

desde entonces se llama ñandutí, en recuerdo (*remembrance*) de la agradecida arañita blanca que, haciéndola, permitió a Guazú casarse con la linda muchacha.

ADAPTED FROM FRANCISCO BARNOYA GÁLVEZ (*Guatemala*)

PALABRAS NUEVAS

3	**agradecido**	grateful		**guaraní** (*m. and f.*)	Indian of Paraguay
3	**ahogarse**	to drown	3	**lágrima**	tear
	el águila (*f.*)	eagle	4	**lucha**	struggle
	araña (-**ita**)	spider		**ñandutí** (*m.*)	Guaraní word for spider, or spider-web lace
3	**el ave** (*f.*)	bird		**palmera**	palm tree
	cántaro	pitcher, jug		**paraguayo**	Paraguayan
2	**digno**	worthy		**pretendiente** (*m.*)	suitor
2	**entregar**	to deliver	3	**tierno**	tender

EXPRESIONES

a consecuencia de, as a result of
llegar a, to succeed in, come to
para con, to, toward
poner mala cara, to pout

¿VERDAD O NO?

1. Guazú vivía en el Perú en una humilde cabaña. 2. El padre de Guazú le enseñó a ser bueno para con todos. 3. Los guaraníes creen que los animales y las plantas tienen alma y corazón como los hombres. 4. Cuando su madre le pidió que fuese por agua, Guazú no quería hacerlo. 5. En el río vió ahogarse a un águila. 6. El animal prometió no olvidar nunca la ayuda de Guazú. 7. Guazú le salvó tres veces la vida a la araña. 8. La linda muchacha le lavó las manos a Guazú en la fuente. 9. Guazú se enamoró de la joven. 10. Sus padres dijeron que el que le trajese más dinero podría casarse con ella. 11. Guazú halló en el bosque una pieza delicada de ñandutí. 12. La ñandutí es algo verdaderamente maravilloso.

Paraguay's boys have to do men's work as traffic officers, policemen, and sanitary inspectors. Two of these boys are fifteen years old, the other is eighteen.

PREGUNTAS

1. ¿Quién le enseñó a Guazú el amor y la bondad? 2. ¿Ponía mala cara el muchacho cuando ayudaba a su madre? 3. ¿Qué vió en las aguas de la fuente? 4. ¿Cómo salvó a la araña blanca? 5. ¿Sabía hablar con él la ñandutí? 6. ¿Comió el águila a la arañita? 7. ¿Dónde encontró Guazú a la linda muchacha? 8. ¿Cómo le ayudó ella? 9. Desde ese día, ¿con qué soñaban los dos? 10. ¿Fué Guazú a ver a los padres de su novia para pedirles su mano? 11. ¿Había otros pretendientes? ¿Por qué? 12. ¿Qué le trajeron los otros a Picazú? 13. ¿Creía Guazú al principio que la araña pudiese ayudarle? 14. ¿Cómo termina el cuento?

PREGUNTAS PERSONALES

1. ¿Aprende Vd. sus lecciones bajo la sombra de una palmera? 2. ¿Pone Vd. mala cara alguna vez cuando sus padres le mandan hacer algo? 3. ¿Tiene Vd. siempre ganas de obedecer a sus padres? 4. ¿Obedece Vd. a su hermanito? 5. ¿Tiene Vd. que llevar de una

fuente toda el agua para la casa? 6. ¿Salvaría Vd. de morir a una araña? 7. ¿Ha estado Vd. para ahogarse alguna vez? 8. ¿Le gustaría a Vd. tener una lucha con un águila grande? 9. ¿Ha robado Vd. alguna vez estrellas al cielo? 10. ¿Sabría Vd. hacer una pieza de ñandutí? 11. ¿Espera Vd. algún día recibir muchos regalos de bodas?

PARA COMPLETAR

1. Guazú vivía .... 2. Todos los días, su madre .... 3. El muchacho nunca ponía mala cara cuando .... 4. Si Guazú no hubiese obedecido a su madre, nunca habría .... 5. La linda muchacha ayudó a Guazú a .... 6. La muchacha era tan bella como .... 7. Todas las tardes los jóvenes .... 8. Picazú lloró porque creía que .... 9. Picazú no podía casarse sin que sus padres .... 10. Un pretendiente le trajo .... 11. Otro le trajo .... 12. Guazú temía no poder hallar ....

REPASO DE VERBOS

I. Using the verbs **traducir, consentir, suceder, construir, suponer, contener,** *and* **devolver,** *give the following verb forms:*

I translated, he consented, it may happen, he built, we supposed, it will contain, they have returned it, they are building (*prog.*), we might suppose, they contained, we shall return it, translate!, we may consent, has it happened?, we have built, he would suppose, it would contain, they used to return them, he had consented, he would have consented

II. Give the infinitive, and then translate each of the following verb forms carefully:

se acercó, coja Vd., han cubierto, se calló, se detuvo, se convirtió en, lo colgué, me despediré de, léalo Vd., se casase con, empecemos, encontrasen, aprendan, compraran, compraron, me faltaba, huyendo, paguen, servimos, sirvamos, siguió, jueguen, rió, riendo, sonreí

ALGO NUEVO

59. Definite Article Used as Demonstrative

los de su familia, *those of his family*
los que hablan demasiado, *those who talk too much*
lo que quiere, *that which he wants*
mi sombrero y el que Vd. tiene, *my hat and that which (the one) you have*

English *that, those, the one, that which* (*what*), are usually expressed by the definite articles (***el, la, los, las, lo***) when followed by ***de*** or ***que.***

EJERCICIO I. *Translate carefully:*

1. Los que no tratan de hacerlo, no ganan. 2. Es imposible darle lo que pide. 3. No tengo el que Vd. busca. 4. Aquel cura (*priest*) es el que hizo el milagro. 5. Las que invitó no pudieron aceptar. 6. El que se declaró vencido no ganó la batalla. 7. Los que contaba Paucar eran cuentos interesantes. 8. ¿Qué es lo que cuentas? 9. Lo que Vd. debe buscar es un hombre rico. 10. No quiero los de plata, sino los de oro. 11. Esta india es la que le mostró el camino.

EJERCICIO II. *Complete in Spanish:*

1. ¿Por qué no invita Vd. a *those who* saben cantar? 2. Pienso invitar solamente *those of* mi clase. 3. *Those of* su clase no podrían ir. 4. ¿Dónde está *the one who* (*f.*) canta bien? 5. Ella es *the one who* está cerca del piano. 6. Nunca sabe *what* quiere. 7. *Those who* (*f.*) hablan demasiado no tienen muchos amigos. 8. ¡Tampoco *the ones who* tienen dos caras! 9. *The one who* nunca hace *what* quieren los demás, no es muy popular. 10. Y no queremos como amigo *the one who* no puede guardar secretos. 11. Sabemos las costumbres de México, pero no sabemos *those of* Guatemala.

60. *The Perfect (Compound) Infinitive*

Es preciso haberlo visto para creerlo. *It is necessary to have seen it to believe it.*

¡Cuánto me alegro de haberlo oído! *How glad I am to have heard it!*

The perfect (compound) infinitive is very commonly used. An object pronoun must be attached to this infinitive as to any other.

EJERCICIO III. *Translate carefully:*

1. Después de haber comido, salió a la calle. 2. A pesar de haber visto el tren, el automovilista no se detuvo. 3. Antes de haber chocado (*collide*) con él, consiguió evitar el peligro. 4. Siente mucho no habérselo entregado. 5. Sin habérnoslo dicho, se fué. 6. Temía haberlo perdido. 7. Después de haberle dado el dinero, no le dió nada más. 8. Para haberlo terminado, habría tenido que trabajar toda la noche.

ESTUDIO DE PALABRAS[1]

I. Here you have a dinner menu from which to choose your meal, and since your Mexican waitress does not speak English, you will have to guess, and if you make a mistake, eat what you get!

The following items are somewhere on the menu: potato salad, crackers, olives, oysters, clam chowder, (green) peas, steak, fruit ice, lemon pie (tart), strawberry sundae, creamed corn, cold chicken, chicken and rice, creamed carrots. If you can't find some of them, read Exercise II, which furnishes clues, for many of the words are not in the general vocabulary.

Choose a good dinner and find out how much it will cost you at five *pesos* to the dollar. The prices are given in Mexican *pesos.*

[1] Optional section, since words used here are not repeated unless introduced in the regular way.

Salón de Refrescos Sanborn

MENÚ[1]

Desayunos Sanborn's entre semana de 7:30 a 11:00
Domingos de 8:00 a 11:00
Lunch Comercial, de 12:30 a 15:00; Te, de 16:00 a 18:00
Comida, de 18:00 a 21:30

FIAMBRES	Pollo frío	1.25	Jamón frío	1.00
	Aceitunas negras o verdes	.40	Lengua fría	1.00
	Pickles "Dill"	.40	Pickles, mixto	.40
	Carnes frías con ensalada de papa 2.00			
SOPAS	Sopa de pollo	1.25	Crema de jitomate	.60
	Consommé con huevo	.75	Crema de espárragos	.60
	Servimos galletas con los pedidos de sopa			
PESCADOS	Langosta a la Newburg	2.00	Puchero de almejas	1.00
	Pescado acremado	1.00	Ostiones (docena)	2.00
	Croquetas de pescado	1.00	Pescado con pan tostado	.75
	Sardinas en salsa de jitomate .75			
LEGUMBRES	Espárragos c/ mantequilla	1.00	Papas a la francesa	.60
	Papas Saratoga	.60	Espinaca	.50
	Chícharos	.60	Elote en crema	.50
	Ejotes	.60	Zanahorias en crema	.50

CARNES	Filete con papas a la francesa	2.00
	Hamburguesa con ensalada de papa	1.75
	Pollo con salsa de limón y espárragos	2.50
	Pollo con arroz y curry	2.00
	Pollo acremado con pan tostado	1.50
	Frankfurters con choucrout	1.45
	Corned beef hash con huevo	1.15
	Jamón importado	1.50
PASTELES Y POSTRES	Shortcake de fresa	.75
	Tartaleta de limón, perón o calabaza	.40
	Panqués	.35
	Helado de chocolate o vainilla	.40
	Helado con fresas	1.00
	Nieve de fruta	.50

[1] For your drink and bread, see the breakfast menu in Chapter 23. Mexicans would order an egg course also, after the soup.

II. Estas frases describen algunos alimentos del menú. Si Vd. las entiende, le será fácil escoger su comida.

1. Los ***fiambres*** se llaman en francés *hors d'oeuvres*; sirven para abrir el apetito al principio de una comida. 2. El ***pescado*** no tiene patas (*legs*) y vive en el agua. Se llama pez antes de sacarse del agua, pero después, es pescado. Muchas personas comen pescado los viernes. 3. Las ***legumbres*** son plantas, y se comen diferentes partes de varias legumbres, como las hojas (*leaves*), las pepitas (*seeds*), o la raíz (*root*). Los ***chícharos*** son pepitas verdes; los ***ejotes*** son una clase de frijol verde; las ***zanahorias*** son raíces de color de naranja. 4. Los ***postres*** se comen al fin de una comida. 5. Las ***aceitunas*** son chicas, y crecen en un árbol llamado olivo. 6. Sin las dos primeras letras y la última, la palabra ***ensalada*** es muy fácil de adivinar (*guess*). 7. Las ***galletas*** casi siempre se comen con la sopa. Son una clase de pan seco, en pedazos pequeños. 8. Una ***langosta*** vive en el océano, tiene patas, y tiene un color rojo después de cocerse (*cook*). 9. El ***puchero de almejas*** es un plato que se come mucho en los estados del nordeste (*northeast*) de nuestro país. Las ***almejas*** son una clase de pescado que no nada y no tiene patas. 10. El ***filete*** algunas veces se llama *biftec*. 11. Los chinos comen mucho ***arroz***. 12. Las ***fresas*** se parecen a corazoncitos rojos. 13. Una ***tartaleta*** es una clase de pastel lleno de fruta. 14. El ***perón*** también se llama *manzana*. 15. La ***tartaleta de calabaza*** se come mucho en nuestro Día de Acción de Gracias. 16. Los ***jitomates*** algunas veces se llaman *tomates*.

III. Conteste Vd. en español, buscando las palabras en el menú, porque muchas no están en el vocabulario:

1. ¿Cuándo le gusta a Vd. mandar carne fría con ensalada de papa (patata)? 2. ¿Pide Vd. sopa cuando se desayuna? 3. ¿Podría Vd. comer una docena de ostiones? 4. ¿Quién come siempre su espinaca y después se pone muy fuerte? 5. ¿Come Vd. muchas hamburguesas cuando asiste a un juego de fútbol? 6. ¿Le gusta a Vd. comer helado cuando hace mucho frío? 7. ¿Come Vd. pescado los viernes? 8. ¿Hace Vd. sandwiches con jamón frío alguna vez? 9. ¿Come Vd. pollo todos los días? 10. ¿Cuál es más barato, el filete o la hamburguesa? 11. ¿Son rojos o verdes los espárragos? 12. ¿Qué hacemos con el arroz cuando asistimos a las bodas de unos amigos? 13. ¿Cuál le gusta más, la tartaleta de limón o de calabaza?

14. ¿Servimos panqués[1] aquí como postre o como alimento de desayuno? 15. ¿Qué clase de sopa le gusta más?

REPASITO

I. Make a sentence using each group of words or expressions:

1. obedecer, padres, en casa, porque 2. cuanto más, tener, más, querer 3. llamar, médico, enfermo, para que, curar 4. guerra, es preciso, combatir, perder 5. hacer frío, tener frío, ponerse, abrigo 6. pedir prestado, dinero, devolverlo 7. comida, sopa, carne, legumbres, postre 8. desayuno, cereal, huevos, pan, café 9. cabeza, boca, nariz, ojos, cara 10. llevar, zapatos, pies, sombrero, cabeza, traje 11. todos los días, ir, volver, acostarse 12. gustar, hacer un viaje, países, para, lo que, hacer 13. burlarse de, amigos, enojarse 14. manejar, coche, cuidado, peligro 15. ratón, queso, gato, coger, comer

II. Here are some expressions which second-year Spanish students have wanted to use but have used incorrectly. *Can you give them correctly?*

1. another horse
2. yesterday afternoon
3. he came to see me
4. with Mrs. García
5. after cleaning house
6. I saw him go
7. at Mary's
8. I took a walk
9. we went swimming
10. the water was cold
11. I was cold
12. that night
13. I drank some milk
14. I worked all morning
15. I was very tired
16. she was there
17. it rained hard
18. we went riding

III. Tell in simple Spanish sentences what you did last night after school. Keep a list of the things you wanted to say and with which you had to be helped.

[1] *Panqueques* is also used.

PARA LEER SIN ESTUDIAR

Algo más acerca del Paraguay

En el Paraguay se ve bien la influencia de la Argentina, porque para los paraguayos, Buenos Aires es la capital del mundo. Se usa el dinero argentino tanto como el del Paraguay, porque éste vale muy poco. ¡Cuesta $5, dinero paraguayo, tomar un tranvía (*streetcar*)!

El movimiento de automóviles de Asunción ya no toma la izquierda,* sino la derecha, y aunque no hay muchos automóviles, la policía trabaja todo el día en las esquinas (*street corners*).

Todas las tiendas y oficinas se cierran entre las 11:30 y las 15:00 para la siesta, y muchos toman mate [1] con bombilla [2] de plata. Se come mucha mandioca [3] en las comidas, en vez de patatas, porque las patatas son muy caras.

Hay siete mujeres en el Paraguay para cada hombre, porque además de los que murieron en la guerra de 1870, murieron muchos

* Until recently, automobiles in many Latin American countries drove on the left; now all South American traffic moves to the right.

[1] See general vocabulary. [2] A *bombilla* is a silver sipper (picture, page 153).

[3] A root from which tapioca is made.

Asunción, capital of Paraguay, located on the winding Paraná River, can be reached by boat in three days from Buenos Aires.

Galloway

paraguayos en la guerra del Chaco con Bolivia entre 1932 y 1935.

Para llamar la atención en el Paraguay, como en España, todos dan palmadas (*clap hands*). Cuando los vapores (*boats*) del río están para salir para Buenos Aires, todos los empleados (*employees*) empiezan a dar palmadas, y siguen haciéndolo hasta que hayan bajado los que no van a hacer el viaje.

Los paraguayos hablan dos lenguas, el español y el guaraní, porque cuando llegaron los conquistadores, no pudieron vencer a los valientes indios que vivían allí. Se encuentran muchas canciones guaraníes que son muy bonitas. Y todos aprenden las antiguas leyendas y fábulas (*fables*) de los indios, porque casi todos llevan en sus venas (*veins*) sangre india.

Aquí tiene Vd. unas palabras guaraníes, para que Vd. pueda percibir la diferencia entre el español y el guaraní:

membira	*madre*	ibotís	*flores*
caá-aná	*bosque*	ara-ra-cá	*águila*
cunumí	*muchacho*	miní	*chico*
cunatai	*muchacha*	bé-tarará	*flauta*

¿Se parece el guaraní al español?

TEMA

Two girls met after school, and if they had only thought of it, they could have carried on their whole conversation in Spanish. How could they have said the following? (The expressions in italics are at the end of the exercise.)

"Hello! Going *home* now?"

"No, I have to *go down town.*"

"*Are you taking a street car?*"

"*I will* if you'll lend me a *nickel.*"

"*Okay. Here it is.* Did you get your *report card*?"

"Yes, but I didn't *do so well.* Did you *get good grades*?"

"*Pretty good.* And *listen, darling*! Mom said I could have a *party* if I passed. But I'm not going to invite that Lupe Ramírez."

"*You don't say!* Why not?"

"She's *two-faced.* Listen, can you keep a secret?"

"Well, maybe. What happened?"

"Well, that *sourpuss* told the teacher that I asked her to help me write yesterday's lesson, and now I have to *stay after school.*"

"*The very idea! Here comes* my car. *See you later.*"

"'*Bye.*"

obtener buenas notas	un cinco	ir al centro
quedarme después de las clases	ya viene	sí
	tiene dos caras	bueno
adiosito	tomar un tranvía	regular; más o menos
tarjeta (*card*)	salir bien	fiesta (reunión)
*a casa	*hasta luego	*aquí lo tiene Vd.
cara de limón	¡Qué barbaridad!	¡No me diga!
mire, preciosa		

CAPÍTULO 26

Optional Chapter[1]

Dos fábulas guaraníes

Long before the Spaniards came to Paraguay, the Guaraní Indians had created their own folklore and stories of the forests where they lived. The animals of their stories had certain human characteristics and were always getting mixed up in interesting situations, sometimes tragic, sometimes humorous. The white deer, the black tiger (really a puma), the armadillo, the crocodile, the tapir, the hawks and the hummingbirds, all figure in tales that would be a credit to a modern author.

Here are two of the fables.

[1] Note to teacher: This chapter may be omitted in order to finish Chapter 27 by the end of the third quarter if there is not time for both. Chapter 27, however, should be completed, since it is a final review of Chapters 19–25, inclusive.

I. El venado blanco y el tigre negro

El venado blanco, buscando un lugar para construir su casa, lo halló en el bosque cerca de un río. Al tigre negro le ocurrió lo mismo. Y ambos, por casualidad, escogieron el mismo sitio, poco frecuentado (*visited*) y con abundante agua.

Al día siguiente, antes de salir el sol, el venado cortó los arbustos y aserró (*sawed*) los árboles. Cuando el tigre negro llegó y vió estas preparaciones constructivas, exclamó, — ¡Es Tupá [1] que viene a ayudarme!

Y empezó a trabajar con los árboles cortados. Cuando el venado llegó al día siguiente, exclamó a su vez, — ¡Sin duda Tupá ha venido a ayudarme! — Y empezó a techar (*roof*) la casa. La dividió en dos habitaciones y se instaló en una de ellas.

Al llegar el tigre vió la casa terminada. Creyó que fué Tupá que la había hecho y se instaló en la otra habitación.

Pero al día siguiente se encontraron los dos animales y comprendieron lo ocurrido. El venado dijo, — Ha de ser Tupá que hizo esto para que viviésemos juntos. ¿Quieres que vivamos juntos?

El tigre aceptó, diciendo, — Vivamos juntos, sí. Hoy salgo yo a buscar comida, mañana saldrás tú. — Y se fué.

Regresó a medianoche, trayendo un venado rojo. Lo dividió en dos partes, y le dijo a su compañero — Toma; haz la comida.

El venado blanco, temblando de miedo y de horror, hizo la comida, pero no comió un bocado (*mouthful*) de ella. Más aun, no durmió en toda la noche. Temía que su peligroso compañero se despertara con hambre.

Al día siguiente el venado blanco tenía que buscar la comida para ambos. Salió al bosque. ¿Qué hacer? De pronto vió un tigre dormido, un tigre más grande y más poderoso que su compañero, y se le ocurrió una idea. Fué en busca del oso negro.

[1] *Tupá* is the old Guaraní word for God. In the Guaraní fables, even the animals believe in God.

— Oso negro, — le dijo, — ¿ves aquel tigre dormido? Ese tigre anda diciendo que tú no eres fuerte.

El oso negro, que es muy fuerte, silenciosamente fué a donde estaba el tigre, le cogió entre sus poderosos brazos y le apretó (*squeezed*) hasta ahogarle (*strangle*).

Entonces el venado cogió al tigre muerto y, llevándolo hasta su casa, lo tiró en medio de ella y dijo a su compañero con desdén: — Toma, come. ¡Es todo lo que he podido encontrar!

El tigre no dijo nada, pero tenía mucho miedo. No comió tampoco. Esa noche no durmió ninguno de los dos compañeros. El venado esperaba la venganza (*vengeance*) del tigre; éste temía que aquél le matara como había hecho con el otro tigre más grande y más poderoso que él.

Ya de día, muerto de sueño, el venado dejó caer la cabeza contra la pared que separaba ambas habitaciones. Creyendo el tigre que su compañero venía a atacarle, salió corriendo. Pero hizo ruido con sus garras (*claws*), y, suponiendo el venado que el tigre venía a matarle, también salió de prisa.

Y la casa quedó abandonada.

II. El Árbol misterioso

Había un árbol misterioso, cuyas frutas eran guardadas por un fantasma. Nadie que no supiese su nombre podía cogerlas. Sólo el fantasma sabía el nombre de las frutas. Era preciso sorprenderle durmiendo y escucharle mientras soñaba. Pero el fantasma tenía un oído muy fino, y se despertaba fácilmente.

El armadillo [1] hizo un túnel subterráneo y así pudo llegar cerca del fantasma sin que éste le oyera. Sorprendióle durmiendo y le oyó decir, — Boií, boií,[2] quizama, quizú; boií, boií, quizama, quizú.

[1] An armadillo is a small tropical animal with a jointed hard shell or armor. The name itself is Spanish, meaning *little armored one*. In Guaraní fables, the armadillo is a pretty clever fellow, always playing a flute. To picture him as musical is perhaps natural, for many an armadillo shell has been made into a small guitar.

[2] Nonsense syllables, like our "abracadabra."

El armadillo cogió su flauta y comenzó a cantar, — Boií, boií, quizama, quizú.

El fantasma, sorprendido su secreto, había perdido el poder, y desapareció.

Las frutas misteriosas eran del armadillo ahora.

Entonces apareció un puma y dijo, — Tú no puedes subir al árbol. Dime a mí el nombre, y yo subiré y las cogeré para ti y para mí.

El armadillo le dió el nombre de la fruta misteriosa. Subió el puma, cogió varias frutas, y al bajar, empezó a correr con ellas sin dar ninguna al armadillo.

Éste, que, además de listo, es obstinado (*stubborn*), corrió tras él, y le alcanzó cerca de un río. El puma, cargado como iba, no se atrevía a cruzar.

El armadillo, disimulando (*hiding*) su indignación, se le acercó, como si no hubiese comprendido la acción del puma, y se ofreció, ya que era un nadador más experto, a llevar la carga al otro lado, diciéndole que allí le esperaría.

El puma le miró receloso (*suspiciously*), pero vió sólo ino-

Tough-shelled armadillos are meat-eaters and live in the deserts as well as the jungles of South America. Guitars or sewing baskets are often made of their armored hides.

Black Star

cencia en los ojos del armadillo. Le entregó las frutas, y el armadillo, al llegar al otro lado del río, corrió a esconderse en su cueva para comerlas.

Y el puma sólo podía bramar (*roar*) de rabia (*anger*) al verse burlado.

ADAPTED FROM ERNESTO MORALES (*Argentina*)

PALABRAS NUEVAS [1]

2 **cortar**	to cut	1 **el poder** (*m.*)	power
fábula	fable	**venado**	deer
oso	bear		

NEW WORDS RELATED TO OTHERS YOU KNOW

atacar (**ataque**), to attack
en busca de (**buscar**), in search of
lo ocurrido (**ocurrir**), what had occurred
nadador (**nadar**), swimmer
4 **peligroso** (**peligro**), dangerous
3 **poderoso** (**poder**), powerful

EXPRESIONES

***a su vez,** in his turn
hacer la comida, to get dinner
***lo mismo que,** the same as
ya que, since

¿VERDAD O NO?

Change these statements to make them true if they are false.

I. 1. El venado negro buscó un lugar para construir su casa. 2. Por casualidad, ambos escogieron un lugar lejos del río. 3. El tigre cortó los árboles para construir la casa. 4. Cada animal creía que Tupá estaba ayudándole a construir la casa. 5. La casa tenía tres cuartos. 6. A los dos animales les gustaba vivir juntos. 7. Cada uno escogió una comida que le gustó al otro. 8. El venado blanco consiguió matar a un tigre más poderoso que su compañero. 9. Ambos durmieron bien en su casa nueva. 10. El oso negro ayudó al tigre negro. 11. El tigre temía que el venado le matase. 12. El venado trató de hacer correr al tigre.

[1] Since this is an optional chapter, all words not used in Book II are given here, but are repeated in vocabularies if introduced later, since this chapter will be omitted by many classes.

II. 1. Para coger las frutas misteriosas, era preciso pagar al fantasma. 2. El fantasma no podía oír bien. 3. El armadillo era más listo que el fantasma. 4. El armadillo no tenía ninguna dificultad en subir al árbol para coger las frutas. 5. El puma tocaba bien la flauta. 6. El puma quería ayudar al armadillo a coger las frutas. 7. El armadillo no podía cruzar el río con la carga de frutas. 8. Al fin el puma se llevó las frutas y se escondió en su cueva para comerlas.

PREGUNTAS

I. 1. ¿Qué se les ocurrió al venado y al tigre? 2. ¿Qué hicieron, por casualidad? 3. ¿Por qué escogieron aquel sitio? 4. ¿Cuándo cortó el venado los árboles? 5. ¿Cuándo trabajó el tigre, de día o de noche? 6. ¿Qué creían ambos? 7. ¿Cuándo se encontraron los dos animales? 8. ¿Por qué decidieron vivir juntos? 9. ¿Qué trajo el tigre para la primera comida? 10. ¿Comió mucho el venado blanco? 11. ¿Qué hizo el oso por el venado blanco? 12. ¿Le dijo la verdad el venado? 13. ¿Creía el tigre que el venado pudiese matarle? 14. ¿Por qué no durmieron bien los dos compañeros? 15. Al fin, ¿cuál de los dos animales siguió viviendo en la casa nueva?

II. 1. ¿Quién guardaba las frutas misteriosas? 2. ¿Cómo sería posible cogerlas? 3. ¿Hablaba el fantasma mientras dormía? 4. ¿Qué decía? 5. ¿Cómo consiguió el armadillo llegar cerca del fantasma sin despertarle? 6. ¿Qué cantó el armadillo? 7. ¿Qué quería hacer el puma? 8. ¿Le dijo el armadillo las palabras misteriosas? 9. Sin ellas, ¿podría haber cogido el puma las frutas? 10. ¿Cuál sabía nadar mejor, el puma o el armadillo? 11. ¿Le entregó el puma la carga al armadillo?

PARA COMPLETAR

I. 1. El venado blanco escogió .... 2. Antes de salir el sol, el venado empezó a .... 3. El tigre negro también .... 4. Los dos animales .... 5. Cada uno iba a .... 6. Cada uno temía que .... 7. El venado blanco le dijo al oso que .... 8. El oso negro era muy .... 9. No durmieron bien los dos porque temían

.... 10. El venado despertó al tigre cuando .... 11. Después, la casa ....

II. 1. Las frutas del árbol encantado eran .... 2. Para cogerlas, era preciso .... 3. El armadillo llegó sin hacer ruido .... (*use a gerund*). 4. En su sueño, el fantasma decía, ... 5. El puma quería que el armadillo .... 6. Después de coger las frutas, el puma .... 7. El armadillo se le acercó y ofreció a .... 8. Al llegar al otro lado del río, el armadillo ....

PREGUNTAS PERSONALES

1. ¿Qué clase de sitio escogería Vd. para una casa? 2. ¿Ha cortado Vd. muchos árboles en un bosque? 3. ¿Regresa Vd. a casa a medianoche muchas veces? 4. ¿Tiene Vd. que salir en busca de comida cada día? 5. ¿Le gusta a Vd. ayudar a su madre a hacer la comida? 6. ¿Tiene Vd. compañeros peligrosos? 7. ¿Se le ocurren a Vd. muchas ideas? 8. ¿Quisiera Vd. coger un oso entre los brazos? 9. ¿Cuál es más poderoso, Vd. o un oso? 10. ¿Se cae Vd. de sueño en la clase de español? 11. Cuando suena la campanilla, ¿sale Vd. de prisa de la clase? 12. ¿Qué dice Vd. mientras sueña? 13.

Iguazú ("Great Waters") Falls cut through the jungle between Brazil and Paraguay. They are higher and wider than Niagara, and are surrounded by tropical ferns, orchids, begonias, and palms.

Gendreau

¿Habla Vd. en la clase sin que el profesor le oiga? 14. ¿Es fácil aprender a tocar la flauta? 15. ¿Es Vd. muy obstinado? 16. ¿Se atrevería Vd. a cruzar un río con una carga? 17. ¿Se ha escondido Vd. en su cuarto algunas veces para comer dulces? 18. ¿Se enoja Vd. mucho al verse burlado?

LO CONTRARIO

The opposites of these expressions were used in the two stories. *If you cannot give them without help, see if you can find them.*

1. lejos de un río
2. después de salir el sol
3. vió la casa empezada
4. vivamos separados
5. temblando de valor
6. tú no eres débil
7. salió despacio
8. otro tigre más débil
9. todos podían cogerlas
10. el fantasma apareció
11. yo bajaré
12. ya que no sabía nadar

¿CÓMO SE DICE?

You should be able to say these expressions in your own words in Spanish. Change the wording all you need to in order to express the idea; for example: ***un sitio poco frecuentado: un lugar a donde iba poca gente.***

se instaló en una de las habitaciones, comprendieron lo ocurrido, temía que su compañero se despertara con hambre, ¿Qué hacer?, vió un tigre dormido, cayéndose de sueño, la casa quedó abandonada, era preciso sorprenderle durmiendo, sorprendióle durmiendo, las frutas eran del armadillo, era un nadador más experto, dime a mí el nombre (*polite*), fué en busca del oso

REPASO DE VERBOS

I. Conjugate in the present indicative: traducir, traer, servir, coger, seguir, reír.

II. Conjugate the same verbs in the preterite indicative.

III. Give the first person present subjunctive of each of the same verbs.

IV. Give these forms in Spanish:

he translated, that we may serve, he laughed, laugh!, take hold of!, follow me!, that they may follow, that she may bring, don't bring it!, we serve, they follow, we translate, that we may translate, they laugh, you bring, he takes hold of

ESTUDIO DE PALABRAS

I. ¿Verdad o no?[1]

1. Durante la conquista de la América del Sur, fué fácil ganar pacíficamente la gloria sin combates ni batallas. 2. Un barbero rústico siempre gana su salario tomando parte en una procesión. 3. Había mucha animación en la plaza cuando el Inca se presentaba con sus nobles y heraldos. 4. Los dos compañeros arrogantes e impetuosos, en una discusión con el primitivo quichua, querían hacerle decir el secreto de la magnífica cadena de metal. 5. Con violenta indignación, el aristocrático monarca de los incas observó el plan de los conquistadores. 6. La niña tenía un par de ojos como dos torpedos cargados de dinamita. 7. En conmemoración de una gloriosa batalla, es costumbre tener una fiesta espléndida en un cementerio. 8. Un espectador de una conversación ininteligible puede ponerse impaciente y abandonar el grupo. 9. Un insecto insignificante forma un monumento artístico. 10. Con frecuencia, la curiosidad femenina puede causar una situación complicada. 11. La gratitud por un servicio experto inevitablemente nos da completa satisfacción.

II. Use each of these words in a short sentence which will show that you know its meaning:

llevar	sonar	envolver	desaparecer	despedirse
llover	soñar	devolver	parecer	impedir
lluvia	sueño	volver	aparecer	pedir

[1] This exercise is made up almost entirely of cognates used in Chapters 17 to 25, inclusive. They are not all in the vocabulary. Guess!

III. Are these pairs synonyms or antonyms?

jamás, nunca	último, primero	alhaja, joya
estrecho, ancho	vivo, muerto	suceder, pasar
obtener, conseguir	vencer, conquistar	entender, comprender
alegre, infeliz	acabar, terminar	dirigirse a, ir a
bello, hermoso	recordar, acordarse de	marido, esposo
pertenecer a, ser de	afuera, dentro	regresar, volver

PARA DIVERTIRSE

I. «Consejos para todos». Escriban Vds. en un pedazo de papel un buen consejo para cualquier otro, como «Lávese Vd. las manos antes de comer», etc. Después cambien Vds. los papeles y lean en voz alta lo que los otros hayan escrito.

II. ¿«Qué letra escoge»? El líder indica a uno de sus compañeros y dice una letra del alfabeto, como ***d***. El jugador (*player*) indicado tiene que decir en seguida (*at once*) algo como, — Soy ***D***iego, de ***D***urango, y me gusta ***d***esaparecer. — O si el líder dice, — ***c***, — entonces otro contesta en seguida. — Soy ***C***onsuelo, de ***C***uernavaca, y me gusta ***c***omer.

PARA LEER SIN ESTUDIAR

Gratis

La mayoría (*majority*) de la gente no sabe que existe un servicio social completamente gratuito (*free*), recientemente instalado por la Compañía de Teléfonos Ericsson. Con sólo llamar al 18–18–60, se puede obtener un médico a medianoche, si un enfermo lo necesita; se puede conseguir informes sobre salida (*departure*) de aviones y trenes, o recetas (*recipes*) de cocina, etcétera. Cualquier pregunta que Vd. haga, se le contestará inmediatamente, sin costo alguno. Este servicio se hace durante veinte y cuatro horas, y en la oficina no hay día de descanso (*rest*).

From «*Todo*», A MAGAZINE OF MEXICO

BUENOS VECINOS

Con motivo de celebrar el cumpleaños del Presidente de los Estados Unidos, Franklin D. Roosevelt, tuvo lugar en el Pabellón (*pavilion*) Nacional un gran baile al cual asistió una selecta concurrencia (*group*) de la ciudad.

El Pabellón era bello bajo la suave iluminación y con la fila (*line*) de muchachas bonitas ricamente vestidas que asistieron en honor del Primer Ciudadano (*citizen*) de América y del Mundo.

Su Excelencia, el Embajador de los Estados Unidos, Dr. Francisco Córrigan, asistió al festival con todos sus amigos, que lo son también de su gran patria.

From «*Billiken*», A MAGAZINE OF CARACAS, VENEZUELA[1]

TEMA

1. The white deer and the black bear chose a place near the forest. 2. The next day the deer cut [down] the trees. 3. Upon seeing this, the bear believed that Tupá was helping him. 4. Finally the house was built by both, and they went to live there. 5. They thought Tupá wanted them to live together. 6. Each one was to look for food and get dinner. 7. At midnight the deer brought [some] milk, but the bear didn't drink a mouthful (**bocado**) of it. 8. He didn't like milk, but water. 9. The bear went to look for a meal for both. 10. Suddenly he saw a tiger and became so frightened that he returned home without anything. 11. That night they made so much noise while they were dreaming that they had to leave the house. 12. The deer ran after the bear and both reached the other side of the river.

[1] Does it sound as if Venezuela is friendly to the United States?

CAPÍTULO 27

Quarterly Review

I. Las monedas y la historia

Not all countries have as commonplace names for their money as we do, with our unimaginative "dollar." Latin-Americans are poets at heart, even when it comes to financial affairs, and so we may expect to find interesting names given to their coins. In most of the Latin-American countries monetary units have significant names, such as *soles* (suns) or the names of birds or heroes, Indian or Spanish.

Here is the story of some of the coins you will carry in your pockets when you visit your Good Neighbors.

La moneda nacional de muchos países lleva en su nombre un recuerdo de la historia del país. Es interesante considerar las monedas diferentes, para recordar lo que pasó hace muchos años en el país de su uso. Como ya saben Vds., los dólares de Guatemala se llaman quetzales, porque el quetzal era el emblema de la libertad entre los indios y todavía lo es entre los guatemaltecos. En Guatemala también se acepta el dinero norteamericano, porque vale lo mismo que el guatemalteco.

En México usan pesos, pero la pieza de diez pesos oro se llama el hidalgo, en honor del «Wáshington de México», que inició (*started*) la revolución de la independencia.

Viajando por Centroamérica, hallamos que dos países — Costa Rica y El Salvador — usan colones, en memoria de Cristóbal Colón, que descubrió estas tierras. La suma de cinco colones se escribe «¢ 5», o «₡ 5» en vez de $5, como lo escribimos nosotros.

La moneda de Honduras se llama el lempira, en honor de un joven héroe indio llamado Lempira, que se rebeló valientemente contra los españoles después de la conquista, tratando de devolver a su país la libertad perdida. El lempira vale unos cincuenta centavos de nuestro dinero.

En Nicaragua la moneda nacional se llama el córdoba, en honor del conquistador del mismo nombre, que exploró el país en 1522.

En Panamá la moneda nacional se llama el balboa, y cada uno lleva una imagen de la cara del famoso explorador (*explorer*), porque fué en Panamá que Balboa descubrió el Océano Pacífico. Por supuesto, viviendo tantos norteamericanos cerca del Canal, allí se acepta nuestro dólar como el suyo, que vale lo mismo.

En Colombia la moneda nacional se llama el peso, y se usa el mismo símbolo, $, como el nuestro. Pero en Venezuela, país donde cuesta más la vida que en cualquier otra parte del mundo, la moneda se llama el bolívar. Sin duda recuerdan Vds. al Libertador, cuyo nombre se ha dado a tantos lugares, así como a las monedas de Venezuela y de Bolivia. En ésta, se llaman bolivianos, aunque muchas personas los llaman «billetes», y los de habla inglesa dicen "*bills*."

En el Ecuador se encuentran sucres, en honor de Sucre, héroe nacional que ayudó a Bolívar a libertar al país de los españoles. Un sucre vale poco, y el costo de la vida en el Ecuador es el más barato del mundo, valiendo un sucre sólo siete centavos norteamericanos, más o menos. La moneda de oro que vale veinte y cinco sucres se llama el cóndor, y lleva la imagen del ave poderosa de los Andes.

En el Perú la moneda nacional se llama el sol en honor de los incas, que adoraban el sol, y que se llamaban Hijos del Sol. El sol vale como diez y seis centavos nuestros. Diez soles se llaman un inca, conmemorando (*commemorating*) así a los indios del gran imperio que existía antes de la llegada de los conquistadores.

Chile tiene el peso, como lo tienen México, el Uruguay, la Argentina, y antes, el Paraguay; en Chile diez pesos oro se llaman el cóndor, en vez de veinte y cinco, como en el Ecuador.

El dinero paraguayo vale tan poco, siendo el país muy pobre, que se usa el dinero argentino en grandes sumas. Los paraguayos no tienen dinero de metal, sino de papel. Hasta la pieza más pequeña, de valor de cinco pesos, es de papel. Ésta vale para nosotros como un centavo y medio, pero allí sirve para ir en tranvía. Todos estos billetes se imprimen en los Estados Unidos del Norte, y al viajero le parece muy curioso encontrar allí, tan lejos de su patria, dinero hecho por una compañía de Nueva York.

El peso argentino vale como veinte y cinco centavos, y no tiene nombre especial. Pero como ya han visto Vds., la mayor parte de los países de habla española han dado a sus monedas nombres que tienen un significado histórico, porque allí la historia es una cosa viva que existe fuera de los textos de escuela y en la cual piensa todo el mundo casi diariamente.

COUNTRY	COIN	NAMED FOR	SIGN	VALUE TO US[1]
México	peso, hidalgo	pesar, *to weigh* Father Hidalgo	$	About 5 for $1
Guatemala	quetzal	Jungle bird	Q	About 1 for $1
El Salvador	colón	Cristóbal Colón	₡	About 2½ for $1
Nicaragua	córdoba	Hernández de Córdoba	C$	About 5 for $1
Honduras	lempira	Lempira, Indian hero	L	About 2 for $1
Costa Rica	colón	Cristóbal Colón	₡	About 6 for $1
Panamá	balboa	Balboa	B	About 1 for $1
Venezuela	bolívar	Simón Bolívar	B	About 3 for $1
Colombia	peso cóndor	 Andean bird	$	Less than 2 for $1
Ecuador	sucre cóndor	Sucre Andean bird	S/	About 14 for $1
Perú	sol inca	Incan sun worship, ruler	S/	About 6 for $1

[1] As of 1943, official rate.

COUNTRY	COIN	NAMED FOR	SIGN	VALUE TO US
Bolivia	boliviano	Simón Bolívar	B	About 46 for $1
Paraguay	guaraní (papel) (formerly peso)		$	About 333 for $1
Chile	peso		$	About 19 for $1
	cóndor	Andean bird		
Argentina	peso (papel)		$	About 4 for $1
Uruguay	peso		$	About 2 for $1
Brasil	cruzeiro		1$000	About 20 for $1
Cuba	peso		$	About 1 for $1
Santo Domingo	dólar	dollar	US$	(Our money)
Puerto Rico	dólar	dollar	$	(Our money)

1. From which country would you rather have "$5"? 2. From which country would you rather have S/5? 3. From which country would you rather have B5? 4. How much is 20$000 worth to us? 5. Why does Puerto Rico use our money? 6. Which would you rather have, C$5 or Q5? 7. In which country do you get the most of their "dollars" for one of ours? 8. In which countries is their "dollar" worth about the same as ours? 9. Why do Ecuador and Chile name a coin after a bird? 10. Which coins are named for revolutionary heroes? 11. Which are named for explorers? 12. Which ones have pre-conquest names?

II. El Brasil, otro buen vecino

Un país más grande que nuestros Estados Unidos, cubriendo casi la mitad de un gran continente, con más ríos que cualquier otro país del mundo, y que tiene miles de millas de territorio inexplorado, y a la vez la ciudad más hermosa del mundo, limpia y moderna, aunque tiene trescientos años, — éste es el Brasil.

Por el lado del Atlántico, este país inmenso tiene ciudades modernas; dentro de sus selvas se esconden indios primitivos que nunca han visto al hombre blanco. Por estas selvas corre el Río Amazonas, tan ancho al llegar al mar que en su boca ¡hay una isla más grande que toda la república de El Salvador! Para cruzar allí este río en avión, volando a ciento sesenta millas por hora, ¡se necesita una hora y diez minutos!

Hace cien años que el Brasil y los Estados Unidos del Norte son amigos, y en Rio [1] de Janeiro, capital de la inmensa república, se ve por todos lados la influencia norteamericana. El movimiento de vehículos toma la derecha en vez de la izquierda, como antes en la Argentina;[2] en el distrito de teatros llamado «Cinelandia», se ven nuestros cines modernos; en las tiendas y boticas se venden nuestros periódicos, nuestras medicinas, y nuestros productos manufacturados.

Las palabras «Ordem e progresso» (*order and progress*), se ven en la bandera verde, amarilla, y blanca, y por todas partes se ve que es un buen lema (*motto*), sobre todo en la capital.

«Rio», con sus aceras (*sidewalks*) de piedrecitas blancas y negras, tiene detrás de sí, riscos grises y una selva verde, y delante, la bahía azul con sus cien islas. Con todo esto, es el puerto más pintoresco del mundo. En su calle principal, la Avenida Rio Branco, hay autobuses aerodinámicos (*streamlined*), hay edificios modernos de plata y negro y cristal, y hay señoras y señoritas guapas, vestidas a la última moda. Y en cada cuadra (*block*) se ven puestos donde se venden tacitas de café negro, porque a todos los brasileños les gusta tomar café

[1] ***Rio de Janeiro,*** Portuguese for *January River,* does not have an accent because it is not Spanish. Portuguese is the language of Brazil.

[2] Traffic regulations were changed in Argentina only recently.

varias veces al día, quizás porque éste constituye la cosecha (*crop*) principal.

Ningún turista que visite a «Rio» se va sin comprar recuerdos típicos: joyas con brillantes, amatistas (*amethysts*) y esmeraldas; platos y bandejas (*trays*) adornados con las alas azules de la mariposa (*butterfly*) brasileña; curiosidades hechas de las maderas preciosas de la selva. Y el recuerdo que uno se lleva, más que cualquier otro, es la memoria de un pueblo simpático, amistoso, culto y bien educado, — el pueblo de un país que es uno de los mejores de nuestros buenos vecinos.

PALABRAS NUEVAS

	amistoso	friendly
	bahía	bay
	balboa (*m.*)	coin of Panama
	bolívar (*m.*)	coin of Venezuela
	boliviano	coin of Bolivia
1	**como**	about
	cóndor (*m.*)	bird of the Andes
	córdoba (*m.*)	coin of Nicaragua
4	**culto**	cultured
	gris	gray
4	**imprimir** (*p.p.* **impreso**)	to print
	lempira (*m.*)	coin of Honduras
	llegada	arrival
3	**mitad** (*f.*)	half
2	**ocupar**	to occupy
3	**poderoso**	powerful
	rebelarse	to revolt
3	**recuerdo**	remembrance, souvenir
1	**sí** (*reflexive*)	itself, himself
	significado	meaning
2	**sol** (*m.*)	coin of Peru
	sucre (*m.*)	coin of Ecuador
4	**suma**	amount, sum
	tranvía (*m.*)	streetcar
	viajero	traveler

PREGUNTAS

1. ¿Qué es el quetzal? 2. ¿Dónde se usan colones y por qué? 3. ¿Se usa el símbolo $ en Costa Rica? 4. ¿Quién fué Lempira? 5. ¿Por qué se llaman balboas las monedas de Panamá? 6. ¿Dónde cuesta más la vida? 7. ¿Dónde cuesta menos? 8. ¿Qué país tiene el dinero de tan poco valor que usa el de otro país? 9. ¿Qué es un cóndor? 10. ¿Cuánto cuesta ir en tranvía en el Paraguay? 11. ¿Dónde se imprimen los billetes del Paraguay? 12. ¿Qué país tiene

Galloway

Rio, the magnificent, is regal at night in black velvet with diamonds. Famous "Sugar Loaf" mountain, in the center, towers over the calm bay with its hundred islands.

más ríos que cualquier otro? 13. ¿Qué hay en las selvas del Brasil? 14. ¿Qué hay en la boca del Río Amazonas? 15. ¿A cuántas millas por hora vuelan algunos aviones comerciales? 16. ¿Cuántos años hace que son amigos el Brasil y nuestro país?

PARA COMPLETAR

1. Un incidente de la historia de un país muchas veces se ve en .... 2. Cristóbal Colón es conmemorado en las monedas de .... 3. El héroe indio, Lempira, trató de .... 4. La vida cuesta más en Venezuela que .... 5. El cóndor es un .... 6. El dinero paraguayo vale muy poco porque .... 7. Un billete de cinco pesos en el Paraguay sirve para .... 8. Los billetes son impresos por

.... 9. En el Brasil hay miles de millas de .... 10. Rio de Janeiro tiene .... 11. En las selvas del Brasil hay .... 12. Hace cien años que el Brasil .... 13. En las tiendas de «Rio» se venden .... 14. «Rio» es muy .... 15. El color gris es una combinación de .... 16. Una persona culta sabe ....

PREGUNTAS PERSONALES

1. ¿Cuál le gustaría a Vd. más, tener S/5 o Q5? 2. ¿Cuál le gustaría a Vd. más, tener S/5 (del Ecuador) o B5 (de Panamá)? 3. ¿Podría Vd. comprar más dulces con cinco bolivianos o con cinco lempiras? 4. ¿Cuál es el emblema de su libertad? 5. ¿Quisiera Vd. ver la imagen de su cara en una moneda? 6. ¿Cómo podría Vd. conseguir eso? 7. ¿Cuál le gustaría a Vd. más, el costo de la vida en el Ecuador, en Venezuela, o aquí? 8. ¿Ha visto Vd. alguna vez un cóndor? 9. ¿Sabe Vd. imprimir billetes? 10. Si fuese Vd. indio, ¿se escondería en la selva o viviría en una ciudad? 11. ¿Ha volado Vd. a ciento sesenta millas por hora? 12. ¿Hace cien años que tiene Vd. el mismo amigo? 13. Si estuviese Vd. en el Brasil, ¿tomaría con frecuencia una tacita de café? 14. ¿Qué compraría Vd. en «Rio» si hiciese una visita allí? 15. ¿Quién es uno de los mejores de sus buenos amigos?

LO CONTRARIO

Find the opposites of these expressions in the reading.

1. quedándose en casa
2. cuesta menos la vida
3. sin duda olvidan Vds.
4. el más caro del mundo
5. después de la llegada
6. dinero de papel
7. ir a pie
8. una cosa muerta
9. tierras exploradas
10. por su interior
11. tan estrecho
12. toma la izquierda

REPASO DE PALABRAS

Give an English word which is related to each of these Spanish words, yet is not the actual meaning. Example: ***encontrar*** means *to find,* and looks like *encounter.*

sol, luna, lavar, esposo, necesitar, cine, tarde, viaje, fin, médico, enfermo, durar, beber, voluntad, tierra, ocupado, volar, caballo, igual, amar, encantado, varios, cuerpo, obedecer, voz, libre, diario

REPASO DE MODISMOS

These are the commonly used idioms from recent chapters. *Find the one which completes each sentence, using each idiom only once.* They are all in the general vocabulary.

sobre todo	por entonces	hacer pedazos
sin embargo	darse cuenta de	ocho días
por último	tener ganas de	hacerse el sordo
por lo tanto	poner mala cara	hacia atrás
al principio	llegar a	volverle la espalda a

1. *At the time,* el sobrino tenía que comprarlo todo al fiado. 2. *He didn't realize* lo que sucedía en el puente. 3. El esclavo no se atrevió a *turn his back on* su soberano. 4. Salieron a medianoche sin mirar *backward.* 5. El criado *broke* (*in pieces*) el abanico de la condesa. 6. Hace *a week,* fuimos a la tienda de cinco y diez. 7. El que no quiere oír, *plays deaf.* 8. El joven héroe *succeeded in* salvar la vida a la araña (*spider*). 9. *Nevertheless,* el águila le hirió severamente. 10. *Therefore,* tuvo que volver a la fuente para lavarse el hombro. 11. El Marqués no *felt like* casarse con una limeña que se ocupaba demasiado de sus joyas. 12. *At first,* los incas creían que hombre y caballo eran un solo ser. 13. *Finally* supieron la triste verdad. 14. Le deseamos *especially* la felicidad. 15. Un buen niño nunca *pouts* cuando su madre le pide que haga algo.

REPASO DE VERBOS

I. Conjugate in the present subjunctive: caer, buscar, dormir, leer.

II. Conjugate in the past subjunctive: poner, traer, oír, ser, dar.

III. Conjugate in the preterite: entregar, huir, hacer, contar, sentir.

IV. Conjugate in the future: hacer, querer, andar.

V. Give the past participles of: volver, romper, cubrir, hacer, ver, poner, decir, creer, leer, matar. (§ 96)

VI. Give the familiar commands, singular and plural, of these verbs: pagar, creer, dormir, poner, venir, decir, seguir, tener.

VII. Give the following expressions in Spanish, using the proper forms of each of these verbs: comprar, vender, entender, leer, ir, decir, poner.

Mosaic sidewalks of Rio are copied from those of Lisbon, Portugal. Their miles of tiny sharp black and white stones are easier to look at than to walk on.

Galloway

1. he —— s
2. ¡—— Vd.!
3. he —— yesterday
4. I used to ——
5. he will ——
6. they would ——
7. she has ——
8. we had ——
9. I want you to ——
10. I wanted you to ——
11. if you —— (*contrary-to-fact*)
12. until you —— tomorrow
13. it is possible that we ——
14. let us ——
15. upon —— ing
16. we were —— ing (*prog.*)

VIII. Give the infinitive of each of these verbs, then translate each of these forms as rapidly as possible. (How much is an incorrect verb form worth?)

1. escogieron
2. tropecé
3. hiriendo
4. obedecían
5. obtengamos
6. obtuvimos
7. entregue
8. entregué
9. se reunirán
10. mejoramos
11. sufrirían
12. curasen
13. niegue
14. envuelto
15. fué herido
16. arrojo
17. sucedió
18. consintieron
19. se dirigió a
20. cumplimos
21. no recuerdo
22. pertenece a
23. ¡vamos!
24. han vuelto
25. curaré
26. obtendrían
27. había sufrido
28. ha herido
29. venderé
30. vendré

IX. Give the Spanish infinitive of each of these verbs from Exercise VIII; then the correct form:

1. we chose
2. he wounded
3. he may deny
4. we shall obtain
5. let us deliver
6. I have thrown
7. it will happen
8. they went to
9. he will fulfill
10. they have suffered
11. it belonged to
12. do you remember?
13. will they consent?
14. we were cured
15. he had denied
16. she wraps
17. we shall meet
18. they had thrown

REPASO DE COSAS NUEVAS[1]

I. If you can complete these statements, you know your rules of grammar. (A dash stands for one word; dots stand for

[1] Note to teacher: This exercise combines the TEMA with the grammar review, and even if the TEMA is not ordinarily assigned, it should be used here.

several.) *Then, if you can give the examples correctly in Spanish, you know how to apply the rule.*

1. *For* is expressed by ***por*** when it means ....; by ***para*** when it means .... (§ 47, 1)

for two months, a shoe box, it is for you, for [the sake of] *the class, he gave me this one for that one, for a week*

2. *By* is expressed by ***por*** when it means ....; by ***para*** when it means .... (§ 47, 2)

It will be made by Pedro, and will be ready by Tuesday. I shall travel by plane, and arrive by ten o'clock.

3. ***Por*** also means ....; ***para*** also means .... (§ 47, 3 and 4)

He was walking through the garden on account of being tired. Four times five are twenty, or fifty per cent of forty. He searched along the road in order to find the horse. He is about to go because he has no more things to sell.

4. In literary word order, the .... is often found attached to a conjugated verb, especially after a ..... (§ 48)

Most popular souvenirs of Rio de Janeiro are made of gorgeous blue butterfly wings mounted under glass in trays, plates, and costume jewelry. The butterflies are caught in the jungles behind the city.

Galloway

Translate: *Aconsejóme que fuese temprano; díjolo por estar cansado.*

5. ***La*** and ***una***, before feminine nouns beginning with stressed ***a*** or ***ha***, are changed to —— and ——. (§ 49)

the cold water, a black wing, the white bird, the innocent soul, the old grandmother, the beautiful jewel, a precious friendship

6. The —— article is used in Spanish with a title except in —— ——. (§ 50)

"Mrs. López is here." "Good morning, Mrs. López. Have you seen Dr. Moreno?"

7. Nouns used in a —— sense must have the —— article. (§ 50)

Bread is worth more than gold. Gentlemen prefer blondes.

8. An expression of time, when —— requires the —— article. (§ 50)

Last year we said we would go next year, but now we intend to go next month.

9. The indefinite article is often omitted after a ——. (§ 51) In this case, the English word —— is often used in the translation.

He hasn't a horse, and he can't walk without a cane (**bastón**), *so he hasn't any way to go.*

10. When ***hace*** means *for*, the other verb in the sentence is in the —— tense. (§ 52)

We have been waiting for two hours. It has been on the desk for a week.

11. ***Lo*** can mean —— or ——. (§ 53)

Translate in two ways: *Lo ví en la calle. Lo envié a la sala.* In one way: *Le dí la manzana; les dieron las naranjas.*

12. The "dative of interest" is an —— —— pronoun, which shows a person's —— in a matter. (§ 54)

Translate and point out the extra word: *Espero que no se nos acabe la gasolina. El criado le hizo pedazos el abanico.*

13. An indirect object instead of a —— is used in Spanish with verbs that imply ——. (§ 55)

We buy shoes from the shoemaker. He took John's hat [away] *from him. He asked Carmen for five cents.*

14. The true passive is formed by —— plus the —— ——, and is used for ——. (§ 56)

The house was sold by the Spaniard. It was bought by his friend. We were invited to dine with them.

15. ***Estar*** plus the —— —— is used for ——, to show a —— or ——. (§§ 56; 123, 124–2)

The house is made of wood. It is well made. The door is closed, but the windows are open(ed).

16. After ***ver*** and ***oír***, one may use the —— of another verb. (§ 57)

We often hear her say it. They saw him do it. She will see us eating in class.

17. Instead of the true passive, Spanish prefers to use the —— substitute, especially in speaking of ——. (§ 58)

The dog was sold yesterday. "The room will be filled with gold," said Atahualpa. The money was not paid.

18. The —— article is used instead of the demonstratives when followed by —— or ——. (§ 59)

Those who don't know, think it is easy. He has the one you want. Those (f.) whom I invited couldn't go.

PARA TRADUCIR SIN ESTUDIAR

I. Here are some easy but useful little expressions that some second-year Spanish pupils have tried to say but have missed. Can you give them correctly without looking up the words? There is a "catch" in every one!

they had a good time
he was afraid
he was looking for something
he took the money home
the girl who went
Robert's aunt
within two hours
Antonio died
he wanted to marry her
he heard a man say
upon leaving the house
it was going to rain
there were two dogs
he thought he saw Tinita
they had to go home
when he came to the plaza
the girl who said it
by putting; by saying (§ 7)
he wanted the men to go
after he left
they were in Lima
he heard me say

Armstrong Roberts

Rio's sunny beaches around its warm blue bay are popular with young and old. Compare the height of "Sugar Loaf" in the distance with that of the tall buildings below it.

II. ¿Sabía Vd. esto?

Since Portuguese is spoken in Brazil and like Spanish is a language derived from Latin, you might like to see just how much like Spanish it is and yet how different. When you travel in Brazil, in an emergency you can speak Spanish and the Brazilians will understand enough to answer you in Portuguese, of which you will be able to guess enough to come back again in Spanish. Of course the Brazilians do not particularly care for this type of conversation, since they rightly feel that their language is as worthy of study as Spanish, but being polite, they will do their best to help the stranger.

If you know Spanish really well, an hour's study of the connecting words and irregular verbs of Portuguese will make it possible for you to read a newspaper with little difficulty, although you must not try to speak the language on such short notice, for Portuguese pronunciation is much more complicated than Spanish.

In the street cars of Rio de Janeiro you often see a sign reading, "He who speaks two languages is worth two men: he who speaks English is worth three." What does this indicate about Brazil's friendship with our country?

Here is a short story told in both Spanish and Portuguese. Compare the two carefully, and you can tell what the Portuguese means.

O JUIZO DO MENINO

Um menino estava assentado uma vez á mesa e pediu um pouco de carne. Seu pai disse-lhe que não era conveniente que pedisse cousa alguma, e que devia esperar até que lhe dessem. O pobre menino, vendo que todos comiam e que não lhe davam nada, disse a seu pai:

"Querido paizinho, faz favor de me dar um pouco de sal."

"Que queres fazer com o sal?" perguntou o pai.

"Vou deita-lo na carne que me der," respondeu o menino. Todos admiraram o juizo do menino, e o pai, vendo que não tinha nada, lhe deu carne sem que êle pedisse tal.

EL JUICIO DEL MUCHACHO

Un muchacho estaba sentado una vez a la mesa y pidió un poco de carne. Su padre le dijo que no era conveniente que pidiera cosa alguna, y que debía esperar hasta que se la diesen. El pobre muchacho, viendo que todos comían y que no le daban nada, dijo a su padre,

— Querido padrecito, hazme el favor de darme un poco de sal (*salt*).

— ¿Qué quieres hacer con la sal? — preguntó el padre.

— Voy a ponerla en la carne que me darás, — respondió el muchacho. Todos admiraron el juicio del muchacho, y el padre, viendo que no tenía nada, le dió carne sin que él la pidiera.

COURTESY OF "LAS AMÉRICAS"

Part Four

Chile, Argentina, and Uruguay

Principal avenue of Montevideo, Uruguay, is considered one of the finest boulevards in South America. In the distance the twenty-six story Palacio Salvó contrasts with the more modern apartment house in the foreground.

Galloway

When Pan American Airways plans a trip around South America for you, its agent is likely to suggest that you go south along the west coast and return by the east coast. When you ask why, you are told that most travelers like to keep the easiest part of a long trip for the last, so that they will be more comfortable on the way home when they are becoming a little weary. Not that one will be "roughing it" anywhere along the line, but in the "modern" countries of Chile and Argentina and Uruguay there is more than a little of the luxury to which we are accustomed; and soft beds, plenty of hot water, and central heating make any tired traveler happy.

This does not mean that there is nothing modern anywhere else in South America, for even in Paraguay and Bolivia you will see modern Hollywood-style buildings being erected next to gems of colonial architecture with patios and balconies, but they are the exception rather than the rule.

The "modern" countries of Argentina and Uruguay are the ones which have no Indian problem because the Spaniards killed or isolated the few primitive natives they found there four hundred

Buenos Aires, Argentina, the largest city in the southern hemisphere, has subways as well as surface cars, and a thundering traffic problem that automatic signals cannot control.

Sawders

Gendreau

Newest thoroughfare of Buenos Aires, popularly called the Diagonal Norte, cuts across the heart of the city. There is always room along Latin-American streets for trees and statues.

years ago. This was cruel treatment but we should remember that it was no different from our ancestors' treatment of the North American Indians. Chile neither conquered nor destroyed the Araucanian Indians whom the settlers found, but finally made peace with them and left them to live on undisturbed in the South. Consequently Chile, as well, has no Indian problem; and these three countries, settled like our own by thrifty and hard-working Europeans, have been able to grow up unhindered by a large native population that, it must be admitted, would have made modern progress difficult.

We find in each of these republics a program of up-to-date social legislation to protect the working classes, which, you must remember, is not the usual thing in much of Latin America, where the troubles of the poor have often concerned the rich even less than they have here. For instance, the tall, good-looking Chileans, sometimes called the "Yankees of South America," have some of the world's most advanced laws, including such modern ideas as old-age pensions, labor insurance, socialized medicine, and eight-hour days.

Powerful Argentina, a country almost half as large as continental United States, and our South American rival in climate, products, and ambitions, is a wealthy republic with noticeable French and British influence in the capital. Menus are printed in French, traffic for many years moved on the left,[1] everyone takes afternoon tea — even at work — and narrow Florida Street, where the wives and daughters of the plutocratic cattle raisers buy their luxuries, is closed to traffic from 16 to 20 o'clock each afternoon, to make it safe for smart window displays to hold the shoppers' attention.

Across the wide estuary from Argentina is little Uruguay, quite as smart and up-to-date as her neighbor. Her strong, handsome people are not too rich nor too poor; there is less illiteracy than in most countries; women can vote — and, like everyone else, are fined if they don't; there are laws providing an eight-hour day, a minimum wage, an old-age pension, and free medical service for the poor, all of which were adopted long before we introduced them in this country.

In countries like these, with their roaring traffic, their smart skyscraper apartments, and their well-dressed people, the *norte-americano* cannot help but feel at home. Name almost any popular product or preparation that you are accustomed to use, and here you can buy one like it of local manufacture, for these countries do

[1] In the 1940's traffic rules like those in the United States were adopted.

Ranchers of cold and stormy southern Chile go about their work on horseback because of the great distances they must cover. Why are January and February the warmest months in Chile?

Sawders

Galloway

High-school athletic events are held in the great stadium in Buenos Aires with enormous crowds attending. Girls take a more strenuous part in interscholastic games than they do here.

not need to import everything. Their great department stores carry displays of sophisticated magnificence that rival Fifth Avenue in New York or Sunset Boulevard in Hollywood, and their fashions are six months ahead of ours, they say, because of the difference in seasons. When you miss the beautiful handicrafts of the Indian countries which you admired all the way down the West Coast, you realize that their absence is but another indication of progress, for when manufactured goods replace primitive arts and crafts, the standard of living for the whole population is likely to be higher.

And when, as in Córdoba, Argentina's oldest Spanish city, a visitor from the United States sees a lovely weathered stone façade being torn from a colonial building to be replaced by one of glittering modernistic design, he realizes at last that our neighbors know as much as we do about chromium, plate glass, red leather, and neon, and that he has at last discovered the part of South America that is the most like home.

Interesting Books to Read

Chile: HANSON, EARL P.: LAND OF PROGRESS. Reynal and Hitchcock. (*Chile explained sympathetically by a man who knows and loves it*)

Argentina: GUEDALLA, PHILIP: ARGENTINE TANGO. Harper. (*Essays and anecdotes on Argentine life*) — CHILDS, HERBERT: EL JIMMY, OUTLAW OF PATAGONIA. Lippincott. (*Life in the bleak country of southern Argentina and Chile*)

Uruguay: CLAR, SYDNEY A.: EAST COAST OF SOUTH AMERICA. Prentice Hall. (*A personalized guidebook*) — HUDSON, W. H.: THE PURPLE LAND. Grosset and Dunlap. (*Life on the pampas of Uruguay*)

All countries: CRANSTON, CLAUDIA: SKY GYPSY. Lippincott. (*A woman's flight around South America and her impressions*) — ROTHERY, AGNES: SOUTH AMERICA: WEST COAST AND EAST. Houghton Mifflin. (*Interesting and easy to read*) — PECK, ANNE M.: ROUNDABOUT SOUTH AMERICA. Harper. (*Life and culture of South American countries told in an enjoyable manner*) — GUNTHER, JOHN: INSIDE LATIN AMERICA. Harper. (*An interpretation as interesting as it is clear*) — STRODE, HUDSON: SOUTH BY THUNDERBIRD. Random House. (*A travel book with meat in it*)

CAPÍTULO 28

Con días — y ollas — venceremos

Beside Simón Bolívar in South American history stands another general — José de San Martín — who accomplished as much for that continent as did the Liberator. In fact, some say he accomplished more, for he did a thing so sporting that it is hard to believe. San Martín had freed the southern part of the continent from Spain while Bolívar was freeing the north, and then the two equally powerful generals met. Which

was to be the leader in the vast territory they had liberated? If San Martín had insisted on ruling the continent, as Bolívar did, many lives would have been lost; but when San Martín saw that his colleague was determined to be the leader, he generously turned over to Bolívar his forces and supplies, and went quietly back to Argentina to die at last unsung and penniless in France.

The story of how San Martín, after liberating Argentina, crossed the Andes with his army to free Chile, makes Hannibal's trip over the Alps look easy, and the feat is commemorated now by an astounding group of life-sized bronze figures piled on top of the "Hill of Glory" in Mendoza, Argentina, at the foot of the Andes. There you actually see blindfolded bronze horses falling off the Andean trails, and weary, half-frozen men pulling desperately at heavy cannons as they struggle over the mountain pass, just as they did with San Martín in 1817. Over that heart-breaking monument today fly silver passenger planes as they cross the Andes over San Martín's route, all of them stopping at Mendoza before they spiral up and up to make the great jump.

This is not the only monument to San Martín, for every place you go in South America, if it isn't Bolívar you see riding a bronze horse in the plaza, it's San Martín, although, since he left the glory to Bolívar, his name has not been given to so many places.

Here is the story of how San Martín outwitted the Spanish loyalists near Lima and gave Peru her independence just after he had freed Chile, and in it you will learn how a great general could see a joke even in the midst of an historic struggle.

En el mes de junio de 1821,[1] cuando se empezaron las famosas negociaciones entre el virrey en Lima y el general San

[1] San Martín had crossed the Andes from Argentina, freed Chile, and was putting the finishing touches on Peru, the last royalist stronghold in South America.

Pan American Union

José de San Martín did as much for the cause of independence in South America as the colorful Bolívar, then nobly withdrew and left the laurels to his compatriot in order to avoid trouble.

Martín, recibieron las tropas revolucionarias, acantonadas (*quartered*) en Huaura, el siguiente santo y seña:[1] Con días — y ollas — venceremos.

Para todos exceptuando unos pocos, el santo y seña era una frase estúpida, y hasta los amigos de San Martín alzaban los hombros murmurando, —¡Tonterías (*foolishness*) del general!

Sin embargo, el santo y seña tenía significado, e hizo su papel en un gran incidente histórico. Y de eso me propongo (*propose*) hablar hoy.

San Martín no quería ocupar a Lima por medio de una batalla, sino por los manejos (*cunning*) de la política (*politics*).

[1] A countersign is a secret word or phrase which must be given in order to pass a sentry, to prove that one is not a spy.

Sus tropas estaban impacientes, pero lo que le importaba más al héroe argentino era salvar la vida a sus soldados.

Estaba en correspondencia secreta y constante con los patriotas de la capital, pero con frecuencia, los espías españoles conseguían interceptar las comunicaciones entre San Martín y sus amigos, frustrando (*defeating*) no pocas veces sus planes. Además, los españoles tenían la costumbre de fusilar (*shoot*) a quienes sorprendían con cartas en cifra (*code*). Era preciso encontrar inmediatamente un medio seguro de comunicación.

Preocupado (*worried*) con este pensamiento, pasaba una tarde el general San Martín por la única calle de Huaura, cuando, cerca del puente, se fijó en una casa vieja que en el patio tenía un horno para alfarería (*pottery making*). En aquel tiempo, la vajilla (*dishes*) de uso diario, como los utensilios de cocina, era de barro cocido.[1]

Al ver el horno, San Martín tuvo una misteriosa inspiración y exclamó para sí, — ¡Eureka![2] ¡Ya está resuelta la X (*equis*) del problema!

El dueño de la casa era un indio viejo, inteligente, leal, y amigo de los insurgentes (*rebels*). Después de una conversación larga, el alfarero prometió hacer una olla con doble fondo, tan bien preparada que el ojo más experto no pudiera descubrir la trampa (*trick*).

El indio hacía cada semana un viajecito a Lima, conduciendo dos mulas cargadas de platos y ollas de barro. Entre estas últimas iba la «olla revolucionaria», llevando en su doble fondo importantísimas cartas. Camino de Lima, el indio se dejaba registrar (*search*) por los españoles, respondía de buen humor a sus preguntas, se quitaba el sombrero cuando el oficial pronunciaba el nombre de Fernando VII,[3] y los españoles lo dejaban seguir su viaje. ¿Quién iba a

[1] Cheap clay pots and kettles are still used in many homes of Latin America and although they are a nuisance to use, food cooked in them has a really good flavor.

[2] *¡Eureka!* Greek word meaning *I have found it.*

[3] Fernando VII, King of Spain at that time, was a tyrannical ruler who suppressed liberties in South America, and even drove many liberals from Spain.

imaginar que ese pobre indio hacía un papel tan importante en cosas revolucionarias?

Vivía el señor don Francisco Javier de Luna Pizarro en Lima, y él fué el patriota nombrado por San Martín para tratar con el alfarero. Pasaba éste a las ocho de la mañana por la calle, gritando con toda la fuerza de sus pulmones (*lungs*), — ¡Ollas y platos! ¡Baratos! ¡Baratos! — Apenas terminaba su pregón en cada esquina, cuando salían a la puerta todos los vecinos que querían comprar utensilios de cocina.

Pedro Manzanares, mayordomo del señor Luna Pizarro, era un negrito muy leal a su amo. Al oír el pregón no dejaba nunca de salir y pagar un real por una olla de barro. Pero todas las semanas volvía a presentarse en la puerta, utensilio en mano, gritando, — Oiga usted, cholo [1] ladrón, con sus ollas que se rompen toditas... Ya puede usted cambiarme ésta que le compré la semana pasada antes que yo se la rompa en la cabeza para enseñarle a no engañarme a mí. ¡Sinvergüenza!

Y tanto se repitió la escena de cambios de ollas y palabrotas, contestadas siempre con paciencia por el indio, que el barbero de la esquina le dijo al negrito una mañana, — ¡Caramba! ¡Yo, que soy pobre, no hago tanto ruido por un miserable real! Oye. Las ollas de barro y las mujeres no se pueden devolver, y el que se lleva chasco (*gets gypped*) que calle el pico [2] y no moleste a los vecinos con gritos y lamentaciones.

— Y usted, ¿quién le dió vela en este entierro? [3] — contestó el negrito Pedro. — Vaya usted a desollar [4] barbas, y no se meta en lo que no le va ni le viene.

[1] ***Cholo*** means a *lower-class person*, and is considered quite an insulting word in some countries.

[2] ***que calle el pico,*** *let him keep still* (slang).

[3] ***¿quién le dió vela en este entierro?***, *who gave you a candle* (*to carry*) *in this funeral?* In other words, *what business is it of yours?*

[4] ***Vaya usted a desollar barbas, y no se meta en lo que no le va ni le viene,*** *go on and skin chins and don't meddle in what doesn't concern you.*

Al oír esto, se puso enojado el barbero, y echando mano a la navaja (*razor*), estaba para atacar a Pedro, que, sin esperar, huyó a la casa de su amo.

¡Quién sabe si la riña entre el barbero y el mayordomo habría servido para despertar sospechas (*suspicion*) sobre las ollas, pues de pequeñas causas han salido grandes efectos! Afortunadamente (*fortunately*), la riña tuvo lugar en el último viaje que hizo el alfarero trayendo «olla revolucionaria». Al día siguiente abandonó el virrey la ciudad, de la cual tomaron posesión los patriotas en la noche del nueve de julio.

La victoria fué ganada sin perderse un soldado; «con días — y ollas,» vencieron los patriotas, y gracias a las ollas que llevaban en el fondo ideas más formidables que los cañones modernos, el 28 de julio se declaró en Lima la independencia del Perú.

Adapted from Ricardo Palma (*Peru*)

Christ of the Andes, on the old Spanish trail crossing from Argentina to Chile, guards the peace of the two countries. Planes flying the pass always dip a wing in salute above it.

Galloway

PALABRAS NUEVAS

	alfarero	pottery maker	**horno**	oven
3	**alzar**	to raise	**leal**	loyal
2	**amo**	master	**mayordomo**	butler
	atacar	to attack	**olla**	pot *or* jug
	barro	clay	**palabrota**	harsh word
	¡caramba!	Gracious! Good heavens!	**pregón** (*m.*)	call (of a vendor)
4	**doble**	double	**riña**	quarrel
3	**engañar**	to deceive	**sinvergüenza** (*m.* or *f.*)	shameless one, rascal
	espía (*m.*)	spy	**tropas**	troops
	esquina	(street) corner	**virrey** (*m.*)	viceroy
2	**fuerza**	force		

Expresiones

de buen humor, good-humoredly
echar mano a, to lay hold of
hacer el (un) papel, to play the (a) part
para sí, to himself
por medio de, by means of
santo y seña, password
tratar con, to deal with

PREGUNTAS

I. Contéstese en inglés:

1. ¿Por qué quería entrar en Lima el general San Martín? 2. ¿Era leal o «patriota» el general? 3. ¿Qué es un virrey? 4. ¿De qué quería San Martín libertar al Perú? 5. ¿Por qué? 6. ¿Por qué era preciso enviar las cartas en el doble fondo de una olla? 7. ¿Por qué salió bien la trampa (*trick*)?

II. Contéstese en español:

1. ¿Quién cuenta esta historia? 2. ¿Cuál era el santo y seña de San Martín? 3. ¿Entendían todos su significado? 4. ¿Qué querían hacer las tropas? 5. ¿Por qué no quería San Martín librar (*fight*) una batalla? 6. ¿Qué hacían algunas veces los espías españoles? 7. ¿Era leal el alfarero? 8. ¿Cuántas veces a la semana hacía el indio un viajecito a Lima? 9. ¿Qué llevaba consigo? 10. ¿Hacía un papel importante el indio? 11. ¿Quién compraba siempre una olla al alfarero? 12. ¿Por qué la cambiaba cada semana? 13. ¿Sabía el barbero el secreto de las ollas? 14. ¿Era muy cortés el negrito para con el barbero? 15. ¿Cuándo declaró el Perú su independencia?

PARA COMPLETAR

1. Las negociaciones del general se empezaron en .... 2. Hasta los amigos de San Martín creían que .... 3. Los españoles tenían la costumbre de .... 4. En el patio de una casa vieja San Martín vió .... 5. El ojo más experto no podía .... 6. El indio tenía que quitarse el sombrero al oír .... 7. El señor don Francisco Javier de Luna Pizarro había de .... 8. El pregón del alfarero era .... 9. Pedro Manzanares era .... 10. Éste decía siempre que las ollas .... 11. El barbero creía que no era preciso .... 12. El barbero estuvo para .... 13. Los patriotas tomaron posesión de Lima .... 14. San Martín ganó la victoria por medio de ....

PREGUNTAS PERSONALES

1. ¿Ha tenido Vd. que usar santo y seña? 2. ¿Dice Vd. muchas frases estúpidas? 3. ¿Está Vd. en correspondencia secreta con alguien? 4. ¿Ha usado Vd. utensilios de barro? 5. ¿Es fácil siempre resolver la X de un problema? 6. ¿Tiene Vd. un ojo experto para descubrir trampas (*tricks*)? 7. ¿Cuándo se quita Vd. el sombrero? 8. ¿Ha hecho Vd. un papel muy importante en una comedia? 9. ¿Cuándo grita Vd. con toda la fuerza de sus pulmones? 10. ¿Es Vd. muy leal a sus amigos? 11. ¿Les rompe Vd. la cabeza a muchas personas para enseñarles algo? 12. ¿Hace Vd. mucho ruido en sus clases? 13. ¿Se mete Vd. en lo que no le va ni le viene? (See footnote 4, page 396.) 14. ¿Tiene Vd. muchas riñas con su novio (-a)?

REPASO DE VERBOS

I. What tense or verb form do these endings show?

-ía	-aba	-ó	-(r)é	-aren	-(r)emos
-ió	-aron	-(er)ían	-ido	-(ar)án	-iendo
-é	-iese	-yendo	-ído	-íamos	-(ar)ía
-yó	-o (2)	-ado	-aran	-ieran	-(ir)íamos

II. Conjugate in present subjunctive and preterite indicative: entregar, sacar, empezar. *In what way are these two tenses alike for these verbs?*

III. Conjugate (like **conocer**) *in the present indicative:* parecer, crecer, ofrecer, obedecer, pertenecer. *What is the first person plural present subjunctive of each?*

IV. Conjugate in the preterite and give the gerund to match: creer, caer, leer, oír, huir,[1] destruir.

ALGO NUEVO

61. Augmentatives

cambios de ollas y palabrotas, *exchanges of pots and harsh words*

¡Ay, qué hombrón! *My, what a big man!*

Spanish augmentatives, like Spanish diminutives (§ 41), add a great deal of color to colloquial speech. Of the many endings that may be used to increase or decrease the size or importance of a word, only a few can be given here. The endings ***-ón*** (***-ona***) and ***-ote*** (***-ota***) are called augmentatives, because they increase the size of the object or person referred to. At the same time they frequently add an idea of clumsiness or disrespect.

The ending ***-azo,*** although neither an augmentative nor a diminutive, is often used to give the idea of a blow with the object to which the ending is added: ***bala,*** *bullet;* ***balazo,*** *a shot;* ***zapato,*** *shoe;* ***zapatazo,*** *a blow with a shoe.*

EJERCICIO I. *Translate these words, showing the force of the endings as clearly as possible, even by using a different word entirely:* **silla,** *chair;* **sillita,** *little chair;* **sillón,** *armchair.*

sala (*living room*), salita, salón
caja (*box*), cajita, cajón [2]
zapatos, zapatitos, zapatones
guitarra, guitarrita, guitarrón (*bass guitar which plays a cello part*)
cuchara, cucharita, cucharón (*ladle*)

[1] Verbs ending in *-uir* have only two written accents, in the preterite, since the last of two weak vowels automatically gets the stress.

[2] One meaning is *an orchard picking box.*

botella, botellita, botellón [1]
flores, florecitas, florones [2]
oreja (*ear*), orejita, orejón [3]

EJERCICIO II. *Translate these expressions:*

1. ¡Ay, qué grandote! (*What the Indians in Mexico say when they see a very tall tourist.*) 2. ¡A mí no me diga palabrotas! 3. Me dió un manotazo. 4. En México hay un edificio con máscaras (*masks*) en las paredes, que se llama «Mascarones». 5. En las procesiones de fiesta se llevan figuras grandes que se llaman gigantones. 6. También se llevan en los hombros, para divertir a la gente, una cabeza falsa que se llama cabezota. 7. ¿Qué quiere ese inglesote? 8. ¡Cuidado que no te des un cuchillazo! (*Said to a man who was dancing* «**Los cuchillos**» *in Mexico.*) 9. El hombre murió de un escopetazo.

ESTUDIO DE PALABRAS

I. You have had a verb which is closely related to each of these nouns and adjectives. Give the verb and its meaning.

lluvia	vendedor	costumbre	paso
pintura	cruz	permiso	libertador
una caída	cambio	adorno	muerte
la ayuda	sonrisa	inolvidable	sueño
encantador	sorpresa	pensamiento	triste
camino	el costo	gobierno	falta
baile	visita	tarde	seco

II. You have had several common idioms with **en.** *Find the one which best completes each sentence, using each idiom only once.*

en vano, en casa, en todas partes, en seguida, en pie, en cambio, en casa de, en efecto, en cuanto, en voz alta

[1] One meaning is *a water jug* (for the table).

[2] One meaning is *big paper flowers* (used for fiesta decorations).

[3] The Inca nobles were called *orejones* because, according to one legend, after one Inca had lost an ear in battle and replaced it for vanity's sake with a gold shell, the other nobles tactfully covered theirs in the same way, and it came to be the accepted style. In pre-Inca civilizations enlarged and ornamented ears were a sign of the warrior's profession.

1. ¡Venga Vd. a casa ....! 2. No quiere ir; .... quiere quedarse con él. 3. Era muy difícil seguir; .... era casi imposible. 4. Quédate ...., porque es peligroso salir. 5. Háblale ...., porque es un poco sordo. 6. Allí estuvimos .... delante de toda la gente. 7. Fué ....; el capitán no pudo salvar al valiente soldado. 8. ¿Dónde está? Está ahora .... Pedro. 9. .... se encuentra el nombre de Simón Bolívar. 10. Iremos a la escuela .... llegue Pablo.

III. Here are some popular colloquial and slang expressions of Mexico that you will enjoy using in talking to your friends. Some of them would be used in other Spanish-speaking countries, while others would be recognized only in Mexico, since slang varies with the locality. These are not in the general vocabulary; when you want to find them again, look under "slang" in the index. *Choose five and make it a point to use them before the next class time.*

¡Ay, qué piocha!, *Swell!*
ahora es cuando, *now's your chance*
¡Pórtese bien! *Be good!*
¡Qué barbaridad! *The very idea!*
felicidades, *congratulations*
¡Chile verde! *Hot stuff!*
estoy bruja, *I'm "broke"*
no le hace, *it doesn't matter*
consentido (-a), *"pet" (teacher's!)*
¡Sinvergüenza! *Shame on you!*
estilo alemán, *Dutch treat*
¡Qué fastidio! *What a nuisance!*
abrir el pico y meter la pata, *to open your mouth and "put your foot in it"*
hacerle la primera curación, *to give first aid*
tirarle la plancha (*iron*), *to "stand him up"*
ésta es su casa, *make yourself at home*
me toma el pelo, *he is kidding me*
me tiene en el horno, *I'm "in the doghouse"*
me hace pedazos, *it thrills me to pieces*
salúdemela Vd., *tell her "hello" for me*
águila o sello; águila o sol; cara o cruz, *heads or tails*

REPASITO

Complete these sentences, using adjectives or pronouns as nouns (§ 12):

1. *The sick* no pueden andar sin ayuda. 2. *The blind* no pueden ver y *the deaf* no pueden oír. 3. *The lazy* no tienen ganas de trabajar. 4. Ganó el tercer premio, pero quería *the first one.* 5. Ese *crazy fellow* trata de lavar el gato. 6. Queremos *the fresh one* en vez del *old one.* 7. *The faithful* siempre son leales. 8. No le dé Vd. *the last one.* 9. *My folks* ya han escogido una nueva máquina de lavar. 10. — Tráigame Vd. una olla de barro. — ¿Quiere Vd. *the red one* o *the blue one*? 11. No me gustan *the red ones,* porque *the blue ones* son más grandes. 12. *This one* es bastante barata, aunque *that one* [*over there*] cuesta aun menos.

PARA LEER SIN ESTUDIAR

Notas sobre unos héroes de Chile

En la historia de Chile hay cuatro nombres famosos de los días de la conquista. Dos son españoles; dos son araucanos, indios que vivían allí cuando llegaron los españoles, y que todavía viven en el sur del país sin haber sido vencidos jamás.

El primer conquistador que llegó a Chile, en 1535, fué Almagro, compañero de Pizarro en la conquista de los incas, que gastó su parte del tesoro de Atahualpa buscando un imperio como el de su amigo. Los araucanos, cuando llegaron los extranjeros, eran amistosos, creyendo que los hombres blancos eran de una raza superior, pero tan crueles eran los españoles que pronto aprendieron los indios a usar de la misma crueldad y aun más.

Cuando supieron los araucanos que tendrían que combatir con los hombres blancos, decidieron escoger un jefe (*chief*) nuevo, que había de ser el más fuerte de todos. Los hombres tenían que llevar sobre los hombros un tronco (*trunk*) grande de árbol cuanto tiempo pudieran, y el que consiguiera llevarlo más horas sería el jefe. Un joven fuerte, llamado Caupolicán, después de mirar a su competidor (*competitor*) mientras lo llevaba por treinta y seis horas, lo cogió y lo llevó por dos días con sus noches sin descansar ni dormir, ganando así el derecho de ser jefe de su pueblo.

Este Caupolicán, que hoy es un héroe nacional de Chile, convenció a Almagro de que sería mejor declararse vencido, y Almagro volvió a Lima. Muchos años más tarde murió Caupolicán horriblemente a manos de sus enemigos, sin dar grito alguno.

Bernardo O'Higgins, of Irish blood, helped win Chile's independence and was its first president. Santiago's wide Avenida de las Delicias is often called O'Higgins Avenue, after the monument erected there to him.

Después de Almagro, llegó Pedro de Valdivia al sur de Chile, y fundó la ciudad de Santiago, hoy día capital del país. Aunque Valdivia quería colonizar el país en vez de conquistarlo, tenía que combatir de vez en cuando con los enojados araucanos. Tenía un joven esclavo araucano, llamado Lautaro, que al fin se escapó y, con algunos caballos, volvió a reunirse con sus amigos. En poco tiempo les enseñó todas las costumbres de los españoles para que ellos pudiesen vencerlos en sus batallas. Al fin Lautaro capturó a su amo antiguo, Valdivia, y la muerte de éste es un cuento horrible.

— ¡Pues es oro lo que quieres! — le dijeron los araucanos a Valdivia. — Bueno, ¡toma esto! — Y le echaron oro fundido (*melted*) en la boca para darle la muerte.

Pero así los araucanos vengaron (*avenged*) la muerte de sus amigos, y después de eso, nadie trató más de vencerlos. Hasta la fecha estos indios viven pacíficamente en el sur de Chile, cuidando su ganado (*livestock*), haciendo sus choapinos (*rugs*) de lana (*wool*) y sus joyas de plata, para venderlos en la capital. Como los guaraníes del Paraguay, los araucanos nunca fueron vencidos.

TEMA

1. General San Martín wanted to save his soldiers. **2.** The Spaniards frequently succeeded in shooting (**fusilar**) those who carried letters. **3.** Near the bridge he noticed an old oven in which clay jugs were made. **4.** Upon seeing it, he asked the pottery maker (**alfarero**) to make some with a double bottom (**fondo**). **5.** These would serve to carry very important letters between Lima and Huaura. **6.** The old Indian went to Lima once a (**la**) week to sell his jugs. **7.** The butler (**mayordomo**) always bought one, and then exchanged it the following week. **8.** The barber thought it was foolish to make so much noise. **9.** If the quarrel (**riña**) had happened sooner, someone might (**podría**) have found out the secret of the jugs. **10.** But the next day San Martín took possession of Lima, without losing a soldier.

CAPÍTULO 29

Por una docena de huevos duros

In the northern part of long narrow Chile, a stretch of desert has known practically no rain for a thousand years. In the south it rains most of the time, but in the lush green central valley Nature has compromised with a perfect climate, and there Pedro de Valdivia founded the capital city of Santiago in 1541. Today it is a smart queen of a city, definitely modern, with skyscrapers, and snappy traffic officers who do a wooden-soldier routine as the signals change on the busy boulevards.

In the heart of the city towers the four-hundred-foot rock that is Santa Lucía Hill, on top of which Valdivia once built a fort for protection from the Araucanians. His statue is there now, as well as that of the husky Indian Caupolicán, a

respected opponent of the Spaniards. The entire hill is now one great landscaped park with paths and benches, flowers, trees, and lily pools, serving at the same time as the campus for the University at its foot. Over the hill the students stroll, books in hand, mumbling aloud the paragraphs they are memorizing. And there one may find, too, young people interested in things other than books, for on the stone side of a fern-hung nook there is a little inscription cut by some student's knife, «*Aquí encontré a mi amor.*»

Chileans have written many short stories, and Ernesto Montenegro, the author of the story given here, is one of their favorites as well as one of ours, for he lived for many years in New York and worked for newspapers there. The following incident of the hard-boiled eggs is supposed to have taken place not so many years ago, although it could have happened only yesterday.

Un hombre que era muy pobre resolvió irse a las minas para probar su suerte, dejando lo poquito que quedaba en la casa para su mujer y los niños. Después de caminar largo tiempo, pasó por un pueblo donde tuvo que pedir que le dieran algo de comer para no caerse muerto de hambre. Al fin llamó a la puerta de una casa, donde había una señora solita junto al brasero [1] con su gato y sus gallinas.

— Por la mucha necesidad que tengo, patroncita, le pido que me dé siquiera unos cuantos huevitos, que cuando vuelva de las minas se los pagaré bien.

En ese tiempo los huevos costaban tan poco que muchas veces ni siquiera valía la pena de ir a buscar en los nidales

[1] A *brasero, charcoal-burner,* serves as a simple stove for poor people.

(*nests*); y como la señora tenía el agua hirviendo [1] para tomar mate,[2] tomó una docena de huevos de la cesta (*basket*) y los echó en la olla a cocer.

El hombre se fué muy agradecido con su docena de huevos duros. Le bastaron para llegar hasta la Descubridora,[3] donde decían que se estaba ganando mucha plata.

Diez años más tarde el minero, viéndose ya rico, pensó que lo mejor era volver a su tierra a ayudar a su familia. Pero no se olvidó de pasar por el pueblo a cumplirle la palabra a la señora que tenía las gallinas. Así pues se detuvo con la tropilla (*herd*) de burros que venía conduciendo.

Ta, ta, ta (*knock-knock*). — ¿Qué, ya no me conoce, abuelita? ¿No se acuerda de lo que le prometió aquel pobre que

[1] This is an exception to the rule that the present participle is not used as an adjective. Note that *hirviendo* does not agree with the noun.

[2] *Mate*, often called *yerba mate*, is South America's most popular "tea," especially in Argentina, Paraguay, Brazil, and Uruguay. This story is laid in Chile, which shows that *mate* is common there, too.

[3] ***la Descubridora,*** *the Discoverer*, is the name of a silver mine.

Looking across Santiago from Santa Lucía Hill, one sees the fourth largest city of South America, a modern capital full of business, traffic problems, and skyscrapers.

Armstrong Roberts

pasó por aquí sin nada que comer para su viaje y que usted le dió una docena de huevos? Bueno, una de estas cargas de plata es para usted; escoja la que más le guste.

Y echó unas cuantas al suelo.

A la vieja le comenzaba a fallar (*fail*) la vista y estaba muy sorda. Pero le pasaba lo mismo que a otros, que con la edad se ponen avarientos (*greedy*).

— ¿Y dice usted, joven, que es plata todo lo que llevan esos burros? ¿Y usted fué a ganar toda esa plata después que me pidió al fiado los huevos a mí?

La vieja no quería que le diera a ella una, no más, ¡cuando los burros eran tantos! ¡Y si ella no hubiera sido de buen corazón, buena minita que se habría encontrado!

— ¿Cuánto tiempo hace que le dí esos huevos?

— Diez años por lo menos. Fué antes del Temblor Grande.[1]

— Entonces, caballerito, ¡toda esa plata es mía! ¿Cree usted que yo esté satisfecha con una carguita? Si yo guardo los huevos y se los doy a mis gallinas, ¿cuántas docenas de miles de huevos y pollos cree que tendría yo ahora? No, señor, no venga a engañarme a mí. Porque me ve vestida de lana,[2] no ha de tomarme por oveja. Ayúdeme a meter esos burros en el corral (*yard*), le digo.

E hizo entrar a los burros y cerró la puerta con llave.

El minero, que era un alma de Dios, no sabía qué hacer con aquella vieja loca. Echarle la puerta abajo, cuando a él no le conocían ni los perros, sería tanto peor, es lo que pensó.

Andando otra vez para el centro, pasito a pasito y con la cabeza baja, oyó que le decían, — ¿No me dirá, amigo, qué es lo que ha perdido?

Era un hombrecito con la nariz bien colorada, que andaba con el sombrero al ojo y un poco como con vino.[3]

[1] The ***Temblor Grande,*** *Great Earthquake,* almost entirely wrecked Valparaíso, Chile, in 1906. The author of this story was living there at the time.

[2] ***Porque me ve vestida de lana, no ha de tomarme por oveja,*** an adaptation of a proverb: *because you see me dressed in wool, you needn't take me for a sheep.* Implying that she isn't so dumb!

[3] ***como con vino,*** *as if he had had some wine.*

Sawders

At the foot of Santa Lucía Hill a great double stairway starts the climb to the lovely park above, where students from the near-by University stroll over the paths as they study aloud.

El minero le contó lo que le había pasado.

— No tenga cuidado, amigo. Mire, yo soy abogado, y le prometo que mañana ganamos el pleito. Haga usted que le manden una citación [1] a la vieja para las dos de la tarde, y espéreme en el juzgado.[2] — Y le pidió al minero el último peso que le quedaba para «curar su enfermedad».

Al día siguiente estaba la vieja muy tiesa (*stubborn*) ante el juez, y el tinterillo sin llegar.

— ¿Qué hace su abogado que no viene? — le dijo de muy mal humor el juez al pobre minero. — Le digo que si no llega a tiempo, le condeno (*sentence*) a usted con costas.

Estaban dando las dos cuando entró el tinterillo, con la nariz como un tomate.

— Su Señoría me perdonará el atraso (*delay*) — le dijo al juez, — pero estaba muy ocupado cociendo unas semillas para plantarlas.

[1] ***Haga usted que le manden una citación,*** *see to it that they send a summons.*

[2] ***juzgado,*** *court.* Our slang word "hoosegow," jail, came from this.

— ¡Vaya a contarle eso a su abuela![1] — le gritó el juez, dando un golpe a la mesa. — ¡El caballerito nos tiene esperándole, y luego viene a burlarse de nosotros! ¿Dónde se ha visto cocer la semilla antes de plantarla?

— Me sorprende que se enoje conmigo Su Señoría cuando le digo que estaba cociendo unas semillas para plantarlas. ¿No ha venido esta señora a contarle que podía haber ganado miles de pesos en huevos y pollos de una docena de huevos duros que le dió a este buen hombre hace como diez años?

— ¡Cómo! ¿Estaban cocidos los huevos, señora? ¡Jure usted decir la verdad! — le gritó el juez.

— Así fué, Su Señoría. Se los dí duritos, — contestó la vieja.

— Entonces, joven, — le dijo el juez al minero, — páguele su real y medio a esta vieja sinvergüenza y llévese su plata, que bastante le ha costado ganarla.

[1] "Tell that to your grandmother" is as old Spanish slang as it is English.

Chilean youngsters of Santiago like to play around the fountains in the many parks. As well as parks, there are wide avenues with flowering center parkways and friendly shade trees.

Gendreau

El minero le dió una carga de plata al tinterillo por su ayuda en ganar el pleito, y se fué con sus burritos para su casa, contento como unas Pascuas.[1]

ADAPTED FROM ERNESTO MONTENEGRO (*Chile*)

PALABRAS NUEVAS

	abogado	lawyer	2	**junto a**	near
4	**cocer** (ue)	to cook, boil		**pleito**	lawsuit
	colorado	red		**pollo**	chicken
2	**duro**	hard	3	**probar** (ue)	to try (out)
	gallina	hen		**semilla**	seed (small)
4	**hervir** (ie, i)	to boil		**tinterillo**	shyster lawyer (slang)
4	**juez** (*m.*)	judge			

EXPRESIONES

al ojo, over one eye
a tiempo, on time
cerrar con llave, to lock
dar un golpe a, to strike
echar abajo, to knock down
huevos duros, hard-boiled eggs
no tener cuidado, not to worry
para el (**al**) **centro,** "downtown"
paso a paso, step by step
***por lo menos,** at least
Su Señoría, Your Honor
un alma de Dios, a good fellow

¿VERDAD O NO?

Change these sentences to make them true if they are false.

1. El señor de este cuento quería probar su suerte en un lugar lejano. 2. Llevaba consigo en el camino todo lo que necesitaba para comer. 3. Trató de comprar a una señora rica una docena de huevos. 4. En ese tiempo los huevos eran muy caros. 5. La señora estaba hirviendo el agua para hacer café. 6. El hombre prometió pagarle cuando volviera de las minas. 7. Después de diez años el minero se olvidó de pagar los huevos. 8. Al detenerse en el pueblo, supo que la vieja había muerto. 9. Cada burrito llevaba una carga de plata que valía mucho. 10. El minero le ofreció a la vieja dos cargas de plata para pagarle. 11. La vieja podía ver y oír bien. 12. La señora quería que le diese tres cargas de plata. 13. El

[1] *contento como unas Pascuas*, "*happy as a lark.*"

Armstrong Roberts

Traffic halts in front of Mapocho Railway Station in Santiago while everyone stares at the celebrities who have just arrived. Note the elaborate decoration of the building's façade.

abogado tenía la nariz colorada porque había tomado mucho mate. 14. Al día siguiente, la vieja tuvo que devolver la plata al minero porque los huevos cocidos no dan pollitos.

PREGUNTAS

1. ¿Por qué fué el hombre pobre a las minas? 2. ¿Por qué pidió algo de comer en el pueblo lejos de su casa? 3. ¿Qué tenía la señora que vivía solita? 4. ¿Para qué tenía el agua hirviendo? 5. ¿Valía mucho la docena de huevos? 6. ¿Se comió el hombre todos los huevos a la vez? 7. ¿Cuánto tiempo después volvió el minero a su casa? 8. ¿Cómo llevaba la plata que había hallado? 9. ¿Cuánta plata iba a darle a la vieja para pagar los huevos? 10. ¿Era mucha? 11. ¿Por qué quería aun más la vieja? 12. ¿Creía la vieja que el minero trataba de engañarla? 13. ¿Por qué no echó abajo la puerta para recobrar (*recover*) sus burritos? 14. ¿Qué nombre se da a un abogado algunas veces? 15. ¿Era verdad que el tinterillo había estado cociendo semillas? 16. ¿Salen los pollitos

de los huevos duros? 17. ¿Cómo le pagó el minero al abogado? 18. ¿Cuánto tuvo que pagar a la vieja?

PREGUNTAS PERSONALES

1. ¿Le gusta a Vd. ir a buscar en los nidales (*nests*) de las gallinas? 2. ¿Cuándo come Vd. huevos duros? 3. Si tuviese Vd. mucha plata, ¿la llevaría Vd. en burros? 4. ¿Pide Vd. algunas veces algo de comer al fiado? 5. ¿Ha echado Vd. abajo una puerta? 6. ¿Cuándo cierra Vd. su puerta con llave? 7. ¿Va Vd. al centro con frecuencia? 8. ¿Lleva Vd. el sombrero al ojo? 9. ¿Quisiera Vd. ser abogado, minero, o juez? 10. ¿Cuida Vd. muchos pollos y gallinas? 11. ¿Está Vd. siempre de mal humor? 12. ¿Cuece Vd. las semillas antes de plantarlas para hacerlas crecer mejor?

REPASO DE VERBOS

I. Here are some irregular verb stems of different tenses. *Can you identify the infinitive and tense they represent?*

sup-	dir-	har-	vin-	estuv-
mur-	hic-	pud-	pid-	tendr-
dij-	pus-	quis-	tuv-	traj-

II. Give a synopsis in the first person plural of contener, conseguir, *and* destruir *according to this outline:*

Infinitive, Gerund, Past Participle
Present Indicative, Present Subjunctive
Preterite Indicative, Past Subjunctive
Future, Conditional
Present Perfect Indicative, Present Perfect Subjunctive
Past Perfect Indicative, Past Perfect Subjunctive

III. Give the first person present subjunctive and preterite indicative of these verbs: sacar, colgar, entregar, rogar, buscar, significar, pagar, obligar. *How do they differ?*

IV. Give the following expressions in Spanish, using the

proper forms of **dormir.** *Then repeat, substituting the verbs* **servir, oír, pagar,** *and* **venir** *for* **dormir.**

1. she sleeps 2. Sleep! 3. we slept yesterday 4. he used to sleep 5. they will sleep 6. he would sleep 7. he has slept 8. they had slept 9. he wants me to sleep 10. he wanted me to sleep 11. if they slept (*contrary-to-fact*) 12. until he sleeps tomorrow 13. it is necessary that we sleep 14. let us sleep 15. before sleeping 16. they were sleeping (*prog.*)

ESTUDIO DE PALABRAS

I. You have had a verb related to each of these words. *Give the infinitive and its meaning.*

llegada	mejor	ataque	abrazo
viajero	obediente	ofrecimiento	amor
recuerdo	deseo	recibimiento	respuesta
consejo	honradez	alimento	nacimiento
vivo	préstamo	conquista	lejos de

II. You have had these word families:

zapato, *shoe*; **zapatero,** *shoemaker*; **zapatería,** *shoeshop*
carne, *meat*; **carnicero,** *butcher*; **carnicería,** *butcher shop*

What word ending is used for the name of a person who works at a certain trade? What ending means his shop or store?

Give the meanings of these words by associating them with some you know (many of them are not in the vocabulary):

gallinero,[1] dulcería, platero (from *plata*), joyería, relojero, cristalería, cafetería, nevería (from *nieve*, ice cream in Mexico), tintorería (*tinte* means color or dye), panadero, cochero, mueblería, botonería,[2] juguetería (from *jugar*), lechero, lechería, barbería (from *barba*, beard or chin), pajarero, carpintería,[3] ollero, pastelería, carnicero, papelería, librería, peluquería (from *pelo*)

[1] This also means a *chicken house*, as well as a *ladies' sewing circle*!

[2] In many towns of South America there are tiny shops which sell only buttons and buckles.

[3] This also means a *lumber yard*.

Sawders

Araucanian Indian girl of southern Chile wears heavy silver jewelry of her tribe as well as modern shoes. Behind her is the primitive family loom on which blankets are woven.

III.[1] Spanish-speaking people usually call their shops and stores something more colorful than "Smith's Grocery" or "Jones' Drygoods." Here are some interesting shop names found in various Latin-American countries. *Cover up the right hand column and try to guess what kind of store the name indicates, then look to see if you were right.* (If you find a word not in the vocabulary, you are supposed to be able to guess its meaning.)

Name of Shop	Kind of Shop
La Gran Panadería del Gallo (*rooster*)	panadería
Tienda la Gallina	tienda mixta
Las Quince Letras	abarrotes (*groceries*, Mex.)
La Nueva Victoria	abarrotes
El Rocío (*dew*)	fábrica (*factory*) de aguas gaseosas

[1] Optional exercise.

La Penumbra (*shadow*)	carbón de leña (*charcoal*)
La Vaquita	lechería
La Gota (*drop*) de Agua	reparaciones (*repairs*) de paraguas (*umbrellas*)
El Polo Norte	dulces y refrescos
La Flecha (*arrow*) Roja	línea de camiones (*bus*)
La Sonrisa	línea de camiones
El Buen Gusto	panadería
La Juventud (*youth*)	barbería
La Guerra Mundial (*world*)	carnicería
La Campanita de Plata	tienda mixta
El 18 de Marzo [1]	gasolinera
Otra Vez Nuevos	reparaciones de zapatos
La Boca del Río	pescado (*fish*)
La Espiga (*head of grain*) de Oro	panadería
El Dragón de Oro	recuerdos de China
El Infierno	carnicería
Mi Cámara Dirá las Bellezas de la Tierra	fotografías
La Vera (*true*) Paz	inhumaciones (*mortuary*)

IV. The following diminutive forms are used in this chapter. *Translate them and give the original word.*

poquito	abuelita	pasito	burritos
solita	minita	hombrecito	vaquita
patroncita	caballerito	tinterillo	campanita
huevitos	carguita	duritos	tropilla (*herd*)

REPASITO

I. Give the equivalent demonstrative or possessive pronouns which could be substituted for each of these expressions and translate. Example: **este libro: éste,** *this one;* **mi libro: el mío,** *mine.*

aquel camino, este balcón, esos árboles, la bandera de Vd., nuestro lugar, sus iglesias, esta cueva, aquellas aves, la fuente de ella, estos esclavos, nuestra felicidad, sus consejos, tu imagen, esta desgracia, aquel valle, estas tazas

[1] Mexico expropriated the oil properties of many foreigners on March 18, 1938.

II. Express in Spanish (§ 37):

that [which is] good, what he wants, the best [thing], the worst [thing], this is impossible, that isn't true, do you know this?, that [which is] new, the important [thing] is, the sad [part of it] is, the only [thing] that he wants, that [which is] Mexican, do you know what happened?, what we do is necessary, the easiest [thing] is to go

III. Put the verbs into Spanish. (***¡Cuidado!*** You may find subjunctives lurking anywhere!)

1. ¿Ha visto Vd. un indio que *is* altote? 2. No, nunca he encontrado uno que *is* grandote. 3. Si *they were* más altos, no se sorprenderían tanto al ver a los turistas. 4. ¿Hay indios que *are* rubios? 5. Sí, los hay, pero no creo que *they live* aquí. 6. Espero que los *we find* más tarde. 7. Vamos a quedarnos aquí hasta que *we find out* la hora. 8. No beba Vd. agua que no *see.* 9. Si *I had* más tiempo, iría al centro con Vd. 10. Mientras yo *live,* seré siempre amigo tuyo. 11. Si *you want* que su novia le *love,* cómprele flores. 12. Quisiera que Vd. *come* temprano. 13. Vió a una chica que *had* los ojos azules como el mar. 14. Pero iba buscando una chica que *had* los ojos como tinteros (*inkwells*).

IV. Why did you use the subjunctive or indicative in each of the sentences in Exercise III?

PARA LEER SIN ESTUDIAR

In Santiago de Chile there is published a household magazine, much like our "Good Housekeeping," called «Margarita», which contains things of interest to the whole family. In a column called *Sugerencias* (Suggestions), one finds some very familiar advice showing that our boys aren't the only ones who like such things as dirty "cords." Read what the Chilean columnist thinks about it!

¿QUÉ OCURRE CON LOS MUCHACHOS DE COLEGIO? [1]

Los muchachos andan con pañuelos sucios. Cuando uno les pide por casualidad un pañuelo, sacan del bolsillo unas pelotillas (*wads*)

[1] *Colegio* corresponds to our high school, not college.

sucias que han estado usando durante días, y con las que quizás han limpiado los zapatos.

Andan con sweaters[1] *sucios.* Las niñas dicen que hasta los muchachos de clases superiores andan a veces con sweaters que no reciben un lavado (*washing*) en todo el año. Y es increíble lo mal que piensan de eso las niñas. Un sweater sucio no es ninguna ayuda a la popularidad, y estamos seguras de que las madres se mueren de ganas de conseguir ese sweater y lavarlo bien.

Son tan económicos con el corte de pelo. ¿Es cierto que los muchachos esperan estar hirsutos (*long-haired*) para cortarse el pelo? ¿Que cuando van al peluquero (*barber*) insisten en que se lo corten tan corto que casi parezca afeitado (*shaved*)? A las niñas no les gusta ninguno de los dos extremos. Y por fin, desearían que los muchachos trajeran peinetas (*combs*) de bolsillo y las usaran con más frecuencia.

Andan con las manos sucias. Hasta los que más se cuidan dejan sucias las manos. Raro, porque todo el mundo se fija en las manos. Si el cuidado del auto o de la bicicleta tiene la culpa, recomendamos un poco de grasa (*grease*) para quitar la mugre (*dirt*), después un buen jabón (*soap*). Las manos bien cuidadas son una gran ventaja (*advantage*).

Son descuidados (careless) *en los detalles.* Aunque esperan que las muchachas que los acompañan vayan bien vestidas, ellos, sin embargo, son negligentes, especialmente en el vestir. Tiran los ternos (*suits*) por cualquier parte en vez de colgarlos, y luego se los ponen arrugados (*wrinkled*). No les importan los zapatos sin lustre (*shine*). Tal vez las niñas no digan nada, pero lo ven todo.

TEMA

1. The man had to leave what little he had for his family. 2. He asked the old woman to give him something. 3. She lived all alone near the road. 4. After waiting [for] a long while, she cooked a dozen eggs. 5. He was very grateful, and promised to pay her when he should return. 6. He did not forget to stop in the village in order to keep his word. 7. The woman was getting blind and deaf

[1] Chileans have adopted many English words, because many of them are of British ancestry.

as well as greedy (**avarienta**). 8. She said that all the silver ought to be hers. 9. If she had kept the eggs, she would have had thousands of chickens. 10. She locked the door, and he did not dare to knock it down. 11. The lawyer was a big fellow with large ears. 12. He told the miner not to worry. 13. He told the judge that one always planted cooked seeds. 14. The judge made the miner pay the old lady a dollar and a half.

CAPÍTULO **30**

Empampado

"Lost on the pampas" sounds like an Argentine story, for we usually think of Argentina as the country of pampas, but in this story the plains referred to are in Chile. The northern part of Chile is a jagged heap of unfinished "geography" where the Andes swoop down into coastal mountains that fade into a rolling sandy desert so dry that even cactus almost gives up the struggle. This is the copper and nitrate country that made Chile wealthy until a scientist discovered how to make artificial nitrates. Although the nitrate business in Chile isn't what it used to be, it is still important, and here in the desert country the *salitreros* — nitrate workers — still live in bleak towns so dry that at one time wine was cheaper and easier to get than water. Yet no one wants it to rain, for rain would ruin the valuable nitrate beds.

This story, although the author does not say so, is probably laid in the Atacama Desert near Antofagasta, the seaport of the nitrate country. There is not a great deal of action in the tale, but it gives a clear picture of what it means to be lost in the terrible rainless Chilean desert.

Tuvo sus palabras con el jefe de máquinas, por no sé qué disputa del trabajo, y, como era un roto [1] fuerte y nada perezoso, resolvió ir a otra oficina. Él no era esclavo; ¿por qué iba a ser el perro de nadie? Tenía sus dos brazos buenos, y en la Pampa no hay quien se muera de falta de trabajo.

Así pensaba Hipólito Pizarro, mientras se daba un baño al fin del día. Se dirigió a su cuarto, se puso sus prendas de domingo, hizo un lío pequeño con su vicuña,[2] y al anochecer, sin decir a nadie una palabra, se fué de allí. Ya se podían ver las luces de todos los establecimientos salitreros,[3] pero Hipólito pensó, con razón, que sería inútil ir a buscar trabajo en cualquiera de ellos, pues pertenecían todos a la misma compañía. Entonces se dirigió hacia el Norte, hacia la Pampa libre, con la esperanza de encontrar una oficina donde no le conocieran.

Llevaba para el viaje una botella de agua, otra de coñac, dos sandwiches [4] y un puñado (*handful*) de coca [5] y ceniza. Cantando una canción de sus tierras del Sur, tomó el camino, y pronto su figura se perdió en la sombra de la noche.

Hacía frío, un frío cortante (*cutting*) y duro, traído por el viento de los Andes. No tuvo más guía (*guide*) que la luz de

[1] A ***roto***, literally *ragged one*, is of the lower class in Chile, and, before the days of social reforms, led a miserable existence.

[2] A *vicuña* is a small wild animal of the camel family that lives in the high Andes. Its tawny fur is so valuable that an American coat made of thread spun from it is worth $900. People who live in and near the Andes use coverlets made of the skins without realizing their value, as Hipólito did.

[3] The nitrate mines in the desert are miserable places to work, but the wages are so high that men are always willing to endure the hardships for a while.

[4] Other English words commonly used in Chile are ***el overall, el garaje, el living, el hall, el porch, el shampoo, aló*** (*hello*).

[5] ***coca y ceniza,*** *coca and ashes.* The Indians of the Andes are not the only ones who chew coca leaves, since any native traveler of desert or mountain knows that they may save his life. They are usually chewed with ashes or unslaked lime.

Flat desert country of Chile brings in tremendous wealth from the nitrate which lies almost at the surface of the ground.

las estrellas, en un cielo sin nubes. El alba le sorprendió en medio del desierto, sin un camino, sin una senda por delante; y el sol, que recibió al principio como un calor confortante (*comforting*), pronto empezó a hacérsele insoportable (*unbearable*).

Anduvo, anduvo ... No quería tocar su ración de agua, y decidió echarse a la boca unas hojas secas de coca, yerba (*herb*) boliviana de uso popular. Pronto se produjeron los efectos de la droga (*drug*); no sentía hambre ni sed.

Anduvo, anduvo ... Sonreía ante los espejismos (*mirages*), acostumbrado a esa cosa de los desiertos. Sobre las tierras lejanas aparecían tropas en combate, trenes, ciudades mágicas y visiones de lagos transparentes bordeados (*bordered*) de árboles.

Sonreía, pensando en los viajeros que se habrían dejado engañar por tales ilusiones. Siguió andando, hora tras hora, hasta que sintió las primeras sensaciones de la sed. Mezcló un poco de coñac con agua y lo tomó. Como empezaba a sentir el peso del lío, lo puso en el suelo y lo convirtió en asiento (*seat*) para descansar.

No había más que soledad (*solitude*) y silencio. Ni una senda, ni una huella de hombre o de animal. Nada más que el desierto seco bajo el cielo con su luz ardiente.

Anduvo así el día todo, tomando de vez en cuando líquido o coca, y por la tarde, sintió alegría al descubrir huellas humanas. Pensó que no debía hallarse muy distante de alguna oficina; pero mayor que su alegría fué su desilusión (*disappointment*) cuando se dió cuenta de que caminaba sobre sus propias huellas, que después de diez horas de caminar, hallábase en el mismo sitio donde se había detenido a descansar.

No quiso andar más aquella noche, ni tampoco habría podido. Sus zapatos estaban rotos y cada paso le dolía como si anduviera sobre agujas (*needles*). Para el hambre y la sed no le quedaba más que un poquito de agua con coñac. Tendió (*unfolded*) la vicuña, se cubrió, y, de cara al cielo, se puso a dormir. Sólo le despertó el alba, con su frío. Hipólito, lleno ya del terrible miedo de los empampados, tuvo que decidirse a seguir su marcha. Débil ahora, ya no pudo sonreír ante los espejismos (*mirages*), y marchaba con los ojos cerrados.

A mediodía, aplastado (*crushed*) por el fuego del sol ardiente, acabada su ración de coca y de agua, habría deseado caerse allí a esperar la muerte, que veía ahora como una liberación. Por todas partes, no veía más que la eterna pampa, extendiéndose hasta lo infinito. Sabía que en el desierto, caer es morir. ¡Había oído tantos cuentos de empampados que habían muerto por no tener valor de dar unos cuantos pasos más . . . !

Siguió andando . . . No sabía ya si soñaba o estaba despierto (*awake*) . . . De pronto, al dar un paso, sintió un choque brutal en todo el cuerpo, y, sin fuerzas para quedarse en pie, cayó al suelo y perdió el sentido.

Cuando volvió en sí, un líquido tibio y salado (*salty*) le llenaba la boca. Abrió los ojos y se encontró junto a un poste telefónico, con el cual había tropezado sin saber. Aquel líquido era su propia sangre ... La desesperación (*desperation*) le inspiró entonces una idea: romper los alambres, cortar la comunicación y quedarse esperando. Pero, ¿cómo? ¿De dónde sacar fuerzas para echar el poste abajo?

De pronto, como si algo misterioso hubiese llegado a iluminar (*enlighten*) su imaginación, sacó su cuchillo. Se arrodilló (*knelt*) junto al poste y comenzó a cavar (*dig*) violentamente ... Se hubiera dicho que un perro acababa de descubrir una ardilla (*squirrel*). Aquello no duró más que unos cuantos minutos. El roto dejó caer su cuchillo y se echó sobre el poste, que se vino pesadamente (*heavily*) al suelo. Rompió en seguida los alambres a cuchillazos, y volvió a perder el sentido...

Hipólito Pizarro fué llevado al hospital del puerto,[1] como reo. Los trabajadores de la Compañía de Teléfonos le habían encontrado junto al poste. En la presencia del juez, el roto lo confesó todo. Estaba listo a sufrir la condena (*sentence*) que se le diese; pero él creía que todo hombre en su caso tenía derecho a hacer lo mismo.

— Yo no quisiera ver a Su Señoría en la situación en que yo me encontraba, — dijo, dirigiéndose al juez. — Pero me parece que Su Señoría no se dejaría morir por no echar un poste abajo o no romper un alambre ...

La historia interesó a los periódicos, y fué publicada (*published*) con muchos detalles. Hubo sensación. Un joven abogado tomó la defensa del reo, y la justicia le perdonó.

Al salir Hipólito de la cárcel, un periodista (*reporter*) se acercó a él y le preguntó, — Y ahora, hombre, ¿qué vas a hacer? ¿A dónde te vas a ir?

Y el roto, con una sonrisa fatalista de hombre que ha aceptado valientemente esta vida de miserias, le respondío, — ¿Y a onde [2] hey d'ir, patrón? A la pampa ...

ADAPTED FROM VÍCTOR DOMINGO SILVA (*Chile*)

[1] The port is probably Antofagasta.

[2] — ***¿Y a onde hey d'ir? = ¿Y a dónde he de ir?*** *where do you suppose I am going?* ***Haber de*** can often be translated quite freely.

PALABRAS NUEVAS

	alambre (*m.*)	wire
	el alba (*f.*)	dawn
	coca	herb chewed by Indians
	coñac (*m.*)	brandy
	empampado	lost on the pampas
2	**fuego**	fire
	huella	footprint
3	**inútil**	useless
	lío	bundle
3	**mezclar**	to mix
	oficina	office, shop
	pampa	plain
2	**producir**	to produce
	reo	criminal
	roto	Chilean laborer
2	**sentido**	consciousness
	tibio	warm

Expresiones

a mediodía, at noon
***no sé qué,** a kind of
ponerse a, to begin to
por delante, ahead
***volver en sí,** to regain consciousness

PREGUNTAS

1. ¿Cómo se llamaba el roto? 2. ¿Por qué resolvió el roto ir a otra oficina? 3. ¿Cómo llevó consigo su ropa usada? 4. ¿Por qué no buscaba trabajo en otro establecimiento? 5. ¿Qué llevaba para el viaje? 6. ¿Cuándo abandonó la oficina? 7. ¿Hace frío siempre en el desierto chileno? 8. ¿Hay muchos caminos y sendas en este desierto? 9. Después de diez horas de caminar, ¿a dónde llegó el roto? 10. ¿Qué pasó con sus zapatos? 11. ¿Dónde durmió? 12. ¿Cómo estaba Hipólito a mediodía? 13. ¿Por qué perdió el sentido? 14. ¿Por qué cortó los alambres? 15. ¿Tenía derecho a hacer esto?

PARA COMPLETAR

1. Al fin del día, Hipólito Pizarro .... 2. Salió con la esperanza de .... 3. Para el viaje llevaba .... 4. No tuvo más guía (*guide*) que .... 5. En vez de tomar agua, el roto .... 6. Muchas veces se ven en el desierto espejismos (*mirages*) que se parecen .... 7. Cuando estaba cansado, Hipólito .... 8. Después de diez horas de caminar, el roto .... 9. Pasó la segunda noche .... 10. Había oído muchos cuentos de empampados que .... 11. Al

chocar (*collide*) con el poste, ... 12. Para romper los alambres, era preciso .... 13. Los trabajadores encontraron .... 14. La historia fué publicada (*published*) en .... 15. Al salir de la cárcel, Hipólito se dirigió a ....

PREGUNTAS PERSONALES

1. ¿Tiene Vd. palabras algunas veces con su jefe? 2. ¿No quiere Vd. ser el perro de nadie? 3. ¿Es inútil buscar trabajo en su pueblo? 4. ¿Tiene Vd. la esperanza de cruzar un desierto? 5. ¿Se deja Vd. engañar por ilusiones? 6. ¿No hay nada más que silencio en esta clase? 7. Si estuviera Vd. empampado, ¿sentiría alegría al descubrir huellas humanas? 8. ¿Ha dormido Vd. de cara al cielo? 9. ¿Teme usted hallarse empampado? 10. ¿Tiene Vd. valor para dar unos cuantos pasos más? 11. ¿Ha visto Vd. un choque de automóviles? 12. ¿Quisiera Vd. cortar los alambres de la Compañía de Teléfonos? 13. ¿Tiene Vd. derecho a echar abajo los postes? 14. ¿Se dejaría Vd. morir antes de romper un alambre? 15. ¿Lee Vd. lo que se publica en los periódicos?

REPASO DE VERBOS

I. Make a sentence for each of these combinations, starting with **Si yo** (*contrary-to-fact*).

tener un cuchillo, cortar
tener hambre, comer
saber cocer, preparar
estar enfermo, mejorar pronto
ayudar a mi padre, estar agradecido
perder mi reloj, tratar de hallar
escribir una carta, firmarla
dejar caer un plato, hacer pedazos

II. Write in Spanish, using the first person for each main verb:

I begin to run, stop running, can't run, want to run, don't dare to run, prefer to run, dream of running, feel like running, don't have to run, continue running, rest after running, know how to run, promise to run, hear him run, want him to run, would run if I could

III. Each of these verbs is conjugated like ***conocer*** (***conozco***) (§ 95). *Give the first person singular and plural of each one:*

parecer, ofrecer, obedecer, pertenecer, desaparecer, crecer, perecer (*to perish*), entristecer

IV. Change these verb forms to the singular and translate:

nos quitaremos, repitieron, habían envuelto, obedecemos, estamos hirviéndolo, hiérvanlo Vds., contuvieron, váyanse Vds., pertenecemos, os dirigiréis, tengamos, ofrecemos, lavad vosotros, cargamos (*pret.*), destruyeron, éramos, ríanse Vds., produjeron

V. Make a sentence containing each of these verbs in the preterite tense:

(yo) probar	(nosotros) mezclar	(Vds.) envolver
(Vd.) hervir	(ellos) obedecer	(yo) entregar
(ella) cocer	(él) obtener	(nosotros) escoger
(tú) hacer	(ella) impedir	(Vd.) repetir

ESTUDIO DE PALABRAS

I. Can you write these first-year expressions in Spanish without an error?

Good day. How are you? Very well, thank you. And you? What is your name? My name is ——, at your service. How old are you? I am —— years old. What is the date? Today is Monday, April first. What time is it? It is 8:35 P.M. Do you like apples? I like oranges better (more). Where is he going? He is going home with me. Where is he now? He is not here. Who is he? He is a friend of mine. Give it to me. With pleasure. Thank you very much. You're welcome.

II. Give the preposition, if any, that is often used with each of these verbs; then give the meaning (§ 98):

acabar	poder	venir	parecerse	dejar
suceder	rodear	pensar	despedirse	fijarse
llenar	casarse	bajar	acercarse	tardar
dirigirse	tratar	subir	atreverse	soñar

III. Using the first word of each family as a clue, tell what you think the others mean. Some of them are not in the vocabulary.

1. ***jugar:*** juego, juguete, jugador 2. ***buscar:*** buscador, búsqueda 3. ***esperar:*** esperanza, en espera de, desesperar 4. ***conquistar:*** conquista, conquistador 5. ***perder:*** una pérdida, perdición, imperdible (*a safety pin*) 6. ***rey:*** reina, reinar, reino, virrey 7. ***pintar:*** pintor, pintura, pintoresco 8. ***campo:*** campar, campesino, acampar, campestre (*adj.*) 9. ***necesario:*** necesitar, necesidad, innecesario 10. ***enfermo:*** enfermedad, enfermera, enfermería 11. ***cruz:*** cruzar, crucero, encrucijada (*crossroads*) 12. ***cambio:*** cambiar, cambiador 13. ***volver:*** devolver, revolver, viaje de vuelta 14. ***llamar:*** una llamada, llamador (*on a door*)

IV. Over forty cognates were used in telling this story. *Make a list of thirty of them, noticing how their spelling differs from the English.*

REPASITO

I. Here is a review of first-year expressions that you should be able to give without even thinking. *See how quickly and accurately you can put them into Spanish.*

a year ago	on Wednesdays	in the afternoon
tonight	we are hungry	tomorrow morning
I have just eaten	we are hot	as pretty as you
everywhere	of course	taller than you
at 9 o'clock	what a pity!	without knowing it
I am at home	without talking	come here!
I am going home	he liked money	next month
let's eat	I ought to go	last week
I haven't anything	everyone	be careful!
the next day	every day	please study

II. Supply **por** *or* **para** *to complete these expressions.* Try to do them "by ear," but if neither one sounds familiar, see section 47 for the rules.

salimos *for* Santiago	mira *through* la ventana
estudié *for* dos años	fué vendido *by* Carlos
estoy *about to* ir	viajamos *by* avión
tengo que llegar *by* las dos	son cuentos *for* niños

dos *times* tres son seis
me dió uno *for* dos
lo hago *for the sake of* mi padre
estamos listos *to* ir
pagan siete *per* ciento
on account of estar enfermo, no fué
anda *along* el camino
¿*For* qué sirve?

PARA LEER SIN ESTUDIAR

¿Sabía Vd. esto?

In all Latin America one finds signs showing that people want to make their country an agreeable place. Here are some you might see if you were traveling. Guess the new words.

1. La civilización de un estado se revela (*reveal*) por su limpieza (*from* limpio). (Chilpancingo, Guerrero, Mexico)
2. En una fuente antigua: «Construida por el muy ilustre Ayuntamiento (*city government*) de esta ciudad de Allende. Año de 1828» (San Miguel de Allende, Guanajuato, Mexico)
3. No dañe (*harm*) los arbolitos. Demuestre su cultura. (Guatemala City)
4. Por respeto a nosotros mismos y en señal de cultura y educación, cuidemos este edificio. (Railroad station, Guanajuato, Mexico)
5. Por orden de la autoridad, se prohibe tirar basura (*rubbish*) en este lugar. (Pátzcuaro, Michoacán, Mexico)
6. Se prohibe a las señoras quedarse en el cine con el sombrero puesto. (Santiago de Chile)
7. Lávese las manos antes de comer. (Soap advertisement)
8. Las legumbres, la leche y el agua pueden llevar la tifoidea (*typhoid*). ¡Hiérvalas! (Mazatlán, Mexico)
9. Enseñe a los niños a cuidar las plantas y las flores. La municipalidad gasta una gran suma en la atención de los jardines. Ayude a cuidarlos. (Santa Lucia Hill, Santiago de Chile)
10. Fresh-paint signs from different countries:
    Pintura fresca
    Cuidado con la pintura
    No se pinte Vd.
    Está acabadita de pintar (acabar de = *to have just*)
    No se pegue (*get close*), que está fresca la pintura

TEMA

1. The "*roto*" was no slave; why must he work? 2. He put on his Sunday clothes and left without speaking to anyone. 3. To cross the plain, one should carry water in a bottle. 4. On the pampa[s] it is hot by day and cold by night. 5. One feels neither thirst nor hunger when one uses coca. 6. Many travelers let themselves be deceived by mirages (**espejismos**). 7. Those-who-are-lost-on-the-plains (**empampados**), after hours of walking, find themselves in the same place. 8. Their shoes wear out and each step pains them. 9. They die on account of not being able to take a few more steps. 10. If they could find the posts (**postes**), they could cut the wires (**alambres** [*m.*]). 11. If you found yourself in that situation, would you let yourself die? 12. Where do you suppose I am going, boss? (See footnote 2 on page 423.)

CAPÍTULO **31**

El tigre de Macuzá

Draw a line with a ruler across a piece of paper, color the upper part of the paper sky blue and the lower part green for spring or brown for autumn, and you have a picture of the most publicized part of the Argentine landscape. Plow a furrow west from glittering Buenos Aires to the Andes 600 miles away as the plane flies, and you will rarely uncover a stone in the rich red soil. This is the pampa, so flat that the raindrop stays where it

falls, and so rich that crops grow abundantly without fertilizer and cattle feed so lazily on such luxuriant grass that Argentine *bife* (beefsteak) is some of the tenderest in the world.

The Indians who were found in Argentina by the Spanish settlers did not have the high civilization of the Aztecs or Incas. They heckled the newcomers with vicious raids until they brought about their own extermination, which made the vast plains safe for the cattle men. In the early days there were little army outposts along the frontier of civilization in the pampas, where life was so hard and the Indians so likely to massacre the whole garrison that soldiers and civilians were sent there for punishment instead of being sent to prison. Manuel Ugarte, a writer of Argentina, in *Tales of the Pampa* tells this blood-curdling horror story of a young fellow who in the old days was sentenced to one of these outposts.

— Confieso que a pesar del calor que secaba la tierra, la primera sensación que sentí al llegar a Macuzá [1] fué un gran frío.

— ¿Es preciso contar los errores juveniles que me habían llevado hasta aquel lejano fortín, último puesto de la civilización en la pampa? Basta saber que me condenaron a aquella pequeña guarnición por seis meses.

— Imaginaos — y aquí la voz de nuestro amigo tembló con emoción, — bajo el cielo uniformemente azul, en medio de la pampa interminable, una pobre habitación. Contra una pared, sentados en el suelo, bebían mate [2] unos soldados medio vestidos, un grupo hostil de ladrones de caballos que pagaban aquí su crimen (*crime*) como en una cárcel. En sus caras duras de aventureros (*adventurers*) se veían pasiones que contrastaban con su docilidad (*meekness*) bajo una disciplina brutal.

— Pero una cara se destacaba (*stood out*) entre todos: la del sargento Linch, nuestro jefe. Duro, atlético, altote (*somewhat tall*), parecía reinar como un Dios sobre sus prisioneros.

[1] Macuzá was the name of a frontier fort of the old days.

[2] People drink *mate* everywhere in the Argentine, and workers always carry their *bombilla* and gourd with them.

Galloway

Flat Argentine pampa just outside Buenos Aires is covered with rich grass which fattens cattle and sheep. Trees are not native to the pampa, but are planted around homes.

Sus ojos brillantes mostraban más que crueldad; en ellos se veía algo de locura (*insanity*); su paso hacía temblar a aquellos hombres perdidos como el de un animal más fuerte entre los débiles. Detrás de él se arrastraba Zug, un negro de cara brutal que parecía ser su asistente. Desde el primer instante sentí miedo en la atmósfera de salvajismo (*savagery*) que reinaba en aquel pequeño puesto donde nunca llegaba un inspector militar.

«Todo consiste,» me dije, «en aceptar la aventura. Seis meses no duran toda la vida.» [1]

— Aquella tarde hablaban los diez prisioneros sólo de un tigre [2] que visitaba la guarnición, llevándose las víctimas. Todos hablaban de la muerte del que la noche anterior había desaparecido, como tantos otros, sin que quedaran rastros (*traces*) . . .

[1] The story is told in the first person, and re-told by the friend who heard it, making quotation marks necessary where the characters speak. These are used in the same way as our single quotes in English.

[2] The most dreaded animal of the *pampa* in the early days was the "tiger," really a puma, which migrated from the Andes to the plains to feed upon the cattle. The Argentine *gaucho* — cowboy — used to kill a "tiger" singlehanded with his long knife, using his heavy *poncho* — blanket — in his left hand as a shield.

Black Star

Teatime is yerba mate time, whether traveling or at home. Everyone carries his own gourd, *bombilla* and tea, and hot water is furnished for all. This is a second-class coach.

«Volveremos a encender las hogueras, y el tigre se alejará,» declaró el más optimista.

—¿Es preciso decir que cuando nos acostamos, de cara al cielo, no pude cerrar los ojos? Bajo la luz de las hogueras que habían de impedir la llegada del tigre sentí una emoción inexplicable. No podía olvidar un incidente que por mis pensamientos seguía pasando sin que yo supiera por qué: la extraña mirada del sargento Linch, que al recibirme, sólo dijo en voz baja, «Entonces somos trece[1] otra vez...»

—Mientras todos dormían bajo la noche, me pareció que se levantaba una sombra. Fué imposible dudar... Linch pasó junto a mí con una pala (*shovel*) al hombro, y se detuvo como para despertar a alguien... Otra sombra se levantó. Era el negro Zug. Se alejaron hacia un pequeño grupo de árboles que se veía a lo lejos bajo la luz de la luna...

—Me pareció inexplicable. ¿En qué podían trabajar a

[1] Thirteen is considered unlucky among many Latin Americans, just as it is with some of us.

aquellas horas? Sin hacer el menor ruido, como un reptil, me arrastré por el campo en la misma dirección.

— Cuando llegué al pie de los árboles, ambos estaban cavando (*digging*) una hoya con el vigor de los que desean terminar pronto. Al fin murmuró el sargento locamente, «La cama no puede ser mejor y el huésped (*guest*) dormirá como nunca . . .»

— Ambos se dirigieron a unos arbustos, de donde sacaron algo grande como un hombre, que echaron brutalmente a la hoya.

«No quiero que quede sangre,» murmuró el sargento, «es preciso que nadie sospeche lo que ocurre.»

«¿Cuántos van?» [1] preguntó Zug.

«Nueve con el de hoy.»

«Y todavía no hemos concluido . . .»

«Ellos tienen [2] la culpa, que siempre nos mandan uno a

[1] *«¿Cuántos van?»* "*How many does that make?*"

[2] *Ellos* refers to the authorities who sentenced the criminals to be sent to the frontier.

Argentinian gaucho lives in the saddle most of his life. Although the typical dress is not so picturesque as it once was, the *gaucho's* long cape and bright neckerchief lend color.

Keystone

la vez. Mientras llegan así, siempre será el mismo número — trece, y el último tendrá que desaparecer... Porque hay que evitar una desgracia. ¿Recuerdas lo que pasó hace algún tiempo cuando éramos trece?»

«¿La tempestad que nos dejó sin habitación y sin caballos?» preguntó Zug estúpidamente.

«Sí. Y «el tigre» tendrá que seguir haciendo desaparecer al último que llegue... ¿No ves que somos trece otra vez? Esta misma noche resuelvo la cosa...»

— Entonces comprendí que lo que acababa de oír era mi sentencia de muerte. ¿Huir? ¿Cómo? A pie por la pampa interminable (*endless*) era imposible, y sólo acercarse a un caballo sería morir, en aquel lugar donde todos vivían con la idea constante de escaparse...

— Una tempestad venía hacia nosotros.[1] Dentro de pocos minutos caería la lluvia, y todos se habían despertado para correr a la habitación.

«Ensilla (*saddle*) dos caballos,» gritó el sargento a Zug. Y en cuanto estuvieron listos, montó sobre uno de ellos y me llamó al otro. «Vamos a explorar un poquito,» me dijo. «No quiero que los indios aprovechen la tempestad para hacer un ataque.»

— Era un pretexto para llevarme campo afuera y matarme. Preferí fingir obedecer, listo a defenderme, si podía. Pero mi resistencia a ese hombrón tendría que ser insignificante. El sargento era más fuerte que yo, y más valiente... Linch parecía ignorar, al principio, mi presencia, ocupado en maldecir (*curse*) la tempestad. Estuve para creer que me había olvidado; sin embargo, esperé con la mano en el sable. Pero cuando llegamos ante los árboles, Linch detuvo su caballo y fingió examinar el suelo, donde empezaban a caer las primeras gotas (*drops*) de lluvia.

«Bájate,» me dijo, «y mira bien. Me parece que han pasado indios por aquí.»

— Era el momento fatal. Entonces resolví jugar el todo

[1] The part of the story telling how they went back to the fort has been omitted.

por el todo (*to gamble everything*). Y mientras el loco bajaba la cabeza para indicar el lugar, saqué el sable y le dí un golpe con toda la fuerza del brazo. Después cerré los ojos para esperar la muerte... Pero el sargento había caído del caballo y allí murió el «tigre» de Macuzá.

— Entonces, bajo la lluvia torrencial, con el sable todavía en la mano como si combatiera con el recuerdo, lancé (*rush*) mi caballo a carrera (*at full speed*) por la pampa. Y aquí me tenéis, después de muchas aventuras, en Europa,[1] desde hace diez años... Pero la imagen del sargento Linch me persigue todavía...

Y nuestro amigo se pasó las manos por los ojos, como si quisiera quitar una visión infeliz.

Adapted from Manuel Ugarte (*Argentina*)

PALABRAS NUEVAS

3	**anterior**	preceding		**guarnición**	garrison
3	**aprovechar**	to take advantage of		**hoguera**	bonfire
3	**arrastrarse**	to crawl		**hoya**	hole, grave
3	**condenar**	to condemn	4	**perseguir** (i)	to pursue
3	**confesar** (ie)	to confess		**puesto**	outpost
3	**dudar**	to doubt		**sable** (*m.*)	sword
3	**encender** (ie)	to light		**sargento**	sergeant
4	**fingir**	to pretend	4	**sospechar**	to suspect
	fortín (*m.*)	small fort		**tempestad** (*f.*)	storm
3	**golpe** (*m.*)	blow		**tigre** (*m.*)	(*here*) puma

PREGUNTAS

I. Answer in English to see if you understood the story:

1. Why did the young man go to the frontier? 2. Why did the prisoners blame a "tiger" for the mysterious disappearances? 3. What sort of person was Sergeant Linch? 4. Who was the killer and why? 5. Explain the title of the story.

[1] Many Argentinians often went to Europe to travel or live before the first World War, when they discovered the United States!

II. Contéstese en español:

1. ¿Por qué sintió frío el joven al llegar a Macuzá? 2. ¿Fué a Macuzá para divertirse? 3. ¿Qué hacían los soldados que estaban sentados en el suelo? 4. ¿Eran guapos y simpáticos los soldados? 5. ¿Cómo reinaba el jefe sobre sus prisioneros? 6. ¿Quién era Zug? 7. ¿Cuánto tiempo tendría nuestro joven que quedarse allí? 8. ¿De qué hablaban los prisioneros? 9. ¿Por qué no pudo dormirse nuestro joven? 10. ¿Qué hicieron el sargento y su asistente durante la noche? 11. ¿Cómo los siguió el joven? 12. ¿Qué echaron a la hoya? 13. ¿Por qué mataba el sargento supersticioso siempre al último que llegase? 14. ¿Iba el sargento a matar a nuestro joven? 15. ¿Por qué no lo hizo?

PARA COMPLETAR

1. El fortín de Macuzá era el último .... 2. El grupo de soldados estaba .... 3. El sargento Linch era .... 4. Los prisioneros creían que un tigre .... 5. Nuestro joven no pudo dormirse porque .... 6. El sargento y el negro fueron a .... 7. El sargento no quería que .... 8. El sargento supersticioso creía que .... 9. El joven quería huir porque .... 10. Durante la tempestad, el sargento le mandó .... 11. El joven tuvo que .... 12. Después, se escapó y fué a .... 13. «El tigre de Macuzá» había sido ....

¿VERDAD O NO?

Change these statements to make them true if they are false.

1. Los indios de la pampa eran muy civilizados. 2. El fortín de Macuzá estaba cerca de Buenos Aires. 3. Los criminales fueron llevados a una guarnición lejana. 4. Los soldados tomaban mate con frecuencia. 5. El jefe de los prisioneros era más débil que ellos. 6. Los prisioneros temían a Zug. 7. Los prisioneros sospecharon que el sargento había muerto a sus compañeros. 8. El jefe aprovechó la tempestad para tratar de matar al joven. 9. Linch y el negro enterraron a sus víctimas lejos de los árboles. 10. Linch creía que el número trece le traería buena suerte. 11. Sería fácil cruzar la pampa a pie. 12. Los indios podrían aprovechar la noche de luna

para hacer un ataque. 13. El joven, después de matar al «tigre de Macuzá,» fué a los Estados Unidos.

PREGUNTAS PERSONALES

1. ¿Siente Vd. un gran frío a pesar del calor? 2. ¿Quisiera Vd. pasar seis meses en una cárcel? ¿Por qué? 3. ¿Hay muchos ladrones de caballos en su pueblo? 4. ¿Es Vd. duro (-a) y atlético (-a)? 5. ¿Cuándo hacen Vds. una hoguera? 6. ¿Ha dormido Vd. muchas veces de cara al cielo? 7. ¿Le gusta a Vd. dar un paseo a la luz de la luna? 8. ¿Se ha arrastrado Vd. en el suelo como un reptil? 9. En caso de un choque, ¿tiene Vd. siempre la culpa? 10. ¿Cree Vd. que el número trece traiga mala suerte? 11. ¿Aprovecha Vd. una tempestad para montar a caballo? 12. ¿Le persigue a Vd. la imagen de alguien?

REPASO DE VERBOS

I. Give the first person plural present and past subjunctive of pagar, sacar, creer, dormir, traer, traducir, saber, poner, decir, ir, hacer.

II. Give the following expressions in Spanish, using the proper forms of **ver.** *Then repeat, substituting the verbs* **conocer, andar, hacer** *and* **caer** *for* **ver.**

1. I see (*pres.*) 2. See! 3. we saw yesterday 4. we used to see 5. they will see 6. we would see 7. she has seen 8. we had seen 9. we want them to see 10. we wanted them to see 11. if you saw (*contrary-to-fact*) 12. although you may see 13. in order that we might see 14. let's see 15. before seeing 16. they were seeing (*prog.*)

III. Say in Spanish (§ 1):

We see each other, they look at each other, you (*pl.*) touch each other, we write to one another, speak to each other!, they don't tell each other the truth

Sawders

Argentinian gaucho game called *Pato* (duck) is a kind of rough polo-basketball played with a leather "ball" equipped with handles for picking it up from the ground at a full gallop.

ESTUDIO DE PALABRAS

I. Here are some of the most common Spanish words, which you should know perfectly by now. *Give the meanings as quickly as you can.*

acá	bien	cuánto	jamás	mejor	quizás
algo	cierto	cuyo	luego	mismo	solo
allá	como	deber	llegar	nadie	tal
así	cómo	dejar	llevar	peor	tan
aún	cuál	entre	mas	quedar	tanto
ayer	cualquier	irse	mayor	quien	ya

II. Make adverbs from these adjectives and translate (§ 118):

triste, leal, débil, humilde, tierno, digno, fiel, cómodo, seco, ciego, milagroso, cierto, frío, loco, atento, dulce, ligero, útil

REPASITO

I. Choose the story you have liked best this semester, and put it into simple "first-grade" Spanish sentences. When your teacher has corrected it, read it aloud and have the class name it.

II. Make a sentence in Spanish identifying each of the following names found in stories beginning with Chapter 19. Or make a sentence describing each, omitting the name itself, and have the class complete the sentence. Example: Los indios que vivían en México cuando llegó Cortés se llamaban ——.

mayas	quichua	Paraná	un colón
Cortés	Lima	Asunción	Rio de Janeiro
Pizarro	guaraní	Bolívar	Buenos Aires
Titicaca	araucano	San Martín	Atahualpa

PARA LEER SIN ESTUDIAR

El famoso poema de Martín Fierro

The wide, flat Argentine pampa, ideal for grazing, brought into being the *gaucho,* who herded his little flock of cattle and lived happily and simply far from civilization with his family. All the vast *pampa* was his — until someone invented barbed wire. Then came the tragedy of the *gaucho* and his extermination, for from the city came men in oxcarts with rolls of the bristling stuff, to fence off thousand-acre pastures, and to burn the hut of the *gaucho* who was to them only a squatter.

Once a romantic figure, the traditional *gaucho* was always to be found either on horseback, drinking *mate,* singing his own verses to the accompaniment of his guitar, or sleeping under the stars. There was poetry in his blood, and the best-seller among the Argentinians is a long poem called *Martín Fierro,* written in 1872 by one who for a few years in his youth lived the life of a *gaucho.* It tells of the tragedy of the plains, and aroused the nation to do something about its human problem.

Every Argentinian is familiar with the famous poem; *gauchos* of the old days who could not read bought copies of it to carry around in the hope that someone would read it aloud to them; new editions for young people come out today, and the poem has been translated into English. At the 1939 World's Fair in San Francisco, the Argentine Pavilion featured a beautiful restaurant called the "Martín Fierro."

Here are a few stanzas of the beloved poem, written as they were supposed to have been sung with his guitar by the imaginary *gaucho* hero, Martín Fierro. The paraphrase at the right explains each stanza in case you do not understand the original.

The *gaucho,* Martín Fierro, consoles himself for his hard life by singing:

Aquí me pongo a cantar
Al compás de la vigüela,
Que al hombre que lo desvela
Una pena estraordinaria,[1]
Como la ave solitaria
Con el cantar se consuela.

Me siento aquí para cantar al son (*sound*) de mi guitarra, porque el hombre que no duerme por tener una pena extraordinaria puede consolarse con su canción, como el pájaro solitario.

The *gaucho* sings of how he loves his liberty:

Mi gloria es vivir tan libre
Como el pájaro del cielo,
No hago nido en este suelo
Ande hay tanto que sufrir;
Y naides me ha de seguir
Cuando yo remuento el vuelo.

Mi gloria es vivir tan libre como el pájaro del cielo. No hago nido (*nest*) en este suelo donde hay tanto que sufrir. Y cuando vuelo por los aires, nadie puede seguirme.

The *gaucho,* driven from his home on the pampa, decides to go to live with the Indians, and sings sadly that man with his intelligence should not be so cruel as they:

Dios formó lindas las flores,
Delicadas como son —

Dios formó las flores lindas y delicadas y les dió toda la per-

[1] The following words in the poem are different from current Spanish: *estraordinaria* (extraordinaria), *la ave* (el ave), *ande* (donde), *naides* (nadie), *remuento* (remonto, I soar), *ansí* (así), *ajuera* (afuera), *vigüela* (vihuela).

Les dió toda perfección —
Y cuanto él era capaz —
Pero al hombre le dió más
Cuando le dió el corazón.

fección posible. Pero dió más al hombre cuando le dió el corazón.

Martín Fierro gives some advice to his sons before he leaves them:

Un padre que da consejos,
Más que padre es un amigo,
Ansí como tal les digo
Que vivan con precaución —
Naides sabe en qué rincón
Se oculta el que es un enemigo.

Un padre que da consejos es amigo, así como padre. Así, como amigo les digo que tengan mucho cuidado, porque nadie sabe en qué rincón (*corner*) se esconde el que es su enemigo.

The *gaucho* warns them against laziness:

Debe trabajar el hombre
Para ganarse su pan;
Pues la miseria en su afán
De perseguir de mil modos —
Llama a las puertas de todos
Y entra en las del haragán.

El hombre debe trabajar para ganarse su pan, porque la miseria, que tiene muchos modos de perseguir a uno, llama a las puertas de todos, y entra en las puertas del perezoso.

The *gaucho* tells his sons to be united:

Los hermanos sean unidos
Porque ésa es la ley primera.
Tengan unión verdadera
En cualquier tiempo que sea —
Porque si entre ellos pelean
Los devoran los de ajuera.

Los hermanos deben ser unidos, porque ésa es la primera ley (*law*). Deben tener siempre una unión verdadera porque si combaten entre sí, los de afuera los devorarán.

The *gaucho* tells why his advice should be respected:

Estas cosas y otras muchas
Medité en mis soledades —
Sepan que no hay falsedades
Ni error en estos consejos —
Es de la boca del viejo
de ande salen las verdades.

He pensado en estas cosas y en otras muchas mientras estaba solo. No hay mentiras ni errores en estos consejos, porque las verdades salen de la boca del viejo.

TEMA

1. The *gauchos* used to live on the plain[s] of Argentina. 2. They rode horseback all day, caring for the cattle (**ganado**). 3. They carried with them only a *poncho*, salt, *mate*, a gourd (**calabaza**), a sipper (**bombilla**), and sometimes a guitar. 4. At night they sat on the ground, ate meat cooked over a little fire, and drank *mate*. 5. With their long knives (**facón** [*sing.*]), they killed "tigers" or Indians. 6. Wrapped in their *poncho*[*s*], they slept under the stars after they had finished the day's work. 7. In the evening they played the guitar and sang verses about love, the horse, the cow, the plains and the great solitude (**soledad**). 8. There was nothing else of which to sing. 9. Sometimes two singers (**payadores**) used to have a song contest (**payada**) in which one would sing a composition (**paya**) asking a question, and the other would answer him. 10. So they sang all night while the other *gauchos* listened. 11. Nowadays the *gauchos* work for the rich landowners (**estancieros**), to whom all the great pampa belongs. 12. The romantic *gaucho* of long ago (**antaño**) has disappeared.

CAPÍTULO 32

La yegua mora[1]

Modern Buenos Aires, the largest city in all Latin America, was for three centuries a village on a mud flat beside the estuary that the Spaniards called the Silver River. For all the treasure-like names (*argent* means "silver" in Latin), Argentina disappointed the explorers, for it turned out to have no

[1] The meaning of *moro*, as applied to horses, varies in different countries. Sometimes it means a black horse with four white "stockings," or one of any color with white markings, or vice versa. In Argentina it is a black horse with white spots.

mines, and Spain ignored it and developed her golden favorite, Peru.

Then in 1860 the country began to be developed, and now Buenos Aires is the wealthy capital of the country, whose city dwellers are called *porteños* — people of the port — and make up about a fifth of the total population. The *campesinos* — people of the *campo* — lead quite different lives, but enjoy themselves quite as much as their more sophisticated city cousins, as you will see by this clever little tale by Hugo Wast, one of Argentina's most popular authors. When two country neighbors put on an amateur horse race just because some rumors have been going around, almost anything can happen, whether in Argentina or Timbuctoo!

A la orilla del arroyo vivía ña Audelina, en un rancho de paja con un corral. Era dueña de tres vaquitas, y vendía su leche a los veraneantes.[1] Era dueña, además, de una yegua mora, que uno de ellos le regaló al volver a la ciudad, y que pasaba por ser yegua de carrera.

En el campo, poseer un animal de carrera, aunque no se le haga correr, es una distinción que da fama a su dueño, como en la ciudad poseer un diploma de doctor, aunque no se ejerza (*practice*) la profesión.

Pero es el caso que en Los Molinos [2] había otro caballo de carrera, el malacara,[3] de don Nicandro Bustos. Éste era un campesino entrado en años que vivía en otro rancho, junto

[1] The smart set from Buenos Aires often goes to the foothills of the Andes, where there are many expensive summer resorts. Look up *verano* and guess what *veraneantes* are.

[2] ***Los Molinos,*** *The Mills*, is in the northern part of Argentina, where there are many windmills which pump water from the ground.

[3] A *malacara* (Argentine word) is a horse with a white stripe on its face. **What does the word mean literally?**

Galloway

President's Palace in Buenos Aires is called the *Casa Rosada* (Pink House) because of its color, and is noted for its outdoor statuary, its luxurious furnishings, and its complete libraries.

al camino real,[1] sin otra ocupación que cuidar al malacara.

En los pueblitos vecinos no faltaban carreras, a las cuales asistía don Nicandro con su caballo. Pero siempre volvía como fué, sin haber corrido. Lo cual no hacía ningún daño a la fama del malacara; al contrario, los campesinos decían con fe, — El día que el malacara corra . . . ¡hum!

Cierto día, sin saberse cómo, nació una calumnia (*slander*), que empezó a correr de rancho en rancho, haciéndose pronto motivo de muchas disputas. Se decía que la yegua mora era de mejor sangre y más ligera que el malacara, y que le había ganado una carrera.

Como la gente estaba ya un poco cansada de su ídolo, empezó a creer que la yegua mora, aunque era muy flaca, tenía, en efecto, mejor sangre que el malacara.

Don Nicandro lo supo.[2] ¡Eso sí que no podía tolerarse

[1] South America, as well as Mexico and the United States, had its *caminos reales* built by Spain.

[2] Remember what *saber* often means in the preterite tense.

(*tolerate*)! Montó a su caballo[1] y llegó hasta el rancho de ña Audelina.

— Vengo a proponerle una carrera con mi malacara.

—¡Jesús, con lo que sale![2] ¡Y quién le va a correr a su malacara, que es más ligero que un relámpago (*lightning*)!

— ¡Su yegua mora, por supuesto! ¿No andan diciendo que me ha ganado una carrera? ¡Para que vuelva a ganar!

Ña Audelina miró a don Nicandro, que encendía un cigarrillo (*cigarette*) con cara de satisfacción.

— ¿Y para cuándo será la carrera?

— Para de aquí a dos domingos, si le gusta.

— ¿Y por cuánto la apuesta?

— ¡Por diez pesos!

— ¡Santa suerte! ¡Qué dineral (*fortune*)! ¡Y mi yegua

[1] Travel by automobile across the dirt roads of the *pampa* is easy enough in the dry season, but when it rains, even today everyone goes horseback on account of the mud. As they say, "Distances are still great in Argentina."

[2] — *¡Jesús, con lo que sale!* "*My goodness, what an idea he comes out with!*"

Modern traffic officer of Buenos Aires stands in a safety box and wears white sleeve covers so his signals can be seen. The sign says, "This policeman watches over your safety. Do your part."

Gendreau

mora va a perder! ¡Como si lo viera![1] Está más flaca que la sopa de los prisioneros... Pero, ya que insiste usted, don Nicandro.

— ¡Así me gusta la mujercita! — respondió el otro, tendiéndole la mano; y, cuando ya se iba, dió media vuelta, titubeando (*stammering*), — Después de la carrera he de hablarle, ña Audelina... Porque tengo una cosa... que decirle...

Y ña Audelina, bajando los ojos, — Lo que guste, don Nicandro.

Ña Audelina fué en busca de su yegua mora, y, al pasar por el almacén (*store*), compró veinte centavos de maíz para darle ese día la primera ración. Pero la vió tan flaca y tan sin esperanzas de que ganara una carrera en dos semanas, que decidió cocer la mitad del maíz, y echó la otra mitad a las gallinas.

— ¡De todos modos, la yegua mora va a perder, porque eso de que tiene sangre de carrera son cuentos de no sé quién! — exclamó para sí.

A la mañana siguiente buscó quien le fiara un cerdo (*pig*) gordo, lo carneó (*butchered*) ella sola, y empezó a hacer chorizos.

La noticia de la carrera corrió como por radiotelefonía de rancho en rancho, y el domingo convenido asistió más gente a la iglesia que en los días de la misión.[2]

La pista de trescientos metros[3] fué preparada en el camino real, que el malacara conocía como su propio corral. La gente se agolpó (*crowded*), a eso de las dos de la tarde, a lo largo del camino. Hombres, mujeres, niños, todos se interesaban por la carrera, y todos apostaban al uno o al otro animal.

Desde temprano ña Audelina se había instalado cerca de la pista con dos grandes bateas (*trays*) llenas de empanadas y

[1] ***¡Como si lo viera!*** *As surely as if I could see it!*

[2] ***días de la misión,*** days when there are special services.

[3] The metric system is used for measurements in many countries. A meter is 39 inches.

de chorizos crudos (*uncooked*), y había hecho un buen fuego, donde borbotaba (*bubbled*) una olla de grasa. Ella parecía ser la única a quien no le interesaba un piñón[1] la emocionante (*thrilling*) carrera.

Se le acercó un soldado, echó una mirada hambrienta sobre los chorizos y empanadas, y ña Audelina se la pescó al vuelo.[2] — Las empanadas son a real; los chorizos, a medio. ¿De cuáles quiere?

— De ninguno; todavía no nos han pagado.

— Le fío entonces.

— Si me fía, bueno... Déme un par de chorizos y una empanada.

Ña Audelina tomó media docena de empanadas y las dejó caer en la grasa hirviente (*boiling*), alzándose de ésta un olorcito delicioso.

Gente de a caballo y de a pie rodearon a ña Audelina y empezó a comprar.

— ¡A real las empanadas! ¡A medio los chorizos! ¿De cuáles quieren? — Con un tenedor ofrecía las empanadas calientes, y con un cuchillo separaba los chorizos dos o cuatro o seis, según la compra (*purchase*).

Al fin de una hora se alzó un grito, — ¡Ahí viene el malacara!

Y llegó el malacara, rodeado de un grupo de admiradores (*admirers*). La yegua mora se hizo esperar todavía un buen rato, que ña Audelina aprovechó para vender más empanadas y llenarse de plata el bolsillo.

Nombraron al juez de paz, juez de la carrera, y el soldado hambriento fué a colocarse al final de la pista para servir también de juez. Montaron los dos jockeys,[3] el juez dió la señal,[4] y los dos caballos salieron entre los gritos de la gente. A cien metros eran una sombra entre una nube de polvo; a los

[1] A ***piñón*** is a tiny *pine nut*, therefore signifies something unimportant.

[2] ***se la pescó al vuelo***, *caught it* (*the look*) *on the fly*.

[3] The Argentinians use many English words.

[4] The starting signal for a horse race is usually — *¡Santiago!* — which was the old Spanish war cry. Do you remember when Pizarro used it? (Chapter 21)

Sawders

"Good Humor Man" on business street of Buenos Aires sells "frozen creams" to a good-looking young Argentinian. Shuttered show window in background indicates that siesta time approaches.

doscientos metros no eran más que una nube de polvo; un poco más allá la tierra pareció tragárselos (*swallow*), y hubo un momento de silencio, hasta que, al final de la pista se oyeron los vítores (*cheers*) al malacara, ganador.

Empezaron a pagar las apuestas. Don Nicandro se acercó a ña Audelina a pedirle los diez pesos, y ella metió la mano en el bolsillo y sacó un imponente (*imposing*) puñado (*handful*) de plata y pagó sin regatear (*haggle*).

— ¡Caramba! — dijo el dueño del malacara, sorprendido. — No la creía tan rica.

— ¡Qué quiere, don! He ganado bastante con las empanadas y los chorizos.

Don Nicandro se quedó pensativo (*thoughtful*). Él había ganado diez pesos en la carrera, pero había gastado en preparar su caballo cuarenta o cincuenta pesos de maíz. Verdaderamente, aquella mujercita valía un Potosí. — ¡Ña Audelina!

— Mande, don Nicandro.

— Voy a decirle una cosa que estoy pensando.

Ña Audelina bajó los ojos y respondió, — Diga lo que guste, don. . . .

Al domingo siguiente, el cura, en la misa, les publicó las amonestaciones,[1] y quince días después, la yegua mora comía su ración de maíz en el corral del malacara.

Ña Audelina había perdido la carrera, pero en ese caso salió cierto aquello de que «quien pierde gana».

ADAPTED FROM HUGO WAST (*Argentina*)

PALABRAS NUEVAS

4	**ahí**	there (*where you are*)		**flaco**	thin
				ganador (*m.*)	winner
	arroyo	ravine		**grasa**	grease
	carrera	race		**ña**	"sister" (*Arg.*)
	colocarse	to locate oneself		**pista**	race track
	corral (*m.*)	yard (for stock)	3	**proponer**	to propose
	chorizo	sausage	3	**tender** (ie)	to extend
	empanada	small fried meat pie		**tenedor** (*m.*)	fork
4	**fiar**	to trust		**yegua**	mare

EXPRESIONES

a lo largo de, along

***dar (media) vuelta,** to turn (halfway) around

de aquí a dos domingos, two weeks from Sunday

en busca de, in search of

entrado en años, aging

rancho de paja, thatched hut

¿VERDAD O NO?

Change these statements to make them true if they are false.

1. Un veraneante (*see footnote 1 on page 443*) había regalado a don Nicandro una yegua mora. 2. La posesión de un caballo de carrera

[1] *amonestaciones, banns.* The notice of a coming marriage is read in a Catholic church two weeks before the wedding.

da fama a su dueño. 3. Don Nicandro asistía a todas las carreras para hacer correr a su caballo. 4. Todos los campesinos creían que si corría el caballo, ganaría. 5. Don Nicandro quería una carrera con la yegua mora para poder ganar diez pesos. 6. El malacara estaba más flaco que la sopa de los prisioneros. 7. Ña Audelina dió mucho maíz a su yegua porque creía que así ganaría la carrera. 8. La noticia corrió por radiotelefonía de rancho en rancho. 9. Todos apostaban al uno o al otro caballo. 10. Ña Audelina llevó sus chorizos y empanadas a la carrera para regalárselos a sus amigos. 11. Servía las empanadas calientes con un cuchillo. 12. El juez de paz servía de jockey. 13. Había mucho polvo en el camino durante la carrera. 14. Ña Audelina no quería pagar su apuesta. 15. La carrera había costado a don Nicandro como treinta o cuarenta pesos. 16. Ña Audelina ganó bastante dinero y a la vez un marido.

PARA COMPLETAR

1. Los Molinos es un pueblo de .... 2. Dos habitantes de Los Molinos tenían .... 3. Se decía que la yegua mora era .... 4. Cuando don Nicandro oyó esto, fué a .... 5. La carrera tendría lugar dentro de .... 6. Ña Audelina echó la mitad del maíz .... 7. Ella compró al fiado un cerdo (*pig*) para .... 8. El domingo convenido, mucha gente .... 9. Hombres, mujeres y niños apostaban .... 10. Entretanto, ña Audelina se ocupaba .... 11. El primero que le compró algo, fué .... 12. El juez de la carrera fué .... 13. El dueño del ganador se sorprendió cuando .... 14. Ña Audelina perdió la carrera, pero ....

PREGUNTAS PERSONALES

1. ¿Ganaría Vd. mucho si fuese dueño (-a) de tres vaquitas? 2. ¿Le gustaría a Vd. ser dueño (-a) de un diploma? 3. ¿Vive Vd. junto a un camino real? 4. ¿Asiste Vd. a muchas carreras de caballos? 5. ¿Es Vd. más ligero (-a) que sus amigos (-as) en una carrera? 6. ¿Cuál le gustaría a Vd. más, — una empanada gorda o una flaca? 7. ¿Corre la noticia por esta escuela como por radiotelefonía? 8. ¿Apuesta Vd. mucho dinero en los juegos de béisbol?

9. ¿Podría Vd. comer ahora un par de chorizos? 10. ¿Come Vd. la carne con su tenedor o su cuchillo? 11. ¿Quisiera Vd. llenarse de plata los bolsillos?

REPASO DE VERBOS

I. Put these expressions into Spanish as quickly as possible, using the **usted** *form wherever a subject is required:*

you learn to fly, begin to fly, can't fly well, dare to fly, prefer to fly, dream of flying, feel like flying, don't have to fly, like to fly, continue flying, know how to fly, before flying, see me flying, want him to fly, would fly if you could

II. Complete each sentence in three ways, using the verbs suggested:

1. Iré al centro cuando Vd. (*volver, tener tiempo, vestirse*). 2. Esperaré hasta que Vd. (*comer, terminar, encender el fuego*). 3. Pablo andaba como si (*estar cansado, tener prisa, ser perezoso*). 4. No volveré a su casa aunque Vd. (*invitarme, pagarme, servirme una comida*). 5. Yo aceptaría la invitación si (*recibirla, no estar ocupado, poder*). 6. Es lástima que Vds. ([*pres. perf.*] *romper la ropa, perder el camino, ponerse enfermos*). 7. Ojalá que nosotros (*ganar la carrera, obtener buenas notas* [grades], *encontrar un buen cine*). 8. Me pide que yo (*escoger un regalo, obedecer a mi padre, entregar la leche*). 9. Temían que ella (*seguirlos, dormirse, apostar demasiado dinero*).

III. Give the polite command, singular, of each verb, adding the pronouns suggested:

envolver (*it for me*), echar (*it to him*), obtener (*them*), entregar (*it, f.*), curar (*her*), reírse de (*him*), no robar (*them*), pensar en (*this*), no perder (*it*), seguir (*me*), devolver (*it to her*), hacer (*it for us*), lavar (*them for him*)

ESTUDIO DE PALABRAS

There are varied shades of meaning in many Spanish words, just as there are in ours. You have been using the following verbs correctly, although perhaps you did not realize it. *Find the verb in List B which accurately translates each one in List A.* Try to choose the Spanish verbs without referring to the Spanish-English vocabulary, although they are all there.

A

to look for	to put	to stop (*detain oneself*)
to look at	to put in	to stop (*doing something*)
to look out (*be careful*)	to put on (*clothing*)	to laugh
to ask (*a question*)	to go (*no destination*)	to laugh at
to ask for	to go (*to a destination*)	to give
to take off (*clothing*)	to go away	to give (*as a gift*)
to take away	to go to (*toward*)	to give (*deliver, hand over*)
to take out	to go near (*approach*)	
to take (*carry*)	to go away from (*far*)	
to take (*internally; often used for* beber)	to return (*two verbs*)	
	to return (*an object*)	

B

entregar	regalar	dar	reírse de	reír
dejar de	detenerse	devolver	regresar	volver
andar	irse	dirigirse a	acercarse a	alejarse de
ir	ponerse	meter	poner	tomar
llevar	sacar	quitar a	quitarse	pedir
preguntar	buscar	mirar	tener cuidado	

REPASITO

I. The following words or expressions may cause the subjunctive, as you know. *Tell why each does* (*causing, emotion, etc.*).

esperar	aunque	querer	sentir
aconsejar	puede ser	es lástima	por — que
cuando	es preciso	no creo	alegrarse de
hasta que	decir	temer	antes que

II. If each of the following is the main verb in a sentence containing a subjunctive, in what tense will the subjunctive

Sawders

Argentine farmer wears a beret (and probably *alpargatas*), like his ancestors who came over from Spain. The tree-covered hills are in the northwest of Argentina, beyond the flat pampa.

verb probably be? (The verb itself need not cause the subjunctive.)

he oído	esperaban	fueron	había estado
aconsejó	¿cree Vd.?	no creería	era posible
irá	pienso	propongo	hemos poseído

III. Answer these questions in Spanish, using pronouns instead of nouns in your answer.

1. ¿Cuándo va Vd. a encender el fuego? 2. ¿Ha perdido Vd. el sentido muchas veces? 3. ¿Qué ha hecho Vd. con su llave? 4. ¿Sabe Vd. cocer huevos? 5. ¿Lleva Vd. muchos pensamientos en la cabeza? 6. ¿Compran los turistas muchos recuerdos para sus amigos? 7. ¿Se puede saber la edad de las aves por los dientes? 8. ¿Arrojó Vd. su libro en la fuente? 9. ¿Puede Vd. comprar medicinas en una botica? 10. ¿Ha roto Vd. muchos platos en la cocina?

PARA LEER SIN ESTUDIAR

¿Sabía vd. esto?

La Argentina tiene muchas cosas notables. El pico (*peak*) más alto de los Andes, Aconcagua, con una altura de casi veinte y cuatro mil pies, está en el paso entre Chile y la Argentina, y pertenece a ésta.

Es el primer país que obtuvo su independencia, gracias a San Martín, y en muchas ciudades hoy día, el hotel principal se llama «Hotel San Martín».

Una canción patriótica que sabe cada niño de escuela de la Argentina es la «Marcha de San Lorenzo», que trata del héroe nacional, San Martín.

Éste es el país de habla española más grande y más poderoso de la América del Sur, y también uno de los más modernos. Pero su capital no tiene señales mecánicas de tránsito, porque a los independientes argentinos no les gusta obedecerlas. Así es muy peligroso tratar de cruzar las calles entre los «matagentes», como se llaman los enormes autobuses.

Buenos Aires tiene la calle más ancha del mundo, llamada «9 de julio», que antes era tres calles. Debajo de esta calle hay un sitio de estacionamiento (*parking*) en donde se puede dejar el automóvil gratis.

Entre los automóviles que se encuentran en las calles se ven muchos de Europa, por ejemplo, el Wanderer, el Mercedes Bentz, el Opel, el Renault, y el Fiat. Y un gran Cadillac, con placa (*license plate*) de oro y el número 1, pertenece al presidente, que vive en un palacio llamado «La Casa Rosada (*pink*)».

Todos los niños, así como las niñas, tienen que llevar a la escuela un guardapolvo (*smock*) blanco para protegerse la ropa. Y hace muchos años, para mejorar las escuelas, el gran educador (*educator*), Sarmiento, hizo venir de los Estados Unidos a sesenta maestras norteamericanas, que pasaron toda la vida allí, enseñando a los argentinitos como antes habían enseñado a nuestros norteamericanitos.

Y cada niño de escuela de toda la «república de plata» sabe de memoria un poema acerca del gran árbol de la pampa, su árbol nacional, llamado el ombú, que da la sombra en que descansan los viajeros y los gauchos. Aquí tienen ustedes un verso del poema:

El ombú

Cada comarca en la tierra
tiene un rasgo prominente:
el Brasil su sol ardiente,
minas de plata el Perú,

[Cada parte de la tierra tiene algo de importancia: el Brasil tiene su sol caliente, el Perú tiene sus minas de plata, Monte-

Montevideo su cerro,
Buenos Aires, patria hermosa,
tiene su pampa grandiosa;
la pampa tiene el ombú.

video (*capital of Uruguay*) tiene su cerro (*hill*), Buenos Aires, nuestra patria hermosa, tiene la gran pampa; y la pampa tiene el ombú.]

LUIS L. DOMÍNGUEZ (*Argentina*)

TEMA

1. *Ña* Audelina was the owner of a mare (**yegua**) of good blood. 2. Her neighbor, who lived near the highway, also had a race horse. 3. She said hers was better than his and could win a race from him. 4. He bought a great deal of corn to give his horse because it was thin. 5. She bought a pig (**cerdo**) and made meat pies to sell at the race. 6. Many of the men who attended were hungry and bought sausages. 7. The judge rode one of the horses in a cloud of dust, and his won. 8. Don Nicandro paid his bet, although he was not worth a Potosí. 9. He said he had something to tell her. 10. Say what you like, sometimes he who loses, wins.

School boys and girls of Argentina are required to wear clean white smocks to school every day. This is a nature study class on a field trip in a Buenos Aires park.

Armstrong Roberts

CAPÍTULO 33

Las medias de los flamencos

One of the friendliest of our Good Neighbors in South America — the smallest one and even so, larger than England — is Uruguay, which owes its existence to the fact that Brazil wouldn't let Argentina have it and Argentina wouldn't let Brazil have it. Land of rolling — not flat — pampas of rich black soil, its *estancias* (farms) are like Argentina's, but its roads are better because there is plenty of rock and gravel with which to pave them.

The broad streets of Montevideo, the capital, flow peacefully over a group of rocky knolls, and much space is given to plazas and parks. Because of its fine climate, Argentina uses it for a summer resort, and mother and the children take a bright-colored villa for the season while father commutes by plane across the hundred-and-twenty-five-mile estuary. The smart beach hotels are the last word in modern design, and the casino, run by the government, accepts the summer visitors' money and uses it for public charity, much as the lotteries in most Latin-American countries provide money for the poor.

Among Uruguay's writers is one of Spanish America's greatest story-tellers, Horacio Quiroga, whose *Cuentos de la Selva* rates with Kipling's *Jungle Book* in its tales of wild life. Here is one of the stories, which explains why flamingos have red legs and are always standing around in the water, told in a humorous way that you will enjoy whether you believe the tale or not!

Cierta vez las víboras dieron un gran baile. Invitaron a las ranas (*frogs*) y los sapos, a los flamencos, y a los cocodrilos y los peces. Los peces, como no caminan, no pudieron bailar; pero siendo el baile a la orilla del río, los peces estaban asomados (*watching*) a la arena (*sand*), y aplaudían con la cola.

Los cocodrilos, para adornarse bien, se habían puesto en el pescuezo (*neck*) un collar de bananas, y fumaban (*smoke*) cigarros paraguayos.[1] Los sapos se habían pegado (*stuck*) escamas (*scales*) de pez en todo el cuerpo, y caminaban como si nadaran. Y cada vez que pasaban junto a la orilla del río, los peces les gritaban, burlándose de ellos.

Pero las que estaban hermosísimas eran las víboras. Todas estaban vestidas con traje de bailarina (*dancer*), del mismo color de cada víbora. Las víboras coloradas llevaban una falda de tul (*tulle*) colorado; las verdes, una de tul verde; las amarillas, otra de tul amarillo.

Y las más espléndidas de todas eran las víboras de coral, que estaban vestidas con larguísimas faldas rojas, blancas y negras, y bailaban en serpentinas. Cuando las víboras danzaban y daban vueltas apoyadas (*leaning*) en la punta (*end*) de la cola, todos los invitados aplaudían como locos.

Sólo los flamencos, que entonces tenían las patas blancas, estaban tristes, porque como tienen muy poca inteligencia, no habían sabido adornarse. Envidiaban el traje de todos, y sobre todo el de las víboras de coral.

Un flamenco dijo entonces, — Yo sé lo que vamos a hacer. Vamos a ponernos medias coloradas, blancas y negras, y las víboras de coral se van a enamorar de nosotros.

Y todos juntos echaron a volar, cruzaron el río y fueron a llamar a la puerta de un almacén del pueblo.

— ¡Tan-tan (*knock-knock*)! — llamaron con las patas.

— ¿Quién es? — respondió el almacenero, porque era de noche.

— Somos los flamencos. ¿Tiene medias coloradas, blancas y negras?

[1] **Paraguayan cigars are big black ones.**

— No, no tengo, — contestó el almacenero. — ¿Están locos? En ninguna parte van a encontrar medias así.

Los flamencos fueron entonces a todos los otros almacenes, y de todas partes los echaban por locos.

Entonces un armadillo [1] que había ido al río a tomar agua, se quiso burlar de los flamencos y les dijo, — ¡Buenas noches, señores flamencos! Yo sé lo que ustedes buscan. No van a encontrar medias así en ningún almacén. Tal vez haya en Buenos Aires, pero tendrán que pedirlas por encomienda postal.[2] Mi cuñada (*sister-in-law*), la lechuza, tiene medias así. Pídanselas, y ella les va a dar las medias coloradas, blancas y negras.

Los flamencos le dieron las gracias, y se fueron volando a la cueva de la lechuza. Y le dijeron, — ¡Buenas noches, lechuza! Venimos a pedirte medias coloradas, blancas y negras. Esta noche es el gran baile de las víboras, y si nos ponemos esas medias, las víboras de coral se van a enamorar de nosotros.

— ¡Con mucho gusto! — respondió la lechuza. — Esperen un segundo, y vuelvo en seguida.

Y echando a volar, dejó solos a los flamencos. Dentro de un rato volvió con las medias. Pero no eran medias, sino cueros de víboras de coral, lindísimos cueros recién quitados a las víboras que la lechuza se había comido.

— Aquí están las medias, — les dijo la lechuza. — No se preocupen de nada, sino de una sola cosa: bailen toda la noche, bailen sin parar un momento, porque si paran, en vez de bailar van entonces a llorar.

Pero los flamencos, como son tan tontos, no comprendían bien el gran peligro que había para ellos en eso, y locos de alegría, se pusieron los cueros de las víboras de coral como

[1] Remember the armadillo story from Paraguay? Apparently even in Uruguay he is considered a trouble-maker. The three countries of the Paraná River basin (Argentina, Uruguay, and Paraguay) have in common the river, the *pampa*, the *gauchos*, their fondness for *mate*, and some Indian words. Otherwise modern Uruguay and Argentina are not at all like Paraguay.

[2] ***encomienda postal,*** *parcel post.* Country people of South America send to mail-order houses for supplies just as we do.

medias, metiendo las patas dentro de los cueros, que eran como tubos. Y muy contentos se fueron volando al baile.

Cuando vieron a los flamencos con sus hermosísimas medias, todos los envidiaron. Las víboras querían bailar con ellos únicamente, y como los flamencos no dejaban un instante de mover las patas, las víboras no podían ver bien de qué estaban hechas aquellas preciosas medias.

Pero poco a poco, sin embargo, las víboras comenzaron a desconfiar (*suspect*). Cuando los flamencos pasaban bailando al lado de ellas, se agachaban hasta el suelo para ver bien. Las víboras de coral, sobre todo, estaban muy inquietas. No quitaban la vista de las medias, y se agachaban también, tratando de tocar con la lengua las patas de los flamencos, porque la lengua de las víboras es como la mano de las personas.

Dentro de poco, un flamenco, que ya estaba muy cansado, tropezó con el cigarro de un cocodrilo, y se cayó. En seguida las víboras de coral corrieron a mirar, vieron lo que eran

Downtown skyline around Plaza Independencia of Montevideo shows a prosperous and busy city. Formal gardens surround a statue of José Artigas, the George Washington of Uruguay.

Sawders

aquellas medias, y dieron un silbido (*hiss*) que se oyó desde la otra orilla del Paraná.[1]

— ¡No son medias! — gritaron las víboras. — ¡Sabemos lo que son! ¡Nos han engañado! ¡Los flamencos han muerto a nuestras hermanas y se han puesto sus cueros como medias! ¡Las medias que tienen son de víboras de coral!

Al oír esto, los flamencos, llenos de miedo porque habían sido descubiertos, quisieron volar; pero estaban tan cansados que no pudieron levantar una sola ala. Entonces las víboras de coral se echaron sobre ellos, y les arrancaron las medias a pedazos, enojadísimas, y también les mordieron las patas para que murieran.

Los flamencos, locos de dolor, saltaban de un lado a otro hasta que al fin, viendo que ya no quedaba un solo pedazo de media, las víboras los dejaron libres.

Pero los flamencos no murieron. Corrieron a echarse al agua, sintiendo un grandísimo dolor. Gritaban de dolor, y sus patas, que eran blancas, estaban entonces coloradas por el veneno de las víboras.

Esto pasó hace mucho tiempo. Y ahora todavía están los flamencos casi todo el día con sus patas coloradas metidas en el agua, tratando de calmar el fuego que sienten en ellas. A veces salen a la orilla, y dan unos pasos por tierra, para ver cómo se sienten. Pero el dolor del veneno vuelve en seguida, y los flamencos corren a meterse en el agua. Todos los peces saben por qué es, y se burlan de ellos. Pero los flamencos, mientras se curan en el agua, no pierden la oportunidad de vengarse (*get even*) comiéndose a cada pececito que se acerca demasiado a burlarse de ellos.

ADAPTED FROM HORACIO QUIROGA, CUENTOS DE LA SELVA
(*Uruguay*)

[1] The Paraná River, 2800 miles long, empties into the great estuary of the Río de la Plata, along with the Uruguay River, which divides Uruguay from Argentina. This story is apparently laid in Argentina.

PALABRAS NUEVAS

	agacharse	to stoop		**morder** (ue)	to bite
	almacén (*m.*)	store	3	**parar**	to stop
	almacenero	storekeeper		**pata**	foot (*animal's or bird's*)
	cocodrilo	crocodile		**pez** (*m.*)	fish
	cola	tail		**preocuparse** (de)	to worry (about)
	cuero	skin, hide	3	**recién**	recently
	envidiar	to envy	4	**saltar**	to jump
	flamenco	flamingo		**saludar**	to greet
4	**inquieto**	uneasy		**sapo**	toad
	invitado	guest		**veneno**	poison
	lechuza	owl		**víbora**	viper, snake

Expresiones

echar a volar, to fly away

en ninguna parte, nowhere

¿VERDAD O NO?

Change these statements to make them true if they are false.

1. Los flamencos dieron un gran baile a la orilla del río. 2. Los

Ice wagon of Montevideo is not so much in demand now as it was before the up-to-date Uruguayans started using electric refrigerators just as we do.

Armstrong Roberts

cocodrilos llevaban un collar de cigarros paraguayos. 3. Las víboras vestían traje del mismo color de su cuero. 4. Los invitados aplaudían cuando danzaban los peces. 5. Los flamencos, siendo muy inteligentes, no se habían adornado. 6. Los flamencos envidiaban el traje de las víboras de coral. 7. Los flamencos querían que las víboras se enamoraran de ellos. 8. En un almacén del pueblo los flamencos encontraron medias coloradas, blancas y negras. 9. El armadillo les dijo que la lechuza podría regalarles tales medias. 10. La lechuza había comido muchas víboras de coral. 11. Los flamencos tendrían que bailar todo el día para que nadie pudiese ver bien las medias. 12. Las víboras usan la lengua para tocar las cosas, como nosotros las manos. 13. Cuando se reconocieron los cueros, los flamencos echaron a volar. 14. Los flamencos metieron las patas en el agua para curar el dolor. 15. Los peces no saben por qué hacen esto.

PARA COMPLETAR

1. El gran baile tuvo lugar .... 2. Los sapos fingieron ser .... 3. Las víboras vestían .... 4. Los flamencos envidiaban .... 5. Los flamencos llamaron a la puerta de .... 6. El almacenero creía que los flamencos .... 7. El armadillo quiso .... 8. La lechuza volvió dentro de un rato con .... 9. La lechuza les dijo a los flamencos que .... 10. Los flamencos se pusieron .... 11. Era difícil ver bien las medias porque los flamencos .... 12. Las víboras se agachaban para .... 13. Cuando vieron lo que eran las medias, gritaron .... 14. Los flamencos no pudieron volar porque .... 15. Ahora los flamencos se pasan todo el día ....

PREGUNTAS PERSONALES

1. ¿Ha sido Vd. invitado a un gran baile? 2. ¿Envidia Vd. a sus amigos que tienen traje nuevo? 3. ¿Se preocupa Vd. de sus lecciones de español? 4. ¿Cómo saluda Vd. a sus amigos al encontrarlos? 5. ¿Salta Vd. mucho mientras está bailando? 6. ¿Tiene Vd. patas o pies? 7. ¿Lleva Vd. medias coloradas? 8. ¿Qué hace

un almacenero? 9. ¿Es bueno fumar cigarros paraguayos? 10. ¿Le gustaría a Vd. bailar toda la noche sin parar? 11. ¿Da Vd. muchas vueltas al bailar? 12. ¿Pide Vd. muchas cosas por encomienda postal (*parcel post*)? 13. ¿Le gustaría a Vd. llevar medias hechas de cuero de víbora? 14. ¿Se burlaría Vd. de sus amigos si llevaran medias coloradas, blancas y negras?

REPASO DE VERBOS

I. Conjugate in the preterite tense: saltar, morder (ue), envidiar, preocuparse, aplaudir, pegar (*to stick*), perseguir (i).

II. Conjugate in the imperfect tense: saludar, mover, aplaudir, ser, ir, ver.

III. Give in Spanish these forms of the verbs in Exercises I and II, using the imperfect only for "used to" *or* "was —ing":

he jumped, I bit, they used to envy, they applauded, I stuck, he pursued, they were moving, we went, he saw, we used to be, I used to worry, she used to envy, they were jumping, we bit, we weren't worrying

IV. What tenses or verb forms in Spanish do these words require: may, might, would, used to, have (*auxiliary*), had, —ing, —ed, was —ing, to?

ESTUDIO DE PALABRAS[1]

I. In a certain hotel in Mexico, you will find a laundry list like the one on page 464. *At five pesos to the dollar, figure out how much it would cost you to have your week's supply of laundry done in twenty-four hours.* (New words are found at the end of the list.)

[1] Optional section, since words used here are not repeated unless introduced in the regular way.

HOTEL IMPERIAL LAVANDERÍA

No. ———

Cuarto No. ——— Cantidad $———

México, ——————de 19—

Sr.————————————

ESPECIAL

NO.	LISTA DE SEÑOR		NO.	LISTA DE SEÑORA	
	Camisas	$0.40		Vestidos	$1.75
	Camisas seda	.50		Blusas	.45
	Camisas franela	.50		Blusas seda	.85
	Cuellos agua	.10		Portabustos	.30
	Cuellos almidón	.12		Camisas	.45
	Camisetas algodón	.20		Camisas seda	.85
	Camisetas lana o seda	.40		Camisas dormir	.75
	Calzoncillos algodón	.40		Camisas dormir seda	1.60
	Calzoncillos seda	.40		Batas	1.25
	Camisas dormir	.65		Calzones	.30
	Calcetines, par	.10		Calzones seda	1.25
	Calcetines seda	.20		Medias algodón	.18
	Pañuelos	.06		Medias seda	.35
	Pañuelos seda chicos	.12		Enaguas	.65
	Pañuelos seda grandes	.20			
	Pijamas	.50		LISTA DE NIÑOS	
	Pijamas lana o seda	.85		Vestidos	.45
	Corbatas algodón	.12		Camisas	.30
	Batas	.50		Calzones	.18
	Chalecos	.80		Camisas dormir	.12
	Traje lino	2.50		Medias	.15

Sírvase hacer la lista de su ropa, de otra manera tiene Vd. que aceptar la que hagamos.

Lavamos los encajes (*laces*) y artículos de color a riesgo (*risk*) del interesado (*owner*).

No respondemos (*responsible*) por artículos que se encojan (*shrink*).

Lavado ordinario de ropa se hace en tres o cuatro días.

Lavado especial de ropa se hace en 24 horas.

No responde la casa más que por las prendas especificadas en la lista.

Toda reclamación (*claim*) deberá hacerse en el momento de recibir la ropa.

New words: ***lavandería,*** *laundry*; ***seda,*** *silk*; ***franela,*** *flannel*; ***almidón,*** *starch*; ***algodón,*** *cotton*; ***cuello,*** *collar* (***cuellos agua,*** *unstarched*); ***lana,*** *wool*; ***camiseta,*** *undershirt*; ***calzoncillos,*** *shorts*; ***calcetines,*** *socks*; ***pañuelo,*** *handkerchief*; ***bata,*** *robe*; ***chaleco,*** *vest*; ***lino,*** *linen*; ***blusa,*** *blouse*; ***portabusto,*** *brassière*; ***enaguas,*** *underskirt*

II. Answer in English:

1. Are you expected to make a list of your laundry in Mexico? 2. Is your clothing insured against shrinkage, fading, or tearing? 3. When should you put in a claim for missing articles? 4. How long does it take to get your laundry back if you do not send it "special"? 5. Do you know if these "special" rates are high or low compared with prices here?

III. Contéstese en español: [1]

1. ¿Cuesta más hacer lavar las camisas de seda que las de algodón? 2. ¿Cuál cuesta más: hacer lavar un vestido de señora o un traje de lino de señor? 3. ¿Es más caro hacer lavar los calcetines o las medias? 4. ¿Lleva Vd. camisa o blusa? 5. ¿Usa Vd. pañuelos grandes de seda? 6. ¿Usa Vd. calcetines o medias? 7. ¿Tiene cuello un chaleco? 8. ¿Tiene Vd. muchas camisas de seda?

REPASITO

I. Complete with the proper form of ser *or* estar (§§ 122–24):

1. El cuchillo y el tenedor *are* sobre la mesa. 2. El caballo *was* muy flaco. 3. El caballo negro *was* en el corral. 4. *It was* las doce cuando llegaron. 5. El ladrón pronto *will be* en la cárcel. 6. El fuego *is* muy caliente. 7. El gaucho *was* muy cansado. 8. Los huevos *had been* duros. 9. Las medias *are* coloradas. 10. El abogado *was* muy inteligente. 11. Los burros *were* metidos en el corral por la viejecita. 12. Las semillas en la cesta (*basket*) *were* cocidas. 13. El amo del negro *was* en la esquina. 14. La fuente *was* cerca del bosque. 15. El dinero *is* en su bolsillo. 16. El helado *is* frío. 17. El agua en la taza *is* fría. 18. *It will be* las diez cuando lleguemos. 19. La pobrecita *is* muy grave. 20. Su abanico *was* de París. 21. El abanico *was* de plumas.

[1] These words are not found in the general vocabulary unless used elsewhere in the book.

II. Change the italicized infinitives to the proper forms of the imperfect or preterite (§ 128). (Some will be subjunctives.)

1. Ña Audelina *poseer* una yegua mora. 2. Don Nicandro *proponer* una carrera (*race*). 3. Ña Audelina *hacer* muchas empanadas y las *vender*. 4. Don Nicandro *ganar* la carrera con su caballo. 5. Ña Audelina le *pagar* los diez pesos sin decir nada. 6. Don Nicandro *creer* que ella *ser* muy inteligente, y le *pedir* que *casarse* con él. 7. Ella *aceptar* con mucho gusto.

8. Las víboras *querer* dar un baile. 9. Ellas *invitar* a muchos animales. 10. El cocodrilo *ponerse* un collar de bananas. 11. Los flamencos *envidiar* a las víboras. 12. Los peces *aplaudir* con la cola. 13. Los flamencos *echar* a volar, y *despertar* al almacenero. 14. El almacenero *creer* que ellos *estar* locos porque *querer* medias de tres colores. 15. Ellos *ir* a ver a la lechuza, que les *dar* las medias. 16. La lechuza les *decir* que *bailar* sin parar. 17. Los pobres flamencos *ponerse* muy cansados y *dejar* de bailar. 18. Después, las víboras los *morder*, y las patas *ponerse* coloradas. 19. Los flamencos *ir* al río para curar su dolor. 20. Los peces *burlarse* de ellos.

PARA LEER SIN ESTUDIAR

¿Sabía vd. esto?

«Uruguay» es una palabra india que quiere decir «Río de los pájaros», porque antes de la llegada de los españoles vivían allí miles de pájaros, entre ellos muchos flamencos con patas coloradas.

El «Río de la Plata» ni es río ni tiene plata. Es un estuario (*estuary*) moreno de poca belleza, muy ancho, en donde desaguan (*empty*) los ríos Paraná y Uruguay. Fué llamado «Río de la Plata» por los españoles porque encontraron en sus orillas a unos indios que llevaban joyas de plata.

El nombre de la capital del Uruguay, Montevideo, quiere decir «veo una montaña», porque los marineros (*sailors*) que llegaban hasta aquel lugar en el Río de la Plata siempre veían a lo lejos el cerro (*hill*) alto.

Las casas de los estancieros (*farmers*) del Uruguay no se parecen a las de los estancieros argentinos. En la Argentina es costumbre tener una casa magnífica, algo como un palacio o castillo, a la europea.

Galloway

Uruguayan gauchos go in for fine wool ponchos of delicate pastel colors with fancy neckerchiefs of contrasting color and pattern. Hats are never of the picturesque "cowboy" type we see in our "Western" movies.

En el Uruguay las casas de campo son grandes, pero de un solo piso, con varios patios, y muchos jardines y árboles.

Los gauchos del Uruguay hoy día visten en un estilo más pintoresco que los de la Argentina. Llevan poncho de lana fina de color pastel, y una corbata de seda (como un pañuelo grande) de otro color vivo. En vez del sombrero del gaucho argentino, llevan la boina (*beret*) de España. Toman mate con calabaza (*gourd*) y bombilla, como los argentinos, pero también les gusta el café negro, como a los brasileños (*Brazilians*), porque son vecinos del Brasil.

TEMA

1. The flamingos (**flamencos**) invited their friends to a grand dance. 2. It took place on the bank of the river, so that the fish could see it. 3. Everyone wore very long skirts, which were very pretty when they danced. 4. The flamingos then had white feet, but little intelligence. 5. They envied the rest, and decided to look for [some]

red stockings. 6. They did not have time to order them by parcel post (**encomienda postal**), so they asked the owl (**lechuza**) to lend them some. 7. The owl told them to dance, because if they didn't (dance), they would cry. 8. The snakes (**víboras**) liked to dance with the flamingos, who did not stop moving their feet. 9. In a short time, a tired flamingo tripped on a toad's (**sapo**) cigar (**cigarro**) and fell down. 10. Then the guests could see that the stockings were not made of wool, but of silk.

CAPÍTULO 34

Cartas de nuestros buenos vecinos

Letter-writing among Spanish-speaking people is a fine art, for even an ordinary business letter is full of polite phrases that make our blunt "Dear Sir" and "Yours truly" sound almost insulting. No Latin is ever too busy to use an elaborate and roundabout way of expressing a thought in order to make it more courteous, and when he writes personal letters he often puts in so many solicitous phrases that there is little room for news!

There are endless accepted ways to begin and end a business letter in Spanish, and although it is possible to translate our formal greeting and complimentary close exactly, we are considered a little curt if we do it.[1] For example, "Dear Madam" can be *Muy señora mía*, but most business letters addressed to a lady begin with *Estimada señora*, *Apreciable señora*, *Distinguida señora*, *Respetable señora*, or even *Señora de nuestro respeto.*

[1] If you would like to study Spanish letter-writing in earnest, get a copy of Luria's *Correspondencia Comercial al Día* (Silver Burdett), which is as interesting as it is useful.

Instead of opening bluntly with a business matter, as ours do, Spanish letters acknowledge one received by calling it a "kind" (*atenta*) or "pleasing" (*grata*) or "esteemed" (*apreciable*) favor. And the complimentary close is always such a masterpiece of respect, friendship, and gratitude for favors received that it may be almost embarrassing to us matter-of-fact Anglo-Saxons.

Here are some ordinary examples of business letters actually written to and received from two Central American countries, which show clearly the custom of taking plenty of time to be polite.

Fillmore High School
Fillmore, California
15 de abril de 19—

Ministerio de Fomento
San Salvador, El Salvador, C.A.

Estimados señores:

Me permito escribirles para pedir unos informes acerca de El Salvador. Los socios de nuestro «Club Copa de Oro»[1] leímos en un periódico mexicano hace poco que hay en El Salvador un «Club Popeye» de jóvenes, con unos 1400 socios.

Esto nos interesa mucho, y quisiéramos saber algo del grupo, porque aquí también es muy popular el buen Popeye. Por ejemplo, les rogamos se sirvan decirnos qué hacen los muchachos en sus reuniones, si tienen emblema, si llevan uniforme, cuál es el objeto de la organización, etc.

Rogándoles dispensen la molestia, y anticipándoles[2] las gracias por su atención (*kindness*), quedo de Vds. atto., afmo., y S.S.,

James H. Jones

James H. Jones, Secretario,
«Club Copa de Oro»

[1] *Copa de oro, cup of gold*, is the poetic name sometimes given to the California poppy.

[2] Consult the section in the chapter vocabulary marked *Expresiones para la correspondencia*, or you will have a hard time trying to read these business forms!

CIRCUITO DE TEATROS NACIONALES
OFICINA CENTRAL
San Salvador, El Salvador, C.A.

Abril 25 de 19–

Sr. don
James H. Jones, Secretario
«Club Copa de Oro»
Fillmore High School
Fillmore, California, E. U. A.

Apreciable señor:

Complaciendo sus deseos contenidos en su atenta [carta] de fecha 15 de abril, y dirigida al Ministerio de Fomento de este país, nos es grato suministrar a Vd. a continuación (*herewith*) los informes con respecto al «Club Popeye».

El «Club Popeye» o «Cruzada Infantil Popeye», se compone exactamente de 1642 socios, niños de 10 a 14 años, aficionados al cine. Este número va aumentándose (*increasing*) semanalmente, debido a las grandes facilidades (*facilities*) que se presentan para ingresar en dicho club.

El «Club Popeye» ha sido creado (*created*) por el Circuito de Teatros Nacionales, una institución del Estado que trabaja por la Beneficencia Pública. Actualmente existe sólo en la capital, pero muy pronto se extenderá por todo el país. El objeto de dicho club es conducir a la juventud salvadoreña por el camino de la nueva cultura por medio de la cinematografía moderna. Está compuesto como sigue: un presidente, elegido anualmente por los socios mismos, cuatro vocales (*board members*), un secretario, cincuenta socios fundadores (*charter*), siendo el resto socios activos. No se paga ninguna cuota (*dues*).

Cada socio, con su respectivo carnet (*membership card*), tiene entrada gratis al Teatro en días de entre semana. Se exhiben (*exhibit*) películas (*films*) instructivas, representadas especialmente para ellos y dedicadas a todos los niños en general, las cuales se empiezan y terminan con dibujos animados de Popeye. Tales privilegios cualquier niño puede conseguirlos, pues lo único que se necesita para ingresar en el club, son dos fotografías, sin costo de ninguna otra clase.

El «Club Popeye» no reconoce clases sociales.[1] Niños ricos y pobres se reúnen en él con el único deseo de aprender cosas útiles por medio del cine. Considerando tales condiciones, ha sido eliminado (*eliminated*) el uniforme, pues hay muchos niños que, debido a la situación financiera (*financial*) de sus padres, no pueden comprarlo. Lo único que se demanda es decencia y limpieza en el vestido. El emblema es una figura de Popeye en forma de prendedor (*pin*), que se lleva en la camisa, y que se regala al socio cuando ingresa en el club.

Las reuniones tienen lugar periódicamente en el escenario (*stage*) del Teatro, donde los niños recitan composiciones suyas escritas sobre películas (*films*) instructivas, ganando premios las seis mejores.

El arte[2] es así cultivado en el «Club Popeye», y tiene muchísimos aficionados: pintores, cantores, recitadores, guitarristas, pianistas, violinistas, etc. Para los aficionados al dibujo y a la pintura, se organizan concursos con premios, que consisten en juegos (*sets*) de acuarelas (*water colors*), estuches (*kits*) de carpintería, vestidos, etc. Los demás ofrecen veladas (*evening performances*) en público o transmisiones (*broadcasts*) por la radio, deleitando (*delighting*) al público con conciertos musicales, comedias, etc.

Sin otro particular por el momento y esperando haber complacido sus estimables deseos, nos es grato suscribirnos de Vd., atentos y seguros servidores,

CIRCUITO DE TEATROS NACIONALES,

MANUEL VIEYTEZ,
Gerente

[1] This statement does not sound unusual to us, but it must be remembered that social classes in most Latin-American countries are fixed, and people of different levels do not intermingle socially.

[2] The arts are not considered "sissy" subjects among Latins, who look with horror upon our general ignorance of good music, poetry, and painting.

Calle de Clay, 426
Fillmore, California
25 de febrero de 19—

Sr. don Claudio E. Montealegre, Gerente
Junta Nacional de Turismo de Costa Rica
Apartado 777, San José, Costa Rica, C. A.

Muy estimado señor:

Acuso recibo de su apreciable [*carta*] de fecha 28 del próximo pasado, junto con los folletos (*pamphlets*) de propaganda turística, y quedo muy agradecida por el favor.

Sirve la presente para hacerle unas preguntas acerca de la famosa Isla del Coco, donde se cree que queda escondido un tesoro de mucho valor. Le ruego se sirva avisarme qué consiguió hallar allí Sir Malcolm Campbell, que buscó el tesoro hace pocos años.

Además, ¿puede usted avisarme qué pasó con esa expedición de buscadores de tesoros bajo la dirección de James Forbes y Fred Lewis de California, quienes con su yate (*yacht*) fueron a la Isla del Coco en marzo de 1940? [1]

Otro asunto de Costa Rica que les interesa mucho a mis alumnos de español es el de las carretas decoradas. ¿Cómo se empezó la costumbre de decorarlas, y hay algo de interés que puede usted decirnos acerca de esto?

Dándole de antemano las más expresivas (*kind*) gracias por su contestación, quedo de Vd. afma. atta. y segura servidora,

Edith Moore Jarrett

[1] Chapter 10 quoted from a newspaper article concerning this expedition; so it seemed like a good idea to try to find out what happened to the treasure seekers.

JUNTA NACIONAL DE TURISMO
DE COSTA RICA
SAN JOSÉ

Oficina del Gerente — 7 de marzo de 19— — Apartado 777, Teléfono 3598

Señora doña Edith Moore Jarrett
Calle de Clay, 426
Fillmore, California, E. U. de A.

Estimada señora:

Acusamos recibo de su interesante carta de fecha 25 de febrero ppdo., que con gusto contestamos.

Con respecto a la primera pregunta que se sirve hacernos sobre el señor Malcolm Campbell, le diremos que hizo hace algún tiempo una visita a esta isla, pero ocurrió una explosión de dinamita, a consecuencia de la cual fueron heridos algunos de los tripulantes (*crew*) de esta expedición. Por esto, el señor Campbell terminó la exploración después de sólo quince días. Más tarde escribió un libro que llamó *My Greatest Adventure.*

En la expedición Forbes-Lewis, marzo de 1940, se descubrió la piedra en que John Keating[1] marcó con una «K» y una flecha (*arrow*) el lugar del tesoro, de acuerdo con los planos del Capitán Thompson en 1821. Esto está de acuerdo con los informes de los dos únicos sobrevivientes (*survivors*) de la expedición que robó y escondió el tesoro de la Catedral de Lima.[2]

En la expedición Forbes-Davenport, diciembre de 1939, se encontró el lugar en que se escondió el tesoro, de acuerdo con los planos de Alexander Forbes, en 1825, pero no se encontró el tesoro.

Con respecto a las carretas de Costa Rica, nuestros campesinos toman especial interés en decorar sus carretas, y es para

[1] John Keating was a wealthy man who was supposed to have given a treasure chart to his servant.

[2] The pirate Thompson took the treasures from the Cathedral of Lima, and rumor says he buried the loot on Cocos Island.

ellos motivo de orgullo (*pride*) poseer la más artísticamente pintada. En la capital durante algunos años se han celebrado concursos de carretas en el Día de la Raza, 12 de octubre,[1] con premios para las de la mejor decoración.

Ojalá tengamos el gusto de verla en Costa Rica y poderla informar más de todo aquello que pueda ser de interés para Vd. en este país.

De usted muy atentos y seguros servidores,

JUNTA NACIONAL DE TURISMO
C. E. MONTEALEGRE
Gerente

PALABRAS NUEVAS

	aficionado	"fan," enthusiast		**dibujo**	drawing
	apartado	(mail) box		**dispensar**	to excuse
	apreciable	esteemed	4	**elegir** (i)	to elect
4	**avisar**	to inform		**gerente** (*m.*)	manager
	carreta	oxcart		**informes** (*m.*)	information
4	**complacer**	to comply with		**ingresar en**	to join
3	**componerse**	to be composed		**recitador** (*m.*)	one who recites
	compuesto	*past participle of* **componer**	3	**representado**	presented
	concurso	contest		**socio**	member

NEW WORDS RELATED TO OTHERS YOU KNOW

buscador (*m.*) (**buscar**), seeker
cantor (*m.*) (**cantar**), singer
cinematografía (**cine**), art of the motion picture
contestación (**contestar**), reply
juventud (*f.*) (**joven**), youth
limpieza (**limpio**), cleanliness
molestia (**molestar**), bother
pintor (*m.*) (**pintar**), painter
reunión (**reunirse**), meeting
salvadoreño (**El Salvador**), person of El Salvador
semanalmente (**semana**), weekly

[1] October 12, Day of the Race, is one holiday celebrated in all Spanish-speaking countries. What do we call that day?

Abbreviations

afmo., afectísmo
atto., atento
C. A., Centroamérica
E. U. (de) A., Estados Unidos de América
ppdo., próximo pasado
S. S., seguro servidor

Expresiones para la correspondencia

acusar recibo, to acknowledge receipt
anticipándoles las gracias, thanking you in advance
de antemano, beforehand
de momento, at present
nos (me) es grato (suministrar), we are (I am) pleased to (furnish)
próximo pasado (ppdo.), last month
quedo de Vd(s). atto. afmo. y S. S., I remain, yours sincerely
sin otro particular, without anything further
sirve la presente para, the object of this letter is
suscribirnos de Vd., atentos y seguros servidores, to remain yours sincerely

Otras expresiones

Beneficencia Pública, Public Welfare
como sigue, as follows
Cruzada Infantil Popeye, Popeye Children's Crusade
de acuerdo con, in accordance with
días de entre semana, week days
dibujos animados, animated cartoons
Junta Nacional de Turismo, National Tourist Board
junto con, along with
Ministerio de Fomento, Department of Public Works
propaganda turística, tourist information

¿VERDAD O NO?

Change these statements to make them true if they are false.

1. La clase de español pidió a su secretario que escribiese a San Salvador con respecto al «Club Copa de Oro». 2. El gerente del Circuito de Teatros Nacionales contestó a la carta en vez del Ministerio de Fomento. 3. Todos los socios del «Club Popeye» son ricos. 4. Los socios del Club son aficionados al béisbol. 5. El Club existe por todo el país de El Salvador. 6. El objeto del Club es enseñar a los jóvenes por medio de lecciones. 7. El Club tiene un presidente, elegido semanalmente. 8. La cuota (*dues*) se paga anualmente. 9. Cada socio tiene un carnet (*card*) que le admite al teatro gratis los domingos. 10. Los socios llevan en la camisa un

prendedor (*pin*) que los cuesta cincuenta centavos. 11. Las reuniones tienen lugar en la escuela. 12. Los socios escriben composiciones sobre sus juegos. 13. Los premios consisten en juguetes (*toys*). 14. Los niños de habla española son aficionados al arte.

PREGUNTAS

1. ¿Por qué escribió el secretario del «Club Copa de Oro» al Ministerio de Fomento de El Salvador? 2. ¿Dónde está El Salvador? 3. ¿Es un país muy grande? 4. ¿Cuántos socios tiene el «Club Popeye»? 5. ¿Por qué no llevan uniforme? 6. ¿Tienen emblema? 7. ¿Cuál es el objeto de la organización? 8. ¿Tienen todos que pagar una cuota? 9. ¿Qué es preciso llevar consigo para entrar gratis en el teatro? 10. ¿Cuánto cuesta ingresar en el club? 11. ¿Qué es lo único que se demanda en vez de uniforme? 12. ¿Cuáles son los premios que se regalan a los ganadores? 13. ¿Qué clase de aficionados puede ganar premios? 14. ¿Escribió el gerente de los Teatros Nacionales una carta interesante?

15. ¿Por qué escribió la profesora a la Junta Nacional de Turismo de Costa Rica? 16. ¿Por qué van tantas expediciones a la Isla del Coco? 17. ¿Qué pasó con la expedición del señor Malcolm Campbell? 18. ¿Qué pasó con la expedición Forbes-Lewis? 19. ¿Por qué decoran sus carretas los campesinos de Costa Rica? 20. ¿Cómo las decoran? 21. ¿Cuándo tiene lugar el concurso de carretas?

PARA COMPLETAR

1. El secretario del «Club Copa de Oro» escribió a .... 2. Escribió para saber qué .... 3. El Ministerio de Fomento no le contestó, sino .... 4. El Circuito de Teatros Nacionales trabaja por .... 5. El objeto del «Club Popeye» es enseñar a los niños por medio de .... 6. Las películas (*films*) que se exhiben son .... 7. Las funciones se empiezan y terminan con .... 8. Para obtener un carnet (*card*), hay que tener .... 9. Ingresan en el Club niños .... 10. Ha sido eliminado el uniforme porque .... 11. El emblema del Club es .... 12. Las reuniones tienen lugar en .... 13. Los aficionados del arte son .... 14. Algunos miembros ofrecen transmisiones (*broadcasts*) ....

PREGUNTAS PERSONALES

1. ¿Sería fácil escribir una carta en español? 2. ¿Conoce Vd. al buen Popeye? 3. ¿Le gustaría a Vd. ser miembro de un «Club Popeye»? 4. ¿Hay en su escuela un Club Español? 5. ¿Es Vd. aficionado al cine? 6. ¿Es fácil aprender por medio del cine? 7. ¿Quiere Vd. que sus clases se empiecen y terminen con dibujos animados? 8. ¿Podría Vd. ingresar en el «Club Popeye» si viviese en San Salvador? 9. ¿Le gusta a Vd. pagar su cuota (*dues*) en un club? 10. ¿Quién es su estrella favorita del cine? 11. ¿Cree Vd. que sea preciso tener limpieza en el vestido? 12. ¿Cuál le gustaría a Vd. más: ser pintor, cantor, guitarrista o violinista? 13. ¿Le gustaría tomar parte en una transmisión (*broadcast*) por la radio? 14. ¿Ha ganado Vd. un premio en un concierto musical?

15. ¿Quisiera Vd. obtener folletos (*pamphlets*) de propaganda turística de varios países? 16. ¿Ha buscado Vd. alguna vez un tesoro escondido? 17. ¿Le gustaría a Vd. dar un paseo en una carreta? 18. ¿Ha decorado Vd. artísticamente su automóvil? 19. ¿Han ocurrido muchas explosiones de dinamita en su pueblo? 20. ¿Dice Vd., — Dispense — cuando hace un error?

ESTUDIO DE PALABRAS

I. Many names of countries take the definite article at all times. Here is a list of those of the Western Hemisphere which require the article. *Say them aloud several times to accustom your ear to the sound.*

El Salvador	la Argentina	el Uruguay
el Ecuador	el Paraguay	las Guayanas
el Perú	el Brasil	los Estados Unidos
la República Dominicana	el Canadá	

II. Put these phrases into Spanish without referring to the list in Exercise I; then check to see if you used the article with the right ones.

Republic of Paraguay	near Bolivia
in Brazil	far from Venezuela

the capital of Ecuador	I have seen Canada
the pampa of Argentina	to leave for Uruguay
in the United States	to enter Santo Domingo
Peru, country of the Incas	near Costa Rica
I like Guatemala	I like Panama
a club of El Salvador	the Andes of Chile

III. Here are some greetings which you may use in writing letters: [1]

BUSINESS LETTERS

Muy señor mío (señora mía)	Dear Sir (Madam)
Muy estimado señor y amigo	(*More friendly form*)
Estimada señora Fulano	Dear Mrs. So-and-So
Muy apreciable señora / **Distinguida señora** / **Respetable señora**	Dear Madam
Muy apreciable y fina señora	(*More courteous*)
Muy señora nuestra y de todo nuestro respeto	(*Very elaborate form*)

PERSONAL LETTERS

Muy amigo mío	My dear friend
Querido amigo	Dear friend (*More familiar*)
Querida María	Dear Mary
Inolvidable amiga / **Estimable e inolvidable amiga mía**	(*Even more affectionate*)

Choose the greeting you would use in writing to the following: (1) a strange man, (2) a strange woman, (3) your pal, (4) your "girl friend," (5) a woman friend of your mother's.

IV. Translate these closing sentences used in different countries:

BUSINESS LETTERS

1. Sin más por ahora y en espera de sus noticias, quedo como siempre su afmo. atto. y S.S., (Mexico)

[1] Optional section for reference in letter-writing.

2. Sin otro particular de momento, me es grato repetirme como siempre de Vd. afmo. atto. y S.S., (Guatemala)
3. Sin más de momento y en espera de verle pronto por ésta su casa, quedo de Vd. su afmo. atto. amigo y S.S., (Mexico)
4. Aprovecho la ocasión para ponerme a su entera disposición y para suscribirme su muy atento y obsecuente (*obedient*) servidor, (El Salvador)
5. Esperando que éste le sea de la utilidad (*usefulness*) deseada, quedo de V. muy atentamente, (Santo Domingo)
6. Con un atento saludo, quedamos de V. sus seguros servidores, (Costa Rica)
7. Me es grato anticiparle a usted nuestro deseo de ofrecerle todas las atenciones que le sean menester (*necessary*) durante su visita en nuestro país. De usted atentamente, (Venezuela)
8. Muy agradecidos de antemano por su atención (*kindness*), nos repetimos de usted afmos. amigos y atentos seguros servidores, (California)
9. Nos es grato ofrecernos a sus órdenes como sus afmos. attos. y respetuosos servidores, (Mexico)
10. Sin más me repito de V. su atta. y Sa. Sa. quien está a sus órdenes. De usted, (California)

Personal letters

1. Como siempre su más leal y mejor amigo,
2. Reciba como siempre el sincero afecto de su atto. y S.S.,
3. Le saluda con cariño su amigo,
4. Créame siempre su leal amigo,
5. Se despide tierna y cariñosamente quien espera su próxima contestación,
6. Se despide quien mucho la quiere y adora y desea verla,
7. Muy cariñosamente como siempre se despide su amigo que muchos deseos tiene de verla, quedando su más sincero y leal amigo,
8. Se despide quien te adora hasta el delirio (*delirium*),

V. Write a short simple letter in Spanish about what you are doing these days, and send it to some unsuspecting friend after your teacher has corrected it.

TEMA

Note how the headings of the four model letters vary from the English form, and change the wording here as necessary. The wording of this letter may sound old-fashioned in English, but it would be rude to phrase it much less elaborately in Spanish.

The formal correspondence expressions are not in the English-Spanish vocabulary. You will have to find them in the chapter vocabulary or the model letters.

1408 Arapahoe Street
Los Angeles, California
June 15, 19—

Mr. Lorenzo Gómez Medina, Manager
Hotel Belmar
Mazatlán, Sinaloa, Mexico

Dear Mr. Gómez:

I acknowledge receipt of your esteemed [favor] of [the] date 29th of last month, and am pleased to be able to inform you that I shall arrive in Mazatlán on the first of July with a group of ten tourists, to spend a week at your charming hotel.

Please reserve (**separar**) for us five outside (**exterior**) rooms with two beds each, with meals. We prefer the rooms which face the patio instead of those facing the ocean, at the rate of $10 each, in accordance with your letter.

Without anything further at present, and thanking you in advance for your kindness (**atención**), I am pleased to remain yours sincerely,

K. H. JAMES

CAPÍTULO 35

Optional Chapter [1]

Como nos ven nuestros vecinos

It's always a little startling, and often a little disagreeable, to "see ourselves as others see us." We are so accustomed to looking at the rest of the world as if we alone knew the proper standards of conduct that it's a shock to find that each of our neighbors is inclined to look at us in the same critical way.

By this time you have learned that people of other nationalities are not necessarily peculiar because they are not just like us, and that no two peoples think or act exactly alike in identical situations. For instance, our Spanish-speaking neighbors are very fond of elaborate courtesy and we aren't; we shake hands heartily and they don't. If we can all learn to accept each other's "peculiarities" charitably, we will soon be good neighbors culturally as well as commercially.

The following two sketches should help us to be more tolerant of others by showing us humorously how we are regarded by a Spaniard, whose point of view is much like that of any Latin. Julio Camba, a Spanish humorist who traveled all through Europe and the United States, caricatured Americans as he saw them abroad and at home, and although he exaggerates as all cartoonists do, his sketches point out whimsically what some of our weaknesses are in the sight of the gentle Latin.

I. El turista yanqui

El turista yanqui mira todas las cosas con aire de comprador.[2] Ante una catedral como ante una montaña, yo siempre

[1] Note to teacher: This chapter may be omitted in order to finish Chapter 36 by the end of the year if there is not time for both. Chapter 36, however, should be completed, since it is a final review of Chapters 28–34 inclusive. Chapter 37 is also optional, the essentials of the year's work being completed with Chapter 34.

[2] This was written before the day of cheap travel, at a time when the only Americans who went to Europe were millionaires who could buy anything they liked. One wealthy man actually bought a medieval stone church and had its aged stones shipped in boxes to California to reassemble on his country estate.

me imagino que van a preguntar lo que cuestan. El otro día he oído a uno preguntar cuánto valía la casa de Voltaire.[1] Miran el lago Lemán [2] como si fueran a decir,

— Aquí tiene Vd. el cheque (*check*). Mándennoslo ustedes a Cincinnati.

Le presenta usted un duque a un turista yanqui — un duque tronado (*penniless*), naturalmente, que uno no encuentra otra clase de duques —, y si el turista yanqui tiene hijas casaderas (*marriageable*), es capaz (*capable*) de preguntarle a usted,

— Y ese duque que usted me ha presentado, ¿cuánto cree usted que puede costar?

Han comprado duques nobilísimos, pinturas hermosísimas, castillos historiquísimos.

Cuando los otros turistas se extasían (*"rave"*) ante las ruinas, el yanqui los desprecia (*despises*) como gente poco práctica, que pierde el tiempo en palabras inútiles, y dirigiéndose al guía le pregunta,

— Estas ruinas, ¿qué es lo que valen?

— ¡Oh! Estas ruinas, sabe usted...

— Nada, nada. ¿Cuánto valen?

— Mire usted. Estas ruinas tienen un gran valor histórico, un gran valor artístico...

— Pero, en fin, ¿cuánto valen en dinero? ¿Cuántos miles de dólares?

Si los turistas yanquis no han comprado ya el Mont Blanc [3] es porque piensan hacer en Chicago uno mucho más grande, con mucha más nieve, con muchas más *crevasses*, y en el que muera mucha más gente. [4]

Físicamente (*physically*) el turista yanqui es más grande

[1] Voltaire was a famous French writer whose house tourists often went to see.

[2] Lake Lemán (Geneva) is one of the lakes of Switzerland, famous for its beauty, and a great tourist attraction.

[3] Mont Blanc, over 15,000 feet in altitude, is the highest peak of the Alps. Mt. Aconcagua (Argentina), the highest peak of the Andes, is almost 24,000 feet high. Had you realized how immense the Andes are?

[4] Mountain-climbing is a dangerous but popular sport of the Swiss Alps, and many people have disappeared into deep cracks in the eternal ice.

que el turista inglés. Viste esos trajes yanquis que le dan la apariencia de un globo, y ha suprimido (*discarded*) el chaleco (*vest*) como un ornamento inútil.

Destroza (*destroys*) las manos de sus compañeros de mesa en *handshakes* de una cordialidad primitiva.[1] Pregunta si hay cuarto de baño en estos trenes suizos (*Swiss*) que atraviesan (*cross*) todo el territorio federal en unas cuantas horas. En el hotel toma el ascensor (*elevator*) para subir al primero, no porque pueda cansarle (*tire*) una docena de escaleras (*steps*), sino porque los yanquis tienen la costumbre de ir al cuarto con mucha maquinaria (*machinery*) y de un modo muy moderno. Luego hace a pie la ascensión del Mont Blanc o de la Jungfrau.[2]

— Usted es norteamericano, ¿eh? — se le pregunta al turista yanqui. — ¿Es usted súbdito norteamericano?

— Yo — contesta el turista yanqui, — soy *ciudadano* de los Estados Unidos de América.[3]

No sé qué significado ponen los yanquis en eso de ciudadano. Es que se llaman ciudadanos llenándose la boca con la palabreja (*strange, odd word*), y que nunca se anuncian como súbditos, sino como ciudadanos.

El turista yanqui no abunda (*is not so numerous*) como el turista inglés, pero tiene mucho más dinero. Un viaje de placer (*pleasure*) es para él tanto mejor cuanto más dinero le ha costado.

— ¿Se divirtió usted mucho en su excursión por Suiza? — le preguntan al turista yanqui cuando regresa a Filadelfia.

— Sí, mucho. Ha sido una excursión deliciosa. Cinco mil dólares . . .

II. Los Estados Engomados [4]

Se ha dicho que el francés es un hombre muy condecorado

[1] Latins shake hands much more often than we do, but usually rather limply, and our hearty handclasp rather startles them.

[2] The Jungfrau is another Swiss mountain popular with expert climbers.

[3] This was written while Spain was still a monarchy. Can you sense the writer's lack of understanding of people who say proudly that they are *citizens*, not *subjects*? Which would you prefer to be?

[4] ***Los Estados Engomados,*** *The Stuck-Together States.*

(*decorated with honors*) y que come mucho pan. El americano, a su vez, es un hombre sin condecoraciones y que masca mucha goma.[1]

Mascar goma: he aquí el gran vicio nacional de los Estados Unidos de Norteamérica. Los americanos mascan goma así como los chinos (*Chinese*) fuman (*smoke*) opio (*opium*). En el tranvía o en el ferrocarril yo he visto a veces frente a mí quince o veinte personas en fila (*row*), abriendo y cerrando la boca, como si fueran peces, y con una expresión contentísima en los ojos.

El año pasado, los americanos han mascado goma por valor de treinta millones de dólares.[2] Es decir, que han gastado en mascar muy poco menos de lo que un pueblo como España gasta en comer.

Yo no sé si ustedes han oído hablar de la mandíbula ame-

[1] The word for *chewing gum* in Latin America is not ***goma,*** but ***chicle,*** the name also given to the sapota tree, from which chewing gum is made.

[2] Camba wrote this several years ago; the figure is much larger now.

Mexican chiclero climbs a *zapote* tree to slash its bark for the *chicle* sap from which our chewing gum is made.

Sawders

ricana, esta mandíbula prominente, de la que se envanecen (*are proud*) los americanos, considerándola un signo de gran energía. Pues, para mí, la mandíbula americana se forma por medio de mascar goma. Todo el mundo masca goma en América, los ricos y los pobres, los negros y los blancos y los amarillos. Y aquí es donde aparecen la utilidad y la importancia social y política de la goma de mascar. La costumbre da algo común para las diferentes razas que viven en los Estados Unidos, y a la vez algo que los diferencia (*makes them different*) de los ciudadanos de otros países. Poco a poco la goma va creando (*creating*) una cara típicamente americana, en que predomina (*predominates*) la mandíbula, como he dicho antes. Si en el porvenir (*future*) llega a existir un tipo americano tan característico como lo son hoy el tipo inglés o el francés o el español, los americanos podrán decir que, para formarlo, se han gastado en goma millones y millones de dólares. Los Estados Unidos, como pueblo, puede decirse que están pegados (*stuck together*) con goma. Son los Estados Engomados.[1]

ADAPTED FROM JULIO CAMBA (*Spain*)

PALABRAS NUEVAS[2]

castillo	castle	**mandíbula**	jaw
ciudadano	citizen	**mascar**	to chew
comprador (*m.*)	buyer	**súbdito**	subject
duque (*m.*)	duke	**yanqui** (*m.*)	Yankee (applied by Spaniards to any North American)
2 **francés** (*m.*)	French, Frenchman		
goma (de mascar)	gum (chewing)		
guía (*m.*)	guide		

EXPRESIONES

***en fin,** in short **a su vez,** in his turn **frente a,** facing

[1] Does the author approve of our gum-chewing habit?

[2] Note to teacher: Since this is an optional chapter, *all* words except cognates not yet used in this book are given here, but are repeated in vocabularies if used later, since this chapter will be omitted by many classes.

¿VERDAD O NO?

Change these statements to make them true if they are false:

I. 1. Según este escritor (*writer*) español, todos los turistas yanquis son ricos. 2. Un turista yanqui quiere casar a sus hijas con duques. 3. Los norteamericanos quieren saber el valor de todas las ruinas. 4. Las ruinas tienen un gran valor en dólares. 5. Los turistas creen que lo que tienen en su propio país es mejor que lo europeo. 6. El turista inglés es más grande que el turista yanqui. 7. Muchos turistas norteamericanos son flacos. 8. Al español le gusta un apretón de manos (*handshake*) de una cordialidad primitiva. 9. El turista yanqui prefiere subir a su cuarto a pie. 10. Los yanquis se llaman súbditos norteamericanos. 11. El turista inglés tiene más dinero que el turista yanqui. 12. El turista francés se divierte más cuando gasta mucho dinero en su viaje.

II. 1. El francés come mucho pan. 2. El inglés masca mucha goma. 3. El vicio nacional de los yanquis es hablar demasiado. 4. Los que mascan goma, abriendo y cerrando la boca, se parecen a los peces. 5. Los españoles gastan mucho dinero en mascar goma. 6. La mandíbula inglesa es muy prominente. 7. Viven muchas razas en los Estados Unidos. 8. La cara típica de los yanquis pronto tendrá una mandíbula fuerte.

PREGUNTAS

I. 1. ¿Cómo mira todas las cosas en Europa el turista yanqui? 2. ¿Tienen mucho dinero la mayor parte de los turistas? 3. ¿Por qué quiere saber el yanqui cuánto vale un duque? 4. ¿Creen los yanquis que valen mucho las ruinas? 5. ¿Por qué no ha comprado algún turista el Mont Blanc? 6. ¿Pierde tiempo el yanqui en palabras inútiles? 7. ¿Por qué tiene el yanqui la apariencia de un globo? 8. ¿Por qué toma el ascensor (*elevatcr*) para subir a su cuarto? 9. ¿Por qué no toma el ascensor para subir al Mont Blanc? 10. ¿Por qué no somos súbditos norteamericanos? 11. ¿Cuándo se divierte más en su viaje un yanqui?

II. 1. ¿Por qué se llama nuestro país «Los Estados Engomados»? 2. ¿Qué se ve a veces en el tranvía? 3. ¿Cuánto dinero se gasta por goma en un año en los Estados Unidos? 4. ¿Por qué se gasta tanto? 5. ¿Quiénes mascan goma? 6. ¿Tiene la goma de mascar alguna importancia social y política? 7. ¿Qué predomina (*predominates*) en la cara típicamente norteamericana? 8. ¿Cómo se ha formado esta clase de cara? 9. ¿Cómo se llama la goma en México? (*See footnote 1, page 484.*)

PARA COMPLETAR

I. 1. El turista yanqui siempre va preguntando .... 2. El yanqui paga todo con un .... 3. Algunas hijas de yanquis quieren .... 4. Los yanquis han comprado hasta .... 5. Un grupo de turistas generalmente tiene un .... 6. Las ruinas tienen un valor .... 7. El turista yanqui no lleva chaleco (*vest*) porque cree que .... 8. Los trenes suizos (*Swiss*) atraviesan (*cross*) el país en .... 9. A los turistas les gusta subir al .... 10. Al norteamericano no le gusta llamarse .... 11. Al norteamericano le gusta más un viaje si ....

II. 1. El americano es un hombre que .... 2. El gran vicio nacional de los Estados Unidos es .... 3. Los que mascan goma se parecen a .... 4. En un año, los americanos mascan goma por valor de .... 5. La costumbre da algo común para .... 6. La mandíbula americana es muy .... 7. Poco a poco la goma va creando (*creating*) ....

REPASO DE VERBOS

I. Change these present subjunctive forms to the past subjunctive and translate:

salga, caigamos, digan, Vd. esté, hagan, vayamos, yo oiga, pongas, yo quiera, rían, yo siga, gane, cuesten, empiece, yo pague, toquemos, cruces, durmamos

II. Change these present tense forms to the preterite and translate:

pongo, hacemos, estamos, cae, Vd. da, voy, oye, pueden, ella quiere, sé, salen, sigo, cojo, conozco, leen, duermen

III. Change these polite commands to the familiar and translate:

dispense Vd., elijan Vds., salúdela Vd., no lo muerda Vd., salten Vds., confiéselo Vd., no lo dude Vd., pruébelo Vd., hiérvalos Vd., mándennoslo Vds., quíteselo Vd., obedézcame Vd., entréguenmelo Vds.

IV. Make these commands negative and translate:

salúdele Vd., confiéselo Vd., persígale Vd., enciéndalo Vd., pruébalos tú, quítatelo tú, repítelas tú, escójalo Vd., arrójalos tú, envolvedlo vosotros, aceptadla vosotros

ESTUDIO DE PALABRAS

I. About thirty cognates were used in this chapter. *Make a list of at least twenty of them, classifying them as to type, as far as possible.*

II. Here are some easy expressions which you should be able to give without hesitation. *Say them in Spanish as fast as possible.*

some boy	to strike ten	it is hot (weather)
next year	to thank the girl	to ask a question
a good book	to the right	many years ago
on horseback	to say good-by to	to be afraid of
from house to house	on the next day	this one is mine
from time to time	please come here	at first

PARA DIVERTIRSE

Play the game «*Comida, cuerpo, o color*» as you play "Beast, Bird, or Fish" in English. Here are lists of words you will want:

COMIDA [1]	CUERPO	COLORES
la carne	cara	rojo
los dulces	la frente (*forehead*)	verde
huevo	boca	morado
el pan	labio	negro

[1] See the menus in Chapters 23 and 25 for names of more foods.

vino
el te
el café
queso
los frijoles
sopa
pescado
el pastel
el postre
el biftec
pollo
empanada

oreja (*ear*)
los dientes
brazo
mano
el pie
pierna
dedos (*fingers*)
el corazón
la nariz
ojos
barba (*chin*)
cuello (*neck*)
hombro
pelo

blanco
color de naranja
color de rosa (*pink*)
violeta
azul
amarillo
moreno
colorado
gris

PARA LEER SIN ESTUDIAR

Have you ever read the "Personal" column in the advertising section of a large newspaper? In it you find humor and sorrow, foolishness and tragedy, as told by the people who pay for the advertisements in the hope of making their lives more pleasant. There are "agony columns," as they are sometimes called, in Latin-American newspapers, too, and to show you some of the human problems of the people of those countries, here are some typical items. Some will make you smile, and one of them should almost make you cry. In order not to offend the country in which these appeared, you are not told where they were printed, but all are authentic.

From a column called «*¿Quiere Vd. casarse?*»:

1. Desearía tener correspondencia, cambiar estampillas de correo, fotos, libros, con jóvenes de cualquier país sudamericano. Margarita.

2. Señorita, educada, seria, buena familia, desea conocer caballero mayor de 25 años, católico, serio y educado. Ojalá extranjero. Solita.

3. Caballero sincero y de buena presencia (*appearance*) desea tener amiga seria, discreta, simpática, de 20 a 23 años. Extranjero.

4. Caballero soltero (*bachelor*), joven, buena presencia, culto, educado, sin vicios, desea conocer señorita que sea blanca, pelo ondulado (*curly*), culta, educada, trabajadora, aficionada al hogar (*home*). La deseo entre los 22 a 25 años, fines muy serios. Solitario.

5. Soy estudiante, moreno, alto, y deseo amistad con chiquilla sincera hasta 18 años. Domingo.

6. Joven simpático de 28 años, serio, sin vicios, desea amistad con señorita profesora. Alberto.

7. Dos amigas, de 17 y 22 años, desean amistad con jóvenes de 25 y 35 años; ellas no buscan actores de cine, sino amigos simpáticos, amantes (*lovers*) de todo lo bello. Anita y Elena.

8. Quiero encontrar joven moreno, simpático, de 25 a 30 años. Ojalá sea alto, moreno, cariñoso. Yo, bajita, ojos verdes, simpática, según dicen; trabajadora e inteligente. Paloma.

9. Joven moreno, culto y sin vicios, desea conocer con fines serios, rubia, simpática, cariñosa, sincera y honorable, hasta 25 años. Pedro.

10. Deseamos conocer dos jóvenes de 25 a 30 años, buen físico (*physique*) y buena situación, con fines serios; ojalá profesionales. Rosa, 19 años, estatura (*height*) 1.65;[1] Helen, rubia, ojos verdes.

11. Lector (*reader*) amigo, examina tu corazón, y si eres bueno y cariñoso, contesta a morena de 28 años. Peggy.

12. ¿Te gustan las noches de luna y canciones de amor? Contéstame. Soy rubio, alto, y sé cantar. Ramón.

From a column called «*Escúchame*»:

1. Ruego a las lectoras de este periódico si alguna me puede facilitar un terno (*suit*) y zapatos usados, pues me encuentro muy necesitado de estas prendas. Soy el único sostén (*support*) de mi pobre madre anciana (*old*). Hace ocho días que trabajo, ganando solamente para vivir. Quisiera andar mejor presentado (*appearing*) en mi trabajo. Dirigirse a Félix Latorre, Calle Girardi 1348.

2. Náufrago (*shipwreck*) de la vida, busco entre las lectoras de este periódico alguna que se digne (*deign*) llevar hasta mi soledad (*solitude*) una palabra de consuelo en mi desgracia. Es todo lo que pido. Gracias. Eladio Avendaño, Cárcel-Presidio (*penitentiary*).

3. Soy ciego y sin recursos (*resources*). Me ganaba la vida con mi guitarra, pero hace algunos meses me la robaron y me he encontrado

[1] Her height is 1.65 meters, and a meter is 39 inches. How tall is she?

en la necesidad de pedir limosna (*alms*), lo que me hace sufrir, pues, a más de (*besides*) no conseguir bastante para comer, no estoy acostumbrado a mendigar (*beg*). Agradeceré (*be grateful*) enormemente si alguna persona generosa pudiera facilitarme una guitarra, aunque esté en mal estado. Camilo Prieto, San Isidro 1549.

TEMA

1. Tourists travel all over the world (through all the world). 2. Some American tourists talk too loudly. 3. The rich ones want to buy everything (that) they see. 4. The poor ones, such as teachers, have to be very careful with their money. 5. Real travelers do not ask the value of ruins, for they already know it. 6. Some tourists go [around] saying that everything in their own country is better than that of the foreign country. 7. This annoys the natives (**naturales**), because they, too, love their native country. 8. Would you like to hear some stranger say that your country was not so good as his? 9. Remember, when you travel, to make use of the customs of the country. 10. Do not talk loudly, make fun of the food, or boast (**jactarse**) of your own country. 11. If you remember this advice, the people will call you *simpático* and believe that the United States is a fine country. 12. If you are not *simpático*, they will think that all Yankees are like you.

CAPÍTULO **36**

Final Review

Las riquezas de nuestros buenos vecinos

What should you like to see? Dusty deserts or high-piled mountains or steaming jungles? Smoking volcanoes or grassy lowlands or deep, brown rivers? Latin America has them all, and with them an infinite variety of products that man has found and taken for his use.

OCÉANO ATLÁNTICO
VENEZUELA
Petróleo
Café
Cacao
Petróleo
COLOMBIA
Esmeraldas
Sombreros de jipijapa
ECUADOR
Cacao
Petróleo
Nueces
Frutas Tropicales
BRASIL
PERÚ
Algodón
Estaño
Oro
Cobre
BOLIVIA
Cobre
Plata
Quebracho
Café
PARAGUAY
Salitre
Ganado
Grano
Yerba mate
Cobre
OCÉANO ATLÁNTICO
Ganado
Ganado
URUGUAY
Ovejas
CHILE
OCÉANO PACÍFICO
ARGENTINA
Lana
Ovejas
PRODUCTOS PRINCIPALES
LA AMÉRICA DEL SUR

Where the climate is like that of North America, you will find the crops we know and use; where tropical heat lifts rank vegetation from the soil almost overnight, you will find trees and plants and animals strange to us. From jungle trees alone Latin America sends us many curious woods. There is the wild *quebracho* — literally axe-breaker — which furnishes tannic acid for tanning leather; a wood so heavy that it sinks in water, and so hard that even wood-boring insects pass it by. There is the wild balsa, so light and spongy that you could carry a great log on your shoulder, and which comes to this country for you to cut up with a razor blade for your airplane models.

Tropical trees furnish our precious hardwoods, some of our medicines, drinks, and fruits. And one tree of Ecuador buttons our clothes [1] and another provides our "Panama" hats! [2]

In addition to jungle products, South America provides us and the world with minerals and jewels, the precious "black gold" that oozes from the ground, and beef, grains, hides, and wool.

Here is the story of only a little of the wealth of our neighbors.

I. Bebidas

El cacao

¡Imagínese una bebida antigua tan preciosa que se servía en tazas de oro, y que solamente a los nobles se les permitía beberla! Esta bebida se hacía de las pepitas de un árbol, tan estimadas que servían de dinero para ricos y pobres. Pero si un pobre usaba unas pocas pepitas para hacerse una taza de esta bebida magnífica, corría el riesgo (*risk*) de ser castigado (*punished*) severamente.

Cuando los conquistadores probaron esta bebida hace más de cuatrocientos años, les gustó tanto que la introdujeron en España, donde los nobles pronto empezaron a tomarla, y donde hoy día es casi la bebida nacional del país.

[1] The tagua palm, which bears nuts that look like Brazil nuts turned to ivory.

[2] A palm tree with leaves of a fine fiber which is woven into expensive hats, not in Panama, but in Ecuador.

Galloway

Tropical cacao trees supply great pods of cocoa beans for our chocolate. One fine variety of Ecuador was once used only by grandees of the Spanish Court, and still commands fancy prices.

¿No le gustaría a Vd. probar una bebida tan preciosa? Pues, la ha tomado Vd. muchas veces, y sin pensar en lo que valía entre los aztecas de México y los incas del Perú cuando llegaron los españoles. Es el chocolate, hecho de las pepitas del cacao, y que hoy día se produce en todos los países tropicales de la América Latina.[1]

El mate [2]

Imagínese otra bebida, popular con los indios antes de la llegada de los españoles, que hoy día es la favorita de la mayor parte de los sudamericanos, pero que nosotros los norteamericanos desconocemos casi completamente. Esta bebida es el mate, una clase de te hecho de las hojas de un

[1] Ecuador, Venezuela, Colombia, Panama, Costa Rica, Brazil, and Santo Domingo supply the world with chocolate. The large brown seeds grow in deep red pods that cluster on the trees, and must be cleaned, dried, roasted, and ground in order to make commercial chocolate. Aztecs and Incas made the drink with water; the Spaniards improved it by using milk.

[2] *Mate* is spelled *maté* in some countries.

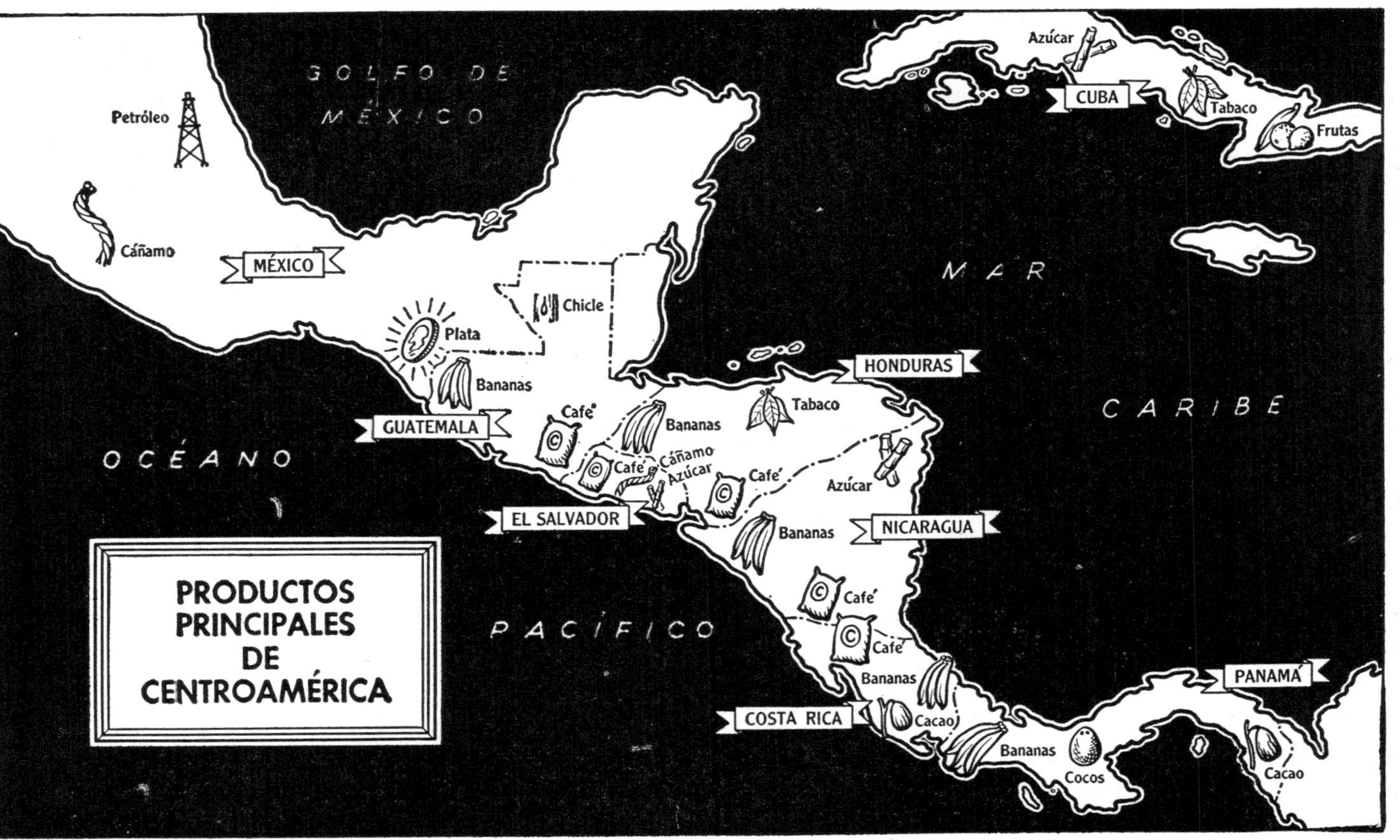
PRODUCTOS
PRINCIPALES
DE
CENTROAMÉRICA
GOLFO DE
MÉXICO
MAR
CARIBE
OCÉANO
PACÍFICO
MÉXICO
GUATEMALA
EL SALVADOR
HONDURAS
NICARAGUA
COSTA RICA
PANAMÁ
CUBA
Petróleo
Cáñamo
Plata
Bananas
Chicle
Café
Café
Bananas
Cáñamo
Azúcar
Tabaco
Café
Azúcar
Bananas
Café
Café
Bananas
Cacao
Bananas
Cocos
Cacao
Azúcar
Tabaco
Frutas

arbolito que se parece a un naranjo (*orange tree*). Como toman te los ingleses, así toman mate los sudamericanos.[1] Todas las tardes, a eso de las cuatro o las cinco en los países ríoplatenses, todos, hasta en las oficinas de los rascacielos (*skyscrapers*) de Buenos Aires, dejan su trabajo un rato para tomar una taza de este te.

Muchos, sobre todo en el Paraguay, lo toman con una calabaza (*gourd*) y bombilla, como los gauchos de la pampa. Una cosa curiosa es que se puede hacer este mate hasta con agua fría, aunque generalmente se prefiere usar agua hirviente.

Nuestros vecinos del sur dicen que esta bebida da más energía que el te negro o el café, que contiene muchas vitaminas, que es más refrescante que ninguna otra bebida, y que nosotros perdemos mucho con no probarla. Tratan de interesarnos en este producto sudamericano, y en un periódico de México (donde tampoco se usa el mate) apareció hace poco este anuncio, ilustrado (*illustrated*) con un gaucho típico:

> Hermano mexicano, más de 50 millones de sudamericanos tomamos mate. En efecto, la Argentina, el Paraguay, Chile y el Uruguay toman mate como toma Vd. te negro. El sabor de esta exquisita e higiénica (*healthful*) bebida ha sido preferido por más de 50 millones de hermanos sudamericanos. ¡Pruébela!
>
> De venta en todas partes.

Sin duda, cuando nosotros los norteamericanos hayamos tenido la oportunidad de probar el mate, se hará tan popular aquí como lo es en los países del sur.

EL CAFÉ

La tercera bebida sudamericana es el café, que no es preciso describir. Éste se produce en el Brasil, así como en Centroamérica, aunque no es natural (*native*) de estos países, habiendo sido introducido allí hace unos cien años.[2]

[1] Countries which drink much *mate* are Brazil, Paraguay, Argentina, Uruguay, and Chile, which means that most of the inhabitants of South America use it.

[2] The chief coffee-producing countries are Brazil, Colombia, Central America, Mexico, and Venezuela.

Monkmeyer

Coffee-drying in Brazil requires the berries to be turned frequently to prevent spoilage. The beans have a thin skin which must be dried before it can be removed by machinery.

Los cafetos (*coffee trees*) crecen en los países tropicales, generalmente a la sombra de árboles grandes. Tienen florecitas blancas y muy fragantes, y después, bonitos racimos (*clusters*) de frutas rojas que se parecen a las cerezas (*cherries*). Los granos (*seeds*) pálidos de estas frutas, después de secarse, se tuestan (*roast*), de donde viene su color obscuro.

¿Qué podríamos servir en nuestro desayuno ordinario si no tuviéramos este producto sudamericano? Quizás aprenderíamos a tomar mate.

II. Drogas

El yodo

Además de las bebidas, la América Latina nos da unas drogas importantísimas, sin las cuales podríamos sufrir mucho.

¿Qué haríamos al hacer la primera curación, si no tuviésemos yodo? No pasa un solo día sin que se use una gran cantidad de esta droga antiséptica, que es uno de los productos de las salitreras (*nitrate mines*) de los desiertos chilenos. Chile nos da la mayor parte del yodo que usamos.

LA QUININA

Y ¿qué haríamos sin la quinina preciosa que les salva la vida a tantos que tienen el paludismo (*malaria*)? Esta droga, que resulta de la corteza de un árbol tropical, es la única que combate esta enfermedad diseminada (*spread*) por los mosquitos.[1] No podría entrar ningún explorador en la selva sin su quinina, y hay miles de personas de países tropicales que tienen que tomarla todos los días para prevenir la enfermedad. Así es que este producto sudamericano es sumamente importante.

[1] You read about the origin of quinine in the *¿Sabía Vd. esto?* section of Chapter 22.

Oxcarts carry Cuban sugarcane from plantation to refining plants, where the stems are crushed between rollers. In some districts the sweet juice is pumped through pipes from the estates to a central refinery.

Sawders

La cocaína

La cocaína, sin la cual sufriríamos mucho a veces, al hacernos sacar un diente, por ejemplo, se hace de la coca del Perú y de Bolivia. Como ya sabe Vd., los indios la usan para prevenir el hambre y la sed en los viajes largos a pie por los Andes o los desiertos. Las hojas de la coca son de un arbusto que crece en los Andes, y se exportan a todas partes del mundo para hacer la cocaína.

El «bálsamo del Perú»

Lo curioso del «bálsamo del Perú» es que no nos viene del Perú sino de El Salvador. Recibió su nombre en los tiempos coloniales cuando todos los productos del Nuevo Mundo se llevaban a Panamá para cargarlos en los galeones españoles, y al llegar a España los tesoros del Perú, se creía que este tesoro también era del país de oro.

Consiste en la savia (*sap*) aromática de un árbol de la selva, y sale al cortarse la corteza del árbol. Se usa en varias medicinas importantes para curar heridas (*wounds*), porque es un antiséptico natural.

El chicle

En esta lista de productos sudamericanos que llenan nuestras boticas, se debe mencionar, aunque no es medicina, el chicle, del cual se hace nuestra popular goma de mascar (*chewing gum*). México y Guatemala nos envían todos los años como seis millones de libras (*pounds*) de chicle, que es una savia (*sap*) que se saca del zapote (*sapota tree*) de la selva.

Hay otras drogas y productos medicinales que obtenemos de nuestros buenos vecinos, pero éstos son los principales.

III. Lo que produce la América Latina

Centroamérica

Costa Rica	café, bananas, oro, cacao
El Salvador	café, «bálsamo del Perú,» oro, plata, azúcar

Guatemala	café, bananas, chicle
Honduras	bananas, café, tabaco
Nicaragua	bananas, azúcar, café
Panamá	bananas, cacao, cocos
	Sudamérica
Argentina	carne, trigo (*wheat*), cueros, lana
Bolivia	estaño (*tin*), oro, plata, cobre (*copper*)
Brasil	café, diamantes, caucho (*rubber*), mandioca (*tapioca*)
Chile	cobre, salitre (*nitrate*), oro
Colombia	café, oro, petróleo, esmeraldas
Ecuador	cacao, petróleo, tagua (*vegetable ivory*), sombreros de jipijapa (*Panama hats*)
Paraguay	quebracho (*ironwood*), carne, cueros, mate
Perú	cobre, plata, petróleo, algodón (*cotton*), quinina
Uruguay	carne, trigo, cueros, lana
Venezuela	petróleo, cacao, café

Hemp fibers on plantations of Yucatán are dried in the sun after the fleshy leaves have been run through rollers to extract the juice. The boy at work is a Mayan Indian.

Sawders

México y las Antillas

Cuba	azúcar, tabaco
México	petróleo, plata, chicle, productos artísticos indígenas (*native*)
Puerto Rico	azúcar, tabaco
Santo Domingo	azúcar, tabaco, cacao

PALABRAS NUEVAS

bombilla	sipper used to drink mate	**pepita**	large seed
cacao	cocoa bean or tree	**prevenir**	to prevent
corteza	bark (of a tree)	**refrescante**	refreshing
chicle (*m.*)	sap of sapota tree	**sabor** (*m.*)	flavor, taste
droga	drug	4 **sumamente**	highly, very
4 **introducir**	to introduce	**yodo**	iodine

New Words Related to Others You Know

bebida (**beber**), drink
3 **desconocer** (**conocer**), to be unacquainted with
4 **herida** (**herir**), wound
hirviente (**hervir**), boiling
ríoplatense (**Río de la Plata**), of the Plata River country
4 **de venta** (**vender**), for sale

Expresión

hacer la primera curación, to give first aid

PREGUNTAS

I. 1. ¿Cómo se llama la bebida más preciosa de los aztecas e incas? 2. ¿De qué se hace? 3. ¿Qué país la usa hoy día? 4. ¿Dónde se producen las pepitas del cacao? 5. ¿Qué otra bebida usaban los indios de la América del Sur antes de la llegada de los españoles? 6. ¿Dónde se usa esta bebida ahora? 7. ¿La hemos probado los norteamericanos? 8. ¿Quieren los sudamericanos que probemos su bebida favorita? 9. ¿A qué se parece el mate? 10. ¿En qué países se produce? 11. ¿En qué países se usa mucho? 12. ¿Por qué anuncian los sudamericanos el mate en los periódicos de México? 13. ¿Qué quiere decir «color café»?

II. 1. ¿De dónde nos viene la mayor parte del yodo? 2. ¿De qué se hace? (*salitre*) 3. ¿Para qué sirve el yodo? 4. ¿Para qué sirve la quinina? 5. ¿En qué clase de clima es preciso tomar quinina todos los días? 6. ¿Qué previene la cocaína? 7. ¿De qué se hace? 8. ¿Saben los indios de los Andes el valor de la coca? 9. ¿Para qué sirve el «bálsamo del Perú»? 10. ¿En qué países se produce? 11. ¿Qué se hace del chicle? 12. ¿Es el chicle un producto necesario para la civilización?

III. 1. Nombre Vd. cinco países en que se dan muchas bananas. 2. Nombre Vd. cinco países que producen café. 3. ¿Qué dos países de la América del Sur producen exactamente las mismas cosas? 4. ¿Dónde se produce el petróleo? 5. ¿Qué país produce tres minerales? 6. ¿De qué países son dos piedras preciosas? 7. ¿De qué se hacen los botones? (*Footnote 1, p. 493*) 8. ¿Dónde se hacen los sombreros de jipijapa? 9. ¿Cuál pesa más, — el quebracho o la balsa? 10. ¿Dónde se produce mucho mate? 11. ¿Por qué son la carne y los cueros productos importantes de los países ríoplatenses? 12. ¿Qué países tienen productos más o menos como los de los Estados Unidos?

PARA COMPLETAR

I. 1. Las pepitas del —— servían de dinero entre los aztecas: 2. Solamente los nobles podían beber el ——. 3. Los pobres no

Narrow-gauge banana "railways" crisscross great tropical plantations of Costa Rica, where the fast-spoiling stems must be gathered while green and loaded for export in a matter of hours.

Galloway

se atrevían a hacerse una taza de ——. 4. Los conquistadores —— esta bebida en España. 5. Allí se ha puesto —— la bebida. 6. La bebida favorita de la mayor parte de los sudamericanos es el ——. 7. Los trabajadores dejan su trabajo todas las —— para tomar ——. 8. En el Paraguay, es costumbre tomar mate con .... 9. Los —— de la pampa beben mate. 10. Se dice que esta bebida da mucha —— y que contiene muchas ——. 11. Un anuncio que apareció en un periódico mexicano decía que el mate tenía un —— exquisito. 12. Los cafetos (*coffee trees*) crecen debajo de .... 13. Las florecitas de los cafetos son ....

II. 1. Sin las drogas que se importan de la América del Sur, nosotros .... 2. El yodo sirve para .... 3. La quinina es necesaria para —— el paludismo (*malaria*). 4. Al sacarnos un diente, el dentista usa una forma de ——. 5. Los indios usan la coca para —— el hambre y la sed. 6. Una herida se cura pronto con el —— del Perú. 7. Este antiséptico resulta de la —— de un árbol de la ——. 8. México y Guatemala nos —— mucho chicle con el cual hacemos nuestra ——.

III. 1. Las «repúblicas de la banana» son las de ——. 2. Los países con productos de la pampa son ——, ——, y ——. 3. El —— y el —— se importan de tres países que son islas. 4. El —— crece solamente en países tropicales. 5. Un país de los Andes que produce muchos minerales es ——. 6. El algodón (*cotton*) crece en el ——. 7. El «oro negro» se encuentra en ——, ——, y ——. 8. El país donde se hacen muchas cosas artísticas es ——. 9. La Argentina y el Uruguay tienen los mismos productos porque ambos países tienen ——.

PREGUNTAS PERSONALES

1. ¿Ha visto Vd. botones que se producen en un árbol? 2. ¿Le parecen a Vd. hermosos los sombreros de jipijapa? 3. ¿Ha cortado Vd. mucha balsa para hacer modelos de aeroplanos? 4. ¿Cuál preferiría Vd. llevar al hombro, — un tronco (*trunk*) de balsa o uno de quebracho? 5. ¿Ha probado Vd. la bebida real de los incas? 6. ¿Le gustaría a Vd. probar la bebida favorita de los sudamericanos? 7. ¿Toman Vds. te todas las tardes, como los ingleses? 8. ¿Preferiría Vd. tomar el mate hecho con agua fría o con agua hirviente? 9. ¿Ha visto Vd. el mate de venta en todas partes?

10. ¿Sabe Vd. hacer la primera curación? 11. ¿Ha tenido Vd. que tomar quinina? 12. ¿Se ha hecho usted sacar un diente? 13. ¿Ha curado Vd. una herida con «bálsamo del Perú»? 14. ¿Ha usado Vd. mucho chicle en sus clases? 15. ¿Le gustaría a Vd. vivir en un país que produjese muchas bananas? 16. ¿Cuál le gustaría a Vd. más, —— tener un collar de brillantes [1] o de esmeraldas? 17. ¿Por qué es preciso tener petróleo para poder manejar un automóvil? 18. ¿Usa Vd. azúcar en su chocolate?

REPASO DE PALABRAS IMPORTANTES [2]

I. Choose the correct meaning of each of these Spanish nouns from the four suggested:

1. fuego: fog, fierce, then, fire
2. mitad: middle, half, friendship, mercy
3. lágrima: lake, lagoon, tear, lottery
4. juicio: judge, game, juice, judgment
5. marido: seasick, ocean, married, husband
6. cuerpo: skin, corpse, body, cave
7. peligro: film, danger, piece, hair
8. guerra: gorilla, warrior, war, grease
9. amo: love, master, amiable, lover
10. sombra: shade, somber, hat, path
11. labio: pencil, lobby, side, lip
12. desgracia: disgrace, misfortune, unlucky, despair
13. obra: work, dark, opera, snake
14. caso: case, almost, house, wedding
15. consejo: consolation, I conserve, advice, with him
16. fuerza: strength, forceful, fort, outside of
17. golpe: gulp, fat, blow, handsome
18. ave: bird, airplane, aviator, he flies
19. sobrino: above, sober, nephew, shadow
20. extraño: extra, foreigner, I exaggerate, strange
21. duro: endure, hard, duration, during
22. tierno: tender, land, store, inkwell
23. digno: dignified, I say, worthy, he said

[1] *Brillantes* are the cut stones; *diamantes* are uncut.

[2] These words are from Buchanan's first 1000, and were all used in the second semester's work.

24. loco: lock, locate, loyal, crazy
25. vivo: hurrah, view, alive, virtue
26. fiel: faithful, feel, trust, fail
27. bello: beauty, kiss, beautiful, pretty
28. roto: rotary, broken, red, surrounded
29. inútil: useful, useless, utility, uneasy

II. Choose the proper translation of the English verb from the three suggested:

1. to propose: prometer, proponer, pronunciar
2. to try (out): tratar, asistir, probar
3. to take off: quitarse, quitar, tomar
4. to deceive: decidir, cocer, engañar
5. to raise: levantarse, alzar, recibir
6. to meet: reunirse, meter, mejorar
7. to hand (over): entregar, manejar, habitar
8. to choose: cumplir, escoger, regresar
9. to wound: hervir, herir, heredar
10. to deny: demostrar, renunciar, negar
11. to happen: honrar, suceder, ocupar
12. to go (to): dirigirse, despedirse, despertarse
13. to fulfil: cumplir, fingir, firmar
14. to belong: bastar, burlarse, pertenecer
15. to remember: recordar, resolver, repetir
16. to threaten: traducir, amenazar, jurar
17. to wrap: rebelarse, envolver, regalar
18. to throw: tocar, arrancar, arrojar
19. to greet: saludar, gritar, guardar
20. to mix: meter, mezclar, molestar
21. to surround: suponer, rogar, rodear

III. Turn back to Chapters 9 and 18, Repaso de palabras importantes, *and do Exercise IV in each one.*

IV. These Spanish cognates are identical with English. *If you can pronounce them correctly in Spanish without being confused by their appearance, you know your rules of pronunciation.*

medicinal, chocolate, popular, tropical, federal, musical, social, club, coral, gratis, notable, final, doctor, unión, vigor, inspector, negro, interminable, error, hospital, fatal, brutal, visión, cruel, superior, formidable, miserable, humor, general, perfume, natural, división, metal, canal, puma, horror, ópera, proverbial, arsenal, probable, explosión, torpedo, noble, plan, original

REPASO DE MODISMOS

I. Choose the idiom which best translates the English: [1]

1. at least: por fin, por lo menos, echar de menos
2. to feel like: querer decir, tener razón, tener ganas de
3. especially: sobre todo, por lo tanto, al principio
4. nevertheless: para siempre, sin embargo, al menos
5. gradually: con frecuencia, por último, cada vez más
6. to realize: darse cuenta de, dar un paso, tener prisa
7. meanwhile: de todos modos, entretanto, en efecto
8. it is necessary to: hace poco, es cierto, hay que

[1] All but three of these idioms are among Keniston's first 200.

Tropical cattle ranch of Venezuela, with its giant palms, flame trees, and shrubbery undergrowth, is quite different from the Argentine pampa, even where the land is level.

Gendreau

9. at any rate: por entonces, de todos modos, por un rato
10. to be about to: estar en pie, haber de, estar para
11. to take a step: dar un paso, estar en pie, dar un paseo
12. forever: por supuesto, por cierto, para siempre
13. affectionately: en efecto, con afecto, caer de rodillas
14. he says so: quiere decir, dice que sí, todo el mundo
15. for this reason: tiene razón, por esto, por cierto
16. at the same time: a la vez, mucho tiempo, tal vez
17. from time to time: con frecuencia, de vez en cuando, de casa en casa
18. at a distance: a la derecha, en cambio, a lo lejos
19. aloud: en voz alta, a pie, en vez de
20. perhaps: quizás, acaso, tal vez
21. at once: en seguida, a la vez, es la una
22. at first: a la una, al principio, al fin
23. to miss: he aquí, le falta, echar de menos
24. see you later: volver a ver, hasta luego, más tarde
25. right here: aquí tiene Vd., aquí mismo, a la derecha

REPASO DE VERBOS

I. Conjugate these tricky verbs as indicated:

present, coger; *pres. perfect,* volver; *future,* tener; *imperfect,* ir; *preterite,* leer; *conditional,* hacer; *past perfect,* romper; *present subjunctive,* pagar; *past subjunctive,* dormir

II. Give the following expressions in Spanish, using the proper forms of **decir.** *Then repeat, substituting the verbs* **caer, tener,** *and* **dar** *for* **decir.**

1. he tells 2. Tell! 3. I told yesterday 4. she used to tell 5. he will tell 6. they would tell 7. you have told 8. we had told 9. I want you to tell 10. I wanted you to tell 11. if you told (*contrary-to-fact*) 12. until you tell tonight 13. it is necessary that we tell 14. let us tell 15. after telling 16. we were telling (*prog.*)

III. Give the infinitive of each of these verbs, then translate this form carefully:

1. saltó
2. engañamos
3. se reunirán
4. saludemos
5. obedezco
6. obtuvieron
7. entregué
8. escojan
9. hiriendo
10. ha arrojado
11. niegue
12. sucede
13. envolvimos
14. amenacé
15. cumplió
16. pertenezca
17. ¿recuerda Vd.?
18. tropiece
19. escogiesen
20. propuso
21. sospechase
22. mezclo
23. ¡pruébelo!
24. han cocido
25. ¡quíteselo!
26. repitiéramos
27. alzaron
28. rodearán
29. haya prometido
30. suframos

REPASO DE COSAS DIFÍCILES

I. For a final review of the year's grammar study, turn back to the Repaso de cosas nuevas *in Chapters 9, 18, and 27, and do those exercises again.* This will give you a good survey of important and catchy points, and prepare you for Exercise II.

II. If you can put these short sentences or phrases correctly into Spanish "by ear," without thinking of rules, so much the better, but if you are not sure, look up the sections indicated. There is a catch in every one; so be wary.

If you do well with these, it will be perfectly safe for you to be stranded alone in a little Mexican town where no one speaks English.

1. Go away, little boy (*fam.*)! (§ 17)
2. Don't go away yet (*fam.*). (§ 24)
3. Bring it to me (*fam.*). (§§ 17, 110)
4. Don't bring it to him (*fam.*). (§§ 17, 110)
5. The dress is silk. (§§ 29, 123)
6. It is Mary's. (§ 123)
7. It is at Anita's. (§ 122)
8. Put on (*pol. pl.*) your hats. (§ 113)
9. Who saw Joseph? (§ 127)
10. Here is mine; where is yours? (§ 114)
11. I don't see anyone. (§ 13)
12. He has probably gone. (§ 14)

13. One can't live without eating. (§§ 34, 16)
14. Let's read the first book. (§ 28, 1–5)
15. Spanish is easier than French. (§ 125, 6)
16. I see her; I will give it to her; I will go with her. (§§ 108, 109, 110, 112)
17. He tells us to go; he tells them to come. (§ 33)
18. He permits her to sing. (§ 33)
19. They are glad we have come. (§ 33)
20. I don't believe they have gone. (§ 36)
21. He wanted us to return. (§ 43)
22. Is it necessary for Peter to leave? (§ 40)
23. He will wait until you go. (§ 44, 1)
24. Even if he wants it, he can't have it. (§ 44, 2)
25. If I were there, I would be happy. (§ 44, 4)
26. You talk as if you were lonely. (§ 44, 5)
27. He wants a friend who is faithful. (§ 45, 1)
28. He doesn't want one who is two-faced. (§ 45, 2)
29. I should like to give it to you. (§ 46, 2)
30. for three years, for me, for 10 cents (§ 47, 1)
31. by Wednesday, by train, by 6 o'clock (§ 47, 2)
32. along the road, 20 per cent, 2 times 3 (§ 47, 3)
33. Where is Dr. López? How are you, Mrs. García? (§ 50)
34. Silver is worth more than bread. (§ 50)
35. Last week is not next week. (§ 50)
36. Haven't you a hat? (§ 51)
37. We have been studying for a week. (§ 52)
38. He bought it from Carmen. (§ 55)
39. Mexico was conquered by Cortés. (§ 56)
40. The box is made of gold. (§ 56)
41. They heard me say it. (§ 57)
42. The letter was written at once. (§ 58)
43. Those who do not go, stay home. (§ 59)

CAPÍTULO 37

Optional Chapter

La nochebuena de los vagabundos

Most of the stories by Latin American authors which you have read in this book were chosen for their plot interest, which is something that all short stories in Spanish do not have. Many Spanish stories are really only short sketches or scenes from life, instead of actual stories, and many of them are pathetic or even tragic, since the Latin realizes even better than we do that in real life one does not always find a happy ending.

This last story or sketch, by a Chilean author, is one which exemplifies the Latin tendency toward pathos, and the reader is supposed to wipe away a tear as he finishes, in sympathy for the unhappy wanderer who is homeless and unloved on Christmas Eve.

Vestía una chaqueta roja y un sombrero adornado con plumas, bajo el cual se veían las delicadas orejas. Con estas prendas danzaba sobre el organillo. Vivía feliz, se llamaba Bibí, y era — como lo habréis comprendido — un mono.

No era un mono esclavo, porque vivía en la libertad de los caminos y porque podía bailar sobre la caja del organillo.

Petersen,[1] su amo, era un hombre joven, aunque de aspecto triste por su larga barba y su flacura (*leanness*). Vestía un traje roto, y en sus ojos azules se veía un gran cansancio (*weariness*).

El hombre y el mono se entendían perfectamente. Bibí

[1] There are many familiar and very un-Spanish names in Chile, due to immigration from many parts of Europe.

tenía su amo y su dios en Petersen. Apenas la música empezaba a sonar,[1] Bibí comenzaba a bailar, no por cumplir una orden, sino por un sentimiento de lealtad y cariño hacia Petersen.

Iban por todos los caminos, el hombre cargado con el organillo y Bibí encima de sus hombros o saltando a su lado. Petersen marchaba con el paso lento de aquél cuyo camino no tiene fin. Dormía al lado del camino, entre los árboles, prefiriendo siempre la vecindad de un río o de un arroyo. Bibí exploraba el campo sin alejarse mucho, pues conocía los peligros de la civilización, tanto como los de la selva.

Llegaron al pueblo una tarde, un pueblo muy pequeño, con una sola calle y algunas casitas entre los árboles.

Petersen descargó su organillo y aún no había terminado de hacerlo cuando ya estaba rodeado de niños. Cuando sonó la música, Bibí empezó su danza.

El corro (*circle*) de los niños crecía, y algunas personas mayores se acercaban también. Un viejo, fumando una enorme pipa, miraba con simpatía (*sympathy*) el espectáculo de Bibí saltando sobre el organillo. Cuando terminó la segunda pieza, el viejo de la pipa se acercó a Petersen. — Tengo un nietecito enfermo, — dijo. — ¿Podría Vd. ir a tocar cerca de su cama para que pueda ver al mono?

Petersen consintió con la cabeza, y echaron a andar por el camino. Entre los árboles hallaron una hermosa casa, rodeada de un enorme jardín. El viejo abrió la verja[2] y siguieron por una senda entre las flores. Subieron los peldaños (*steps*) que conducían a la casa, y apenas pasaron la puerta, Petersen se detuvo asombrado. Se hallaba en un hall[3] grande y elegante, en cuyo centro estaba un hermoso árbol de Navidad, un pino sobre cuyas ramas (*branches*) la

[1] After a clause beginning with *apenas*, the word *cuando* is often understood.

[2] The *verja* is the gate of the beautiful wrought-iron fence which nearly always surrounds the front yard, when there is one. Front yards are most often seen in the more spacious suburbs and country homes. Other homes usually have patios.

[3] Chileans use many English words, as you have noticed before.

nieve estaba figurada (*represented*) por pequeños copos (*tufts*) de algodón.

Petersen quedó inmóvil, mirando el árbol. El pino del Norte, con su nieve de algodón, estaba tan perfumado de recuerdos para el vagabundo como si estuviese bailando en los vientos de los *fiords*.[1]

El vagabundo de los caminos quedó inmóvil.

— Pase usted.

La voz era de una anciana de pelo blanco y una mirada bondadosa. — Pase usted . . . por aquí. . . .

Petersen la siguió. La puerta de una habitación estaba abierta, y por ella pudo ver una cama blanca sobre la cual descansaba la pálida cabeza de un niño.

El vagabundo descargó el organillo y la música empezó a sonar; la misma música, el viejo vals mecánico. Sin embargo, al vagabundo le parecía que el organillo respondía esta vez a su emoción como un instrumento tocado por su mano.

Entretanto, Bibí saltaba alegremente, y el niño enfermo aplaudía con sus débiles manos. Al fin la música terminó, y Petersen cargó el instrumento sobre sus hombros.

Pero en ese instante, por encima de la cabeza de la anciana, dos ojos azules le miraron, dos ojos tiernos que iluminaban una cara de tranquila belleza. Era una mujer alta, elegante. Se le acercó y tendió su mano hacia Bibí. El mono, de pronto quieto, recibió la caricia (*caress*).

La noche había caído. Nueva gente circulaba en torno del árbol iluminado con sus pequeñas velas. Petersen fué invitado a tocar a medianoche, y entretanto se le condujo a las habitaciones de los criados.

Se marchó sin atreverse a mirar de nuevo los ojos azules.

Cuando volvió a aparecer en el hall, el árbol resplandecía (*shone*) como el cielo de verano. Petersen dejó su organillo en un rincón y esperó a que se le mandara tocar.

Por un instante vió los ojos azules sonriendo en un grupo

[1] What country is Petersen from, judging from his name and this word?

de gente. La alegre atmósfera rodeaba a Petersen como un anillo (*ring*), en cuyo centro él estaba sin ser tocado.

Al fin se le indicó que empezara la música. Giró (*turned*) el manubrio (*handle*) del organillo y Bibí se despertó asustado. La gente empezó a bailar al son de los viejos valses que salían de la vieja caja.

La alegría de los bailarines apagaba (*extinguished*) la voz del instrumento, y pronto el organillo fué olvidado. Música diferente lo substituyó (*replaced*), y Petersen quedó en su rincón sin saber qué camino tomar para salir de la casa.

El anciano de la pipa volvió a acercársele y le depositó unas monedas en la mano. Petersen le dió las gracias, se echó sobre los hombros el instrumento y cogió en sus brazos a Bibí, que se había dormido. Se encontraba ya cerca de la puerta cuando volvió a ver los ojos azules.

Le sonreían desde lejos. Toda la cara de la dama le sonreía dulcemente. Petersen se detuvo un instante en la puerta. Él, que en tantos años no tuvo hogar (*home*), él, sin más compañero que un mono, comprendió de pronto que sólo ahora, al no ver más aquellos ojos azules, iba a conocer la verdadera soledad (*loneliness*).

Petersen hizo una reverencia (*bow*) que sólo vió la dama de los ojos azules. Afuera, encontró la noche, con sus grandes estrellas. Los perros ladraban (*barked*) a lo lejos.... Le parecía que por primera vez se encontraba solo en un mundo en que nadie le esperaba.

Dió un paso hacia el camino, pero se detuvo. La puerta acababa de abrirse. Se volvió y vió a la dama de los ojos azules.

— Dispense [1] usted, — dijo ella, — he visto... ¿En qué puedo ayudarle?

Petersen se quedó un segundo inmóvil. Luego, cogió la mano blanca que se extendía hacia él, la tocó con los labios [2] y se volvió. La figura blanca continuaba inmóvil en la

[1] The object pronoun *me* is not often used with this word in Spanish.

[2] Kissing a lady's hand is a respectful gesture quite common among Latins.

puerta, iluminada por la luz de la casa, mientras Petersen echó a andar hacia el camino.

Se oyó el ruido de la puerta al cerrarse. Petersen apuró (*hastened*) el paso, y Bibí, asustado, le echó los brazos al cuello (*neck*).

Entretanto, las campanitas de la iglesia llamaban a la misa de Navidad.... [1]

Adapted from Salvador Reyes (*Chile*)

PALABRAS NUEVAS [2]

algodón (*m.*)	cotton	3 **marcharse**	to go away
4 **anciano**	old man	**mono**	monkey
4 **asombrado**	astonished	**Navidad**	Christmas
3 **aspecto**	appearance	**nieto**	grandson
asustado	frightened	**nochebuena**	Christmas eve
4 **barba**	beard	4 **oreja**	ear
chaqueta	jacket	**organillo**	hand organ
3 **caja**	box	**pino**	pine tree
fumar	to smoke	**pipa**	pipe
4 **iluminar**	to light	4 **rincón** (*m.*)	corner
4 **lento**	slow	**vagabundo**	wanderer

New Words Related to Others You Know

bailarín (*m.*) (**bailar**), dancer
descargar (**cargar**), to unload
inmóvil (**mover**), motionless
lealtad (*f.*) (**leal**), loyalty
2 **sentimiento** (**sentir**), feeling
son (*m.*) (**sonar**), sound
vecindad (**vecino**), vicinity

Expresiones

***de nuevo**, again
echar a, to start out
en torno de, around
por encima de, over

[1] The Christmas Eve mass would be the ***Misa del Gallo***, *Mass of the Cock*, which is celebrated in most Spanish-speaking countries, as well as in parts of the United States where there is much Spanish atmosphere.

[2] New words used in this chapter are not included in the general Spanish-English dictionary.

¿VERDAD O NO?

Change these statements to make them true if they are false:

1. Petersen vestía una chaqueta roja y un sombrero adornado con plumas. 2. El amo del mono era de aspecto triste porque era viejo y gordo. 3. Apenas la música empezaba a sonar, el mono empezaba a cantar. 4. Los dos dormían en los hoteles de los pueblos chicos. 5. Bibí sabía que había peligros en las ciudades. 6. Cuando Petersen empezó a tocar el organillo, los niños le rodearon. 7. El anciano de la pipa quería que los dos vagabundos fueran a su casa. 8. Petersen acompañó al viejo a una casa pobre y miserable. 9. Dentro del hall vió el vagabundo un árbol cubierto de nieve. 10. Petersen era del Norte, y el pino le hizo pensar en los *fiords* de su patria. 11. El niño enfermo no podía aplaudir con sus débiles manos. 12. Los ojos azules de la anciana miraron fríamente a Petersen. 13. Los invitados esperaron en las habitaciones de los criados. 14. Petersen se sentía solo en el grupo de invitados. 15. Cuando tocó el organillo la gente empezó a *foxtrotear.* 16. El niño enfermo le dió unas monedas. 17. Petersen se enamoró de la dama de los ojos negros. 18. El vagabundo creía que nunca la vería más.

PREGUNTAS

1. ¿Era pobre o rico el vagabundo? 2. ¿Era pordiosero? 3. ¿Quería el mono a su amo? 4. ¿Por qué marchaba Petersen con paso lento? 5. ¿Dónde dormían los dos? 6. ¿Cuándo bailaba Bibí? 7. ¿Por qué quería el anciano que Petersen le acompañara? 8. ¿Era rico o pobre el anciano? 9. ¿Qué cosa extraña vió el vagabundo en el hall elegante? 10. ¿Por qué miró Petersen tanto tiempo el árbol? 11. ¿Qué clase de piezas tocaba el organillo? 12. ¿Quién tenía los ojos azules? 13. ¿Dónde esperó Petersen la hora de volver a tocar? 14. ¿Qué hizo la gente al oír los viejos valses? 15. ¿Por qué dejó de tocar Petersen? 16. ¿Por qué se detuvo el hombre en la puerta? 17. ¿Salió la dama para despedirse de él? 18. ¿Qué hizo Petersen al despedirse de ella? 19. ¿Estaba triste el vagabundo al salir de la casa?

PREGUNTAS PERSONALES

1. ¿Ha visto Vd. alguna vez a un mono bailar sobre un organillo? 2. ¿Quisiera Vd. tener en casa un mono que supiera bailar? 3. ¿Comienza Vd. a bailar al oír sonar un vals? 4. ¿Vive Vd. en la vecindad de una iglesia? 5. ¿Tiene Vd. un traje de algodón? 6. ¿Está Vd. sentado (-a) en un rincón? 7. ¿Se queda Vd. inmóvil durante toda la lección? 8. ¿Le asusta a Vd. la selva? 9. ¿Es Vd. un (-a) buen (-a) bailarín (-a)? 10. ¿Quisiera Vd. tener una barba larga y rubia? 11. ¿Es Vd. un buen mecánico cuando se para su automóvil? 12. ¿Tiene Vd. en su casa un árbol de Navidad todos los años? 13. ¿Pone Vd. velas en su árbol de Navidad? 14. ¿Conoce Vd. los peligros de la civilización? 15. ¿Aplaude Vd. con manos débiles los programas de asamblea (*assembly*)? 16. ¿No se atreve Vd. algunas veces a mirar un par de ojos azules?

REPASO DE VERBOS

I. Change the infinitives in italics to the imperfect (indicative or subjunctive), preterite, or conditional according to the meaning:

Todos los días, Pablo *ir* al centro. Ayer *ir* a la tienda de cinco y diez para comprar un regalo para el cumpleaños de su amigo, Alberto. *Tener* que ir a pie porque a su automóvil le *faltar* gasolina. No *querer* ir a pie porque *hacer* mucho calor. *Ponerse* un sombrero para protegerse del sol, aunque no le *gustar* llevar sombrero.

Mientras *andar* por la calle, *hallar* una moneda cerca de una esquina. La *coger* y *decir*, — Si esta pieza de dinero *ser* de oro, *valer* cinco pesos. Si *valer* cinco pesos, yo *poder* comprar un mejor regalo para Alberto, y además, me *quedar* bastante dinero para tomar un refresco (*soft drink*) en la botica. Pero, ¡así es la vida! Algunas personas nunca tienen suerte. Compraré solamente el refresco. ¡Pobre Alberto!

¿Cuánto *valer* la moneda que *hallar* Pablo?

II. Put into Spanish: (§ 98)

I have just laughed, I dared to laugh, I stopped laughing, I began to laugh, I was to laugh, I succeeded in laughing, I used to dream of laughing, I tried to laugh, I laughed again, I was thinking about laughing, I decided not to laugh

III. Put into Spanish: (§ 98)

he approached the house, he remembered to knock, he made fun of the garden, he went to the door, he entered the hall, he paid attention to his friend, he played football, he resembled a monkey, he thought about the tree, he laughed at the servant, he left the room, he was surrounded with friends, he fell in love with two girls, he left town

REPASO DE PALABRAS

I. Here are some words which English has adapted from Spanish. *Tell in English what each means; look up in a dictionary those you do not know.* If you live in a part of the United States where there is much Spanish culture, you will know most of them.

rancho	mesa	tango	mosquito	alforja
hacienda	plaza	tomato	flotilla	potato
corral	cocoa	guerrilla	condor	alfalfa
cafeteria	alpaca	coyote	canyon	tamales
chile	bonanza	sierra	vanilla	vigilante
chocolate	canoe	patio	pinto	cigar
tapioca	fiesta	tobacco	puma	lagoon

II. Which word does not belong in each of these groups?

virtud	peligro	cocer	labio	lindo
mitad	tierno	hervir	boca	bello
juicio	digno	fuego	guerra	hermoso
confianza	agradecido	vergüenza	oído	guapo
bondad	estimado	mezclar	oreja	sagrado

III. Here are some expressions which second-year students have tried to say in Spanish and missed. *Can you say them correctly the first time?*

Galloway

Silky little chinchilla of the Andes is the most valuable fur-bearing animal in the world. About a hundred pelts will make a coat worth $30,000, and few people can own one.

everyone has gone, to wash his clothes, one may buy, for many centuries, the most beautiful city, he had a good time, the people stay home, Louis likes the city, Spaniards like music, among them, he asked them to speak, one of them, he saw another dog, he comes to open it, at midnight, they are like (resemble) us, they were seated, looking for someone, he carried away all the gold, they thought he was a Spaniard, money from his aunt, he gave her some meat, so many things, a friend of ours, he had to return the money

PARA DIVERTIRSE

«HÁGAME OTRA»

I. Copy these questions on slips of paper and pass them out to the members of the class for a review of the cultural material you have had about Spanish-American countries. They may be answered in Spanish if they are simple, or in English if there is much to tell. Under the names of the countries in the index you will find the chapters dealing with them.

1. ¿Cómo se llamaban los indios que vivían en México cuando

llegaron los españoles? 2. ¿Quiénes usaron primero las tortillas? 3. ¿Qué país tenía cuatro capitales? 4. ¿Quiénes hablaban náhuatl? 5. ¿Qué país tiene el quetzal? 6. ¿Qué hizo Cortés? 7. ¿Por qué iba mucha gente a la Isla del Coco? 8. ¿Qué país se llama la tierra de esmeraldas? 9. ¿Cómo se llama el camino más largo del mundo por donde se hablan solamente dos lenguas? 10. ¿Cuál es el país más pequeño de Centroamérica? 11. ¿Cuál es el país más pequeño de la América del Sur? 12. ¿Qué país terminó primero su tramo de la Carretera Panamericana? 13. ¿Cuál es el país donde cuesta más la vida? 14. ¿Cuál es el país donde cuesta menos la vida? 15. ¿Dónde se produce mucho «oro negro»? 16. ¿Qué isla de habla española pertenece a los Estados Unidos? 17. ¿Dónde se estableció el primer pueblo del Nuevo Mundo? 18. ¿Qué país se llama el azucarero (*sugar bowl*) del mundo? 19. ¿Cómo se llaman los indios de Yucatán? 20. ¿Quién hizo las primeras ruedas (*wheels*) del Nuevo Mundo? 21. ¿Cuál es el lago más grande y más alto de la América del Sur? 22. ¿Cómo se llamaban los indios que vivían en el Perú cuando llegaron los españoles? 23. ¿Por qué ofreció un indio llenar de oro un cuarto? 24. ¿Por qué no pudieron los españoles hallar la cadena de oro del lago Titicaca? 25. Nombre usted dos países sudamericanos que se pueden llamar «tierra de mujeres». 26. ¿Qué quiere decir la expresión «vale un Potosí»? 27. ¿Qué ciudad fué capital de toda la América del Sur durante parte de los tiempos coloniales? 28. ¿Por qué valía entonces un gato doscientos duros? 29. ¿Dónde se hacen los sombreros de jipijapa? 30. ¿De dónde se importa el «bálsamo del Perú»? 31. ¿Quiénes fueron dos generales famosos que libertaron de España a los países de la América del Sur? 32. ¿Quién fué el «Jorge Wáshington de la América del Sur»? 33. ¿Qué país exploraron Almagro y Pedro de Valdivia? 34. ¿De qué tribu (*tribe*) de indios eran Caupolicán y Lautaro? 35. ¿En qué países se toma mucho mate? 36. ¿En qué país prefieren tomar café? 37. ¿En qué país tienen desiertos donde casi nunca llueve? 38. ¿Qué es una llama? 39. ¿Qué ciudad tiene la calle más ancha del mundo? 40. ¿Por qué se llamó así la Argentina? 41. ¿Qué «río» famoso no es río? 42. ¿Qué capital sudamericana es muy popular entre los veraneantes (*summer visitors*) de otro país? 43. ¿Cuáles son dos países que tienen muchos gauchos? 44. ¿Qué dos países se parecen más uno a otro? 45. ¿Qué lengua se habla en el Brasil? 46. ¿Cuál es el país más grande de habla española?

II. Complete each sentence with a word or expression from the list at the left.[1]

el Cuzco
llama
balsa
coca
marimba
Xochimilco
Popocatépetl
el sol
bombilla
pampa
el bolívar
quinina
ñandutí
mate
cacao
chicle
gaucho
ombú
guaraníes
araucanos
Martín Fierro
Aconcagua

1. Los indios de Guatemala tocan un instrumento llamado . . . .
2. Los aztecas construyeron jardines flotantes (*floating*) que hoy día llevan el nombre de . . . .
3. Un volcán de México se llama . . . .
4. La capital antigua de los incas se llamaba . . . .
5. Un animal de carga de los Andes es la . . . .
6. Los quichuas cruzan el lago de Titicaca en sus . . . .
7. Para prevenir el hambre y la sed, los indios de los Andes mascan (*chew*) . . . .
8. El «dólar» del Perú se llama . . . .
9. El «dólar» de Venezuela se llama . . . .
10. Una medicina importante que viene de la selva es la . . . .
11. Las indias guaraníes del Paraguay hacen el . . . .
12. La mayor parte de la gente de la América del Sur toma . . . . en vez de te.
13. Para tomar mate se usa una . . . .
14. Los gauchos viven y trabajan en la . . . .
15. Una figura romántica del pasado, con su caballo y su guitarra, era el . . . .
16. En la pampa el único árbol que da sombra es el . . . .
17. El chocolate se hace del . . . .
18. La goma de mascar (*chewing gum*) se hace del . . . .
19. Un poema que trata de la vida del gaucho se llama . . . .
20. El pico (*peak*) más alto de las Américas es . . . .
21. Los indios del Paraguay, que nunca fueron vencidos por los españoles, se llaman . . . .
22. Los indios de Chile, que nunca fueron vencidos por los españoles, se llaman . . . .

[1] For a Spanish club party you could pin one of these words on the back of each member and have him guess what it is according to the things others tell him about it. Or one member could read a sentence and call on another to complete it, who will have to be "It" if he misses.

Galloway

Iguana, great tropical lizard found throughout Central and South America, makes a nice pet, although he will snap like a dog if annoyed. Wild ones live in rocky places and Indians eat them.

PARA LEER SIN ESTUDIAR

Los animales de la América del Sur

1. En la pampa. Había poca vida animal en la pampa cuando llegaron los españoles, pero pronto después los pumas y los jaguares bajaron de los Andes para comerse las vacas y los caballos.

Los habitantes originales de la pampa eran las vizcachas (*prairie dogs*), los armadillos, los avestruces (*ostriches* or *rheas*), y las lechuzas, así como los guanacos (*small llamas*) que vivían en el sur. Hoy día quedan pocas vizcachas, pero en las estancias (*ranches*) parece que hay una lechuza en cada estacón (*fence post*), y de vez en cuando se ve correr por la pampa un avestruz que dejan vivir allí como un elemento romántico del país.

Los gauchos cogen los armadillos con una lata (*tin can*), en que meten un pedazo de carne. Cuando el animal ha bajado para comer la carne, no puede salir.

Los guanacos tienen la piel (*fur*) bonita, usada aquí para hacer chaquetas cortas de señora, que cuestan como sesenta dólares.

Miles de gaviotas (*sea gulls*) siguen el arado (*plow*) por la pampa para comerse los insectos, aunque estén lejos del mar. Y siempre se oyen los gritos del «bienteveo», pájaro de colores vivos que vuela por toda la pampa.

2. En la selva. Hay mucha vida animal en la selva, con sus pájaros, mariposas (*butterflies*) e insectos de colores vivos. Hay bandas de loros (*parrots*) verdes que gritan por todas partes; hay monos que saltan de árbol en árbol, y boas enormes que se cuelgan de las ramas. Allí vive la iguana (*large lizard*), la víbora de coral, y el armadillo; cerca de los ríos se encuentran cocodrilos (*crocodiles*) y caimanes (*alligators*). El puma y el jaguar cazan (*hunt*) al hombre y al venado, y en los ríos hay peces feroces (*ferocious*) que se comen a cualquier animal que caiga al agua.

3. En los Andes. Las llamas y las alpacas, «camellos de los Andes», ya no existen en un estado salvaje (*wild*), pero la vicuña, animal más chico y con piel (*fur*) más fina, todavía vive en las alturas. Nadie puede acercarse a la tímida vicuña para cogerla viva;

Andean alpacas look like overstuffed llamas, with their thick, tangled wool which is sheared yearly. They live at altitudes above 12,000 feet, and were domesticated by Andean Indians centuries ago.

Sawders

siempre es preciso matarla a lo lejos con escopeta. Su piel es de tanto valor que entre los incas sólo se les permitía a los nobles llevarla. Hoy día está prohibido cazar (*hunt*) la vicuña en el Perú, aunque en Bolivia se permite pagando un impuesto (*tax*).

La llama es la bestia de carga (*beast of burden*) del indio, y bien se sabe que no se le puede dar una carga demasiado pesada, pues se niega a (*refuses*) andar. Otra cosa de interés es que la llama no puede vivir mucho tiempo sino en las alturas. Si baja al nivel del mar, muere pronto.

La alpaca, algo más grande que la llama, da lana de mucho valor. Pero la pequeña chinchilla de los Andes tiene la piel (*fur*) más preciosa del mundo, pues un abrigo de su piel cuesta miles de dólares, y hay muy pocas mujeres que pueden poseer uno.

El cóndor que vuela por los picos (*peaks*) es para los sudamericanos lo que es el águila para nosotros. Sus alas son tan enormes que puede coger y llevarse un venado chico, y tres países han dado a sus monedas el nombre de esta ave poderosa.

TEMA

1. The monkey's little ears could be seen beneath his red hat. 2. His master was young, and the two understood each other well. 3. They traveled slowly, sleeping in the forest near a river. 4. Hardly [had] Petersen dropped his hand organ, [when] the monkey began to dance. 5. The old man's little grandson was ill, and the old man wanted Petersen to go home with him. 6. The house was surrounded by trees, and inside, there was a Christmas tree. 7. It made Petersen think of his own country. 8. The little sick boy wanted Bibí to dance. 9. While he was dancing, Petersen saw that two blue eyes were looking at him. 10. He was invited to play again (**volver a**) at midnight. 11. After playing, he sat down in a corner without knowing how to leave the house. 12. He knew that when he left (*subj.*), he would never again (**más**) see those blue eyes. 13. But the beautiful lady followed him to the door and gave him her hand. 14. He kissed (**besar**) it and went out into the night without saying anything. 15. It was the Christmas Eve of the wanderers (**vagabundos**).

LA MAQUINITA

Groups of wandering singers called *mariachis*, like the minstrels of the Middle Ages, still stroll over Mexico singing old folk songs, new love songs, and ballads (*corridos*) about current events. Whenever a startling occurrence happens anywhere in the country, it is immediately told in verse and set to music, and the *mariachis* sing it from village to village, even though nowadays they have competition from the radio.

This ballad about the "little engine" is still popular although it was composed long ago, and tells rather facetiously of a famous wreck in the early days of railroading. The fact that it mentions an airplane merely shows that some singer has brought it up to date, just as gossip grows as it spreads from person to person.

The same melody or a very similar one is still used to sing of modern calamities, such as the cloudburst and flood near Xochimilco, the death of an aviator, or the sinking of a ship.

Verses are marked A or B and are to be sung with the music with the same marking.

[1]1840

[2]Tula and Guanajuato are two cities of central Mexico.

3. (A) El tren que corría sobre la ancha vía (*track*)
de pronto se fué a chocar (*collide*)
contra un aeroplano que estaba en el llano (*plain*)
volando sin descansar.

4. (A) Quedó el maquinista (*engineer*) con los ojos fuera
mirando tal aviador,
que ya sin cabeza, buscaba el sombrero
para librarse (*protect*) del sol.

5. (B) Los pocos supervivientes (*survivors*) los contemplaban llorando,
y la máquina seguía, pita, (*whistle*) pita, y caminando.

6. (A) Llegó la Cruz Blanca, llegó la Cruz Roja,
a ayudar a los heridos,
y allí descubrieron que todos los muertos
de miedo ya habían corrido.

7. (A) Ahora ya no quiero seguir esta historia
para no cansar a ustedes;
rueguen (*pray*) por aquéllos que allí se murieron,
hombres, niños, y mujeres.

8. (B) Al recordar tanta muerte, todos están vacilando (*overcome*)
porque la máquina sigue pita, pita, y caminando.

Serenata de Guanajuato

PERSONAJES

JIMMIE, *joven norteamericano que está pasando el verano en Guanajuato, México, practicando su "high-school Spanish."*

PEDRO, *joven mexicano de Guanajuato.*

SUSIE, *jovencita morena, a quien* JIMMIE *ve en Guanajuato.*

BELLE, *hermana mayor de* SUSIE.

BOLERO,[1] *que trabaja en el Jardín de la Unión.*

VENDEDOR DE FLORES.

RANCHERO,[2] *que está celebrando el día de su santo con el* MARIACHI.[3]

ACTO PRIMERO

Escena primera

El Jardín de la Unión[4] *de Guanajuato, México. Árboles y flores. Hay dos bancos de hierro en la banqueta a la sombra de unos árboles. Son las cinco de la tarde. A levantarse el telón,* PEDRO *está sentado en uno de los bancos, leyendo un libro. Sale*[5] JIMMIE *por la derecha y se sienta en el otro banco. Le ha seguido el* BOLERO.

BOLERO — Chine, meester? (*Indica los zapatos de* JIMMIE.)

JIMMIE — (*Mirándolos.*) Well, maybe I do need one. ¿Cuánto me cobra (*charge*) Vd.?[6]

BOLERO — ¡Ah! ¡Vd. habla español! Veinte y cinco centavos, joven.

JIMMIE — Bueno. (*El* BOLERO *se sienta en la banqueta y empieza a limpiar los zapatos de* JIMMIE.)

Escena II[7]

Sale el VENDEDOR DE FLORES, *que lleva a* (on) *la cabeza una cesta* (basket) *de flores blancas atadas* (tied) *en ramitos pequeños.*

VENDEDOR — ¡Flores de San Juan ¡Frescas y fragantes! (*Ve a* JIMMIE.) ¿Flores de San Juan, joven? Diez centavos el ramito.

[1] The bootblack should wear bib overalls, a cap with a visor, a cotton work shirt, and have a tight leather belt around his middle on top of the overalls.

[2] A *ranchero* should wear tight trousers, a big hat, and a tan cotton jacket with a design embroidered on the back.

[3] A *mariachi* is a group of at least three wandering musicians, playing violin, guitar, and cello or bass guitar (*guitarrón*). They often wear *charro* costumes.

[4] The Jardín de la Unión is a popular park where people of all classes find time to sit awhile on the benches.

[5] ***Sale*** in a play means *enter;* ***vase*** (***vanse***) means *exit* (*exeunt*).

[6] In Mexico you always find out beforehand what things are going to cost.

[7] Spanish plays are divided into "scenes," not on the basis of a change of scenery or a break in the play, but with the entrance or exit of any of the principal players.

JIMMIE — Gracias.[8] What would *I* do with a bunch of flowers?

VENDEDOR — ¿Mande Vd.?

JIMMIE — Well, I suppose I can say it in Spanish if I have to. Digo, ¿para qué quiero yo flores?

VENDEDOR — Ah, joven, estas flores curan enfermedades, y con ellas uno puede hacer que una damita le quiera.

JIMMIE — ¡No me diga! Pero no estoy enfermo, y no quiero novia.[9]

VENDEDOR — ¿Verdad? Pues otro día, ¿eh, joven? Con permiso.

JIMMIE — Vd. lo tiene.

VENDEDOR — (*Pregonando* [calling out].) ¡Flores de San Juan! ¡Frescas y fragantes! (*Vase.*)

Escena III

PEDRO — (*Que ha estado escuchando la conversación desde su banco, se levanta y se acerca a* JIMMIE. *Indicando el banco.*) ¿Con permiso?

JIMMIE — Siéntese Vd.

BOLERO — (*Terminando.*) Ya,[10] joven.

JIMMIE — (*Sacando dinero del bolsillo.*) ¿Puede Vd. cambiar un dolor?

BOLERO — ¿Mande Vd.? ¿Qué dice?

JIMMIE — Aquí tiene Vd. un dolor. (*Le muestra una moneda.*)

BOLERO — ¡Un dolor! ¡Ay! (*Ríe a carcajadas* [heartily], *y* PEDRO *no puede menos de* [cannot help] *reír un poco también.*) ¡Eso es un peso! ¡Debe Vd. decir *dólar* en vez de *dolor*, y además, nuestros dólares se llaman pesos!

JIMMIE — (*Aparte.*) Leave it to me! I remember now, — it's *dolor de cabeza*, and so on. (*Al* BOLERO.) Bueno. Aquí tiene Vd. el peso.

BOLERO — Gracias. (*Lo toma y le devuelve el cambio.*) Listo, señor. (*A* PEDRO, *indicando los zapatos de éste.*)

PEDRO — Gracias.[11] Más tarde, quizás. (*Vase el* BOLERO.)

PEDRO — (*A* JIMMIE, *hablando con mucha dificultad.*) You have [12] joost arrive een Guanajuato?

JIMMIE — Yes, I came yesterday. So you speak English!

[8] ***Gracias*** in response to an invitation or suggestion means *no, thank you.* Jimmie would wag a forefinger to emphasize the negative.

[9] See note 8.

[10] *Ya* is a very handy word indicating that something is ready or finished.

[11] See note 8.

[12] Pedro pronounces all his *a's* as *ah.*

PEDRO — I estudy[13] eet een my eschool, but eet ees very difícil. You practice eet weeth me?

JIMMIE — I'll be glad to. I've been studying Spanish in school, so I know just what you mean. And you can help me practice, too.

PEDRO — Con todo gusto. We should perhaps present ourselves the one to the other. (*Se levanta.*) Pedro Flores, a sus órdenes.

JIMMIE — (*Levantándose.*) James Fansler, de Fillmore, California, servidor de Vd. (*Se dan la mano y después se sientan.*)

PEDRO — ¡Ah, California! There ees where Hollywood, ¿no?

JIMMIE — Sí; vivo a unas cincuenta millas de Hollywood.

PEDRO — ¡Qué bonito (*how nice*)! You speak Espaneesh very well.

JIMMIE — Favor que Vd. me hace.[14] But I feel like a dope when I don't know how to say some things.

PEDRO — Thees *dope*, what you mean?

JIMMIE — Dope? Well, a dumb cluck, you know, well, a heel.

PEDRO — A heel? Ah, sí, I onderstan' the heel. There are many heels een Guanajuato.

JIMMIE — There are? Why, I thought folks here seemed pretty nice.

PEDRO — (*Sin entender.*) Ah, sí. The ceety ees surround' weeth heels. (*Indica las montañas.*)

JIMMIE — (*Riendo.*) Oh, I get it! You mean *hills!* You don't pronounce an English *i* like *ee* the way you do in Spanish. Now I'm even for that *dolor* business you thought was so funny.

PEDRO — Es cierto. Se me había olvidado. Now I am the what-you-call dope, too. (*Ríen los dos.*)

Escena IV

Sale el MARIACHI *por la derecha, tocando y cantando, siguiendo a un* RANCHERO *muy contento, que lleva el sombrero al ojo. Vanse por la izquierda.*

JIMMIE — (*Mirándolos con mucho interés.*) Well, what do you make of that! ¿Por qué iban siguiendo los músicos a aquel señor?

PEDRO — Eet ees without doubt the birthday of the señor, and he pay the mariachi that they follow heem all the day for honor heem.

JIMMIE — Well, I'll be darned! Wouldn't Fillmore love that!

PEDRO — ¿Mande Vd.?

[13] Spanish-speaking people find it difficult to pronounce words beginning with an *s* followed by a consonant, so they put an *e* in front of it.

[14] ***Favor que Vd. me hace,*** *you flatter me.* Proper reply to a compliment.

JIMMIE — Digo que eso les divertiría mucho a los habitantes de mi pueblo, porque allí no tenemos la costumbre de hacer tal cosa.

PEDRO — ¡No me diga! ¡Qué país tan curioso es el de Vd.!

Escena V

Salen SUSIE *y* BELLE *por la izquierda, dando un paseo, y pasan despacio por el escenario* (stage), *viendo a los jóvenes sin mirarlos. Vanse por la derecha.*

PEDRO — (*Al pasar de cerca las muchachas, mirándolas con admiración.*) ¡Ay, qué preciosas chicas! ¡Más divinas no hay!

JIMMIE — (*Con reproche, después de pasar las muchachas.*) Gosh, I'll bet those girls heard you!

PEDRO — Sí, claro (*of course*). ¿Cómo no?

JIMMIE — You don't mean you *wanted* them to hear, do you?

PEDRO — ¿Cómo no? Es costumbre. Las chicas se enojan si los chicos no les echan flores.

JIMMIE — ¿Echan flores? You didn't throw any flowers.

PEDRO — Es una expresión que tenemos. Eet mean that we say what you call compliment to the girls. They like eet, but they no answer. No es costumbre.

JIMMIE — Hm! Voy a hacer uso de esa costumbre. Esas chicas me agradan. Especially the little one. (*Silba quedito* [softly].) Wait till I see *her* again! This Good Neighbor Policy is beginning to appeal to me!

PEDRO — ¿Vd. la conoce?

JIMMIE — Never saw her before. ¿Cómo consigo conocerla? Me gustaría llevarla a *ella* al cine un día de éstos.

PEDRO — (*Con horror.*) ¡Ah, pero es imposible llevar a una muchacha al cine! ¡No es costumbre! Pero si quiere Vd., puede seguirla a casa para saber dónde vive, y en la noche puede ir a su balcón [15] para cantar y después platicar con ella.

JIMMIE — Me sing! Gosh, I can't sing! I'd sound pretty sour warbling love songs under a balcony!

PEDRO — Pues no le hace (*never mind*). El mariachi le acompañará al balcón para tocar y cantar para ella.

JIMMIE — (*Pensando.*) Might be fun at that. Say, I think I'll walk around the Jardín and see if I meet those girls again. Sure like that little one. ¿Quiere Vd. acompañarme?

[15] ***Balcón*** means either a *balcony* or a big barred *window.*

PEDRO — Gracias. Tengo que estudiar esta lección.

JIMMIE — Pues, con permiso.

PEDRO — Vd. lo tiene. (*Vase* JIMMIE *por la derecha.*)

Escena VI

Sale el BOLERO *por la izquierda.*

BOLERO — (*A* PEDRO.) ¿Grasa (*shine*), señor?

PEDRO — Pues, sí. (*El* BOLERO *se sienta y empieza a trabajar, mientras* PEDRO *lee su libro.*)

Escena VII

Salen el MARIACHI *y el* RANCHERO *por la derecha y vanse por la izquierda, aquél cantando como antes.* PEDRO *los mira y vuelve a leer.*[16]

Escena VIII

Sale JIMMIE *por la derecha y se sienta cerca de Pedro.*

JIMMIE — Well, I saw those girls —

PEDRO — ¡En español! ¡Debe Vd. practicar!

JIMMIE — Pues, ví a esas chicas a la vuelta y me acerqué y traté de platicar con ellas.

PEDRO — ¡Qué barbaridad! ¡No debía Vd. haber hecho eso!

JIMMIE — But you said things about them that they could hear, and they didn't care. Why can't I just go up and speak to them?

PEDRO — Pero eso es otro cantar.[17] No es costumbre platicar con las muchachas excepto a la reja.

JIMMIE — Funniest country I ever saw!

PEDRO — ¿Qué contestaron las chicas cuando Vd. les habló?

JIMMIE — (*Con mucho disgusto.*) No contestaron nada. Se rieron como locas. Pareció que no entendieron lo que les dije. I guess my high-school Spanish must be pretty bad. ¿Sabe Vd. dónde viven?

PEDRO — No sé. Son recién llegadas a Guanajuato.

BOLERO — Yo sé donde viven. Son hermanas, y su casa está cerquita, — a la vuelta en la Calle de Sopeña.

JIMMIE — Gracias. (PEDRO *le paga al* BOLERO, *que se va por la derecha.*)

Escena IX

JIMMIE — A ver, Pedro. Si Vd. me cita (*engage*) el mariachi para esta noche, llevo una serenata a la reja de esa chica. ¿Le gustaría acompañarme?

[16] Both of the *mariachi-ranchero* scenes may be omitted if a shorter play is desired.

[17] **otro cantar,** "*a horse of another color.*"

PEDRO — Con todo gusto. Entonces aquí nos encontramos como a las diez, ¿eh? [18]

JIMMIE — Sí, con el mariachi. Sin falta, ¿eh?

PEDRO — Sin falta. (*Mirando el reloj.*) Pues, tengo clases esta tarde y debo irme. Con permiso. (*Se levanta.*) Hasta las diez.

JIMMIE — Vd. lo tiene. Hasta luego. (*Vase* PEDRO *por la izquierda.*)

Escena X

Sale el VENDEDOR DE FLORES *por la derecha.*

VENDEDOR — ¡Flores de San Juan! ¡Frescas y fragantes!

JIMMIE — ¡Psst! [19] Say, gimme a bunch of those.

VENDEDOR — ¿Mande Vd., joven?

JIMMIE — Digo, déme un ramito, por favor. (*Le da una moneda y escoge un ramito.*)

VENDEDOR — (*Sonriendo.*) Buena suerte, joven.

JIMMIE — (*Sonriendo.*) Gracias. (*Aparte.*) Well, he said these flowers would do the trick. No harm trying. And that little one sure is cute. (*Vase por la derecha, oliendo las flores.*)

ACTO SEGUNDO

Escena primera

Es de noche. La Calle de Sopeña. Al fondo, la casa de SUSIE *y* BELLE, *con una puerta grande y ventana con reja. Salen* JIMMIE *y* PEDRO, *seguidos por el* MARIACHI.

JIMMIE — Ésta es la casa. Creo que aquella ventana es la de ella. ¿Qué hago ahora?

PEDRO — Bueno, puesto que (*since*) Vd. no la conoce todavía y no piensa platicar con ella esta noche, esperamos al otro lado de la calle mientras toca el mariachi.

JIMMIE — (*Al* MARIACHI.) ¡Bueno, muchachos! Por acá (*this way*). Canten Vds. And sing it pretty! I don't spend ten pesos on music for a slick chick every day! (JIMMIE *y* PEDRO *cruzan la calle; el* MARIACHI *se estaciona cerca de la ventana y canta una canción popular de amor. No pasa nada dentro de la casa.*)

[18] Most serenades take place after midnight or even at four or five o'clock in the morning, but we must have this one early for a particular reason! It is quite correct for a fellow to take friends with him.

[19] You call people this way in Mexico. Jimmie must also wave his hand at the vendor as if swatting a fly to signify, "Come here."

PEDRO — (*Al terminar el* MARIACHI.) Parece que la señorita no oye la música. Debe prender (*light*) la luz un momentito.

JIMMIE — ¿Para qué?

PEDRO — Para indicar que oye y le agrada la serenata.

JIMMIE — Gosh, I hope she's home! I'd hate to have all this fiddling wasted on the desert air, so to speak.

PEDRO — (*Al* MARIACHI.) Toquen otra, muchachos. (*El* MARIACHI *vuelve a tocar y cantar. Al terminar el* MARIACHI, *se abren las puerta-ventanas* [shutters] *y salen al balcón,* SUSIE *y* BELLE *murmurando y riéndose.*)

Escena II

PEDRO — ¡Qué curioso! Una señorita nunca debe salir al balcón durante una serenata.

JIMMIE — ¿No? ¿Qué debe hacer?

PEDRO — Es costumbre quedarse en su cuarto sin decir nada.

JIMMIE — Well, this *is* funny! Esas chicas deben saber la costumbre.

PEDRO — Por supuesto. Platicar y reír durante una serenata, — ¡qué cosa!

JIMMIE — Están mirándonos. Quizás deba yo acercarme a platicar con la morenita. Quizás tendré mejor suerte con mi español esta vez. Espéreme un momentito. Con permiso. (*Se acerca a la reja y se dirige* [addresses] *a las chicas, haciendo una reverencia profunda* [deep bow] *y hablando con mucha dignidad.*) Buenas noches, señoritas. Espero que les agrade la música que les he traído. ¿Qué otra canción quieren Vds.?

(*Las chicas siguen riendo y murmurando y no le contestan nada.*)

JIMMIE — El mariachi puede tocar la canción que les guste.

SUSIE — (*Después de mucha risa, y pronunciando las palabras con mucho cuidado.*) No . . . entiendo.

JIMMIE — (*Aparte.*) Dawggone it! My accent certainly must be lousy. (*Tratando una vez más, pronunciando las palabras con cuidado exagerado.*) Espero . . . que . . . les . . . guste . . . la . . . música. . . . ¿Quieren . . . Vds. . . . que . . . los . . . músicos . . . les . . . canten . . . otra? (*Las dos muchachas murmuran y ríen.*)

SUSIE — No . . . entiendo. (*A su hermana, en voz alta.*) Oh, Sis, isn't he just too heavenly for words! If he could only talk English wouldn't it be fun to date him!

BELLE — You're telling me! Well, I told you not to flunk Spanish.

SUSIE — Oh, I'll get acquainted with him somehow. Don't you worry!

JIMMIE — Holy cow! You don't sound like any *señorita*! Don't tell me you're an American!

SUSIE — (*Chillando* [squealing].) Oh! Why, of course I am!

BELLE — (*A* SUSIE.) What you said just now! (*Muerta de risa.*)

SUSIE — (*A* JIMMIE.) And f'goodness' sake, you don't sound much like a Mexican yourself!

JIMMIE — Who said I was?

SUSIE — But you were talking Spanish to us in the plaza today! Or anyway, we thought it was Spanish.

JIMMIE — It was my most reasonable facsimile. And *I* thought you couldn't understand me because my accent was all wet! Do you live here?

SUSIE — No, Sis and I just came down to spend the summer with our Aunt. And maybe you think we haven't been bored! We haven't met anyone who can speak English and all we do is sit around. Will you be here long?

JIMMIE — Couple of months. Dad's a mining engineer, and he brought me along when he came to inspect the mines for one of the companies here.

SUSIE — Isn't that just too heavenly! I mean, — well — Auntie's still up, and it's only eleven o'clock, and wouldn't you and your friend like to come in for a little while?

JIMMIE — No kiddin'. Come on, Pedro! The girls want us to come in.

PEDRO — (*Acercándose a la reja.*) But one cannot go een to veeseet the señoritas! ¡No es costumbre!

JIMMIE — That's what you think! This may be Mexico, but the girls and I are Americans, and good old United States customs are okay by us. Come on, muchachos! Let's have some music inside.

(*Las muchachas van a abrir la puerta de adentro. Los jóvenes entran en la casa, seguidos del mariachi. Se oyen risas, y exclamaciones alegres, y música.*)

Se baja despacio el telón.

PALABRAS NUEVAS: **agradar,** to please, to suit; **a la vuelta,** around the corner; **aparte,** aside; **banco,** bench; **banqueta,** sidewalk; **bolero,** bootblack; **murmurar,** to whisper; **platicar,** to chat; **reja,** barred window; **risa,** laughter; **serenata,** serenade; **sin falta,** without fail.

Facts About Our Latin-American Neighbors

COUNTRY	CAPITAL	COMPARATIVE SIZE	POPULATION	IMPORTANT PRODUCTS
Argentina	Buenos Aires	Almost $\frac{1}{2}$ as large as continental United States	13,518,239	cattle, sheep, grains
Bolivia	La Paz [1]	Over twice as large as Texas	3,426,296	tin, gold, silver, copper
Brazil	Rio de Janeiro	Larger than continental United States	44,120,000	coffee, tropical fruits and nuts
Chile	Santiago	Larger than Texas	5,000,782	copper, nitrates, wool
Colombia	Bogotá	$1\frac{3}{4}$ times Texas	9,523,200	coffee, oil, emeralds
Costa Rica	San José	Slightly smaller than West Virginia	656,129	coffee, bananas, cacao
Cuba	Habana	Slightly smaller than Pennsylvania	4,199,952	sugar, fruits, tobacco
Ecuador	Quito	About Texas plus Maryland	3,200,000	cacao, "Panama" hats
Guatemala	Guatemala	About size of Louisiana	3,284,000	coffee, bananas, chicle
Honduras	Tegucigalpa	Slightly smaller than Pennsylvania	1,105,504	bananas, coffee, tobacco
México	México	Almost 3 times Texas	19,473,741	oil, silver, hemp
Nicaragua	Managua	Somewhat larger than Georgia	1,380,287	bananas, sugar, coffee
Panamá	Panamá	Somewhat smaller than Indiana	635,836	bananas, coconuts, cacao
Paraguay	Asunción	Over twice as large as Idaho	1,014,773	quebracho, cattle, yerba mate
Perú	Lima	Over 3 times California	7,023,111	copper, cotton, oil
Puerto Rico	San Juan	Smaller than Connecticut	1,869,255	sugar, embroideries, tobacco
El Salvador	San Salvador	Somewhat larger than Maryland	1,744,535	coffee, hemp, sugar
Santo Domingo	Ciudad Trujillo	Less than $\frac{1}{2}$ Ohio	1,616,561	sugar, cacao, tobacco
Uruguay	Montevideo	Slightly larger than North Dakota	2,146,545	cattle, sheep
Venezuela	Caracas	$1\frac{1}{2}$ times Texas	3,492,747	oil, cacao

[1] Sucre is the official capital, but La Paz is usually called the capital.

More About Spanish-Speaking Countries

I. IF YOU LIKE MOVIES [1]

The following companies or agencies will sell, rent, or lend films and slides showing Spanish-speaking countries, which you can use in class, assembly, or for your Spanish Club.

De Vry Corporation. 1111 Armitage Ave., Chicago, Ill. Catalogue 25¢.

EDUCATIONAL FILM CATALOG. H. W. Wilson Co. 950 University Ave., New York City.

Metropolitan Motion Picture Council. Room 75, 100 Washington Square, New York City. List 50¢.

U. S. Film Service. Washington, D.C.

Pan American Union. Division of Intellectual Cooperation. Washington, D.C.

Bell and Howell Co. 1801 Larchmont Ave., Chicago, Ill.; 30 Rockefeller Plaza, New York City; 716 N. La Brea Ave., Hollywood, Calif.

Erpi Classroom Films, Inc. Rochester, New York.

Burton Holmes, Inc. 7510 N. Ashland Ave., Chicago, Ill.

Slides and Strip Film

American Museum of Natural History. Educational Dept., 77th and Central Park West, New York City.

Cambosco Scientific Co. Chicago, Ill.

Will H. Dudley. 736 S. Wabash Ave., Chicago, Ill.

Keystone View Co. Educational Dept., Meadville, Pa.

Society for Visual Education. 100 E. Ohio St., Chicago, Ill.

II. IF YOU WANT PICTURES

Acme. 220 E. 42d St., New York City.

International News Service. 235 E. 45th St., New York City.

Wide World. 229 W. 43d St., New York City.

Banks Upshaw & Co. 707 Browder St., Dallas, Texas (post cards).

Sanborn's. Av. Francisco I. Madero, Mexico, D.F. (post cards).

III. IF YOU LIKE MUSIC

R.C.A. Manufacturing Co., Camden, New Jersey. Catalogue of DISCOS VICTOR, Catálogo Internacional (phonograph records).

[1] Write the Extension Division or Division of Visual Aids of your state university for catalogues or information regarding nearby sources of films and slides. *The Other Americas Through Films and Records*, published by the American Council on Education, Washington, D.C., contains many sources for pictures and records.

ÁLBUM DE MÚSICA POPULAR MEXICANA. Wagner & Levien, Mexico, D.F.

ÁLBUM POPULAR NO. 2. Repertorio de Música de Angela Peralta, V. Carranza 20, Mexico, D.F.

MOLINA, CARLOS: ALBUM OF SPANISH FAVORITES. Edward B. Marks Music Corporation, New York City.

TOOR, FRANCES: EL CANCIONERO MEXICANO. Manchester 8, Mexico, D.F.

CANTEMOS. Penny Press, 366 Greenwich St., New York City.

HAGUE, E.: FOLKSONGS FROM MEXICO AND SOUTH AMERICA. American Folk-lore Society, Augustin, Inc., 141 East 29th St., New York City.

THE OTHER AMERICAS. Edward B. Marks Music Corporation, New York City.

IV. IF YOU LIKE TO DANCE

HARRISON, SALOMAY, and GILSTRAP, OPAL: CLAVELITO. Tardy Publishing Co., Dallas, Texas. *Cucaracha* and *Jarabe Tapatío.*

MEXICAN FOLK DANCES (colored folder, 25¢). Banks Upshaw, Dallas, Texas.

SHAMBAUGH, MARY EFFIE: FOLK FESTIVALS. A. S. Barnes.

V. IF YOU LIKE TO COOK

MEXICAN COOKERY FOR AMERICAN HOMES. Gebhardt's, San Antonio, Texas. Free pamphlet. (Recipes for *tortillas, tamales, tacos*; menus for Mexican meals and teas.)

BROWN, CORA, ROSE, and BOB: SOUTH AMERICAN COOK BOOK. Doubleday Doran.

SCOTT, NATALIE: YOUR MEXICAN KITCHEN. Putnam.

VI. IF YOU ARE REALLY GOING TO SPANISH AMERICA

BRENNER, ANITA: YOUR MEXICAN HOLIDAY. Putnam. Guidebook.

TERRY, PHILIP: GUIDE TO MEXICO. Houghton Mifflin Co.

Pemex Travel Club, Bucareli 35, Mexico, D.F. Write for free folders.

CONSOLIDATED VISITOR'S GUIDE. Av. 5 de Mayo 11, Mexico, D.F. Free booklet.

THE SOUTH AMERICAN HANDBOOK. Trade and Travel Publications, Ltd.

FRANCK, HARRY A., and LANKS, HERBERT C.: THE PAN AMERICAN HIGHWAY. Appleton-Century. (Central America.)

VII. IF YOU LIKE TO READ SPANISH

LA LUZ. Banks Upshaw & Co., Dallas, Texas. Periodical.

EL ECO. The Odyssey Press, New York City. Periodical.

HARRISON, SALOMAY L.: LINDAS TIERRAS DE MÉXICO. Heath.

FORRESTER, K. T., and LOLY, K. D.: VAMOS A MÉXICO. Heath.

WEISINGER, NINA, and JOHNSTON, MARJORIE: LOS OTROS AMERICANOS. Doubleday Doran.

DEVITIS, M. A., and TORREYSON, DOROTHY: TALES OF SPANISH AMERICA. Macmillan.

SHAPIRO, A., and HURLEY, F. J.: COSAS DE ESPAÑA Y DE LA AMÉRICA ESPAÑOLA. Holt.

TORRES-RIOSECO, A., and MORBY, E. S.: CARTILLA MEJICANA. Crofts.

VIII. IF YOU LIKE TO ACT

BROOMHALL, E.: SPOKEN SPANISH. Allyn & Bacon.

HENRY, RUTH: PIECECITAS ESPAÑOLAS FÁCILES. Allyn & Bacon.

HARRISON, SALOMAY, and GILSTRAP, OPAL: CLAVELITO. Tardy Pub. Co., Dallas, Texas.

JARRETT, EDITH MOORE: SAL Y SABOR DE MÉXICO. Houghton Mifflin Co.

IX. IF YOU LIKE TO MAKE THINGS

JARRETT, EDITH MOORE: SAL Y SABOR DE MÉXICO. Houghton Mifflin. Directions for making Mexican costumes, etc.

X. IF YOU WANT CURIOS FROM SPANISH-AMERICAN COUNTRIES

Banks Upshaw & Co., 707 Browder St., Dallas, Tex. Catalogue of favors, post cards, maps, figurettes, etc., from Mexico.

Dextre Shop, 1401 Mason St., San Francisco, Calif. Curios from all Spanish-speaking countries.

Estrellita Shop, 527 Pacific Ave., San Francisco, Calif. Curios.

XI. OTHER THINGS YOU MAY LIKE

JONES, WILLIS KNAPP: CALENDAR OF SPANISH ANNIVERSARIES. Tardy Pub. Co., Dallas, Texas.

ESPINOSA, J. M.: ROMPECABEZAS ESPAÑOLES (Crossword Puzzles), Allyn & Bacon.

Verb Appendix

62. Regular Verbs

	FIRST CONJUGATION	SECOND CONJUGATION	THIRD CONJUGATION
INDICATIVE MOOD			
INFINITIVE	ganar *to earn*	responder *to answer*	vivir *to live*
GERUND	ganando *earning*	respondiendo *answering*	viviendo *living*
PAST PARTICIPLE	ganado *earned*	respondido *answered*	vivido *lived*
PRESENT INDICATIVE	*I earn, am earning, do earn* gano ganas gana ganamos ganáis ganan	*I answer, am answering, do answer* respondo respondes responde respondemos respondéis responden	*I live, am living, do live* vivo vives vive vivimos vivis viven
IMPERFECT INDICATIVE	*I was earning, used to earn, earned* ganaba ganabas ganaba ganábamos ganabais ganaban	*I was answering, used to answer, answered* respondía respondías respondía respondíamos respondíais respondían	*I was living, used to live, lived* vivía vivías vivía vivíamos vivíais vivían
PRETERITE INDICATIVE	*I earned, did earn* gané ganaste ganó ganamos ganasteis ganaron	*I answered, did answer* respondí respondiste respondió respondimos respondisteis respondieron	*I lived, did live* viví viviste vivió vivimos vivisteis vivieron

	First Conjugation	Second Conjugation	Third Conjugation
FUTURE INDICATIVE	*I shall earn, I will earn* ganaré ganarás ganará ganaremos ganaréis ganarán	*I shall answer, I will answer* responderé responderás responderá responderemos responderéis responderán	*I shall live, I will live* viviré vivirás vivirá viviremos viviréis vivirán
CONDITIONAL INDICATIVE	*I should earn, I would earn* ganaría ganarías ganaría ganaríamos ganaríais ganarían	*I should answer, I would answer* respondería responderías respondería responderíamos responderíais responderían	*I should live, I would live* viviría vivirías viviría viviríamos viviríais vivirían
PRESENT PERFECT INDICATIVE	*I have earned* he ganado has ganado ha ganado hemos ganado habéis ganado han ganado	*I have answered* he respondido has respondido ha respondido hemos respondido habéis respondido han respondido	*I have lived* he vivido has vivido ha vivido hemos vivido habéis vivido han vivido
PAST PERFECT INDICATIVE	*I had earned* había ganado habías ganado había ganado habíamos ganado habíais ganado habían ganado	*I had answered* había respondido habías respondido había respondido habíamos respondido habíais respondido habían respondido	*I had lived* había vivido habías vivido había vivido habíamos vivido habíais vivido habían vivido
FUTURE PERFECT INDICATIVE	*I shall have earned* habré ganado habrás ganado habrá ganado habremos ganado habréis ganado habrán ganado	*I shall have answered* habré respondido habrás respondido habrá respondido habremos respondido habréis respondido habrán respondido	*I shall have lived* habré vivido habrás vivido habrá vivido habremos vivido habréis vivido habrán vivido

	First Conjugation	Second Conjugation	Third Conjugation
CONDITIONAL PERFECT INDICATIVE	*I should have earned* habría ganado habrías ganado habría ganado habríamos ganado habríais ganado habrían ganado	*I should have answered* habría respondido habrías respondido habría respondido habríamos respondido habríais respondido habrían respondido	*I should have lived* habría vivido habrías vivido habría vivido habríamos vivido habríais vivido habrían vivido
	SUBJUNCTIVE MOOD		
PRESENT SUBJUNCTIVE	*(that) I (may) earn* (que) gane ganes gane ganemos ganéis ganen	*(that) I (may) answer* (que) responda respondas responda respondamos respondáis respondan	*(that) I (may) live* (que) viva vivas viva vivamos viváis vivan
PAST SUBJUNCTIVE (*-se* form)	*(that) I (might) earn* (que) ganase ganases ganase ganásemos ganaseis ganasen	*(that) I (might) answer* (que) respondiese respondieses respondiese respondiésemos respondieseis respondiesen	*(that) I (might) live* (que) viviese vivieses viviese viviésemos vivieseis viviesen
PAST SUBJUNCTIVE (*-ra* form)	ganara ganaras ganara ganáramos ganarais ganaran	respondiera respondieras respondiera respondiéramos respondierais respondieran	viviera vivieras viviera viviéramos vivierais vivieran
FUTURE SUBJUNCTIVE (*rare*)	ganare ganares ganare ganáremos ganareis ganaren	respondiere respondieres respondiere respondiéremos respondiereis respondieren	viviere vivieres viviere viviéremos viviereis vivieren

	First Conjugation	Second Conjugation	Third Conjugation
PRESENT PERFECT SUBJUNCTIVE	*(that) I (may) have earned* haya ganado hayas ganado haya ganado hayamos ganado hayáis ganado hayan ganado	*(that) I (may) have answered* haya respondido hayas respondido haya respondido hayamos respondido hayáis respondido hayan respondido	*(that) I (may) have lived* haya vivido hayas vivido haya vivido hayamos vivido hayáis vivido hayan vivido
PAST PERFECT SUBJUNCTIVE	*(that) I (might) have earned* hubiera (-se) ganado hubieras ganado hubiera ganado hubiéramos ganado hubierais ganado hubieran ganado	*(that) I (might) have answered* hubiera (-se) respondido hubieras respondido hubiera respondido hubiéramos respondido hubierais respondido hubieran respondido	*(that) I (might) have lived* hubiera (-se) vivido hubieras vivido hubiera vivido hubiéramos vivido hubierais vivido hubieran vivido
IMPERATIVE MOOD (*Familiar Commands*)			
AFFIRMATIVE	*earn!* gana tú ganad vosotros	*answer!* responde tú responded vosotros	*live!* vive tú vivid vosotros
NEGATIVE	*don't earn!* no ganes (tú) no ganéis (vosotros)	*don't answer!* no respondas (tú) no respondáis	*don't live!* no vivas (tú) no viváis
SUBJUNCTIVE IMPERATIVE			
POLITE COMMANDS	*earn!* gane Vd. ganen Vds.	*answer!* responda Vd. respondan Vds.	*live!* viva Vd. vivan Vds.

Irregular Verbs

Note: Only the irregular forms are given here; those not given are regular. (The future subjunctive is not included.)

63. **andar** *to walk*
PRETERITE: anduve, anduviste, anduvo; anduvimos, anduvisteis, anduvieron
PAST SUBJUNCTIVE: anduviera (-se), anduvieras, anduviera; anduviéramos, anduvierais, anduvieran

64. **caer** *to fall*
GERUND: cayendo
PAST PARTICIPLE: caído
PRESENT: caigo, caes, cae; caemos, caéis, caen
PRETERITE: caí, caíste, cayó; caímos, caísteis, cayeron
PRESENT SUBJUNCTIVE: caiga, caigas, caiga; caigamos, caigáis, caigan
PAST SUBJUNCTIVE: cayera (-se), cayeras, cayera; cayéramos, cayerais, cayeran
POLITE COMMANDS: caiga Vd., caigan Vds.

65. **dar** *to give*
PRESENT: doy, das, da; damos, dais, dan
PRETERITE: dí, diste, dió; dimos, disteis, dieron
PRESENT SUBJUNCTIVE: dé, des, dé; demos, deis, den
PAST SUBJUNCTIVE: diera (-se), dieras, diera; diéramos, dierais, dieran
POLITE COMMANDS: dé Vd., den Vds.

66. **decir** *to tell, to say*
GERUND: diciendo
PAST PARTICIPLE: dicho
PRESENT: digo, dices, dice; decimos, decís, dicen
PRETERITE: dije, dijiste, dijo; dijimos, dijisteis, dijeron
FUTURE: diré, dirás, dirá; diremos, diréis, dirán
CONDITIONAL: diría, dirías, diría; diríamos, diríais, dirían
PRESENT SUBJUNCTIVE: diga, digas, diga; digamos, digáis, digan
PAST SUBJUNCTIVE: dijera (-se), dijeras, dijera; dijéramos, dijerais, dijeran
FAMILIAR COMMANDS: di tú
POLITE COMMANDS: diga Vd., digan Vds.

67. **estar** *to be*
PRESENT: estoy, estás, está; estamos, estáis, están
PRETERITE: estuve, estuviste, estuvo; estuvimos, estuvisteis, estuvieron
PRESENT SUBJUNCTIVE: esté, estés, esté; estemos, estéis, estén
PAST SUBJUNCTIVE: estuviera (-se), estuvieras, estuviera; estuviéramos, estuvierais, estuvieran
POLITE COMMANDS: esté Vd., estén Vds.

68. **haber** *to have* (auxiliary verb)
PRESENT: he, has, ha; hemos, habéis, han

PRETERITE: hube, hubiste, hubo; hubimos, hubisteis, hubieron
FUTURE: habré, habrás, habrá; habremos, habréis, habrán
CONDITIONAL: habría, habrías, habría; habríamos, habríais, habrían
PRESENT SUBJUNCTIVE: haya, hayas, haya; hayamos, hayáis, hayan
PAST SUBJUNCTIVE: hubiera (-se), hubieras, hubiera; hubiéramos, hubierais, hubieran

69. **hacer** *to do, to make*
PAST PARTICIPLE: hecho
PRESENT: hago, haces, hace; hacemos, hacéis, hacen
PRETERITE: hice, hiciste, hizo; hicimos, hicisteis, hicieron
FUTURE: haré, harás, hará; haremos, haréis, harán
CONDITIONAL: haría, harías, haría; haríamos, haríais, harían
PRESENT SUBJUNCTIVE: haga, hagas, haga; hagamos, hagáis, hagan
PAST SUBJUNCTIVE: hiciera (-se), hicieras, hiciera; hiciéramos, hicierais, hicieran
FAMILIAR COMMAND: haz tú
POLITE COMMANDS: haga Vd., hagan Vds.

70. **ir** *to go*
GERUND: yendo
PRESENT: voy, vas, va; vamos, vais, van
IMPERFECT: iba, ibas, iba; íbamos, ibais, iban
PRETERITE: fuí, fuiste, fué; fuimos, fuisteis, fueron
PRESENT SUBJUNCTIVE: vaya, vayas, vaya; vayamos, vayáis, vayan
PAST SUBJUNCTIVE: fuera (-se), fueras, fuera; fuéramos, fuerais, fueran
FAMILIAR COMMAND: ve tú
POLITE COMMANDS: vaya Vd., vayan Vds.

71. **oír** *to hear*
GERUND: oyendo
PAST PARTICIPLE: oído
PRESENT: oigo, oyes, oye; oímos, oís, oyen
PRETERITE: oí, oíste, oyó; oímos, oísteis, oyeron
PRESENT SUBJUNCTIVE: oiga, oigas, oiga; oigamos, oigáis, oigan
PAST SUBJUNCTIVE: oyera (-se), oyeras, oyera; oyéramos, oyerais, oyeran
POLITE COMMANDS: oiga Vd., oigan Vds.

72. **poder (ue, u)** *to be able, can*
GERUND: pudiendo
PRESENT: puedo, puedes, puede; podemos, podéis, pueden
PRETERITE: pude, pudiste, pudo; pudimos, pudisteis, pudieron
FUTURE: podré, podrás, podrá; podremos, podréis, podrán
CONDITIONAL: podría, podrías, podría; podríamos, podríais, podrían
PAST SUBJUNCTIVE: pudiera (-se), pudieras, pudiera; pudiéramos, pudierais, pudieran

73. **poner** *to put, to place*
PAST PARTICIPLE: puesto

PRESENT: pongo, pones, pone; ponemos, ponéis, ponen
PRETERITE: puse, pusiste, puso; pusimos, pusisteis, pusieron
FUTURE: pondré, pondrás, pondrá; pondremos, pondréis, pondrán
CONDITIONAL: pondría, pondrías, pondría; pondríamos, pondríais, pondrían
PRESENT SUBJUNCTIVE: ponga, pongas, ponga; pongamos, pongáis, pongan
PAST SUBJUNCTIVE: pusiera (-se), pusieras, pusiera; pusiéramos, pusierais, pusieran
FAMILIAR COMMAND: pon tú
POLITE COMMANDS: ponga Vd., pongan Vds.

74. **querer** (ie) *to wish, to want; to love* (with **a**)
PRESENT: quiero, quieres, quiere; queremos, queréis, quieren
PRETERITE: quise, quisiste, quiso; quisimos, quisisteis, quisieron
FUTURE: querré, querrás, querrá; querremos, querréis, querrán
CONDITIONAL: querría, querrías, querría; querríamos, querríais, querrían
PAST SUBJUNCTIVE: quisiera (-se), quisieras, quisiera; quisiéramos, quisierais, quisieran
POLITE COMMANDS: quiera Vd., quieran Vds.

75. **reír** (i) *to laugh*
GERUND: riendo
PAST PARTICIPLE: reído
PRESENT: río, ríes, ríe; reímos, reís, ríen
PRETERITE: reí, reíste, rió; reímos, reísteis, rieron
PRESENT SUBJUNCTIVE: ría, rías, ría; riamos, riais, rían
PAST SUBJUNCTIVE: riera (-se), rieras, riera; riéramos, rierais, rieran
POLITE COMMANDS: ría Vd., rían Vds.

76. **saber** *to know, to know how to*
PRESENT: sé, sabes, sabe; sabemos, sabéis, saben
PRETERITE: supe, supiste, supo; supimos, supisteis, supieron
FUTURE: sabré, sabrás, sabrá; sabremos, sabréis, sabrán
CONDITIONAL: sabría, sabrías, sabría; sabríamos, sabríais, sabrían
PRESENT SUBJUNCTIVE: sepa, sepas, sepa; sepamos, sepáis, sepan
PAST SUBJUNCTIVE: supiera (-se), supieras, supiera; supiéramos, supierais, supieran

77. **salir** *to leave, to go out*
PRESENT: salgo, sales, sale; salimos, salís, salen
FUTURE: saldré, saldrás, saldrá; saldremos, saldréis, saldrán
CONDITIONAL: saldría, saldrías, saldría; saldríamos, saldríais, saldrían
PRESENT SUBJUNCTIVE: salga, salgas, salga; salgamos, salgáis, salgan
FAMILIAR COMMAND: sal tú
POLITE COMMANDS: salga Vd., salgan Vds.

78. **seguir (i)** *to follow, to continue*
GERUND: siguiendo
PRESENT: sigo, sigues, sigue; seguimos, seguís, siguen
PRETERITE: seguí, seguiste, siguió; seguimos, seguisteis, siguieron
PRESENT SUBJUNCTIVE: siga, sigas, siga; sigamos, sigáis, sigan
PAST SUBJUNCTIVE: siguiera (-se), siguieras, siguiera; siguiéramos, siguierais, siguieran
POLITE COMMANDS: siga Vd., sigan Vds.

79. **ser** *to be*
PRESENT: soy, eres, es; somos, sois, son
IMPERFECT: era, eras, era; éramos, erais, eran
PRETERITE: fuí, fuiste, fué; fuimos, fuisteis, fueron
PRESENT SUBJUNCTIVE: sea, seas, sea; seamos, seáis, sean
PAST SUBJUNCTIVE: fuera (-se), fueras, fuera; fuéramos, fuerais, fueran
FAMILIAR COMMAND: sé tú
POLITE COMMANDS: sea Vd., sean Vds.

80. **tener** *to have*
PRESENT: tengo, tienes, tiene; tenemos, tenéis, tienen
PRETERITE: tuve, tuviste, tuvo; tuvimos, tuvisteis, tuvieron
FUTURE: tendré, tendrás, tendrá; tendremos, tendréis, tendrán
CONDITIONAL: tendría, tendrías, tendría; tendríamos, tendríais, tendrían
PRESENT SUBJUNCTIVE: tenga, tengas, tenga; tengamos, tengáis, tengan
PAST SUBJUNCTIVE: tuviera (-se), tuvieras, tuviera; tuviéramos, tuvierais, tuvieran
FAMILIAR COMMAND: ten tú
POLITE COMMANDS: tenga Vd., tengan Vds.

81. **traducir** *to translate*
PRESENT: traduzco, traduces, traduce; traducimos, traducís, traducen
PRETERITE: traduje, tradujiste, tradujo; tradujimos, tradujisteis, tradujeron
PRESENT SUBJUNCTIVE: traduzca, traduzcas, traduzca; traduzcamos, traduzcáis, traduzcan
PAST SUBJUNCTIVE: tradujera (-se), tradujeras, tradujera; tradujéramos, tradujerais, tradujeran
POLITE COMMANDS: traduzca Vd., traduzcan Vds.

82. **traer** *to bring, to carry*
GERUND: trayendo
PAST PARTICIPLE: traído
PRESENT: traigo, traes, trae; traemos, traéis, traen
PRETERITE: traje, trajiste, trajo; trajimos, trajisteis, trajeron
PRESENT SUBJUNCTIVE: traiga, traigas, traiga; traigamos, traigáis, traigan
PAST SUBJUNCTIVE: trajera (-se), trajeras, trajera; trajéramos, trajerais, trajeran
POLITE COMMANDS: traiga Vd., traigan Vds.

83. **valer** *to be worth*

PRESENT: valgo, vales, vale; valemos, valéis, valen

FUTURE: valdré, valdrás, valdrá; valdremos, valdréis, valdrán

CONDITIONAL: valdría, valdrías, valdría; valdríamos, valdríais, valdrían

PRESENT SUBJUNCTIVE: valga, valgas, valga; valgamos, valgáis, valgan

FAMILIAR COMMAND: val tú

POLITE COMMANDS: valga Vd., valgan Vds.

84. **venir** *to come*

GERUND: viniendo

PRESENT: vengo, vienes, viene; venimos, venís, vienen

PRETERITE: vine, viniste, vino; vinimos, vinisteis, vinieron

FUTURE: vendré, vendrás, vendrá; vendremos, vendréis, vendrán

CONDITIONAL: vendría, vendrías, vendría; vendríamos, vendríais, vendrían

PRESENT SUBJUNCTIVE: venga, vengas, venga; vengamos, vengáis, vengan

PAST SUBJUNCTIVE: viniera (-se), vinieras, viniera; viniéramos, vinierais, vinieran

FAMILIAR COMMAND: ven tú

POLITE COMMANDS: venga Vd., vengan Vds.

85. **ver** *to see*

PAST PARTICIPLE: visto

PRESENT: veo, ves, ve; vemos, veis, ven

IMPERFECT: veía, veías, veía; veíamos, veíais, veían

PRESENT SUBJUNCTIVE: vea, veas, vea; veamos, veáis, vean

POLITE COMMANDS: vea Vd., vean Vds.

86. **Radical-Changing Verbs of the First or Second Conjugation with o>ue Change**

contar (ue) *to count*

PRESENT: cuento, cuentas, cuenta; contamos, contáis, cuentan

POLITE COMMANDS: cuente Vd., cuenten Vds.

87. **Radical-Changing Verbs of the First or Second Conjugation with e>ie Change**

perder (ie) *to lose*

PRESENT: pierdo, pierdes, pierde; perdemos, perdéis, pierden

POLITE COMMANDS: pierda Vd., pierdan Vds.

88. **Radical-Changing Verbs of the Third Conjugation with e>i Change**

pedir (i) *to ask for*

GERUND: pidiendo

PRESENT: pido, pides, pide; pedimos, pedís, piden

PRETERITE: pedí, pediste, pidió; pedimos, pedisteis, pidieron

PRESENT SUBJUNCTIVE: pida, pidas, pida; pidamos, pidáis, pidan

PAST SUBJ.: pidiera (-se), pidieras, pidiera; pidiéramos, pidierais, pidieran

POLITE COMMANDS: pida Vd., pidan Vds.

89. Radical-Changing Verbs of the Third Conjugation with o>ue and o>u Changes

dormir (ue, u) *to sleep*
GERUND: durmiendo
PRESENT: duermo, duermes, duerme; dormimos, dormís, duermen
PRETERITE: dormí, dormiste, durmió; dormimos, dormisteis, durmieron
PRES. SUBJ.: duerma, duermas, duerma; durmamos, durmáis, duerman
PAST SUBJUNCTIVE: durmiera (-se), etc.
POLITE COMMANDS: duerma Vd., duerman Vds.

90. Radical-Changing Verbs of the Third Conjugation with e>ie and e>i Changes

sentir (ie, i) *to feel*
GERUND: sintiendo
PRESENT: siento, sientes, siente; sentimos, sentís, sienten
PRETERITE: sentí, sentiste, sintió; sentimos, sentisteis, sintieron
PRES. SUBJ.: sienta, sientas, sienta; sintamos, sintáis, sientan
PAST SUBJUNCTIVE: sintiera (-se), etc.
POLITE COMMANDS: sienta Vd., sientan Vds.

91. Orthographical-Changing Verbs Ending in -gar

pagar *to pay*
PRETERITE: pagué, pagaste, pagó; pagamos, pagasteis, pagaron
PRESENT SUBJUNCTIVE: pague, pagues, pague; paguemos, paguéis, paguen
POLITE COMMANDS: pague Vd., paguen Vds.

92. Orthographical-Changing Verbs Ending in -car

tocar *to play*
PRETERITE: toqué, tocaste, tocó; tocamos, tocasteis, tocaron
PRESENT SUBJUNCTIVE: toque, toques, toque; toquemos, toquéis, toquen
POLITE COMMANDS: toque Vd., toquen Vds.

93. Orthographical-Changing Verbs Ending in -ger or -gir

coger *to take hold of, to pick up*
PRESENT: cojo, coges, coge; cogemos, cogéis, cogen
PRESENT SUBJUNCTIVE: coja, cojas, coja; cojamos, cojáis, cojan
POLITE COMMANDS: coja Vd., cojan Vds.

94. Orthographical-Changing Verbs Ending in -zar

cruzar *to cross*
PRETERITE: crucé, cruzaste, cruzó; cruzamos, cruzasteis, cruzaron
PRESENT SUBJUNCTIVE: cruce, cruces, cruce; crucemos, crucéis, crucen
POLITE COMMANDS: cruce Vd., crucen Vds.

95. Verbs Ending in -cer or -cir preceded by a vowel (Inceptive)

conocer *to know*
PRESENT: conozco, conoces, conoce; conocemos, conocéis, conocen
PRESENT SUBJUNCTIVE: conozca, conozcas, conozca; conozcamos, conozcáis, conozcan
POLITE COMMANDS: conozca Vd., conozcan Vds.

96. Verbs with Irregular Past Participles

abrir	abierto	hacer	hecho
componer	compuesto	imprimir	impreso
cubrir	cubierto	morir	muerto
decir	dicho	poner	puesto
describir	descrito	resolver	resuelto
descubrir	descubierto	romper	roto
devolver	devuelto	satisfacer	satisfecho
envolver	envuelto	ver	visto
escribir	escrito	volver	vuelto

97. Second and Third Conjugation Verbs with the Stem Ending in a Vowel

leer *to read* (**huir**, *to flee*; PRESENT: huyo)

GERUND: leyendo

PAST PARTICIPLE: leído [1]

PRETERITE: leí, leíste,[1] leyó; leímos,[1] leísteis,[1] leyeron

PAST SUBJUNCTIVE: leyera (-se), leyeras, leyera; leyéramos, leyerais, leyeran

98. Verbs Requiring a Preposition [2]

acabar de, to have just
acercarse a, to approach
acordarse de, to remember
acostumbrarse a, to become accustomed to
alegrarse de, to be glad to
alejarse de, to go (farther) away
aprender a, to learn to
atreverse a, to dare to
burlarse de, to make fun of
cargar de, to load with
casarse con, to marry
cesar de, to cease
comenzar a, to commence
convenir en, to agree upon
decidirse a *or* —, to decide to
dejar de, to stop
depender de, to depend on
despedirse de, to say good-by to
dirigirse a, to go to
empezar a, to begin to
enamorarse de, to fall in love with
enseñar a, to teach, show
entrar en, to enter
fijarse en, to pay attention to
haber de, to be to
insistir en, to insist on
ir a, to go to
jugar a, to play
libertar a, to liberate
llegar a, to succeed in
llenar de, to fill with
ocuparse de, to attend to
olvidarse de, to forget
parecerse a, to resemble
pasar con, to happen to
pensar en, to think about
reírse de, to laugh at
rodear de, to surround with
salir de, to leave
soñar con, to dream of
suceder con, to happen to
tardar en, to delay in
tratar de, to try to
venir a, to come to
volver a, to —— again

[1] **-uir** verbs do not need the written accent on this form.

[2] Before an object or a dependent infinitive. This list includes only verbs used in this book.

Grammar Appendix

99. Formula for Making Polite Commands

Take the first person singular of the present tense if it ends in *-o*, remove the *-o*, add the "opposite vowel" and *usted*: ***comprar: compro: compre Vd.*** (The "opposite vowel" for *-ar* verbs is *-e*; for *-er* and *-ir* verbs, *-a*.)

100. Numerals

1 uno	8 ocho	15 quince
2 dos	9 nueve	16 diez y seis
3 tres	10 diez	17 diez y siete
4 cuatro	11 once	18 diez y ocho
5 cinco	12 doce	19 diez y nueve
6 seis	13 trece	20 veinte
7 siete	14 catorce	21 veinte y uno (-a)

30 treinta	80 ochenta
40 cuarenta	90 noventa
50 cincuenta	100 ciento, cien
60 sesenta	101 ciento uno (-a)
70 setenta	120 ciento veinte

200 doscientos (-as)	800 ochocientos
300 trescientos	900 novecientos
400 cuatrocientos	1000 mil
500 quinientos	1500 mil quinientos
600 seiscientos	2000 dos mil
700 setecientos	1.000.000 un millón (de)

1st primero	6th sexto
2nd segundo	7th séptimo
3rd tercero	8th octavo
4th cuarto	9th noveno
5th quinto	10th décimo

The numbers 2 to 100 do not agree with their nouns (except 21, 31, etc.). *Ciento* becomes *cien* before a noun or *mil*: ***cien caballos, cien mil personas.***

The numbers 200–900 agree with their nouns.

Mil **must never have the article, and does not change for gender:**

mil personas, *one thousand persons.* When plural, it requires *de* before the noun: ***miles de personas,*** *thousands of persons.*

Un millón always takes *de* before a noun: ***un millón de personas.***

The decimal point (9.5) is a comma in Spanish: 9,5; the comma (5,000) is a period in Spanish: 5.000.

101. Days, Months, and Dates

Los días: *domingo, lunes, martes, miércoles, jueves, viernes, sábado.* All are masculine. ***El*** or ***los*** with a day of the week means *on*: ***el lunes,*** *on Monday*; ***los lunes,*** *on Mondays.*

Los meses: *enero, febrero, marzo, abril, mayo, junio, julio, agosto, septiembre, octubre, noviembre, diciembre.*

In giving dates, the day must precede the month, and is usually used with the article except in letters or diaries: ***el cuatro de julio,*** *July fourth.*

Cardinal numerals (two, three, four) are used except for *first*, when **primero** is used: ***el primero (el dos) de enero,*** *January first (second).*

102. Telling Time

The verb *ser*, with *la* or *las* and a number, is used for telling time: ***es la una; son las dos.***

Minutes up to 30 *after* the hour are expressed by *y*: ***son las tres y veinte,*** *it is 3:20.*

Half-past is ***y media.***

Minutes *before* the next hour are expressed by the hour toward which the small hand is moving, and *menos:* ***son las tres menos quince,*** *it is 2:45 (three minus fifteen).*

A.M. and P.M. are expressed by ***de la mañana, de la tarde (noche).***

103. Agreement of Adjectives

Adjectives must agree with their nouns (expressed or understood) in gender and number: ***el libro negro, la pluma roja.***

An adjective which modifies two masculine nouns must be masculine plural: ***el libro y el papel blancos.***

An adjective which modifies two feminine nouns must be feminine plural: ***la pluma y la bandera amarillas.***

An adjective which modifies several nouns must be masculine plural if any *one* of them is masculine: ***el papel, la mesa, la pluma, y la bandera blancos.***

104. Position of Adjectives

Descriptive adjectives usually follow their nouns: ***la casa grande.*** Numbers, limiting adjectives (*mucho, poco*), possessive and demonstrative adjectives, precede their nouns: ***cuatro niños, mucho dinero, mi casa, este libro.***

Two adjectives often follow their noun and are connected with *y*: ***el hombre rico y bueno.***

Some adjectives have different meanings according to their position: ***el muchacho pobre,*** *the poor* (*not rich*) *boy;* ***el pobre muchacho,*** *the poor* (*to be pitied*) *boy.*

105. Shortened (apocopated) Adjectives

Seven common adjectives drop the final ***-o*** when they stand before a masculine singular noun: ***uno, primero, tercero, bueno, malo, alguno, ninguno.*** (*Alguno* and *ninguno* become *algún* and *ningún.*)

Grande becomes *gran* when it stands before any noun, and the meaning of ***gran*** then changes to *great*: ***un hombre grande,*** *a large man*; ***un gran hombre,*** *a great man.*

Ciento becomes *cien* before any noun or *mil* (§ 100).

106. Subject Pronouns

yo	I	**nosotros**	we
tú	thou	**vosotros**	you (*fam.*)
Vd.	you (*pol.*)	**Vds.**	you (*pol.*)
él	he	**ellos**	they (*m.*)
ella	she	**ellas**	they (*f.*)

Subject pronouns are usually necessary only for clearness or emphasis, and are omitted whenever possible.

107. Reflexive Pronouns

me	myself	**nos**	ourselves
te	thyself	**os**	yourselves (*fam.*)
se	himself, herself, yourself, itself	**se**	themselves, yourselves (*pol.*)

Reflexive pronouns must be used with a verb when its infinitive ends in *-se*: ***sentarse: me siento, te sientas,*** etc.

Many verbs change in meaning when they are made reflexive (Ch. 4): ***ir,*** *to go*; ***irse,*** *to go away.*

The plural of the reflexive pronouns often has a reciprocal

meaning: ***nos vemos,*** *we see each other;* ***Vds. se escriben,*** *you write to each other;* ***ellos se miran,*** *they look at one another.*

108. Direct Object Pronouns

me	me	**nos**	us
te	thee	**os**	you (*fam.*)
le	him; you (*pol.*)	**los**	them; you (***pol. m.***)
lo	it (*m.*)	**los**	them
la	her or it (*f.*); you (*pol.*)	**las**	them; you (*pol. f.*)

When ***le, la, los*** and ***las*** mean *you* (*pol.*), they are often explained by *a Vd.* or *a Vds.* for courtesy and clearness: *le veo a Vd., Juan.*

Lo is sometimes used instead of ***le*** meaning *him,* although in this text ***lo*** ordinarily means *it* and ***le*** means *him.*

109. Indirect Object Pronouns

me	to *or* for me	**nos**	to *or* for us
te	to *or* for thee	**os**	to *or* for you
le . . . a Vd.	to *or* for you	**les . . . a Vds.**	to *or* for you (*pol.*)
le . . . a él	to *or* for him	**les . . . a ellos**	to *or* for them
le . . . a ella	to *or* for her	**les . . . a ellas**	to *or* for them

All indirect object pronouns mean *to* or *for.* Since they do not change for gender, the explanations are often required for clearness. This double construction is used even when the indirect object is a noun: ***Le doy a Juan el libro.***

The double construction is extended to the direct object only for emphasis or contrast: ***Yo te veo a ti y tú me ves a mí.***

110. Position of Object Pronouns

All object pronouns — reflexive, direct, and indirect — precede a verb unless it is an infinitive, gerund, or affirmative command, then they follow it and are attached to it:

Me da el libro; quiere darme el libro; está dándome el libro; déme Vd. el libro; no me dé Vd. el libro (negative command).

Or one may say that object pronouns precede a conjugated verb or a negative command, and follow and are attached to all other verb forms.

When one object pronoun is attached to a gerund or an affirmative command, count the vowels, beginning at the end, and write an accent on the third one: ***dándome; cómprelo Vd.***
3 2 1 3 2 1

When you attach two object pronouns to a verb, keep the accent in the same place as before: ***dándomelo; cómpremelo Vd.***

One pronoun attached to an infinitive requires no accent; with two pronouns, accent the third vowel as before; ***darme; dármelo.***

111. Two Object Pronouns

When two object pronouns are used with the same verb, the indirect always precedes the direct: ***démelo Vd.,*** *give it to me.*

If one is a reflexive, it must precede the other.

If both object pronouns begin with *l*, the first one (the indirect) always changes to *se*: ***déselo Vd.,*** *give it to him* (*them*).

dé + le + lo = déselo; dé + les + lo = déselo

Thus *se* as a substitute form has six possible meanings, or all the combined meanings of *le* and *les*.

112. Prepositional Pronouns

(*para*) **mí**	(*for*) me	(*para*) **nosotros**	(*for*) us
(*para*) **ti**	(*for*) thee	(*para*) **vosotros**	(*for*) you
(*para*) **Vd.**	(*for*) you (*pol.*)	(*para*) **Vds.**	(*for*) you (*pol.*)
(*para*) **él**	(*for*) him, it (*m.*)	(*para*) **ellos**	(*for*) them (*m.*)
(*para*) **ella**	(*for*) her, it (*f.*)	(*para*) **ellas**	(*for*) them (*f.*)

Note that these pronouns have the same meanings as the direct object list (§ 108), but that they must be used with prepositions instead of with verbs.

With the preposition *con*, the first and second persons are *conmigo* and *contigo*, and the reflexive is *consigo.*

Note that in form these pronouns are identical with the subject pronoun list except for the first two: ***mí, ti.***

113. Possessive Adjectives, Short Forms

mi	my	**nuestro**	our
tu	thy	**vuestro**	your (*fam.*)
su . . . (de Vd.)	your	**su . . . (de Vds.)**	your (*pol.*)
su . . . (de él)	his	**su . . . (de ellos)**	their (*m.*)
su . . . (de ella)	her	**su . . . (de ellas)**	their (*f.*)

These possessive adjectives always precede their nouns: *mi libro.* Since *su* has six possible meanings, it is sometimes explained: ***su libro de Vd., your book.***

Note that it is better to replace *su* with the article when there is an explanatory phrase: ***el libro de Vd.,*** *your book.*

Note that the definite article often replaces the possessive adjective when used with articles of clothing being worn and with parts of the body: ***me pongo el sombrero,*** *I put on my hat.* However, the possessive adjective may still be used when it is the first word of the sentence, for the article would be ambiguous: ***su sombrero*** (not ***el sombrero***) ***es nuevo.***

114. Possessive Adjectives, Long Forms

mío		(of) mine	(my)	**nuestro**		ours	(our)
tuyo		thine	(thy)	**vuestro**		yours	(your)
suyo *or*	**de Vd.**	yours	(your)	**suyo** *or*	**de Vds.**	yours	(your)
	de él	his			**de ellos**	theirs	(their)
	de ella	hers	(her)		**de ellas**	theirs	(their)

The long forms follow their nouns or some form of *ser*: ***hijo mío*** (in direct address); ***el libro es mío.***

Since ***suyo*** has six possible meanings, it is often *replaced* by ***de Vd., de él,*** etc. Note that *both* ***suyo*** and its explanation cannot be used: ***el libro es suyo; el libro es de él.***

115. Possessive Pronouns

The long forms of the possessive adjectives (§ 114), preceded by the definite article, become pronouns: ***el mío está en la mesa; tengo el mío.***

Just remember that the article is always used with *mío*, etc., except when it follows its noun or *ser*: ***es mío; es un amigo mío.***

116. Demonstrative Adjectives

1. **este**	**(esta)**	this (*which I have*)
2. **ese**	**(esa)**	that (*which you have*)
3. **aquel**	**(aquella)**	that (*which someone else has*)
1. **estos**	**(estas)**	these (*which I have*)
2. **esos**	**(esas)**	those (*which you have*)
3. **aquellos**	**(aquellas)**	those (*which someone else has*)

Ese and ***aquel*** both mean *that,* but ***ese*** could be said to be a second person *that,* referring to that which *you* have: ***Vd. tiene ese libro;*** while ***aquel*** is a third person *that,* referring to that which *someone else* has: ***Juan tiene aquel libro.***

Aquel also means *that distant* or *over there*: ***¿Ve Vd. aquella casa?***

117. Demonstrative Pronouns

Adding an accent to a demonstrative adjective (*éste, ése, aquél*) changes it to a pronoun which stands alone: *tengo este libro; tengo* ***éste***. The meaning then is often *this one, that one* (singular only).

Éste often means *the latter*; ***aquél,*** *the former*.

The definite articles instead of the demonstrative pronouns are used when followed by *de* or *que*:

la de mi hermana, *that of my sister*
los que no ven, *those who do not see*
lo que quiere es fácil, *that which* (*what*) *he wants is easy*

118. Formation of Adverbs

To form an adverb from an adjective (*rich, richly*), change the final ***-o*** to ***-a*** and add ***-mente: rico: rica, ricamente.***

If the adjective does not end in ***-o,*** merely add ***-mente: triste: tristemente.***

119. Comparison of Adjectives

1. Regular

Regular adjectives are compared like the model:

POSITIVE	COMPARATIVE	SUPERLATIVE
nuevo	**más nuevo**	**el más nuevo**
new	*newer*	*newest*

The possessive adjective may take the place of the definite article in the superlative:

mi libro más nuevo, *my newest book*

After a superlative (*richest*) use ***de*** instead of ***en:***

la niña más rica de la escuela, *the richest girl in school*

In comparison, *than* is usually expressed by ***que:***

Vd. es más alto que yo, *you are taller than I.*

Before a number, *than* is expressed by ***de:***

Tiene más de diez, *he has more than ten.*

Comparison of equality is expressed by ***tan*** (*adj.*) ***como.***

Vd. es tan alto como yo, *you are as tall as I.*

2. Irregular

Two common adjectives are irregular:

bueno, good	**mejor,** better	**el mejor,** best
malo, bad	**peor,** worse	**el peor,** worst

(*Mejor* and *peor* often precede their nouns.)

Two common adjectives, *grande* and *pequeño,* may be compared either regularly or irregularly, but with a difference in meaning:

REGULAR: **grande, más grande, el más grande** (size)
pequeño, más pequeño, el más pequeño (size)

IRREGULAR: **grande, mayor** (*older*), **el mayor** (*oldest*)
pequeño, menor (*younger*), **el menor** (*youngest*)

120. Absolute Superlative

When there is no actual comparison, the superlative idea is expressed by attaching ***-ísimo*** (***-a***) to the adjective or by using ***muy*** with the positive form of the adjective:

¡Ay, qué hermosísima! *Oh, how very beautiful!*
Es una mujer muy hermosa. *She is a very beautiful woman.*

121. Comparison of Adverbs

Adverbs are compared like adjectives, except that the superlative is usually the same as the comparative:

pronto	**más pronto**	**más pronto**
soon	*sooner*	*soonest*

Four adverbs are compared irregularly:

mucho	**más**	**más**	**poco**	**menos**	**menos**
much	*more*	*most*	*little*	*less*	*least*
bien	**mejor**	**mejor**	**mal**	**peor**	**peor**
well	*better*	*best*	*badly*	*worse*	*worst*

122. Ser *and* Estar

Here is a simple outline of the principal uses of *ser* and *estar*:

SER:

1. Always used to tell *who* or *what*: ***Juan es alumno; es el libro.***
2. Used with an adjective to express a *permanent* (characteristic) condition: ***La casa es grande; la niña es bonita.***

ESTAR
1. Always used to tell *where*:
¿Dónde está? Aquí está.
2. Used with an adjective to express a *temporary* (accidental) condition: ***El agua está fría; el niño está enfermo.***

123. Other Uses of Ser

1. *Ser* is always used in telling time: ***es la una.***

2. *Ser* is used to express origin: ***es de España;*** to express ownership: ***es de Juan;*** to express material: ***es de papel.***

3. *Ser* is used with a past participle to form the true passive, which expresses action, not description: ***la puerta fué abierta por Juan.*** (See § 129.) The tense most often used for the passive is the preterite, which expresses action in the past: *la carta **fué** escrita por María.*

124. Other Uses of Estar

1. *Estar* is used with the gerund to form progressive tenses: ***está estudiando; estaba estudiando.***

2. *Estar* is used with a past participle for description, not action, to show a state or condition: ***la puerta está abierta.***

125. Uses of the Definite Article

The definite article is used:

1. Instead of the possessive adjective with articles of clothing and parts of the body. (§ 113)

2. With expressions of time modified by *pasado*, etc.:
la semana pasada, *last week* **el año próximo,** *next year*

3. With nouns whose meaning signifies "in general":
El dinero (money in general) **es el rey del mundo.**
Los hombres (men in general) **prefieren a las rubias** (blondes in general).

4. With a title, except when speaking to the person named:
El señor Núñez no está. *Mr. Núñez isn't here.*
Buenos días, Capitán García. *Good morning, Captain García.*

5. With the names of some countries:
la Argentina, el Brasil, el Canadá, el Ecuador, los Estados Unidos, el Paraguay, el Perú, el Uruguay, El Salvador

6. With the name of a language, except after *hablar*, *de*, or *en*:
El español es fácil. Hablo español. La clase de inglés es fácil. Escribe en francés.

126. Omission of the Indefinite Article

The indefinite article is usually omitted:

1. Before an unmodified noun after *ser*:

   es alumno *but* **es un buen alumno**

2. Before a noun in apposition:

   su amigo, famoso profesor inglés
   his friend, a famous English teacher

3. After a negative if the noun is not modified:

   no tiene lápiz; sin pluma; no quiere caballo

127. The Personal a

When the direct object of a verb is (a) a definite person, (b) a proper noun,[1] (c) a personified thing, (d) an intelligent animal, or (e) a pronoun referring to a person, it must be preceded by ***a:***

(*a, b*) **veo a Juan;** (*c*) **honra a su nación;** (*d*) **veo al caballo;** (*e*) **no veo a nadie.**

128. Uses of the Imperfect and Preterite

1. The preterite is used:
   (1.) For a single completed past action: ***Cerró la puerta.***
   (2.) Normally after *nunca*: ***Nunca le vió.***
   (3.) When the action of the verb or a condition is in any way limited by an expression of time: ***Estuvo enfermo dos años.*** This is sometimes called the "preterite of definite duration."
2. The imperfect is used:
   (1.) For description ("stage setting") in the past (often "was — ing"):

   el sol brillaba, *the sun was shining*

   (2.) For repeated or habitual past action (often "used to").
   (3.) Ordinarily with verbs such as believing, knowing, thinking, and wishing, which express a mental idea without definite duration:

   Sabía la lección, pero no podía escribirla.
   He knew the lesson, but he could not write it.

129. True Passive vs. Reflexive Substitute

The true passive (*ser* with the past participle) is generally used for

[1] If a geographical name is preceded by the definite article, the personal ***a*** is not used: *Visité la Habana.*

passive action when the subject is a person, or when the subject is not a person, if the agent is expressed:

> **Él indio fué visto por el conquistador.**
> *The Indian was seen by the conqueror.*
> **La carta fué escrita por la niña.**
> *The letter was written by the girl.*

The reflexive substitute for the passive is preferred, especially when not speaking of persons:

> **fué invitado,** *he was invited* (not **se invitó**)

130. Uses of the Subjunctive

The subjunctive is required in Spanish:

1. In commands:
   All polite commands, first person plural commands, and familiar commands when negative:

   hable Vd., hablemos, no hables (tú), no habléis (vosotros)

2. In noun clauses:
   (1.) After a verb of causing with a change of subject:

   Quiero que Vd. vaya, *I want you to go.*
   Exceptions: dejar, hacer, permitir, mandar

   (2.) After expressions of emotion with a change of subject:

   Espero que tenga razón, *I hope he is right.*

   (3.) After expressions of doubt with a change of subject:

   ¿Cree Vd. que haya tiempo? *Do you believe there is time?*

   (4.) After impersonal expressions:

   Es preciso que Juan vaya, *it is necessary for John to go.*

3. In adverbial clauses:
   (1.) After conjunctions expressing time:

   hasta que se haya ido, *until he has gone*

   (2.) After other conjunctions (*para que*, etc.)
   (3.) After other words (*como*, (*a*) *donde*), when the action in the future is indefinite
   (4.) After *si* when contrary-to-fact
   (5.) After *como si*

4. In adjective clauses:
   (1.) After an indefinite antecedent:

   Quiero un libro que sea nuevo, *I want a book that is new.*

   (2.) After a negative:

   No hay nadie que sepa, *there is no one who knows.*

   (3.) After *whatever, however, whoever*:

   Por bueno que sea, no lo quiero.
   However good it may be, I don't want it.

5. Other subjunctive uses:
   (1.) After *ojalá (que)*:

   Ojalá pudiera ir, *if only he could go.*

   (2.) In softened statements:

   Quisiéramos ir, *we should like to go.*

   (3.) After *perhaps* when future time is implied:

   Quizás pueda aprender a nadar.
   Perhaps he may be able to learn to swim.

131. Words Causing the Subjunctive

1. In noun clauses:[1]
   (1.) Verbs of causing:

   Most common: **querer, decir, pedir, desear**
   Less common: **aconsejar, preferir, rogar**
   Exceptions: **dejar, hacer, permitir, mandar**

   (2.) Expressions of emotion:

   esperar, ser lástima, temer, alegrarse de, sentir

   (3.) Expressions of doubt:

   no creer, ¿creer?, no estar seguro de

   (4.) Impersonal expressions:

   es posible, puede ser, es preciso, es mejor, es necesario, es probable, es importante, importar, convenir

2. In adverbial clauses:
   (1.) Conjunctions expressing time:

   cuando, antes que, mientras (que), hasta que, (a que), en cuanto

[1] Given in the order of their frequency.

(2.) Other conjunctions:

para que, aunque, sin que, a fin de que, de manera que, con tal (de) que

(3.) Other words (when the action in the future is indefinite):

como, (a) donde

(4.) *Si* (past tense only)

(5.) *Como si* (imaginative)

3. In adjective clauses:
   (1.) After any indefinite antecedent
   (2.) After any negative: *no, nada, nadie, ninguno*
   (3.) After *lo que, por — que, quienquiera*
4. Other subjunctive uses:
   (1.) After *ojalá*
   (2.) As in *quisiera* and *debiera*
   (3.) After *quizás, acaso, tal vez*

Pronunciation

132. Vowels

Spanish vowels are pronounced clearly and distinctly. They must not be prolonged as in English when we say *go-u* for *go* and *my-e* for *my*.

LETTER	NEAREST ENGLISH EQUIVALENT	SPANISH EXAMPLE	RULE
A	father, ah!	**casa**	Everywhere
E	1. they (but not *they-e*)	**ese**	In open syllables [1]
		cesta	In syllables closed by ***m, n, s, x***
	2. let	**lección**	In closed syllables unless closed by ***m, n, s, x***
		tierra	Next to trilled ***r***
		mejor	Before ***j, ge, gi***
		rey	In diphthongs ***ei, ey***
I [2]	see	**piso**	
O	1. tone	**todo**	In open syllables [1]
	2. or	**contar**	In closed syllables [1]
		rosa	Next to trilled ***r***
		ojo	Before ***j, ge, gi***
		hoy	In diphthongs ***oi, oy***
U [2]	rule	**puro**	
Y [3]	boy	**doy**	Alone or final

[1] An open syllable is one that ends in a vowel or diphthong; a closed syllable is one that ends in a consonant.

[2] *To the teacher:* The distinction between the two sounds of this letter is slight

133. Semi-Consonants

LETTER	NEAREST ENGLISH EQUIVALENT	SPANISH EXAMPLE	RULE
I	*you*	**bien**	Preceded by a consonant and followed by a vowel in the same syllable
U	*we*	**bueno** **hueso**	*u* or ***hu*** before a vowel in the same syllable

134. Diphthongs

I, y used as a vowel, and *u* are weak vowels; ***a, e, o*** are strong vowels. A diphthong is a combination of (1) a strong and a weak vowel or (2) two weak vowels. They form one syllable which is a combination of the individual sounds.

In a diphthong the strong vowel, regardless of position, or the second of two weak vowels gets the stress. A written accent breaks the diphthong.

Initial ***i*** and ***u*** in a diphthong are semi-consonants.

135. Consonants

LETTER	NEAREST ENGLISH EQUIVALENT	SPANISH EXAMPLE	RULE
B V	1. Weaker than in *boy*	**¡basta!** **¡vamos!** **un hombre** **un vaso**	When initial or after *m* or *n* in a breath group[4]
	2. None (lips not completely closed)	**Cuba** **uva**	All other times
	3. Silent	**obscuro** **substituir**	In these and a very few other words

and difficult for English-speaking pupils to master. It is suggested that only the closed sound be taught and imitation of the teacher be relied upon for the acquisition of the open sound.

[3] *Y* is a semi-consonant, that is, sometimes it is used as a vowel and sometimes as a consonant.

[4] See footnote on page 564.

LETTER	NEAREST ENGLISH EQUIVALENT	SPANISH EXAMPLE	RULE
C, QU	*cat*	cama quema	Takes the place of English *k* *u* is never pronounced after *q*
C(E) C(I) Z	1. *thin* 2. *sin*	veces cinco vez	1. Castilian (*th*) 2. Span. Amer. (*s*)
CH	*church*	techo	Everywhere
D	1. *din* (made against the teeth)	dar	Initial in a breath group [1]
		el día mundo	After *l* or *n* within or between words
	2. None. *d* + *th* made against the teeth. Somewhat like English *this*	padre	All other times and especially between vowels
	3. None	estado usted	Weak when final or in endings *-ado*, *-ido* (Often omitted in careless speech)
F	*fall*	fama	Like English
G	1. *go*	gana grande	Usually
	2. None	agua hago	Between vowels is pronounced very weakly
G(E) G(I) J	*Hey!*	gente jarro	Like a strong English *h* (Similar to German *ch*)
H	None	hasta ahora	Always silent

[1] We do not talk with single words, but with groups of words between slight pauses. For example, we do not say: The | cow | jumped | over | the | moon. We say: The-cow jumped-over the-moon. This grouping of words between slight pauses is called a breath group.

LETTER	NEAREST ENGLISH EQUIVALENT	SPANISH EXAMPLE	RULE
L	*let*	la alto	Tip of tongue to upper gums. Avoid raising back of tongue
LL	1. *William* 2. *you*	silla	1. Castilian (*ly*) 2. Span. Amer. (*y*)
M	*more*	más	Like English
N	1. *more*	invierno	Before *p*, *b*, *v*, *m*
	2. *no*	uno	All other times like Eng.
Ñ	*canyon, onion*	señor	Always
P	1. *push*	palo	Like English but without letting out as much air
	2. *pneumonia*	séptimo septiembre	Silent in a very few words
R	1. None	rosa	When initial it is trilled like *rr* with a rapid vibration of tongue against gums
	2. None	padre	Other times it has a slight trill
RR	None	perro	Trilled (two to five vibrations)
S	1. *rose*	mismo desde asno	Before some consonants such as *m*, *n*, *d*, *g*, *b*, *v*, *l*
	2. *sister*	sala, este	All other times
T	None	tinta patio	Tongue against inside of upper front teeth
X	1. *sir*	explicar	Before a consonant, pronounced *s*
	2. *examine*	examen	Before a vowel, pronounced like Eng. *gs*

LETTER	NEAREST ENGLISH EQUIVALENT	SPANISH EXAMPLE	RULE
Y	*you*	ayer	As a consonant, i.e., not alone or final
K W	Do not appear in Spanish words. Pronounce them as they should be pronounced in the foreign language from which they have been borrowed. Examples: Wáshington, Wágner, kilómetro.		

136. Syllabication

The formal rules for syllabication do not always conform to the way Spanish-speaking people actually divide words when speaking. The following are the rules for orthographic syllabication, that is, for the division of words when writing.

1. There are as many syllables as there are vowels and diphthongs in a word.

a ma ri llo	**au tor**	**pa gas teis**	**ca ca o**
1 2 3 4	1 2	1 2 3	1 2 3

2. A single consonant, *ch*, *ll*, or *rr* between two vowels begins a syllable.

pe-re-zo-so co-me-dor si-lla pi-za-rra mu-cha-cho

3. Two consonants are divided, one remaining and one going with the following syllable.

en-ten-der

4. A consonant plus *l* or *r* is inseparable (except *rl*, *sl*, *tl*, *sr*).

de-trás a-pli-ca-do (at-le-ta)

5. When there are three or more consonants, only the last or an inseparable combination begins a syllable.

sem-brar

6. Prefixes are kept intact regardless of the usual rules.

des-a-pa-re-cer

7. A diphthong is broken by a written accent.

ca-í-do re-ír

8. Weak vowels (*i*, *u*) followed by another vowel become semi-consonants and lose their syllabic value. To retain it they must have a written accent.

siem-pre **en-tien-de** **ha-cia** **ha-cí-a**

Phonetic syllabication: Within a breath group the final consonant of a word goes with the initial vowel or diphthong of the following word and forms a syllable with it. Prefixes are not kept intact.

de español	*des-pa-ñol*
con alegría	*co-na-le-grí-a*
en un año	*e-nu-na-ño*
mis amigos	*mi-sa-mi-gos*

137. Accentuation

1. Words that end in a vowel or *n* or *s* accent the next to the last syllable.

ameri*ca*no **extran*je*ro** ***jo*ven** ***co*sas**

2. Words that end in a consonant except *n* or *s* accent the last syllable.

gene*ral* **ver*dad*** **enten*der***

3. All exceptions have a written accent (′).

úl*timo** **in*glés **lec*ción***

4. The addition of a syllable sometimes causes the insertion or omission of a written accent to preserve the original stress.

lección, lecciones **joven, jóvenes** **dando, dándolo**

5. A written accent is used to distinguish words with similar spelling.

el, él; si, sí; se, sé

138. The Alphabet (*El alfabeto*)

SYMBOL	NAME	SYMBOL	NAME
a	a	n	ene
b	be	ñ	eñe
c	ce	o	o
ch	che	p	pe
d	de	q	cu
e	e	r	ere
f	efe	rr	erre
g	ge	s	ese
h	hache	t	te
i	i	u	u
j	jota	v	ve
k	ka	w	ve doble, doble uve
l	ele	x	equis
ll	elle	y	i griega
m	eme	z	zeta

English-Spanish Dictionary

Numbers following verbs refer to sections in the Appendix where they, or similar verbs, are conjugated. Radical-changing verbs have their present, preterite, and gerund change indicated: *dormir* (*ue, u*).

The gender of nouns ending in ***-o*** is masculine and that of nouns ending in ***-a, -ción,*** or ***-dad*** is feminine unless otherwise marked.

Abbreviations used in both English-Spanish and Spanish-English dictionaries:

abbr.	abbreviation	imperf.	imperfect
adj.	adjective	inf.	infinitive
adv.	adverb	m.	masculine
Arg.	Argentina	n.	noun
aux.	auxiliary	neg.	negative
com.	command	no.	number
cond.	conditional	pers.	person
conj.	conjugated	pl.	plural
dim.	diminutive	p.p.	past participle
exp.	expression	pres.	present
f.	feminine	pret.	preterite
fam.	familiar	subjv.	subjunctive
fut.	future	Urug.	Uruguay
ger.	gerund	w.	with

A

a un, una

about unos (*with a number*); acerca de

at about a eso de

to be about to estar para

accompany, to acompañar

according to según

account: on account of por

advice consejo (*often pl.*)

advise, to aconsejar

affection cariño

afraid: to be afraid of tener miedo de *80*; temer

after después (de); detrás de

afternoon tarde (*f.*)

in the afternoon por la tarde

again otra vez; volver a + *inf.*

never again jamás volver a; nunca más

against contra

age edad (*f.*)

ago hace

not long ago hace poco

ahead: to send on ahead mandar adelante

Albert Alberto

all todo

allow, to permitir, dejar

almost casi

alone solo

all alone solito

along por

already ya

although aunque

always siempre

A.M. de la mañana

ambassador embajador (*m.*)

American americano

among entre
amuse, to (oneself) divertir (se) (ie, i) *90*
and y
Andes Andes (*m.*)
angry: to become angry enojarse
animal animal (*m.*)
annoy, to molestar
another otro
  one another nos; se
answer, to responder, contestar
any ninguno; cualquier (*often omitted after a neg.*)
anyone (a) nadie; cualquier persona
anything nada
appetite apetito
applaud, to aplaudir
apple manzana
approach, to acercarse a *92*
April abril (*m.*)
are son; están; (Vd.) es
arm brazo
around alrededor de
arrange, to arreglar
arrive (at), to llegar (a) *91*
as como
  as if como si
  as much as tanto como
  as pretty as tan bonito como
  as soon as en cuanto (*w. subjv.*)
ask (for), to pedir (i) *88*
  to ask a question hacer una pregunta *69*, preguntar
at a (*telling time*); en
  at Anita's en casa de Anita
  at once en seguida
attend, to asistir (a)
aunt tía
automobile automóvil (*m.*)
away: to go away irse *70*
Aztec azteca (*invariable*)

B

bad malo
bank orilla
barber barbero
be, to ser; estar *79, 67*
  to be able to poder *72*
  to be about to estar para *67*
  to be afraid tener miedo *80*
  to be right tener razón *80*
  to be to haber de *68*
  to be to blame tener la culpa *80*
  to be willing querer *74*
beans frijoles (*m.*)
bear oso
beautiful hermoso
beauty belleza
because porque
become, to ponerse, hacerse *73, 69*
  to become angry enojarse
bed cama
before antes de; antes que
begin (to), to comenzar (ie) (a), empezar (ie) (a) *87*
behaved (well) (bien) educado
behind detrás de
believe, to creer *97*
  believe it or not aunque Vd. no lo crea; créase o no
belong, to pertenecer *95*
beneath bajo, debajo de
beside al lado de
best mejor
bet apuesta
better mejor
  to get better mejorar
between entre
bicycle bicicleta
big grande
bird pájaro, ave (el) (*f.*)
bite, to morder (ue) *86*
black negro
blame: to be to blame tener la culpa *80*
blind (man) ciego
blond rubio
blood sangre (*f.*)
blue azul

boatman canoero
body cuerpo
book libro
borrow, to pedir prestado *88*
boss patrón (*m.*)
both ambos
bother, to molestar
bottle botella
box caja
boy niño (*little*), muchacho
brave valiente
bread pan (*m.*)
break, to romper (se) *96*
bride novia
bridge puente (*m.*)
bring, to traer *82*
broken roto
brother hermano
  little brother hermanito
brown moreno
build, to construir *97*
built: to have built mandar construir
bury, to enterrar (ie) *87*
but pero; sino (*after neg.*)
buy, to comprar
by por, para; *sometimes expressed by the ger. alone*

C

call, to llamar; **be called** llamarse
can poder (ue) *72*
canal canal (*m.*)
candle vela
candy dulces (*m.*)
cantaloupe mélon (*m.*)
capital capital (*f.*)
captain capitán (*m.*)
car (*auto*) coche (*m.*); (*street*) tranvía (*m.*)
care for, to cuidar (de)
  I don't care no me importa
careful cuidadoso
  to be careful tener cuidado *80*
carefully cuidadosamente, con cuidado
carnation clavel (*m.*)
carry (away), to llevar (se)
Castilian castellano
cat gato
cave cueva
cent centavo
century siglo
certain (a) cierto
certainly ciertamente
  That certainly is it! ¡Eso sí que es!
chain cadena
chair silla
change, to cambiar, convertir (ie, i) *90*
chapel capilla
charming encantador
cheap barato
chicken pollo
chief jefe (*m.*)
child niño
children niños
choose, to escoger, elegir (i) *93*
Christ Cristo
Christmas Navidad
  Christmas Eve nochebuena
  Christmas tree árbol de Navidad
church iglesia
cistern cisterna
city ciudad
civilization civilización
class clase (*f.*)
clay barro
clean, to limpiar
climb, to (down) bajar; **(up)** subir
clock reloj (*m.*)
close, to cerrar (ie) *87*
clothes prendas, ropa
cloud nube (*f.*)
club club (*m.*)
coconut coco
Cocos Island la Isla del Coco
coffee café (*m.*)
cold frío

to be cold (*persons*) tener frío *80*
to be cold (*weather*) hacer frío *69*
come, to venir *84*
to come into entrar en
to come out salir *77*
to come out to meet salir a (su) encuentro *77*
to come to (*a place*) llegar a *91*
comfortable cómodo
command, to mandar
company compañía (*abbr.*) Cía
complain, to quejarse
conflict conflicto
conquer, to conquistar
conqueror conquistador (*m.*)
conquest conquista
consent, to consentir (ie, i) *90*
continue, to seguir (i) *78*
cook, to cocer (ue) *95*
cordially cordialmente
corn maíz (*m.*)
corner rincón (*m.*)
count, to contar (ue) *86*
country país (*m.*); (*native*) patria
course, of por supuesto
courteous cortés
courtesy cortesía
cover, to cubrir *96*
covered cubierto
cow vaca
crazy loco
credit: on credit al fiado
crop cosecha
cross, to cruzar *94*
cry grito
cry, to llorar
to cry out gritar
cure, to curar
curious curioso
the curious thing lo curioso
curtain cortina
custom costumbre (*f.*)
cut (down), to cortar
cute (little) -ito, -cito

D

daily diario
dance baile (*m.*)
dance, to bailar
danger peligro
dare (to), to atreverse **(a)**
dark obscuro
date fecha
day día (*m.*)
all day todo el día
by day de día
every day todos los días
good day buenos días
the next day al día siguiente
to this day hasta hoy, hasta la fecha
dead muerto
deaf sordo
deal: a great deal of mucho
death muerte (*f.*)
deceive, to engañar
decide, to decidir
deer venado
delicate delicado
deliver, to entregar *91*
deny, to negar (ie) *91*
desert desierto
desk mesa
destroy, to destruir *97*
die, to morir (ue, u) *89*
dine, to comer
disagreeable desagradable
disappear, to desaparecer *95*
discover, to descubrir *96*
distant lejano
do, to hacer *69*
doctor médico; doctor (*title*)
dog perro
dollar (*U.S.*) dólar (*m.*); peso; (*Sp.*) duro
don't *sign of neg. com.*
door puerta
double doble
down hill cuesta abajo
dozen docena

dream (of), to soñar (con)
dress vestido
drink, to beber
drive, to manejar
drop gota
drop, to dejar caer
drown, to ahogarse
dry seco
dry (up), to secar (se) *92*
dust polvo

E

each cada (*invariable*)
  each one cada uno
  each other nos; se
ear (*inner*) oído; (*outer*) oreja
  large ear orejón (*m.*)
early temprano
earn, to ganar
easy fácil
  easiest el más fácil
eat, to comer
  to eat up comerse
egg huevo
either tampoco
  either —— or o —— o
eleven once
else más
emblem emblema (*m.*)
embrace abrazo
embrace, to abrazar *94*
emerald esmeralda
Emperor emperador (*m.*)
empire imperio
end, to terminar
English inglés (*m.*)
enjoy oneself, to divertirse (ie, i) *90*
enough bastante
  to be enough bastar
enter, to entrar
envy, to envidiar
escape, to escaparse
especially sobre todo
even hasta
  even if aunque
evening: in the evening por la noche
every todo
  every day todos los días
everyone todo el mundo
everything (that) todo (lo que)
everywhere por (de) todas partes
exactly exactamente
exceedingly -ísimo
exchange, to cambiar
expression expresión
eye ojo

F

face cara
face, to dar a *65*
faithful fiel
fall, to caer *97*
  to fall down caerse *97*
  to fall in love with enamorarse de
family familia
far lejos
  far from lejos de
farmer campesino
farther más lejos
father padre
fear miedo
fear, to temer
feather pluma
feel, to sentir (ie, i) *90*
  to feel like tener ganas de *80*
feeling sentimiento
feet pies (*m.*); pata (*animal's*)
fellow hombre
  big fellow hombrón
  young fellow joven
few pocos
  a few unos cuantos
field campo
fifty cincuenta
fight, to combatir
fill (with), to llenar (de)

finally al (por) fin
find, to hallar
  to find oneself encontrarse (ue) *86*
  to find out saber *76*
fine bueno
finish, to terminar, acabar
fire lumbre (*f.*)
first primero
  at first al principio
fish pescado; pez (*m.*)
five cinco
  five hundred quinientos
  "the five and ten" tienda de cinco y diez
flee, to huir *97*
float, to flotar
flower flor (*f.*)
fly, to volar (ue) *86*
folks (young) los jóvenes
  my folks los míos
  your folks los suyos
follow, to seguir (i) *78*
following siguiente
food alimento, comida
foolish tonto
foot pie (*m.*)
football fútbol (*m.*)
for por, para (*47*); porque; hace; que
foreign, foreigner extranjero
forest bosque (*m.*)
forget, to olvidar
  to forget to olvidarse de
fortune fortuna
forty cuarenta
four cuatro
fourteen catorce
freight carga
French francés (*adj. or m. noun*)
frequently con frecuencia
fresh fresco
Friday viernes (*m.*)
friend amigo
friendship amistad (*f.*)
frightened asustado
from desde; de; a (*with dative of separation*)
  from —— to —— de —— en ——
fruit fruta (*often pl.*)
fulfill, to cumplir
fun: to make fun of burlarse de
furniture muebles (*m.*)

G

garden jardín (*m.*)
gardenia gardenia
general general
gentlemen caballeros, señores
George Jorge
get, to conseguir (i) *78*; recibir
  to get better mejorar
  to get dinner hacer la comida *69*
  to get married casarse
  to get rich hacerse rico *69*
  to get up levantarse
gift regalo
girl muchacha, niña, señorita
give, to dar *65*
glad: to be glad (of) alegrarse (de)
go, to ir; (*with no destination*) andar *70, 63*
  to go away irse *70*
  to go for a walk *or* **ride, go walking** dar un paseo *65*
  to go near acercarse a *92*
  to go out into salir a *77*
  to go to sleep dormirse (ue, u) *89*
  to go toward dirigirse a
god dios (*m.*)
goddess diosa
gold oro
golden de oro
good bueno
good-by: to say good-by to despedirse de (i) *88*
government gobierno
gradually cada vez más
grand gran (*before a noun*)
grandmother abuela

grandson nieto
grateful agradecido
great gran (*before a noun*)
  a great deal of mucho
ground suelo
group grupo
grow, to crecer *95*
grown-up, a un grande
guest invitado
guitar guitarra

H

had *imperfect tense of* haber *or* tener *68, 80*
half medio
hall salón (*m.*), hall (*m.*) (*Chile*)
hand mano (*f.*)
handsome guapo
happen, to pasar, suceder
happy contento
hard mucho
harder más difícil
hardly apenas
hat sombrero
have, to tener; haber *80, 68*
  to have a good time divertirse (ie, i) *90*
  to have just acabar de
  to have to tener que *80*
  what little he had lo poco que tenía
he él (*usually omitted*)
  he who el que, quien
head cabeza
headache dolor (*m.*) de cabeza
hear, to oír *97*
heart corazón (*m.*)
hello hola
help, to ayudar
her ella; su —— de ella; la
  to her le —— a ella, la
here aquí; acá (*with verb of motion*)
hers el de ella, suyo
hide, to esconder
high alto
  to be —— feet high tener —— pies de altura
highway camino, carretera, camino real
him, to him, from him le; él
himself se; mismo
his el suyo, (el) de él, su
history historia
home: to go home ir a casa *70*
  at home en casa
hope, to esperar
horse caballo
  race horse caballo de carrera
horseback (on) a caballo
  to ride horseback montar a caballo
hospitality hospitalidad
hot caliente
  to be hot tener calor (*persons*); hacer calor (*weather*) *80, 69*
hotel hotel (*m.*)
hour hora
house casa
how cómo
however por —— que
hundred (one) ciento, cien
hunger hambre (*f.*)
hungry hambriento
  to be hungry tener hambre (*f.*) *80*
hurt, to hacer daño a *69*

I

I yo
idea idea
if si
ill enfermo
immediately inmediatamente, en seguida
important importante
  very important importantísimo
  to be important to importar
impossible imposible
in en; de (*after a superlative*)
Inca, Incan inca (*m.*) (*invariable*)

Indian indio
innocent inocente
inside (of) dentro (de)
inspector inspector (*m.*)
instead of en vez de
intelligence inteligencia
intelligent inteligente
intend, to pensar (ie) *87*
into en
  to fall into caer a *97*
invite, to invitar
iron hierro
is es, está
  there is hay
island isla
it *as subject, omitted; as object* lo, la
  it is es, está
Italian italiano

J

jade jade (*m.*)
jewel joya, alhaja
Joe Pepe
John Juan
  John's (el) de Juan
Johnny Juanito
Joseph José
judge juez (*m.*)
jug olla
July julio
jump, to saltar
June junio

K

keep, to guardar
  one keeps on se va + *ger.*
  to keep —— ing ir + *ger.* *70*
  to keep (one's word) cumplir (la palabra)
kill, to matar
king rey
kiss, to besar
knife cuchillo
knock, to llamar
  to knock down echar abajo
know, to conocer (*people*); saber (*facts*) *95, 76*
  to know how to saber *76*

L

lack falta
lack, to faltar (*used like* gustar)
lady dama
  old lady vieja
lake lago
land tierra; país (*m.*)
large grande
largest el más grande
last último; pasado (*w. exp. of time*)
  at last al fin, por fin
last, to durar
later más tarde
latter éste
laugh, to reír *97, 88*
  to laugh at reírse de
lawyer abogado
lazy perezoso
learn (to), **to** aprender (a)
least: at least siquiera
leave, to salir (de) *77*; dejar
  to leave for salir para *77*
leg pierna
legend leyenda
lend, to prestar
less menos
lesson lección
let, to dejar
  to let oneself dejarse
let's *sign of first pers. com.*
  let's go vamos
letter carta
like como
like, to (*be pleasing to*) gustar
  to be like parecerse a *95*
  they would like quisieran
lip labio

listen, to escuchar; oír (*as a com.*) *71*
little pequeño; poco (*in quantity*)
little by little poco a poco
little old lady viejecita
live, to vivir
loan préstamo
loan, to prestar
lock, to cerrar con llave (ie) *87*
lonely solito
long largo; mucho tiempo
not long ago hace poco
to be long tardar mucho (*time*
very long larguísimo
longer: no longer ya no
look (at), to mirar
to look for buscar *92*
to look out tener cuidado *80*
lose, to perder (ie) *87*
loudly en voz alta
too loudly muy fuerte
Louis Luis
love amor (*m.*)
love, to amar, querer a *87*
to fall in love with enamorarse de
luck suerte (*f.*)

M

make, to hacer *69*
to make fun of burlarse de
to make use of hacer uso de *69*
make yourself at home ésta es su casa
man hombre
old man viejo
young man joven
many muchos
Margaret Margarita
marry, to casarse (con)
Mary María
master amo
matter, to importar
may poder (ue) *72*; *often the sign of the pres. subjv.*
Maya maya (*m.*) (*invariable*)
maybe quizás
me me, mí
to me me
with me conmigo
meal comida
meals asistencia
mean, to significar, querer decir
meat carne (*f.*)
meat pie empanada
medicine medicina
meet, to (*become acquainted with*) conocer *95*; encontrar; (*to gather, join*) reunirse
meeting . reunión, mitín (*m.*)
melon melón (*m.*)
metal metal (*m.*)
Mexican mexicano
Mexico México
midnight medianoche (*f.*)
at midnight a medianoche
might *often the sign of the past subjv.*
milk leche (*f.*)
million millón (*m.*)
mine mío, el mío, los míos
miner minero
minute minuto; *omitted when telling time*
miracle milagro
miraculous milagroso
misfortune desgracia
miss, to echar de menos
mistake error (*m.*)
to make a mistake equivocarse
modern moderno
"Mom" mamacita
moment: at that moment en ese momento
Monday lunes (*m.*)
money dinero
monkey mono
month mes (*m.*)
moon luna
it was moonlight había luna

more más
more than (*w. a no.*) más de
the more —— the more cuanto más —— más
morning mañana
all morning toda la mañana
good morning buenos días
tomorrow morning mañana por la mañana
most más
most of la mayor parte de
mother madre
mountain montaña
mouth boca
move, to mover (ue) *86*
movies cine (*m.*)
Mrs. (la) señora
much mucho
so much tanto
too much demasiado
music música
must deber, tener que *80*, haber de *68*
my mi, mío

N

name nombre (*m.*)
to be named llamarse
what is your name? ¿cómo se llama Vd.?
national nacional
native (country) patria
near cerca de, junto a
necessary preciso, necesario
to be necessary ser preciso
neighbor vecino
neither —— nor ni —— ni
neither do I ni yo tampoco
nephew sobrino
never nunca
new nuevo
news noticia
newspaper periódico
next próximo, siguiente
nice (little) -ito, -cito
night noche (*f.*)
all night toda la noche
at night por la noche
by night de noche
nine nueve
nine hundred novecientos
no no; ninguno
noise ruido
none ninguno
no one nadie
not no
nothing nada
nothing else nada más
notice, to fijarse en
now ahora
nowadays hoy día

O

obtain, to obtener *80*
occur, to ocurrir
ocean océano
o'clock la *or* las *with a number*
October octubre (*m.*)
of de
offer, to ofrecer *95*
often muchas veces
old viejo
how old are you? ¿cuántos años tiene Vd.?
to be ten years old tener diez años
older, oldest mayor
on en, sobre; (*with a day*) el, los
"on" (*article of clothing*) puesto
on account of por
on top of encima de
once una vez
at once en seguida
one uno; se (*with 3d pers. verb*)
one another nos, se
one may speak se puede hablar
one who quien
the one who el que
the rich ones los ricos

only único; solamente
open, to abrir *96*
open(ed) abierto
or o, ni (*after a neg.*)
orange naranja
order: in order to para
in order that para que
order, to mandar, pedir (i)
organ (hand) organillo
other otro
ought to deber
our nuestro
ours nuestro, el nuestro
ourselves (we) nosotros mismos
outside afuera (de)
oven horno
over sobre
own propio
owner dueño

P

page página
pain, to doler (ue) *86*
painting pintura
pair par (*m.*)
palace palacio
Panama Panamá (*m.*)
paper papel (*m.*)
parents padres
part parte (*f.*)
pass, to pasar
Paul Pablo
pave, to pavimentar
pay (for), to pagar *91*
to pay attention to fijarse en
peace paz (*f.*)
pencil lápiz (*m.*)
people gente (*f.*) (*usually singular*); pueblo
per cent por ciento
permission permiso
permit, to permitir
person persona
Peru Perú (*m.*)
Peter Pedro
pick up, to coger *93*
pie: meat pie empanada
piece pedazo
pirate pirata (*m.*)
pity lástima
what a pity! ¡qué lástima!
place lugar (*m.*), sitio
to take place tener lugar *80*
plain pampa
plane avión (*m.*)
plant, to plantar
play, to jugar (ue) (*a game*); **tocar** (*an instrument*) *91, 92*
please haga Vd. el favor de, favor de, tenga Vd. la bondad de
pleasure gusto
plenty bastante
P.M. de la tarde; de la noche
poor pobre
possession posesión
possible posible
precious precioso
prefer, to preferir (ie, i) *90*
prepare, to preparar
pretty bonito, lindo
prettiest el más bonito (lindo)
priest padre
prize premio
probably *sign of fut. or cond. tense*
promise, to prometer
proof prueba
public público
punish, to castigar *91*
pupil alumno
pursue, to perseguir (i) *78*
put, to poner *73*
to put into meter
to put on ponerse *73*
pyramid pirámide (*f.*)

Q

question pregunta
quickly pronto

R

race carrera
radio radio (*m. or f.*)
rain lluvia
rain, to llover (ue) *86*
ranch rancho
rate: at any rate de todos modos
  at the rate of con tarifa de
Raymond Ramón
reach, to llegar a *91*
read, to leer *97*
ready listo
real verdadero
realize, to darse cuenta de *65*
really? ¿verdad?
receive, to recibir
recognize, to reconocer *95*
red rojo, colorado
  reddest el más rojo
regret, to sentir (ie, i) *90*
remain, to quedarse
remember, to acordarse de (ue) *86*
republic república
resemble, to parecerse a *95*
resolve, to resolver (ue) (*p.p.* resuelto) *86*
rest, the los demás
rest, to descansar
restaurant restaurante (*m.*) (*sometimes* restaurant)
return, to volver (ue); devolver (ue) (*an object*) *86, 96*
  return trip viaje de vuelta
  returned vuelto
rich rico
  to get rich hacerse rico *69*
richest el más rico
ride, to montar (a caballo)
  to go for a ride (riding) dar un paseo, pasearse
right derecho
  one's right la derecha
  to be right tener razón *80*
  to give the right of way dar el paso *65*
  to the right (hand) a la derecha
river río
road camino
Robert Roberto
romantic romántico
room cuarto
ruin ruina
run, to correr

S

sacred sagrado
sad triste
saint santo
sake: for the sake of por
salt sal (*f.*)
same mismo
Saturday sábado
save, to salvar
say, to decir (i) *66*
  they say se dice
  to say good-by to despedirse de (i) *88*
  to say so decir que sí *66*
school escuela
scorpion alacrán (*m.*)
sea mar (*m. or f.*)
search: in search of en busca de
search, to buscar *92*
seated, to be estar sentado *67*
second (*date*) dos
secret secreto
see, to ver *85*
seed semilla
seem, to parecer *95*
seen visto
sell, to vender
send, to mandar, enviar
  to send on ahead mandar adelante
September septiembre (*m.*)
servant criado, -a
serve, to servir (i) *88*
  to serve to (*be good for*) servir para
service: at your service servidor (-a) de Vd.
seven siete
seventh (*date*) siete

several varios
severely severamente
shake hands, to dar la mano *65*
shall *sign of fut. tense*
sharp: six o'clock sharp las seis en punto
shirt camisa
shoe zapato
shoemaker zapatero
shore orilla
short (time) rato
  (with)in a short time dentro de poco
should *sign of cond. tense; sometimes of past subjv.*
shout, to gritar
show, to enseñar; mostrar (ue) *86*
sick enfermo
side lado
sign (*traffic*) señal (*f.*)
silently silenciosamente
silk seda
silver plata
since desde
sincerely: very sincerely yours soy de Vd. su atento amigo y seguro servidor
sing, to cantar
"single thing" nadita
sister hermana
sit (down), **to** sentarse (ie) *87*
situation situación
six seis
skirt falda
sky cielo
slave esclavo
sleep, to dormir (ue, u) *89*
slowly despacio
small pequeño
snow nieve (*f.*)
so así; tan (as); lo
  so-and-so street la calle tantos más cuantos
  so many tantos
  so much tanto
  so that para que, a fin de que
soft suave
soldier soldado
some alguno (*often omitted*); las
someone alguien
something algo, una cosa
sometimes algunas veces, a veces
son hijo
soon pronto
  as soon as en cuanto
  sooner más pronto
soul alma (el) (*f.*)
South America la América del Sur
Spain España
Spaniard español (*m.*)
Spanish español (*m.*)
speak, to hablar
spend, to gastar (*money*); pasar (*time*)
spite: in spite of a pesar de
standing en pie
star estrella
stay (home), **to** quedarse (en casa)
steal, to robar
step paso
  to take a step dar un paso
stick, to pegar *91*
still todavía
  to be still callarse
stocking media
stone piedra
stop, to cesar, detenerse *80*, dejar de
store tienda
  five- and ten-cent store tienda de cinco y diez
story cuento
strange curioso
stranger extranjero
street calle (*f.*)
  streetcar tranvía (*m.*)
strike, to (the hour) dar (la hora) *65*
strong fuerte
study, to estudiar
succeed (in), **to** conseguir (i), llegar a *78, 91*

such (a) tal
such as como
suddenly de pronto
suffer, to sufrir
sun sol (*m.*)
Sunday domingo
suppose: where do you suppose *See footnote 1 of story, Ch. 31, p. 434*
surround (with), to rodear (de)
swim, to nadar

T

table mesa
take, to (*along*) llevar; (*away*) llevarse; (*carry*) llevar; (*away from*) quitar; (*off*) quitarse
to take care of cuidar
to take for a walk llevar a pasear
to take out sacar *92*
to take place tener lugar *80*
to take possession of tomar posesión de
to take a step dar un paso *65*
to take (go for) a walk *or* **ride** pasearse
talk, to hablar
tall alto
taller más alto
tea te (*m.*)
teach, to enseñar
teacher profesor, -a
teaspoon cucharita
tell, to decir (i) *66*; (*a story*) contar (ue) *86*; cantar
ten diez
than que; (*before a number*) de
thank, to dar las gracias a *65*
thank you (very much) (muchas) gracias
that eso; que
so that para que, a fin de que
that of lo de
that one ése, aquél
that which lo que
the el, la, los, las
thee te
their su (de ellos), suyo
theirs los de ellos
them ellos, ellas; los, las
themselves se
with them consigo
then entonces
there allí, allá
there has been ha habido
there is (are) hay
there was había
these estos, éstos
they ellos (*usually omitted*)
they say se dice
thief ladrón (*m.*)
thin flaco
thing cosa
the only thing lo único
think (about), to pensar (ie) (en) *87*; (*believe*) creer
third tercero
one third la tercera parte
thirst sed (*f.*)
thirsty, to be tener sed (*f.*) *80*
thirty treinta
at ten-thirty a las diez y media
this este, esto
this one éste
those esos, ésos; aquellos, aquéllos; los (*followed by* de *or* que)
thousand mil
three tres
through por
throw, to echar, arrojar
Thursday jueves (*m.*)
thus así
tiger tigre (*m.*)
till hasta
ten till two las dos menos diez
time hora, tiempo, vez (*f.*)
from time to time de vez en cuando
to have a good time divertirse (ie,i) *90*
(with) in a short time dentro de poco

times por
tired cansado
to a; que; para
toad sapo
  little toad sapito
today hoy
together juntos
tomorrow mañana
tonight esta noche
too también; muy
tooth diente (*m.*)
top: on top of encima de
torn roto
touch, to tocar *92*
tourist turista (*m. or f.*)
toward hacia
town pueblo, ciudad
traffic tránsito
train tren (*m.*)
travel, to caminar, viajar
traveler viajero
treasure tesoro
tree árbol
trip viaje (*m.*)
  return trip viaje de vuelta
trip on, to tropezar con *94*
trousers pantalón (*m.*)
trousseau ropa de novia
true: it is true es verdad
truth verdad
try (to), **to** tratar (de)
Tuesday martes (*m.*)
turquoise turquesa
twelve doce
twenty veinte
  twenty-one veinte y uno
two dos
  two-faced, to be tener dos caras *80*

U

ugly (little) -illo, -cillo
uncle tío
under bajo
uniform uniforme (*m.*)
United States los Estados Unidos
unless sin que
unpleasant (little) -illo, -cillo
until hasta (que)
up: to eat up comerse
upon (*with a ger.*) al + *inf*
us nos, nosotros
use uso
use, to usar
used to *sign of imperf. tense*

V

value valor (*m.*)
various varios
vegetable legumbre (*f.*)
vendor vendedor (*m.*)
verse verso
very muy, mismo
village pueblo
Virgin Virgen (*f.*)
visit, to visitar
voice voz (*f.*)

W

wait (for), **to** esperar
walk, to andar *63*, caminar
  to take (go for) **a walk** pasearse
want (to), **to** querer (ie) *74*
was *imperf. or pret. of* ser, estar, *or* haber *79, 67, 68*
  was —— ing *sign of imperf. tense*
wash, to lavar
watch reloj (*m.*)
water agua (el) (*f.*)
wave ola
way (to) manera (de)
we nosotros (*usually omitted*)
  we Americans nosotros los americanos
weak débil
wealthiest el más rico
wear, to llevar
  to wear out romperse *96*

Wednesday miércoles (*m.*)
week semana; ocho días
the following week a la semana siguiente
weep, to llorar
welcome: you're welcome de nada
well bien; pues (*at beginning of sentence*)
as well as así como
were: there were había
what? ¿qué?
what a! ¡qué!
what (that which) lo que; cuál
what is the date? ¿cuál es la fecha?
what little he had lo poquito que tenía
whatever lo que
when cuando; ¿cuándo?
where donde; ¿dónde?
which que; el cual, la cual
while mientras; *often expressed by the ger. alone*
a long while largo rato
to be worth while (to) valer la pena (de) *83*
white blanco
who que; ¿quién?
whoever quienquiera
whom: those whom los (las) que
to whom a quien
whose? ¿de quién?
why ¿por qué?; si
wife esposa
will *sign of fut. tense*
willing: to be willing querer (ie) *74*
win, to ganar
wind viento
window ventana
wing ala (el) (*f.*)
winter invierno
wish, to querer (ie) *74*
with con
within dentro de
without sin; sin que (*with subjv.*)
woman mujer
old woman vieja
wood madera
wooden de madera
wool lana
word palabra
work trabajo
work, to trabajar
world mundo
worry, to preocuparse
not to worry no tener cuidado *80*
worst peor
worth, to be valer *83*
to be worth while (to) valer la pena (de)
would *often sign of cond. tense*
wound, to herir (ie, i) *90*
wrap, to envolver (ue) *86, 96*
wrapped envuelto
write, to escribir *96*
to write to each other escribirnos escribirse
written escrito

Y

Yankee yanqui (*m.*)
year año
yes sí
yesterday ayer
yesterday's de ayer
yet todavía
you usted
young joven
a young fellow un joven
youngest menor
your su —— de usted
yours (el, los) de usted, de ustedes, suyo(s)

Spanish-English Dictionary

To the pupil:

Why waste time looking here for words which you could guess with very little effort? To encourage you to *think* as you read the stories and therefore to make it easier for you in the long run, many cognates (words similar to English) used after the first five chapters have intentionally been omitted from this dictionary. In the early chapters you are taught how to recognize the different types of cognates, and the kinds omitted are listed here as a reminder.

Remember, if you do not find a certain word in this dictionary, the chances are that you should never have looked for it, but should have guessed!

Cognates frequently omitted are those which:

1. Are identical with English: ***federal, admirable, hotel.***
2. Are unmistakable (long enough to be easily guessed, no matter what variations they may have): ***automóvil, aeroplano, cigarro, paciente.***
3. End in ***-dad*** instead of *-ty*: ***electricidad, cordialidad, crueldad.***
4. End in ***-ción*** instead of *-tion*: ***acción, institución, liberación.***
5. End in a different final letter from English or add ***-a, -o,*** or ***-e*** to the English: ***argentino, cemento, contraste.***
6. Add verb endings to forms exactly or almost exactly like English: ***alarmar, presentar, observar.***
7. End in ***-cia, -cía,*** or ***-cio*** instead of *-y* or *-ce*: ***ceremonia, violencia.***
8. End in ***-oso*** instead of *-ous*: ***glorioso, religioso.***
9. Are unmistakable cognates ending in ***-mente*** instead of *-ly*: ***curiosamente.***
10. Are unmistakable cognates ending in ***-ado*** or ***-ido*** instead of *-ed*: ***civilizado, manufacturado.***
11. Begin with ***es-*** instead of *s-*: ***especial, esplêndido.***
12. Begin with ***in-*** instead of *un-*: ***inexplorado, innecesario.***
13. Are spelled with ***t*** instead of *th* (***autor***), ***f*** instead of *ph* (***foto***), ***c*** instead of *ch* (***cristiano***), ***i*** instead of *y* (***Egipto***).
14. Are spelled with single consonants instead of double: ***recomendar, colosal.***

Word markings:

Numbers preceding words refer to their frequency in Buchanan's *Graded Spanish Word Book.* Those marked **1** are in the first 189; **2,** 190–500; **3,** 501–1000; **4,** 1001–1500.

Words and idioms starred were used in Book I of *El camino real.*

Numbers following verbs refer to sections in the Appendix where they, or similar verbs, are conjugated. Radical-changing verbs have their present, preterite, and gerund change indicated: *preferir* (*ie, i*).

The gender of nouns ending in ***-o*** is masculine and that of nouns ending in ***-a, -ción,*** or ***-dad*** is feminine unless otherwise marked.

Omitted forms:

In general, words omitted from the Spanish-English dictionary are:

1. Regular past participles and gerunds unless they have new meanings: ***cuidado,*** *be careful.*
2. Regular adverbs ending in ***-mente*** and formed from adjectives which are listed: ***ricamente.***
3. Regular adjectives ending in ***-ísimo*** when the adjective is listed: ***muchísimo.***

4. Feminine forms of masculine nouns (or masculine forms of feminine nouns) which are listed: ***esposa, profesora.***
5. Words translated in parentheses in stories unless used subsequently.
6. Proper nouns similar to or identical with English or explained in the reading matter.
7. Unusual plot words given in chapter vocabularies but used only in that chapter: ***alacrán, pejerrey, yegua.***

A

*1 **a** to, at
  ***a las** + *number* at (*telling time*)
  a que until (*followed by a conj. verb*)
  ***¿a dónde?** where (*with verb of motion*)
3 **abajo** below; down
  cuesta abajo down hill
  de abajo below
  echar abajo to knock down
  para abajo down below
* **abanico** fan
*2 **abierto,** *p.p. of* **abrir** opened, open
abogado lawyer
3 **abrazar** to embrace; accept *94*
3 **abrazo** embrace
abrigo coat
*2 **abrir** to open
* **abuelo** grandfather
*1 **acá** here (*with verb of motion*)
1 **acabar** to finish
  ***acabar de** to have just
  acabarse to be finished, "all gone"
3 **acaso** perhaps
*3 **aceptar** to accept
*4 **acerca de** about, concerning
*2 **acercarse a** to approach, go near *92*
*2 **acompañar** to accompany
4 **aconsejar** to advise
3 **acordarse de (ue)** to remember *86*
* **acostarse (ue)** to go to bed *86*
acostumbrar to be in the habit of
*3 **acostumbrarse (a)** to become accustomed (to)
4 **actualmente** at present, nowadays
  de acuerdo con in accordance with
3 **adelante** onward, forward
  mandar adelante to send on ahead
  seguir adelante to go on ahead
*2 **además (de)** furthermore, besides
*3 **adiós** good-by
  adiosito bye-bye (*informal farewell*)
* **adobe** (*m.*) *mud bricks used for building material*
1 **adonde** where, to which
3 **adorar** to adore
* **adornar (se) (con)** to adorn (oneself) (with)
adorno ornament, adornment
aeropuerto airport
3 **afecto** affection, affectionate
  con afecto affectionately
aficionado "fan," enthusiast
afmo. *abbr. for* **afectísimo**
* **afortunado** lucky
afuera (de) outside (of)
*3 **agradable** agreeable
3 **agradecido** grateful
*2 **(el) agua** (*f.*) water
(el) águila (*f.*) eagle
agujero hole
4 **ahí** there
3 **ahogarse** to drown
*1 **ahora** now
*2 **aire** (*m.*) air
  por los aires through the air
*1 **al** to the; (+ *inf.*) on, upon, while
* **(el) ala** (*f.*) wing
alambre (*m.*) wire
2 **alcanzar** to reach; overtake *94*
4 **alegrarse (de)** to be glad to

* 3 **alegre** happy, merry (*used with* **estar**)
* 3 **alegremente** happily
* 3 **alegría** happiness, joy
de alegría for joy
3 **alejarse (de)** to go (*farther*) away
* 1 **algo** something; somewhat
* 1 **alguien** someone
* 1 **alguno** some
***alguna vez** ever
***algunas veces** sometimes
alhaja jewel
alimentarse (con) to feed (on)
alimento food
* 1 **(el) alma** (*f.*) soul
(de) mi alma darling
un alma de Dios a good fellow
almacén (*m.*) store
almorzar (ue) to eat lunch (*Mex.*) *86, 94*
* 4 **alrededor de** around
* 2 **alto** high; tall; stop (*traffic*)
***en voz alta** aloud
3 **altura** height, altitude
tener —— pies de altura to be —— feet high
* **alumno** pupil
Alvarado *blond Spanish conqueror who assisted Cortés in the conquest of Mexico and then conquered Guatemala (See Ch. 9, 17)*
3 **alzar(se)** to raise *94*
* 1 **allá** there, back there
más allá beyond
* 1 **allí** there
* 2 **amar** to love
* **amarillo** yellow
2 **ambos** both
3 **amenazar** to threaten *94*
* **la América del Sur** South America
* 4 **americano** American (*we are usually called* **norteamericanos** *in Spanish-speaking countries*)
* 1 **amigo** friend
amiguita little friend (*f.*)
3 **amistad** (*f.*) friendship
amistoso friendly
2 **amo** master
* 2 **amor** (*m.*) love
hacer el amor a to make love to
* 3 **ancho** wide
* 2 **andar** to go (*no destination*); to walk *63*
* 2 **anduv-** *pret. stem of* **andar**
3 **animar** to cheer up
anoche last night
anochecer to grow dark
al anochecer at nightfall
ansiosamente anxiously
1 **ante** before
ante todo before all, above all
* 3 **anterior** preceding
* 1 **antes (de)** before
antes (de) que before (*followed by a conj. verb*)
Antigua *name given to third capital of Guatemala to distinguish it from modern Guatemala City*
2 **antiguamente** formerly
* 2 **antiguo** old
3 **anunciar** to announce; advertise
anuncio advertisement
* 1 **año** year
***tener —— años** to be —— years old
2 **aparecer** to appear *95*
apariencia appearance
apartado (*mail*) box
2 **apenas** hardly
* **apetito** appetite
con buen apetito with a good appetite
apetitoso appetizing
apoderarse de to overpower, overcome
apostar (a) (ue) to bet *86*
* 3 **aprender (a)** to learn (to)

3 **aprovechar** to take advantage of
apuesta bet
* 1 **aquel** that
* 1 **aquél** that one, the former
* 1 **aquí** here
aquí mismo right here
***aquí tiene Vd.** here is
he aquí here is, are
***por aquí** around here; this way
araucano Araucanian, *Indian of Southern Chile*
* 3 **árbol** (*m.*) tree
arbusto bush
4 **ardiente** burning
3 **(el) arma** (*f.*) weapon
3 **arrancar (se)** to draw out, to pull out, tear out, off *92*
3 **arrastrarse** to crawl
* **¡arre!** go on! get up! (*to animal*)
* 3 **arreglar** to arrange; to settle (*a bill*)
* 3 **arriba** above, up
cuesta arriba uphill
* 3 **arrojar** to throw
arroz (*m.*) rice
* 1 **así** thus, so; like that (this)
así como as well as, just as
* 3 **asistir (a)** to attend
* 3 **asunto** matter, affair
* **asustado** frightened
atacar to attack *92*
Atahualpa *last ruler of the Incan Indians of Peru, who filled a room with gold for his ransom (See Ch. 21, 24)*
ataque (*m.*) attack
4 **atento** attentive, kind
aterrado terrified
3 **atrás: hacia atrás** backward
2 **atreverse (a)** to dare (to)
4 **atto.** *abbr. for* **atento**
1 **aun** even, still
1 **aún** yet
* 1 **aunque** although, even if

automovilista (*m. or f.*) motorist
3 **autoridad** authority
3 **(el) ave** (*f.*) bird
* 4 **aventura** adventure
avión (*m.*) airplane
por avión by plane
4 **avisar** to inform
* **¡ay!** oh! alas!
¡Ay de él! Alas for him, too bad for him!
***¡Ay de mí!** Alas for me!
* 1 **ayer** yesterday
ayuda help, aid
* 3 **ayudar (a)** to help, aid (to)
* **azteca** (*m. or f.*) Aztec, *Indian who lived in Mexico when the Spaniards arrived (See Ch. 7, 12)*
* 3 **azúcar** (*m.*) sugar
* 3 **azul** blue

B

bahía bay
* 4 **bailar** to dance
* 4 **baile** (*m.*) dance
* 2 **bajar** to lower; climb down
bajar a to come, (go) down to
bajar por to climb down
bajar(se) de to get out (*of car*), get down, go down
* 2 **bajo** beneath, under; low; short
* 4 **balcón** (*m.*) balcony
balsa *reed boat of Lake Titicaca*
bálsamo del Perú *sap of a tree of El Salvador, used for its healing properties*
* **bandera** flag
* **bandido** bandit
* **baño** bathroom; bath
* **barato** cheap
barbaridad: ¡qué barbaridad! How ridiculous! The idea!
* **barra** bar, stripe
* **barro** clay

* 2 **bastante** quite, plenty, enough
2 **bastar** to be enough
4 **batalla** battle
* 2 **beber** to drink
bebida drink
béisbol (*m.*) baseball
3 **belleza** beauty
2 **bello** beautiful
4 **beso (-ito)** kiss
bicicleta bicycle
* 1 **bien** well; *with adj.*, quite
***estar bien** to be all right
* **billete** (*m.*) **(de lotería)** (*lottery*) ticket
billete de banco bank bill
bisabuelo great-grandfather, ancestor
* 2 **blanco** white
* 2 **boca** mouth
4 **bodas** wedding (*usually pl.*)
boliviano Bolivian; coin of Bolivia
* **bolsillo** pocket
bombilla *silver or bamboo sipper used to drink* **mate**
3 **bondad** kindness
***tener la bondad de** to please to
* 3 **bondadoso** kind
* 1 **bonito** pretty
4 **bosque** (*m.*) forest
* **botella** bottle
botica drugstore
botón (*m.*) button; bell-boy
brazo arm
4 **brillante** (*m.*) diamond; (*adj.*) brilliant
brisa breeze
* 1 **bueno** good; all right; fine (*sarcastic*)
***buenos días** good morning, good day
burlarse de to make fun of
* **burro** donkey
busca: en busca de in search of
* 2 **buscar** to look for; to get *92*

C

C. A. *abbr.* **Centroamérica**
2 **caballero** gentleman; knight (*old meaning*)
* **caballo** horse
***a caballo** on horseback
* 2 **cabeza** head
Cabeza de Vaca *Spanish explorer who walked across what is now the United States*
cacao *cocoa bean from which chocolate is made*
* 1 **cada** (*invariable*) each
cada vez más gradually
4 **cadena** chain
* 1 **caer(se)** to fall (down) *64*
caer a to fall into
caer de rodillas to fall on one's knees
***dejar caer** to drop
* 3 **café** (*m.*) coffee; (*adj.*) brown (*Mex.*) (*chief product of Brazil*)
4 **caída** (*n.*) drop, fall; end (*of the afternoon*)
calabaza pumpkin, gourd
* **caliente** warm, hot
3 **calor** (*m.*) heat
***hacer calor** to be hot (*weather*)
***tener calor** to be hot (*persons*)
2 **callar(se)** to be quiet
* 2 **calle** (*f.*) street
* 2 **cama** bed
3 **cambiar** to change; exchange
* 3 **cambio** change; exchange
***en cambio** on the other hand
4 **caminar** to travel, go, walk
* 1 **camino** road
camino de on the way to
* **camisa** shirt; slip
4 **campana** bell
campanilla little bell
* **campesino** farmer, country person
* 2 **campo** field; country; **"camp"** (***Arg.***)

* **canción** song
canoa canoe
* 3 **cansado** tired
3 **cansarse** to get tired
* 2 **cantar** to sing
3 **cantidad** quantity, amount (*money*)
cañón (*m.*) canyon; cannon
capilla chapel
4 **capitán** (*m.*) captain
* 4 **capítulo** chapter
* 2 **cara** face
 ***tener dos caras** to be "two-faced"
¡caramba! *exclamation of disapproval or surprise*
* **caray: ¡Ay, caray!** My goodness!
* 4 **cárcel** (*f.*) jail
3 **carga (de)** load (of); freight
3 **cargar (de)** to load (with), to carry *91*
* 3 **cariño** affection
* **carne** (*f.*) meat; flesh
* **carnicería** butcher shop
caro expensive, dear
carreta oxcart
carretera highway (*Pan American Highway, see Ch. 11*)
* 2 **carta** letter
* 1 **casa** house
 ***a casa** (*w.* **ir** *or* **volver**) to go home
 ***de casa en casa** from house to house
 ***en casa** at home
 ***en casa de (María)** at (Mary's)
casar to marry (*off*)
* 2 **casarse con** to marry (*someone*)
* 2 **casi** almost
2 **caso** case, fact; affair; situation
3 **castellano** Castilian
casualidad chance
 por casualidad by chance
* 1 **catorce** fourteen
* 1 **cayendo** *ger. of* **caer**

* 3 **celebrar** to celebrate; observe
* **centavo** cent
* 3 **centro** center
 para el (al) centro "downtown"
Centroamérica Central America
* 2 **cerca de** near
 cerca nearby
 más cerca nearer
* 2 **cerrar (ie)** to close *87*
 cerrar con llave to lock
 cerrar el paso to block one's way
3 **cesar (de)** to cease
Cía *abbr.* **compañía**
3 **ciego** blind
* 2 **cielo** sky; heaven
* 1 **ciento (cien)** (one) hundred
 por ciento per cent
* 1 **cierto** certain
 es cierto it is true
 por cierto certainly, for certain
cima summit, top
* 1 **cinco** five; a "nickel"
* 1 **cincuenta** fifty
* **cine** (*m.*) movies; motion-picture house
* 1 **ciudad** city
* 3 **clase** (*f.*) class; kind
 toda clase de all kinds of
clavel (*m.*) carnation
clima (*m.*) climate
coca *leaves of a plant from which cocaine is made, chewed by Indians of Peru and Bolivia*
* 4 **cocer (ue)** to cook, boil *86*
* **cocina** kitchen
coco coconut
cocodrilo crocodile
4 **coche** (*m.*) car (*auto*); carriage
* 2 **coger** to pick up; pick; take hold of; catch; seize *93*
* 3 **colgar (ue)** to hang (up) *86, 91*
colón (*m.*) *coin of Costa Rica and El Salvador*

Colón, Cristóbal Christopher Columbus
* 2 **color** (*m.*): **de colores** colored
colorado red
colorete (*m.*) rouge
collar (*m.*) necklace
4 **combatir** to fight, to combat
* **comedor** (*m.*) dining room
2 **comenzar** (**ie**) to commence *87, 94*
* 2 **comer** to eat
  comerse to eat up (*all*)
* **comida** meal, dinner; food
  en la comida for dinner
* 1 **como** like, (such) as, as if; since; (*with a number*) about
  así como as well as
  como si as if (*with subjv.*)
  ***tan —— como** as —— as
* 1 **¿cómo?** how?
  ¿cómo le va? how goes it?
  ***¿cómo no?** why not?
cómodo comfortable
* 2 **compañero** companion
3 **compañía** company
* 4 **complacer** to comply with *95*
completar to complete
* 3 **componerse** (**de**) to be composed (of)
* 3 **comprar** to buy
  comprar a to buy from
2 **comprender** to comprehend
* 3 **compuesto** *p.p. of* **componer**
3 **común** common
* 1 **con** with
  con frecuencia frequently
3 **condenar** to condemn
4 **condesa** countess
cóndor (*m.*) *bird of the Andes; coin of Chile and Ecuador*
3 **conducir** to lead, drive, conduct *81*
3 **confesar** (**ie**) to confess
3 **confianza** confidence
* 1 **conmigo** with me
* 1 **conocer** to know; meet (*in pret.*) *95*
* **conquistador** (*m.*) conqueror
4 **conquistar** to conquer (*territory*)
4 **consecuencia: a consecuencia de** as a result of
3 **conseguir** (**i**) to obtain, get, attain; succeed in (*doing something*) *78*
3 **consejo**(**s**) advice (*often used in pl.*)
4 **consentir** (**en**) (**ie, i**) to consent *90*
* 2 **conservar** to keep, conserve
2 **considerar** to consider
1 **consigo** with him, himself, herself, yourself, themselves; *1st pers. pres. of* **conseguir**
* 4 **construir** to build *97*
4 **Consuelo** Consolation (*girl's name*)
consultar to consult
* 2 **contar** (**ue**) to count; tell *or* relate *86*
* 3 **contener** to contain *80*
* 3 **contento** (**de**) happy (to, with) (*used with* **estar**)
* 2 **contestar** to answer, reply
* 1 **contigo** with you (*fam.*)
* 3 **continuar** to continue
3 **continuo** continuous
* 2 **contra** against
* 2 **contrario: lo contrario** the opposite
  ***al contrario** on the contrary
4 **convencer** (**de**) to convince
conveniente fitting, suitable
3 **convenir** to be fitting *or* proper *84*
  convenir (**en**) to agree (upon)
3 **convertir**(**se**) (**en**) (**ie, i**) to convert, to change (into) *90*
* 1 **corazón** (*m.*) heart
* **corbata** necktie; neckerchief
corral (*m.*) *pen for livestock*

*2 **correr** to run; run around; race
2 **cortar** to cut
3 **corte** (*f.*) court; (*m.*) cut (*hair*)
* **cortés** courteous
Cortés, Hernando *conqueror of Mexico in 1519* (See Ch. *17*, *19*)
* **cortesía** courtesy
cortina curtain
*3 **corto** short
*1 **cosa** thing; affair, matter
  otra cosa something (anything) else
3 **costa** coast; (*pl.*) costs
*3 **costar (ue)** to cost *86*
*3 **costumbre** (*f.*) custom
  ***no es costumbre** it "isn't being done"
*3 **crecer** to grow *95*
*1 **creer** to believe *97*
  creer que sí to think so
  creerse to believe oneself
*1 **creyendo** *ger. of* **creer**
*2 **criado** servant
4 **cristal** (*m.*) glass
Cristo Christ
*4 **cruz** (*f.*) cross
3 **cruzar** to cross *94*
cruzeiro *monetary unit of Brazil*
*1 **el cual** which, who
  ***¡cuál!** how great, what!
  ***¿cuál?** what, which?
  cuál no fué su sorpresa what was his surprise
*1 **cualquier** any
*1 **cuando** when
  ***de vez en cuando** from time to time
*1 **¿cuándo?** when?
*1 **cuanto** how much, as much
  cuanto más —— más the more —— the more
  en cuanto as soon as
  ***en cuanto a** as for, concerning
  unos cuantos a few
*1 **¿cuánto?** how much?
  ¿cuánto tiempo? how long?
  ¿cuántos? how many?
*1 **cuarenta** forty
*2 **cuarto** room; fourth
*1 **cuatro** four; a few
*1 **cuatrocientos** four hundred
*2 **cubierto** *p.p. of* **cubrir**
*2 **cubrir** to cover *96*
cuchara spoon
* **cuchillo** knife
*4 **cuento** story
cuero skin, hide
*2 **cuerpo** body
cuesta hill
  cuesta abajo down hill
  cuesta arriba up hill
* **cueva** cave
*2 **cuidado** care
  al cuidado de in care of
  ***con mucho cuidado** carefully
  cuidado con (el tren) look out for (the train)
  no tener cuidado not to worry
  ***tener cuidado** to be careful
*3 **cuidar (de)** to take care of
*3 **culpa** fault
  ***tener la culpa** to be to blame
4 **culto** cultured
4 **cumbre** (*f.*) peak
* **cumpleaños** (*m.*) birthday
*2 **cumplir** to fulfill, keep (*a promise*)
4 **cura** (*m.*) priest
curación: hacer la primera curación to give first aid
4 **curar** to cure
*4 **curiosidad** souvenir; curiosity
*4 **curioso** curious, strange, "funny"
custodia custody
1 **cuyo** whose
Cuzco *capital of Incan Indians in Peru*

CH

* **charro** *horseback rider or costume (Mex.) (See Ch. 7)*
* **chicle** (*m.*) *sap of sapota tree used to make chewing gum*
* **chico** little
  chiquilla little girl
  los chicos the little folks
chicha *drink of Peruvian Indians*
* **chiste** (*m.*) joke
* **chófer** (*m.*) chauffeur
choque (*m.*) collision; shock

D

3 **dama** lady, girl
*1 **dame** give me (*fam.*)
danzar to dance *94*
3 **daño** harm
  ***hacer(le) daño a** to harm, injure
*1 **dar** to give *65*
  *** dar a** to face
  dar el paso a to give the right-of-way to
  dar la mano to shake hands
  ***dar las (cuatro)** to strike (four)
  ***dar las gracias a** to thank
  ***dar (media)** *or* **(una) vuelta** to turn (halfway) around
  dar muerte a to kill
  dar un golpe a to strike
  dar un grito (de alarma) to cry out (in alarm)
  dar un paseo to go for a walk, ride *or* drive
  dar un paso to take a step
  darse cuenta de to realize, pay attention to
*1 **de** of; from
  ***de (casa) en (casa)** from (house) to (house)
  de diez en diez by tens
  ***de prisa** fast, quickly
  de pronto suddenly
  ***de vez en cuando** from time to time
  ser de to belong to
*3 **debajo de** beneath, below, under
*1 **deber** ought; to owe; must (*probability*)
  debido a due to
  se debe a is due to
4 **débil** weak
*3 **decidir(se)** to decide, make up one's mind
*1 **decir (i)** to say, tell *66*
3 **declarar(se)** to declare (oneself); find oneself
  declararse vencido to give up
3 **defender (ie)** to defend *87*
*1 **dejar** to let, allow; leave
  ***dejar caer** to drop
  dejar de to fail to; to stop (*doing something*)
*2 **delante (de)** in front of, before
  por delante ahead
3 **delicado** delicate
*1 **del** of the (*m.*)
*2 **los demás** the rest
*3 **demasiado** too, too much; *pl.*, too many
3 **demostrar (ue)** to show *86*
*1 **dentro (de)** within, inside (of)
depender (de) to depend (on)
*2 **derecho** right
  ***a la derecha** to the right
  tomar la derecha to turn to the right
* **desagradable** disagreeable
*3 **desaparecer** to disappear *95*
* **desayunarse** to eat breakfast
* **desayuno** breakfast
3 **descansar** to rest
3 **desconocer** to be unacquainted with *95*
descortés discourteous
*4 **describir** to describe
4 **descrito** *p.p. of* **describir**

*2 **descubierto** uncovered; discovered *p.p. of* **descubrir**
*2 **descubrir** to discover *96*
*1 **desde (que)** since, from
desde entonces since then
desde hace diez años since ten years ago
desde —— hasta from —— till
desdén (*m.*) disdain
*2 **desear** to desire, want
2 **deseo** desire
deseoso desirous
*4 **desesperado** desperate
4 **desesperar** to despair, give up
3 **desgracia** misfortune
3 **desgraciado** unfortunate, unlucky (*one*)
deshonrado disgraced
*4 **desierto** desert; deserted
* **despacio** slowly
*3 **despedirse (de) (i)** to take leave (of), say good-by (to) *88*
*2 **despertar(se) (ie)** to wake, awaken *87*
*1 **después (de)** after; afterwards
3 **destino** destination
con destino a en route to
3 **destruir** to destroy *97*
detalle (*m.*) detail
*2 **detener(se)** to stop *80*
*3 **detrás de** behind
devolver (ue) to return (*an object*) *86*, *96*
*1 **dí,** *etc.* *pret. of* **dar**
1 **di** *fam. com. of* **decir**
*1 **día** (*m.*) day
***al día siguiente** on the following day
al otro día the next day
***buenos días** good day
***de día** by day
***día del santo** Saint's day
días de entre semana weekdays
***hoy día** nowadays
ocho días a week
***todos los días** every day
tres veces al día three times a day
4 **diablo** devil
*3 **diario** daily; daily paper
* **dibujo** drawing
dibujos animados animated cartoons
*1 **dice** he says
dice que sí he says so
***se dice** "they say," one says
*1 **dicho** (*p.p. of* **decir)** said, told; aforesaid
* **diciembre** (*m.*) December
Diego James
*3 **diente** (*m.*) tooth
*1 **diez** ten
de diez en diez by tens
*3 **diferente** different
*3 **difícil** difficult
*4 **dificultad** (*f.*) difficulty
*1 **diga Vd.** (*com. of* **decir)**
dígame Vd. tell me
dignidad dignity
2 **digno** worthy
*1 **dij-** *pret. stem of* **decir**
se dijo he said to himself
*2 **dinero** money
*1 **Dios** God; (**dioses** gods); ***diosa** goddess
¡Dios mío! my goodness!
por Dios for goodness' sake
un alma de Dios a good fellow
*1 **dir-** *fut. stem of* **decir**
3 **dirección** address
2 **dirigirse a** to go to, toward; address
dispensar to excuse
*3 **distancia: a distancia de** at a distance of
3 **distinto** different
*4 **divertir(se) (ie, i)** to amuse; enjoy oneself *90*

4 **doble** double
* 1 **doce** twelve
* **docena** dozen
* **dólar** (*m.*) dollar (*U.S.*)
doler (ue) to ache; pain *86*
* 2 **dolor** (*m.*) pain; sorrow
dolor de cabeza headache
* **domingo** Sunday
de aquí a dos domingos two weeks from Sunday
* 1 **don** (*m.*) *courteous title used with given names*
* 1 **donde** where
* 1 **¿dónde?** where?
¿a dónde? where? (*with verb of motion*)
en donde in which
* 1 **doña** *courteous title used with given names*
* 2 **dormir (ue)** to sleep; **dormirse** to go to sleep *89*
* 1 **dos** two; **los dos** we *or* they both, you two
* 1 **doscientos** two hundred
* 1 **duda: sin duda** doubtless
3 **dudar** to doubt
* 2 **dueño** owner
* 2 **dulce** sweet; (*m. pl.*) candies
* 2 **durante** during
* 3 **durar** to last
* 2 **durmiendo** *ger. of* **dormir**
* 2 **duro** dollar (*Spanish*); (*adj.*) hard
huevos duros hard-boiled eggs

E

* 1 **e** and (*before* **i** *or* **hi**)
* 2 **echar** to throw; throw out; pour; cast
echar a volar to fly away
echar abajo to knock down
echar de menos to miss
echar flores to pay a compliment
echar mano a to lay hold of
echar sangre to bleed
* 2 **edad** age
mayores de edad older persons
* 4 **edificio** building
educado educated
bien educado well behaved, brought up
2 **efecto: en efecto** really, actually, in fact
* **¿eh?** isn't that so? won't you? aren't you? is he? *etc.*
* 2 **ejemplo: por ejemplo** for example
* **ejercicio** exercise
* 1 **el** the, that (*followed by* **de** *or* **que**)
***el que, el cual** who, which, he who, the one who
* 1 **él** he; him
4 **elegir (i)** to elect *88*, *93*
* **Elena** Helen
* 1 **ella** she; her
* 1 **ellas** they; them
* 1 **ellos** they; them
embajador (*m.*) ambassador
* 1 **embargo: sin embargo** nevertheless
empanada *small fried meat pie or turnover*
emperador (*m.*) emperor
* 2 **empezar (ie) (a)** to begin (to) *87*, *94*
* 2 **emplear** to employ, use
* 1 **en** in, on, upon
* 3 **enamorado de** in love with
* 3 **enamorarse de** to fall in love with
* 3 **encantado** haunted; charmed
4 **encantador** charming
* 3 **encanto** enchantment; charm
* 3 **encender (ie)** to light *87*
3 **encerrar (ie)** to lock up, shut up *87*
* 3 **encima (de)** on top (of), above
* 2 **encontrar(se) (ue)** to find, meet; find oneself, be *86*

4 **encuentro: volver al encuentro de** to go back to meet
enemigo enemy
4 **enfermedad** illness
* 4 **enfermo** ill, sick
3 **engañar** to deceive
enojarse to become angry
* 3 **enorme** enormous
* **Enrique** Henry
* 3 **enseñar** to teach; show
* 1 **entender** (ie) to understand *87*
* 2 **entero** entire
* **enterrar** (ie) to bury *87*
* 1 **entonces** then
por entonces at the time
* 3 **entrada** entrance; admission
* 1 **entrar** to enter
* 1 **entre** between, among
entre semana on week days
2 **entregar** to deliver, hand over *91*
entretanto meanwhile
entristecer to sadden *95*
2 **enviar** to send
envidiar to envy
3 **envolver** (ue) to wrap *86*, *96*
* 3 **envuelto** (*p.p. of* **envolver**) wrapped
equipaje (*m.*) luggage
equivocarse to be mistaken
* 1 **era** *imperf. of* **ser**
* 1 **eres** (**tú**) it's you (*from* **ser**)
* 3 **escaparse** to escape
* 2 **escena** scene; stage
4 **esclavo** slave
* 3 **escoger** to choose *93*
* 3 **esconder** (se) to hide
* **escopeta** gun
* 1 **escribir** to write *96*
* 1 **escrito** *p.p. of* **escribir**
* 2 **escuchar** to listen (to)
* 3 **escuela** school
* 1 **ese** that; **ése** that one
esmeralda emerald (*found in Colombia*)
* 1 **eso** that (*neuter*)
***a eso de** at about (*telling time*)
eso sí que es that certainly is it, that's just it
3 **espalda: volver la espalda a** to turn his back on
* **España** Spain
* 1 **español** (*m.*) Spaniard; (*adj.*) Spanish
2 **esperanza** hope
* 1 **esperar** to wait (for); hope; expect
esperar a que to wait until
espero que sí I hope so
* 2 **esposo** husband
* **es que** the fact is that
esquina (*street*) corner
* 1 **esta** this
***esta noche** tonight
* **estación** station; (**de calores**) (hot) season
estacionarse to park
* **estado** state
Estados Unidos United States
estampillas de correo postage stamps
* 1 **estar** to be *67*
***estar bien** to be all right
***estar de moda** to be in style
estar para to be about to
* 4 **estatua** statue
* 1 **este** this; **éste** this one; the latter
estilo style
3 **estimado** esteemed, valued
* 1 **esto** this (*neuter*)
* 3 **estrecho** narrow
* 3 **estrella** star
* 3 **estudiar** to study
3 **estudio** study
* 1 **estuv-** *pret. stem of* **estar**
2 **eterno** eternal
* **E. U.** (de) **A.** *abbr.* **Estados Unidos de América**
* **europeo** European
a la europea European style
3 **evitar** to avoid

*4 **exactamente** exactly
exagerar to exaggerate
* **examen** (*m.*) examination
*3 **exclamar** to exclaim
*2 **existir** to exist
*3 **explicar** to explain *92*
3 **expresión** expression, idiom
*3 **extranjero** foreigner; (*adj.*) foreign
3 **extraño** strange
3 **extremo** extreme

F

*3 **fácil** easy
facilitar to facilitate, make easy; supply
*4 **falda** skirt
*2 **falta** lack
*2 **faltar** to lack, need
  no faltaba más that was the last straw
3 **fama** fame
*2 **familia** family
*3 **famoso** famous
fantasma (*m.*) ghost
*2 **favor: por favor** please; **favor de** + *inf.* please
2 **fe** (*f.*) faith
* **fecha** date
  ***¿cuál es la fecha?** what is the date?
  hasta la fecha up to the present time
3 **felicidad** happiness
*2 **feliz** happy (*used with* **ser**)
*3 **feo** ugly
ferrocarril (*m.*) railroad
4 **fiado: al fiado** on credit
4 **fiar** to trust
*3 **fiel** faithful
3 **fijar** to fix
  fijarse (en) to notice, pay attention to
*1 **fin** end; object
  a fin de que so that
  ***al fin** at last, after all
  por fin at last, after all
  un sin fin de an endless amount of
finca farm
*4 **fingir** to pretend *93*
firmar to sign
flaco thin
flauta flute
*2 **flor** (*f.*) flower
  echar flores to pay a compliment
flotar to float
2 **fondo** bottom; depths; back (*of a room*)
fórmula (de cortesía) expression (of courtesy)
fortaleza fortress
3 **fortuna** fortune
*2 **francés** (*m.*) Frenchman; (*adj.*) French
3 **frase** (*f.*) sentence; phrase
Fray Brother (*name of priest*)
  Fray Marcos de Niza *a priest who tried to find the mythical Seven Cities of Cíbola in New Mexico*
frecuencia: con frecuencia frequently
*3 **fresco** fresh; cool
  hacer fresco to be cool (*weather*)
* **frijol** (*m.*) bean
2 **frío** cold
  ***hacer frío** to be cold (*weather*)
  ***tener frío** to be cold (*person*)
frontera border, frontier
*1 **fu-** *pret. stem of* **ser** *or* **ir**
2 **fuego** fire
*3 **fuente** (*f.*) fountain
*2 **fuera (de)** outside (of), out
2 **fuerte** strong; heavy; loud
2 **fuerza** force, strength
* **Fulano (-a) (de Tal)** So-and-So
4 **función** performance

3 **fundar** to found
fútbol (*m.*) football

G

4 **galán** (*m.*) courtier, gallant
galeón (*m.*) galleon
* **galería** gallery
gallardo gallant
* **gallina** hen
* 2 **ganar** to gain; win; earn
4 **gana**(s) (**de**) desire (to)
  tener ganas de to feel like
* 4 **gastar** to spend; use up
* **gato** cat
gaucho cowboy (*Arg. and Urug.*) (*See Ch. 31, 33*)
* 2 **gente** (*f.*) people (*usually used in sing.*)
  gente de razón "nice people"
3 **gobierno** government
* 3 **golpe** (*m.*) blow
  dar un golpe a to strike
* **gordo** fat
4 **gota** drop
* **gracias** thanks, thank you
  ***dar las gracias a** to thank
3 **grado** degree (*of education*) grade
gramática grammar
* 1 **gran** great
* 1 **grande** large, great
  los grandes grown-ups
  un grande a grown-up
gratis free
2 **grave** ill
gris gray
* 3 **gritar** to shout; cry out; scream (at)
* 3 **grito** cry; shout
grueso thick; heavy
* 3 **grupo** group
guapo handsome
guaraní (*m. or f.*) *Indian of Paraguay; the language* (*See Ch. 25, 26*)
* 2 **guardar (silencio)** to keep (quiet); guard
guardia (*m.*) policeman, guard
guatemalteco Guatemalan
2 **guerra** war
guerrero warrior
* 2 **gustar** to be pleasing (to)
  ***¿gusta Vd.?** would you care to?
  ***le gusta** he likes (to)
  ***me gustaría** I should like **(to)**
* 2 **gusto** pleasure; liking; taste
  con todo gusto with the greatest of pleasure

H

* 1 **haber** to have (*auxiliary*) *68*
  haber de to be to, must
  ***había** there was *or* were
  ***habrá** there will be
hábil skilled
3 **habitación** room; dwelling
* **habitante** (*m.*) inhabitant
* **habla: de habla española** Spanish-speaking
* **hablar** to speak, talk
* 1 **habr-** *fut. stem of* **haber**
* 1 **hacer** to make; do; **hacerse** to become, get (*rich*) *69*
  ***hace** ago; for (*w. exp. of time*)
  ***hace poco** not long ago
  hacer el amor a to make love to
  ***hacer buen (mal) tiempo** to be good (bad) weather
  ***hacer calor** to be hot (*weather*)
  ***hacer (le) daño a** to harm, injure, damage
  ***hacer el favor de** to please to
  ***hacer fresco** to be cool (*weather*)
  ***hacer frío** to be cold (*weather*)
  ***hacer el oso** to play the bear (*make love*)
  ***hacer (otra) pregunta** to ask (another) question

hacer el papel to play the part
hacer pedazos to break in pieces
hacer la primera curación to give first aid
hacerse el sordo to play deaf
***hacer un viaje** to take a trip
hacer viento to be windy
no hace muchos años que it has not been many years since
* 2 **hacia** toward
hacia atrás backward
4 **hacienda** large ranch
* 1 **hag-** *pres. subjv. stem of* **hacer**
***haga Vd. el favor de** please
* 2 **hallar** to find
* 3 (el) **hambre** (*f.*) hunger
***tener (mucha) hambre** to be (very) hungry
hambriento hungry
* 1 **hasta** even; until; as far as; as many as
desde —— hasta from —— to
¿hasta cuándo? how long?
***hasta la vista** until we meet again, until I see you
***hasta luego** see you later
hasta que until (*followed by a conj. verb*)
* 1 **hay** there is, there are
***hay lodo** it is muddy
hay luna it is moonlight
***hay neblina** it is foggy
***hay polvo** it is dusty
***hay que** it is necessary to, one must
***hay sol** (*or* **hace**) it is sunny
* 1 **he** *pres. tense of* **haber** *68*
he aquí here is, are
3 **hecho** (*m.*) fact
* 1 **hecho** *p.p. of* **hacer** made, done
* **helado** ice cream; (*adj.*) iced
* 1 **hemos** we have (**haber**)
heredar to inherit
4 **herida** wound
3 **herir (ie, i)** to wound *90*
* 1 **hermano** brother; *pl.* brothers and sisters
* 1 **hermoso** beautiful
4 **hervir (ie, i)** to boil *90*
* 1 **hic-** *pret. stem of* **hacer**
3 **hierro** iron
* **higuera** fig tree
* 1 **hijo** son; junior (Jr.)
* 2 **historia** history; story
* 1 **hizo** *pret. of* **hacer**
* 3 **hoja** leaf
* 1 **hombre** (*m.*) man
4 **hombro** shoulder
a hombros on his back
al hombro on his shoulder
honradez (*f.*) honesty
* **honrado** honest
3 **honrar** to honor
* 1 **hora** hour; time
¿a qué hora? at what time?
por hora an hour
horno oven
hospitalidad hospitality
* 1 **hoy** today
***hoy día** nowadays
hoy mismo this very day
* 1 **hub-** *pret. stem of* **haber**
* 3 **huevo** egg
huevos al plato shirred eggs
huevos duros hard-boiled eggs
huevos tibios soft-boiled eggs
2 **huir** to flee *97*
* 3 **humilde** humble
humor (*m.*): **de buen humor** good-humoredly, in a good humor

I

* 1 **iba** *imperf. of* **ir**
* 3 **iglesia** church
3 **ignorar** to ignore
* 1 **igual** similar, equal

***igualito** exactly alike, just like it, identical
3 **imagen** (*f.*) image
* 3 **imaginarse** to imagine, fancy
imaginaos *2d pers. pl. fam. com.*
3 **impedir** (i) to prevent *88*
4 **imperio** empire
* 2 **importar** to matter, be important (to)
***no importa** it doesn't matter
4 **imprimir** to print (*p.p.* **impreso**)
inca (*m. or f.*) *ruler of the Indian tribes of pre-conquest Peru (see Ch. 20, 21); (m.) coin of Peru*
* 2 **indicar** to indicate *92*
indignado indignant
* **indio** Indian
Inés Inez
3 **infeliz** unhappy; unpleasant
informes (*m.*) information
Inglaterra England
* 3 **inglés** (*m.*) English, Englishman; (*adj.*) English
3 **inmediatamente** immediately
* 3 **inmenso** immense
inolvidable unforgettable
4 **inquieto** uneasy
insistir (en) to insist (on)
2 **instante: en ese instante** at that instant
3 **interés** (*m.*) interest
* 4 **interesante** interesting
* 4 **interesar(se)** to interest
4 **introducir** to introduce *81*
4 **introduj-** *pret. stem of* **introducir**
3 **inútil** useless
* 3 **invierno** winter
invitado guest
* **invitar (a)** to invite
* 1 **ir** to go (*to a destination*); **irse** to go away *70*
***ir a caballo** to ride horseback
va (trabajando) he keeps on (working)
3 **isla** island
Isla del Coco Cocos Island (*Costa Rica*)
* 3 **izquierdo** left
***a la izquierda** to the left
tomar la izquierda to turn to the left

J

* 1 **jamás** never, ever
* 3 **jardín** (*m.*) garden
* **jardinero** gardener
4 **jefe** (*m.*) chief
* **Jorge** George
* **José** Joseph
* 1 **joven** young; young person
jóvenes young people
* **joya** jewel; (*piece of*) jewelry
* **Juan** John
* **Juana** Jane
* 4 **juego** game
* **jueves** (*m.*) Thursday
* 4 **juez** (*m.*) judge
* 3 **jugar a** (ue) to play; gamble *91*
3 **juicio** judgment
* **julio** July
* **junio** June
2 **junto a** near
junto con along with
* 2 **juntos** together
3 **jurar** to swear
3 **juventud** (*f.*) youth

K

km. *abbr.* **kilómetro** *about 5/8 of a mile*

L

* 1 **la** the; her, it; which, that (*followed by* **de** *or* **que**)
***es la (son las)** it is (*telling time*)
3 **labio** lip
4 **labrador** (*m.*) working man

* 2 **lado** side
a ambos lados on both sides
***al lado de** beside
al otro lado on (to) the other side
* 4 **ladrón** (*m.*) thief
lago lake
3 **lágrima** tear
lana wool
* **lápiz** (*m.*) pencil; lipstick
* 2 **largo** long
a lo largo de along
millas de largo miles long
* 1 **las** the; them; those (*before* **de** *or* **que**)
* 4 **lástima** pity
***¡qué lástima!** too bad! what a pity!
***ser lástima** to be too bad
* 4 **lavar** to wash
* 1 **le** him; to him, to her, to you, to it
leal loyal
* **lección** lesson
* **leche** (*f.*) milk
lechuza owl
* 2 **leer** to read *97*
* **legumbre** (*f.*) vegetable
4 **lejano** distant
* 2 **lejos de** far from
a lo lejos in the distance
* 2 **lengua** language; tongue
* 1 **les** them; you; to them, to you
* 2 **letra** letter (*of the alphabet*); words of a song
* 1 **levantar** to raise, lift; **levantarse** to get up
leyenda legend
2 **libertad** (*f.*) liberty
libertador (*m.*) liberator
libertar (a) to liberate
* 2 **libre** free; open
* 1 **libro** book
3 **ligero** swift, fast
limeño *inhabitant of Lima*
limpiabotas (*m.*) bootblack
* **limpiar** to clean
limpieza cleanliness
* 3 **limpio** clean
* 4 **lindo** pretty
* **lista** (*n.*) roll; list; menu
listo (*adj.*) ready; clever
* 1 **lo** it; so
lo (curioso) the (curious) thing
lo mexicano that which is Mexican
***lo mismo que** the same as
lo mucho que how much
***lo (que)** that which, what (*neuter*)
* 2 **loco** crazy
* **lodo: hay lodo** it is muddy
* 1 **los** the; them; *with* **hay,** some *or* any
* **lotería** lottery
4 **lucha** struggle
* **Lucita** *dim. of* **Lucía** Lucy
1 **luego** then
***hasta luego** see you later
* 2 **lugar** (*m.*) place
en lugar de instead of
tener lugar to take place
* **Luis** Louis
* 4 **luna** moon
hay luna it is moonlight
***noche de luna** moonlight night
* **lunes** (*m.*) Monday
* 2 **luz** (*f.*) light

LL

4 **llama** (*m. or f.*) *pack animal of the Andes, belonging to the camel family*
* 1 **llamar** to call; knock; ring
llamar por teléfono to "call up"
llamarse to be called *or* named
* 4 **llave** (*f.*) key
cerrar con llave to lock
llegada arrival

* 1 **llegar** to arrive; **llegar a** to reach, come to; succeed in *91*
llegar a ser to become
* **llenar (de)** to fill (with)
* 2 **lleno (de)** full (of)
* 1 **llevar** to take, carry; wear; bear (*name*)
llevar a pasear to take for a walk
llevarse to take *or* carry away
2 **llorar** to weep, cry
* **llover (ue)** to rain *86*
* **lluvia** rain

M

* **madera** wood
* 1 **madre** (*f.*) mother
3 **maestro** teacher (*elementary*)
* 4 **magnífico** magnificent
maíz (*m.*) corn
4 **mal** (*m.*) illness
* 1 **mal** badly, not so good
* 1 **malo** bad
* 2 **mandar** to command; order; send
mandar adelante to send on ahead
mandar hacer to have made
***mande Vd.** *reply when one is called or addressed*
* **manejar** to drive
* 2 **manera** manner, way
de manera que so that (*usually followed by subjv.*)
de otra manera otherwise
* 1 **mano** (*f.*) hand
dar la mano to shake hands
echar mano a to lay hold of
* **manzana** apple
* 1 **mañana** morning; tomorrow
***de la mañana** in the morning, A.M.
mañana mismo tomorrow (*no later*)
***por la mañana** in the morning
toda la mañana all morning
mapa (*m.*) map
* 4 **máquina (-ita)** engine; machine
* 2 **mar** (*m. or f.*) sea
* 4 **maravilla** marvel
* **maravilloso** marvelous
* 4 **marcar** to mark *92*
* **Margarita** Margaret; daisy
2 **marido** husband
marimba *musical instrument of Guatemala, similar to a xylophone* (*See Ch. 9*)
* **martes** (*m.*) Tuesday
* **marzo** March
1 **mas** but
* 1 **más** more; any more
cuanto mas, —— más the more, —— the more
más allá beyond
***más de** more than (*before a number*)
***más —— que** —— er than
***más tarde** later
***no —— más que** only
* 2 **matar** to kill (*p.p.* **muerto** *when used with aux.* **haber** *only*)
mate (*m.*) (*sometimes called* **yerba mate**) *popular Argentine "tea" used in several South American countries, mainly Brazil, Uruguay, Argentina, Paraguay, and Chile*
maya (*m. or f.*) *Indian of southern Mexico and Guatemala;* (*m.*) *the language* (*See Ch. 12, 19*)
* **mayo** May
* 1 **mayor** greater, greatest; older, oldest
la mayor parte de most of
mayores de edad older (*persons*)
mayordomo superintendent; butler
* 1 **me** me; to me
* **media** stocking

* **medianoche: a medianoche** at midnight
* 4 **médico** doctor; medical
* 2 **medio** half; method, means
a mediodía at noon
en medio de in the midst (middle) of
por medio de by means of
***y media** half-past
* 1 **mejor** better, best
lo mejor the best (thing)
4 **mejorar** to get better
* **menor** younger, youngest; least
* 1 **menos** except; minus; less, least
***al menos** at least
echar de menos to miss
***las nueve menos cinco** five minutes to nine
lo menos the least
más o menos more or less
por lo menos at least
* 3 **mentira** (*f.*) lie; (*adj.*) not true
* 1 **mes** (*m.*) month
* 2 **mesa** table
mesero waiter
* 2 **meter** to put (in)
método method
* **metro** meter (*39 inches*)
* **mexicano** (*spelled* **mejicano** *in some countries*) Mexican
lo mexicano that which is Mexican
3 **mezclar** to mix
* 1 **mi** my
* 1 **mí** me
***¡ay de mí!** alas for me!
* 3 **miedo** fear
de miedo from fear
***tener miedo de (a)** to be afraid of
miembro member
* 2 **mientras** while
* **miércoles** (*m.*) Wednesday
* 1 **mil** (one) thousand
milagro miracle
* **milagroso** miraculous
milla mile
* 4 **minuto** minute
* 1 **mío** mine; my
3 **mirada** look
* 1 **mirar** to look (at)
* 3 **misa** mass
* 1 **mismo** same, very; oneself, himself, myself
aquí (allí) mismo right here (there)
***hoy mismo** this very day
***lo mismo que** the same as
4 **misterio** mystery
3 **mitad** (*f.*) half
* **moda** style
***estar de moda** to be in style
pasado de moda out of style
modismo idiom, expression
modo manner
de todos modos at any rate
* 4 **molestar** to annoy, bother
* **molestia** bother, annoyance
* 2 **momento** moment
monarca (*m.*) monarch
* **moneda** coin (*coins of Spanish-American countries, see Ch. 27*)
* 3 **montaña** mountain
montañoso mountainous
* 4 **montar** to mount; ride
***montar a caballo** to go horseback riding
morado purple
ojo morado "black eye"
morder (ue) to bite *86*
moreno brown; dark-complexioned
* 1 **morir (ue, u)** to die *89*
* **moro** Moor, Moorish; (*Arg.*) *black horse with white spots*
* 2 **mostrar (ue)** to show *86*
* 1 **muchacho** boy; **muchacha** girl
* 1 **mucho** much, great; **muchos** many

lo mucho que how much
***muchas veces** often
mucho tiempo a long time
* **mueble** (*m.*) (*piece of*) furniture
muela tooth
* 2 **muerte** (*f.*) death
dar muerte a to kill
* 1 **muerto** *p.p. of* **morir** died, dead; *p.p. of* **matar** killed
el muerto the dead man
* 1 **mujer** (*f.*) woman; wife
* 1 **mundo** world
***todo el mundo** everyone
* 1 **mur-** *pret. stem of* **morir**
murió he died
muralla wall
* 4 **murmurar** to whisper; murmur
* 3 **música** music
* **músico** musician
* 1 **muy** very

N

* 2 **nacer** to be born *95*
* **nacimiento** birth
nacionalidad nationality
* 1 **nada** nothing; (*with adj.*) not at all; (*as exclamation*) never mind!
*** de nada** you're welcome
nadar to swim
* 1 **nadie** no one
náhuatl (*m.*) *language spoken by the Aztecs of Mexico*
* **naranja** orange
nariz (*f.*) nose
* **neblina** fog
hay neblina it is foggy
2 **necesidad** need, necessity
* 2 **necesitar** to need
2 **negar** (ie) to deny *87, 91*
* 2 **negro** black
* 1 **ni —— ni** neither —— nor
***ni yo tampoco** neither have (do) I
nieve (*f.*) snow; ice cream (*Mex.*)
* 1 **ninguno** none, any
en ninguna parte nowhere
* 1 **niño** boy; child
nivel (*m.*) level
* 1 **no** no; not
* 1 **noche** (*f.*) night
buenas noches good evening; good night
*(es) **de noche** it is night; **at** night; by night
***esta noche** tonight
***por la noche** at night
Nochebuena Christmas Eve
3 **nombrar** to name, appoint
* 2 **nombre** (*m.*) name
* 4 **norte** (*m.*) north
la América del Norte North America
* **norteamericano** North American
* 1 **nos** us; to us; ourselves
* 1 **nosotros** we; us
nosotros los mexicanos we Mexicans
* 3 **noticia** (*piece of*) news; notice
* **noviembre** (*m.*) November
* 4 **novio** fiancé, sweetheart; (*f.*) bride
* 3 **nube** (*f.*) cloud
* 1 **nuestro** our, ours
* 1 **nueve** nine
* 1 **nuevo** new
* 2 **número** number
* 1 **nunca** never, ever

O

* 1 **o** or
* 1 **o —— o** either —— or
* 3 **obedecer** to obey *95*
2 **objeto** object
* **obligatorio** required
2 **obra** work (*of art*)
4 **obscuridad** darkness
* 2 **obscuro** dark
* 4 **obtener** to obtain *80*

occidental western; west
Hemisferio Occidental Western Hemisphere
* 1 **ocho** eight
ocho días a week
* 2 **ocupado** busy
* 2 **ocupar** to occupy
ocuparse de to attend to
3 **ocurrir** to occur, happen; to apply
oeste west
* **oficina** office
* 2 **ofrecer** to offer *95*
¿ se le ofrece a Vd. algo? can I do anything for you (offer you anything)?
ofrecimiento offer
3 **oído** ear (*inner*); hearing
* 1 **oír** to hear *71*
ojalá oh that, would that (*usually followed by subjv.*)
* 1 **ojo** eye
al ojo over one eye
ola wave
oler (ue) to smell (*1st pers. pres.* **huelo**) *86*
4 **olor** (*m.*) odor
* 2 **olvidar (se) (de)** to forget
ombú (*m.*) *great shade tree of the Argentine pampa, the only tree native to the plains* (*See Ch. 32*)
* 1 **once** eleven
* 2 **orden** (*m.*) order
a sus (tus) órdenes at your service
3 **origen** (*m.*) origin
4 **orilla** shore, bank
* 2 **oro** gold
de oro golden
«oro blanco» sugar (*Cuba*)
«oro negro» oil (*Venezuela*)
* 1 **os** you; to you
* **oso: hacer el oso** to play the bear (*make love*)
* 1 **otro** other; another
al otro día (domingo) the next day (Sunday)
otra cosa something (anything) else
***otra vez** again

P

* **Pablo** Paul
* 1 **padre** (*m.*) father; priest
***padres** parents
* 2 **pagar** to pay (for) *91*
* 4 **página** page
* 2 **país** (*m.*) country
* 4 **pájaro** bird
* 1 **palabra** word
pálido pale
palmera palm tree
* **paloma** dove
pampa plain (*particularly of Argentina and Uruguay*)
* 2 **pan** (*m.*) bread
¡Pan! ¡Pan! Dingdong!
panamericano Pan American
* **Pancho** Frank, *nickname for* **Francisco**
* **pañuelo** handkerchief
* 1 **papel** (*m.*) paper
hacer el (un) papel to play the (a) part
3 **par** (*m.*) pair
* 1 **para** for, in order to, to
estar para to be about to
para con to, toward
para que in order that, so that (*followed by a conj. verb*)
***¿para qué?** what for?
***para sí** to himself
para siempre forever
paraguayo Paraguayan
paralizado paralyzed
3 **parar(se)** to stop
* 1 **parecer** to seem *95*
* 1 **parecerse a** to resemble *95*
* 3 **pared** (*f.*) wall

*2 **parte** (*f.*) part
de todas partes from everywhere
en ninguna parte nowhere
en otras partes in other places
en todas partes everywhere
la mayor parte de most of
la tercera parte one third
***por todas partes** everywhere
*1 **pasado** last; past
pasado de moda out of style
pasado mañana day after tomorrow
pasajero passenger
*1 **pasar** to go, pass; happen; spend (*time*)
pasar con to happen to
pasar lista to call the roll
***pase Vd.** come in
*4 **pasear: llevar a pasear** to take for a walk
*4 **paseo** drive; walk
dar un paseo to go for a drive, ride *or* walk
2 **paso** way, right-of-way; step; pass
cerrar el paso to block one's way
dar el paso to give way to
dar un paso to take a step
paso a paso step by step
* **pastel** (*m.*) pastry, cake; pastel (*light color*)
* **pastelería** pastry shop
pata foot (*animal's or bird's*)
* **patata** potato
* **patio** courtyard
3 **patria** native country
patrón (*m.*) patron; boss; owner
patroncita "lady"
santo patrón patron saint
pavimentar to pave
*2 **paz** (*f.*) peace
juez de paz justice of the peace
*3 **pedazo** piece
a pedazos in pieces
hacer pedazos to break in pieces
*1 **pedir** (i) to ask (for); order *88*
pedir prestado to borrow
* **Pedro** Peter
3 **peligro** danger
peligroso dangerous
*3 **pelo** hair
2 **pena** trouble, sorrow
no valer la pena (**de**) not to be worth while (to)
*2 **pensamiento** thought
*1 **pensar** (ie) (**en**) to think (about); intend to
*1 **peor** worse, worst
* **Pepe** Joe, *nickname for* **José**
*1 **pequeño** little, small
pera pear
percibir to perceive
*1 **perder** (ie) to lose; miss *87*
4 **perdón** (*m.*) pardon
* **perezoso** lazy
*4 **periódico** newspaper, periodical
* **perla** pearl
3 **permanecer** to remain
* **permiso** permission
2 **permitir** to permit
*1 **pero** but
*3 **perro** dog
4 **perseguir** (i) to pursue *78*
*2 **persona** person
3 **pertenecer** to belong *95*
peruano Peruvian
2 **pesado** heavy
2 **pesar** to weigh
a pesar de in spite of
* **pescado** fish
*3 **peso** dollar (*monetary unit of several Latin-American countries*); weight
pez (*m.*) fish
*2 **pie** (*m.*) foot
***a pie** on foot
en pie standing

tener —— pies de altura to be —— feet high
* 2 **piedra** stone
* **pierna** leg
4 **pieza** piece
* 3 **pintar** (de) to paint (with)
pintoresco picturesque
* **pintura** painting; paint
pirámide (*f.*) pyramid
4 **pisar** to step (on), tread, set foot on
* **piso** story, floor (*of buildings*)
el primer piso the second floor
plano chart
* 3 **plata** silver
* 4 **plato** dish
huevos al plato shirred eggs
* 2 **plaza** park, "square"
* 3 **pluma** pen; feather
plumafuente (*f.*) fountain pen
* 4 **población** town
* 1 **pobre** poor
pobreza poverty
* 1 **poco** little (*amount*); *with adj.*, not very
*__hace poco__ not long ago
*__poco a poco__ little by little
poco tiempo después a short time after
pocos few
por poco almost
* 1 **poder** (ue) to be able (*ger.* **pudiendo**) *72*
3 **poderoso** powerful
* **pollo** chicken
polvo dust; (*pl.*) powder
*__hay polvo__ it is dusty
poncho *blanket with a slit for the head, worn by cowboys of Argentina, Chile, and Uruguay*
* 1 **poner** to put; **ponerse** to put on; become *73*
poner mala cara to pout
ponerse a to begin to
ponerse (**pálido**) to turn (pale)
Popocatépetl (*m.*) *volcano of Mexico*
* 1 **por** for; through; along; in exchange for; by; for the sake of
por + *inf.* on account of
*__por aquí__ around here; this way
por ciento per cent
por cierto certainly
por entonces at the time
por esto for this reason
por fin at last, after all
*__por la mañana__ in the morning
*__por la noche__ at night
por poco almost
por lo tanto therefore
*__por la tarde__ in the afternoon
por —— que however
*__¿por qué?__ why?
*__por supuesto__ of course
*__por todas partes__ everywhere
por último finally
* **pordiosero** beggar
* 1 **porque** because
portugués (*m.*) *Portuguese language or person* (*See Ch. 27*)
* 3 **poseer** to possess
4 **posesión** possession
* **postre** (*m.*) dessert
Potosí (*m.*) *mining town of Bolivia, from which so much bullion was taken to Spain in colonial days that the name came to be applied to any wealth-producing region*
vale un Potosí (it) is worth a mint
* **práctico** practical
* 3 **precio** price
* 4 **precioso** precious; "darling"
precipicio precipice
2 **preciso** necessary
* 4 **preferir** (ie, i) to prefer *90*
* 4 **pregunta** question
*__hacer__ (**una**) **pregunta**(**s**) to ask (a) question(s)

*2 **preguntar** to ask (*a question*)
*4 **premio** prize
*4 **prenda (de vestir)** article of clothing
preocuparse (de) to worry (about)
*3 **preparar** to prepare
préstamo loan
3 **prestar** to lend
pedir prestado to borrow
prevenir to prevent *84*
*1 **primero** first
el primer piso the second floor
3 **príncipe** (*m.*) prince
*2 **principio** beginning
***al principio** at first
*4 **prisa: de prisa** fast, quickly; hastily
***tener prisa** to be in a hurry
*3 **probar (ue)** to try (out), test *86*
2 **producir** to produce *81*
2 **produj-** *pret. stem of* **producir**
* **profesor (-a)** teacher (*high school*)
prohibir to prohibit
se prohibe it is forbidden
*3 **prometer** to promise
*2 **pronto** soon, quickly
de pronto suddenly
3 **pronunciar** to pronounce
*2 **propio** own
3 **proponer** to propose *73*
proteger to protect *93*
provenir to come from *84*
*4 **próximo** next
3 **prueba** proof
*1 **pud-** *pret. stem of* **poder**
*2 **pueblo** town; a people
puente (*m.*) bridge
*1 **puerta** door
4 **puerto** port
*1 **pues** well, then; for; since
pues bien well, then
puesta: puesta del sol sunset
*1 **puesto** *p.p. of* **poner**; (*n.*) stand; place; barracks; (*adj.*) "on"
4 **punta** point
Punta Guijarros Cobblestone Point (*old name of Point Loma, San Diego, California*)
***punto: a punto de** on the point of
*1 **pus-** *pret. stem of* **poner**

Q

*1 **que** who, which, what, that; than; for (*like* **porque**)
dice que sí he says so
***es que** the fact is that
más —— que —— er than
*1 **¿qué?** what?
¿Qué tal? How's everything?
*1 **¡qué!** what!, what a
quebracho ironwood
1 **quedar** to be; to be left
le queda (un peso) he has left (a dollar)
me queda I have left
*1 **quedarse** to stay, remain; to be
*1 **querer (ie)** to want; **querer a** to love *74*
***querer decir** to mean
*3 **querido** dear, darling
* **queso** cheese
quetzal (*m.*) *national bird, emblem and coin of Guatemala*
quichua (*m. or f.*) *Indian of Peru;* (*m.*) *the language he speaks*
*1 **quien** he who, one who, who
***a quien** whom
*1 **¿quién?** who?
¿de quién? whose?
1 **quienquiera** whoever
*1 **quince** fifteen
*1 **quinientos** five hundred
*1 **quis-** *pret. stem of* **querer**
*2 **quitar** to remove, take away; **quitarse** to take off
*1 **quizás** perhaps

R

* **radio** (*m. or f.*) radio
* 4 **ramo** (-ito) bouquet; branch
* **Ramón** Raymond
rancho ranch
* 3 **raro** rare, strange
* 3 **rato** short time, while
* **ratón** (*m.*) mouse
4 **raza** race
* 1 **razón** (*f.*) reason
***tener razón** to be right
* 2 **real** royal; *old Spanish coin;* **El camino real,** the King's Highway (*name of main roads built by the State in Spanish-speaking countries in colonial times; now applied to "Old Spanish Trail" between St. Augustine, Florida, and Sonoma, California, via Santa Fe and San Diego, and to colonial roads of Latin America*)
* 2 **recibir** to receive
* 3 **recién** recently
* 3 **reconocer** to recognize *95*
* 2 **recordar** (**ue**) to remember, recall *86*
* 3 **recuerdo** remembrance, souvenir; (*pl.*) regards
2 **referir** (**ie, i**) to refer *90*
* **refrán** (*m.*) proverb
refrescante refreshing
refresco soft drink, refreshments (*Mex.*)
4 **regalar** to present, give (*as a gift*)
* **regalo** gift
regar (**ie**) to irrigate *87*
3 **regla** rule
regresar to return
3 **reina** queen
4 **reino** kingdom
* 3 **reír** (i) to laugh; **reírse de** to laugh at *75*
* **reloj** (*m.*) watch *or* clock
renunciar to renounce
repasar to review
* **repaso** review
repentino sudden
* 2 **repetir** (i) to repeat *88*
* 3 **representado** presented
3 **resolver** (**ue**) (*p.p.* **resuelto**) to solve; remedy; resolve *86*
respecto: con respecto a with respect to
2 **respeto** respect
* 2 **responder** to answer
* 4 **respuesta** answer, reply
3 **resuelto** *p.p. of* **resolver**
4 **reunión** (*f.*) meeting; party
* 3 **reunir** to gather up; **reunirse** to meet
* 2 **rey** (*m.*) king
* 2 **rico** rich
* 3 **riendo** *ger. of* **reír**
* 2 **río** river
Río de la Plata *a wide estuary between Uruguay and Argentina into which the Paraná and Uruguay Rivers flow* (*See Ch. 33*)
* 3 **rió** *pret. of* **reír**
3 **riqueza** wealth, (*pl.*) riches
risco cliff
3 **robar** to steal, rob
roca rock
3 **rodear** (**de**) to surround (with)
4 **rodilla: caer de rodillas** to fall on one's knees
3 **rogar** (**ue**) to beg *86*
* 3 **rojo** red
romance Romance (*any language based upon Latin*)
* 2 **romper** (*p.p.* **roto**) to break; tear; wear out
* 3 **ropa** clothing, clothes
ropa de novia trousseau
* 2 **roto** (*p.p. of* **romper**) broken; torn
roto (*n.*) Chilean laborer

4 **rubio** blond
* 3 **ruido** noise

S

* **sábado** Saturday
  ***el sábado** on Saturday
* 1 **saber** to know (how to); to find out (*especially in pret.*) *76*
* 2 **sacar** to take out, pull out *92*
4 **sacerdote** (*m.*) priest
4 **sagrado** sacred
* 4 **sala** living room; room
* 1 **salir (de)** to leave, go out; come out *77*
  salir bien (mal) en un examen to do well (badly) in an examination
  salir para to go out to
  with **billete de lotería** to win
4 **salón** (*m.*) hall, large room
4 **saltar** to jump
* 3 **salud** (*f.*) health
  estar bien de salud to be in good health
  ¡Salud! *wish for good health made when someone sneezes*
3 **saludar** to greet
  salúdeme say "hello" for me
3 **salvar** to save
2 **sangre** (*f.*) blood
  echar sangre to bleed
* 2 **santo** holy, saintly; saint
  ***día del santo** Saint's day
  ***en su santo** on your Saint's day (*birthday*)
  santo patrón patron saint
  santo y seña password
sapo toad
3 **satisfacer** to satisfy (*p.p.* **satisfecho**) *69*
* 3 **satisfecho** satisfied (*p.p. of* **satisfacer**)
* 1 **se** (to) himself, yourself, oneself; each other; (*impersonal*) one
  se puede one can
  se vende for sale
* 1 **sé** *1st pers. pres. of* **saber**
  no sé qué a kind of; goodness knows what
secar(se) to dry (up), be dried
3 **seco** dry
sed (*f.*) thirst
  ***tener sed** to be thirsty
seda silk
* 3 **seguida: en seguida** at once, immediately
* 1 **seguir (i)** to follow; continue *78*
  como sigue as follows
  seguir adelante to go on ahead
  seguir (trabajando) to keep on (working)
* 2 **según** according to
  según dicen so they say
* 1 **segundo** second
4 **seguridad** safety
2 **seguro** sure; constant
* 1 **seiscientos** six hundred
selva jungle
* 4 **semana** week
  días de entre semana week days
semanalmente weekly
semilla (*small*) seed
senda path
* 2 **sentarse (ie)** to sit down *87*
2 **sentido** consciousness
* 1 **sentir (ie, i)** to feel; regret, be sorry *90*
4 **señal** (*f.*) sign, signal
  en señal de as a sign of
  señales de tránsito traffic signs
* 1 **señor** gentleman; sir; master; Mr.
* 1 **señora** lady; madam; Mrs.
Señoría: Su Señoría Your Honor
* 3 **separar(se)** to separate
* **septiembre** (*m.*) September
* 1 **ser** to be *79*
  ***es que** the fact is that
  llegar a ser to become

ser de to belong to
***ser lástima** to be too bad, a pity
somos we are
son they are
soy I am
1 **ser** (*m.*) being
* 3 **serio** serious
* **servidor** (*m.*) servant (*in the sense of "at your service"*)
* 2 **servir** (i) to serve; **servirse** please, to be pleased *88*
no servir de nada to be good for nothing
***para servir a Vd.** at your service
* 1 **sesenta** sixty
* 1 **setecientos** seven hundred
* 1 **si** if; why (*in exclamation*)
* 1 **sí** yes; certainly; himself, **itself**
creo (**digo, espero**) **que sí** I think (say, hope) so
eso sí que es that certainly is it
para sí to himself
sí (**que lo hará**) he will (do it)
volver en sí to regain consciousness
* 1 **siempre** always
para siempre forever
* 1 **siesta** nap
dormir una siesta to take a nap
siga go (*traffic*)
2 **siglo** century
significado meaning
4 **significar** to mean, signify *92*
* 2 **siguiente** following
***al día siguiente** on the following day
* 2 **siguieron** *pret. of* **seguir**
* 2 **siguió** *pret. of* **seguir**
silencioso silent
* 3 **silla** chair
* **simpático** "nice," congenial
* 1 **sin** without
sin que unless, without (*followed by a subjv.*)
* 1 **sino** but (*after a neg.*); except
sinvergüenza (*m. or f.*) shameless one; shame on you
3 **siquiera** even, at least
ni siquiera not even
2 **sírvase** please (*formal*) (*from* **servir**)
* 2 **sitio** place, site
4 **soberano** sovereign
* 1 **sobre** over, above, on; concerning
sobre todo especially
* 3 **sobrino** nephew
socio member
* 2 **sol** (*m.*) sun; *monetary unit of Peru*
***hay** (**hace**) **sol** it is sunny
* 1 **solamente** only
3 **soldado** soldier
solito all alone; lonely
* 2 **solo** alone; single
* 1 **sólo** only
* 2 **sombra** shadow; shade
* 4 **sombrero** hat
3 **sonar** (**ue**) to ring; sound *86*
3 **soñar** (**ue**) (**con**) to dream (of) *86*
3 **sonreír** (i) to smile *75*
* **sonrisa** smile
* **sopa** soup
4 **sordo** deaf
hacerse el sordo to play deaf
* 3 **sorprender**(**se**) to surprise, be surprised
* 4 **sorpresa** surprise
con gran sorpresa de to the great surprise of
4 **sospechar** to suspect
S. S. *abbr.* **seguro servidor** (your) constant servant (yours truly)
* 1 **su** his, her, your, its, their
3 **suave** soft
* 2 **subir** (**a**) to climb up; get into; rise
2 **suceder** (**con**) to happen (to)

sucio dirty
* **sudamericano** South American
* 2 **suelo** floor; ground
* 2 **sueño** dream; sleep
* 2 **suerte** (*f.*) luck
tener suerte be lucky
* 2 **sufrir (de)** to suffer (from)
4 **suma** amount, sum
4 **sumamente** highly, very
4 **sumo** greatest; very (*as adv.*)
* 1 **sup-** *pret. stem of* **saber**
supo he found out
* 3 **superior** superior; upper; high (*school*)
* 2 **suponer** to suppose *73*
* **supuesto: por supuesto** of course
* **sur** (*m.*) south
* 1 **suyo** (of) his, (of) hers, (of) theirs
los suyos his people

T

tacita: taza + ita little cup
* 1 **tal** such (a); the said
con tal (de) que provided that (*usually followed by subjv.*)
***¿Qué tal?** (*informal greeting*) How's everything?
***tal vez** perhaps
* 1 **también** also, too
* 3 **tampoco** either, neither
***ni yo tampoco** neither do (have) I
* 1 **tan** as
***tan —— como** as —— as
* 1 **tanto** so much, as much; (*pl.*) so many
por lo tanto therefore
tanto como as well as
¡tanto mejor! so much the better!
3 **tardar en** to be long in; to spend (*time*)
* 2 **tarde** late; (*f.*) afternoon
***de la tarde** P.M.
más tarde later
***por la tarde** in the afternoon
* **taza** cup
* **te** (*m.*) tea
* 1 **te** thee, you; to thee, to you; yourself, thyself
* 2 **teatro** theater
tela cloth; material
* **teléfono** telephone
llamar por teléfono to "call up"
tema (*m.*) theme, composition
* 3 **temblar (ie)** to tremble *87*
* 2 **temer** to fear
tempestad (*f.*) storm
* 4 **templo** temple
* 4 **temprano** early
3 **tender** to extend
* 1 **tendr-** *fut. stem of* **tener**
tenedor (*m.*) fork
* 1 **tener** to have *80*
***aquí tiene Vd.** here is
***tener —— años** to be —— years old
***tener la bondad de** to please to
***tener calor** to be warm (*persons*)
***tener cuidado** to be careful, look out
no tener cuidado not to worry
***tener la culpa** to be to blame
***tener dos caras** to be "two-faced"
***tener frío** to be cold (*persons*)
tener ganas de to feel like (*inclined to*)
***tener hambre** to be hungry
tener lugar to take place
***tener miedo (de, a)** to be afraid (of)
tener —— pies de altura to be —— feet high
***tener prisa** to be in a hurry
***tener que** to have to

*tener razón to be right
*tener sed to be thirsty
tener suerte to be lucky
* Tenochtitlán (*m.*) *Aztec capital of Mexico, now Mexico City*
* 1 tercero third
la tercera parte one third
* 2 terminar (de) to finish, end
terremoto earthquake
* 4 tesoro treasure
* 1 ti thee
tibio warm
huevos tibios soft-boiled eggs
* 1 tiempo time; weather
a tiempo on time
¿cuánto tiempo? how long?
*hacer buen (mal) tiempo to be good (bad) weather
mucho tiempo a long time
poco tiempo después a short time after
* 4 tienda store
3 tierno tender
* 2 tierra land, country; earth
tierra(s) de temporal unirrigated land(s), dry-farming lands
tinta ink
* 1 tío uncle
* típico typical
* 3 tirar to throw; tirar (de) to pull
* 2 tocar to play (*musical instrument*); touch *92*
* 1 todavía still, yet
* 1 todo all, every
sobre todo especially
*todo el mundo everyone
*todos los días every day
* 1 tomar to take; drink
tomar la derecha to turn to the right
* 4 tonto foolish; fool
* tortilla *corn-meal pancake of Mayas and Aztecs, still popular today in Mexico and Guatemala*
tortilla de huevos omelet
tostón (*m.*) *Mexican fifty-cent piece* (*slang*)
* 1 trabajar to work
* 2 trabajo work
* traducir to translate *81*
* 1 traer to bring *82*
* 1 traj- *pret. stem of* traer
* 3 traje (*m.*) dress; suit
tranvía (*m.*) streetcar
3 tras after
2 tratar con to deal with
* 2 tratar de to try to; to be about
* 1 trece thirteen
* 1 treinta thirty
* tren (*m.*) train
* 1 trescientos three hundred
* 2 triste sad
* 3 tristeza sadness
trono throne
tropas troops
* 4 tropezar (ie) (con) to run into *87, 94*
* 1 tu thy, your
* 1 tú thou, you
* turista tourist
turquesa turquoise
* 1 tuv- *pret. stem of* tener
* 1 tuyo yours, your, (*fam.*) thy, thine

U

1 Ud. *abbr.* usted
* 2 último last
por último finally
* 2 único only; lo único the only thing
2 unir(se) to unite, join
* 1 uno one; a, an
unos, -as some; about (*with number*)
* 2 usar to use
usado used, second-hand
* 4 útil useful

V

* **vaca** cow
* 2 **valer** to be worth *83*
***más vale** is worth more
no valer la pena (**de**) not to be worth while (to)
¡Válgame Dios! Heaven help me!
* 3 **valiente** brave
* 2 **valor** (*m.*) value; courage
4 **valle** (*m.*) valley
vals (*m.*) waltz
* 1 **vamos** come
***vamos a** let's
3 **vano: en vano** in vain
* 2 **varios** (*before noun*) several; (*after noun*) various, assorted
varios de several
* 1 **vaya Vd.** *com. of* **ir**; **vaya Vd. con Dios** *polite way to say good-by*
* 1 **Vd.** *abbr.* **usted** you (*polite*); (*pl.*) **Vds.**
* 3 **vecino** neighbor; resident; (*adj.*) near-by
* 1 **veinte** twenty
* 4 **vela** candle
4 **velar** to watch over
velitas little candles (*to put on a cake*)
velocidad speed
* 1 **ven** *fam. com. of* **venir**
3 **vencer** to conquer (*persons*)
declararse vencido to give up
* **vendedor** (*m.*) vendor
* 3 **vender** to sell
se vende is sold, for sale
1 **venir** to come *84*
4 **venta** sale
de venta for sale
* 3 **ventana** window
* 1 **ver** to see; **verse** to be, find oneself *85*
a ver let's see
* 4 **verano** summer
* 4 **veras: de veras** really
* 1 **verdad** truth; **¿era verdad?** was it true?
***es verdad** it is true
***¿verdad?** is that so, *etc.*?
* 2 **verdadero** true, real
* 3 **verde** green
* 4 **vergüenza** shame, embarrassment
* 3 **vestido** dress, suit, clothes; dressed
vestido de charro dressed as a charro (*See* **charro**)
vestido de domingo dressed in Sunday best
* 2 **vestir**(**se**) (**i**) (**de**) to dress; to wear *88*
* 1 **vez** (*f.*) time
***a la vez** at the same time
***alguna vez** ever
***algunas veces** sometimes
a veces sometimes
cada vez más gradually
***de vez en cuando** from time to time
dos veces twice
***en vez de** instead of
***muchas veces** often
***otra vez** again
***por primera vez** for the first time
***tal vez** perhaps
tres veces al día three times a day
***una vez** once
una y otra vez time after time
* 2 **viaje** (*m.*) trip, journey
***buen viaje** pleasant journey
***hacer un viaje** to take a trip
viaje de vuelta return trip
* **viajero** traveler
vicuña (*m. or f.*) *small wild animal of the camel family living in the Andes and valued for its soft fur*
* 1 **vida** life; living (*cost*)
¡por vida mía! on my life!

* 1 **viejo** old
* 3 **viento** wind
  ***hacer viento** to be windy
* **viernes** (*m.*) Friday
* 1 **vin-** *pret. stem of* **venir**
2 **vino** wine
* 4 **virgen** (*pl.* **vírgenes**) virgin; **Virgen de Guadalupe** *Patron Saint of Mexico and, recently, of all Latin America*
virrey (*m.*) viceroy
2 **virtud** (*f.*) virtue
* 3 **visitar** to visit
* 2 **vista** sight; gaze
  ***hasta la vista** (*informal good-by*) until we see each other again
* 1 **visto** *p.p. of* **ver**
* 1 **¡viva!** (*com. of* **vivir**) Long live —! Hurrah for —!
* 1 **vivir** to live
* 2 **vivo** alive, living; bright (*color*)
* 3 **volar (se) (ue)** to fly (away) *86*
  echar a volar to fly away
volcán (*m.*) volcano
* 2 **voluntad** (*f.*) will
* 1 **volver (ue)** to return; to turn *86*
  volver a to do again
  volver a casa to go home
  volver al encuentro de go back to meet
  volver en sí to regain consciousness
  volver la espalda a to turn one's back on
  volverse to turn around
* 1 **vosotros** you
* 2 **voz** (*f.*) voice
  ***en voz alta** aloud
3 **vuelta** turn (around)
  ***dar (media) (una) vuelta** to turn (halfway) around
  viaje de vuelta return trip
* 1 **vuelto** *p.p. of* **volver**
* 1 **vuestro** your (*fam. pl.*)

X

Xochimilco *site of "floating gardens" of the Aztecs near Mexico City*

Y

* 1 **y** and
* 1 **ya** already; now
  ***¡ya lo creo!** I should say so!
  ***ya no** no longer
  ya que since
* 1 **yendo** *ger. of* **ir**
* 1 **yo** I
Yucatán *State of Mexico originally inhabited by Mayan Indians (See Ch. 19)*

Z

* **zapatero** shoemaker
* **zapato** shoe

Index

INDEX

NOTE: See Spanish-English Dictionary for cultural material not given here.

Numbers refer to pages unless otherwise marked.